PHILIP'S

STREE...S

Edinburgh

and **East Central Scotland**

D0245526

www.philips-maps.co.uk
First published in 1995 by Philip's
a division of Octopus Publishing Group Ltd
www.octopusbooks.co.uk
Endeavour House 189 Shaftesbury Avenue
London WC2H 8JY
An Hachette UK Company
www.hachette.co.uk

Fourth colour edition 2010
First impression 2010
EDIDA

ISBN 978-1-84907-131-4 (pocket)

© Philip's 2010

Ordnance Survey®

This product includes mapping data licensed from
Ordnance Survey® with the permission of the
Controller of Her Majesty's Stationery Office.
© Crown copyright 2010. All rights reserved.
Licence number 100011710.

No part of this publication may be reproduced,
stored in a retrieval system or transmitted in any
form or by any means, electronic, mechanical,
photocopying, recording or otherwise, without the
permission of the Publishers and the copyright
owner.

While every reasonable effort has been made to
ensure that the information compiled in this atlas is
accurate, complete and up-to-date at the time
of publication, some of this information is subject
to change and the Publisher cannot guarantee its
correctness or completeness.

The information in this atlas is provided without
any representation or warranty, express or
implied and the Publisher cannot be held liable
for any loss or damage due to any use or reliance
on the information in this atlas, nor for any
errors, omissions or subsequent changes in such
information.

The representation in this atlas of a road, track
or path is no evidence of the existence of a right
of way.

Ordnance Survey and the OS Symbol are registered
trademarks of Ordnance Survey, the national
mapping agency of Great Britain.

Speed camera data provided by
PocketGPSWorld.com Ltd

Post Office is a trade mark of Post Office Ltd in the
UK and other countries.

Printed in China

Contents

II	Major administrative and Postcode boundaries
III	**Key to map symbols**
IV	**Key to map pages**
VI	**Route planning**
1	**Street maps** at 2⅔ inches to 1 mile
218	**Street maps** at 1⅓ inches to 1 mile
228	**Street map of Edinburgh** at 5⅓ inches to 1 mile
230	**Index** of towns, villages, streets, hospitals, industrial estates, railway stations, schools, shopping centres, universities and places of interest

Digital Data

The exceptionally high-quality mapping found in this atlas is available as digital data in TIFF format, which is easily convertible to other bitmapped (raster) image formats.

The index is also available in digital form as a standard database table. It contains all the details found in the printed index together with the National Grid reference for the map square in which each entry is named.

For further information and to discuss your requirements, please contact
philips@mapsinternational.co.uk

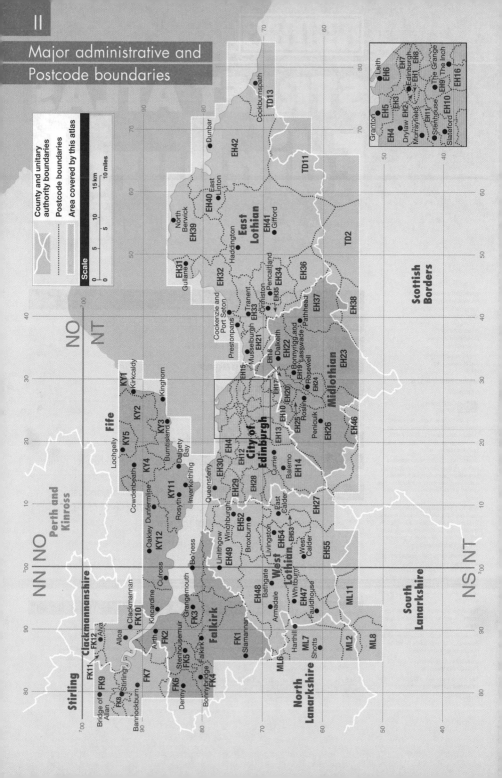

II

Major administrative and Postcode boundaries

Scale

County and unitary authority boundaries
Postcode boundaries
Area covered by this atlas

0   5   10   15 km
0   5   10 miles

Key to map symbols

Motorway with junction number	
Primary route – dual/single carriageway	
A road – dual/single carriageway	
B road – dual/single carriageway	
Minor road – dual/single carriageway	
Other minor road – dual/single carriageway	
Road under construction	
Tunnel, covered road	
Speed cameras – single, multiple	
Rural track, private road or narrow road in urban area	
Gate or obstruction to traffic – may not apply at all times or to all vehicles	
Path, bridleway, byway open to all traffic, restricted byway	
Pedestrianised area	
BS22 Postcode boundaries	
County and unitary authority boundaries	
Railway with station	
Tunnel	
Railway under construction	
Metro station	
Private railway station	
Miniature railway	
Tramway, tramway under construction	
Tram stop, tram stop under construction	
Bus, coach station	

♦	Ambulance station
♦	Coastguard station
♦	Fire station
♦	Police station
✚	Accident and Emergency entrance to hospital
H	Hospital
+	Place of worship
i	Information centre – open all year
	Shopping centre
P	Parking
P&R	Park and Ride
PO	Post Office
X	Camping site
	Caravan site
▶	Golf course
☓	Picnic site
Church	Non-Roman antiquity
ROMAN FORT	Roman antiquity
Univ	Important buildings, schools, colleges, universities and hospitals
	Built-up area
	Woods
River Medway	Water name
	River, weir
	Stream
	Canal, lock, tunnel
	Water
	Tidal water
112, 58, 87	Adjoining page indicators

Abbreviations

Acad	Academy	Meml	Memorial
Allot Gdns	Allotments	Mon	Monument
Cemy	Cemetery	Mus	Museum
C Ctr	Civic centre	Obsy	Observatory
CH	Club house	Pal	Royal palace
Coll	College	PH	Public house
Crem	Crematorium	Recn Gd	Recreation ground
Ent	Enterprise		
Ex H	Exhibition hall	Resr	Reservoir
Ind Est	Industrial Estate	Ret Pk	Retail park
IRB Sta	Inshore rescue boat station	Sch	School
		Sh Ctr	Shopping centre
Inst	Institute	TH	Town hall / house
Ct	Law court	Trad Est	Trading estate
L Ctr	Leisure centre	Univ	University
LC	Level crossing	W Twr	Water tower
Liby	Library	Wks	Works
Mkt	Market	YH	Youth hostel

The small numbers around the edges of the maps identify the 1-kilometre National Grid lines

The dark grey border on the inside edge of some pages indicates that the mapping does not continue onto the adjacent page

The map scale on the pages numbered in green is 1⅓ inches to 1 mile
2.1 cm to 1 km • 1:47 620

```
0        ½ mile        1 mile        1½ miles        2 miles
0    500m    1 km    1½ km    2km
```

The map scale on the pages numbered in blue is 2⅔ inches to 1 mile
4.2 cm to 1 km • 1:23 810

```
0        ¼ mile        ½ mile        ¾ mile        1 mile
0    250m    500m    750m    1km
```

The map scale on the pages numbered in red is 5⅓ inches to 1 mile
8.4 cm to 1 km • 1:11 900

```
0        220yds        440yds        660yds        ½ mile
0    125m    250m    375m    500m
```

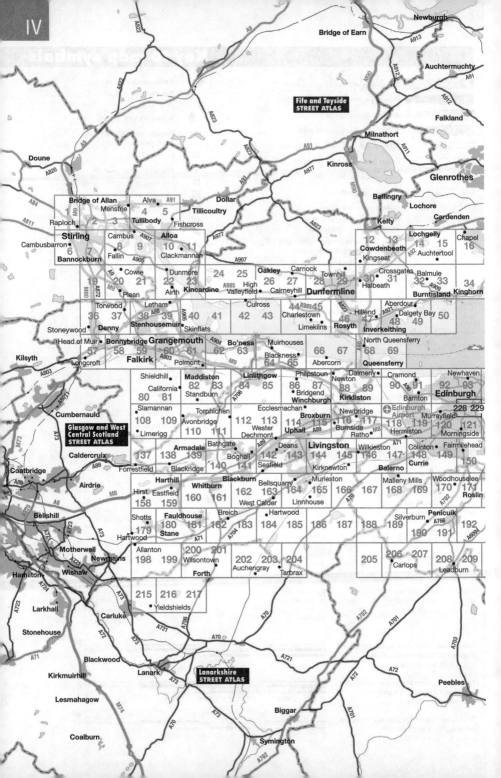

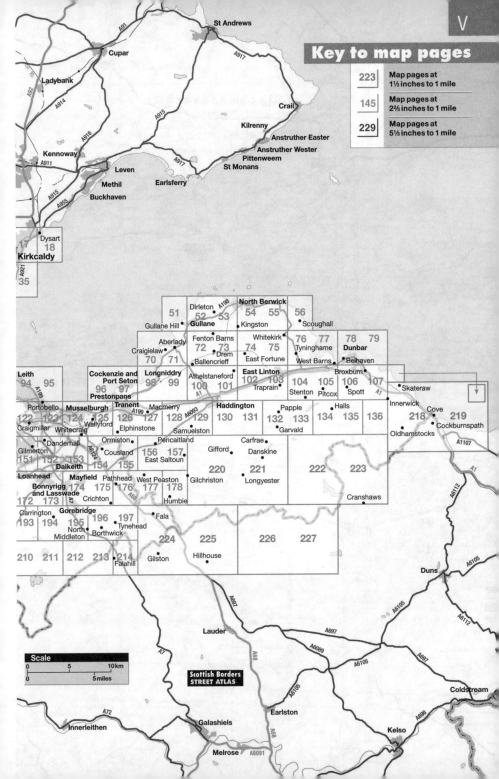

V

Key to map pages

223	Map pages at 1⅓ inches to 1 mile
145	Map pages at 2⅔ inches to 1 mile
229	Map pages at 5⅓ inches to 1 mile

St Andrews
Cupar
Ladybank
Crail
Kilrenny
Anstruther Easter
Anstruther Wester
Pittenweem
St Monans
Kennoway
Leven
Earlsferry
Methil
Buckhaven
Dysart
18
Kirkcaldy
17
35

Dirleton
North Berwick
51
52 **53** **54** **55** **56**
Gullane Hill
Gullane
Kingston
Scoughall
Aberlady
Fenton Barns
Whitekirk
76 **77** **78** **79**
Craigielaw
72 **73** **74** **75**
Tyninghame
Dunbar
Drem
Ballencrieff
East Fortune
West Barns
Belhaven
70 **71**
Athelstaneford
East Linton
Broxburn
Leith
Longniddry
100 **101** **102** **103**
104 **105** **106** **107**
94 **95**
Cockenzie and Port Seton
98 **99**
Traprain
Stenton
Pitcox
Spott
Skateraw
Portobello
96 **97**
Prestonpans
Innerwick
Cove
218 **219**
122 **123** **Musselburgh** **Tranent** Macmerry
Haddington Papple
Halls
Cockburnspath
124 **25** **126** **127** **128** **129** **130** **131** **132** **133** **134** **135** **136**
Craigmillar
Whitecraig
Wallyford
Elphinstone
Samuelston
Garvald
Oldhamstocks
Danderhall
Ormiston
Pencaitland
Carfrae
Gilmerton
151 **152** **153** Cousland
154 **155** East Saltoun
Gifford
Danskine
Loanhead
Dalkeith
Mayfield Pathhead West Peaston
220 **221** **222** **223**
Bonnyrigg and Lasswade
174 **175** **176** **177** **178**
Gilchriston
Longyester
172 **173** Crichton
Humbie
Carrington
Gorebridge
Fala
Cranshaws
193 **194** **195** **196** **197** Tynehead
North Middleton Borthwick
224 **225** **226** **227**
210 **211** **212** **213** **214** Gilston
Hillhouse
Falahill
Duns

Lauder

Scale
0   5   10km
0   5 miles

Scottish Borders STREET ATLAS

Coldstream

Innerleithen
Galashiels
Earlston
Kelso
Melrose

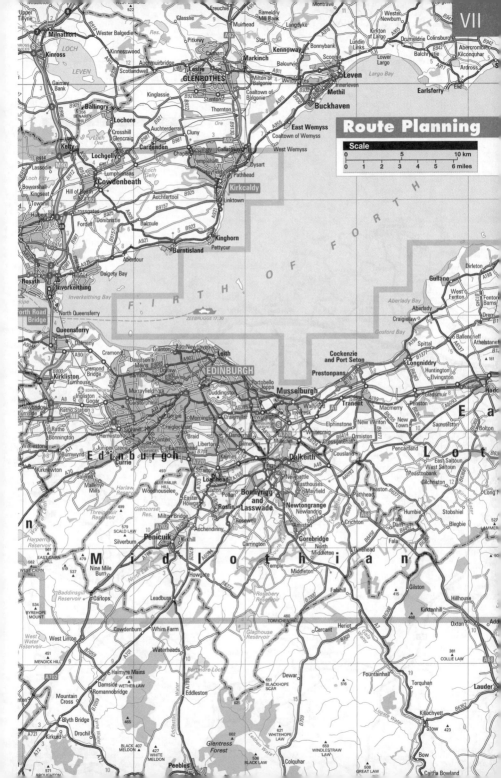

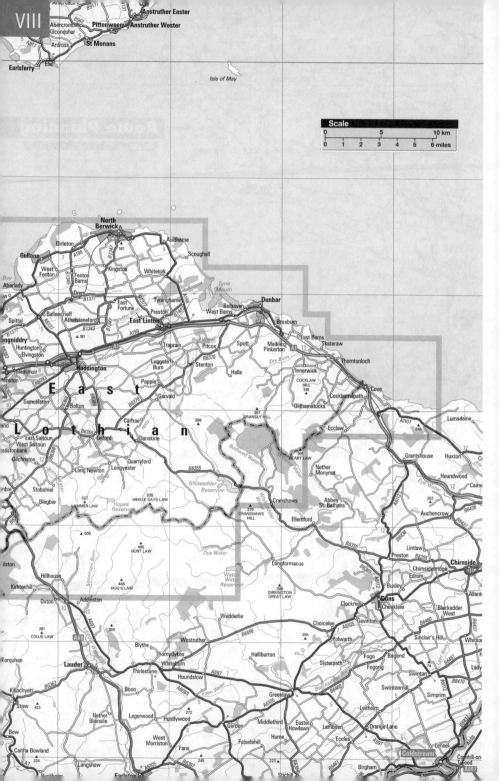

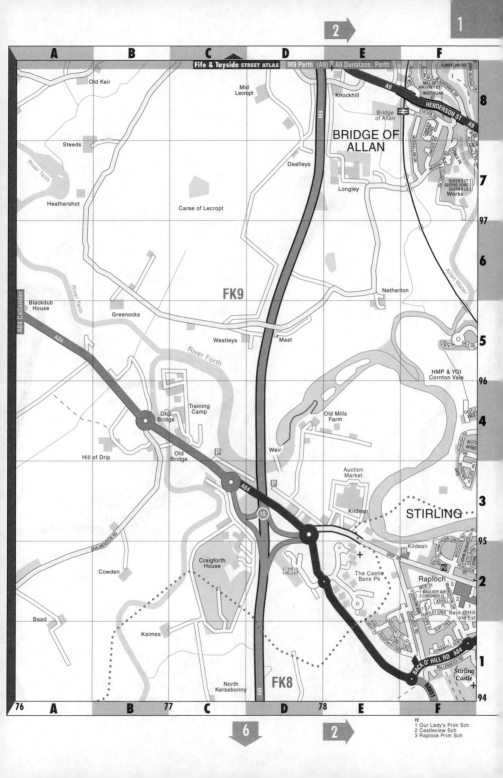

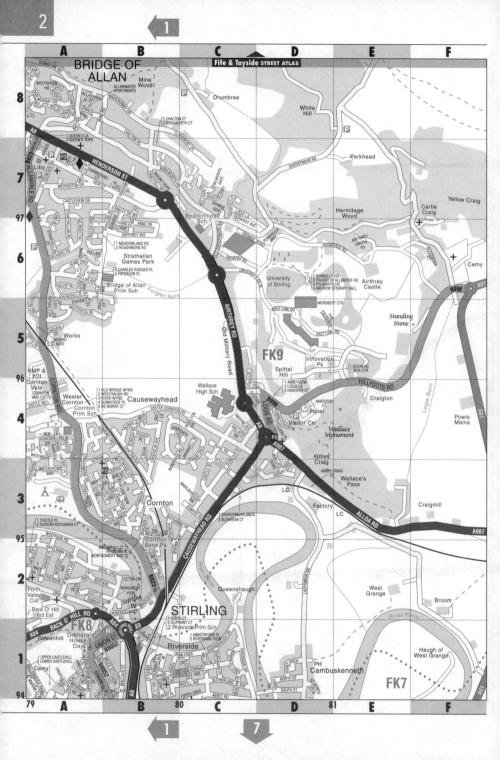

Fife & Tayside STREET ATLAS

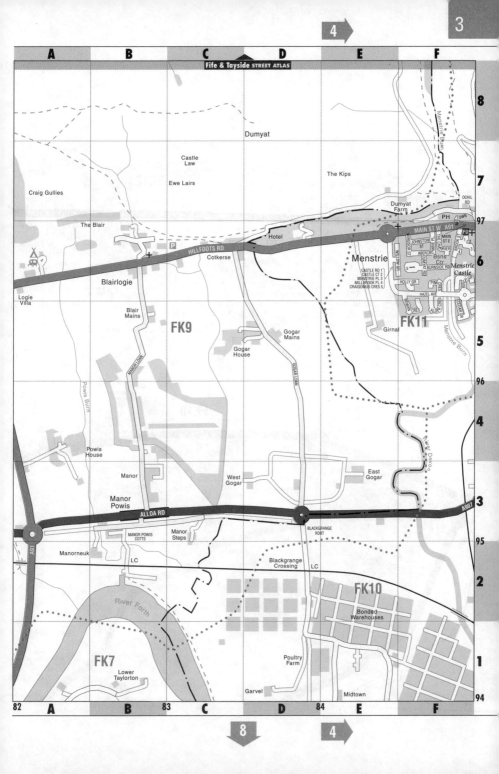

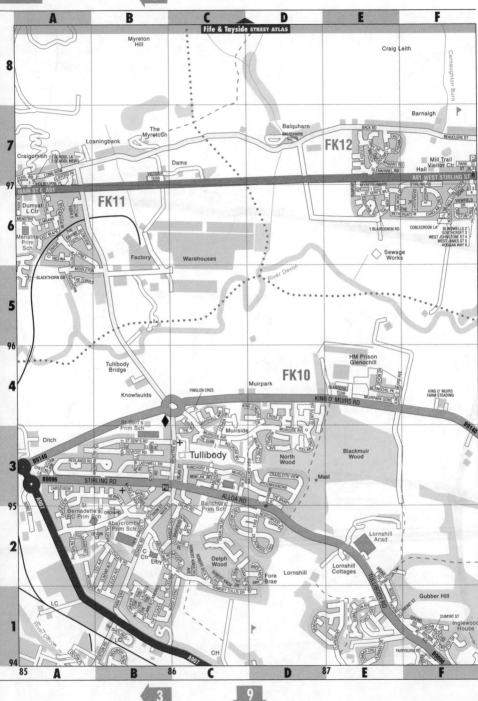

Fife & Tayside STREET ATLAS

| | A | B | C | D | E | F |

8

Myreton Hill

Craig Leith

Carnaughton Burn

Barnaigh

7

The Myretoun

Loaningbank

Balquharn

BALQUHARN COTTS

FK12

BACK RD

Craigomish

1 SCHOOL LA
2 SCHOOL MEWS

Dams

Mill Trail Visitor Ctr

Hall

BEAUCLERC ST

PARK ST

LONG ROW

CLIFFORD PK

VICTORIA TERR

ST HARRY ST

GLENWINNEL RD

DUMYAT

MYRETOUNGATE

ST SERF'S WLK

STIRLING RD

VIEWFIELD DR

97

MAIN ST E A91

OCHIL RD

1 HOLBOURNE PL

A91 WEST STIRLING ST

THE NETHERGATN

CAROL ST

FK11

PARK RD

MENSTRIE

ELMBANK

EAST MAINS

THE CAUSEWAY

1 BLAIRDENON RD

COBLECROOK LA

BLINDWELLS 2
SOUTHCROFT 3
WEST JOHNSTONE ST 4
WEST JAMES ST 5
HOGGAN WAY 6

6

Dumyat L Ctr

Menstrie Prim Sch

COLSNAUR

INCHNA

MIDDLETON

Factory

Warehouses

River Devon

Sewage Works

5

BLACKTHORN GR

THE CLOVES

96

Tullibody Bridge

HM Prison Glenochill

4

Knowfaulds

Muirpark

FINGLEN CRES

FK10

KING O' MUIRS RD

GLENOCHIL TERR

GLENOCHIL PK

MUIRPARK GDNS

KING O' MUIRS FARM STEADING

B9140

Ditch

St Serf's Prim Sch

ST SERF'S RD

DOVECOT RD

MARSHALL WY

MUIRSIDE AVE

THE GLEN

ROSE ST

MUIRSIDE AVE

PINE CT

North Wood

Blackmuir Wood

3

B9140

CHESTNUT

REDLANDS RD

LADYWELL DR

Muirside

Tullibody

BANCHORY

CRAIGLEITH VIEW

BROOMIEKNOWE

Mast

95

B9096

STIRLING RD

CARSEVIEW

NEWLAN

ALLOA RD

PO

MUIRS

THE BRAES

A907

KING ST

St Bernadette's RC Prim Sch

THE ORCHARD

Abercromby Prim Sch

Banchory Prim Sch

DELPH RD

NORTHWOOD PL

Lornshill Acad

2

COCHRIE

ROBERT KNOX

C Ctr

Liby

Delph Wood

Fore Brae

Lornshill

Lornshill Cottages

TULLIBODY RD

Gubber Hill

1

LC

River Devon

THE SHEILINGS

LC

RAMSEY TULLIS DR

DUMYAT ST

Inglewood House

WOODBURN

FAIRBURN

B9096

A907

CH

| **85** | A | **86** B | C | **87** D | E | F |

8

7

97

6

5

96

4

95

3

2

1

94

A B C D E F

88 89 C 90

Fife & Tayside STREET ATLAS

A91 Tillicoultry

A908 Tillicoultry

B9140

WEST STIRLING ST 1
COURTHILL 2
DUKE ST 3
THE GREEN 4
OCHILVIEW 5
BURNSIDE CT 6
CRAIGLEITH TERR 7

Alva Glen
Nature
Trail

Alva Glen

Rhodders
Farm

Silver Glen

Silver Burn

Ochil Hills
Woodland Park

Hotel

The
Roundal

STRUDE
MILL

MAXTON
CRES

Burnside

FK12

CH

Cemy

BEAUCLERC ST

ERSKINE ST

PARK ST

7 Lby

PO

STIRLING ST

EAST STIRLING ST

PROVOST
HUNTER
AVE

OCHIL RD

Alva
Ind Est

FK13

JOHNSTONE ST

WEST
JAMES
ST

STANLEY
ST

JAMES ST

GEORGE ST

BROOKFIELD PL

WEST
JOHNSTONE
ST

ALVA

The
Boll

JOHNSTONE CT

MINTO GDNS

MINTO
CT

Alva
Prim Sch

MEADOW

Alva
Acad

B908

BROOK ST

Spring Burn

Kersiepow

River Devon

FK10

Glenfoot

MARCHGLEN

A908

Westhaugh
Cvn Site

Howetown

BURNVIEW TERR

DANNEL HL VW

Blackfaulds

DEVON VILLAGE

BANKHEAD RD

Twentyfive Acre
Wood

Brandyhill
Wood

Collyland

COLLYLAND RD

PITFAIRN RD

ALLOA RD

Fishcross
Prim Sch

LAWSWELL

COAL POTS
WAY
DEVONBANK

Fishcross

Hamilton
Wood

WHITEYETTS
CRES

DEVON VALLEY

Fairfield

THE
ROWANS

ARNSWELL

ALCHINBA

RIVERSWELL

LOCHBRAE

CRAIGVIEW

WHITEYETTS RD

MILLARS WYND

BIRCHWOOD

FARMOUNT DR

BLAIRDENON DR

Branshill

FAIRFIELD

TEA ACRES

ABBEY CRAIG RD

MEADOW
GDNS

Fairfield
Sch

ALLOA

BRANSHILL PK

HALL PARK RD

MAIN ST RD

PO

A908

Craigbank
Prim Sch

PRESTON
TERR

GREYGORAN

NEWTONSHAW

THE HENN

MARCHSIDE

B908

BRIARS

BOLTON CT

CHURCH GR

PARKHEAD RD

MAIN ST

BIRCHWOOD

SCHAWPARK AVE

MANSFIELD AVE

GARTMORN RD

POSTHILL

ROSEBANK

Sauchie

CH

Schaw Park

Cowpark
Wood

DEERPARK

MOUNT WILLIAM

WOODLANDS

TOWER RD

Deerpark
Prim Sch
&
Lochies Sch

Mount
William

INGLEWOOD
GDNS

WOODLEA ROAD

WOODLEA PK

C1
1 HOLTON CT
2 BAILLE CT

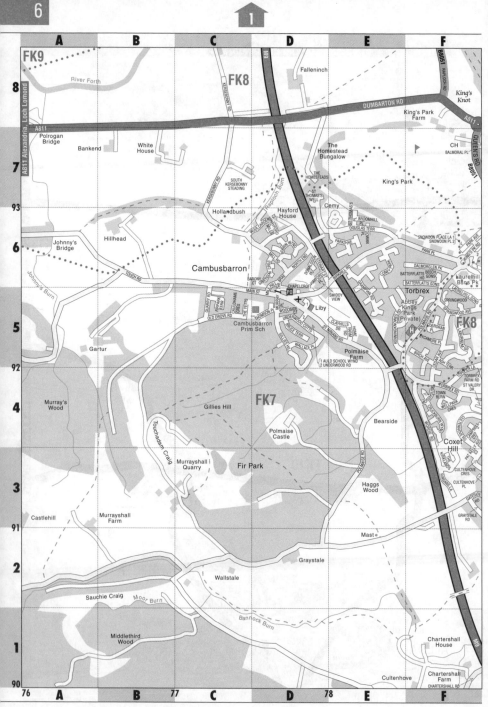

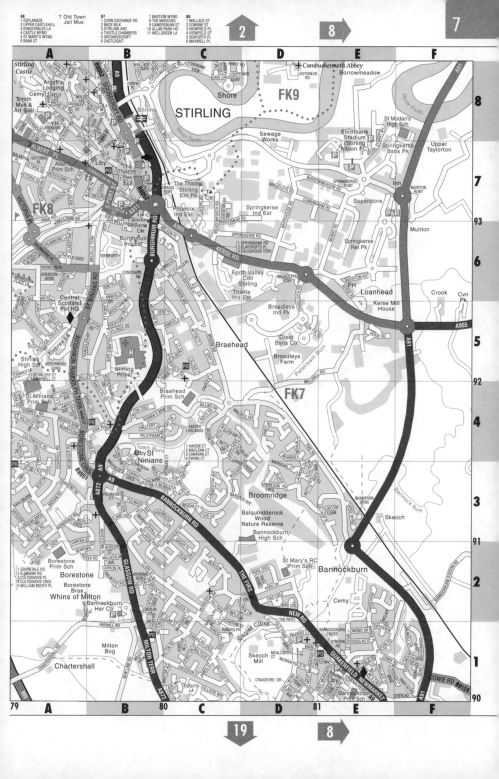

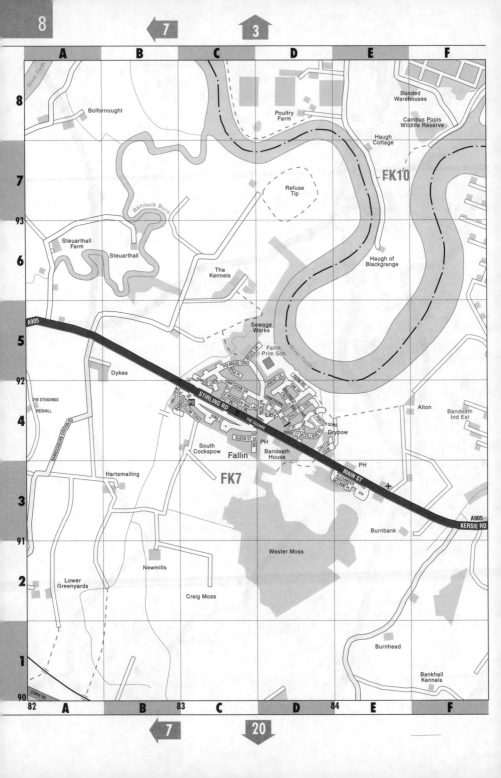

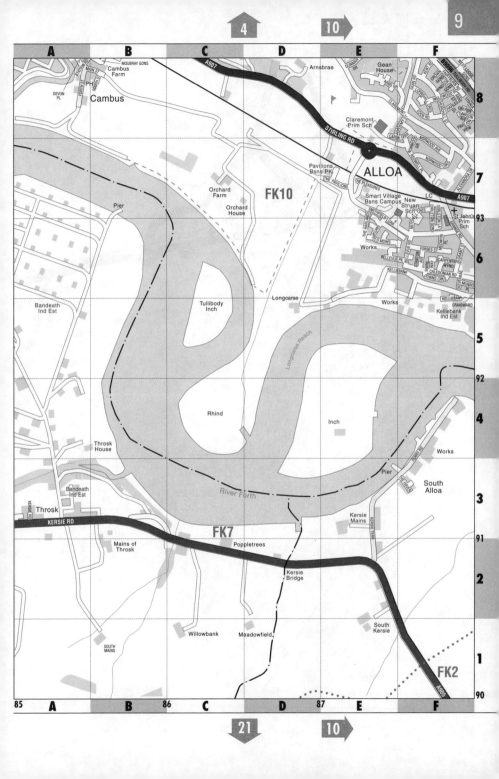

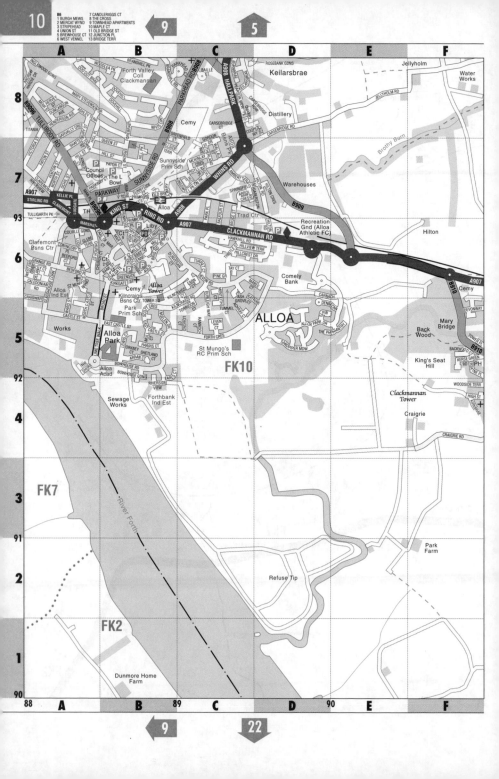

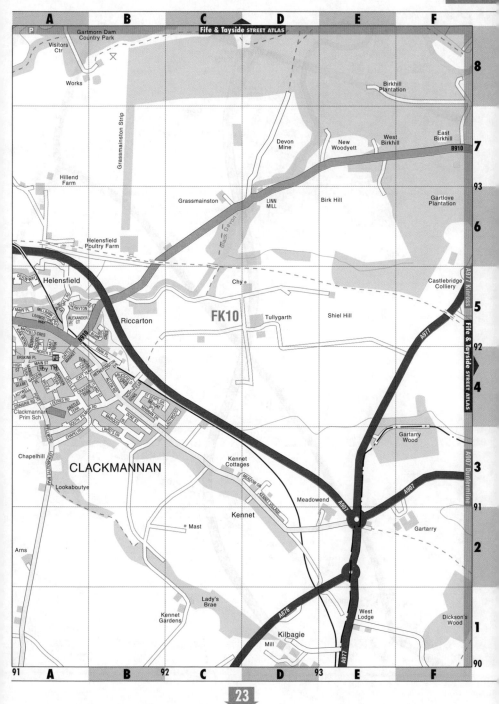

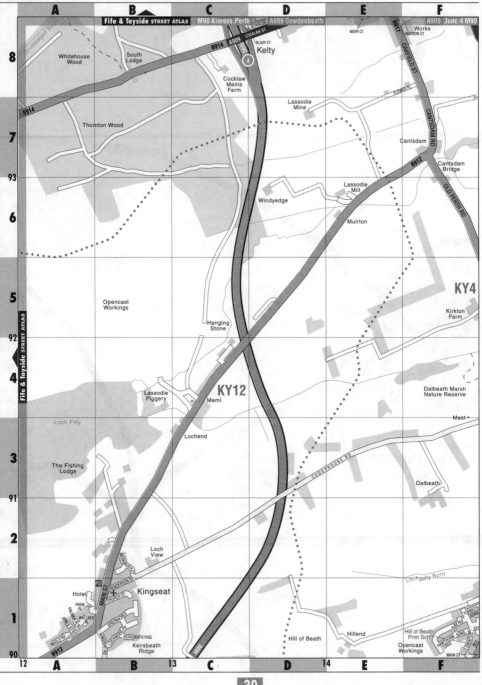

Kelty

MOIR CT
Works
WATSON CT

BLAIR ST
COCKLAW ST

Cocklaw
Mains
Farm

Lassodie
Mine

FLOWER PL

OAKFIELD ST

CANTSDAM RD

Cantsdam

Cantsdam
Bridge

Whitehouse
Wood

South
Lodge

Drummagoff Burn

B914

B914

Thornton Wood

B912

Lassodie
Mill

Windyedge

OLD PERTH RD

Muirton

Opencast
Workings

KY4

Kirkton
Farm

Hanging
Stone

KY12

Lassodie
Piggery

Meml

Dalbeath Marsh
Nature Reserve

Mast

Loch Fitty

Lochend

The Fishing
Lodge

CUDDYHOUSE RD

Dalbeath

Loch
View

Lochgelly Burn

Hotel
PO

FREW
PL

PALMER ST
WALLACE

MAIN ST

HENDERSON ST

CHURCH ST

Kingseat

GREENSIDE

GREENSIDE

NASH RD
JONES ST
KEIR ST

KEIRSBEATH RISE

Keirsbeath
Ridge

Hill of Beath

Hillend

Hill of Beath
Prim Sch

TORBEITH
GDNS

HAWTHORN GDNS
PINES

Opencast
Workings

MAIN ST

B912

A801

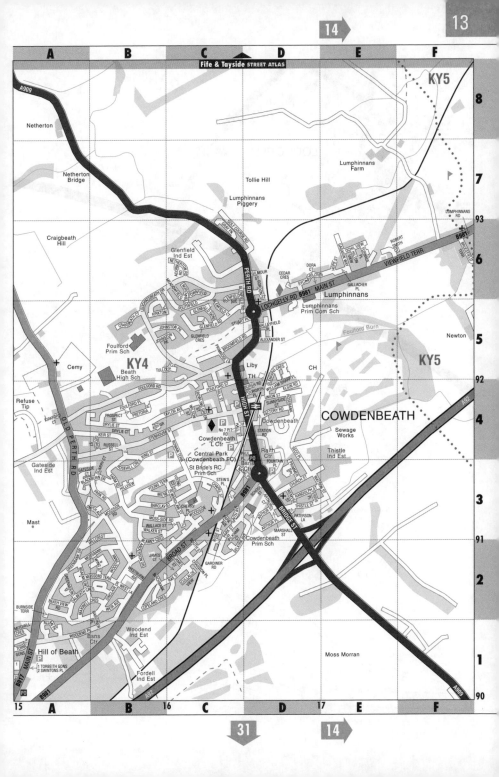

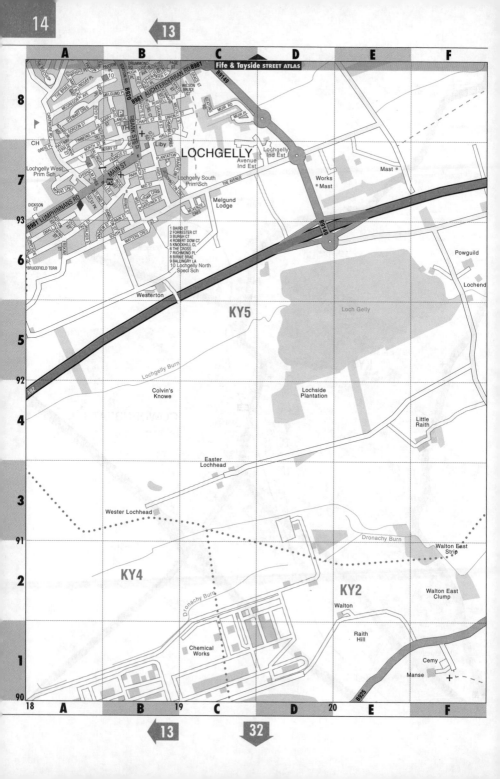

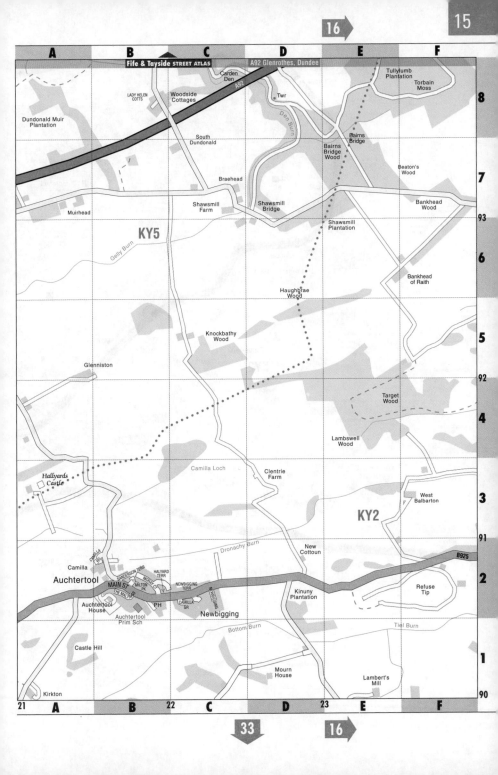

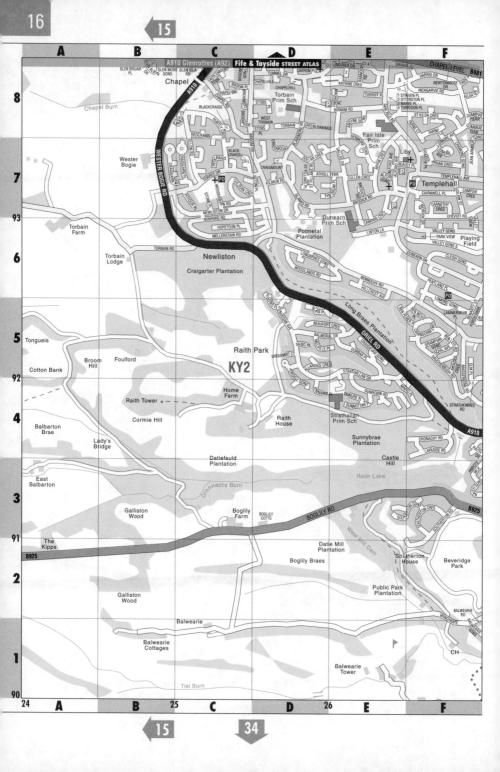

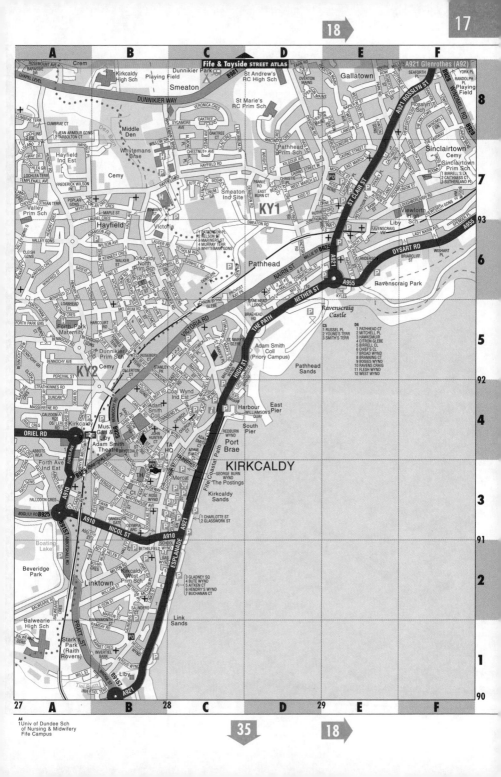

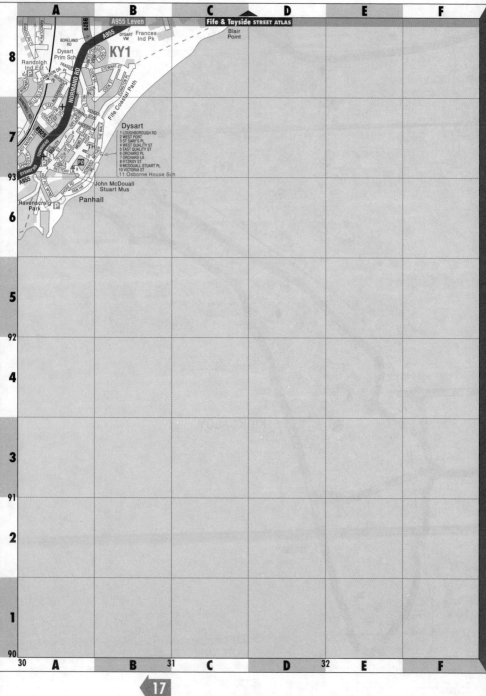

A955 Leven

DYSART Frances
VW Ind Pk

Fife & Tayside STREET ATLAS

Blair
Point

KY1

BORELAND
RD

Dysart
Prim Sch

Randolph
Ind Est

NORMAND RD

STEWART ST

Fife Coastal Path

Dysart
1 LOUGHBOROUGH RD
2 WEST PORT
3 ST SARF'S PL
4 WEST QUALITY ST
5 EAST QUALITY ST
6 ORCHARD PL
7 ORCHARD LA
8 FITZROY ST
9 MCDOUALL STUART PL
10 VICTORIA ST
11 Osborne House Sch

John McDouall
Stuart Mus

Panhall

Ravenscraig
Park

A955

PO

RECTORY LA

A955

8929

8925

30   A   B   31   C   D   32   E   F

8   7   93   6   5   92   4   3   91   2   1   90

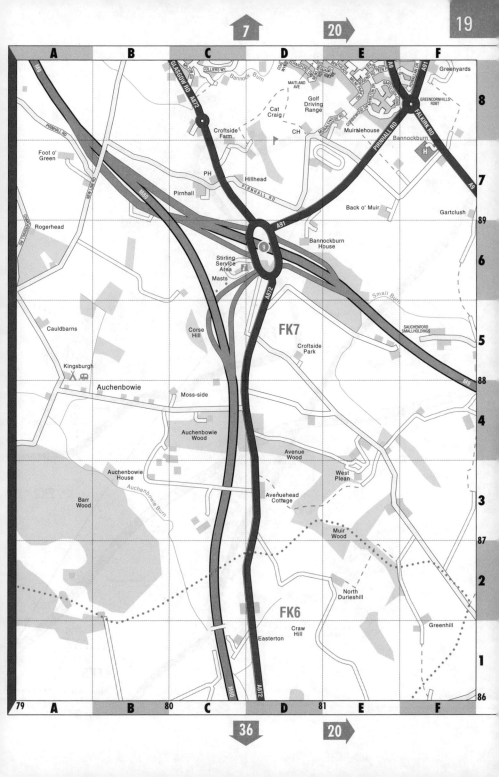

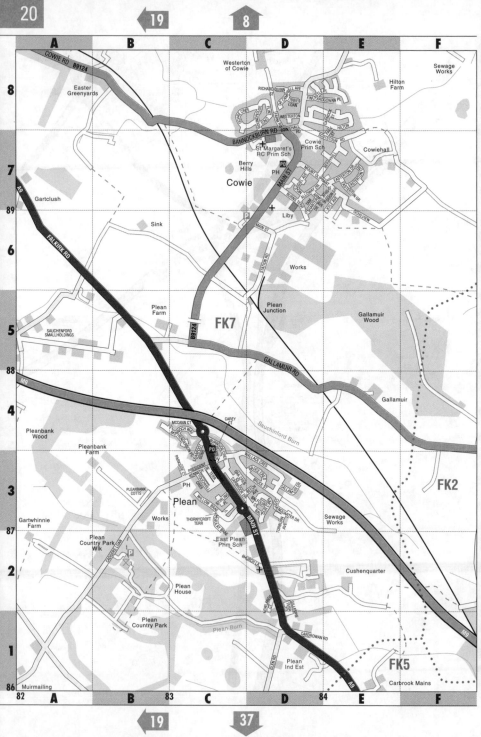

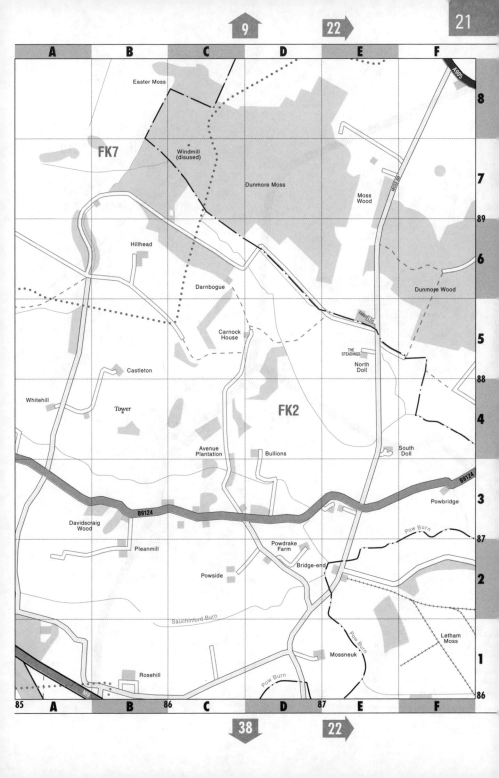

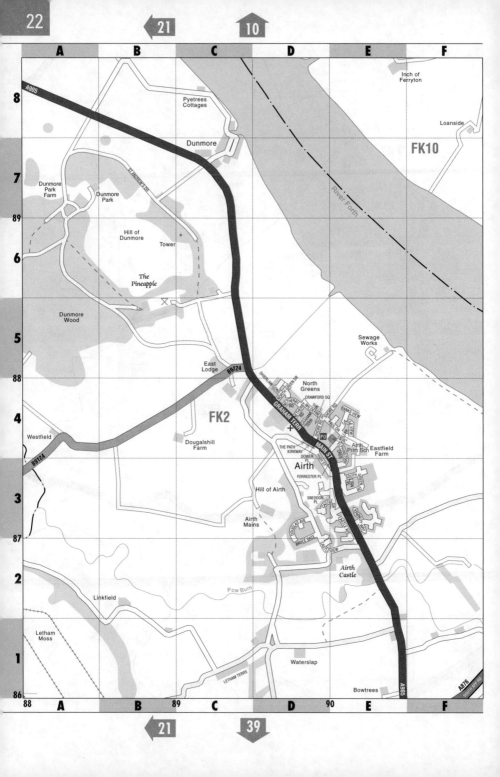

A905

8

PYETREES
COTTAGES

Inch of
Ferryton

Loanside

Dunmore

FK10

7

St ANDREW'S DR

Dunmore
Park
Farm

Dunmore
Park

89

Hill of
Dunmore

Tower

River Forth

6

The
Pineapple

Dunmore
Wood

5

Sewage
Works

East
Lodge

B9124

88

SWARLAND GREEN DR

GREEN DR

North
Greens

CRAWFORD SQ

BANKS VIEW

THERE RD

DEAN RD

FK2

4

GRAHAM TERR

SHORE RD

PARK TERR

Westfield

Dougalshill
Farm

MAIN ST

Airth
Prim Sch

Eastfield
Farm

B9124

THE PATH
KIRKWAY

DOWER

Airth

SOUTH
GREEN RD

FORRESTER PL

3

Hill of Airth

SNEDDON
PL

CASTLE

CASTLE AVE

CASTLE PL

Airth
Mains

DOUGLAS AVE

87

BRUCE GATE

GOLF VIEW

2

CASTLE RD

Linkfield

Pow Burn

Airth
Castle

Letham
Moss

1

Waterslap

86

LETHAM TERRS

Bowtrees

A905

A876

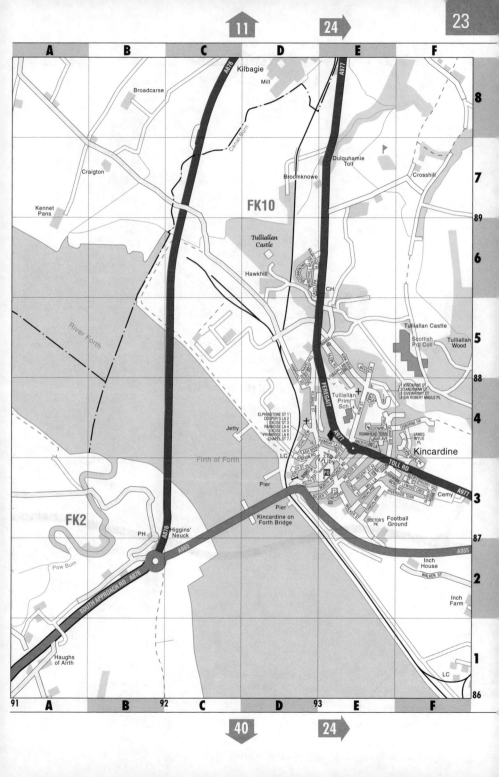

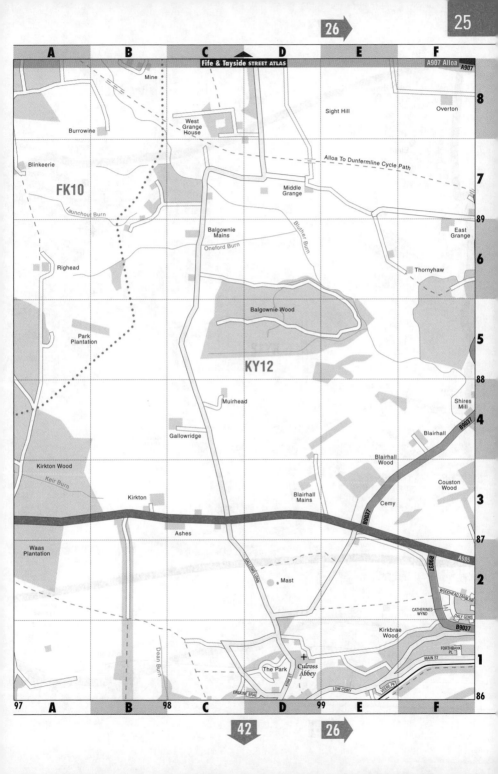

A B C D E F

Fife & Tayside STREET ATLAS

A907 Alloa

8

Overton

Sight Hill

West
Grange
House

Burrowine

Alloa To Dunfermline Cycle Path

7

Blinkeerie

89

FK10

East
Grange

Launchout Burn

Balgownie
Mains

Middle
Grange

Bluther Burn

Thornyhaw

Righead

Oneford Burn

6

Balgownie Wood

Park
Plantation

5

KY12

88

Muirhead

Shires
Mill

B9037

4

Gallowridge

Blairhall

Kirkton Wood

Blairhall
Wood

Keir Burn

Couston
Wood

Kirkton

Blairhall
Mains

Cemy

3

B9037

Ashes

87

Waas
Plantation

A985

B9037

2

WOODHEAD FARM RD

Mast

CATHERINES
WYND

DALY GDNS

B9037

Kirkbrae
Wood

FORTHBANK
PL

Dean Burn

MAIN ST

1

The Park

Culross
Abbey

VETRE PK

ERSKINE BRAE

RICK ST

LOW CSWY

86

97   A   B   98   C   D   99   E   F

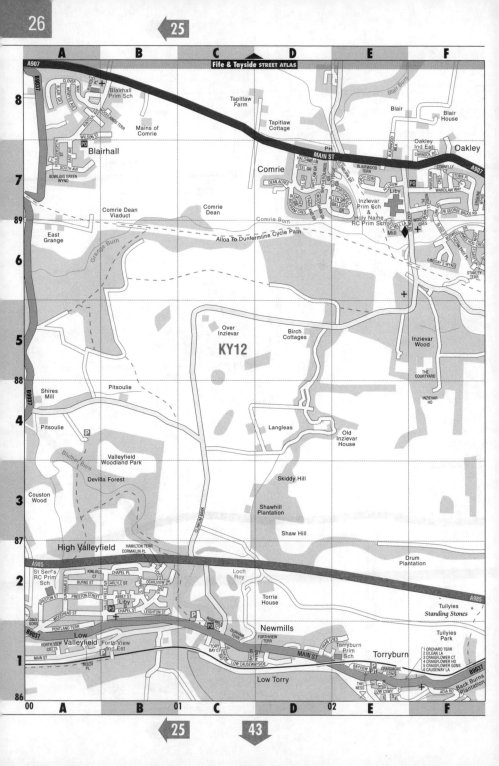

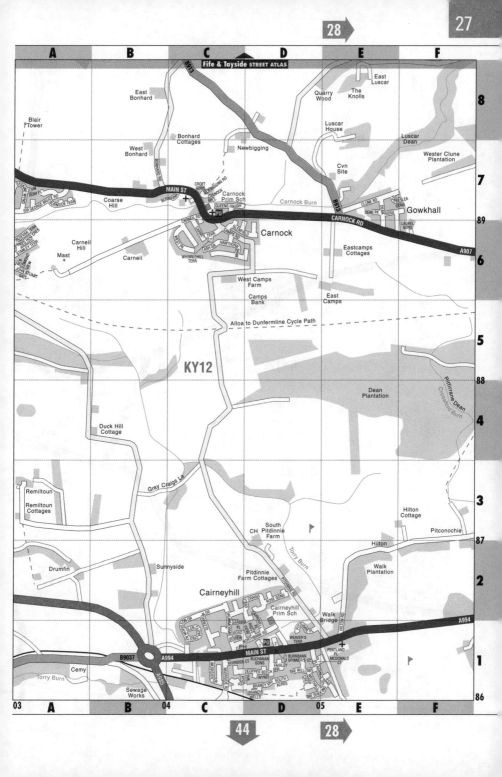

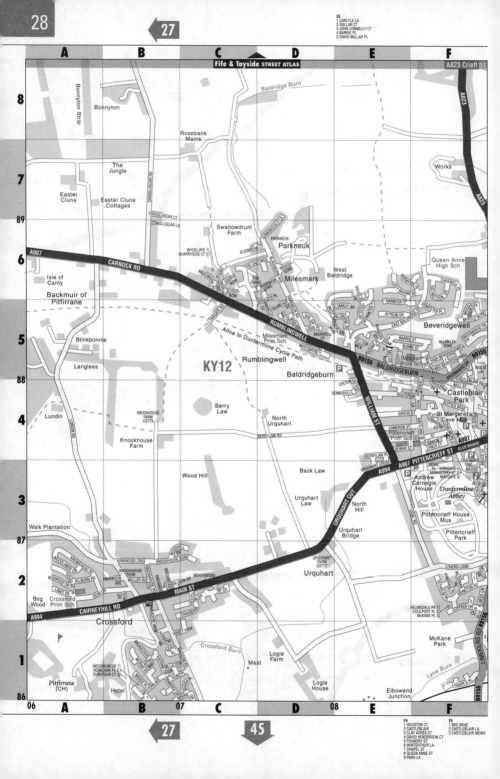

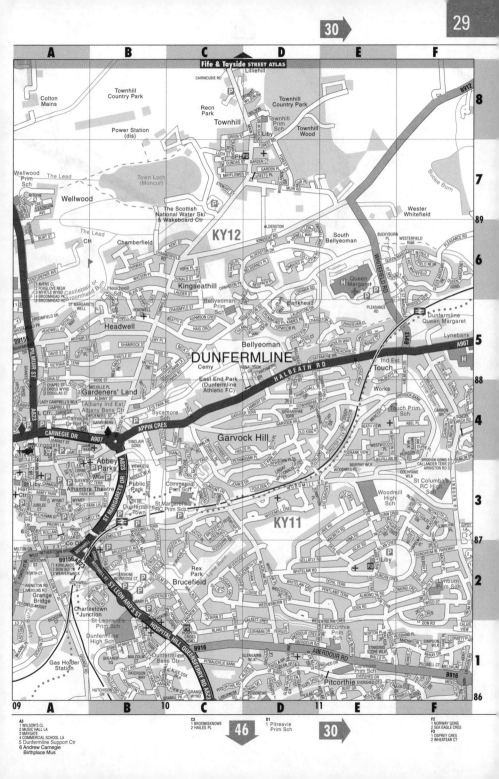

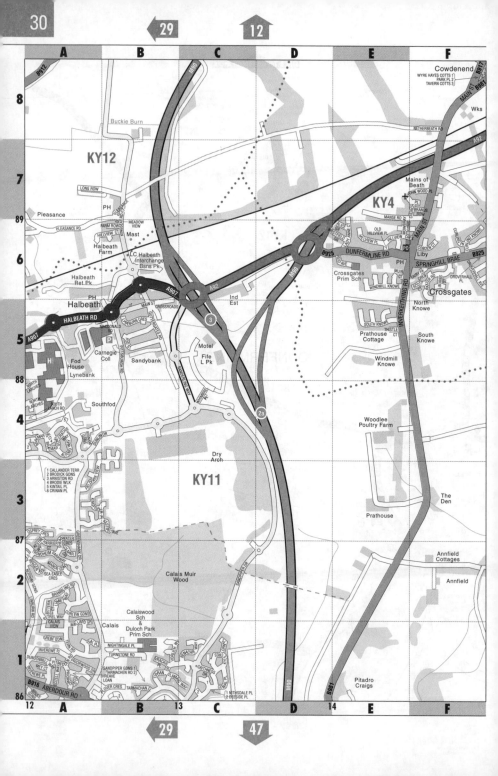

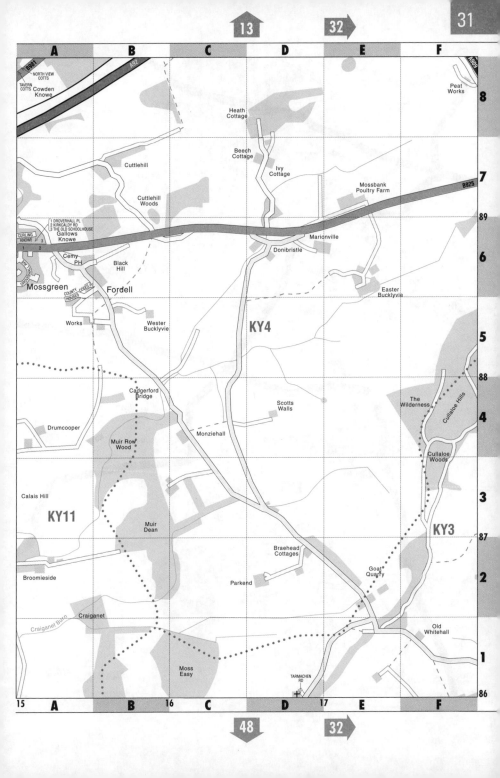

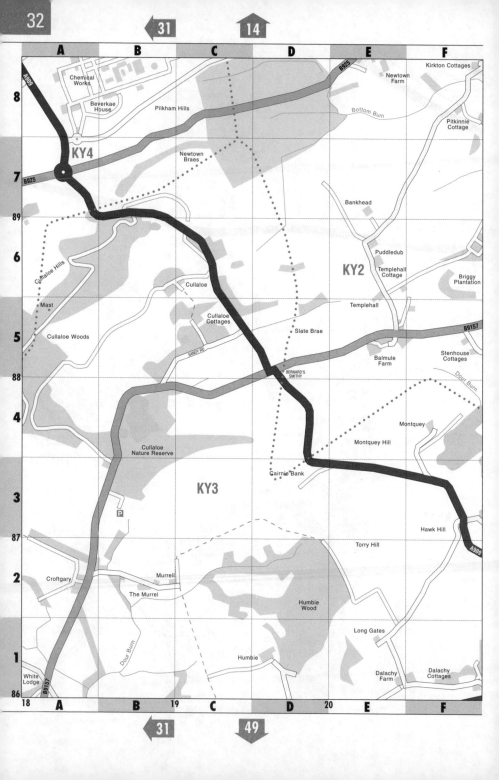

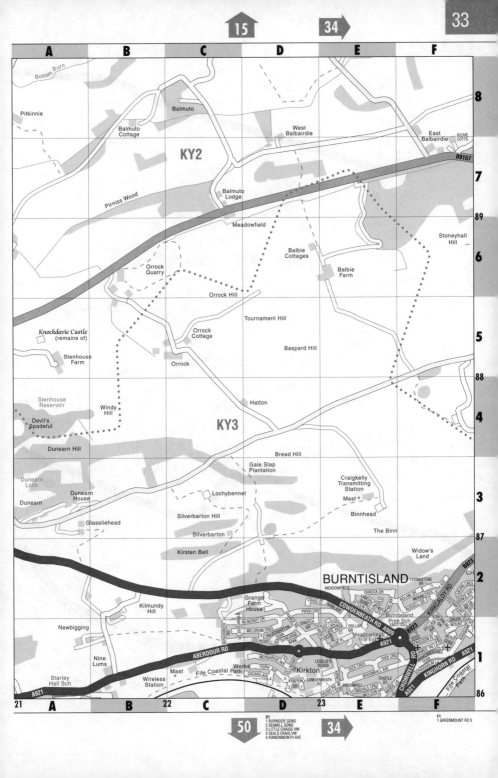

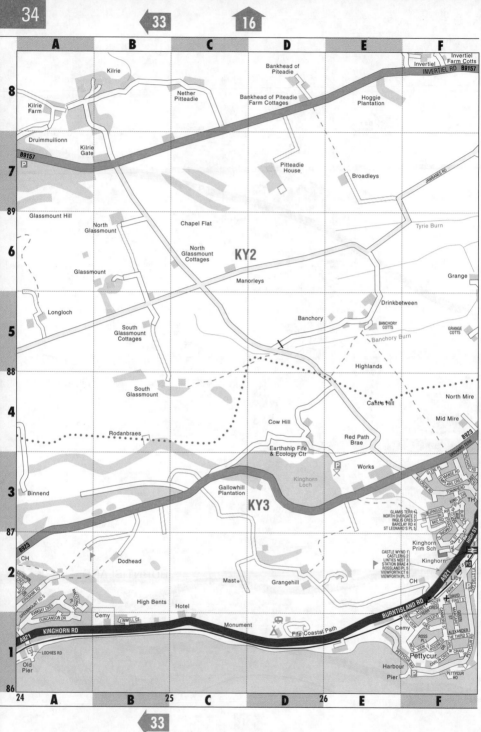

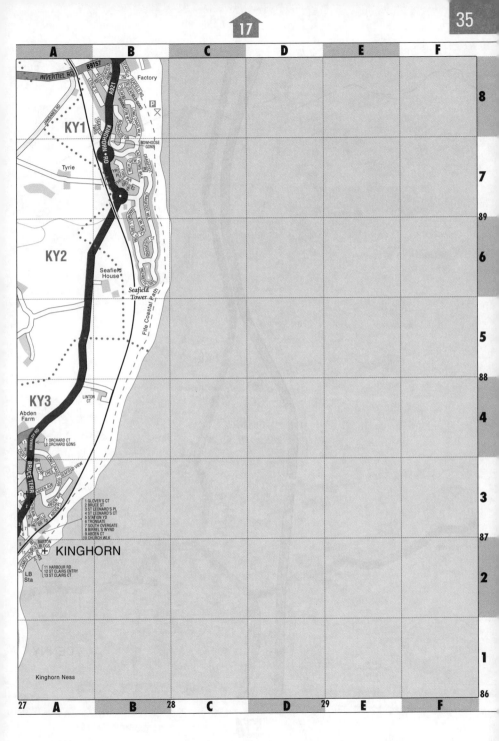

A B C D E F

8

7

89

6

5

88

4

3

87

2

1

86

INVERTIEL RD

B9157

KY1

Tyrie

KY2

Factory

KINGHORN · RD

BOWHOUSE
GDNS

Seafield
House

Seafield
Tower

Fife Coastal Path

KY3

LINTON
CT

Abden
Farm

1 ORCHARD CT
2 ORCHARD GDNS

SEAFIELD VIEW

BRUCE TERR

1 GLOVER'S CT
2 BRUCE ST
3 ST LEONARD'S PL
4 ST LEONARD'S CT
5 STATION YD
6 TRONGATE
7 SOUTH OVERGATE
8 BIRREL'S WYND
9 ABDEN CT
10 CHURCH WLK

KINGHORN

LB
Sta

11 HARBOUR RD
12 ST CLAIRS ENTRY
13 ST CLAIRS CT

Kinghorn Ness

27 A B 28 C D 29 E F

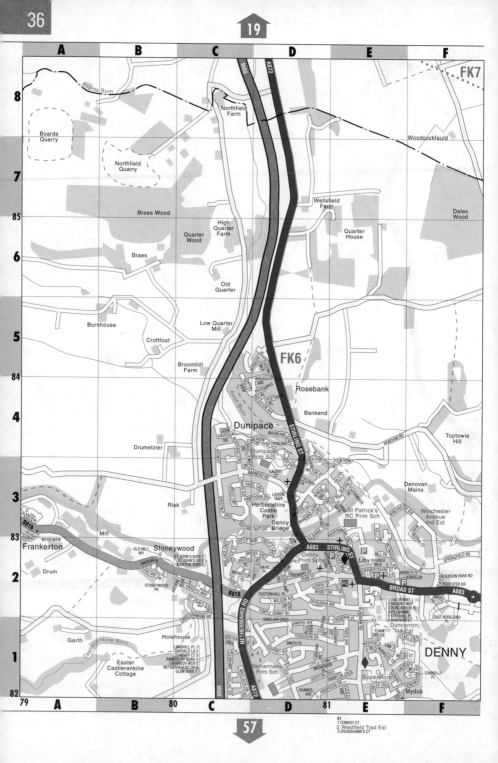

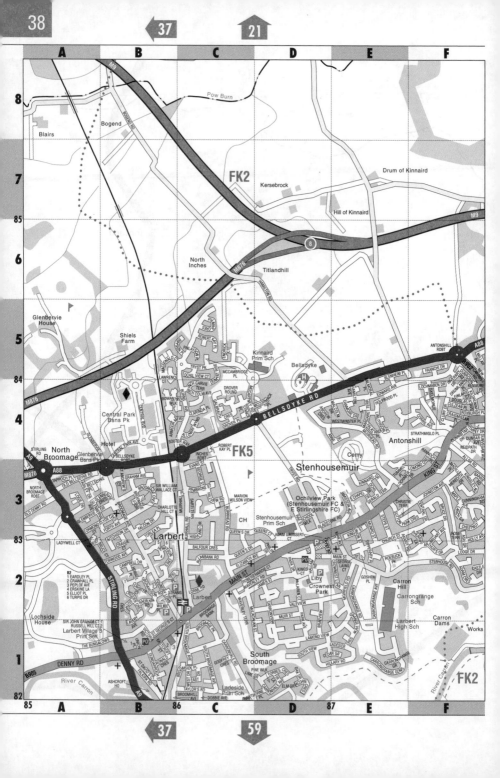

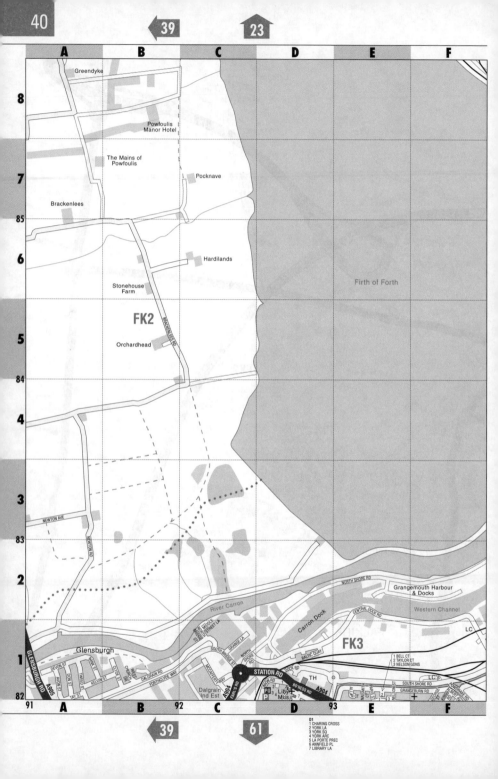

39
23

Greendyke

Powfoulis
Manor Hotel

The Mains of
Powfoulis

Pocknave

Brackenlees

Hardilands

Stonehouse
Farm

FK2

Orchardhead

Firth of Forth

NEWTON AVE

NEWTON RD

River Carron

NORTH SHORE RD

Grangemouth Harbour
& Docks

Western Channel

Carron Dock

CENTRAL DOCK RD

LC

FK3

1 BELL CT
2 TAYLOR CT
3 NELSON GDNS

GLENSBURGH RD

A905

Glensburgh

DEVON ST

AVON ST

TAY ST

YORK ST

KELVIN ST

CLYDE ST

TWEED ST

FORTHCLYDE WAY

DALGRAIN RD

SOUTH BRIDGE ST

GRANGE LA

WEST

MACKENZIE

BRODIE LA

BENNETT LA

NORTH
SHORE
RD

BALDIN QUAY

DOCK RD

SOUTH SHORE RD

GRANGEBURN RD

STATION RD

TH

A904

A904

FARM'S RD

BO'NESS RD

PO

Liby
Mus

P

Dalgrain
Ind Est

LC'S

LC'S

D1
1 CHARING CROSS
2 YORK LA
3 YORK SQ
4 YORK ARC
5 LA PORTE PREC
6 ANNFIELD PL
7 LIBRARY LA

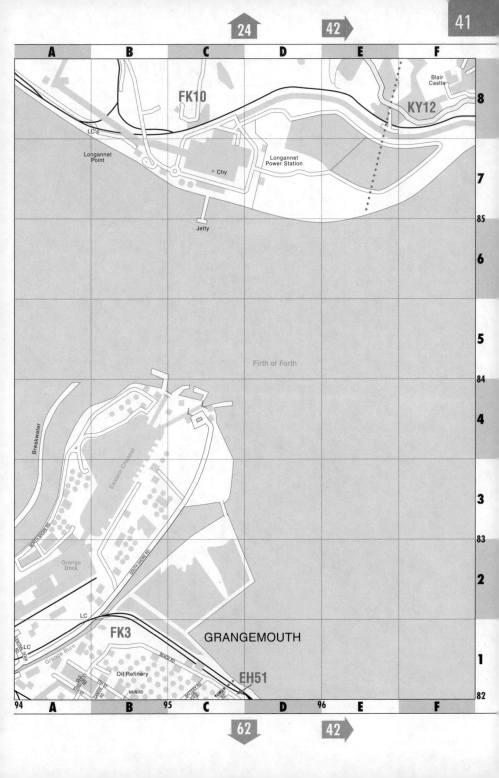

41
25

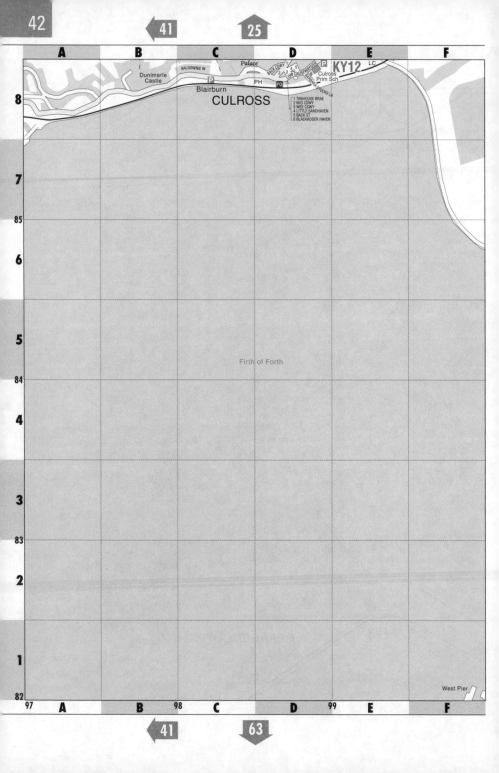

| | A | B | C | D | E | F |

Dunimarle
Castle

BALGOWNIE W

Palace

BACK CSWY

P KY12

LC

Culross
Prim Sch

P

CULROSS

Blairburn

PH

P

1 TANHOUSE BRAE
2 MID CSWY
3 WEE CSWY
4 LITTLE SANDHAVEN
5 BACK ST
6 BLACKADDER HAVEN

8

7

85

6

5

Firth of Forth

84

4

3

83

2

1

82

West Pier

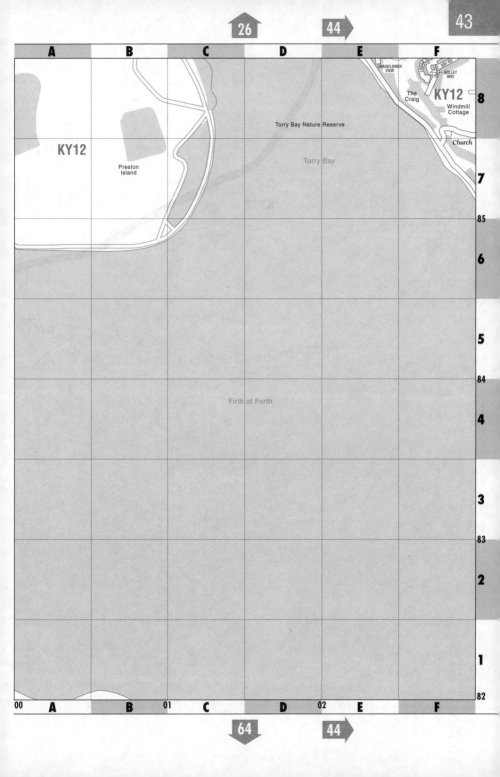

Torry Bay Nature Reserve

CRAIGFLOWER VIEW

The Craig

KY12

Windmill Cottage

Church

KY12

Preston Island

Torry Bay

GOLLET WAY

Firth of Forth

43
27

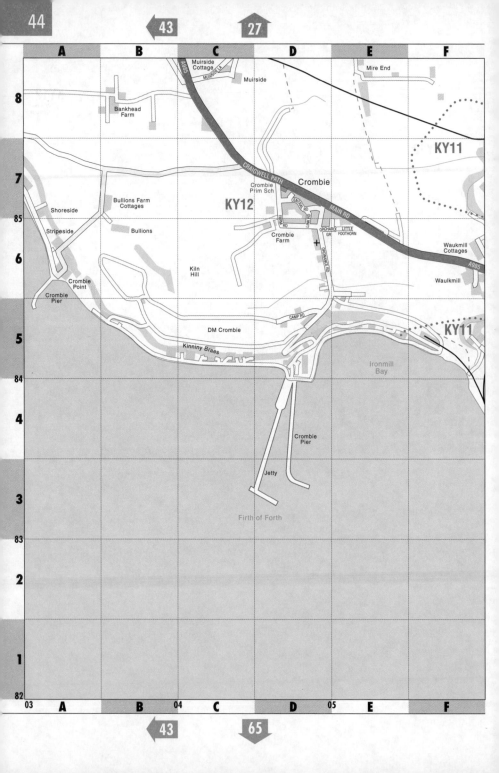

43
65

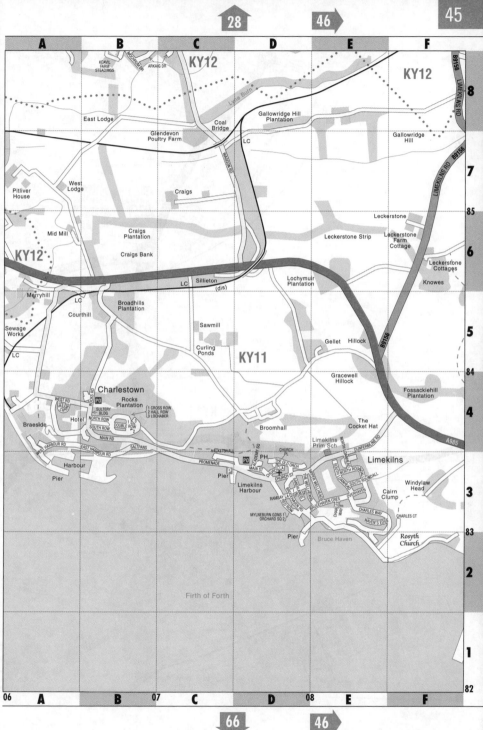

KY12

KY12

B9156
LIMEKILNS RD

East Lodge

Coal
Bridge

Gallowridge Hill
Plantation

Gallowridge
Hill

KEAVIL
FARM
STEADINGS

MOUNTJOY DR

ARKAIG DR

Glendevon
Poultry Farm

LC

WAGGON RD

B9156

LIMEKILNS RD

Pitliver
House

West
Lodge

Craigs

Leckerstone

Leckerstone Strip

Leckerstone
Farm
Cottage

Mid Mill

Craigs
Plantation

Leckerstone
Cottages

KY12

Craigs Bank

Lochymuir
Plantation

Knowes

Merryhill

LC

Sillieton

(dis)

B9156

LC

Broadhills
Plantation

Courthill

Sawmill

KY11

Gellet

Hillock

Sewage
Works

Curling
Ponds

Gracewell
Hillock

Fossackiehill
Plantation

LC

Charlestown

Rocks
Plantation

1 CROSS ROW
2 HALL ROW
3 LOCHABER

The
Cocket Hat

A985

WEST RD

PO

ROCKS RD

SULTERY
BLDG

NORTH ROW

1
2
3

DOUBLE ROW

1
2

Broomhall

Limekilns
Prim Sch

JUNIPER LEA RD

Limekilns

Braeside

Hotel

SOUTH ROW

MAIN RD

SALTPANS

CHURCH
PL

NORTH ROW

SOUTH ROW

ROUNDALL

Windylaw
Head

WEST HARBOUR RD

EAST HARBOUR RD

HALKETSHALL

PROMENADE

MAIN ST

CHURCH

PH

THE OLD ORCH

CHURCH ST

ACADEMY SQ

GREEN WELL PLACE

STREET WILLIAM CO

SOUTH CASTLE

Cairn
Clump

Harbour

Pier

PO

Pier

Limekilns
Harbour

RAMSAY LA

CROSS ST

WALTERS HAVEN RD

BRUCEHAVEN CRES

CHARLES WAY

OVERHAVEN

CHARLES CT

CHARLES CT

MYLNEBURN GDNS 1
ORCHARD SQ 2

HAVEN'S EDGE

Pier

Bruce Haven

Rosyth
Church

Firth of Forth

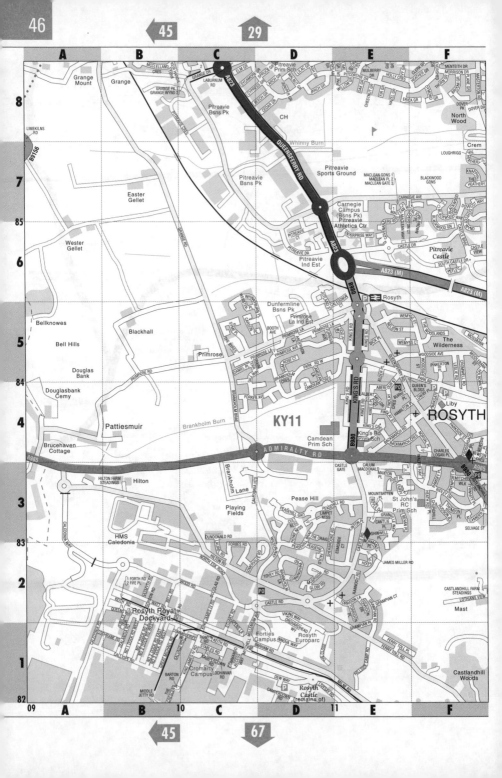

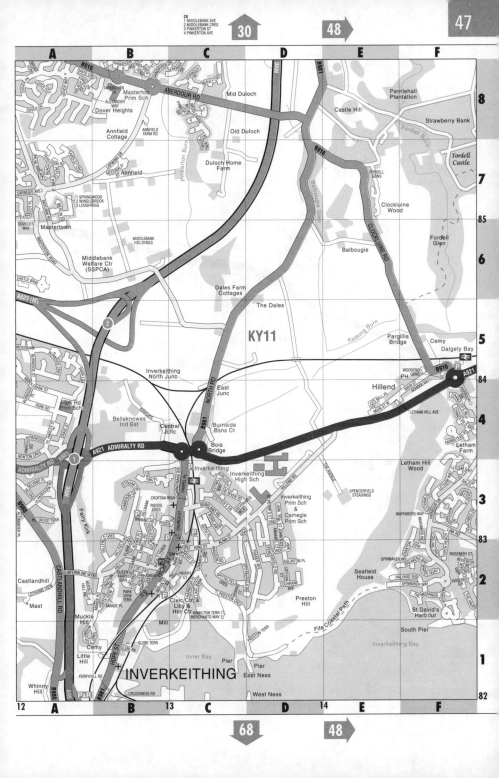

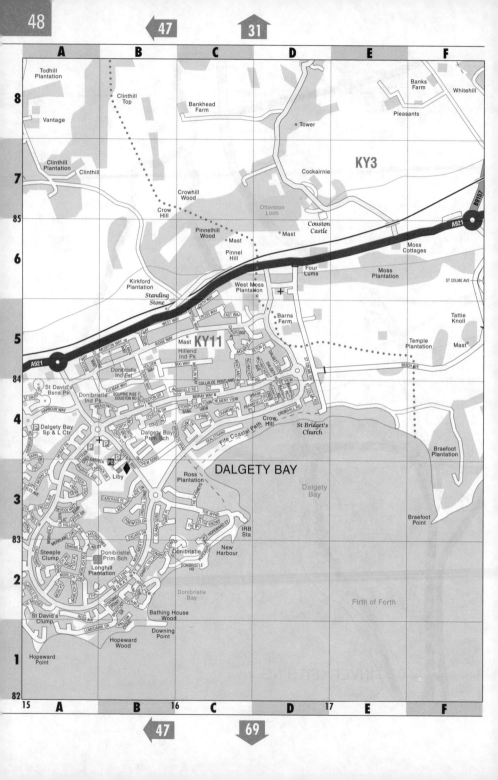

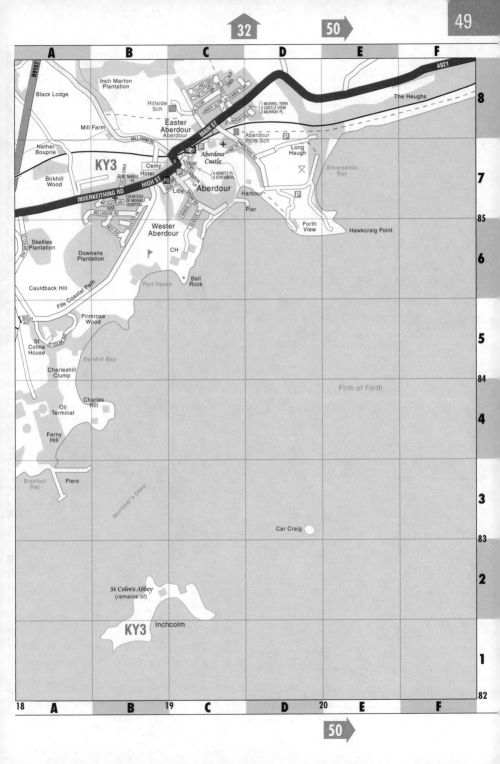

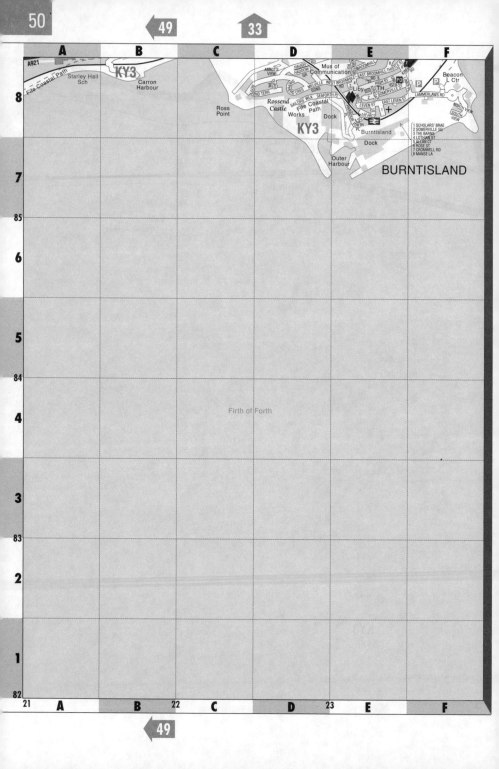

49

33

A921

File Coastal Path

Starley Hall Sch

KY3

Carron Harbour

Ross Point

Rossend Castle

Mus of Communication

ABBOT'S VIEW

HAUGH RD

BROOMHILL

EAST BROOMHILL

THISTLE

HIGH ST

Beacon L Ctr

NORTH VIEW

SOUTH VIEW

LAMMERLAWS RD

Works

Sailors' Wlk

Fife Coastal Path

Dock

Liby

T.H.

EAST LEVEN ST

SOMERVILLE ST

KY3

Burntisland

Dock

Outer Harbour

1 SCHOLARS' BRAE
2 SOMERVILLE SQ
3 THE BARNS
4 LOTHIAN ST
5 ALCAN CT
6 ROSE ST
7 CROMWELL RD
8 MANSE LA

BURNTISLAND

Firth of Forth

A B C D E F

21 22 23

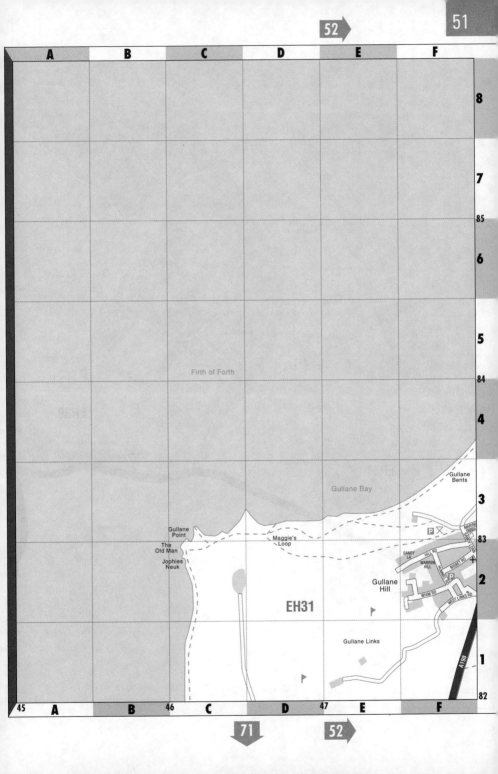

Firth of Forth

Gullane Bay

Gullane Bents

Gullane Point

Maggie's Loop

The Old Man

Jophies Neuk

SANDY LA
HILL RD
WARREN HILL
NISBET RD
SALINE RD
MARINE TERRACE
STATION RD

Gullane Hill

WHIM RD
WEST LINKS RD

EH31

Gullane Links

A198

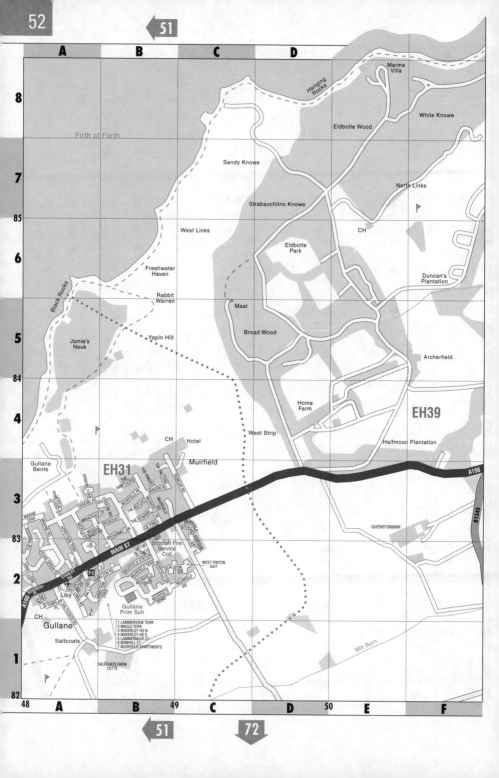

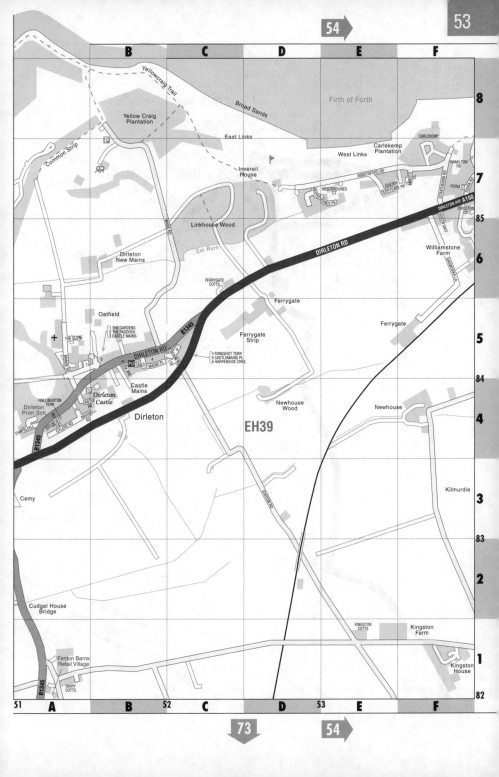

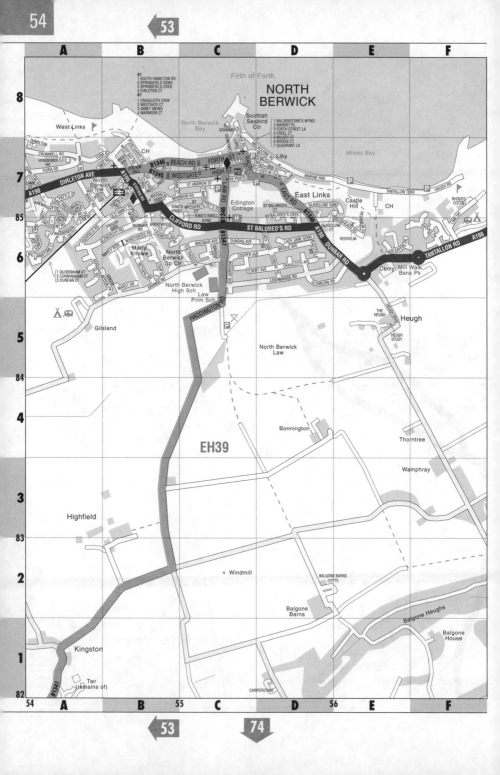

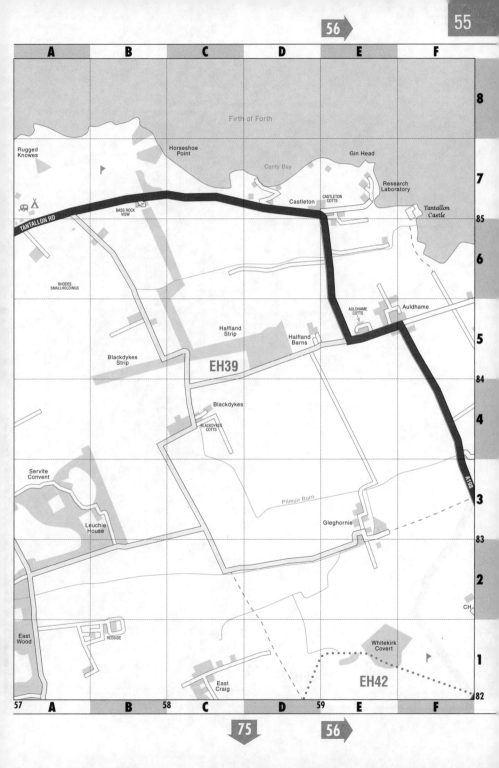

A   B   C   D   E   F

8

Firth of Forth

Rugged
Knowes

Horseshoe
Point

Gin Head

7

Canty Bay

Research
Laboratory

Castleton

CASTLETON
COTTS

TANTALLON RD

BASS ROCK
VIEW

Tantallon
Castle

85

6

RHODES
SMALLHOLDINGS

AULDHAME
COTTS

Auldhame

Halfland
Strip

Halfland
Barns

5

Blackdykes
Strip

EH39

84

Blackdykes

4

BLACKDYKES
COTTS

Servite
Convent

A198

Pilmuir Burn

3

Gleghornie

Leuchie
House

83

CH

2

East
Wood

REDSIDE

Whitekirk
Covert

1

East
Craig

EH42

82

8

7

85

6   Auldhame

Cave

5   SEACLIFF COTTS

Seacliff

84

Chapel Brae

4   Crow Wood

EH39

Pilmuir Burn

SCOUGHALL COTTS

Scoughall

3   A198

83

Coastguard Lookout

2   New Mains

Scoughall Links

Power Burn

Peffer Sands

Pefferside

1

EH42

82

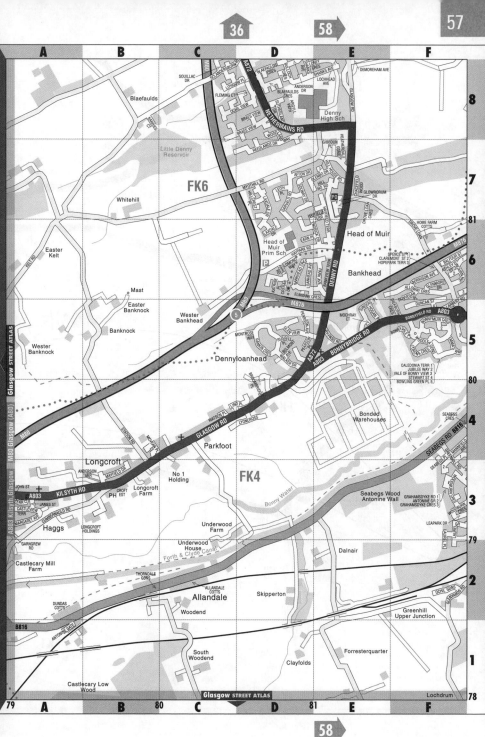

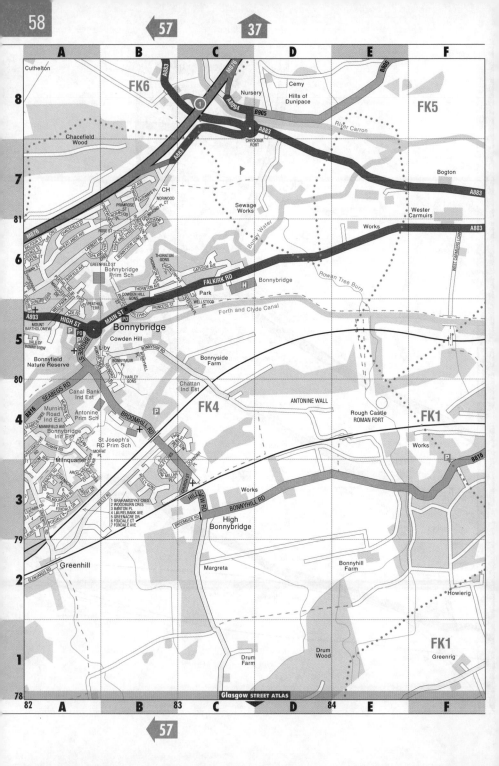

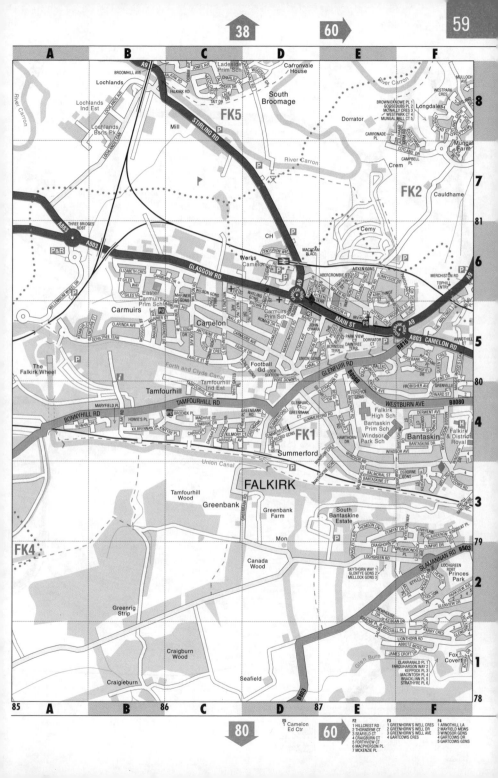

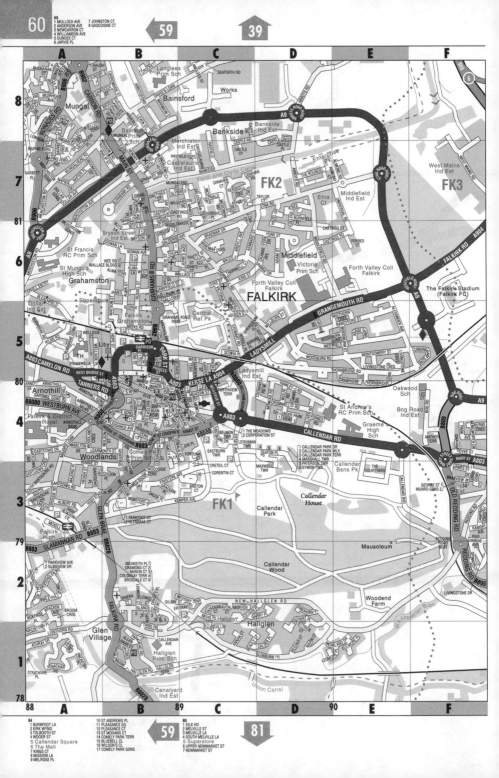

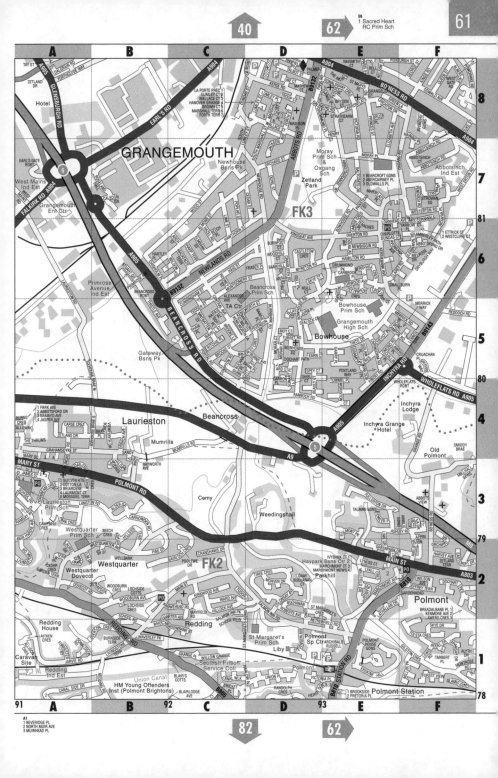

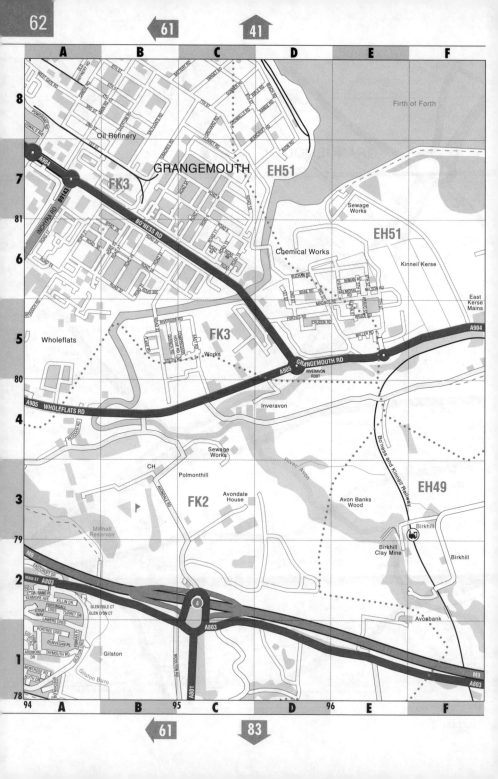

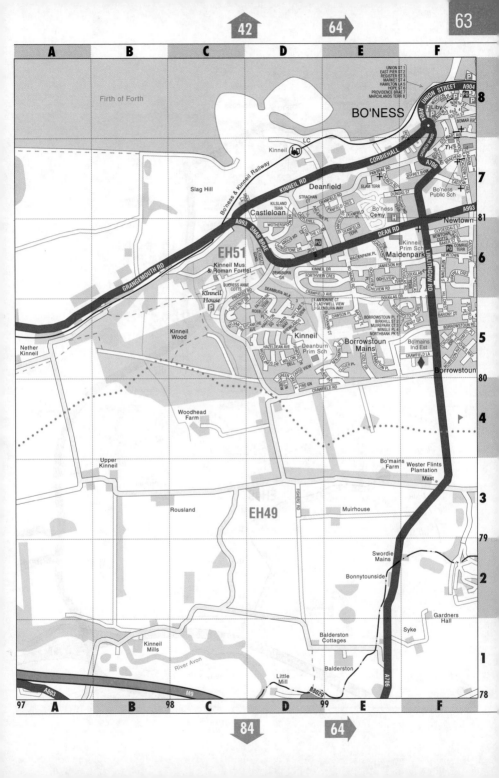

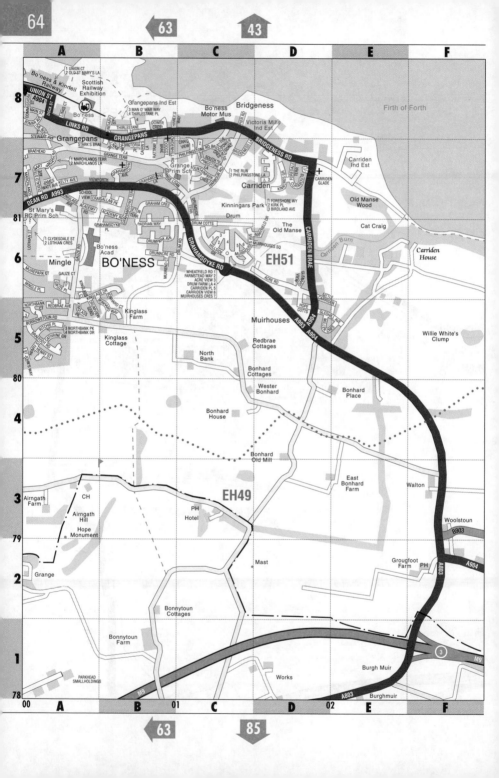

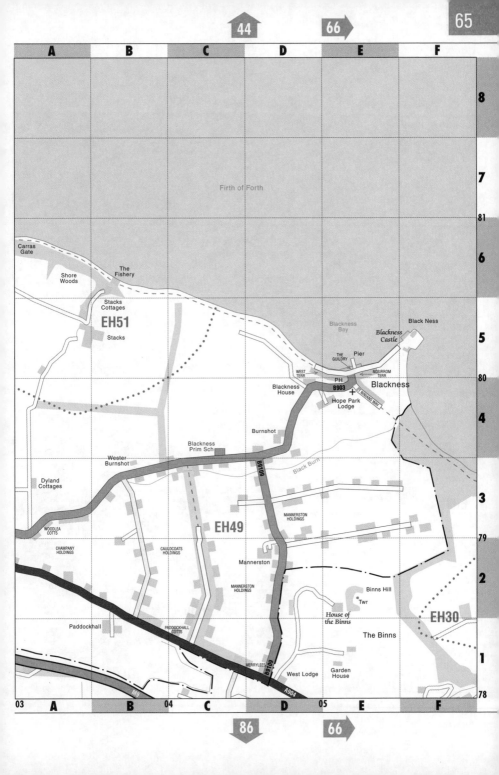

A B C D E F

8

7

Firth of Forth

81

6

Carras
Gate

Shore
Woods

The
Fishery

Stacks
Cottages

EH51

Stacks

Blackness
Bay

Black Ness

Blackness
Castle

5

THE
GUILDRY

Pier

WEST
TERR

NOSIRROM TERR

80

PH

B903

Blackness

Blackness
House

Hope Park
Lodge

ST NINIANS WAY

4

Burnshot

Black Burn

Blackness
Prim Sch

Wester
Burnshot

B9109

Dyland
Cottages

3

WOODLEA
COTTS

MANNERSTON
HOLDINGS

EH49

79

CHAMPANY
HOLDINGS

CAULDCOATS
HOLDINGS

Mannerston

2

MANNERSTON
HOLDINGS

Binns Hill

Twr

EH30

House of
the Binns

The Binns

Paddockhall

PADDOCKHALL
COTTS

1

MERRYLEES

B9109

M9

West Lodge

Garden
House

A904

78

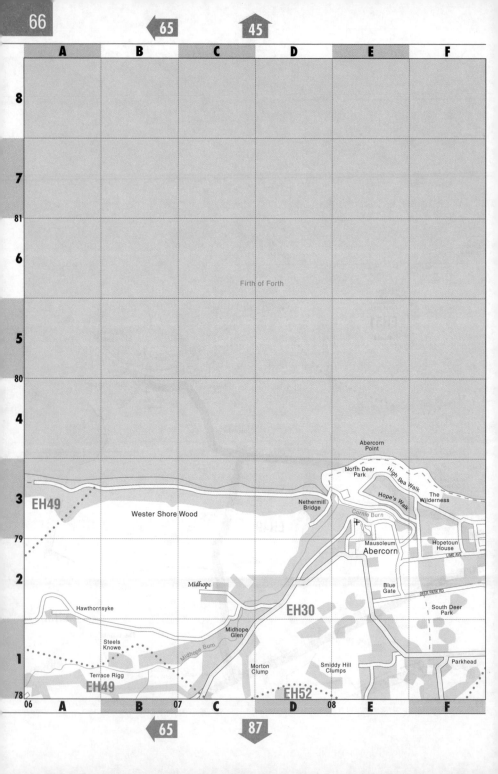

A   B   C   D   E   F

8

7

81

6

Firth of Forth

5

80

4

Abercorn
Point

North Deer
Park

High Sea Walk

3

EH49

Wester Shore Wood

Nethermill
Bridge

Hope's Walk

The
Wilderness

Cornie Burn

79

Mausoleum

Hopetoun
House

Abercorn

LIME AVE

2

Midhope

Blue
Gate

DEER PARK RD

South Deer
Park

EH30

Hawthornsyke

Midhope
Glen

Steels
Knowe

Midhope Burn

1

Terrace Rigg

Morton
Clump

Smiddy Hill
Clumps

Parkhead

EH49

78

EH52

06   A   B   07   C   D   08   E   F

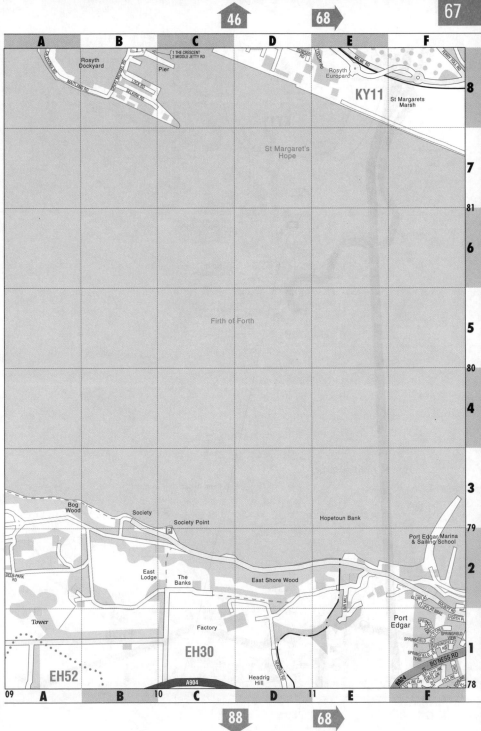

A B C D E F

8

KY11

Rosyth
Dockyard

Pier

1 THE CRESCENT
2 MIDDLE JETTY RD

Rosyth
Europarc

St Margarets
Marsh

CALFFORN RD
MAITLAND RD
WEST MIDDLE RD
LOCK RD
SELKIRK RD
DUNDAS RD
TY550N RD
MILNE RD
FERRY TOLL RD

St Margaret's
Hope

7

81

6

Firth of Forth

5

80

4

3

79

Bog
Wood

Society

Society Point

Hopetoun Bank

Port Edgar Marina
& Sailing School

DEEP-PARK
RD

East
Lodge

The
Banks

East Shore Wood

CLUFFLAT
CLUFFLAT BRAE
SOCIETY RD
FORTH PL

2

Tower

Factory

EH30

Port
Edgar

SPRINGFIELD
SPRINGFIELD
VIEW
SPRINGFIELD
PL
SPRINGFIELD
TERR

1

EH52

A904

Headrig
Hill

HEADRIG RD

LIN MILL

BO NESS RD
B924
ECHLINE DR
ECHLINE
ECHLINE
ESTATE

78

09 A B 10 C D 11 E F

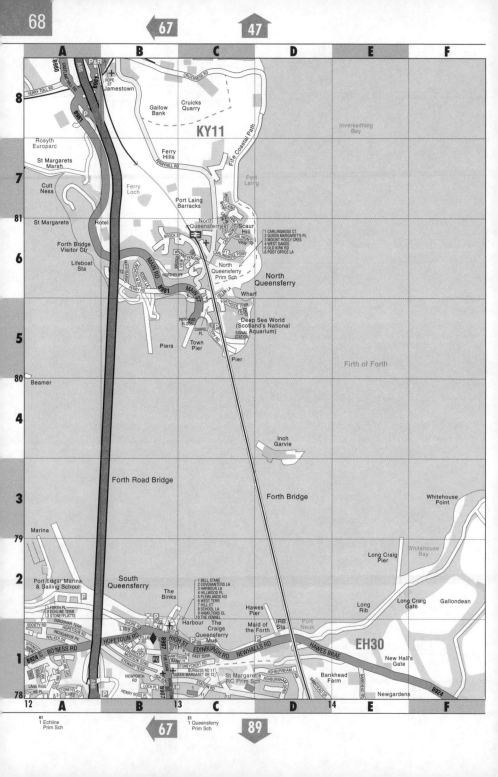

A B C D E F

8

KY11

Inverkeithing
Bay

Cruicks
Quarry

Gallow
Bank

CRUICKS RD

File Coastal Path

B980

EASTFIELD RD

B981

FERRY TOLL RD

Ferry Toll Rd
Jamestown
HOPE ST

P&R

Rosyth
Europarc

7

St Margarets
Marsh

Ferry
Hills

FERRYHILL RD

Port
Laing

Cult
Ness

Ferry
Loch

Port Laing
Barracks

WEST CRAIGS

PORT LAING

81

St Margarets

Hotel

North
Queensferry

Scaur
Hill

1 CARLINGNOSE CT
2 QUEEN MARGARET'S PL
3 MOUNT HOOLY CRES
4 WEST SANDS
5 OLD KIRK RD
6 POST OFFICE LA

BROCK ST

6

Forth Bridge
Visitor Ctr

MAIN RD

FERRY LA

B981

WHINNYKNOWE

NORTHCLIFF

MAIN ST

CARLINGNOSE POINT

North
Queensferry
Prim Sch

North
Queensferry

Lifeboat
Sta

FERRYBANK

Wharf

HELEN LA

FORTHSIDE TERR

PIER-HEAD
BLDGS

5

Piers

Town
Pier

CHAPEL
PL

BATTERY RD

Deep Sea World
(Scotland's National
Aquarium)

SIGNAL
STATION

Pier

80

Beamer

Firth of Forth

4

Inch
Garvie

3

Forth Road Bridge

Forth Bridge

Whitehouse
Point

79

Marina

Whitehouse
Bay

Long Craig
Pier

2

Port Edgar Marina
& Sailing School

South
Queensferry

The
Binks

1 BELL STANE
2 COVENANTERS LA
3 HARBOUR LA
4 HILLWOOD PL
5 WEST TERR
6 WEST TERR
7 HILL CT
8 SCHOOL LA
9 HAMILTONS CL
10 THE VENNEL

Hawes
Pier

Maid of
the Forth

IRB
Sta

Port
Neuk

Long
Rib

Long Craig
Gate

Long Craig
Pier

Gallondean

1 FORTH PL
2 ECHLINE TERR
3 STONEYFLATTS

SOCIETY RD

FARQUHAR TERR

INCHGARVIE PK

HOPETOUN RD

WALKER DR

Liby

SHORE RD

ROSE LA

Harbour

The
Craigs
Queensferry
Mus

EDINBURGH RD

NEWHALLS RD

HAWES BRAE

EH30

New Hall's
Gate

1

B924

BO'NESS RD

HOPETOUN RD

MORISON GDNS

NEW HALLS RD

High St

B907

HAMILTON
BANK

EAST TERR

STONEYCROFT RD

St Margaret's
RC Prim Sch

ASHBURNHAM

ASHBURNHAM LA

Bankhead
Farm

BANKHEAD RD

B924

LANG RIGG

78

STONEYFLATTS
CRES

VIEWFORTH
RD

LOCH PL

HENRY ROSS PL

B907

BURGESS RD
QUEEN MARGARET DR

STATION RD

Newgardens

Newgardens

12 A B 13 C D 14 E F

| A | B | C | D | E | F |

8

7

81

6

5

80

4

Firth of Forth

Tanker
Berths

Hound
Point

Pealdraught
Bay

The
Warrens

Fishery
Cottage

3

79

Leuchold

Leuchold Wood

EH30

Castle Craig
Clump

Castle
Craig

Midlothian
Clump

Crow
Thickets

Barnbougle
Castle

2

Mons Hill

Dalmeny Park

Peacock Ride

New England

Dalmeny
House

Livingston
Clump

1

78

15 A   B 16 C   D 17 E   F

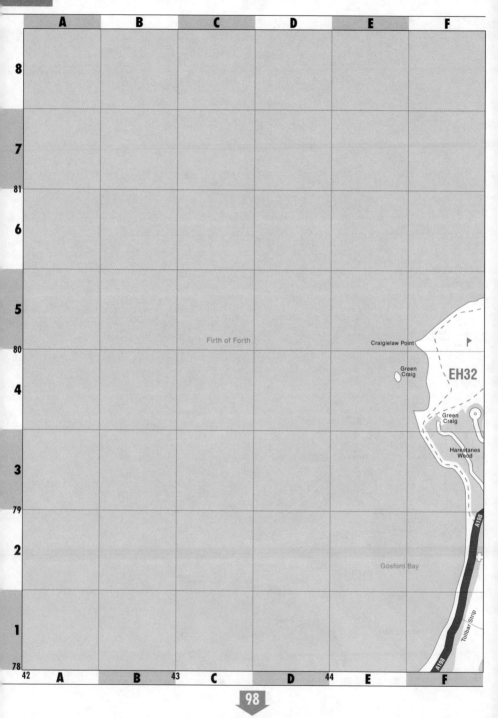

Firth of Forth

Craigielaw Point

Green Craig

EH32

Green Craig

Harestanes Wood

A198

Gosford Bay

A198

Tollbar Strip

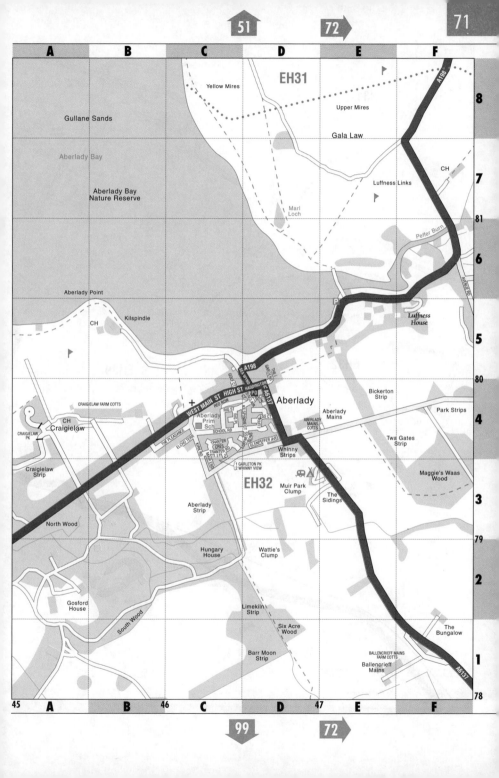

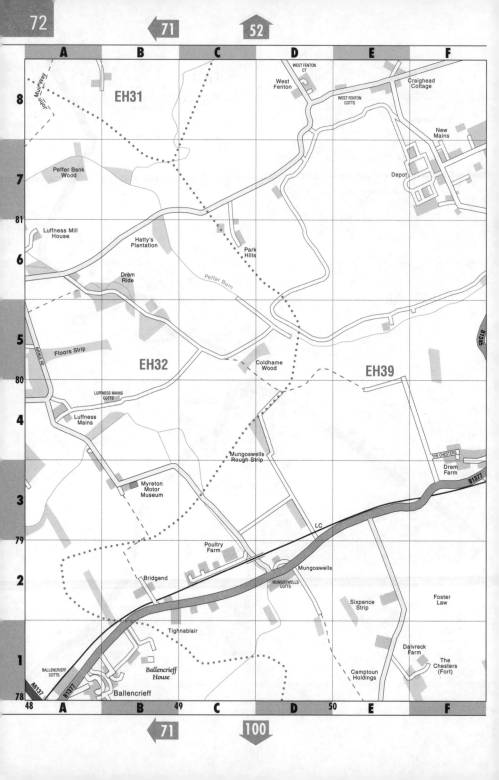

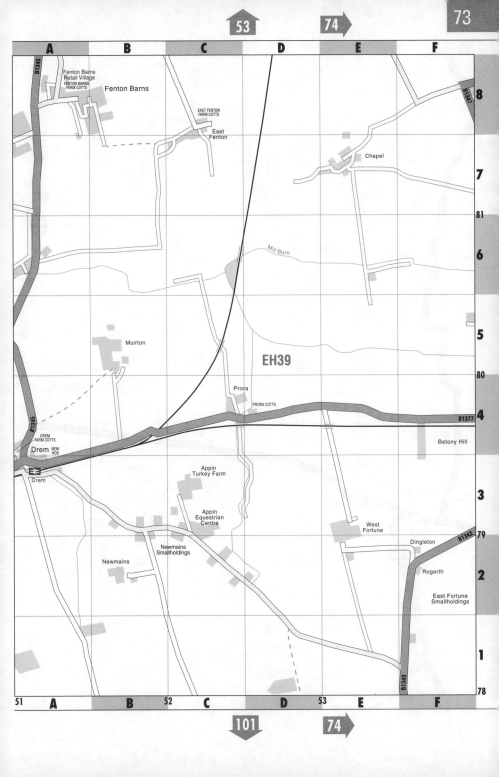

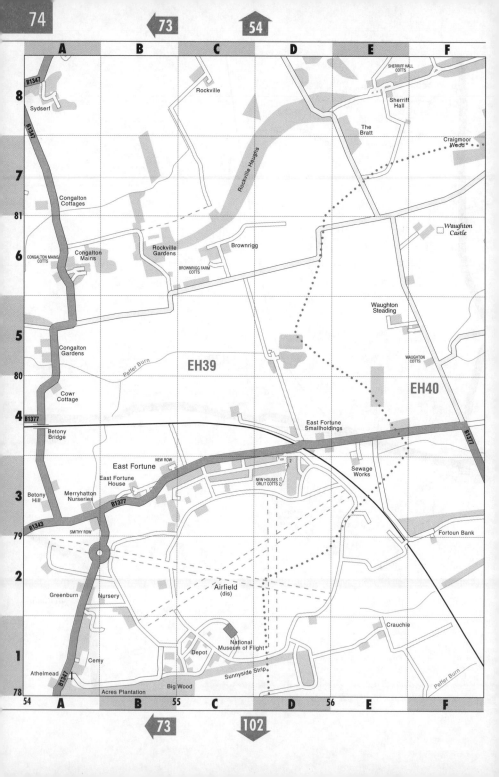

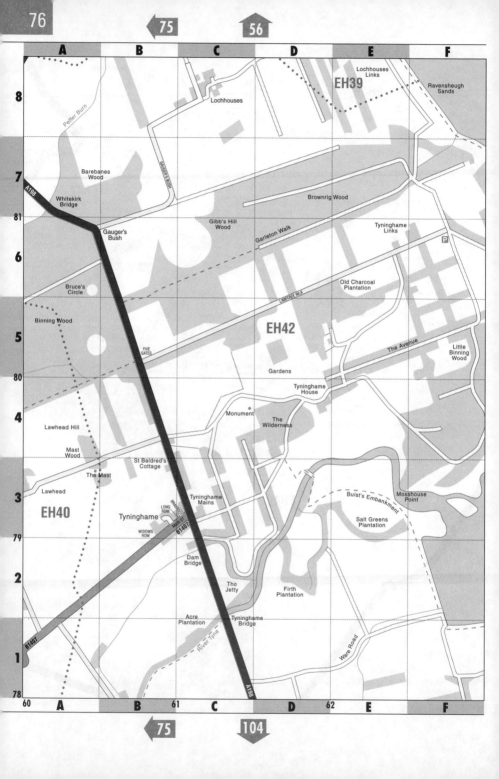

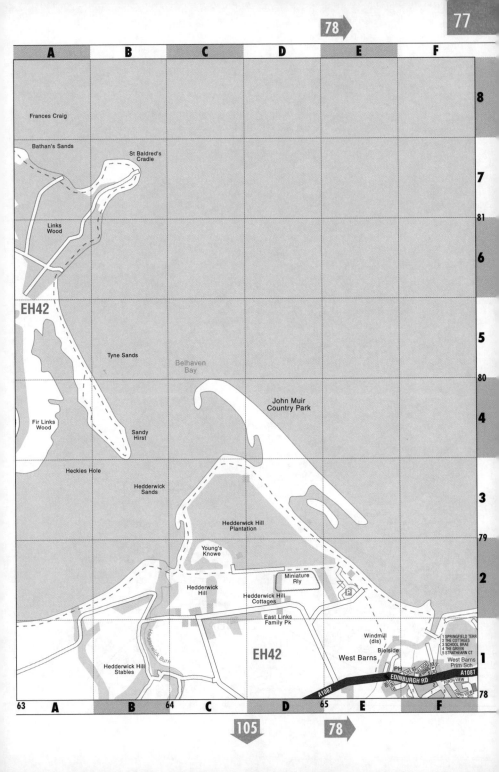

A B C D E F

8

Frances Craig

Bathan's Sands

St Baldred's
Cradle

7

81

Links
Wood

6

EH42

5

Tyne Sands

Belhaven
Bay

80

John Muir
Country Park

Fir Links
Wood

4

Sandy
Hirst

Heckies Hole

Hedderwick
Sands

3

Hedderwick Hill
Plantation

79

Young's
Knowe

Miniature
Rly

2

Hedderwick
Hill

Hedderwick Hill
Cottages

East Links
Family Pk

Windmill
(dis)

1 SPRINGFIELD TERR
2 THE COTTAGES
3 SCHOOL BRAE
4 THE GREEN
5 STRATHEARN CT

EH42

Bielside

West Barns

West Barns
Prim Sch

Hedderwick Hill
Stables

Hedderwick Burn

PH

EDINBURGH RD

A1087

FORTH VIEW

1

78

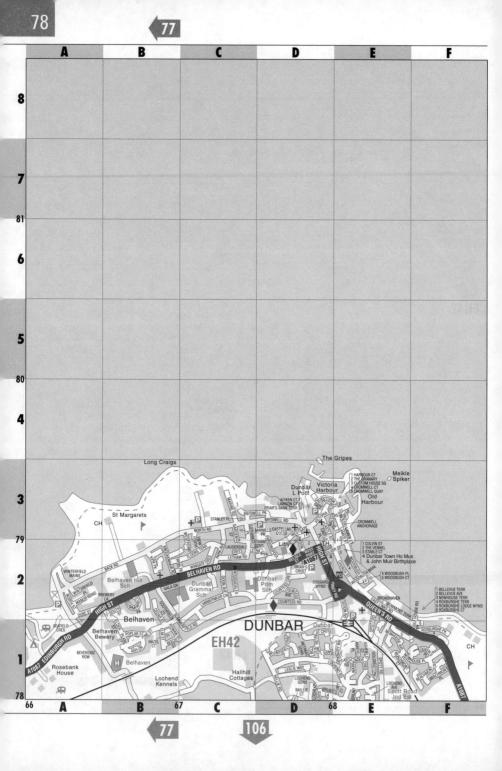

The Gripes

1 HARBOUR CT
2 THE GRANARY
3 CUSTOM HOUSE SQ
4 CROMWELL CT
5 CROMWELL QUAY

Meikle
Spiker

Long Craigs

Dunbar
L Pool

Victoria
Harbour

Old
Harbour

St Margarets

CH

CROMWELL
ANCHORAGE

AITKEN CT
LAWSON CT
FRIAR'S BANK TERR

STANLEY PL

BAYSWELL RD

BAYSWELL PK

NORTH RD

MAYVILLE
COTTS

CASTELLAU

1 COLVIN ST
2 THE VENNEL
3 STABLE CT
4 Dunbar Town Ho Mus
 & John Muir Birthplace

LAUDERDALE
CRES

LETHAM
GDNS

LETHAM

Lib

WINTERFIELD
MAINS

WINGATE

BELHAVEN RD

FRIAR'S
CROFT

4 WOODBUSH PL
5 WOODBUSH CT

BACK RD

Belhaven Hill
Sch

Dunbar
Grammar
Sch

Dunbar
Prim
Sch

COSSARDS
WYND

BROADHAVEN

1 BELLEVUE TERR
2 BELLEVUE AVE
3 NEWHOUSE TERR
4 ROXBURGHE TERR
5 ROXBURGHE LODGE WYND
6 ROXBURGHE CT

SALA GDN

LAMMERMUIR CRES

COUNTESS RD

QUEEN'S RD

BREWERY

WINTERFIELD

POPLAR ST

HAZEL
CT

ASH PK

DUKE ST

HIGH ST

Belhaven

A1087 EDINBURGH RD

SEAFIELD
CRES

Dunbar

COUNTESS RD

DUNBAR

EH42

Rosebank
House

BEVERIDGE
ROW

Belhaven
Bewery

H

Belhaven

Lochend
Kennels

Hallhill
Cottages

LESLIE WAY

BAILLIE
CT

LOCHEND

Spott Road
Ind Est

CH

A1087

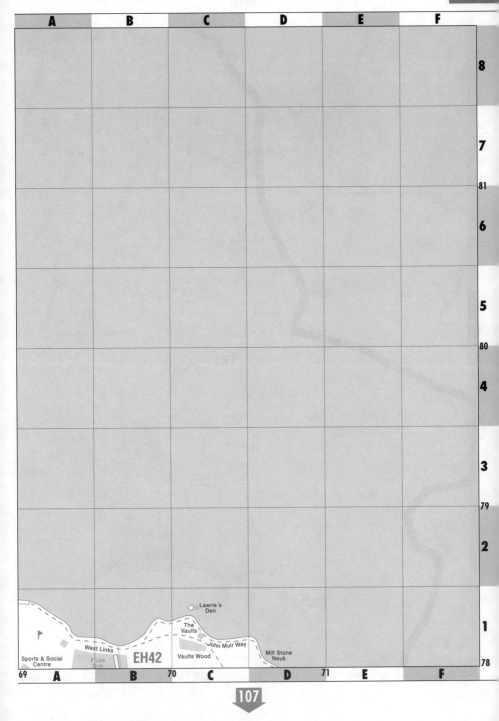

	A	B	C	D	E	F
8						
7						
6						
5						
4						
3						
2						
1						

81

80

79

78

West Links

Sports & Social Centre

Fluke Dub

EH42

The Vaults

Vaults Wood

John Muir Way

Lawrie's Den

Mill Stone Neuk

69   A   B   70   C   D   71   E   F

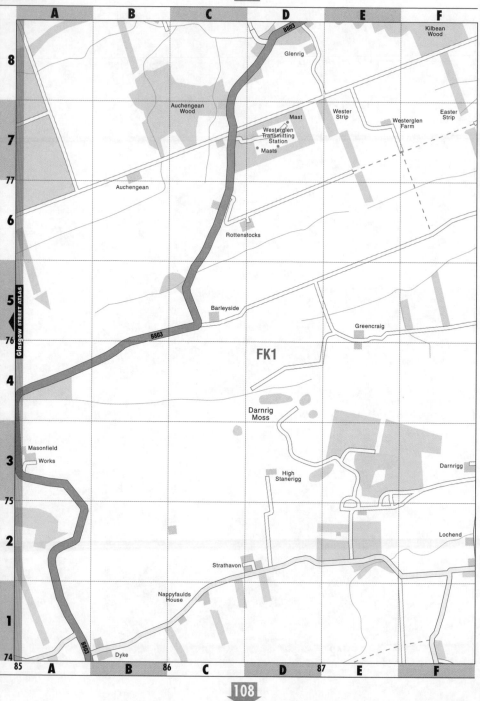

A B C D E F

8

7

77

6

5

76

4

3

75

2

1

74

85 A B 86 C D 87 E F

Glasgow Street Atlas

FK1

B803

Kilbean Wood

Glenrig

Auchengean Wood

Mast

Wester Strip

Westerglen Farm

Easter Strip

Westerglen Transmitting Station

Masts

Auchengean

Rottenstocks

Barleyside

Greencraig

Darnrig Moss

Masonfield

Works

High Stanerigg

Darnrigg

Lochend

Strathavon

Nappyfaulds House

B803

Dyke

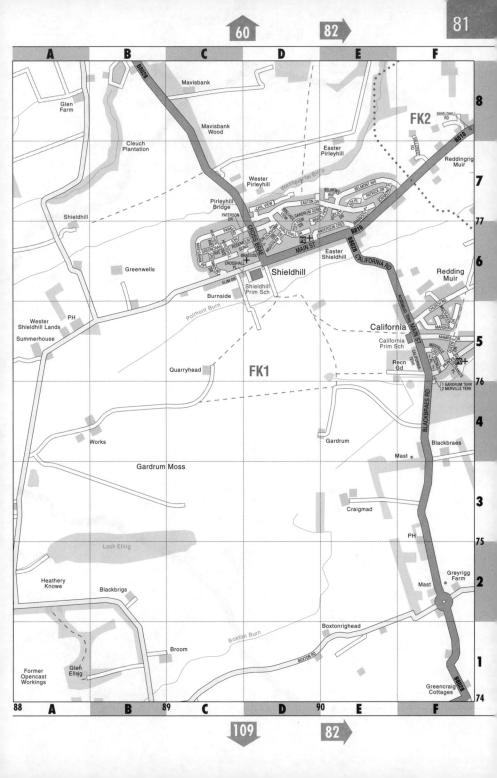

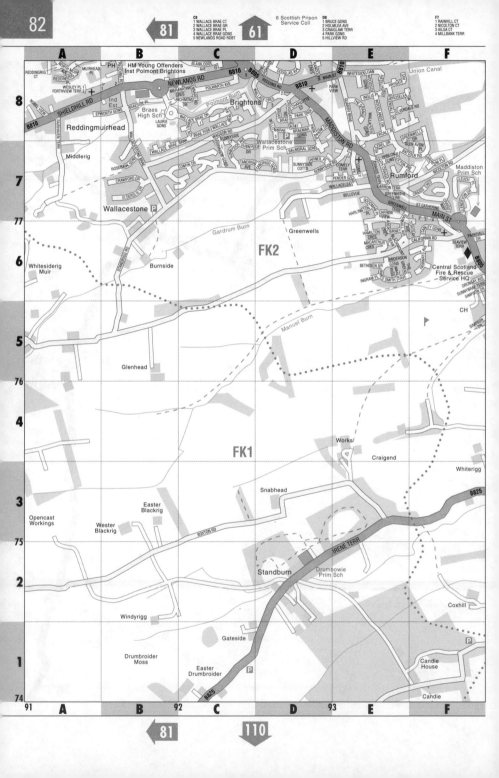

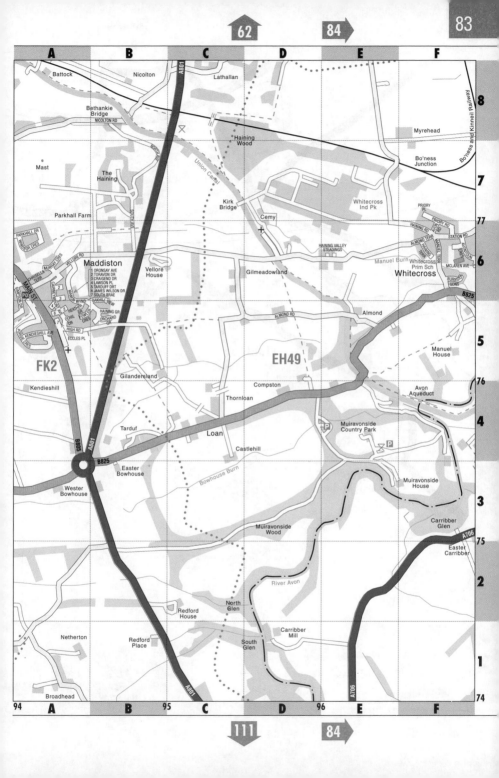

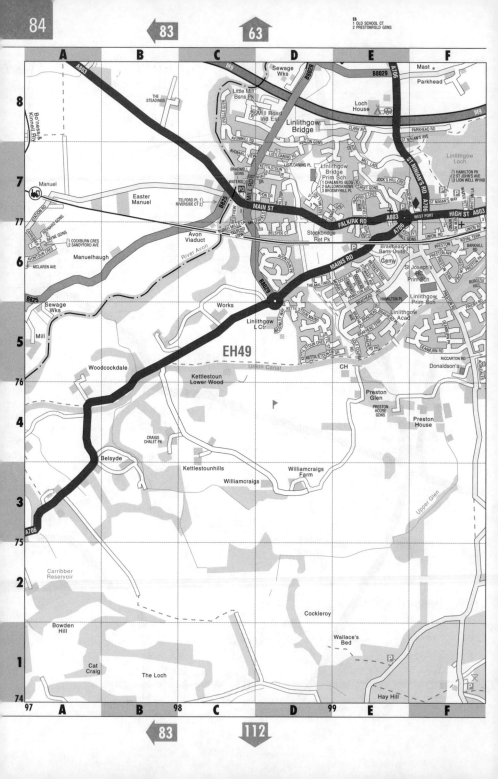

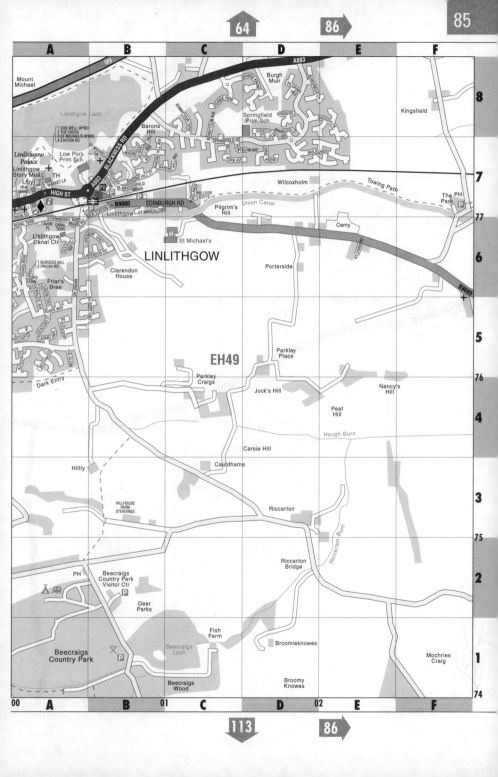

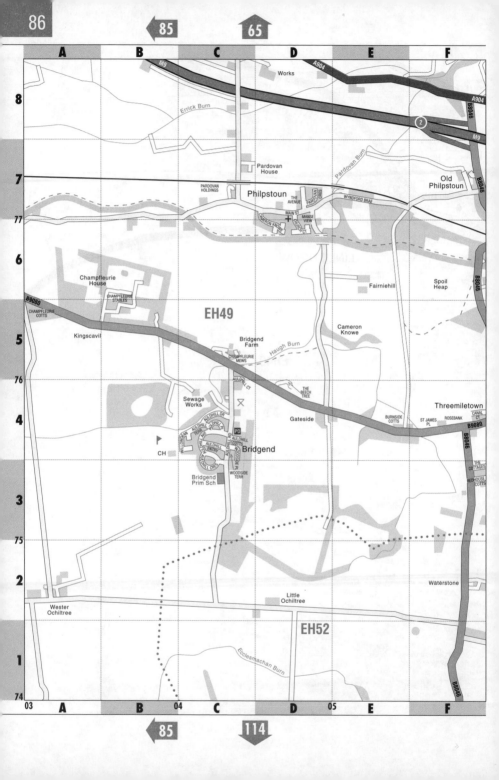

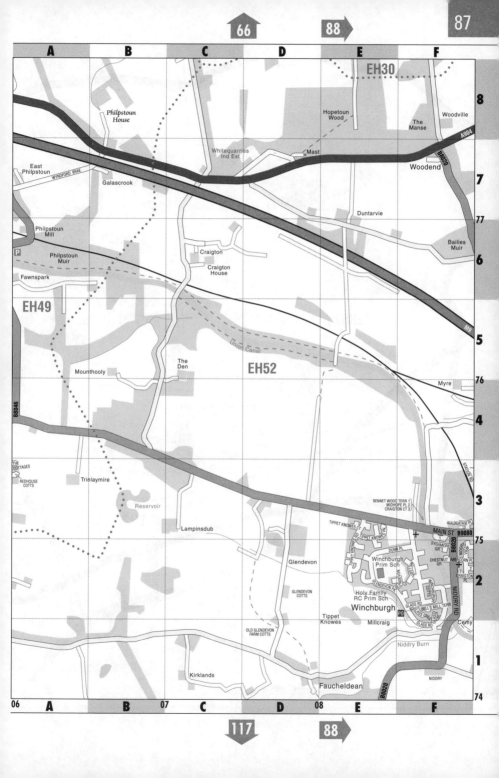

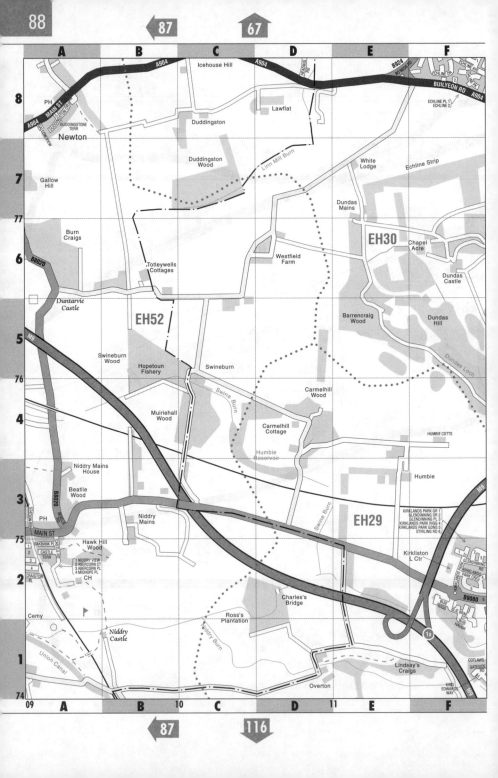

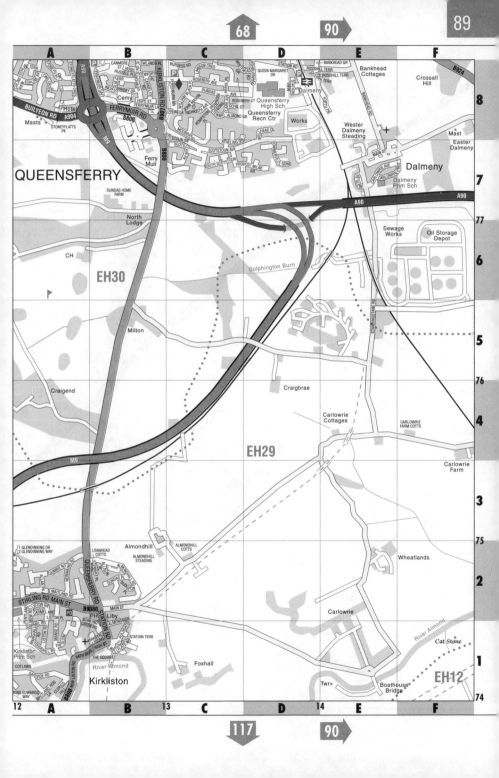

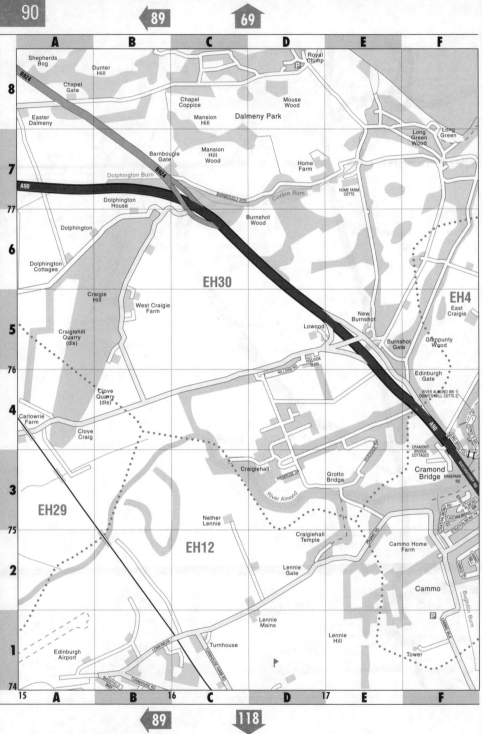

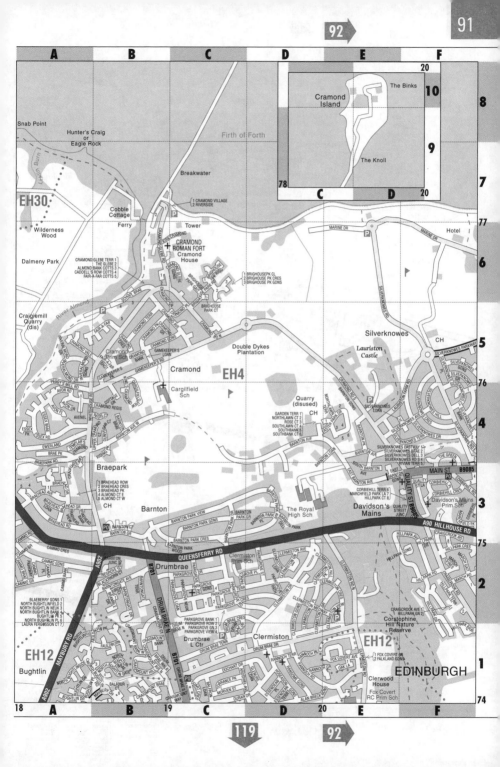

91

C5
1 St David's RC
  Prim Sch
2 Pirniehall
  Prim Sch

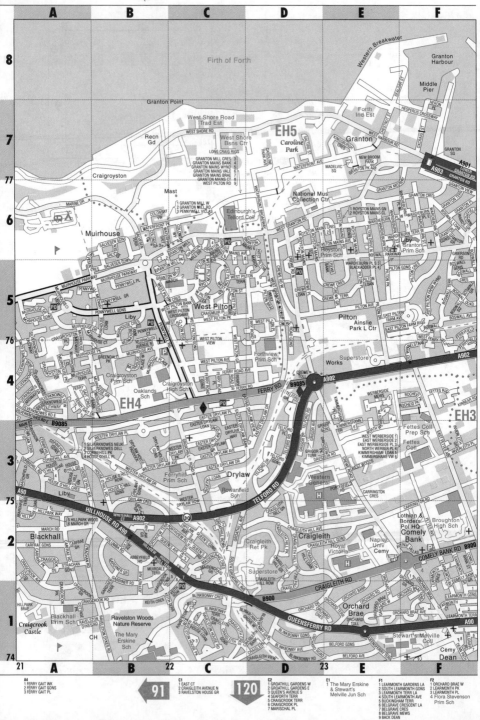

Firth of Forth

Western Breakwater

Granton
Harbour

Middle
Pier

Granton Point

West Shore Road
Trad Est

West Shore
Bsns Ctr

EH5

Caroline
Park

Forth
Ind Est

Granton

Recn
Gd

LONG CRAIG RIGG

GRANTON MILL CRES 3
GRANTON MAINS BANK 4
GRANTON MAINS WYND 5
GRANTON MAINS VALE 6
GRANTON MAINS BRAE 8
GRANTON MAINS CT 8
WEST PILTON RD 1

Craigroyston

Mast

National Mus
Collection Ctr

1 GRANTON MILL W
2 GRANTON MILL RD
3 PENNYWELL VILLAS

COLONSAY
VW

Edinburgh's
Telford Coll

1 ROYSTON MAINS GN
2 ROYSTON MAINS GL

Royston
Prim Sch

Liby
Granton
Prim Sch

Muirhouse

WARDIEBURN PL 3 3
BLACKADDER PL 4 7

West Pilton Bank

West Pilton

WEST PILTON
VIEW

Pilton
Ainslie
Park L Ctr

EAST PILTON
FARM AV

Forthview
Prim Sch

Superstore

Craigroyston
Prim Sch

Oaklands
Sch

Craigroyston
High Sch

EH4

Works

A902

A902

FETTES RIG

WERBERSIDE
MEWS

ROCHEID

ROCHEID

KIMMERGHAME

Fettes Coll
Prep Sch

EH3

Fettes
Coll

Easter Drylaw Pl

1 SILVERKNOWES NEUK
2 SILVERKNOWES DELL
3 CORBIEHILL PL
4 HOUSE O'HILL PL

1 WEST WERBERSIDE 2
2 EAST WERBERSIDE 2
3 EAST WERBERSIDE PL 3
4 NORTH WERBER PL 4
5 KIMMERGHAME LOAN 5
6 KIMMERGHAME VW 6

Ferryhill
Prim Sch

Drylaw

Western
General

Bowanfield
Sch

TELFORD RD

CARRINGTON
CRES

Liby

HILLHOUSE RD A90

A902

Lothian &
Borders
Pol HQ

Broughton
High Sch

Blackhall

WHITEHALL
RD

Craigleith
Ret Pk

Craigleith

Napier
Univ
Cemy

Comely
Bank

COMELY BANK RD

B900

Craigleith
Royal
Victoria

MARCH RD

Blackhall
Prim Sch

Ravelston Woods
Nature Reserve

Superstore

CRAIGLEITH RD

Orchard
Brae

Stewart's Melville
Coll

A90

Craigcrook
Castle

The Mary
Erskine
Sch

QUEENSFERRY RD

ORCHARD
TOLL

B900

Cemy
Dean

BELFORD GDNS

BELFORD AVE

A4
1 FERRY GAIT WK
2 FERRY GAIT GDNS
3 FERRY GAIT PL

C1
1 EAST CT
2 CRAIGLEITH AVENUE N
3 RAVELSTON HOUSE GR

C2
1 GROATHILL GARDENS W
2 GROATHILL GARDENS E
3 QUEEN'S AVENUE S
4 SEAFORTH TERR
5 CRAIGCROOK TERR
6 CRAIGCROOK PL
7 MARISCHAL PL

E1
1 The Mary Erskine
  & Stewart's
  Melville Jun Sch

F1
1 LEARMONTH GARDENS LA
2 SOUTH LEARMONTH GDNS
3 LEARMONTH TERR LA
4 SOUTH LEARMONTH AVE
5 BUCKINGHAM TERR
6 BELGRAVE CRESCENT LA
7 BELGRAVE CRES
8 BELGRAVE MEWS
9 BACK DEAN

F2
1 ORCHARD BRAE W
2 LEARMONTH PK
3 LEARMONTH PL
4 Flora Stevenson
  Prim Sch

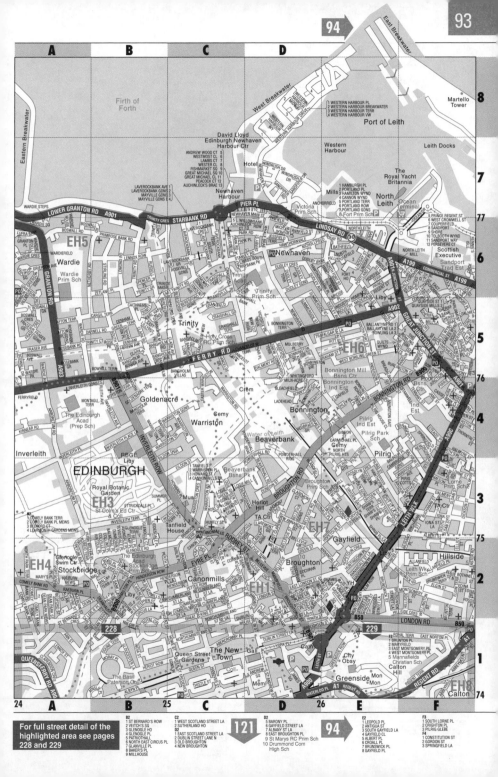

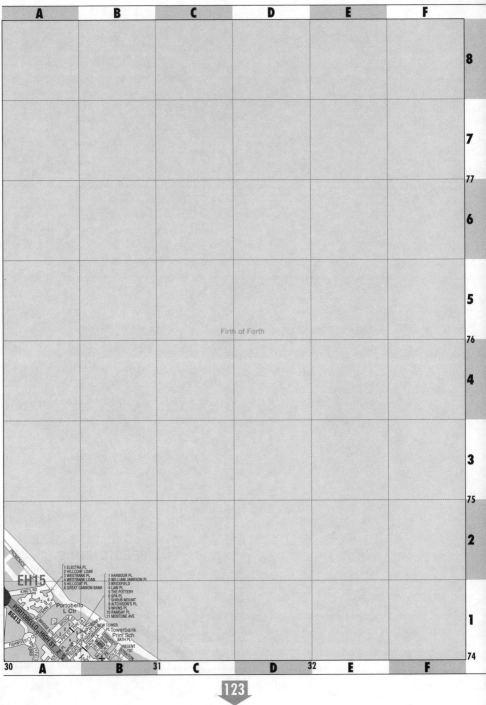

Firth of Forth

EH15

KING'S RD

Portobello
L Ctr

A6415

Towerbank
Prim Sch

1 ELECTRA PL
2 HILLCOAT LOAN
3 WESTBANK PL
4 WESTBANK LOAN
5 HILLCOAT PL
6 GREAT CANNON BANK

1 HARBOUR PL
2 WILLIAM JAMESON PL
3 BRICKFIELD
4 LAW PL
5 THE POTTERY
6 SPA PL
7 SHRUB MOUNT
8 AITCHISON'S PL
9 WHINS PL
10 RAMSAY PL
11 MENTONE AVE

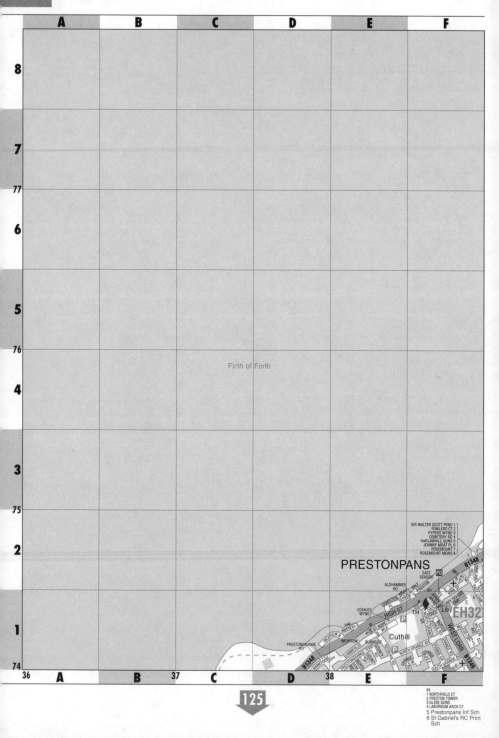

Firth of Forth

SIR WALTER SCOTT PEND 1
FOWLERS CT 2
PYPERS WYND 3
CEMETERY RD 4
HARLAWHILL GDNS 5
JOHNY MOAT PL 6
ROSEMOUNT 7
ROSEMOUNT MEWS 8

PRESTONPANS

EAST
SEASIDE

ALDHAMMER
HO

COOKIES
WYND

HIGH ST

TH

Lby

EH32

THE
POTTERY

INCHVIEW N.
INCHVIEW

BURNSIDE

Cuthill

PRESTONGRANGE
RD

PRESTONGRANGE TERR

B1348

B1349

B1348

F1
1 NORTHFIELD CT
2 PRESTON TOWER
3 GLEBE GDNS
4 LABURNUM ARCH CT
5 Prestonpans Inf Sch
6 St Gabriel's RC Prim
Sch

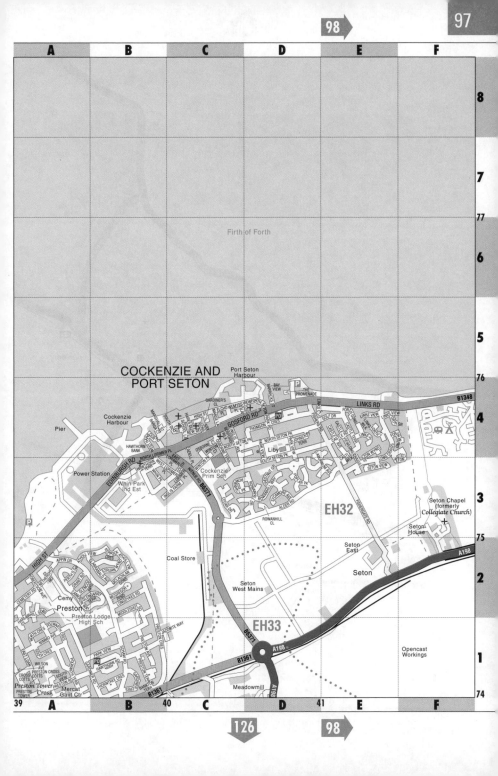

98

COCKENZIE AND PORT SETON

Firth of Forth

Port Seton Harbour

BAY VIEW

THE PROMENADE

LINKS RD

B1348

GARDINER'S

GOSFORD RD

Cockenzie Harbour

Pier

HAWTHORN BANK

Power Station

EDINBURGH RD

NORTH GRIMMER PL

Whin Park Ind Est

Cockenzie Prim Sch

Liby

EH32

Seton Chapel (formerly Collegiate Church)

Seton House

HIGH ST

APPIN DR

Coal Store

A198

Seton East

Seton

Cemy

Preston

Preston Lodge High Sch

ROWANHILL CL

Seton West Mains

EH33

B1361

A198

B1361

A198

Opencast Workings

Preston Tower Cross

Mercat Gait Ctr

Meadowmill

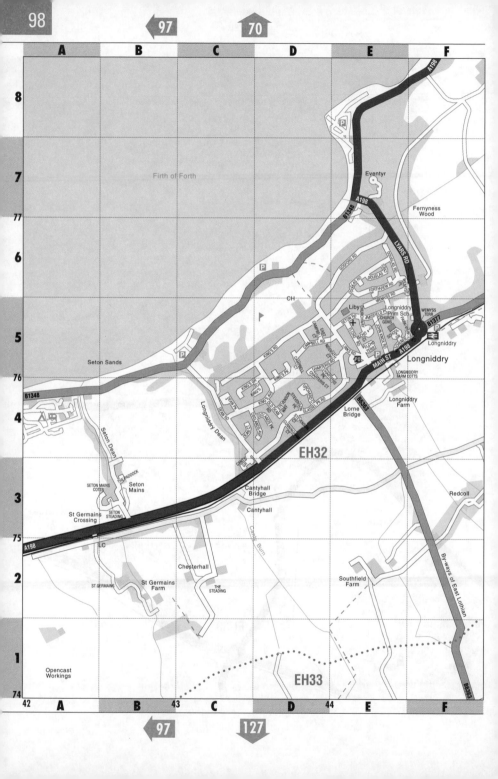

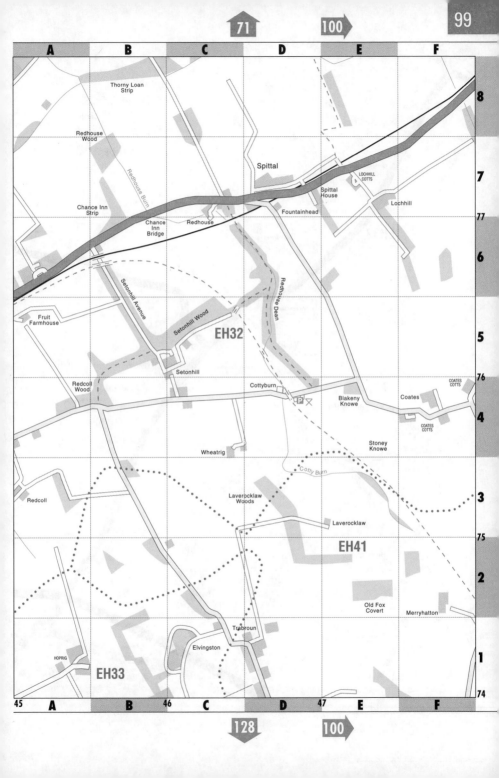

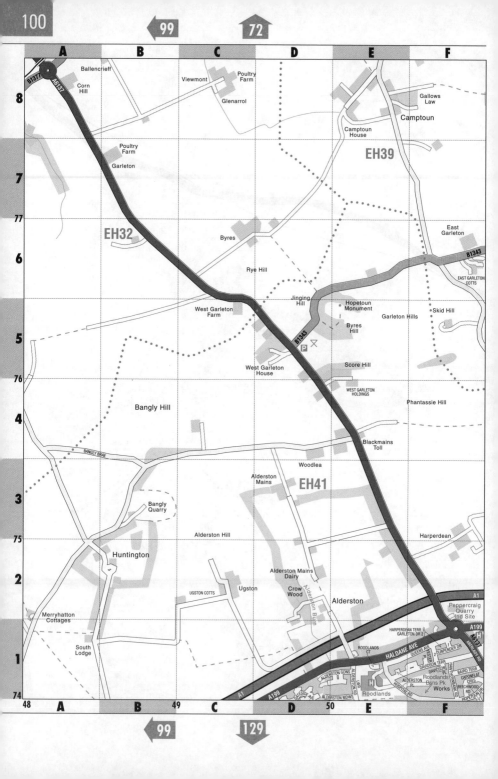

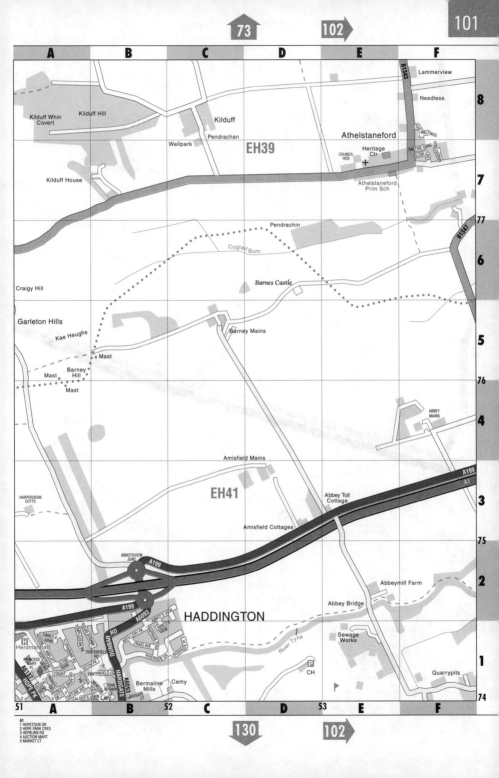

A **B** **C** **D** **E** **F**

8

Kilduff Whin Covert
Kilduff Hill
Kilduff
Pendrachan
Wellpark

B1343
Lammerview
Needless

Athelstaneford

EH39

COUNCIL HOS
Heritage Ctr

Kilduff House

Athelstaneford Prim Sch

7

Pendrachin

Cogtail Burn

B1347

77

6

Craigy Hill

Barnes Castle

Garleton Hills

Kae Heughs
Barney Mains

5

Mast
Barney Hill
Mast
Mast

ABBEY MAINS

76

4

HARPERDEAN COTTS

Amisfield Mains

EH41

Abbey Toll Cottage

A199
A1

3

Amisfield Cottages

75

ABBOTSVIEW JUNC
A199

Abbeymill Farm

2

A199
A6093

HADDINGTON

Abbey Bridge

Sewage Works

H
Herdmanflatt
PRINCESS MARY PL
LYDGAIT
A6137
HOPE PK
DUNBAR RD
HARDGATE
TENTERFIELD HO
CRAIG AVE
RIVERSIDE DR
TENTERFIELD
JOHN BROWN CT
CALDER'S LAWN
A6093
Bermaline Mills
Cemy

River Tyne

P
CH

Quarrypits

1

A1
1 HOPETOUN DR
2 HOPE PARK CRES
3 HEPBURN RD
4 AUCTION MART
5 MARKET CT

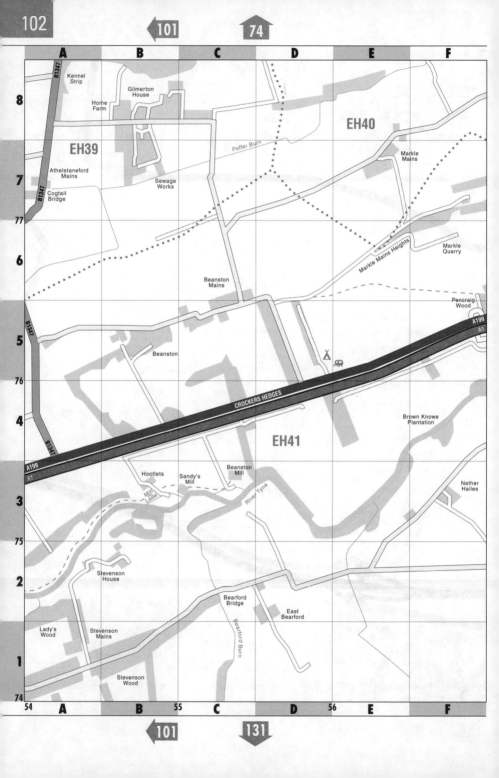

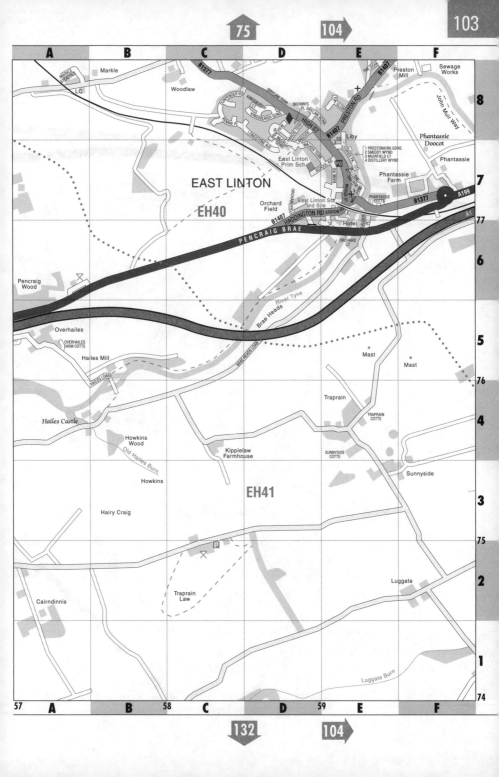

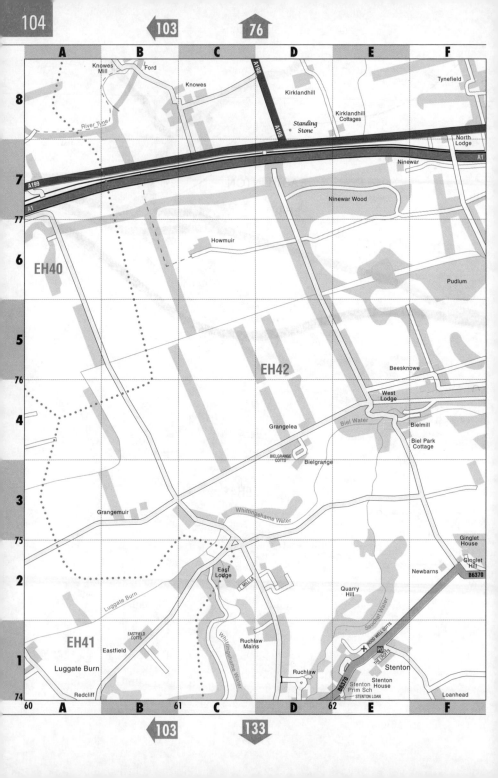

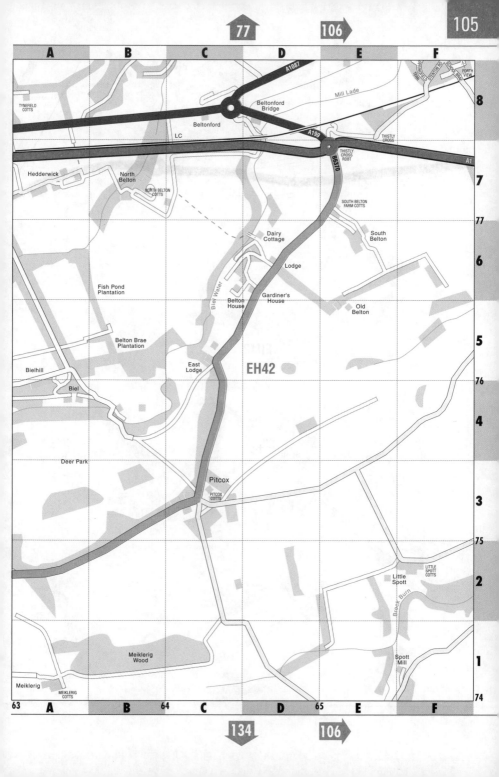

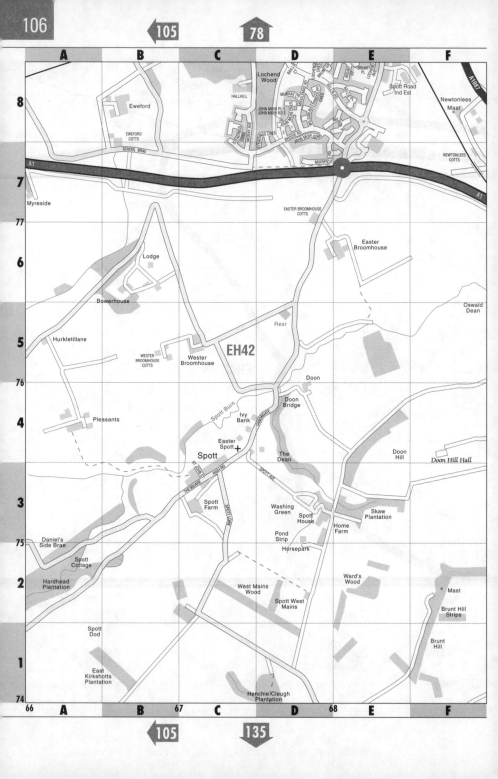

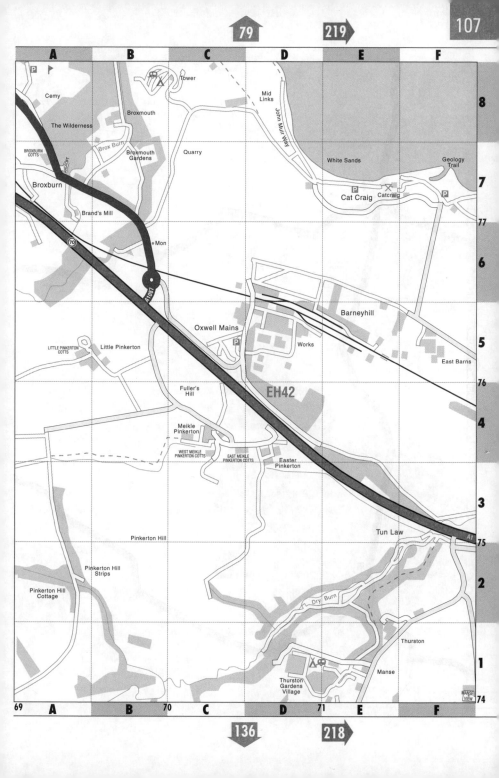

	A	B	C	D	E	F

8

Cemy

The Wilderness

Broxmouth

Tower

Mid Links

John Muir Way

7

BROXBURN COTTS

Broxburn

AIRPORT

Brox Burn

Broxmouth Gardens

Broxmouth

Quarry

White Sands

Geology Trail

Cat Craig

Catcraig

77

Brand's Mill

Mon

A1087

70

6

A1087

Oxwell Mains

Barneyhill

5

LITTLE PINKERTON COTTS

Little Pinkerton

Works

East Barns

76

Fuller's Hill

EH42

4

Meikle Pinkerton

WEST MEIKLE PINKERTON COTTS

EAST MEIKLE PINKERTON COTTS

Easter Pinkerton

3

Pinkerton Hill

Tun Law

A1

75

Pinkerton Hill Strips

2

Pinkerton Hill Cottage

Dry Burn

Thurston

1

Thurston Gardens Village

Manse

MANSE VIEW

74

69	A	B	70	C	D	71	E	F

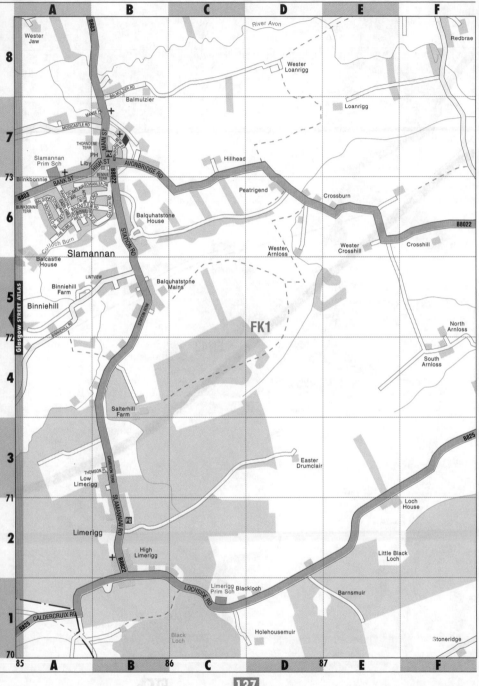

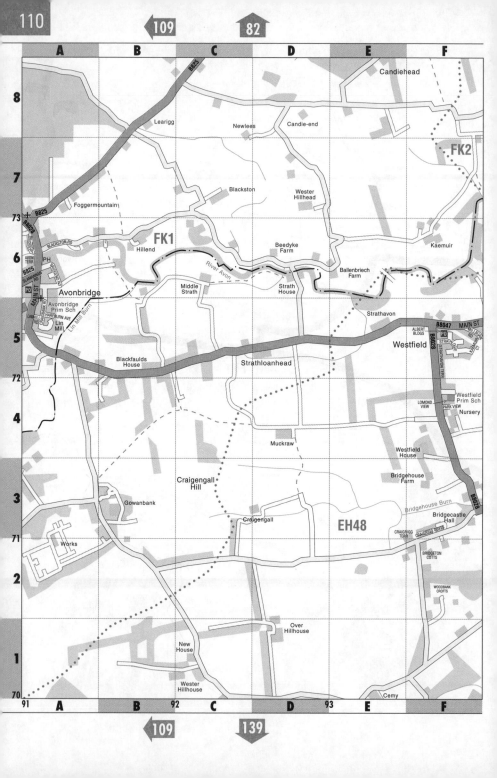

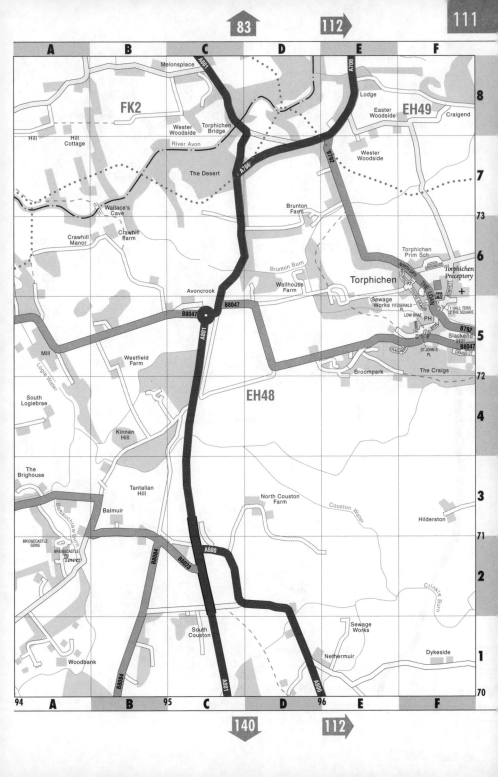

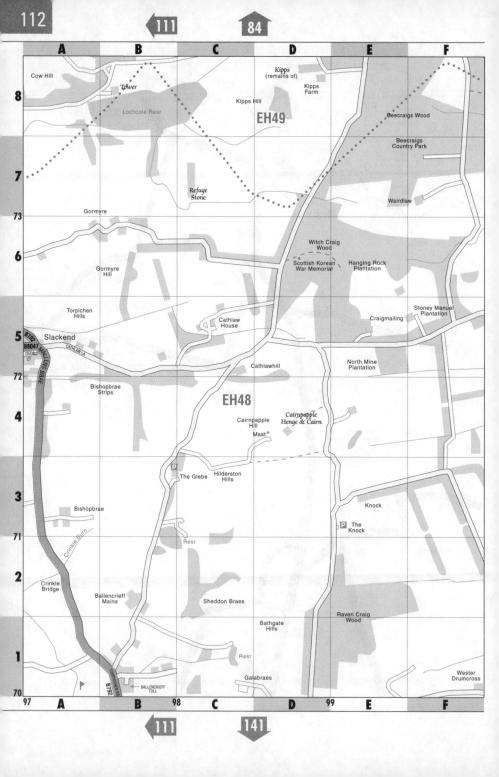

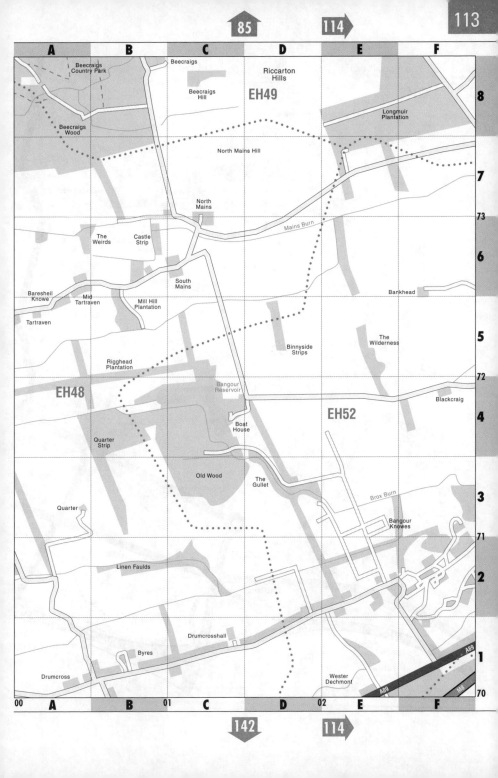

85
114

A **B** **C** **D** **E** **F**

Beecraigs
Country Park

Beecraigs

Riccarton
Hills

Beecraigs
Hill

EH49

Longmuir
Plantation

8

Beecraigs
Wood

North Mains Hill

7

North
Mains

73

Mains Burn

The
Weirds

Castle
Strip

6

Bankhead

South
Mains

Baresheil
Knowe

Mid
Tartraven

Mill Hill
Plantation

The
Wilderness

5

Tartraven

Binnyside
Strips

Rigghead
Plantation

72

EH48

Bangour
Reservoir

Blackcraig

EH52

Boat
House

4

Quarter
Strip

Old Wood

The
Gullet

3

Brox Burn

Quarter

Bangour
Knowes

71

Linen Faulds

2

Drumcrosshall

Byres

1

Drumcross

Wester
Dechmont

A89

A89

M8

70

00 **A** **B** 01 **C** **D** 02 **E** **F**

142
114

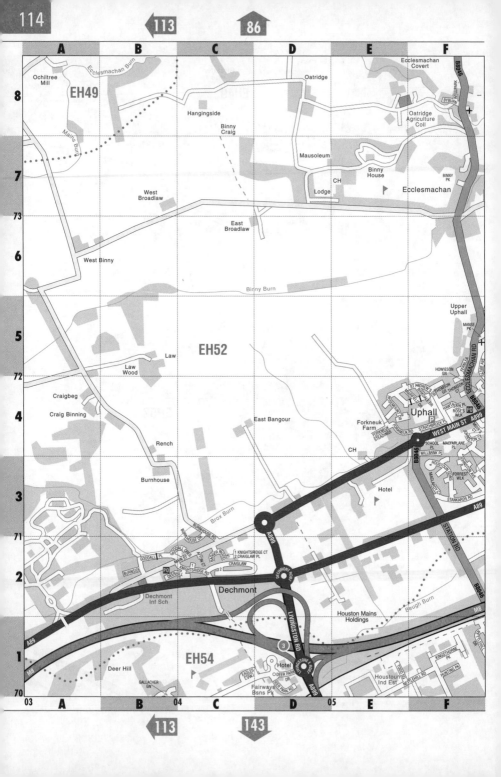

A B C D E F

8

Ochiltree
Mill

EH49

Ecclesmachan Burn

Oatridge

Ecclesmachan
Covert

Hangingside

Binny
Craig

Oatridge
Agriculture
Coll

7

Mains Burn

West
Broadlaw

Mausoleum

Binny
House

Lodge

CH

BINNY
PK

Ecclesmachan

73

East
Broadlaw

6

West Binny

Binny Burn

Upper
Uphall

MANSE
PK

5

EH52

Law

HOWIESON
GN

72

Law
Wood

ST MICHAEL'S
ST THOMSON

Uphall

ROSE'S
WLK

4

Craigbeg

Craig Binning

East Bangour

Forkneuk
Farm

WEST MAIN ST

FORKNEUK
STEADING

A899

SCHOOL
PL

MACFARLANE
PL

MILLBANK PL

Rench

CH

FORREST
WLK

3

Burnhouse

Brox Burn

Hotel

STANKARDS RD

A89

STATION RD

71

BURNSIDE

BURNHOUSE DR

GOODALL
PL

1 KNIGHTSRIDGE CT
2 CRAIGLAW PL

DECHMONT RD

2

BURNSIDE

PO

KNIGHTSRIDGE RD

CRAIGLAW

Dechmont

Houston Mains
Holdings

Beugh Burn

M8

B8046

Dechmont
Inf Sch

1

A89

M8

Deer Hill

EH54

LIVINGSTON RD

3

Hotel

Houstoun
Ind Est

A89

70

GALLACHER
GN

ODEER PARK

Fairways
Bsns Pk

HUNTING PK

03

A

B

04

C

D

05

E

F

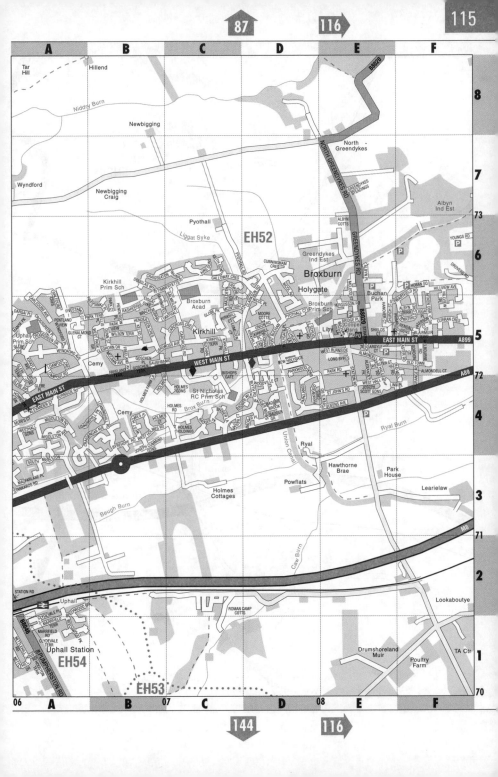

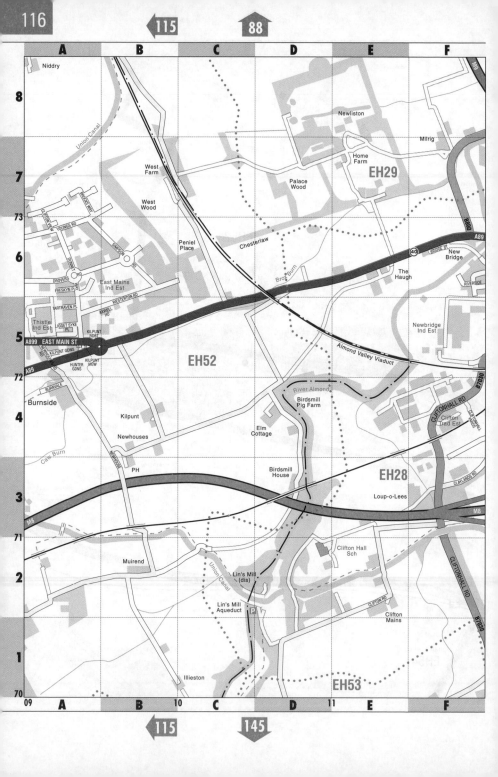

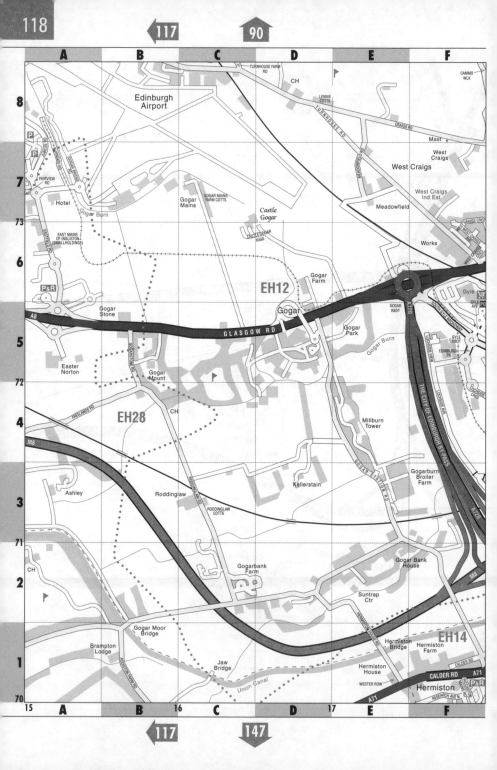

117
90
117
147

A   B   C   D   E   F

8
7
73
6
5
72
4
3
71
2
1
70

15   A   B   16   C   D   17   E   F

TURNHOUSE FARM RD
CH
CAMMO WLK
Edinburgh Airport
LENNIE COTTS
CRAIGS RD
Mast
West Craigs
West Craigs Ind Est
FAIRVIEW RD
Hotel
Gogar Mains
GOGAR MAINS FARM COTTS
Castle Gogar
CASTLE GOGAR RIGG
Meadowfield
CRAIGS CRES
Works
Gogar Burn
EAST MAINS OF INGLISTON (SMALL HOLDINGS)
P&R
EH12
Gogar Farm
Gyle
GYLE RBDT
GYLE AVE
A8
Gogar Stone
GLASGOW RD
Gogar
GOGAR RBDT
A720
GYLE RBDT
EDINBURGH PK
LOCHSIDE VIEW
Easter Norton
Gogar Mount
GODASTONE RD
Gogar Park
Gogar Burn
THE CITY OF EDINBURGH BYPASS
LOCHSIDE CRES
EH28
CH
FREELANDS RD
Millburn Tower
A720
M8
Ashley
Roddinglaw
RODDINGLAW COTTS
Kellerstain
GOGAR STATION RD
Gogarburn Broiler Farm
CH
Gogarbank Farm
Gogar Bank House
M8
CH
Suntrap Ctr
HERMISTON HOUSE RD
EH14
Gogar Moor Bridge
Hermiston Bridge
Hermiston Farm
Brampton Lodge
ROSTER FARM RD
Jaw Bridge
Hermiston House
CALDER RD
A71
P&R
Union Canal
WESTER ROW
Hermiston
A71
RESEARCH AVE N

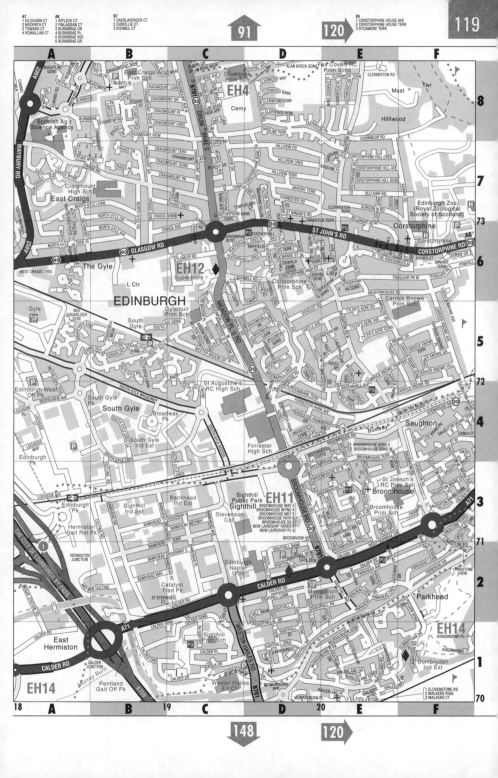

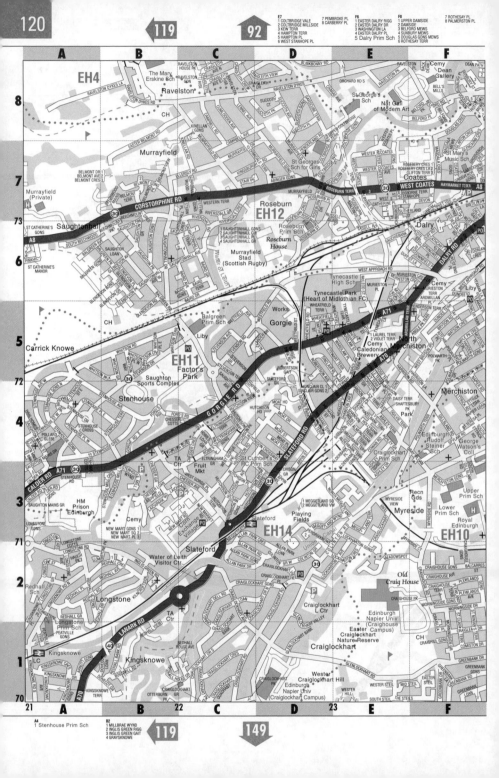

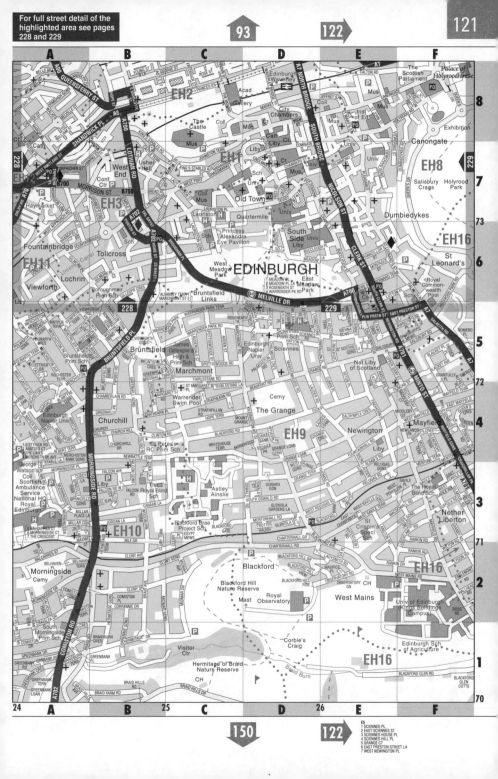

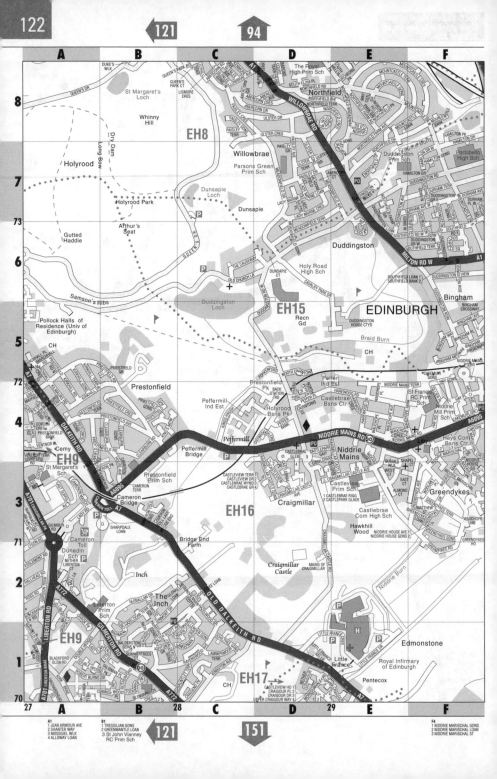

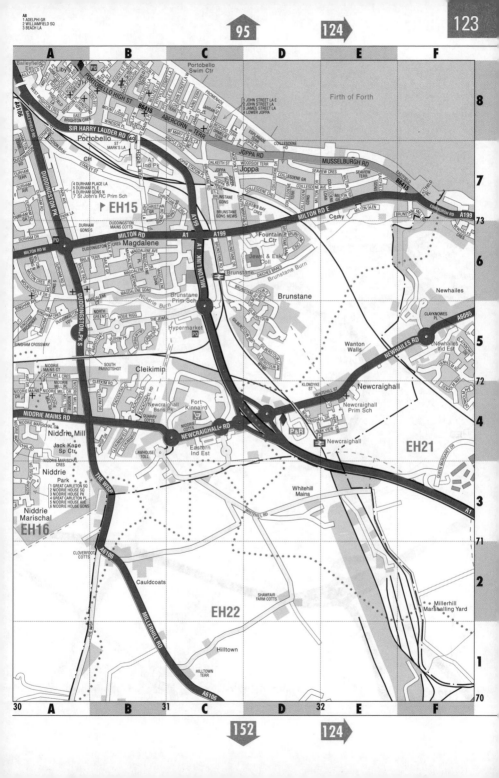

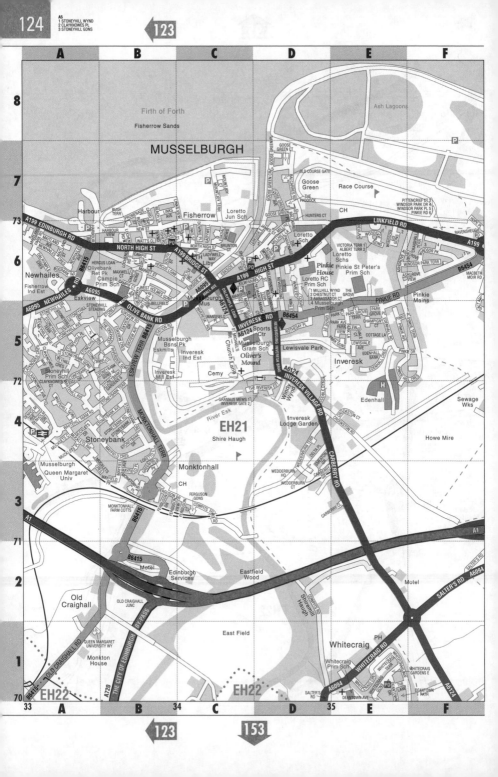

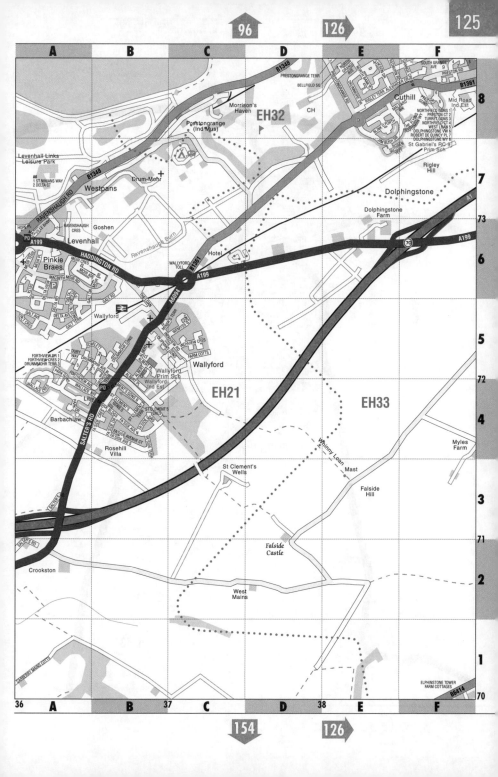

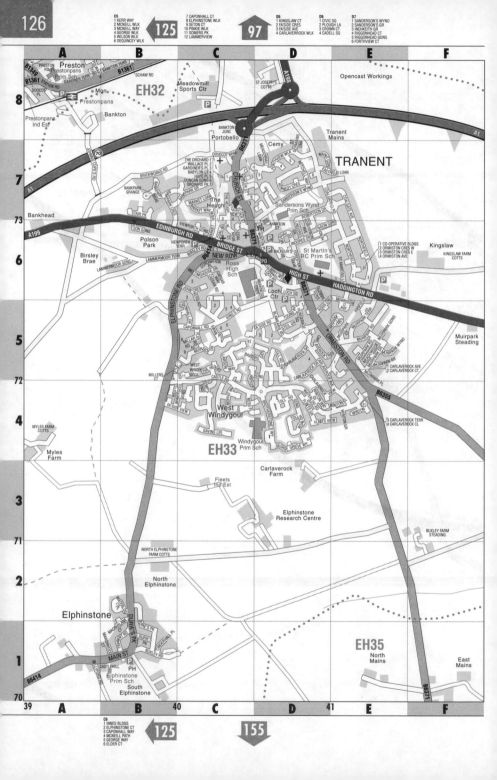

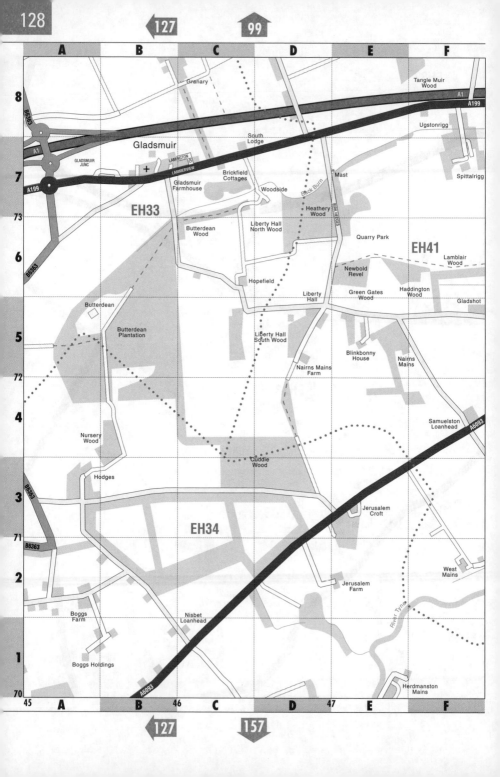

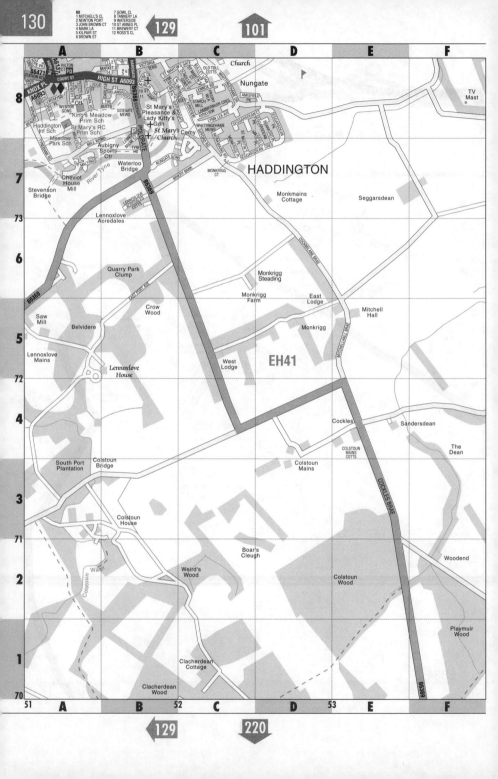

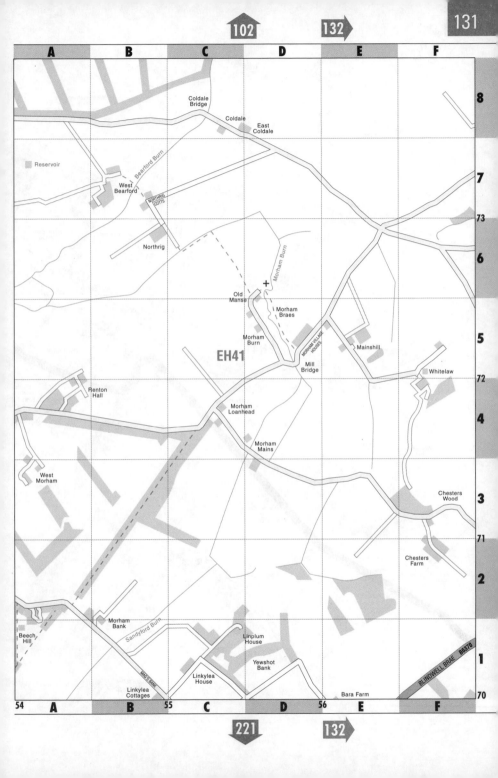

8

Coldale
Bridge

Coldale

East
Coldale

7

Reservoir

Bearford Burn

West
Bearford

NORTHRIG
COTTS

73

Northrig

Morham Burn

6

Old
Manse

+

Morham
Braes

5

Morham
Burn

EH41

MORHAM VILLAGE
HOUSES

Mainshill

Mill
Bridge

Whitelaw

72

Renton
Hall

Morham
Loanhead

4

Morham
Mains

West
Morham

Chesters
Wood

3

71

Chesters
Farm

2

Morham
Bank

Sandyford Burn

Linplum
House

Beech
Hill

Yewshot
Bank

MAIS'S PARK

Linkylea
House

Linkylea
Cottages

Bara Farm

BLINDWELL BRAIE B6370

1

70

54   55   56

A   B   C   D   E   F

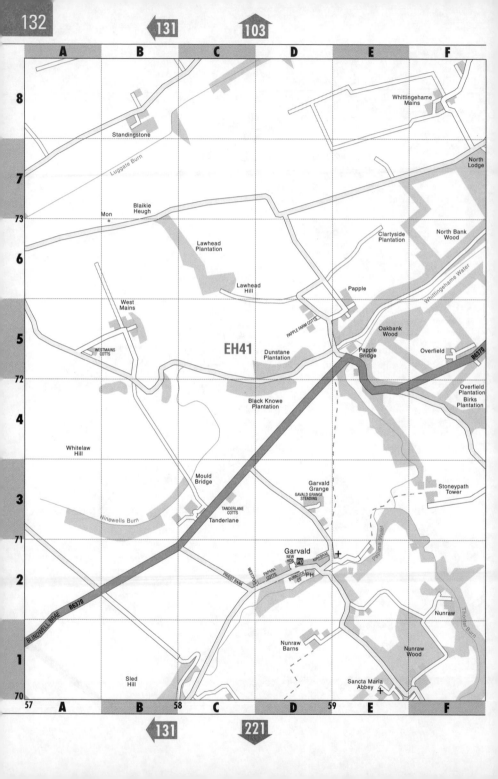

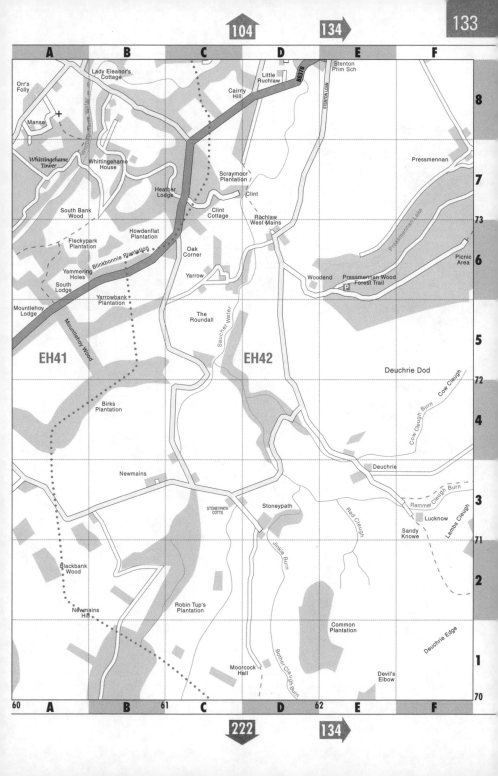

133
105

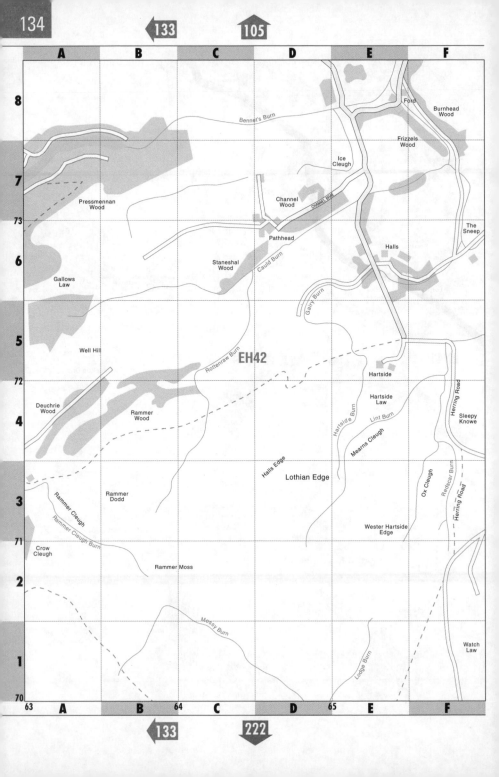

EH42

Bennet's Burn

Ford

Burnhead
Wood

Frizzels
Wood

Ice
Cleugh

Pressmennan
Wood

Channel
Wood

CHANNEL BURN

The
Sneep

Pathhead

Halls

Staneshal
Wood

Cauld Burn

Gallows
Law

Gairy Burn

Well Hill

Rottenraw Burn

Hartside

Hartside
Law

Herring Road

Deuchrie
Wood

Rammer
Wood

Hartside Burn

Lint Burn

Sleepy
Knowe

Mearns Cleugh

Halls Edge

Lothian Edge

Ox Cleugh

Redscar Burn

Herring Road

Rammer
Dodd

Rammer Cleugh

Wester Hartside
Edge

Rammer Cleugh Burn

Crow
Cleugh

Rammer Moss

Messy Burn

Lodge Burn

Watch
Law

133
222

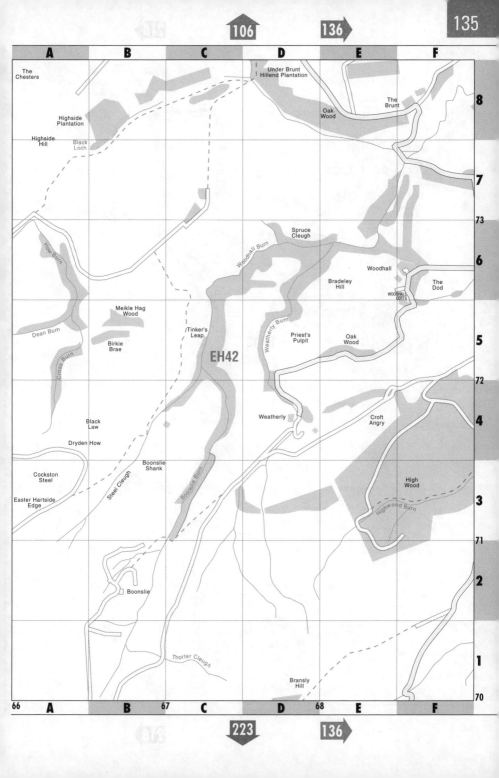

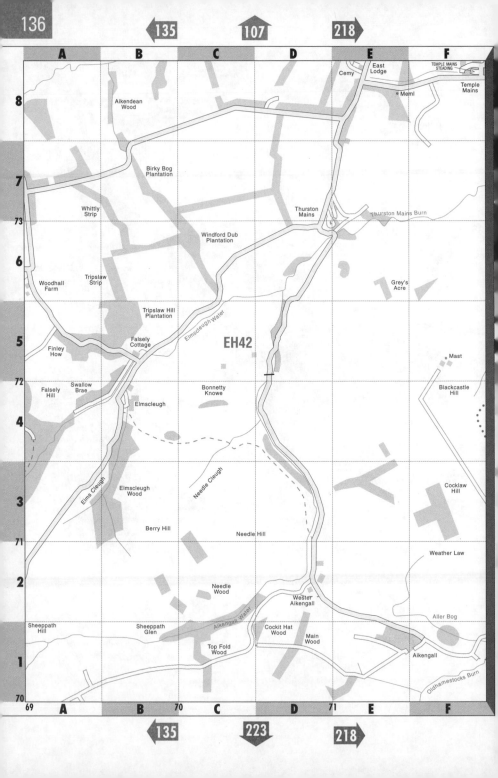

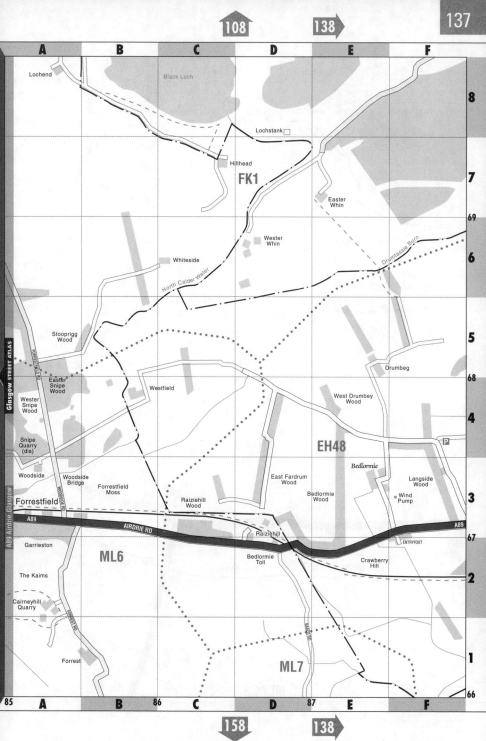

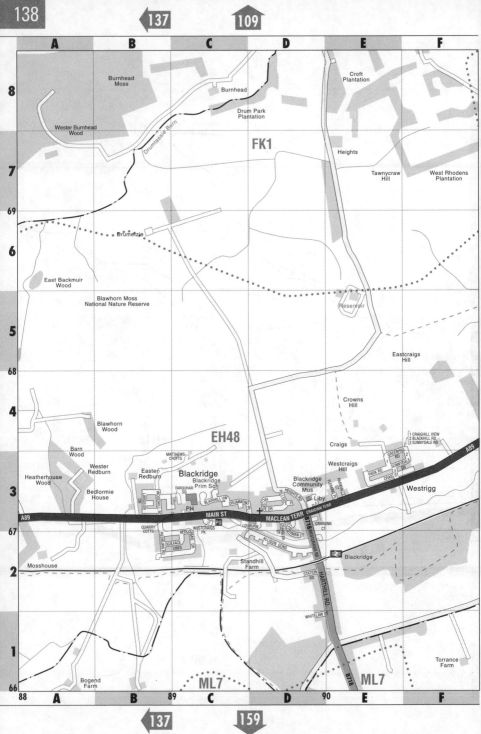

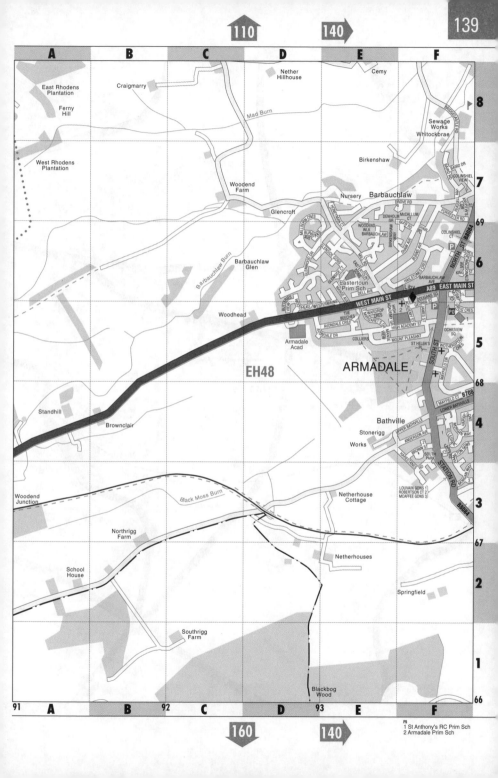

A B C D E F

East Rhodens Plantation

Craigmarry

Nether Hillhouse

Cemy

8

Ferny Hill

Mad Burn

Sewage Works
Whitockbrae

West Rhodens Plantation

Birkenshaw

7

Woodend Farm

Nursery

Barbauchlaw

DROVE RD

69

Glencroft

Barbauchlaw Burn

Barbauchlaw Glen

MILL BURN CRES

DENHOLM

McCALLUM CT

WOODEND WLK
BARBAUCHLAW

6

Eastertoun Prim Sch

EASTERTON

WEST MAIN ST

Liby

A89 EAST MAIN ST

Woodhead

THE BEECHES

WARDROP

High Academy

Mount Pleasant

EH48

Armadale Acad

AVONDALE CRES

AVONDALE DR

COLLIERS LA

St HELEN'S

5

ARMADALE

68

Standhill

Brownclair

Bathville

Stonerigg

Works

UPPER BATHVILLE

ANDERSON AVE

BROWN ST

SOUTH PARK

LOWER BATHVILLE

B8O8

STATION RD

4

Woodend Junction

Black Moss Burn

Netherhouse Cottage

LOUVAIN GDNS 1
ROBERTSON CT 2
McAFFEE GDNS 3

B8O84

3

Northrigg Farm

67

School House

Netherhouses

Springfield

2

Southrigg Farm

1

Blackbog Wood

66

91 A B 92 C D 93 E F

F5
1 St Anthony's RC Prim Sch
2 Armadale Prim Sch

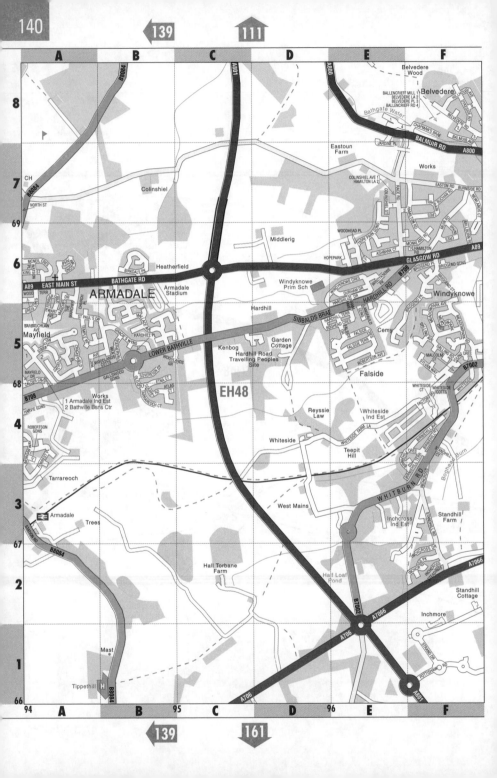

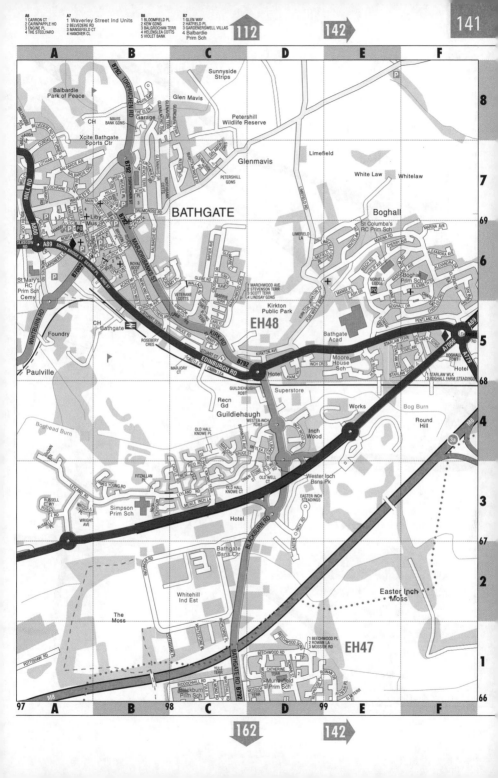

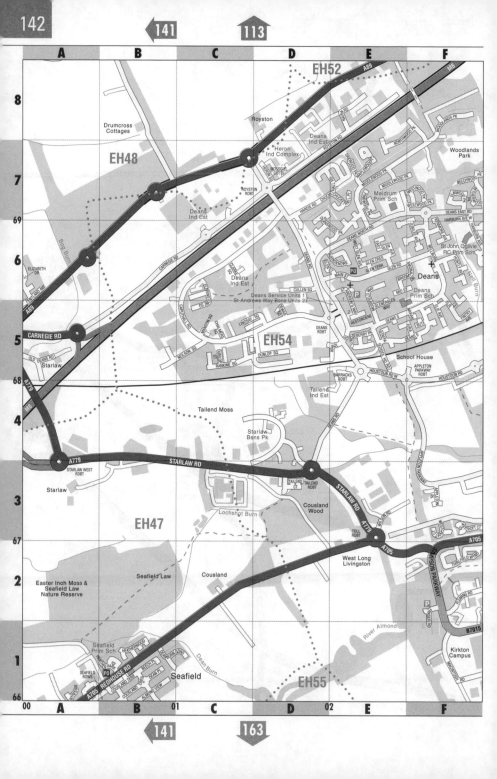

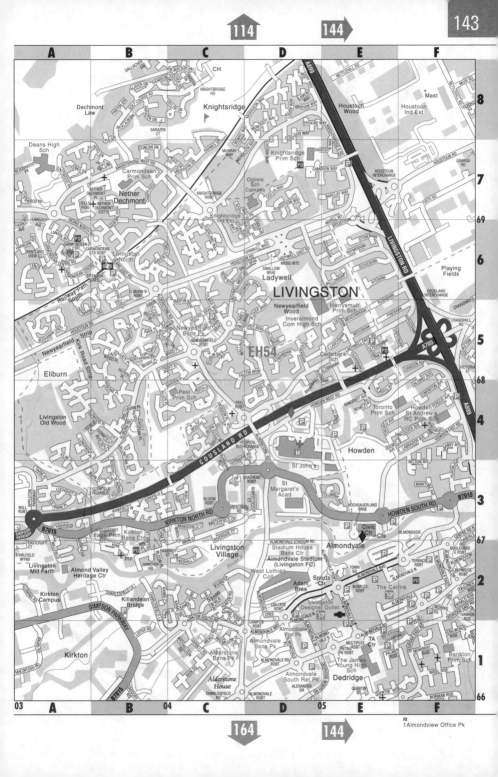

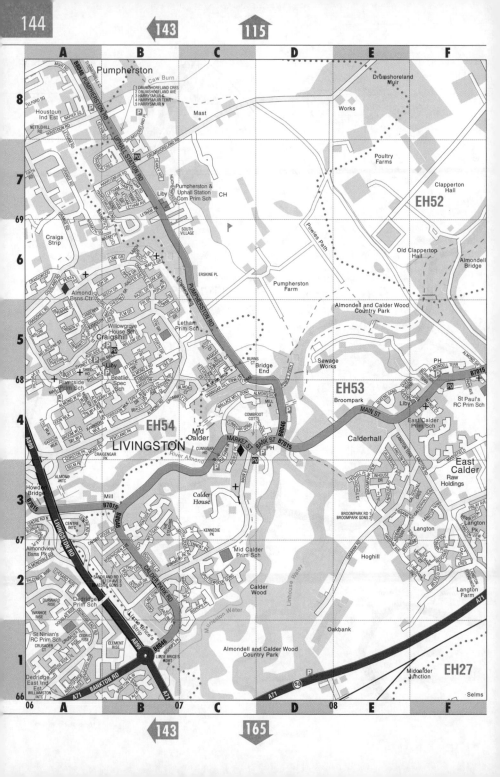

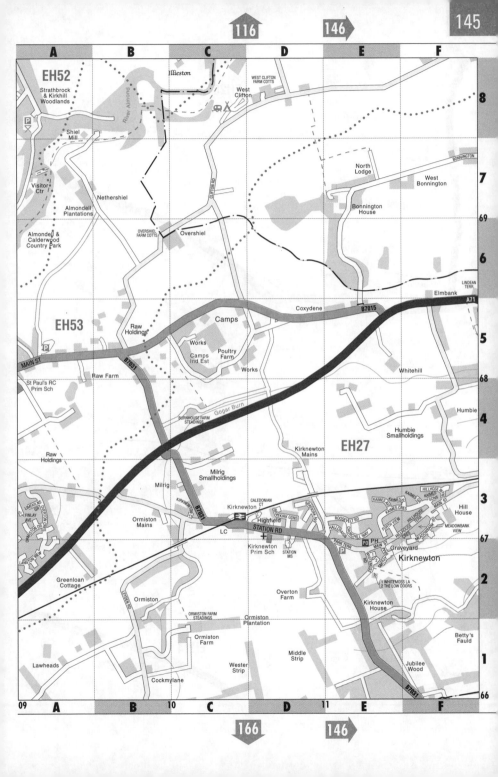

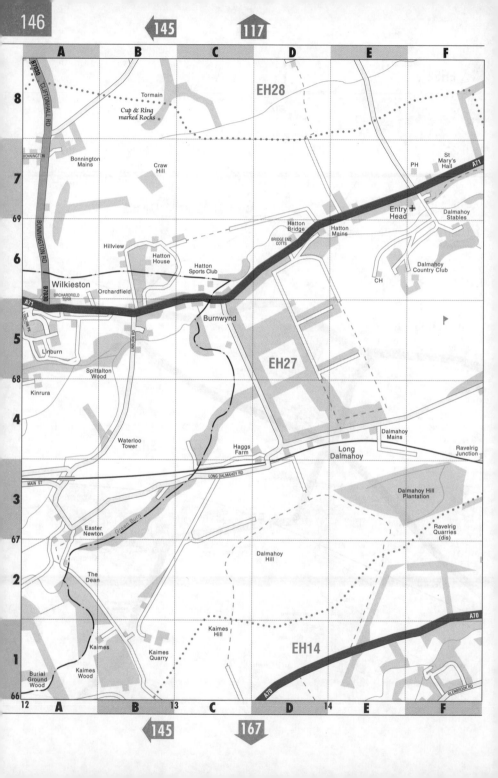

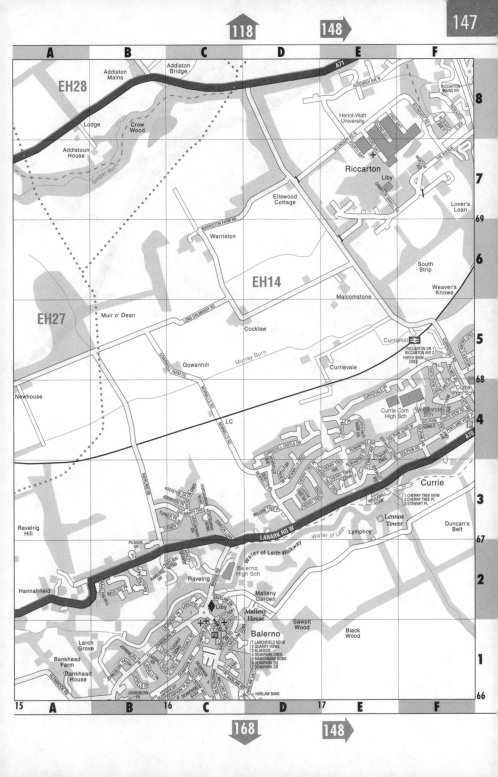

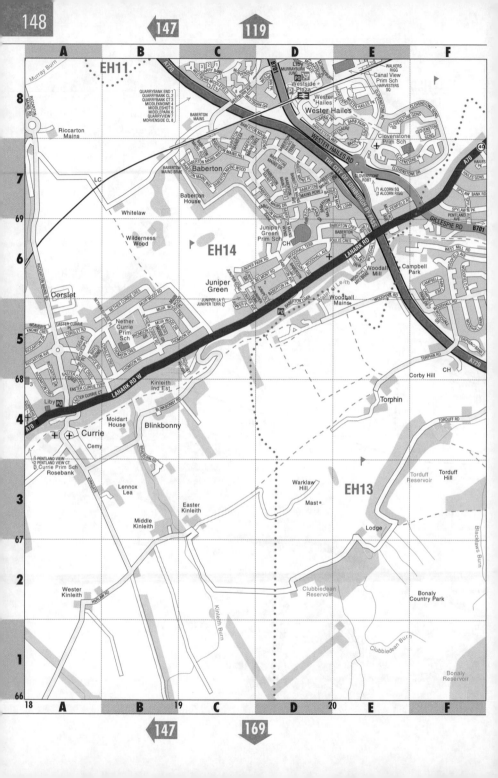

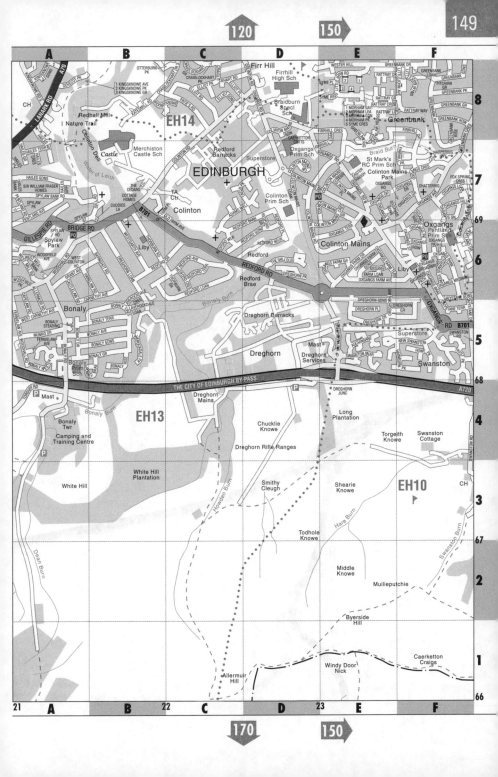

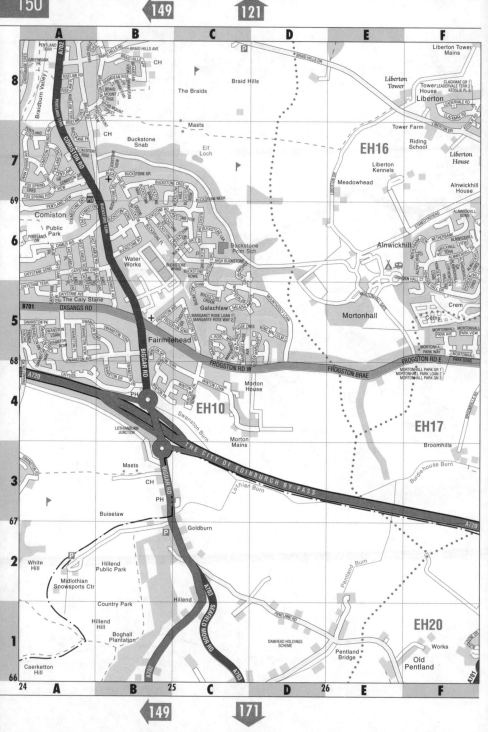

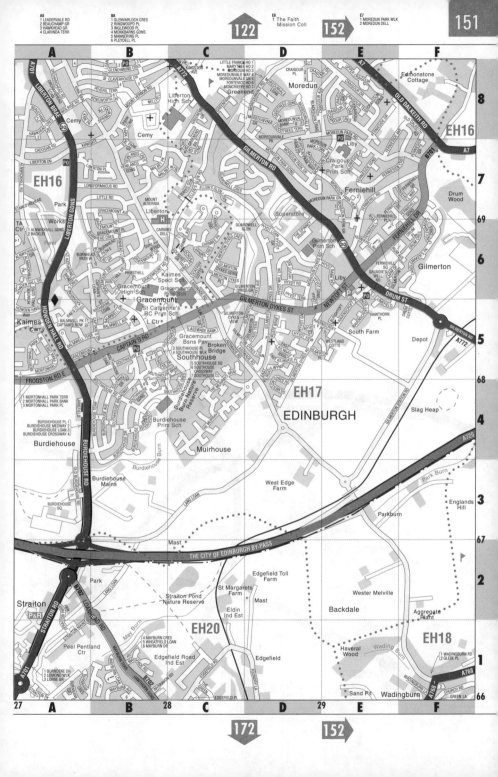

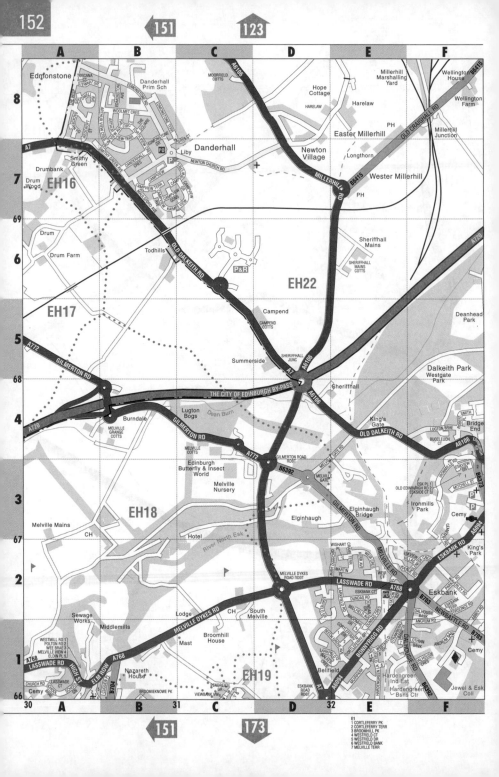

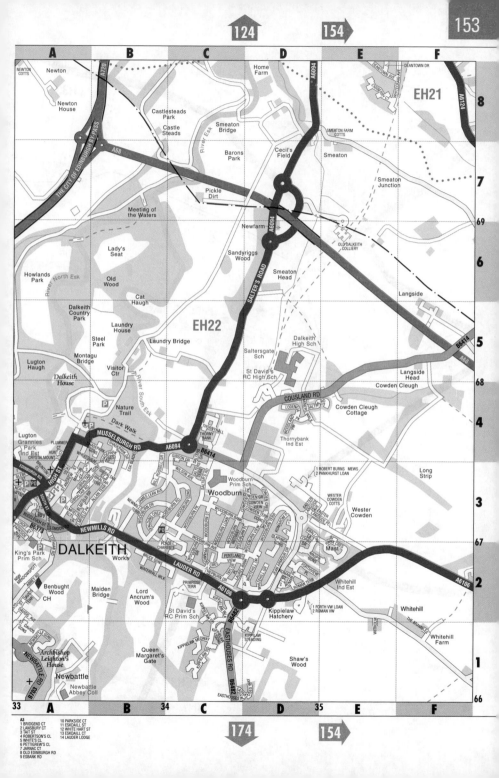

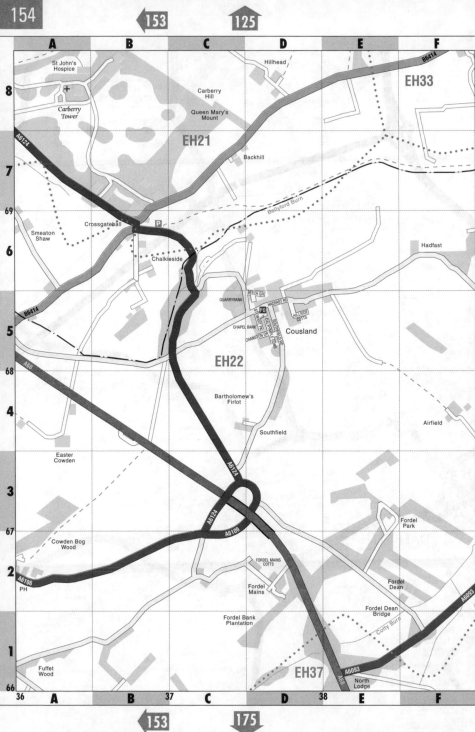

153
125

A B C D E F

8

7

69

6

5

68

4

3

67

2

1

66

St John's
Hospice

Carberry
Tower

EH21

Hillhead

Carberry
Hill

Queen Mary's
Mount

Backhill

EH33

A6124

B6414

Bellyford Burn

Crossgatehall

Smeaton
Shaw

P

Chalkieside

Hadfast

B6414

A68

QUARRYBANK

BEECH GR

HADFAST RD

ST MARGT PL

HILLSIDE
COTTS

CHAPEL BANK

CRANSTON DR

SOUTHFIELD RD

CALDWELL ELMS

Cousland

EH22

Bartholomew's
Firlot

Southfield

Airfield

A6124

Easter
Cowden

Cowden Bog
Wood

A6106

Fordel
Park

A6124

A6106

FORDEL MAINS
COTTS

Fordel
Mains

Fordel
Dean

Fordel Bank
Plantation

Fordel Dean
Bridge

Cotty Burn

A6093

A6106
PH

Fuffet
Wood

EH37

A6

A6093

North
Lodge

A B C D E F

36 37 38

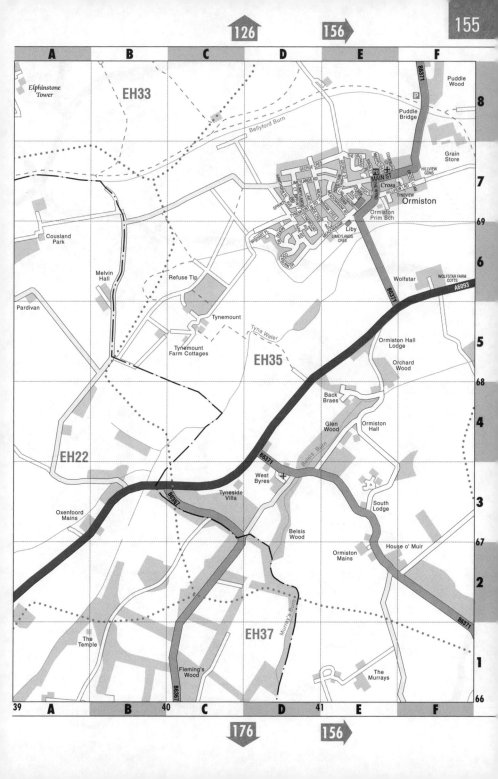

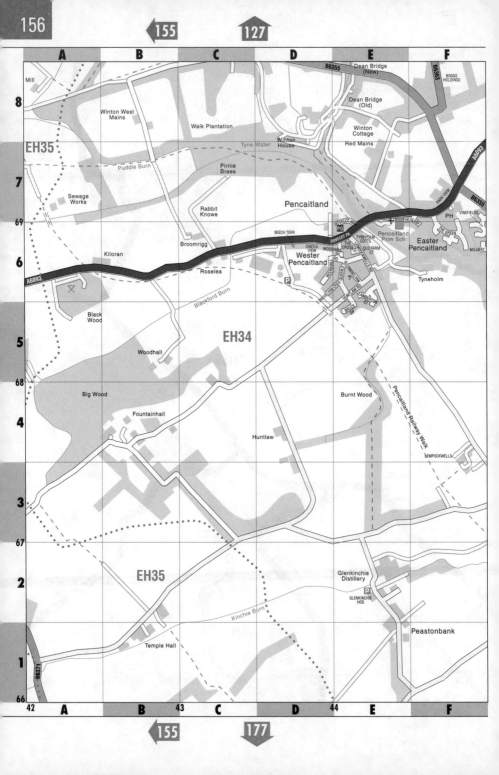

A B C D E F

8

7

69

6

5

68

4

3

67

2

66

1

EH35

Mill

Winton West Mains

Walk Plantation

Puddle Burn

Sewage Works

Pirnie Braes

Rabbit Knowe

Broomrigg

Kiloran

Roselea

Blackford Burn

Black Wood

Woodhall

EH34

Big Wood

Fountainhall

Huntlaw

Tyne Water

Winton House

B6355

Dean Bridge (New)

Dean Bridge (Old)

Winton Cottage

Red Mains

Pencaitland

Wester Pencaitland

BEECH TERR

DOVECOT PK

PO

CASTLE VIEW

WOODHALL

THE CROSS

OLD FARM CT

TYNEHOLM COTTS

Pencaitland Prim Sch

THE GLEBE

PH

VINEFIELDS

THE GREEN

MILLWAY

Easter Pencaitland

Tyneholm

TYNEHOLM DR

OLD FARM CT

P

PARK VIEW

A6093

B6363

BOGGS HOLDINGS

A6093

A6093

B6363

Burnt Wood

Pencaitland Railway Walk

LEMPOCKWELLS

Glenkinchie Distillery

GLENKINCHIE HOS

P

Peastonbank

Kinchie Burn

EH35

Temple Hall

B6371

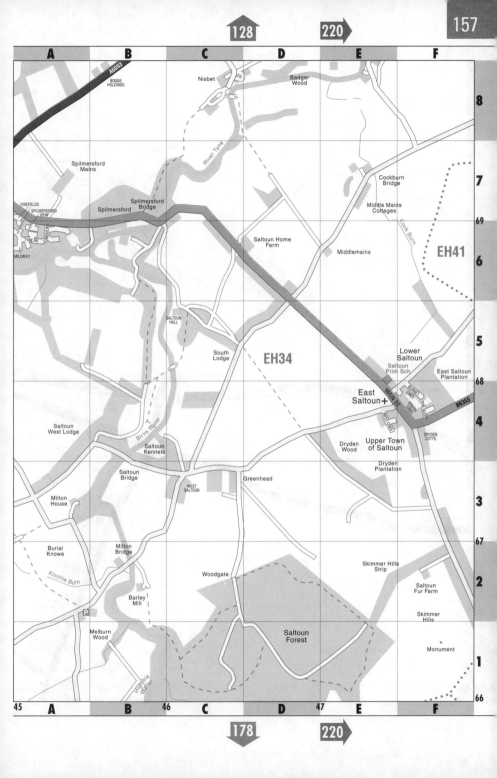

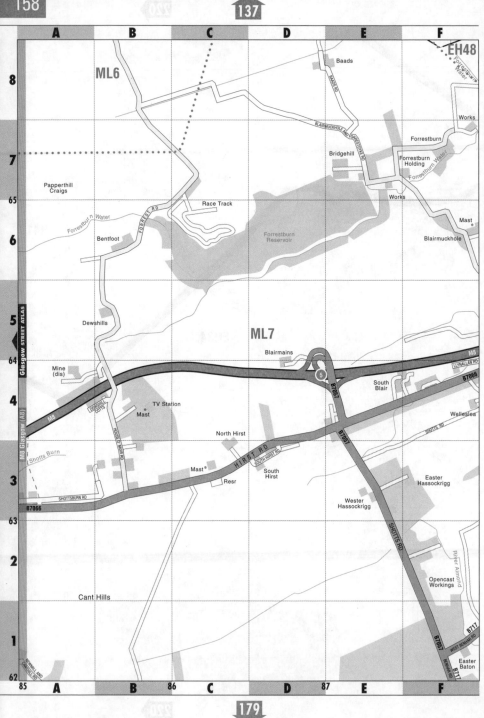

ML6

8

Baads

EH48

Forrestburn Water

Works

BAADS RD

BLAIRMUCKHOLE AND FORRESTDYKE RD

Forrestburn

7

Bridgehill

Forrestburn Holding

Papperthill Craigs

65

Forrestburn Water

Works

FORREST RD

Race Track

Mast

Forrestburn Water

6

Bentfoot

Forrestburn Reservoir

Blairmuckhole

5

Dewshills

ML7

64

Blairmains

M8

LLYNALLAN RD

B7066

4

Mine (dis)

DEWSHILL COTTS

HOUSE O MUIR RD

TV Station

Mast

B7057

South Blair

Welleslea

SHOTTS RD

M8 Glasgow (A8)

M8

Glasgow STREET ATLAS

North Hirst

HIRST RD

SOUTH HIRST RD

South Hirst

B7057

Easter Hassockrigg

Shotts Burn

Mast

Resr

3

SHOTTSBURN RD

63

B7066

Wester Hassockrigg

2

Opencast Workings

River Almond

Cant Hills

SHOTTS RD

1

B7717

B7057

WEST BENHAR RD

Easter Baton

62

BENHAR RD

B7717

NEWMILL AND CANTHILL RD

138
160

A **B** **C** **D** **E** **F**

EH48

Blairhill
Quarry

Loan
Farm

EH48

8

Hill
Farm

Netherton
Farm

Blairmuckhill

7

Knowehead

Mast

M8

65

Harthill
Service
Area

Sewage
Works

Greenrigg
Prim Sch

6

Treesbank
Farm

Service
Area

WESTCRAIGS RD

BURNBRAE RD

WHYTE ST

VIEWFIELD

MILLER ST

HOWBURN RD

HOWBURN

PYTHORN DR

MILLSON

MILLER PL

DUNN TERR

MCFAIL ST

MURDOS

VIEWFIELD
ST

BURNS
CRES

6

How Burn

MOSSBURN AVE

GIBBSHILL PL

ROYTON ST

PAXSTONE DR

CRES

PAXSTONE

BANK RD

FORREST PL

LOAN PL

BRIG WAY

DEER
PATH

EAST MAIN ST

P

B7066

POLKEMMET LA

GREENRIGG
COTTS

B718

B7066

Mossburn Ind Est

WEST MAIN ST

P

VICTORIA RD

BALBAKIE RD

LAUD

MILL RD

Harthill

5

BERTRAM ST

BROOMHILL ST

PEDEN ST

BAIRD TERR

MINTHILL
PL

ALMOND
TERR

B711 CHURCH ST

B711

OLD EASTFIELD
ST

PD

HEATHERBELL
CT

COMBINATION RD

Alexander
Peden
Prim Sch

VICTORIA ST

APSIE RD

5

HIRST RD

Tam's Loup Quarry

Eastfield

LLYNALLAN RD

THISTLE
CONINGBURGH PL

MUIRHEAD PL

Paxtane

64

West
Benhar

PH

ML7

Works

River Almond

4

WEST BENHAR RD

Active
Workings

Spoil
Heap

63

3

Mon

2

Brownhill
Farm

1

62

88 **A** 89 **B** **C** **D** 90 **E** **F**

180
160

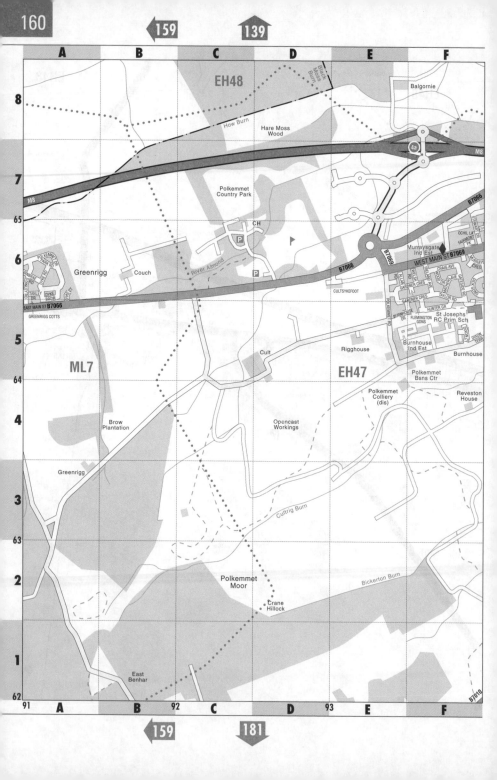

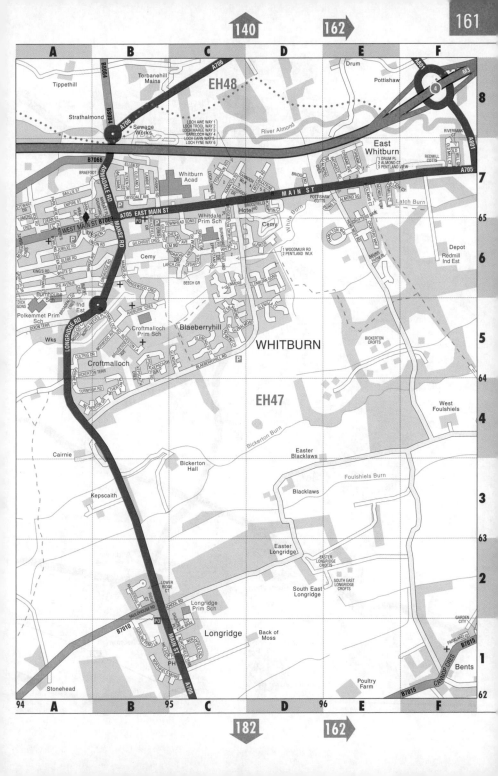

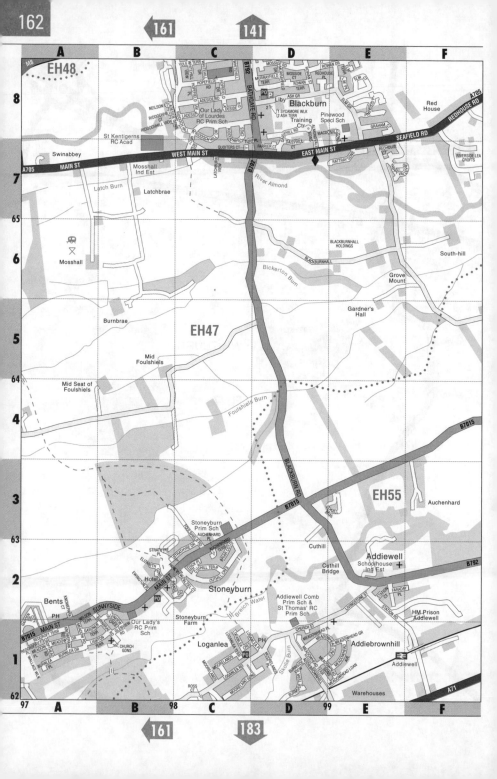

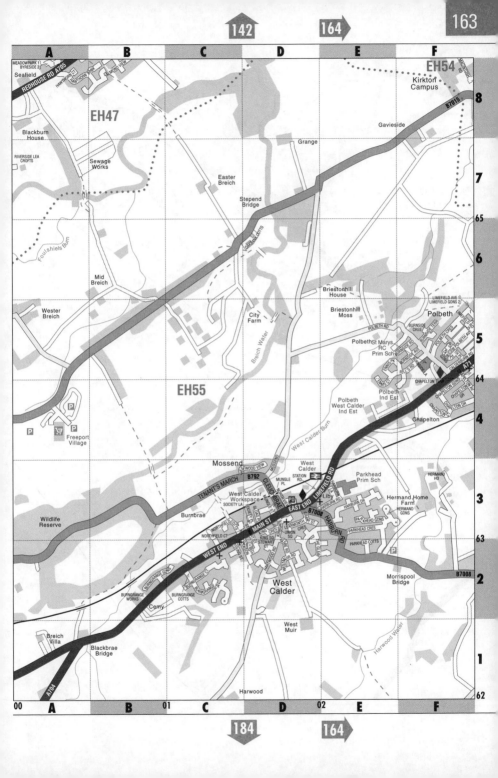

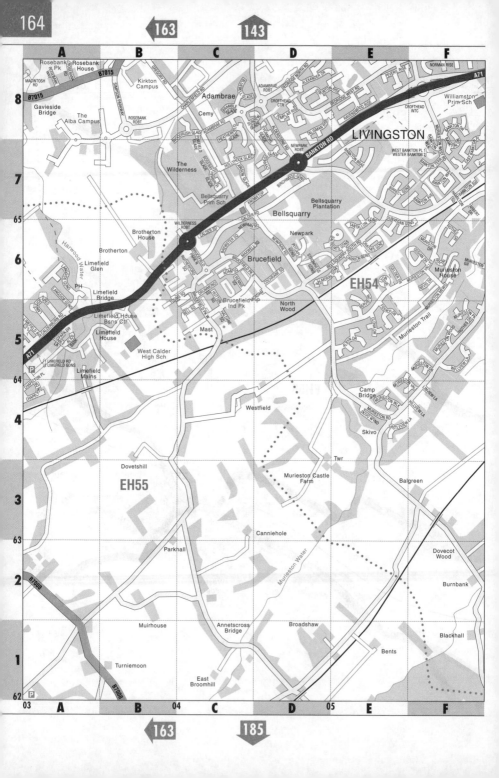

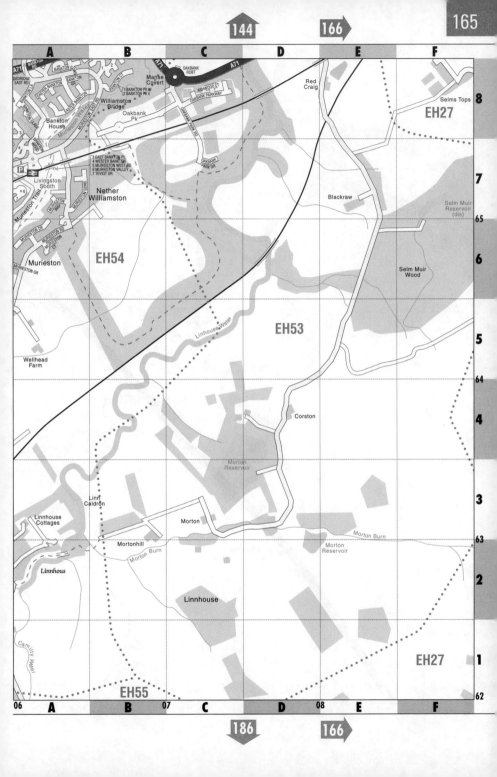

165
145

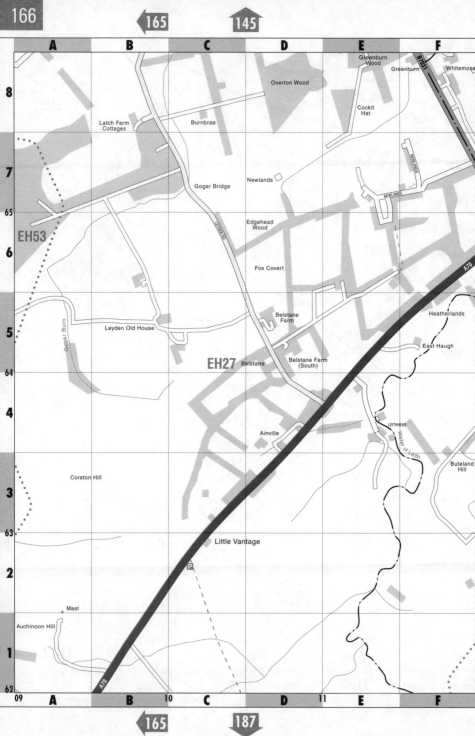

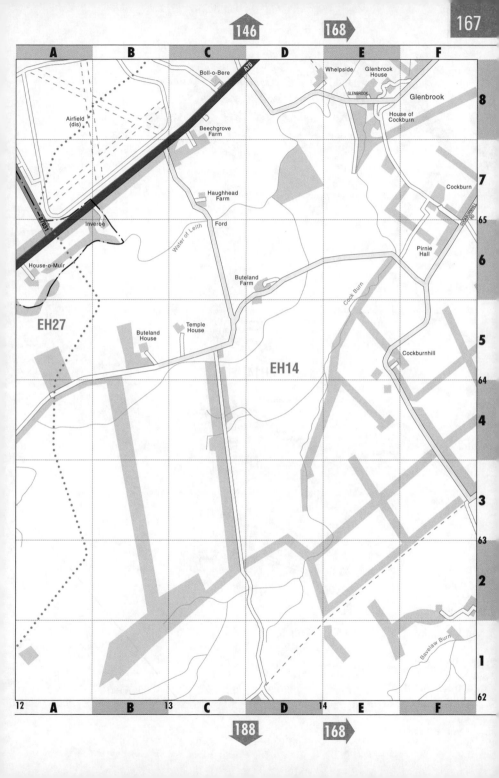

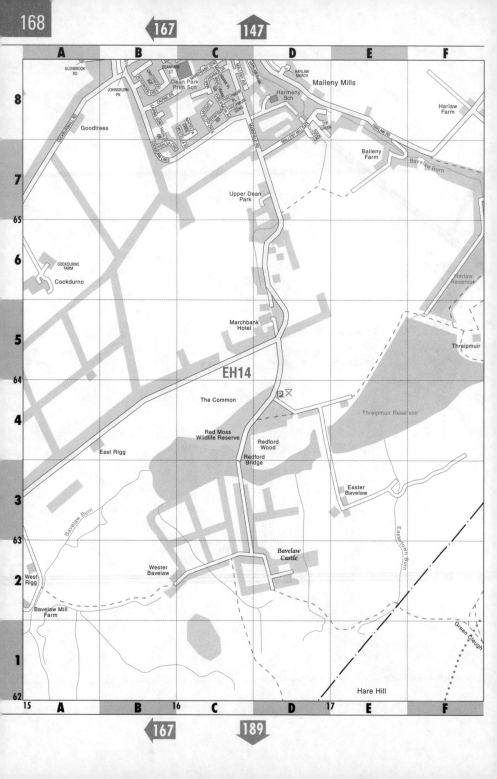

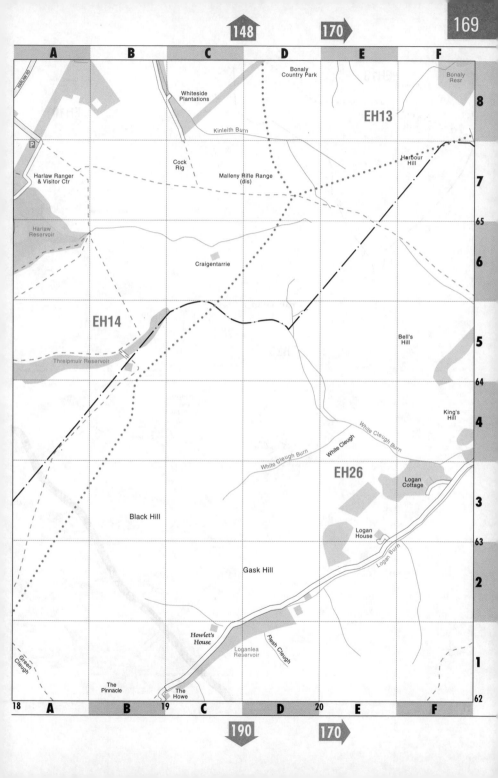

A B C D E F

8

Bonaly
Country Park

Bonaly
Resr

EH13

Whiteside
Plantations

Kinleith Burn

Harbour
Hill

7

Cock
Rig

P

Harlaw Ranger
& Visitor Ctr

Malleny Rifle Range
(dis)

65

Harlaw
Reservoir

6

Craigentarrie

EH14

Bell's
Hill

5

Threipmuir Reservoir

64

King's
Hill

4

White Cleugh Burn

White Cleugh

EH26

Logan
Cottage

3

Black Hill

Logan
House

63

Gask Hill

Logan Burn

2

White Cleugh Burn

Flesh Cleugh

Howlet's
House

Loganlea
Reservoir

1

Green
Cleugh

The
Pinnacle

The
Howe

18   A   B   19   C   D   20   E   F   62

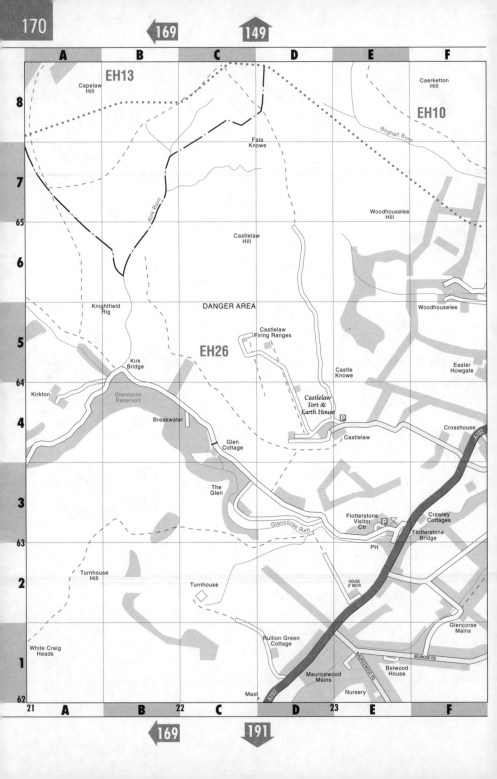

169
149

EH13

Capelaw Hill

Caerketton Hill

EH10

8

Fala Knowe

Boghall Burn

Kirk Burn

7

65

Woodhouselee Hill

Castlelaw Hill

6

DANGER AREA

Knightfield Rig

Woodhouselee

Castlelaw Firing Ranges

5

EH26

Easter Howgate

Kirk Bridge

Castle Knowe

64

Kirkton

Glencorse Reservoir

Castlelaw Fort & Earth House

Breakwater

Castlelaw

Crosshouse

4

A702

Glen Cottage

The Glen

3

Glencorse Burn

Flotterstone Visitor Ctr

Crawley Cottages

Flotterstone Bridge

63

PH

Turnhouse Hill

HOUSE O' MUIR

2

Turnhouse

Glencorse Mains

White Craig Heads

1

Rullion Green Cottage

BELWOOD RD

Belwood House

MAURICEWOOD RD

Mauricewood Mains

Nursery

62

Mast

A702

21 | A | | B | **22** | C | | D | **23** | E | | F

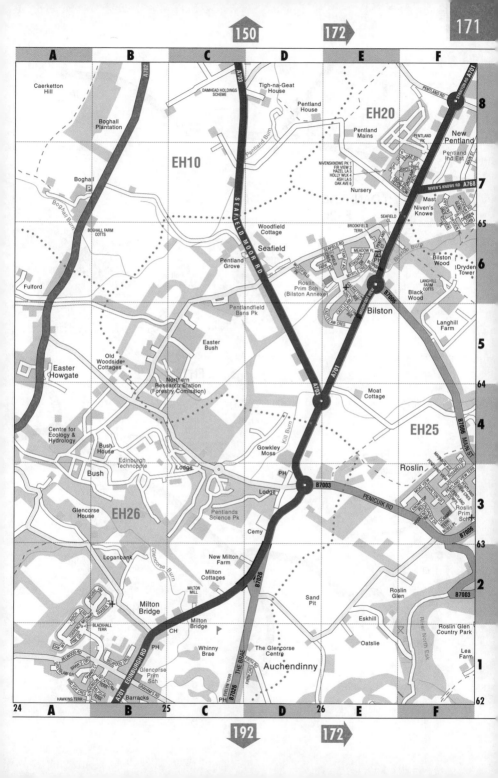

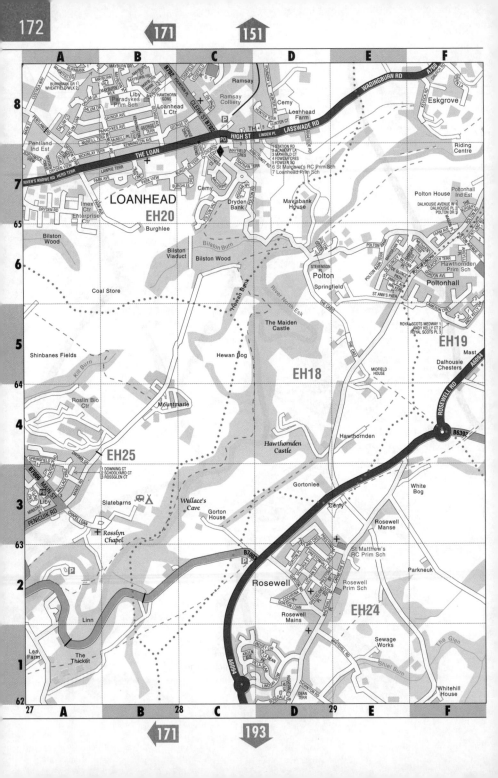

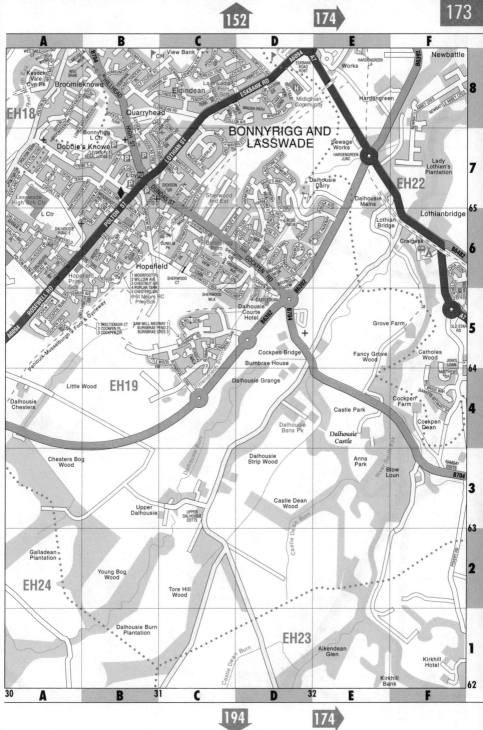

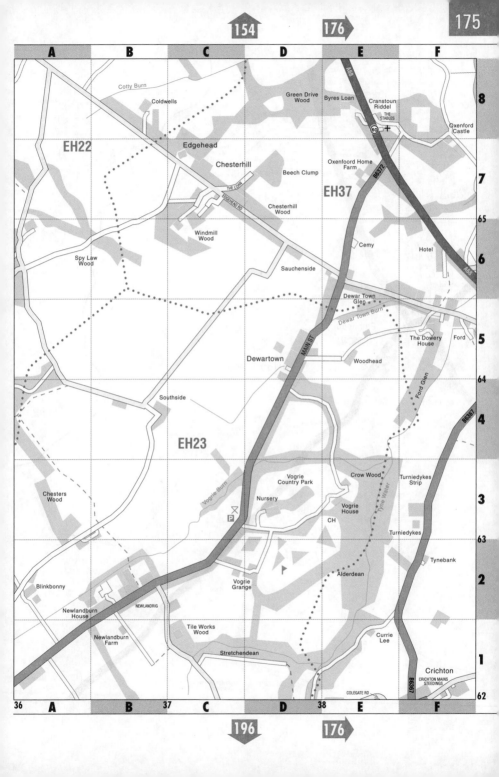

Cotty Burn
Coldwells
EH22
Edgehead
Chesterhill
THE LOAN
EDGEHEAD RD
Beech Clump
Green Drive Wood
Byres Loan
Cranstoun Riddel
THE STABLES
Oxenford Castle
Oxenfoord Home Farm
EH37
Chesterhill Wood
Windmill Wood
Spy Law Wood
Sauchenside
Cemy
Hotel
B6372
A68
Dewar Town Glen
Dewar Town Burn
The Dowery House
Ford
Dewartown
MAIN ST
Woodhead
Ford Glen
Southside
EH23
B6367
Chesters Wood
Vogrie Burn
Vogrie Country Park
Crow Wood
Turniedykes Strip
Nursery
Vogrie House
CH
Tyne Water
Turniedykes
Blinkbonny
Tynebank
Newlandburn House
NEWLANDRIG
Vogrie Grange
Alderdean
Newlandburn Farm
Tile Works Wood
Currie Lee
Stretchendean
Crichton
CRICHTON MAINS STEEDINGS
B6367
COLEGATE RD

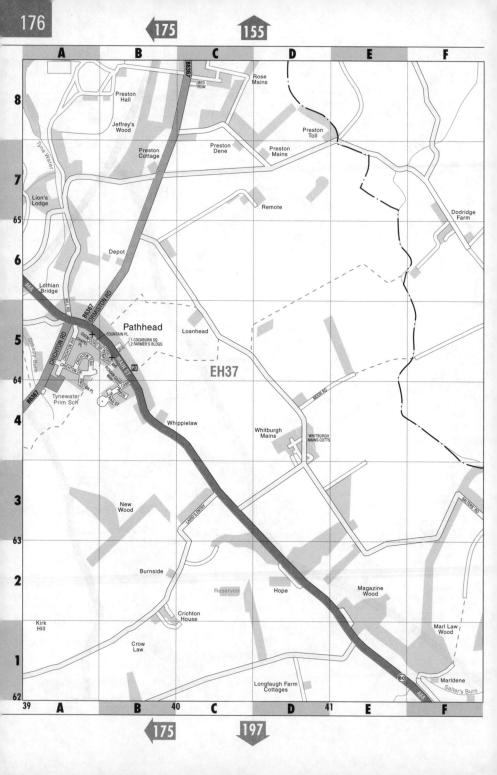

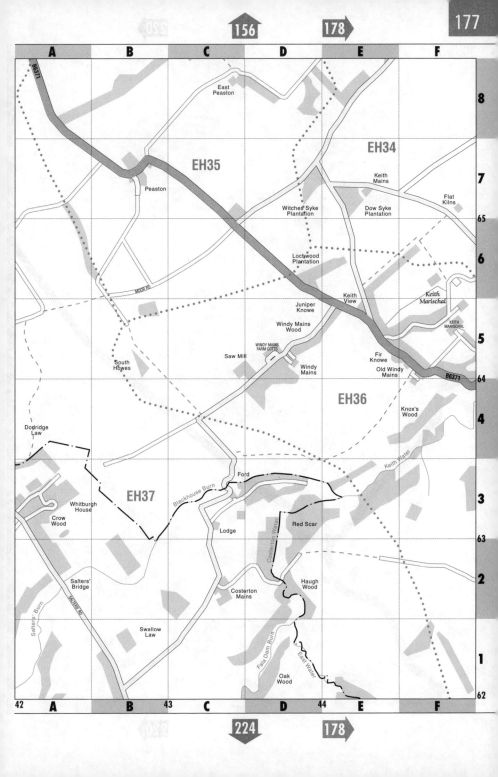

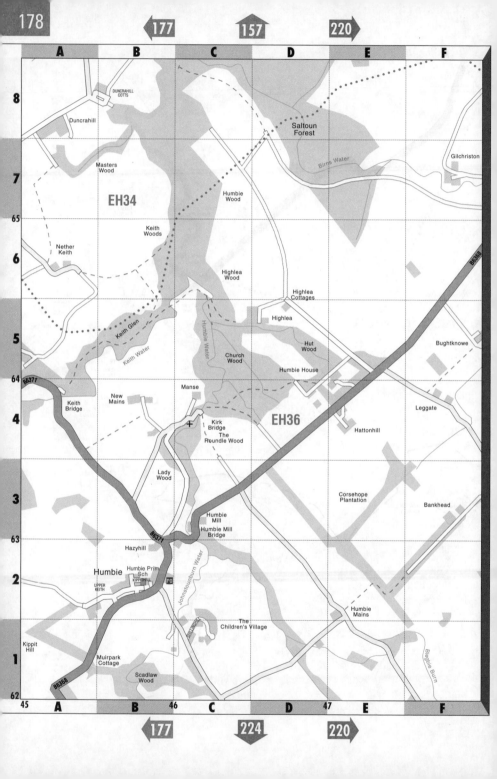

179
159

B717

CH

Starryshaw
Farm

South Calder Water

Stanebent

Spoil
Heap

Cairneyhead

ML7

Stane

STANE RD

HIGH ST

HERBISON
CRES

Stane
Prim Sch

STANE GR

MANSE RD

CROWN AVE

CRES

GOWRIE ST

HAZEL GR

TORBOTHIE RD

CLYDE CRES

KEITH DR

PITLOCHRY DR

CALDER DR

NORTHFIELD

SOUTHFIELD RD

Torbothie

CEMETERY RD

Cemy

B7010

MAIN ST

CHARLOTTE ST

SANDYVALE
PL

SPRINGVALE
PL

STEVENSON PL

Stane

BLINNY CT 1
TARBRAX PATH 2

BRIDGE ST

KNOLL CROFT RD

LOCHEND
CRES

MAITLAND CT

APPIN TERR

LANSDOWNE CRES

LASSODIE ST

NEVIS PL

GARTER

TULLOCH RD

MELFORD RD

LAGGAN AVE

OMOCH DR

WYLIE PL

1 ETIVE WLK
2 JIG WAY
3 GAIR WYND
4 BOWMORE WLK
5 TORRIN LOAN
6 SPRINGHILL VIEW
7 DORNIE WYND
8 MORAR WAY
9 CORE LOAN
10 SUNA PATH
11 SALEN LOAN

SPRINGHILL RD

Springhill

B7010

BLACKHALL ST

BELMONT DRIVE

MULLOCH CT

BERRYHILL
TERR

BROWN'S PL

LARCHFIELD PATH

NORTHFIELD AVE

ELMWOOD RD

Works

Springhill

A71

Works

Knowton
Farm

SPRINGHILL AND LEADLOCH RD

Lingore Linn

EH47

B7010

HEADLESSCROSS RD

B715

A71

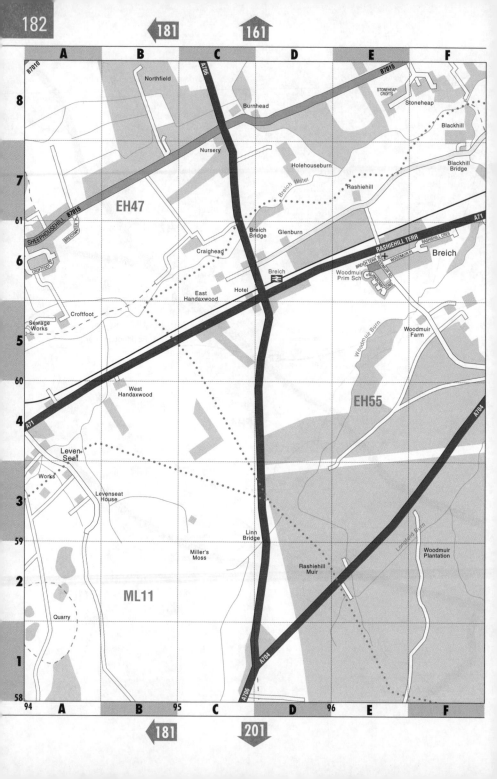

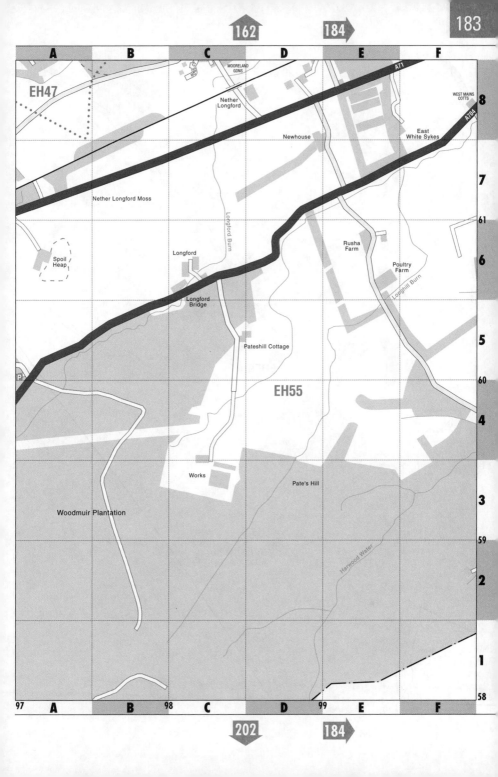

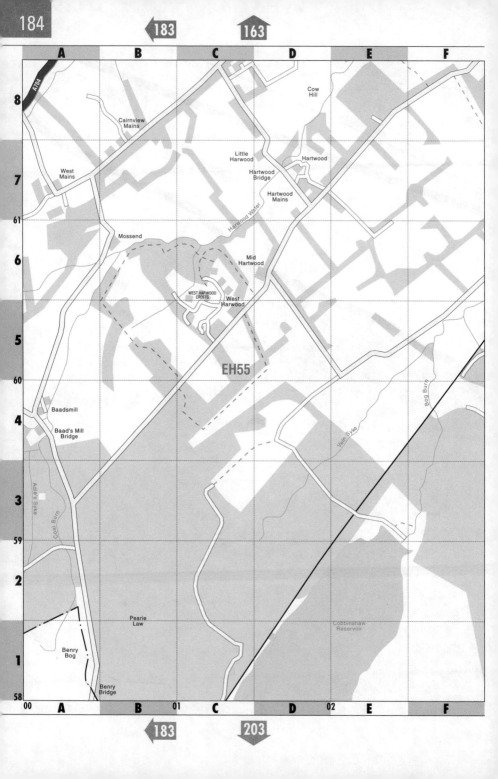

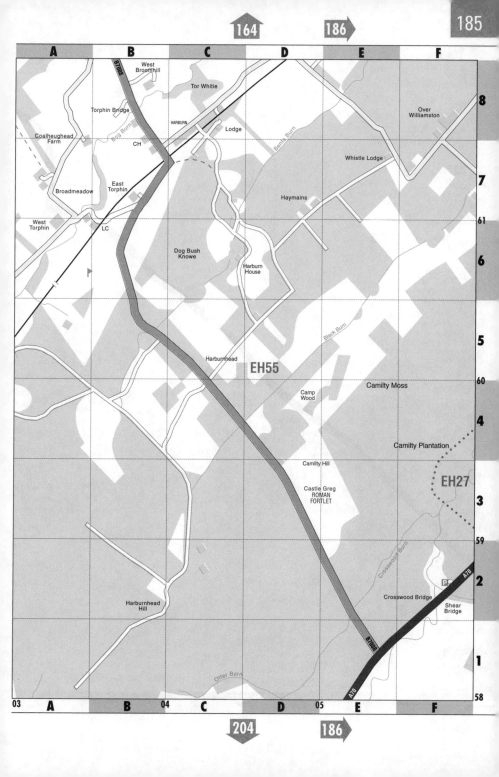

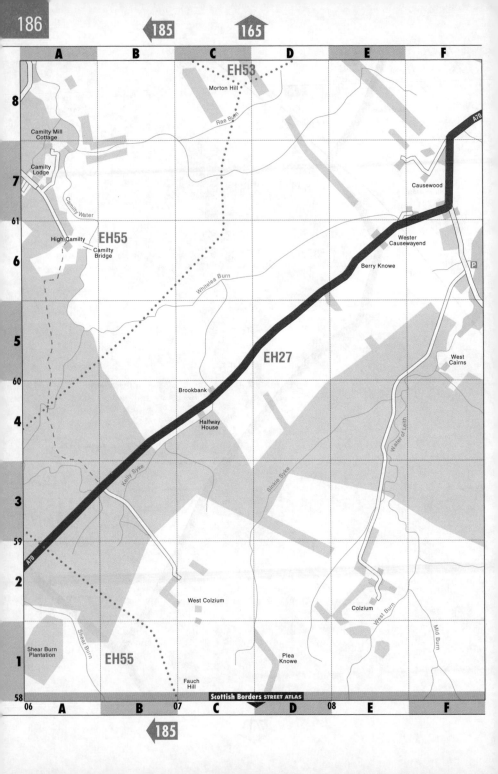

EH53

Morton Hill

Camilty Mill
Cottage

Camilty
Lodge

8

Rae Burn

A70

Causewood

7

Camilty Water

Causewood

61

High Camilty

EH55

Wester
Causewayend

Camilty
Bridge

6

Whitelea Burn

Berry Knowe

P

West
Cairns

5

EH27

Brookbank

60

Halfway
House

4

Kelly Syke

Sinkie Syke

Water of Leith

3

59

West Colzium

Colzium

West Burn

Mid Burn

2

A70

West Burn

Shear Burn
Plantation

EH55

Shear Burn

Plea
Knowe

1

Fauch
Hill

58

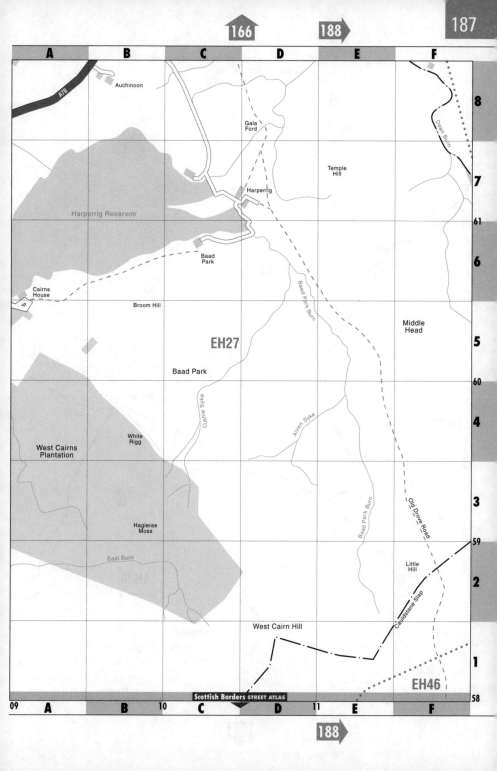

A B C D E F

8

Auchinoon

A70

Gala
Ford

7

Temple
Hill

Harperrig

61

Harperrig Reservoir

Baad Park Burn

Baad
Park

6

Cairns
House

Broom Hill

Middle
Head

EH27

5

Baad Park

60

Cushie Syke

Aiven Syke

4

West Cairns
Plantation

White
Rigg

Baad Park Burn

3

Old Drove Road

Hagierae
Moss

59

East Burn

Little
Hill

2

Cauldstane Slap

West Cairn Hill

1

EH46

58

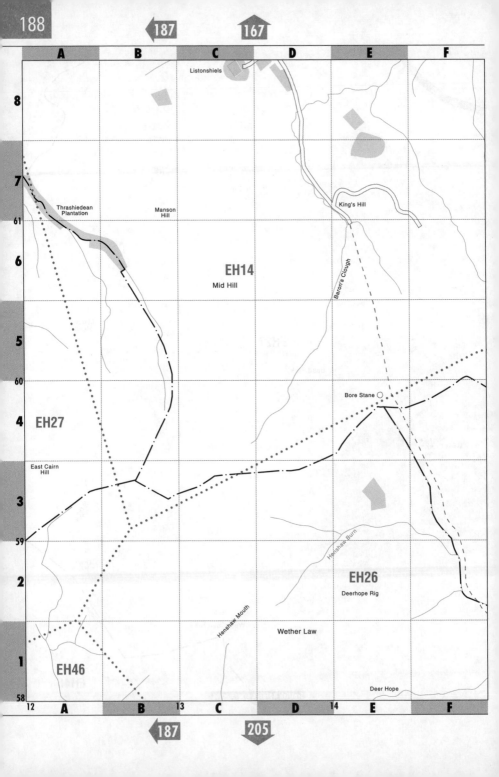

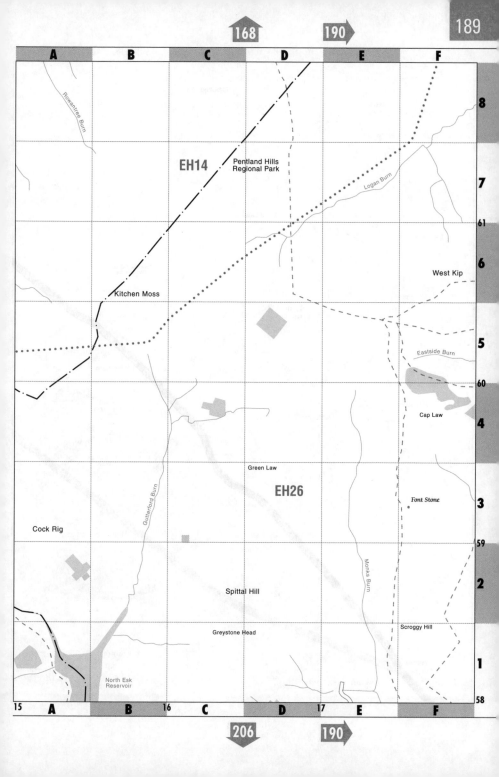

A B C D E F

8

Rowantree Burn

EH14 · Pentland Hills
Regional Park

7

Logan Burn

61

West Kip

6

Kitchen Moss

Eastside Burn

5

60

Cap Law

4

Green Law

EH26

Font Stone

3

Cock Rig

59

Gutterford Burn

Monks Burn

Spittal Hill

2

Greystone Head

Scroggy Hill

1

North Esk
Reservoir

58

15 A B 16 C D 17 E F

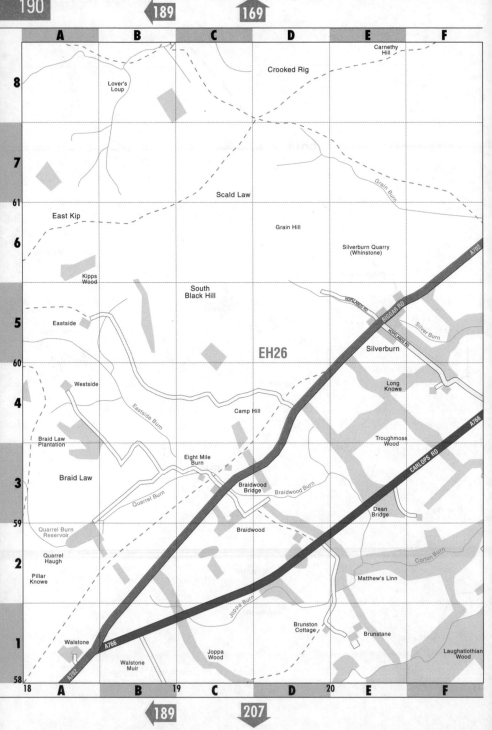

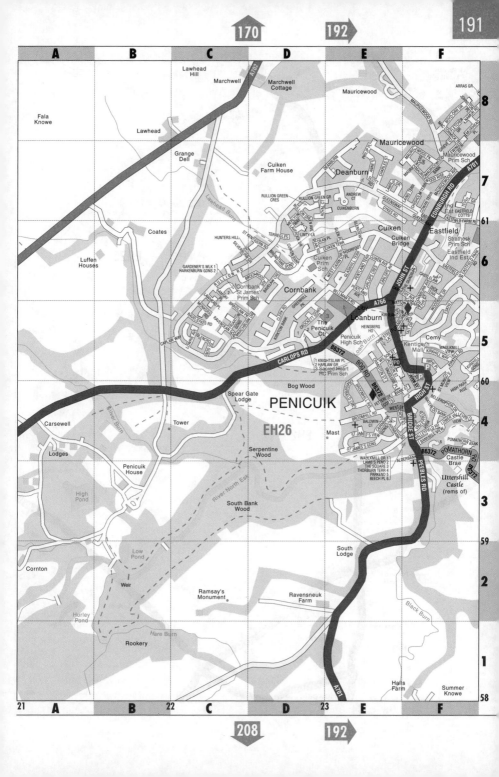

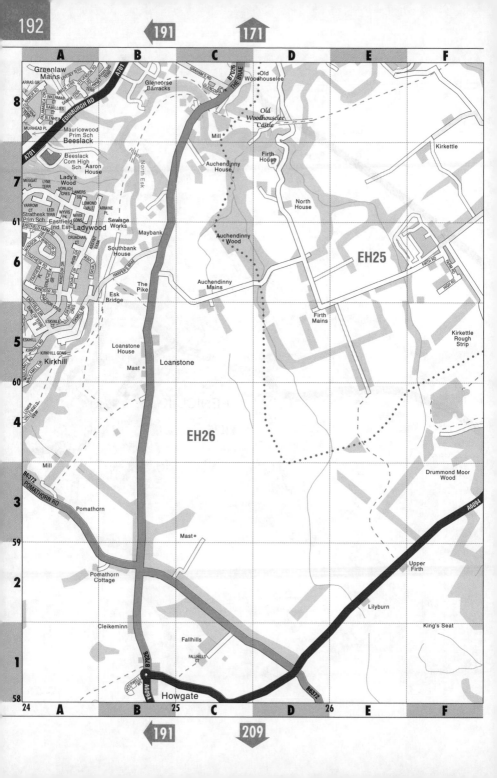

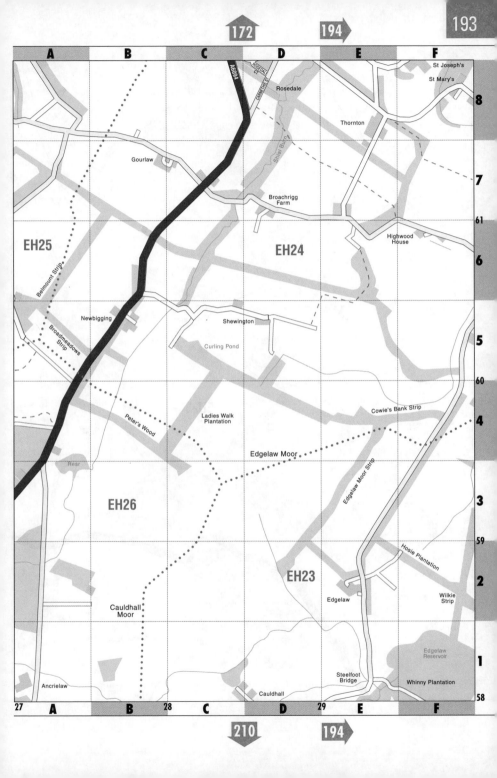

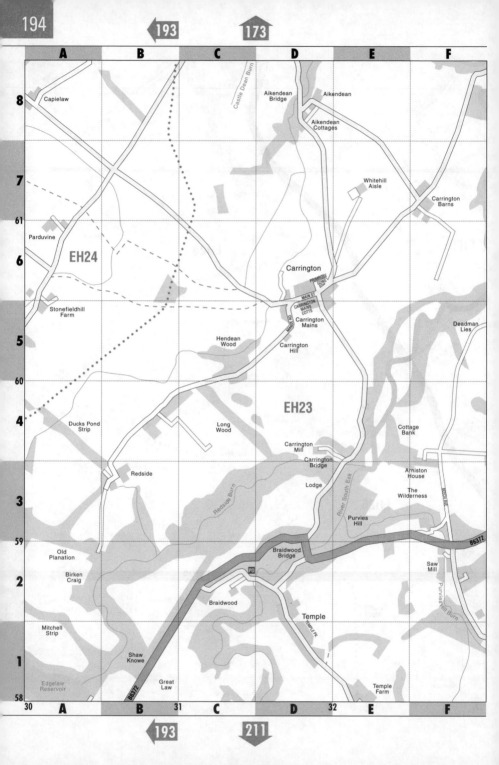

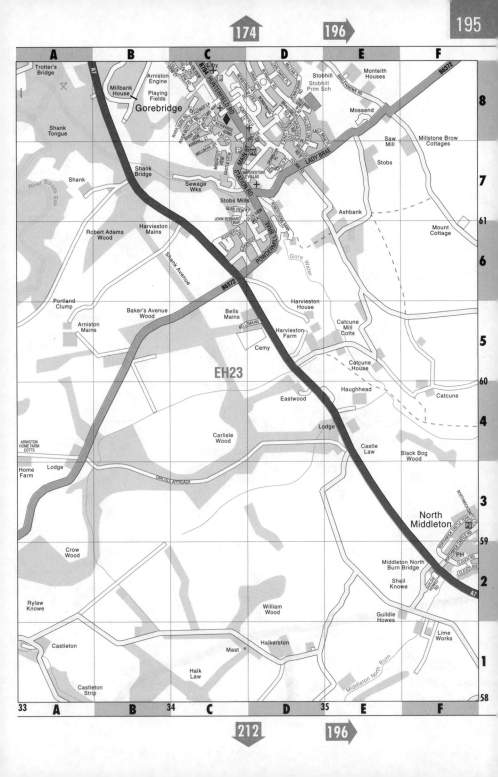

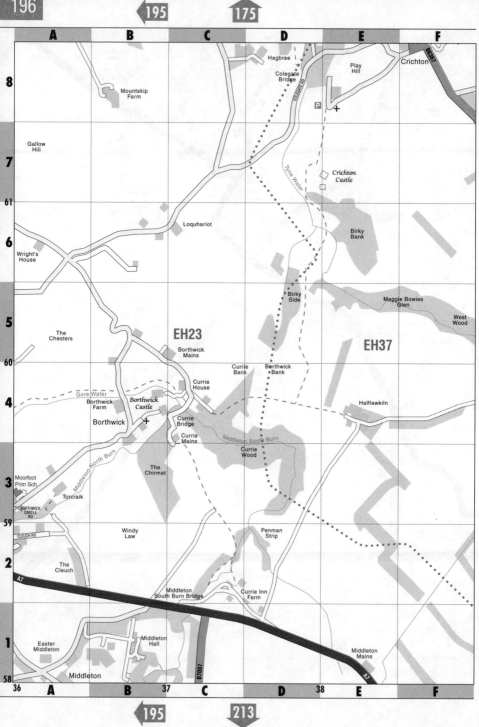

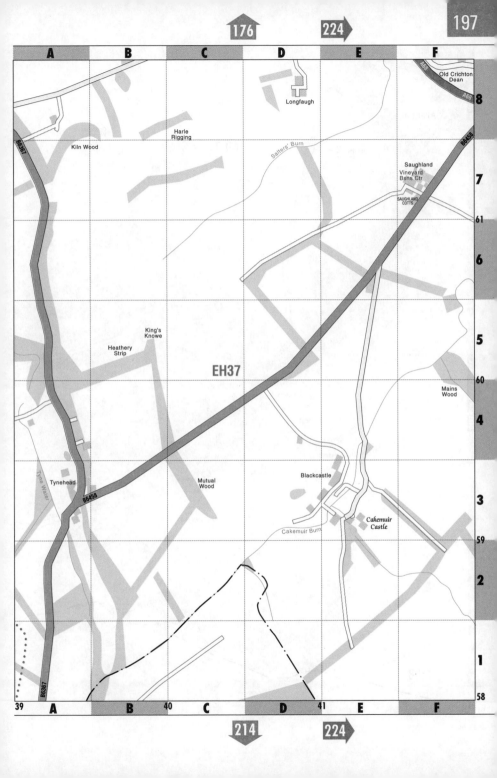

A B C D E F

8

Old Crichton Dean

Longfaugh

Harle Rigging

Salters' Burn

Kiln Wood

Saughland Vineyard Bsns Ctr

7

SAUGHLAND COTTS

61

6

King's Knowe

Heathery Strip

5

EH37

Mains Wood

60

4

Tyne Water

Tynehead

B6458

Mutual Wood

Blackcastle

3

Cakemuir Castle

Cakemuir Burn

59

2

1

58

39 A B 40 C D 41 E F

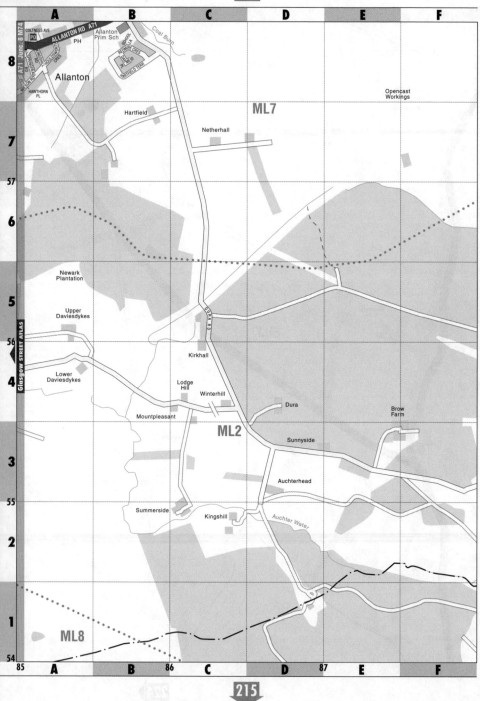

179

A   B   C   D   E   F

COLTNESS AVE
PO
ALLANTON RD A71
PH
Allanton
Prim Sch
A71 Junc. 8 M74
SCHOOL LA
RETMYX CRES
ORHFIELD TERR

Allanton

HAWTHORN PL

8

Hartfield

Coal Burn

ML7

Opencast
Workings

Netherhall

7

57

6

Newark
Plantation

Upper
Daviesdykes

5

DURA RD

56

Kirkhall

Lower
Daviesdykes

4

Lodge
Hill

Winterhill

Dura

Brow
Farm

Mountpleasant

ML2

Sunnyside

3

Auchterhead

55

Summerside

Kingshill

Auchter Water

2

1

ML8

54

85   A   B   86   C   D   87   E   F

Glasgow STREET ATLAS

215

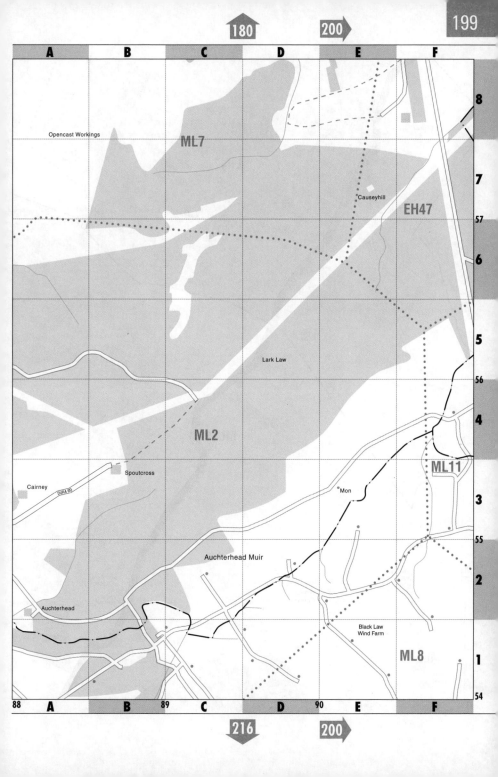

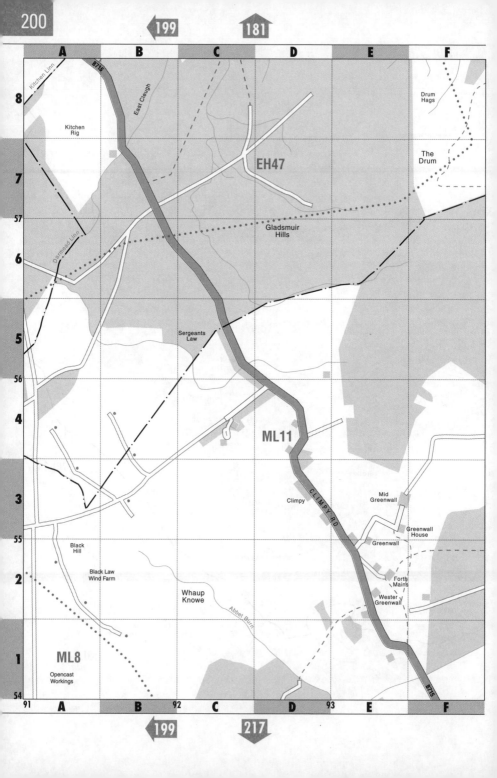

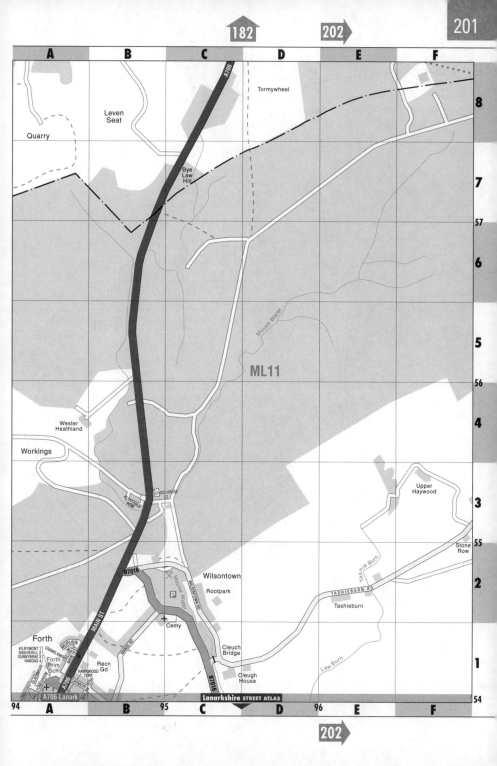

Tormywheel

Leven
Seat

Quarry

8

Bye
Law
Hill

7

57

6

Mouse Water

5

ML11

56

Wester
Heathland

4

Workings

Upper
Haywood

3

SCHOOLHOUSE
CT

55

Stone
Row

PROVIDENCE
ROW

B7016

Wilsontown

Rootpark

2

TASHIEBURN RD

Tashieburn

P

Mouse Water

WILSONTOWN RD

Tashie Burn

Cleuch
Bridge

Cemy

Forth

KILRYMONT 1
RASHIEHILL 2
SUNNYBRAE 3
HANDAX 4

CRAWS KNOWE

Forth
Prim
Sch

HAWKWOOD
TERR

MANSE RD

Recn
Gd

Cleugh
House

Law Burn

1

A706 Lanark

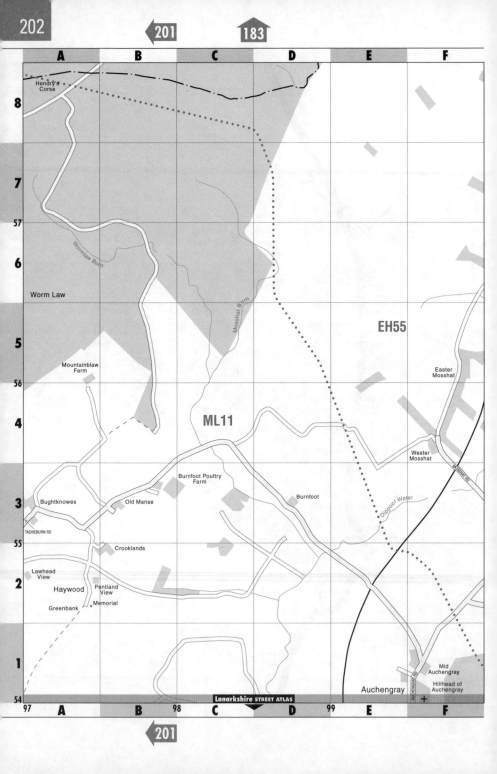

Hendry's Corse

Worm Law

Wormlaw Burn

Mosshat Burn

EH55

Easter Mosshat

Mountainblaw Farm

ML11

Wester Mosshat

MOSSHAT RD

Burnfoot Poultry Farm

Burnfoot

Dippool Water

Bughtknowes

Old Manse

TASHIEBURN RD

Crooklands

Lawhead View

Haywood

Pentland View

Greenbank

Memorial

Auchengray

AUCHENGRAY RD

Mid Auchengray

Hillhead of Auchengray

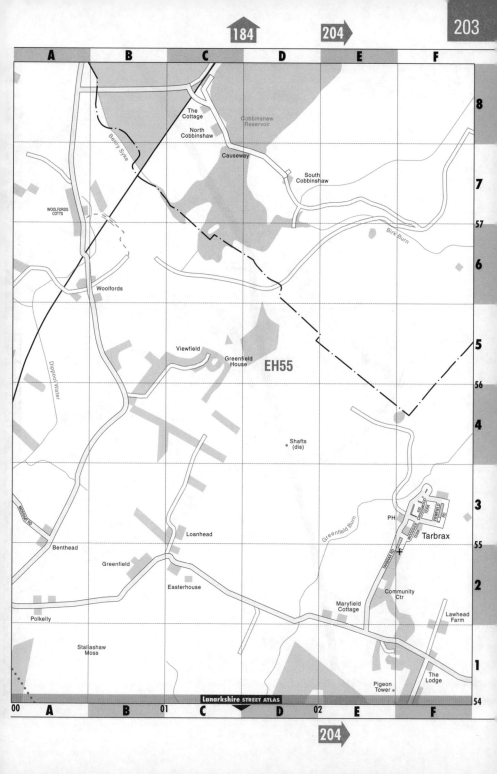

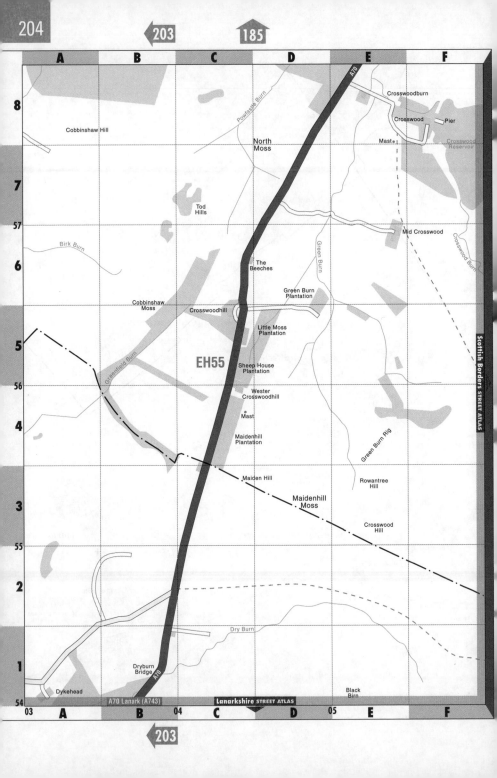

| A | B | C | D | E | F |

8 Cobbinshaw Hill

Powfaside Burn

Crosswoodburn

Crosswood

Pier

North
Moss

Mast

Crosswood
Reservoir

7

Tod
Hills

57

Birk Burn

Mid Crosswood

Crosswood Burn

6

The
Beeches

Green Burn

Cobbinshaw
Moss

Green Burn
Plantation

Crosswoodhill

Little Moss
Plantation

5

EH55

Greenfield Burn

Sheep House
Plantation

56

Wester
Crosswoodhill

4

Mast

Maidenhill
Plantation

Green Burn Rig

Maiden Hill

Rowantree
Hill

3

Maidenhill
Moss

Crosswood
Hill

55

2

Dry Burn

1

Dryburn
Bridge

A70

Black
Birn

54
Dykehead

03 | A | B | **04** | C | D | **05** | E | F

Scottish Borders STREET ATLAS

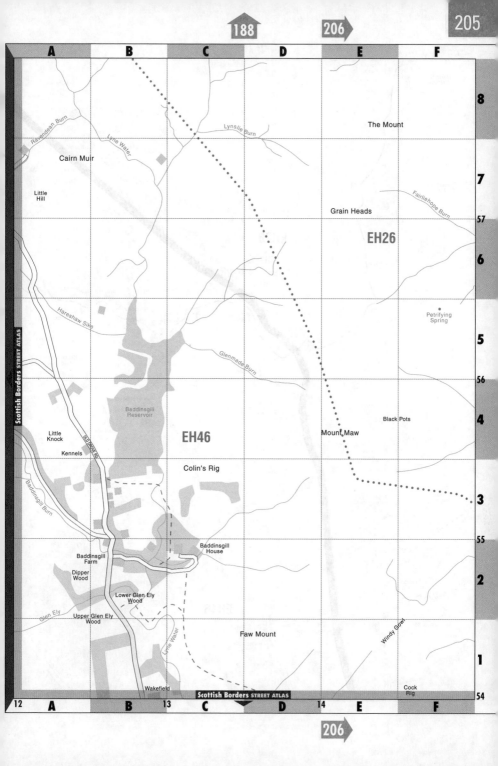

The Mount

Cairn Muir

Lynslie Burn

Ravendean Burn

Lyne Water

Little
Hill

Grain Heads

Fairliehope Burn

EH26

Hareshaw Sike

Petrifying
Spring

Glenmade Burn

Baddinsgill
Reservoir

EH46

Black Pots

Little
Knock

Mount Maw

Kennels

Colin's Rig

Baddinsgill Burn

Baddinsgill
House

Baddinsgill
Farm

Dipper
Wood

Lower Glen Ely
Wood

Glen Ely

Upper Glen Ely
Wood

Lyne Water

Faw Mount

Windy Gowl

Wakefield

Cock
Rig

Scottish Borders STREET ATLAS

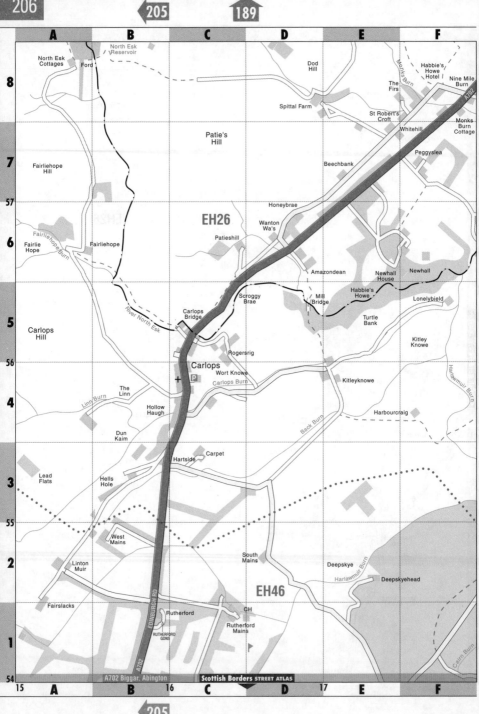

| | A | B | C | D | E | F |

8

North Esk Cottages
Ford
North Esk Reservoir
Dod Hill
Habbie's Howe Hotel
Nine Mile Burn
The Firs
Spittal Farm
St Robert's Croft
Monks Burn Cottage
Whitehill

7

Fairliehope Hill
Patie's Hill
Beechbank
Peggyslea

57

Honeybrae

EH26

Wanton Wa's

6

Fairlie Hope
Fairliehope
Fairliehope Burn
Patieshill
Amazondean
Newhall House
Newhall
Scroggy Brae
Mill Bridge
Habbie's Howe
Lonelybield
River North Esk
Carlops Bridge
Turtle Bank
Kitley Knowe

5

Carlops Hill
Rogersrig

56

Carlops
Wort Knowe
Carlops Burn
Kitleyknowe
Harlawmuir Burn

4

The Linn
Linn Burn
Hollow Haugh
Harbourcraig
Back Burn
Dun Kaim

Hartside
Carpet

3

Lead Flats
Hells Hole

55

West Mains
South Mains
Deepskye
Deepskyehead
Harlawmuir Burn

2

Linton Muir

EH46

Fairslacks
Rutherford
Rutherford Mains
CH
Cairn Burn

1

EDINBURGH RD
RUTHERFORD GDNS
A702

54

| 15 | A | B | 16 | C | D | 17 | E | F |

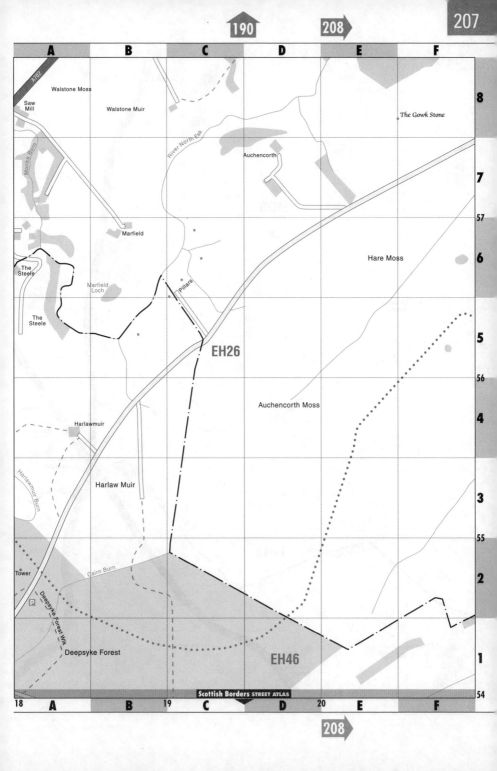

A B C D E F

8

Walstone Moss

Saw
Mill

Walstone Muir

The Gowk Stone

River North Esk

Auchencorth

7

57

Marfield

Hare Moss

6

The
Steele

Marfield
Loch

Pillars

The
Steele

EH26

5

56

Auchencorth Moss

Harlawmuir

4

Harlawmuir Burn

Harlaw Muir

3

55

Tower

Cairn Burn

2

P

Deepsyke Forest Wlk

Deepsyke Forest

EH46

1

54

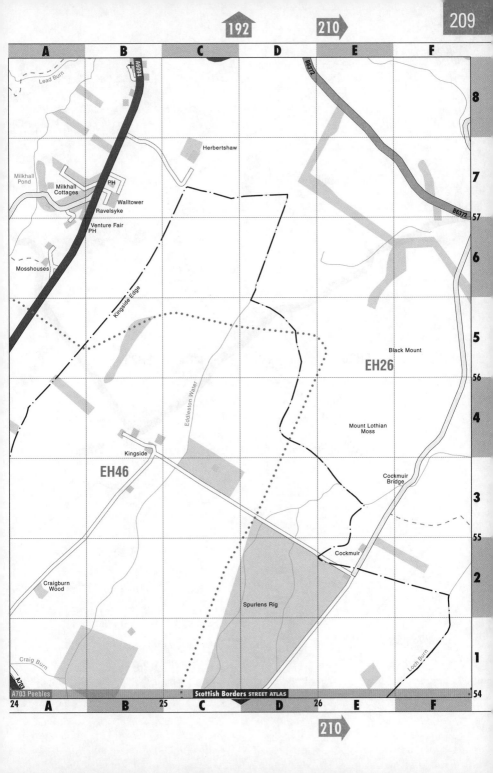

Lead Burn

A6094

B6372

Herbertshaw

Milkhall
Pond

PH

Milkhall
Cottages

Walltower

Ravelsyke

Venture Fair
PH

Mosshouses

Kingside Edge

B6372

57

8

7

6

Black Mount

EH26

5

56

Eddleston Water

Mount Lothian
Moss

4

Kingside

EH46

Cockmuir
Bridge

3

55

Cockmuir

Craigburn
Wood

Spurlens Rig

2

Craig Burn

Loch Burn

1

A703

A703 Peebles

Scottish Borders STREET ATLAS

54

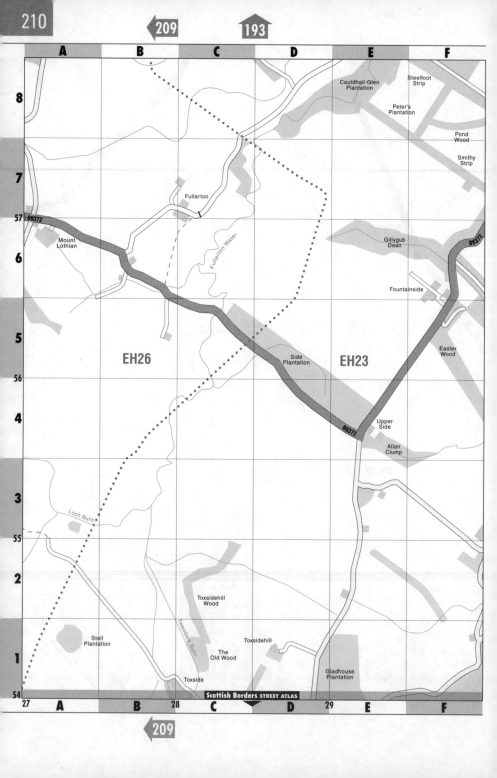

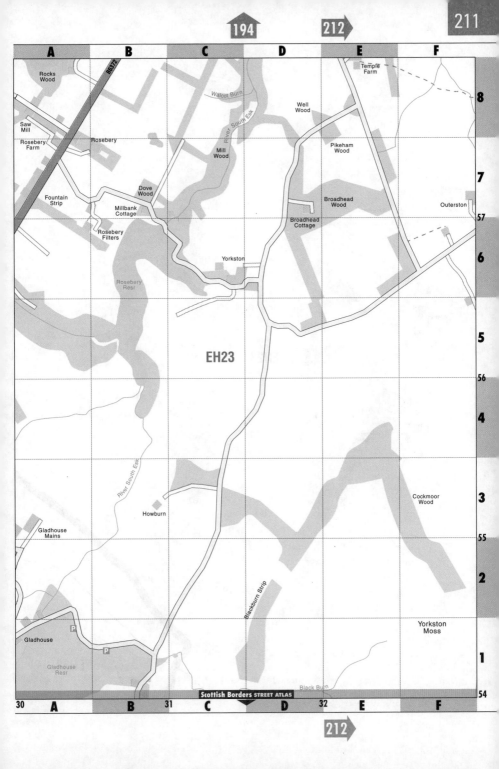

A   **B**   **C**   **D**   **E**   **F**

Rocks
Wood

Temple
Farm

8

Walcot Burn

Well
Wood

Saw
Mill

Rosebery
Farm

Rosebery

Mill
Wood

Pikeham
Wood

7

River South Esk

Dove
Wood

Fountain
Strip

Broadhead
Wood

Outerston

Millbank
Cottage

57

Rosebery
Filters

Broadhead
Cottage

Yorkston

6

Rosebery
Resr

EH23

5

56

4

River South Esk

Cockmoor
Wood

3

Howburn

Gladhouse
Mains

55

Blackburn Strip

2

Yorkston
Moss

P

Gladhouse

P

1

Gladhouse
Resr

Black Burn

54

30   **A**   **B**   31   **C**   **D**   32   **E**   **F**

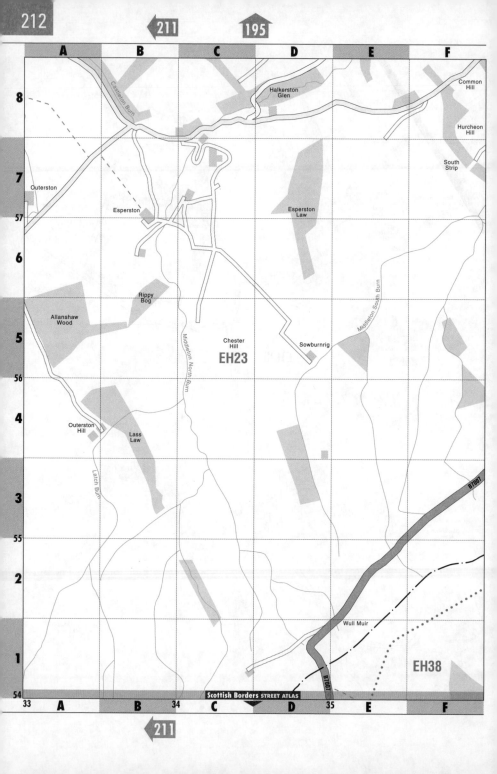

Outerston

Esperston

Halkerston
Glen

Common
Hill

Hurcheon
Hill

South
Strip

Esperston
Law

Castleton Burn

Rippy
Bog

Allanshaw
Wood

Middleton North Burn

Middleton South Burn

Chester
Hill

EH23

Sowburnrig

Outerston
Hill

Lass
Law

Leich Burn

Wull Muir

B7007

B7007

EH38

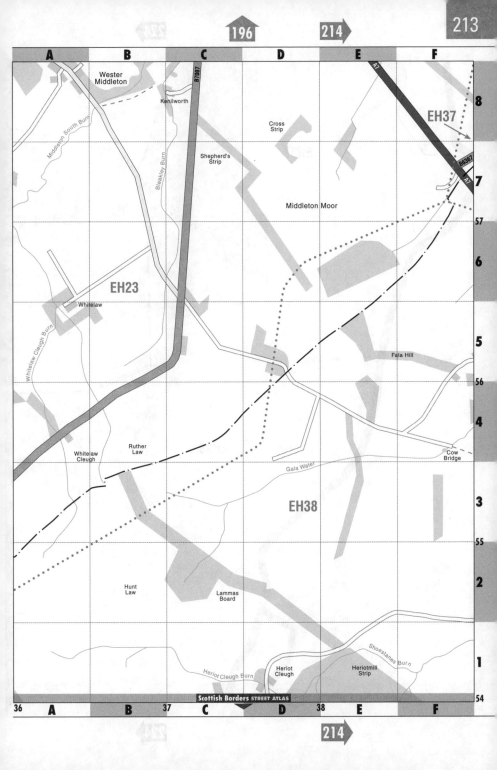

EH37

Wester Middleton
Kenilworth
Cross Strip
Shepherd's Strip
Middleton Moor
EH23
Whitelaw
Whitelaw Cleugh
Ruther Law
Fala Hill
Cow Bridge
Gala Water
EH38
Hunt Law
Lammas Board
Heriot Cleugh Burn
Heriot Cleugh
Heriotmill Strip
Shoestanes Burn

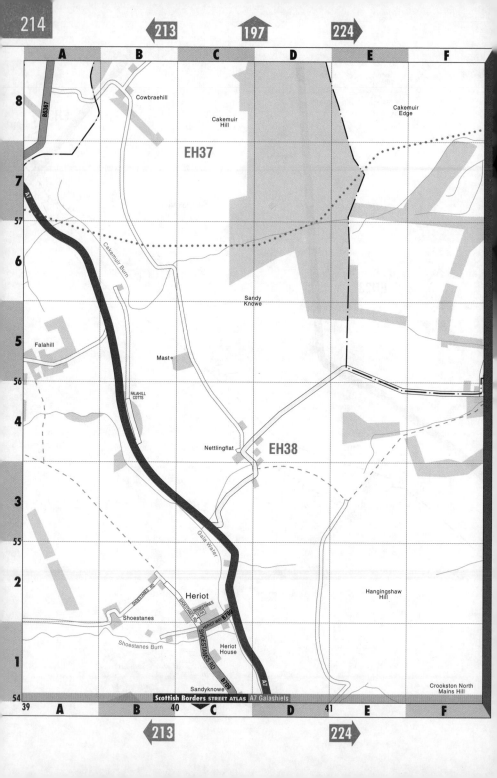

Cowbraehill

Cakemuir
Hill

Cakemuir
Edge

EH37

B6367

A7

Cakemuir Burn

Sandy
Knowe

Falahill

Mast

FALAHILL
COTTS

Nettlingflat

EH38

Gala Water

Hangingshaw
Hill

SHOESTANES RD

Heriot

SHOESTANES RD

Shoestanes

HERIOT WAY

B709

SHOESTANES RD

Shoestanes Burn

Heriot
House

Crookston North
Mains Hill

B709

A7

Sandyknowe

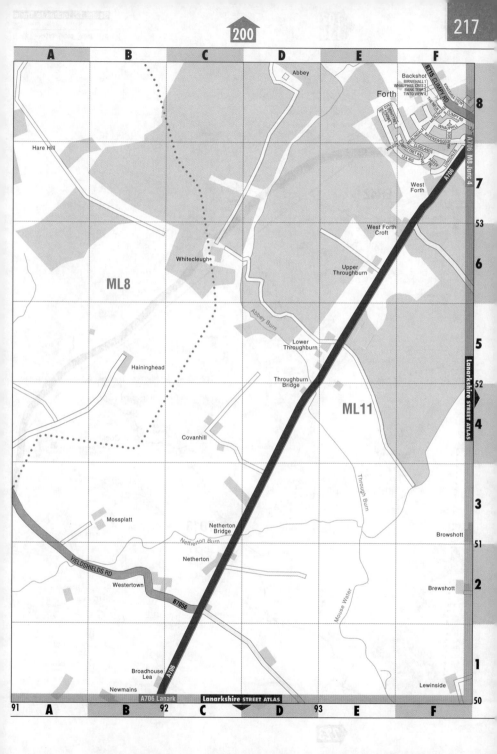

200

ML8

ML11

Abbey

Forth

Backshot

BIRNIEHALL 1
WHAUPHILL CRES 2
BANK TERR 3
TINTO VIEW 4

West
Forth

West Forth
Croft

Upper
Throughburn

Hare Hill

Whitecleugh

Abbey Burn

Lower
Throughburn

Haininghead

Throughburn
Bridge

Covanhill

Through Burn

Mossplatt

Browshott

Netherton
Bridge

Netherton Burn

Netherton

Brewshott

YIELDSHIELDS RD

Westertown

B7056

Mouse Water

Broadhouse
Lea

Newmains

Lewinside

A706 Lanark

Lanarkshire STREET ATLAS

107
136

Scale: 1⅓ inches to 1mile

0   ¼   ½   mile
0   250m 500m 750m 1 km

8

75

7

74

6

73

5

72

4

71

3

70

2

69

1

68

Dry Burn

Mon

Chapel
Point

Skateraw
Harbour

Skateraw

Torness
Power Sta

Torness
Point

Visitor
Ctr

Thorntonloch

Mast

EH42

Crowhill

Innerwick
Prim Sch

Innerwick

BARNS NESS TERR

Innerwick
Castle
(remains of)

THORNTONLOCH
HOLDINGS

Thornton

Thornton Burn

Braidwood Burn

Braidwood

Ogle Burn

Old
Branxton

Branxton

Lawfield

Birnieknowes

Bilsdean

BIRNIEKNOWES
FARM COTTS

Bilsdean
Creek

COASTGUARD
COTTS

Cove

Oldhamstocks
Mains

Dunglass
Mains

Dunglass
Church

Dunglass

Belvidere
Wood

Cockburnspath

Cocklaw

Oldhamstocks Burn

Springfield

Cockburnspath
Prim Sch

Hotel

LADY HALL RD

Dovecot
Hall

THE SQUARE
2, THE CAUSEWAY

Chapelhill

Oldhamstocks

Stottencleugh

Woollands

TD13

Neuk
Farm

Yearn Hope

Ferneylea

Hoprig

Stockbridge

Wightman
Hill

Hoprigshiels

Fulfordlees

FULFORDLEES
COTTS

Heriot Water

Dod
Hill

Falls Burn

Ecclaw

Ewieside
Hill

Scottish Borders STREET ATLAS

223

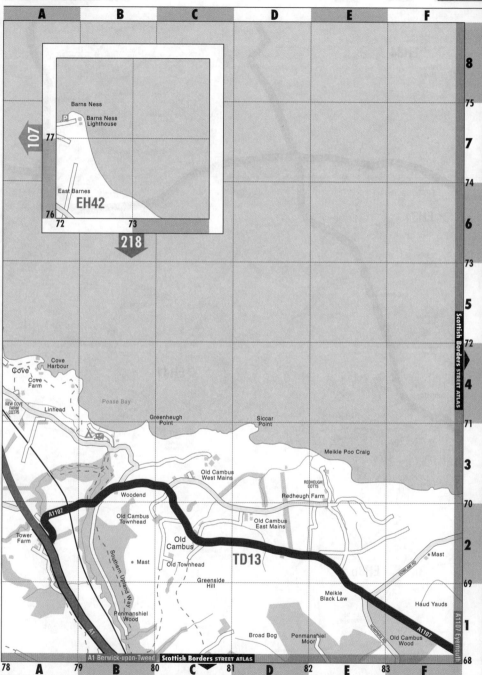

Scale: 1½ inches to 1mile

Barns Ness

Barns Ness
Lighthouse

East Barnes

EH42

218

Cove

Cove
Harbour

Cove
Farm

NEW COVE
FARM
COTTS

Linhead

Pease Bay

Greenheugh
Point

Siccar
Point

Meikle Poo Craig

Old Cambus
West Mains

REDHEUGH
COTTS

Woodend

Redheugh Farm

A1107

Old Cambus
Townhead

Old Cambus
East Mains

Tower
Farm

Old
Cambus

Old Townhead

TD13

Mast

Southern Upland Way

Greenside
Hill

Mast

Penmanshiel
Wood

Meikle
Black Law

Haud Yauds

A1

HOWPARK RD

DOWLAW RD

Broad Bog

Penmanshiel
Moor

Old Cambus
Wood

A1107

A1107 Eyemouth

Scottish Borders STREET ATLAS

A1 Berwick-upon-Tweed

Scottish Borders STREET ATLAS

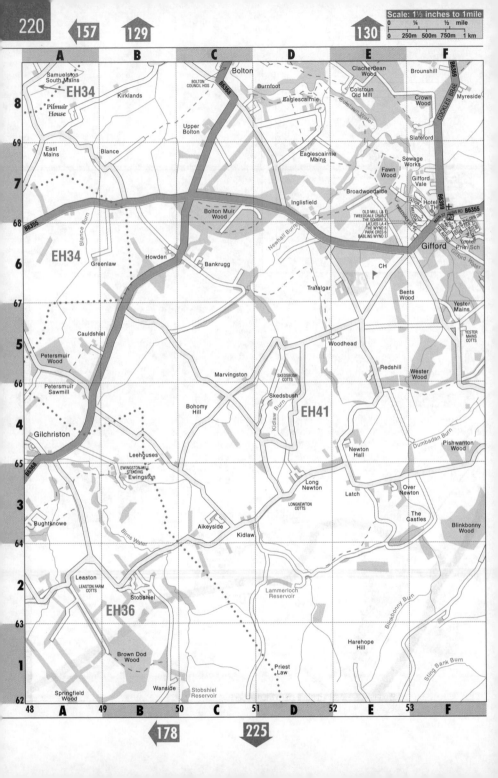

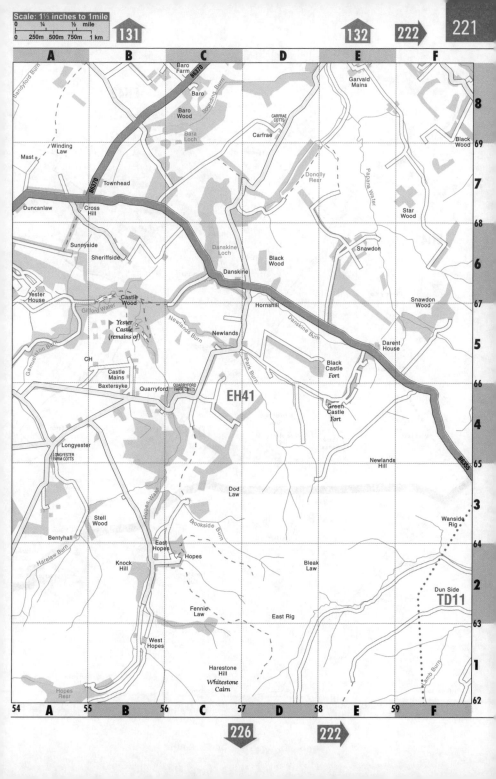

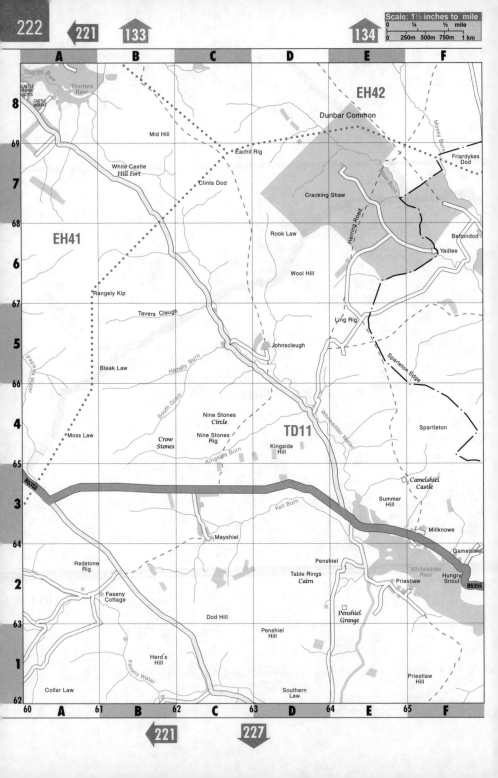

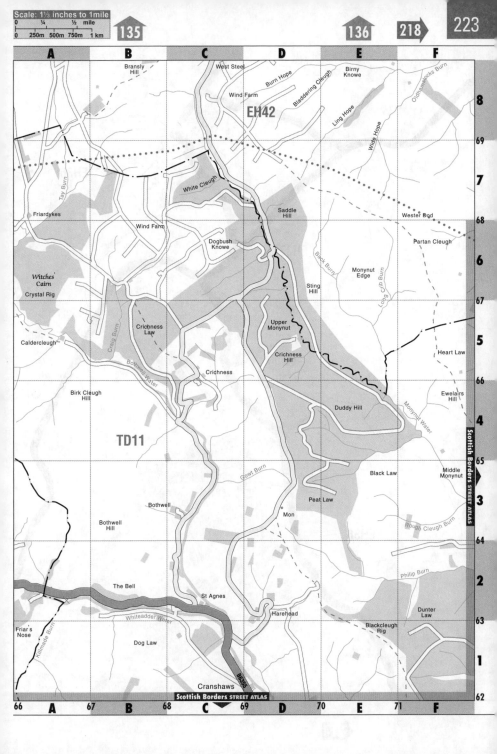

Scale: 1⅓ inches to 1mile

0   ¼   ½   mile
0   250m 500m 750m 1 km

135

136

218

223

West Steel

Bransly Hill

Burn Hope

Birny Knowe

Wind Farm

Bladdering Cleugh

EH42

Ling Hope

Wide Hope

Oldhamstocks Burn

White Cleugh

Saddle Hill

Wester Dod

Friardykes

Tay Burn

Wind Farm

Dogbush Knowe

Partan Cleugh

Witches' Cairn

Back Burn

Monynut Edge

Long Cldb Burn

Crystal Rig

Sting Hill

Crichness Law

Craig Burn

Upper Monynut

Heart Law

Caldercleugh

Bothwell Water

Crichness

Crichness Hill

Birk Cleugh Hill

Duddy Hill

Monynut Water

Ewelairs Hill

TD11

Gowt Burn

Black Law

Middle Monynut

Bothwell

Peat Law

Mon

Rough Cleugh Burn

Bothwell Hill

Philip Burn

The Bell

St Agnes

Dunter Law

Whiteadder Water

Harehead

Blackcleugh Rig

Friar's Nose

Killpade Burn

Dog Law

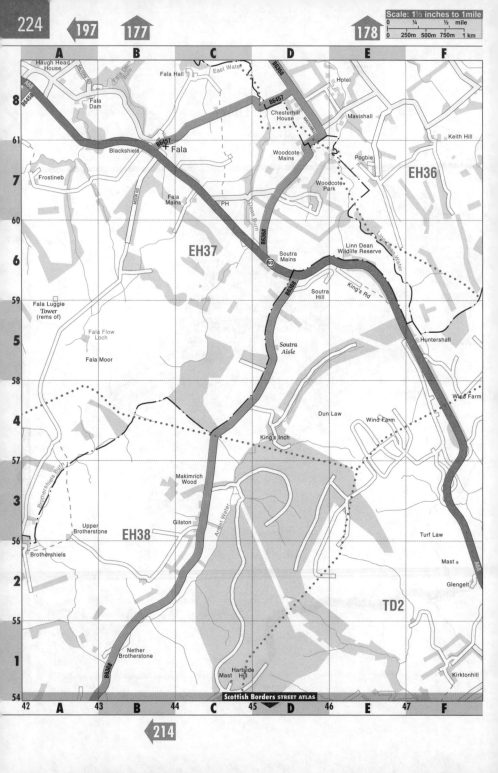

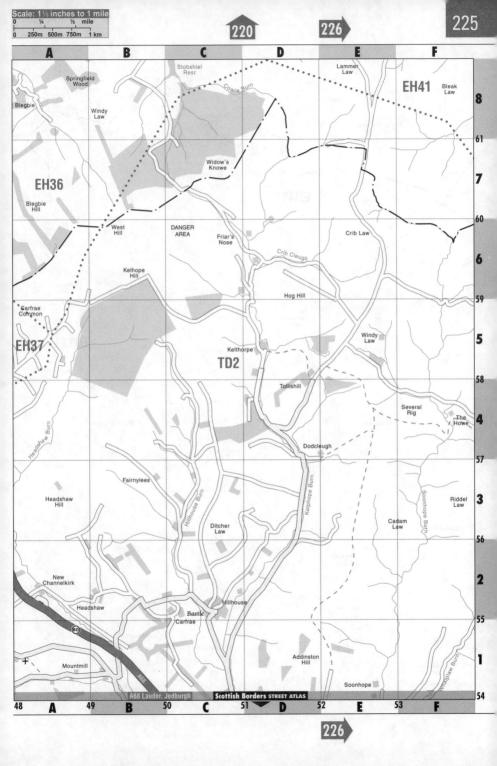

Scale: 1⅓ inches to 1 mile

0 ¼ ½ mile
0 250m 500m 750m 1 km

220
226
225

A   B   C   D   E   F

Springfield Wood
Stobshiel Resr
Lammer Law
EH41
Bleak Law

8

Blegbie
Windy Law
61

EH36

Blegbie Hill
Widow's Knowe
7

West Hill
DANGER AREA
Friar's Nose
Crib Law
60

Kelhope Hill
Crib Cleugh
6

Garfrae Common
Hog Hill
59

EH37
Kelthorpe
Windy Law
5

TD2
Tollishill
58

Several Rig
The Howe
4

Dodcleugh
57

Fairnylees
Headshaw Burn
Riddel Law
3

Headshaw Hill
Hillhouse Burn
Ditcher Law
Cadam Law
Soonhope Burn
56

New Channelkirk
Kelphope Burn
2

Headshaw
Hillhouse
55

Bastle
Carfrae

Mountmill
Addinston Hill
1

Soonhope
54

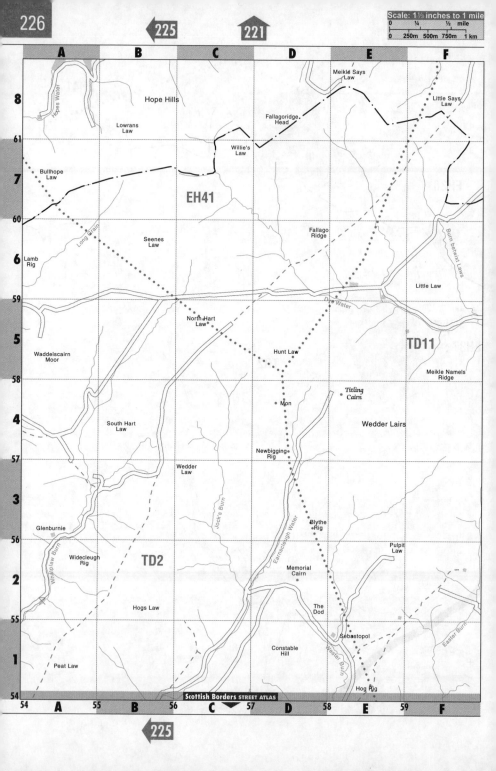

Scale: 1⅓ inches to 1 mile

0   ¼   ½   mile
0   250m   500m   750m   1 km

Hope Hills

Meikle Says Law

Little Says Law

Lowrans Law

Fallagoridge Head

Willie's Law

Bullhope Law

EH41

Hopes Water

Long Grain

Burn betwixt Laws

Seenes Law

Fallago Ridge

Lamb Rig

Little Law

North Hart Law

Dye Water

Waddelscairn Moor

Hunt Law

TD11

Meikle Namels Ridge

South Hart Law

Titling Cairn

Mon

Wedder Lairs

Wedder Law

Newbigging Rig

Jock's Burn

Earnacleugh Water

Blythe Rig

Glenburnie

Pulpit Law

Widecleugh Rig

TD2

Windplaw Burn

Memorial Cairn

Hogs Law

The Dod

Sebastopol

Constable Hill

Wester Burn

Easter Burn

Peat Law

Hog Rig

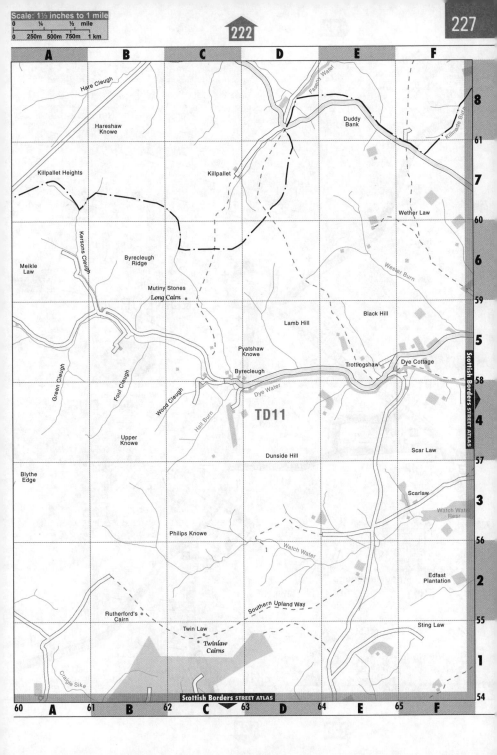

Hare Cleugh

Hareshaw Knowe

Fassny Water

Duddy Bank

Killmade Burn

Killpallet Heights

Killpallet

Wether Law

Kersons Cleugh

Meikle Law

Byrecleugh Ridge

Wester Burn

Mutiny Stones
Long Cairn

Lamb Hill

Black Hill

Pyatshaw Knowe

Green Cleugh

Foul Cleugh

Wood Cleugh

Byrecleugh

Trottlogshaw

Dye Cottage

Dye Water

Hail Burn

TD11

Upper Knowe

Dunside Hill

Scar Law

Blythe Edge

Scarlaw

Watch Water Resr

Philips Knowe

Watch Water

Edfast Plantation

Southern Upland Way

Rutherford's Cairn

Twin Law

Sting Law

Twinlaw Cairns

Cragle Sike

Scottish Borders STREET ATLAS

60   A   61   B   62   C   63   D   64   E   65   F

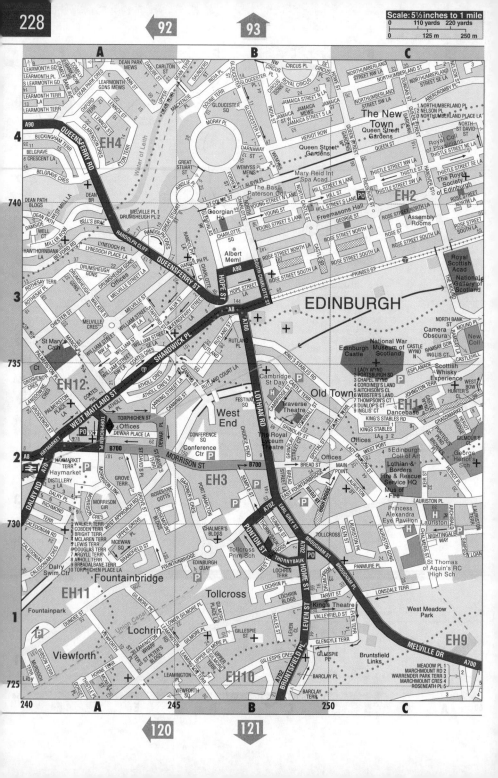

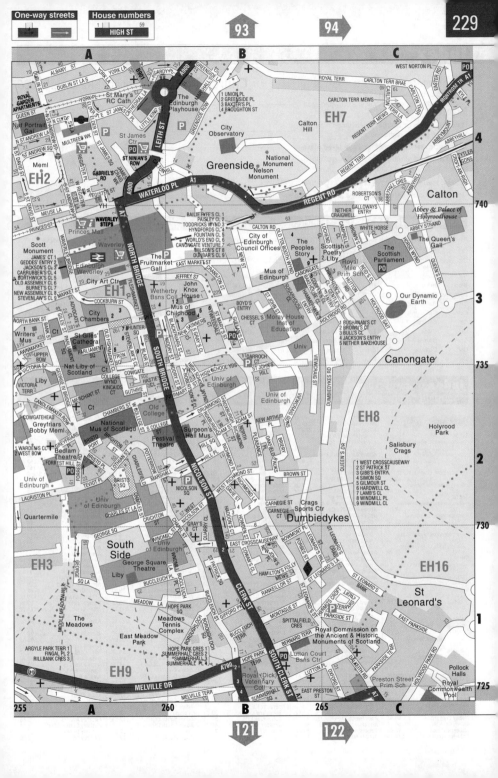

Index

Place name May be abbreviated on the map

Location number Present when a number indicates the place's position in a crowded area of mapping

Locality, town or village Shown when more than one place has the same name

Postcode district District for the indexed place

Page and grid square Page number and grid reference for the standard mapping

Church Rd **6** Beckenham BR2..........**53** C6

Cities, towns and villages are listed in CAPITAL LETTERS

Public and commercial buildings are highlighted in magenta   Places of interest are highlighted in blue with a star *

Abbreviations used in the index

Acad	Academy	Comm	Common	Gd	Ground	L	Leisure	Prom	Promenade
App	Approach	Cott	Cottage	Gdn	Garden	La	Lane	Rd	Road
Arc	Arcade	Cres	Crescent	Gn	Green	Liby	Library	Recn	Recreation
Ave	Avenue	Cswy	Causeway	Gr	Grove	Mdw	Meadow	Ret	Retail
Bglw	Bungalow	Ct	Court	H	Hall	Meml	Memorial	Sh	Shopping
Bldg	Building	Ctr	Centre	Ho	House	Mkt	Market	Sq	Square
Bsns, Bus	Business	Ctry	Country	Hospl	Hospital	Mus	Museum	St	Street
Bvd	Boulevard	Cty	County	HQ	Headquarters	Orch	Orchard	Sta	Station
Cath	Cathedral	Dr	Drive	Hts	Heights	Pal	Palace	Terr	Terrace
Cir	Circus	Dro	Drove	Ind	Industrial	Par	Parade	TH	Town Hall
Cl	Close	Ed	Education	Inst	Institute	Pas	Passage	Univ	University
Cnr	Corner	Emb	Embankment	Int	International	Pk	Park	Wk, Wlk	Walk
Coll	College	Est	Estate	Intc	Interchange	Pl	Place	Wr	Water
Com	Community	Ex	Exhibition	Junc	Junction	Prec	Precinct	Yd	Yard

Index of towns, villages, streets, hospitals, industrial estates, railway stations, schools, shopping centres, universities and places of interest

1st–Air

1st St
Grangemouth, Chemical Works
FK3...............................62 D6
Grangemouth, Oil Refinery
FK3...............................62 A7

2nd St
Grangemouth, Chemical Works
FK3...............................62 D6
Grangemouth, Oil Refinery
FK3...............................62 A8

3rd St
Grangemouth, Chemical Works
EH51..............................62 D6
Grangemouth, Oil Refinery
FK3...............................62 A8

4th St
Grangemouth, Chemical Works
EH51..............................62 E6
Grangemouth, Oil Refinery
FK3...............................62 B8

5th St
Grangemouth, Chemical Works
EH51..............................62 E6
Grangemouth, Oil Refinery
FK3...............................62 B8

6th St
Grangemouth, Chemical Works
EH51..............................62 E6
Grangemouth, Oil Refinery
FK3...............................62 B8

7th St
Grangemouth, Chemical Works
EH51..............................62 E5
Grangemouth, Oil Refinery
FK3...............................62 C8
8th St FK3, EH51.........62 C8
92 Fettes Coll Prep Sch
EH4...............................92 F4

A

A1 Ind Pk EH15...........123 B7
Abbey Craig Ct FK9......2 D3
Abbeycraig Pk FK9.......2 D4
Abbey Craig Rd FK10.....5 B1
Abbey Cres EH39.........54 B7
Abbey Ct EH39.............54 B7
Abbeyfield Ho EH4........92 B2
Abbeygrange EH22.......174 A6
ABBEYHILL.................94 A1
Abbeyhill EH8.............229 C4
Abbeyhill Cres EH8.......229 C4
Abbeyhill Ind Est EH8....94 A1
Abbeyhill Prim Sch 9
EH7...............................94 A1
Abbey Kings Park Hospl
(private) FK7....................6 F5
Abbey La EH8................94 A1
Abbey Mains EH41.......101 A4
Abbey Mews 3 EH39......54 B7
Abbey Mill FK8..............7 C8
Abbeymount EH8.........229 C4
**Abbey & Palace of
Holyroodhouse** EH8....229 C3
Abbey Park Pl KY12........29 A3
Rosewell EH24.............172 C1
ABBEY PARKS..............29 B3
Abbey Pl ML11.............217 F7
Abbey Rd Dalkeith EH22....153 A2
Dunbar EH42................78 D2
North Berwick EH39.......54 B7
Stirling FK8...................2 C1
Abbey Road Pl FK8..........7 C8
Abbey St Edinburgh EH7...94 A1
High Valleyfield KY12....26 B2
Abbey Strand EH8.........229 C3
Abbeyview FK9................2 A2
Abbey View Crossford KY12 28 C1
Dunfermline KY11........29 E2
Abbot Rd FK7.................7 D4
Abbots Cl EH39............53 F7
Abbotsford Cres
Edinburgh EH10...........121 A4
Shotts ML7..................179 F5
Abbotsford Ct EH10.....121 A4
Abbotsford Dr
Grangemouth FK3...........61 F6
Laurieston FK2..............61 A4
Abbotsford Gdns FK2.....39 B1
Abbotsford Pk EH10.....121 A4
Abbotsford Pl FK8...........2 C1
Abbotsford Rd EH39......53 E7
Abbotsford Rise EH54...144 A1
Abbotsford St FK2.........60 B8
Abbotshall Rd
Kirkcaldy KY1, KY2..........17 B3
Kirkcaldy, Linktown KY1,
KY2..............................17 A2
Abbotsinch Ct KY2.........17 A3
Abbotsinch Ind Est FK3...61 F7
Abbotsinch Rd FK3.........61 F7
Abbots Mill KY2.............17 A3

Abbots Moss Dr FK1......59 F1
Abbots Rd
Falkirk, Bankside FK2.......60 D8
Falkirk, Middlefield FK2.....60 D7
Grangemouth FK3............61 D7
Abbots Road Rdbt FK2....60 D8
Abbot St KY12...............29 A3
Abbots View FK2...........61 F3
Abbot's View
Burntisland KY3...............50 D8
Haddington EH41...........101 B2
Abbotsview Junc EH41...101 B2
Abbots Wlk KY2.............16 F3
Abbott Ho Her Ctr * KY12 39 A3
Abden Ave Kinghorn KY3..35 A3
Rosewell EH24.............172 C1
Abden Ct KY3................35 A3
Abden Pl KY3................35 A3
Abel Pl KY11..................29 F4
Abercairney Cres FK2....82 E6
Abercairney Pl FK3.........61 E7
ABERCORN...................66 E2
Abercorn Ave EH8.......122 D8
Abercorn Cres EH8.......122 D8
Abercorn Ct
Edinburgh EH8..............122 D7
Winchburgh EH52............88 A2
Abercorn Dr EH8..........122 D8
Abercorn Gdns EH8........94 D1
Abercorn Gr EH8..........122 D8
Abercorn Pl EH52..........87 F2
Abercorn Rd EH8.........122 C8
Abercorn Terr EH15......123 C8
Abercrombie Pl FK1........3 F6
Abercrombie St FK1.......59 E6
Abercromby Dr FK9........2 B8
Abercromby Pl
Edinburgh EH3..............228 C4
Stirling FK8...................7 A7
Tullibody FK10...............4 B2
Abercromby Prim Sch
FK10...............................4 B2
ABERDOUR..................49 C7
Aberdour Castle * KY3....49 C7
Aberdour Cres KY11......29 D1
Aberdour Pl KY11.........29 D1
Aberdour Prim Sch KY3...49 C8
Aberdour Rd
Burntisland KY3...............33 C1
Dunfermline KY11...........30 A1
Aberdour Sta KY3.........49 C7
ABERLADY...................71 D4

**Aberlady Bay Nature
Reserve** * EH32............71 B7
Aberlady Mains Cotts
EH32.............................71 D4
Aberlady Prim Sch EH32..71 C4
Aberlady Rd EH41.......100 F1
Aberlour St KY11...........46 E4
Abinger Gdns EH12......120 D7
Abington Rd KY12..........28 F2
Aboyne Ave FK9..............2 C4
Aboyne Gdns KY26.......16 E8
Academy La EH20........172 C8
Academy Pk EH6...........94 A4
Academy Pl
Bannockburn FK7.............7 E1
Bathgate EH48............141 B6
Academy Rd Bo'ness EH51..64 A7
Stirling FK8...................7 A8
Academy Sq KY11.........45 D3
Academy St Alloa FK10....9 F8
Armadale EH48............139 F5
Bathgate EH48............141 B6
Edinburgh EH6..............94 A4
Acheson Dr EH32.........125 E8
Achray Ct KY10............10 C5
Achray Dr Falkirk FK1.....60 A1
Stirling FK9....................2 A4
Acklam Path EH20........171 F7
Acorn Cres FK5.............38 D1
Acorn Dr FK10................4 A3
Acorn Rd KY4................13 C6
Acredale EH48.............141 B6
Acredales
Haddington EH41...........129 F7
Linlithgow EH49............85 A5
Acredales Wlk EH41.....129 F8
Acre Rd EH51................64 D6
Acre View EH51............64 C6
ADAMBRAE.................164 C8
Adambrae Rd EH54......164 C8
Adambrae Rdbt EH54....164 C8
Adam Cres FK5..............38 F2
Adam Grossert Ct FK5....38 D3
Adam Pl KY5.................14 A8
Adams Loan FK2............39 A1
Adam Smith Cl KY1........17 C4
Adam Smith Coll KY1......17 C4
Adam Smith Coll (Priory
Campus) KY1...............17 D5
Adam Smith Coll KY1......17 C4
Adam Smith Theatre *
KY2...............................17 B4
Adamson Ave KY26.......17 B6

Adamson Cres KY12.......29 C5
Adamson Pl FK9.............2 B3
Adamson Rd KY5...........14 A8
Adam Sq EH54.............164 C6
Adam St FK2.................60 D6
Adams Well EH13.........149 C7
ADDIEBROWNHILL.......162 E1
Addiebrownhill EH55....162 D1
ADDIEWELL.................162 E2
**Addiewell Comb Prim Sch &
St Thomas' RC Prim Sch**
EH55.............................162 D1
Addiewell Sta EH55......162 E1
Addiston Cres EH14......147 C3
Addiston Farm Rd EH28..118 B1
Addiston Gr EH14.........147 C3
Addiston Pk EH14.........147 C3
Adelaide St EH54..........144 A5
Adelphi Gr **1** EH15.......123 C8
Adelphi Pl EH15............123 A8
Adia Rd KY12.................26 F1
Admiral Terr EH10........121 B5
Admiralty Rd
Inverkeithing KY11...........47 B4
Rosyth KY11.................46 D4
Admiralty St EH6............93 F6
Advocate's Cl EH1.........229 A3
Affleck Ct **1** EH12........119 A8
Affric Dr FK2..................39 C1
Affric Loan ML7............179 E6
Affric Way KY12.............28 E4
Afton Ct Dechmont EH52..7 C2
Stirling FK7....................7 C8
Afton Dr KY6.................57 D7
Afton Gr KY11................29 F5
Afton Pl EH5..................93 A5
Afton Terr EH5...............93 A5
Agnew Terr EH6.............93 D5
Ailsa Ct **3** FK2.............82 F7
Ailsa Gr FK10................16 F8
Ainslie Gdns FK2............61 B3
Ainslie Park L Ctr EH5....92 E5
Ainslie Pl EH3..............228 B4
Airdrie Rd EH48, ML6....137 B3
Airlie Dr FK2.................61 F2
Airlie Pl EH3..................93 C2
Airth Dr FK7....................7 C4
Airth Prim Sch FK2.........22 C4
Airthrey Ave FK9.............2 B6
Airthrey Castle Yd FK9.....2 E6
Airthrey Dr FK5..............38 F4
Airthrey Rd FK9..............2 C5

Aitchison Dr FK5 38 B3
Aitchison Pl FK1 60 B3
Aitchison's Cl EH1 228 C2
Aitchison's Pl EH15 95 A1
Aitken Cres Falkirk FK2 61 A1
Stirling FK7 7 B2
Aitken Ct Dunbar EH42 78 D3
Kirkcaldy KY1 17 B2
Aitken Dr Slamannan FK1 108 A6
Whitburn EH47 161 B7
Aitken Gdns FK1 59 E6
Aitken Orr Dr EH52 115 F5
Aitken Rd FK1 59 D6
Aitken St KY1 17 E7
Aitken Terr FK1 59 D6
Akarit Rd FK5 38 E2
Alan Breck Gdns EH4 91 D1
Alba Campus The EH54 164 A8
Albany Bsns Ctr KY12 29 B4
Albany Ind Est KY12 29 B4
Albany St Dunfermline KY12 29 B4
Edinburgh EH1 229 A4
Albany Street La 7 EH3 93 D2
Alberta Ave EH54 143 E4
Albert Ave FK3 61 F8
Albert Bldgs EH48 110 F5
Albert Cl EH21 125 B5
Albert Cres EH21 125 B5
Albert Pl 5 Edinburgh EH7 93 E2
Stirling FK8 7 A7
Wallyford EH21 125 B5
Albert Rd Edinburgh EH6 94 B5
Falkirk FK1 60 A3
Harthill ML7 159 E5
Albert St Edinburgh EH7 93 F3
Rosyth KY11 46 E4
Albert Terr
Edinburgh EH10 121 A4
Musselburgh EH21 124 E6
Albion Bsns Ctr EH7 94 A2
Albion Gdns EH7 94 A2
Albion Pl EH7 94 A2
Albion Rd EH7 94 A2
Albion Terr EH7 94 A2
Albyn Cotts EH52 115 E6
Albyn Dr EH54 164 E5
Albyn Ind Est EH52 115 F7
Albyn Pl Broxburn EH52 115 E6
Edinburgh EH2 228 B4
Albyn Terr EH52 115 F5
Alcorn Rigg EH14 148 E7
Alcorn Sq EH14 148 E7
Alderbank Livingston EH54 143 E5
Penicuik EH26 191 F4
Alderbank Gdns EH11 120 E4
Alderbank Pl EH11 120 E4
Alderbank Terr EH11 120 E4
Alder Cres FK11 3 F5
Alder Gr Dunfermline KY11 29 D1
Westquarter FK2 61 B3
Alder Rd EH32 97 D3
ALDERSTON 100 E2
Alderston Ct KY12 29 D6
Alderston Dr KY12 29 D6
Alderstone Bsns Pk
EH54 143 C1
Alderstone Rd
Livingston, Adambrae
EH54 164 D7
Livingston, Howden EH54 143 D4
Alderston Gdns EH41 100 E1
Alderston Mdws EH41 100 E1
Alderston Pl EH41 100 E1
Alderston Rd EH41 129 E8
Aldhammer Ho EH32 96 F1
Alemoor Cres EH7 94 B3
Alemoor Pk EH7 94 B3
Alexander Ave Falkirk FK2 60 E5
Grangemouth FK3 61 C5
Alexander Ct
Clackmannan FK10 11 A5
Stirling FK9 2 F6
Alexander Dr
Bridge of Allan FK9 2 A8
Edinburgh EH11 120 D5
Livingston EH54 164 D8
Prestonpans EH32 125 F8
Alexander McLeod Pl FK7 8 E3
Alexander Peden Prim Sch
ML7 159 E5
Alexander Pk EH52 115 E4
Alexander Pl KY11 46 F3
Alexander Rd ML7 179 D5
Alexander St
Cowdenbeath KY4 13 D5
Dysart KY1 18 A8
Uphall EH52 115 A4
Alexander the Third St
KY3 34 F1
Alexander Way KY11 47 B8
Alexandra Ave EH48 141 F6
Alexandra Bsns Pk EH28 117 A5
Alexandra Dr Alloa FK10 9 F7
Bathgate EH48 141 F6
Alexandra Pl FK8 2 C1
Alexandra St
Dunfermline KY12 29 A5
Kirkcaldy KY1 17 C5
Alford Ave KY2 16 E7
Alford Gdns KY2 16 E7
Alford Way KY11 30 A4
Alfred Pl EH9 121 F4
Alhambra Theatre★ KY12 29 A3
Alice Bank EH55 164 A5
Alice Cox Wlk KY11 29 C1
Alice Gr KY4 30 E6
Aline Ct KY11 48 A2
Alison Gr KY12 28 B2
Alison St KY1 17 B2
Allanbank Rd FK5 38 C2
Allan Barr Ct FK1 60 B1
Allan Cres Denny FK6 36 D3
Dunfermline KY11 29 E2
Allan Ct Burntisland KY3 50 E8
Grangemouth FK3 40 E1
ALLANDALE 57 C2
Allandale Cotts FK4 57 C2
Allanfield EH7 93 F2
Allanfield Pl EH7 93 F2
Allan Lea Terr KY12 28 F5
Allan Park Cres EH14 120 C3
Allan Park Dr EH14 120 C2
Allan Park Gdns EH14 120 C2
Allan Park Ho 10 FK8 7 B7
Allan Park Loan EH14 120 D2
Allan Park Rd EH14 120 C2
Allan Pk Cowdenbeath KY4 13 A1
Kirkliston EH29 89 A2
Stirling FK8 7 A7
Allan Pl FK4 58 A4
Allan Rd EH47 160 E6
Allan's Prim Sch FK8 7 A7
Allan St EH4 93 A2
Allan Terr EH22 153 B3
ALLANTON 198 A8
Allanton Prim Sch ML7 198 B8
Allanton Rd ML7 179 D2
Allanvale Rd FK9 1 F7
Allanwater Apartments
FK9 2 A8
Allanwater Gdns FK9 2 A8
Allan Wlk FK9 1 F8
Allanwood Ct FK9 2 A8
Allardice Cres KY2 16 D5
Allen Gr KY12 26 E7
Allen Rd EH54 143 C3
Allermuir Ave EH25 171 E5
Allermuir Rd EH13 149 A6
Aller Pl EH54 143 B4
Allison Cres FK2 61 A4
Allison Gdns EH48 138 D2
Allison Pl EH29 89 B2
ALLOA 10 C5
Alloa Acad FK10 10 B5
Alloa Bsns Pk FK10 10 C7
Alloa Ind Est FK10 10 A6
ALLOA PARK 10 B5
Alloa Park Dr FK10 10 D5
Alloa Rd Clackmannan FK10 11 B4
Fishcross FK10 5 D3
Menstrie FK9 3 B3
Stenhousemuir FK5 38 F4
Stirling FK9 2 E3
Tullibody FK10 4 C3
Alloa Tower★ FK10 10 B6
Alloa Trad Ctr FK10 10 C7
Alloway FK2 61 A4
Alloway Cres FK4 57 F6
Alloway Dr Cowie FK7 20 D7
Kirkcaldy KY2 17 A7
Alloway Loan 4 EH16 122 A1
Alloway Wynd FK5 38 C4
Alma La FK2 60 B6
Alma St Falkirk FK2 60 B6
Inverkeithing KY11 47 C3
Alma Terr FK2 60 B6
Almond Ave EH12 117 F7
Almond Bank Cotts EH4 91 B5
Almondbank Terr EH11 120 E4
Almond Bsns Ctr EH54 144 A6
Almond Court E EH4 91 A3
Almond Court W EH4 91 A3
Almond Cres EH19 173 B6
Almond Ct
East Whitburn EH47 161 E7
Edinburgh EH16 122 E3
Falkirk FK2 60 E7
Livingston EH54 144 C4
Stirling FK7 7 C5
Almond E EH54 144 B4
Almond East Rd EH54 144 B5
Almondell & Calder Wood
Ctry Pk★ EH53 144 E5
Almondell Ct EH52 115 E5
Almondell Rd EH52 115 E5
Almondell Terr EH53 144 F5
Almond Gn EH12 119 A8
Almond Gr
East Calder EH53 144 F5
Queensferry EH30 89 C8
Almondhill Cotts EH29 89 C2
Almondhill Rd EH29 89 B2
Almondhill Steading EH29 89 B2
Almond Intc EH54 144 A3
Almond Pk EH54 144 A4
Almond Pl KY1 17 C7
Almond Rd
Blackburn EH47 141 C1
Dunfermline KY11 29 E2
Falkirk FK2 60 E7
Livingston EH54 144 B4
Ratho Station EH12, EH28 117 F7
Whitecross EH49 83 D5
Almondside Kirkliston EH29 89 B1
Livingston EH54 143 F2
Almond Side EH53 144 D4
Almond South Rd EH53 144 C4
Almond Sq
East Whitburn EH47 161 E7
Edinburgh EH12 119 A8
Almond St FK3 61 C6
Almond Terr Harthill ML7 159 C5
Whitecross EH49 83 F6
ALMONDVALE 143 E2
Almondvale Ave EH54 143 E2
Almondvale Bsns Pk
EH54 143 D1
Almondvale Bvd EH54 143 E2
Almondvale Cres EH54 143 D2
Almondvale Dr EH54 143 F2
Almondvale East Rd
EH54 143 F2
Almondvale Gdns EH47 162 D7
Almondvale N EH54 143 D2
Almondvale Parkway
EH54 143 E2
Almondvale Pl EH54 143 D1
Almondvale Rd EH54 143 E1
Almondvale Rdbt EH54 143 C1
Almondvale Ret Pk EH54 143 D1
Almondvale Road Rdbt
EH54 143 D1
Almondvale S EH54 143 D1
Almondvale South Ret Pk
EH54 143 D1
Almondvale Stadium
(Livingston FC)★ EH54 143 D2
Almondvale Stadium Rd
EH54 143 D2
Almondvale W EH54 143 D1
Almondvale Way EH54 143 D1
Almond Valley Heritage Ctr★
EH54 143 A2
Almondview EH54 143 F2
Almond View EH47 142 B1
Almondview Bsns Pk 1
EH54 143 F2
Almond West Rd EH54 144 A4
Alness Gr KY12 28 F2
ALNWICKHILL 150 E6
Alnwickhill Cres EH16 150 F6
Alnwickhill Ct EH16 150 F6
Alnwickhill Dr EH16 150 F6
Alnwickhill Gdns EH16 150 F6
Alnwickhill Gr EH16 150 F6
Alnwickhill Loan EH16 150 F6
Alnwickhill Pk EH16 151 A6
Alnwickhill Rd EH16 151 A7
Alnwickhill Terr EH16 150 F6
Alnwickhill View EH16 150 F6
Alpha St EH51 62 E5
ALVA 5 A6
Alva Acad FK12 5 B6
Alva Glen Nature Trail★
FK12 5 A8
Alva Ind Est FK12 5 C6
Alvanley Terr EH9 121 B5
Alva Pl EH7 94 A2
Alva Prim Sch FK12 5 A6
Alva St EH2 228 A3
Alyth Dr FK2 62 A1
Ambassador Ct EH21 124 D6
Amberley Path FK3 61 F6
Ambrose Rise EH54 144 A1
Amisfield Pk EH41 130 C8
Amisfield Pl
Haddington EH41 130 D7
Longniddry EH32 98 E5
Amos Path EH20 171 F7
Amulree Pl EH51 63 D7
Ancaster Pl FK1 60 A1
Anchorfield EH6 93 D6
Ancroft EH42 107 A7
Ancrum Bank EH22 152 F1
Ancrum Rd EH22 152 F1
Anderson Ave
Armadale EH48 139 F4
Crossford KY12 28 B2
2 Falkirk FK2 60 A8
Newtongrange EH22 174 B6
Anderson Cres FK1 81 E6
Anderson Dr
Cowdenbeath KY4 13 B2
Denny FK6 36 E1
Falkirk FK2 39 B2
Anderson Gdns FK2 82 E6
Anderson Gn EH54 143 C7
Anderson La
Kincardine FK10 23 E4
Rosyth KY11 46 D5
Anderson Park Rd FK6 36 F2
Anderson Pl Edinburgh EH6 93 E5
Stirling FK7 7 A4
Anderson St
Bonnybridge FK4 58 B5
Dysart KY1 18 A7
Kirkcaldy KY1 17 E6
Anderson Terr FK4 57 B3
Andrew Ave EH48 141 F6
Andrew Carnegie Birthplace
Mus★ 6 KY12 29 A3
Andrew Carnegie House★
KY12 28 F3
Andrew Cres FK5 38 D4
Andrew Ct EH26 191 E7
Andrew Dodd's Ave
EH22 174 E7
Andrew Hardie Dr FK10 10 A8
Andrew St KY5 14 A6
Andrew Stewart Hall FK9 2 D6
Andrew Wood Ct EH6 93 C6
Andy Kelly Ct EH19 172 F5
Andy Kelly View EH19 172 F5
Angle Park Terr EH11 120 F5
Angres Ct EH22 152 C7
Angus Rd Bo'ness EH51 63 D6
Carluke ML8 215 B1
Annabel Ct KY11 47 D2
Annan Ct FK1 60 C1
Annandale St EH7 93 E2
Annandale Street La EH7 93 E2
Anne Dr Bridge of Allan FK9 2 B6
Stenhousemuir FK5 38 E4
Anne St Alloa FK10 9 F8
Bathgate EH48 141 E6
Penicuik EH26 191 E7
Annet Rd FK6 57 D6
Annfield Edinburgh EH6 93 D6
Tranent EH33 126 E5
Annfield Ct EH33 127 C5
Annfield Dr FK7 7 C5
Annfield Farm Rd KY11 47 B7
Annfield Gdns FK8 7 B6
Annfield Gr FK8 7 B6
Annfield Pl 6 FK3 40 D1
Annfield St EH6 93 D6
Ann St EH4 228 A4
Anson Ave FK1 59 E4
Antigua St 2 EH1 93 E2
Antonine Ct EH51 63 D5
Antonine Gate FK4 57 A1
Antonine Gdns FK1 59 C5
Antonine Gr FK4 57 F3
Antonine Prim Sch FK4 58 A4
Antonine St FK1 59 C5
Antonine Wall★ FK4 58 D4
ANTONSHILL 38 E4
Antonshill Rdbt FK5 38 F5
Appin Cres
Dunfermline KY12 29 B4
Kirkcaldy KY2 16 E7
Appin Dr EH32 97 A2
Appin Gr FK2 61 F3
Appin Pl EH14 120 D3
Appin St EH14 120 D4
Appin Terr
Edinburgh EH14 120 D4
Shotts ML7 180 B3
Appleton Parkway EH54 142 F3
Appleton Parkway Rdbt
EH54 142 F5
Appleton Pl EH54 142 F3
Arboretum Ave EH3 93 A2
Arboretum Pl EH3 93 A3
Arboretum Rd EH3 93 A4
Arbroath Cres FK9 2 B4
Arbuthnot Rd EH20 172 C7
Arbuthnot St FK1 59 E6
Archers Ave FK7 7 C4
Archers Ct EH31 52 A2
Archibald Pl EH3 228 C2
Archibald Russell Ct FK2 61 E1
Ard Ct FK3 61 D5
Ardeer Pl KY11 29 C2
Arden St EH9 121 C5
Ardgay Cres FK4 58 A3
Ardgay Dr FK4 58 A3
Ardgay Rd FK4 58 A3
Ardgay Terr FK4 58 A3
Ardgowan Pl Cowie FK7 20 E8
Shotts ML7 179 E6
Ardmillan Pl EH11 120 F5
Ardmillan Terr EH11 120 E5
Ardmore Dr FK2 62 A1
Ardshiel Ave EH4 91 C1
Ardvreck Pl FK2 39 A3
Argyle Cres EH15 123 C7
Argyle Ct EH52 115 E5
Argyle Park Terr EH9 229 A1
Argyle Pl EH9 121 D5
Argyle St EH6 93 E6
Argyll Ave Falkirk FK2 60 C6
Stirling FK8 2 C1
Argyll Ct ML7 159 F5
Argyll Path FK6 57 D8
Argyll Pl Alloa FK10 10 C7
Bonnyrigg and Lasswade
EH19 172 F6
Argyll's Lodging★ FK8 7 A8
Argyll St FK10 10 C7
Argyll Terr EH11 228 A2
Arkaig Dr KY12 28 C1
Arkwright Ct EH39 54 A7
ARMADALE 139 E5
Armadale Acad EH48 139 D5
Armadale Ind Est EH48 140 A5
Armadale Prim Sch 2
EH48 139 F5
Armadale Rd EH47 161 B7
Armadale Sta EH48 140 A3
Armine Pl EH26 192 B7
Armour Ave FK7 20 D7
Armour Mews FK5 38 B4
Arneil Pl FK2 82 D7
ARNISTON 174 B1
Arniston Home Farm Cotts
EH23 195 A4
Arniston House★ EH23 194 F3
Arniston Rd KY11 30 A4
ARNOTHILL 60 A4
Arnothill FK1 60 A4
Arnothill Bank FK1 60 A4
Arnothill Ct FK1 59 F5
Arnothill Gdns FK1 60 A4
Arnothill La 1 FK1 59 F4
Arnothill Mews FK1 60 A4
Arnot St FK1 60 C4
Arnott Gdns EH14 120 A1
Arnprior Rd EH23 195 D8
Arns Gr FK10 9 E8
Arnswell FK10 5 C2
Arran EH54 142 F5
Arran Cres KY2 16 F7
Arran Ct Alloa FK10 10 B5
Grangemouth FK3 61 D6
Arran Pl EH15 123 C8
Arran Terr FK1 59 C4
Arras Gr EH26 192 A8
Arrol Cres FK10 10 C7
Arrol Pl EH30 89 C8
Arrol Sq EH54 142 E5
Arthur Ct KY4 13 D3
Arthur Pl KY4 13 D3
Arthur's Dr FK5 38 F2
Arthur St Cowdenbeath KY4 13 D3
Dunfermline KY12 29 B5
Edinburgh EH6 93 F3
Arthur Street La EH6 93 F3
Arthur View Cres EH22 152 B8
Arthur View Terr EH22 152 B8
Artillery Pk EH41 101 B1
Ashbank Ct EH48 140 E6
Ashbank Terr EH53 144 E3
Ashbrae Gdns FK7 7 B2
Ash Braes FK10 23 D4
Ashburnham Gdns EH30 68 D1
Ashburnham Loan EH30 68 D1
Ashburnham Rd EH30 89 D8
Ashcroft Ho FK5 38 B1
Ashfield Ct EH42 78 E1
Ashfield Pl EH42 78 E1
Ash Gr Alloa FK10 10 C6
Bathgate EH48 141 E6
Blackburn EH47 162 D8
Carnock KY12 27 C6
Cowdenbeath KY4 13 B4
Dunbar EH42 78 B1
Dunfermline KY11 46 D8
Livingston EH54 144 B6
Stenhousemuir FK5 38 F2
Westquarter FK2 61 B2
Ashgrove Mayfield EH22 174 E7
Musselburgh EH21 124 E6
Ashgrove Pl EH21 124 F6
Ashgrove View EH21 124 F6
Ash La EH20 171 F7
Ashley Ct EH49 84 E6
Ashley Dr EH12 120 E3
Ashley Gdns EH11 120 E4
Ashley Gr EH11 120 E4
Ashley Grange EH14 147 C2
Ashley Hall Gdns EH49 84 E6
Ashley Pl EH6 93 E4
Ashley Rd FK2 61 F3
Ashley St FK4 57 F6
Ashley Terr Alloa FK10 10 A8
Edinburgh EH11 120 E4
Ash Terr Blackburn EH47 162 D8
Stirling FK8 6 F5
Ashton Gr EH16 122 B1
Ashville Terr EH6 94 B3
Ashwood Ct EH53 165 C8
Asquith St KY1 17 B3
Assembly St EH6 94 A5
Assynt Bank EH26 192 A6
Astley Ainslie Hospl EH9 121 C3
Atheling Gr EH30 89 C7
ATHELSTANEFORD 101 E8
Athelstaneford Her Ctr★
EH39 101 E7
Athelstaneford Prim Sch
EH39 101 E7
Athol Cres FK2 61 A3
Atholl Cres EH3 228 A2
Atholl Crescent La EH3 228 A2
Atholl Pl Edinburgh EH3 228 A2
Falkirk FK2 60 C5
Stirling FK8 1 F2
Atholl Terr
Edinburgh EH11 228 A2
Kirkcaldy KY2 16 D7
Atholl View EH32 97 A2
Atholl Way EH54 143 E7
Athol Pl Bathgate EH48 141 B7
Dunfermline KY12 29 C4
Athol Terr EH48 141 B7
Atlas Ct EH48 140 B4
Atrium Way FK4 58 A3
Attlee Cres EH22 174 E5
Aubigny Sports Ctr EH41 130 A7
AUCHENBOWIE 19 B4
AUCHENDINNY 171 D1
AUCHENGRAY 202 E1
Auchengray Rd ML11 202 F1
Auchenhard Pl EH47 162 C2
Auchenhard Terr EH47 162 C2
Auchentyre Pl FK2 39 C3
Auchinbaird FK10 5 C2
Auchingane EH10 149 E5
Auchinleck Ct EH6 93 C6
Auchinleck's Brae EH6 93 D6
Auchterderran Rd KY5 14 B8
AUCHTERTOOL 15 A2
Auchtertool Prim Sch KY2 15 B2
Auction Mart 4 EH41 101 A1
Auld Brig Rd FK10 10 B6
Auldcathie Pl EH52 87 F3
Auldgate EH29 89 B1
Auldhame Cotts EH39 55 E5
Auldhill Ave EH49 86 C4
Auldhill Cotts EH49 86 C4
Auldhill Cres EH49 86 C3
Auldhill Ct EH49 86 C5
Auldhill Dr EH49 86 C4
Auldhill Entry EH49 86 C4
Auldhill Pl EH49 86 C4
Auldhill Rd EH49 86 C4
Auldhill Terr EH49 86 C4
Auldkirk Rd FK10 4 C3
Auld Orch EH19 173 C7
Auld School Wynd FK7 6 D5
Avalon Gdns EH49 84 D8
Ava St KY1 17 A2
Aven Dr FK2 60 F3
Avens Cl KY12 29 A5
Avenue Ind Est KY5 14 C7

Avenue Park W EH53....**144** C4
Avenue Pk
  Bridge of Allan FK9........1 F7
  Mid Calder EH53..........**144** C4
Avenue Rd Aberlady EH32 ..72 A5
  Cockenzie & Port Seton
  EH32......................**97** C3
  Dalkeith EH22............**152** E2
Avenue The
  Bridge of Allan FK9........2 A7
  Falkirk FK2................**39** D2
  Gifford EH41.............**220** F6
  Gorebridge EH23.........**174** B1
  Inverkeithing KY11........**47** E3
  Lochgelly KY5.............**14** C7
  Philpstoun EH49..........**86** D7
  Riccarton EH14..........**147** F7
  Whitburn EH47..........**161** A6
Avenue Villas EH4.........**92** F2
Averton ML1...............**201** A1
Avonbank Ave FK3.........**61** E6
Avonbank Gdns FK6........**36** D4
AVONBRIDGE.............**110** A6
Avonbridge Prim Sch
  FK1......................**110** A5
Avonbridge Rd FK1.......**108** B7
Avon Ct FK1...............**60** C2
Avondale Cres EH48......**139** E5
Avondale Dr EH48........**139** E5
Avondale Pl EH13.........**93** B2
Avondale Rd FK2..........**62** B3
Avondhu Gdns FK3........**61** F8
Avon Dr EH49.............**84** D7
Avon Gr Edinburgh EH4 ...**91** A4
  Penicuik EH26...........**192** A6
Avonlea Dr FK2............**61** F3
Avonmill Rd EH49.........**84** C8
Avonmill View EH49.......**84** C7
Avonpark FK1.............**109** F6
Avon Pl Bo'ness EH51......**63** F8
  Edinburgh EH4............**91** A4
  Linlithgow EH49...........**85** A6
Avon Rd Bathgate EH48...**141** A7
  Edinburgh EH4............**91** A4
  Grangemouth EH51.........**62** D7
  Whitecross EH49..........**83** F6
Avonside Dr FK6...........**36** D5
Avon St Denny FK6.........**36** C4
  Grangemouth FK3..........**40** A1
Avon Terr FK1.............**110** A6
Avontoun Pk EH49........**84** D6
Axwell Ho EH52..........**116** B5
Ayres Wynd EH32..........**96** F1
Aytoun Cres KY3...........**33** E2
Aytoun Gr KY12...........**28** E5

B

Baads Rd
  Blackridge EH48, ML7.....**137** D1
  Harthill ML7..............**158** E8
BABERTON................**148** C7
Baberton Ave EH14......**148** D6
Baberton Cres EH14......**148** E6
Baberton Ct EH14.........**148** E6
Baberton Loan EH14......**148** D6
Baberton Mains EH14....**148** C8
Baberton Mains Ave
  EH14.....................**148** D7
Baberton Mains Bank
  EH14.....................**148** D7
Baberton Mains Brae
  EH14.....................**148** C7
Baberton Mains Cres
  EH14.....................**148** D7
Baberton Mains Dell EH14.**148** D7
Baberton Mains Dr
  EH14.....................**148** C7
Baberton Mains Gdns
  EH14.....................**148** D7
Baberton Mains Gn
  EH14.....................**148** D7
Baberton Mains Gr EH14 .**148** D7
Baberton Mains Hill
  EH14.....................**148** C7
Baberton Mains Lea
  EH14.....................**148** C7
Baberton Mains Loan
  EH14.....................**148** E7
Baberton Mains Pk EH14 .**148** D7
Baberton Mains Pl EH14 .**148** D7
Baberton Mains Rise
  EH14.....................**148** C7
Baberton Mains Row
  EH14.....................**148** D7
Baberton Mains Terr
  EH14.....................**148** D7
Baberton Mains View
  EH14.....................**148** D7
Baberton Mains Way
  EH14.....................**148** C7
Baberton Mains Wood
  EH14.....................**148** C7
Baberton Mains Wynd
  EH14.....................**148** D7
Baberton Pk EH14........**148** D6
Baberton Sq EH14........**148** D6
Bablins Wynd EH41.......**220** F6
Babylon Ct EH33..........**126** C7
Back Cswy KY12............**42** D8
BACKDALE................**151** E2
Back Dean EH4............**120** F8
Backdean Rd EH22.......**152** A8

Back La EH32...............**71** D4
Backlee EH16.............**151** A6
Backmarch Cres KY11......**46** E4
Backmarch Rd KY11........**46** E4
BACKMUIR OF
  PITFIRRANE.............**28** A6
Back O' Hill Ind Est FK6...**2** A2
Back O' Hill Rd FK8.........**1** F1
Back O'Yards KY11........**47** B2
Back Rd Alva FK12...........**4** E7
  Dunbar EH42...............**78** B2
Back St KY12...............**42** D8
Back Station Rd
  Edinburgh EH16..........**122** D4
  Linlithgow EH49...........**85** B7
Backwell Ct KY12..........**28** D5
Back Wlk [2] EH8............**7** B7
Backwood Ct FK10.........**10** F5
Badallan Pl EH47.........**181** E6
Badger Brook EH52.......**115** D4
Badger Ct EH52...........**115** C4
Badger Gr EH52...........**115** D4
Badger La EH52...........**115** C4
Badger Mdws EH52.......**115** C4
Badger Pk EH52...........**115** C4
Badger Pl EH52...........**115** C4
Badger Wlk EH52.........**115** C4
Badger Wood EH52.......**114** C2
Baileyfield Cres EH15.....**123** A8
Baileyfield Ct EH15.......**123** A8
Baileyfield Rd EH15........**94** F1
Bailie Fyfe's Cl EH1.......**229** B3
Bailie Gr EH15...........**123** B6
Bailielands EH49...........**85** D7
Bailie Path EH15.........**123** A6
Bailie Pl EH15............**123** B6
Bailie Ct [2] FK10...........**5** C1
Bailie Ave ML7...........**159** F5
Bailie St EH47............**161** A7
Bailie Waugh Rd FK7.......**7** C3
Baingle Brae FK10..........**4** B3
Baingle Cres FK10..........**4** B3
BAINSFORD................**60** B8
Bainsford Prim Sch FK2 ...**60** B8
Baird Ave Edinburgh EH12 .**120** C6
  Edinburgh EH12...........**120** C6
Baird Ct KY5...............**14** A7
Baird Dr Armadale EH48 ..**139** F7
  Edinburgh EH12...........**120** C6
Baird Gdns EH12..........**120** C6
Baird Gr EH12............**120** C6
Baird Rd Armadale EH48 ..**139** F7
  Livingston EH54..........**143** A1
  Ratho EH28................**123** B2
Baird St FK1...............**59** D5
Baird's Way EH19.........**173** D7
Baird Terr
  Edinburgh EH12...........**120** C6
  Haddington EH41..........**100** F1
  Harthill ML7..............**159** F5
Bairns Ford Ave FK2........**60** A7
Bairns Ford Ct FK2.........**60** A7
Bairns Ford Dr FK2.........**60** A7
Bakehouse Cl EH8.........**229** B3
Baker's Pl [8] EH3..........**93** B2
Baker St Bo'ness EH51......**63** F6
  Stirling FK8................**7** A8
Balbakie Rd ML7..........**159** E5
Balbardie Ave EH48.......**141** A7
Balbardie Cres EH48......**141** A7
Balbardie Prim Sch [4]
  EH48.....................**141** B7
Balbardie Rd EH48........**141** B6
Balbirnie Pl EH12.........**120** E7
Balcarres Ct EH10.........**121** A2
Balcarres Pl EH21.........**124** D7
Balcarres Rd EH21........**124** D7
Balcarres St EH10.........**121** A2
Balcastle Rd FK1...........**60** B2
Balderstone's Wynd EH39 .**54** C7
Balderston Gardens N
  EH16.....................**122** B1
Balderston Gdns EH16 ...**122** B1
BALDRIDGEBURN.........**28** D5
Baldridgeburn KY12......**28** D5
Baldwin Cres KY2..........**17** A5
Baldwin St EH26..........**191** E4
BALERNO.................**148** C7
Balerno High Sch EH14 ..**147** C2
Balfour Cres Plean FK7 ....**20** D3
  Stenhousemuir FK5.........**38** C2
Balfour Ct
  Dunfermline KY12..........**29** D5
  Edinburgh EH12............**91** B1
  Plean FK7.................**20** D3
Balfour Pl EH6.............**93** F4
Balfour's Sq EH33.........**126** D6
Balfour St Alloa FK10.......**10** C7
  Bannockburn FK7...........**7** C1
  Bonnybridge FK4...........**57** F6
  Edinburgh EH6.............**93** F3
  Kirkcaldy KY2..............**17** A5
  North Berwick EH39........**54** D7
  Stirling FK8................**1** F2
Balfour Terr EH26.........**171** B1
Balfron Loan EH4...........**91** C1
Balgone Barns Cotts
  EH39......................**54** D2
Balgownie W KY12..........**42** C8
Balgreen Ave EH12........**120** A6
Balgreen Gdns EH12......**120** B6
Balgreen Pk EH12.........**120** B6
Balgreen Prim Sch EH11 .**120** C5
Balgreen Rd EH11........**120** C5
Balgrochan Terr [3] EH48.**141** B6
Baliol St KY3..............**34** F2

Ballantyne La EH6..........**93** F5
Ballantyne Pl EH54........**143** B4
Ballantyne Rd EH6.........**93** F5
Ballast Bank KY11..........**47** C2
Ballater Dr FK9.............**2** C4
BALLENCRIEFF............**72** B1
Ballencrieff Cotts EH32 ...**72** A1
Ballencrieff Mains Farm
  Cotts EH32................**71** F1
Ballencrieff Mill EH48.....**140** E8
Ballencrieff Rd EH48......**140** E8
Ballencrieff Toll EH48.....**112** B1
Ballengeich Pass FK8.......**2** A1
Ballengeich Rd FK8.........**1** F1
Ballingry La KY5...........**14** B7
Ballingry St KY5...........**14** A7
Balloch Rd ML7...........**179** E6
Balmoral Dr Falkirk FK1....**59** E3
  Kirkcaldy KY2..............**16** D5
Balmoral Gdns
  Grangemouth FK2..........**82** D7
  Livingston EH54..........**144** D6
Balmoral Pl Edinburgh EH3 .**93** B2
  Stenhousemuir FK5.........**38** E4
  Stirling FK8................**7** A7
Balmoral Rd EH11..........**62** E6
Balmoral St FK1...........**59** E3
Balmuir Ave EH48.........**140** F8
Balmuir Rd EH48.........**140** F7
Balmwell Ave EH16.......**151** B5
Balmwell Gr EH16.........**151** B5
Balmwell Pk EH16........**151** B5
Balmwell Terr EH16......**151** A5
Balnacraig KY12............**28** B1
Balquharn Cotts FK12......**4** D7
Balquhatstone Cres FK1..**108** A6
Balquhidderock Wood
  Nature Reserve ★ FK7....**7** D3
Balsusney Rd KY2..........**17** B5
Baltic Quay FK3............**40** D1
Baltic St EH6...............**94** A5
Balure Cres FK7............**8** D4
Balvaird Pl KY12...........**29** C6
Balwearie Cres KY2........**17** A2
Balwearie Gdns KY2........**16** F1
Balwearie High Sch KY2 ..**17** A1
Balwearie Rd KY2..........**17** A2
Banchory Cotts KY2........**34** E5
Banchory Pl FK10...........**4** C3
Banchory Prim Sch FK10...**4** C3
Bancroft Ave EH54.......**143** E4
Bandeath Ind Est FK7......**9** A5
Bandeath Rd FK7...........**9** A4
Bandon Ave KY1...........**17** F8
Bangholm Ave EH5..........**93** B5
Bangholm Bower Ave EH5 .**93** B5
Bangholm Gr EH5...........**93** C5
Bangholm Loan EH5........**93** C5
Bangholm Pl EH5...........**93** B5
Bangholm Terr EH3.........**93** B4
Bangholm View EH5........**93** C5
Bangholm Villas EH5.......**93** C5
Bangly Brae EH41, EH32...**100** A4
BANGLY HILL.............**100** B4
Bangor Rd EH6.............**93** F5
Bankfoot EH32.............**96** D1
Bankhead EH14............**57** E6
Bankhead Ave EH11......**119** C3
Bankhead Broadway
  EH11.....................**119** B3
Bankhead Cotts EH40......**75** C6
Bankhead Cres FK4.........**57** D6
Bankhead Crossway N
  EH11.....................**119** C2
Bankhead Crossway S
  EH11.....................**119** C2
Bankhead Dr EH11.........**119** B3
Bankhead Gr EH30..........**68** D1
Bankhead Ind Est EH11 ..**119** C3
Bankhead Medway EH11 .**119** C3
Bankhead Pl EH11.........**119** C2
Bankhead Rd Fishcross FK10 .**5** D3
  Queensferry EH30..........**68** C7
Bankhead Terr EH11......**119** C2
Bankhead Way EH11......**119** B2
Bankhill Ct FK3.............**61** D6
Bankmill View EH26......**191** F4
Bankpark Brae EH33......**126** B7
Bankpark Cres EH33......**126** B7
Bankpark Gr EH33........**126** C7
Bankt Pl ML7..............**179** F4
Bank Rd East Linton EH40.**103** E7
  Harthill ML7..............**159** E5
BANKSIDE.................**60** C8
Bankside FK2..............**60** C7
Bankside Ho FK6............**36** E2
Bankside Ind Est FK2......**60** D8
Bank St Alloa FK10..........**10** B6
  Edinburgh EH1............**229** A3
  Falkirk FK1................**60** B5
  Grangemouth FK3..........**40** A1
  Inverkeithing KY11........**47** C2
  Kincardine FK10...........**23** D3
  Kirkcaldy KY1..............**17** E7
  Lochgelly KY5..............**14** B8
  Mid Calder EH53.........**144** D4
  North Berwick EH39........**54** B7
  Penicuik EH26............**191** E4
  Slamannan FK1............**108** A6
  Stirling FK8................**7** A8
Banks View FK2............**22** E4
Bank Terr ML11...........**217** F8

Bankton Ave EH54........**164** F7
Bankton Brae EH54.......**164** E7
Bankton Ct
  Livingston EH54..........**165** B8
  Tranent EH33.............**126** D6
Bankton Dr EH54.........**164** F7
Bankton Gdns EH54......**165** A8
Bankton Glade EH54......**165** A8
Bankton Gn EH54.........**164** F7
Bankton Gr EH54.........**165** A8
Bankton Junc EH33.......**126** C8
Bankton La EH54.........**165** A8
Bankton Park E EH54.....**144** B1
Bankton Park W EH54....**144** B1
Bankton Prim Sch EH54 ..**143** F1
Bankton Rd EH54.........**164** D8
Bankton Sq EH54.........**164** F7
Bankton Terr
  Livingston EH54..........**164** F7
  Prestonpans EH32..........**97** B1
  Tranent EH33.............**126** B8
Bankton Way EH54.......**164** F7
Bankton Wlk EH54.......**164** F7
Bankton Wood EH54......**165** A7
Bankview Terr FK4..........**57** E6
Bannerman Ave KY11......**47** C3
Bannerman St KY12........**29** A5
Bannock Brae KY12........**29** C3
BANNOCKBURN............**7** E2
Bannockburn Cross FK7....**7** E1
Bannockburn Heritage Ctr ★
  FK7.......................**7** B2
Bannockburn High Sch
  FK7.......................**7** D2
Bannockburn Hosp FK7 ...**19** F7
Bannockburn Prim Sch
Bannockburn Rd
  Cowie FK7.................**20** C8
  Stirling FK7................**7** C3
Bannockburn Station Rd
  FK7.......................**8** A4
Bannock Rd FK7.............**8** C4
BANTASKIN................**59** F4
Bantaskine Dr FK1.........**59** F4
Bantaskine Gdns FK1......**59** E3
Bantaskine Prim Sch FK1 ..**59** E4
Bantaskine Rd FK1.........**59** F4
Bantaskine St FK1.........**59** E3
Banton Pl FK4.............**58** A3
Baptie Pl EH51.............**63** E5
Barassie Dr KY2...........**17** A8
Barbara Stocks La KY12....**42** D8
Barbauchlaw Ave EH48...**139** E6
Barbauchlaw Ave EH48...**139** F6
Barbour Ave FK7............**7** C3
Barbour Dr KY12............**28** E5
Barclay Pl EH10...........**228** B1
Barclay St KY4.............**13** B3
Barclay Terr EH10.........**228** B1
Barclay Way EH54........**143** E7
Barga Ct EH32..............**97** A2
Barham Rd KY11...........**46** D1
Barkhill Rd EH49...........**84** F6
Barkin Ct FK1..............**60** B2
Barlaw Gdns EH48........**140** A6
Barley Bree La EH22......**174** D8
Barley Ct EH22...........**174** D8
Barleyhill FK4..............**58** B5
Barleyhill Terr FK4.........**58** B3
Barleyknowe Cres EH23..**174** C1
Barleyknowe Gdns EH23 .**174** C2
Barleyknowe La EH23.....**174** C1
Barleyknowe Pl EH23.....**174** C1
Barleyknowe Rd EH23....**174** C1
Barleyknowe St EH23.....**174** C1
Barleyknowe Terr EH23...**174** C2
Barnbougle Ride EH30.....**90** C7
Barnego Rd FK6............**36** D3
Barnes Gn EH54..........**143** C7
Barnet Cres KY1............**17** B1
Barnhill Dr FK10.............**4** C2
Barnhill Pl KY11............**48** D4
Barnhill Rd KY11............**48** D4
Barn Park Cres EH14.....**148** E8
Barn Pk EH14.............**148** E7
Barn Pk Cres EH14........**143** B3
Barn Rd FK8................**7** A8
Barns Ct EH47.............**161** E7
Barnsdale Rd FK7...........**7** A3
Barnshot Rd EH13.........**149** B6
Barns Ness Terr EH42.....**218** A6
Barns Pk KY11.............**48** A2
Barns The KY3.............**50** E8
BARNTON..................**91** B3
Barnton Ave EH4...........**91** D4
Barnton Brae EH4..........**91** B4
Barnton Ct EH4............**91** B3
Barntongate Ave EH4......**91** B2
Barntongate Dr EH4.......**91** B2
Barntongate Terr EH4.....**91** B2
Barnton Gdns EH4..........**91** B3
Barnton Gr EH4............**91** B3
Barnton Junc EH4..........**91** B2
Barnton La FK1............**60** B4
Barnton Park Ave EH4.....**91** D3
Barnton Park Cres EH4....**91** C3
Barnton Park Dell EH4....**91** D3
Barnton Park Dr EH4......**91** C3
Barnton Park Gdns EH4...**91** D3
Barnton Park Gr EH4......**91** C3
Barnton Park View EH4...**91** C3
Barnton Park Wood EH4..**91** C2
Barnton Pk EH4............**91** E4

Barnton St FK8..............**7** B8
Barnwell Rd FK9.............**2** C4
Baronscourt Rd EH8.......**94** D1
Baronscourt Terr EH8.....**122** D8
Barons Hill Ave EH49.......**85** B7
Barons Hill Ct EH49........**85** B7
Barony Cr Bo'ness EH51.....**63** F5
  Cambusbarron FK7..........**6** D6
Barony Pl [5] EH3...........**93** D2
Barony St EH3..............**93** D2
Barony Terr EH12.........**119** D7
Barracks Rdbt EH54.......**142** E5
Barracks St EH32...........**97** D4
Barra Pl FK5................**39** A4
Barrie Ct EH54.............**144** C5
Barrie Pl
  [4] Dunfermline KY12......**28** E5
  Grangemouth FK3..........**61** D5
Barrie Rd FK5................**38** F3
Barrie St KY12..............**28** E5
Barrie Terr EH48..........**141** C5
Barton Bldgs KY3...........**35** A2
Barton Ct EH47...........**181** E6
Barton Rd KY11.............**46** B1
Barton Terr EH47.........**181** F6
Basil Paterson Coll The
  EH2......................**228** B4
Bass Rock View EH39.......**55** B7
Bastion Wynd [7] FK8.......**7** B7
Bathfield EH6...............**93** E6
BATHGATE.................**141** C1
Bathgate Acad EH48......**141** E5
Bathgate Bsns Ctr EH48.**141** C2
Bathgate Rd
  Armadale EH48...........**140** B6
  Blackburn EH47..........**162** C8
  East Whitburn EH48......**161** E7
Bathgate Sta EH48........**141** B5
Bath Pl EH15...............**95** B1
Bath Rd EH6................**94** B5
Bath St EH15..............**123** B8
Bath Street La EH15......**123** B8
Bathville Bsns Ctr EH48..**140** A5
Baton Rd ML7.............**179** D6
Batterflatts Gdns FK7......**6** F6
Batterflatts Ho FK7.........**6** F6
Battery Rd
  Grangemouth FK3..........**62** C8
  North Queensferry KY11....**68** C5
Battock Rd FK2.............**82** F7
Bavelaw Cres EH26.......**191** D6
Bavelaw Gdns EH14......**147** C1
Bavelaw Gn EH14.........**147** C2
Bavelaw Rd EH14.........**147** C1
Baxter Cres FK6............**36** C1
Baxter Rd KY4..............**30** F6
Baxters Gate EH33........**126** D5
Baxter's Pl EH1...........**229** B4
Baxter St FK7...............**8** D4
Baxter's Wynd FK1..........**60** B4
Bayne Gdns EH49...........**84** A6
Bayne St FK8................**2** A1
Bayswell Pk EH42...........**78** D3
Bayswell Rd EH42...........**78** D3
Bayview KY12...............**26** E1
Bay View EH32..............**97** D4
Beach La Edinburgh EH15 ...**95** B1
  Musselburgh EH21........**124** B7
Beachmont Ct EH42.........**78** E1
Beachmont Pl EH42.........**78** F1
Beach Rd Grangemouth FK3 .**41** B1
  North Berwick EH39........**54** B7
Beaconcroft FK9.............**2** C7
Beaconhurst Sch FK9.......**2** C6
Beacon L Ctr KY3...........**50** F8
BEANCROSS................**61** C5
Beancross Prim Sch FK3...**61** C5
Beancross Rd FK3..........**61** C5
Beancross Rdbt FK3........**61** B6
Bean Row FK1..............**60** B4
Bearcroft Gdns FK3........**61** E7
Bearford Pl EH41..........**130** D8
Bearside Rd FK7.............**7** A3
Beath High Sch KY4........**13** B5
Beath View KY11...........**29** E4
Beath View Rd KY4.........**13** A2
Beatlie Rd EH52............**115** A8
Beatlie Specl Sch EH54...**144** B5
Beaton Ave FK7.............**7** C1
Beatty Ave FK8..............**2** A2
Beatty Cres KY1............**17** D7
Beatty Ct KY1..............**17** D7
Beatty Pl KY12..............**29** C5
Beauchamp Gr [2] EH16..**151** A8
Beauchamp Rd EH16......**151** A8
Beauclerc St FK12...........**5** A7
Beaufort Cres KY2..........**16** D5
Beaufort Dr FK2.............**39** A3
Beaufort Rd EH9..........**121** D4
Beauly Cres KY11...........**47** C8
Beauly Ct Falkirk FK1.......**60** C1
  Grangemouth FK3..........**61** D4
Beauly Dr EH54............**143** B4
Beauly Pl KY2..............**16** F7
Beaumont Dr FK2...........**39** B2
BEAVERBANK...............**93** D4
Beaverbank Bsns Pk EH7 .**93** C3
Beaverbank Pl EH7.........**93** D3
Beaverhall Rd EH7.........**93** D3
Beck Cres KY12.............**29** C5
Bedford Ct Alloa FK10......**10** A6
  [3] Edinburgh EH4..........**93** A2
Bedford Pl FK10............**10** A6
Bedford St EH4.............**93** A2
Bedford Terr EH15.........**123** C8
Bedlam Theatre ★ EH1 ...**229** A2

Bedlormie Dr EH48 138 C2
Beech Ave
Carrington EH23 194 F3
Dalgety Bay KY3, KY11 48 F5
Mid Calder EH53 144 B2
Plean FK7 20 C3
Beechbank Cres EH53 144 E2
Beech Cres Denny FK6 36 C3
Larbert FK5 59 C8
Westquarter FK2 61 B3
Beeches The
Armadale EH48 139 E5
Dalgety Bay KY11 48 C3
Gullane EH31 52 B3
Lochgelly KY5 14 A8
Newtongrange EH22 174 A7
Beech Gdns FK7 6 F6
Beech Gr Cousland EH22 154 D5
Dunfermline KY12 46 D8
Livingston EH54 144 B6
Whitburn EH47 161 C6
Beech Grove Ave EH22 152 E1
Beechgrove Rd EH22 174 E6
Beech La FK9 2 B4
Beech Loan EH19 173 B6
Beechmount Cres EH12 120 B7
Beechmount Ct ML7 180 B2
Beechmount Pk EH12 120 B7
Beech Pl Dunfermline KY12 26 A1
Grangemouth FK3 61 C6
Livingston EH54 143 C4
Seafield EH47 142 B1
Beech Rd EH48 141 E6
Beech Terr EH34 156 D6
Beech Tree Pk FK6 37 A2
Beech Tree The EH47 86 D4
Beech Way KY11 48 A5
Beechwood Alloa FK10 5 E1
Crossford KY12 28 B2
Linlithgow EH49 85 A5
Sauchie FK10 5 D1
Beechwood Gdns
Blackburn EH47 141 D1
Stirling FK8 7 A5
Beechwood Gr EH54 115 A2
Beechwood Mains EH12 120 B7
Beechwood Pk
Livingston EH54 142 F7
Newtongrange EH22 174 B6
Uphall Station EH54 115 A1
Beechwood Rd
Blackburn EH47 141 D1
Haddington EH41 129 E7
Beechwood Terr EH6 94 B3
Beecraigs Ctry Pk* EH49 85 A1
BEESLACK 192 A7
Beeslack Com High Sch
EH26 192 A4
Begbie Pl EH54 143 B5
Begbie View EH26 171 B6
Begg Ave FK1 59 E4
Beldorney Pl KY12 29 D6
Belfield Ave EH53 144 F2
Belford Ave EH4 92 E1
Belford Gdns EH4 92 E1
Belford Mews 3 EH4 120 F8
Belford Pk EH4 120 F8
Belford Rd EH4 120 F8
Belford Terr EH4 120 F8
Belgrave Cres EH4 228 A4
Belgrave Crescent La
EH4 228 A4
Belgrave Gdns EH12 119 E7
Belgrave Mews 8 EH4 92 F1
Belgrave Pl EH4 92 F1
Belgrave Rd EH12 119 E8
BELHAVEN 78 B1
Belhaven Bewery* EH42 78 B1
Belhaven Hill Sch EH42 78 B1
Belhaven Hospl EH42 78 B1
Belhaven Pl EH10 121 A2
Belhaven Rd EH42 78 C2
Belhaven Terr EH10 121 A2
Bellamond Cres EH47 161 E7
Bell Ct Falkirk FK2 60 C7
Grangemouth FK3 40 E1
Belleknowes Ind Est KY11 92 E4
Bellenden Gdns EH16 122 C1
Bellerophon Dr EH26 191 F4
Bellevue Edinburgh EH3 93 D2
Grangemouth FK2 82 E7
Bellevue Ave EH7 78 E1
Bellevue Cres EH3 93 D2
Bellevue Gdns EH7 93 D3
Bellevue Gr EH7 93 D2
Bellevue Pk FK10 9 E6
Bellevue Rd Alloa FK10 9 E6
Edinburgh EH7 93 D2
Bellevue St Edinburgh EH7 93 D2
Falkirk FK1 59 C4
Bellevue Terr Dunbar EH42 78 C1
Edinburgh EH7 93 D2
Bellfield Ave
Dalkeith EH22 152 E2
Musselburgh EH21 124 B5
Bellfield Cres KY1 18 A8
Bellfield Ct EH21 124 B5
Bellfield La EH15 123 B8
Bellfield Rd
Bannockburn FK7 7 E1
Stirling FK8 7 B5
Bellfield Sq EH32 125 E8
Bellfield St EH15 123 B8

Bellfield Terr EH15 123 B8
Bellfield View EH19 173 D8
Bellhouse Rd KY3 49 B7
Bellman's Rd EH26 191 E6
Bellman Way KY11 48 B5
Bellona Terr EH47 181 F6
Bell Pl EH3 93 B2
Bell Rd KY11 46 B2
Bell's Brae EH4 228 A3
Bells Burn Ave EH49 85 C7
Bellsdyke Hospl FK5 38 D5
Bellsdyke Pl FK5 38 A3
Bellsdyke Rd Falkirk FK2 39 C6
Stenhousemuir FK5 38 D4
Bellsdyke Rdbt FK5 38 B4
Bellsmains EH23 195 D5
Bellsmeadow Rd FK1 60 C4
Bell's Mills EH4 120 F8
Bell's Mill Terr EH52 87 F2
Bell Sq HS4 164 C5
BELLSQUARRY 164 D7
Bellsquarry Prim Sch
EH54 164 E6
Bellsquarry South Rd
EH54 164 E6
Bell Stane EH30 68 B1
Bell's Wynd FK1 60 B4
BELLYEOMAN 29 D5
Bellyeoman La KY12 29 C5
Bellyeoman Prim Sch
KY12 29 C5
Bellyeoman Rd KY12 29 C5
Bellyford Rd EH33 126 A1
Belmont Ave
Bonnybridge FK4 57 D5
Edinburgh EH12 120 B7
Shieldhill FK1 81 E7
Belmont Cres EH12 120 B7
Belmont Dr
Edinburgh EH12 120 B7
Shotts ML7 180 B2
Belmont Gdns EH12 120 B7
Belmont Pk EH12 120 B7
Belmont Rd EH14 148 D6
Belmont St FK1 60 C4
Belmont Terr EH12 120 B7
Belmont Twr FK1 60 C4
Belmont View EH12 120 B7
Belstane Gate ML8 215 A3
Belstane Mews ML8 215 A3
Belstane Pk ML8 215 A3
Belstane Rd ML8 215 A3
Belsyde Ct EH49 84 D6
BELVEDERE 140 F8
Belvedere La EH48 140 F8
Belvedere Pk EH6 93 C6
Belvedere Pl EH48 140 F8
Belvedere Rd
Bathgate EH48 140 F8
2 Bathgate EH48 141 A7
Belwood Cres EH26 171 B1
Belwood Rd EH26 170 F1
Ben Alder Pl KY2 16 E5
Benarty St KY2 16 F5
Bendachin Dr KY12 29 E5
Bendameer Rd KY3 33 C1
Benhar Rd ML7 180 A6
Benjamin Dr EH51 63 E5
Ben Ledi Rd KY2 16 F5
Ben Lomond Dr FK9 2 A4
Ben Lomond View KY12 27 A6
Bennachie Way KY11 30 B1
Bennet Wood Terr EH52 87 F3
Ben Nevis Pl KY2 16 F5
Bennie Mus* EH48 141 A6
Bennie Terr EH51 108 B7
Bennochy Ave KY2 17 A5
Bennochy Ct KY2 17 A5
Bennochy Gdns KY2 17 A5
Bennochy Gr KY2 17 A5
Bennochy Rd Kirkcaldy KY1 17 B4
Kirkcaldy, Templehall KY2 16 E6
Bennochy View KY2 17 A5
Ben Sayers Pk EH39 54 E6
Bentheads FK7 19 E8
BENTS 162 A2
Benview FK7 7 C2
Benview Terr FK10 5 E4
Beresford Gdns EH5 93 C5
Beresford Pl EH5 93 B5
Beresford Rise EH54 144 A1
Beresford Terr EH5 93 C6
Bergen Ave KY11 30 A2
Berkeley St FK7 7 A4
Bernard Shaw St KY12 28 E5
Bernard's Smithy KY3 32 B5
Bernard St EH6 94 A5
Bernard Terr EH8 229 B1
Berryhill FK7 20 E7
Berryhill Cres FK3 61 E6
Berryhill Pl ML7 180 B2
Berrylaw Pl KY12 28 E4
Berrylaw Rd KY12 28 D4
Berry St KY5 14 B7
Bertram Pl ML7 179 D5
Bertram St Harthill ML7 159 C5
Shotts ML7 179 E5
Bervie Dr EH54 164 E5
Berwick Pl Dysart KY1 18 A8
Kirkcaldy KY1 17 C5
Beta Ctr FK2 2 D5
Bethelfield Pl KY1 17 B2
Bethesda Gr EH47 161 E7
Bethlehem Way EH47 94 B3
Beulah EH21 124 E6
Bevan Dr FK12 5 C7
Bevan Rd KY11 46 E3

Bevan Rd EH22 174 D5
Beveridge Ave EH22 174 E5
Beveridge Cl EH22 174 E5
Beveridge Pl 1 FK2 61 A1
Beveridge Rd KY1 17 B3
Beveridge Row 78 A1
Beveridge Sq EH54 143 E1
Beveridge St KY11 29 C2
BEVERIDGEWELL 28 F5
Bickerton Crofts EH47 161 E5
Bickerton Terr EH47 161 A5
Bickram Cres KY12 28 F3
Bielgrange Cotts EH42 104 D4
Bielside Gdns EH42 77 F1
Big Brigs Way EH22 173 F4
Biggar Rd Edinburgh EH10 150 B3
Silverburn EH26 190 E5
Biggin Wa's KY11 17 F7
Bill Russel Gr EH22 153 B3
BILSTON 171 E5
Bingham 122 F6
Bingham Ave EH15 123 A5
Bingham Broadway
EH15 123 A5
Bingham Cres EH15 123 A5
Bingham Crossway EH15 123 A5
Bingham Dr EH15 123 A5
Bingham Medway EH15 122 F5
Bingham Pl EH15 122 F5
Bingham Way EH15 122 F5
Binn Ave KY3 33 E2
Binney Wells KY1 17 F6
Binnie Pl FK2 39 F2
Binniehill Rd FK1 108 A5
Binnie Pl EH47 39 F2
Binning Rd KY11 47 B3
Binning Wood Rd EH42 75 F7
Binns The* EH49 65 E1
Binny Pk EH52 114 F7
Birch Ave FK8 6 F5
Birchbank EH14 13 B2
Birch Cres EH20 171 F7
Birch Ct Edinburgh EH4 91 B2
Livingston EH54 143 C2
Birch Gr Dunfermline KY11 46 D8
Menstrie FK11 3 F6
Birch Terr EH26 171 A2
Birchwood FK10 5 D2
Birchwood Gdns EH54 164 D7
Birdland Ave EH51 64 D7
Birkdale Dr EH52 114 F4
Birkdale Pk EH48 140 B6
Birkenshaw Way EH48 139 C6
Birkenside EH23 195 C6
Birkfield Loan EH48 215 C1
Birkfield Pl ML8 215 C1
Birk Hedges EH41 128 E6
Birkhill Clay Mine* EH49 62 E2
Birkhill Cres EH51 63 F6
Birkhill Rd FK7 6 F6
Birkhill St * EH49 62 F3
Birnam Gdns EH15 30 A4
Birnam Pl FK2 60 C5
Birnam Rd KY2 16 E8
Birnie Brae KY5 14 B7
Birniehall ML11 217 F8
Birniehill Ave EH48 140 F4
Birniehill Cres EH48 140 F4
Birniehill Rd EH48 140 F4
Birniehill Terr EH48 140 F4
Birnieknowes Farm Cotts
EH42 104 B1
Birrell Cl 5 KY1 17 D6
Birrell Dr KY11 29 D1
Birrell Gdns EH54 164 E7
Birrell's La KY1 17 E7
Birrel's Wynd KY3 35 A3
Birsley Rd EH33 126 C6
Bishops Gate EH52 115 C5
Bishops Pk
Livingston EH53 144 B1
Mid Calder EH53 144 C2
Bittern Ct KY11 30 A2
Blackadder Haven KY12 42 D8
Blackadder Pl EH5 92 E6
Blackbarony Rd EH16 122 A7
Blackbraes Rd FK1 81 F4
BLACKBURN 162 D8
Blackburn Ave KY12 28 A1
Blackburn Crag EH14 151 D8
Blackburn Dr KY4 13 A3
Blackburnhall EH47 162 D6
Blackburnhall Holdings
EH47 162 A6
Blackburn Prim Sch
EH47 141 C1
Blackburn Rd
Addiewell EH55 162 D3
Blackburn EH48 141 D3
Blackchapel Cl EH15 123 B4
Blackcot Ave EH22 174 D5
Blackcot Dr EH22 174 D5
Blackcot Pl EH22 174 D5
Blackdykes Cotts EH39 55 C4
Blacket Ave EH9 121 F5
Blacket Pl EH9 121 F5
Blackfaulds Ct EH47 181 E6
Blackfaulds Dr EH47 181 E6
Blackfaulds Pl EH47 181 E6
Blackford Ave EH9 121 D3
Blackford Bank EH9 121 E3
Blackford Brae Project Sch
EH9 121 C3
Blackford Gate EH9 121 C3

Blackford Glen Cotts
EH16 121 F1
Blackford Glen Rd EH16 121 F1
Blackford Hill Gr EH9 121 D2
Blackford Hill Nature
Reserve* EH16 121 D2
Blackford Hill Rise EH9 121 D2
Blackford Hill View EH9 121 D2
Blackford Rd EH9 121 C4
Blackfriars St EH1 229 B3
Blackgrange Rdbt FK5 3 D3
BLACKHALL 92 A2
Blackhall Prim Sch EH4 92 A1
Blackhall St ML7 180 B3
Blackhall Terr EH26 171 A1
Blackhall Rd EH48 138 F3
Blackie Rd EH6 94 B4
Blacklaw Rd KY11 29 D2
Blackmill Cres FK2 39 B3
Blackmount Terr FK2 82 E6
Blackmuir Pl FK10 4 D3
BLACKNESS 65 E4
Blackness Castle* EH49 65 F5
Blackness Prim Sch EH49 65 D4
Blackness Rd EH49 85 B7
Blackraigs KY2 16 C7
BLACKRIDGE 138 C3
Blackridge Com Mus*
EH48 138 D3
Blackridge Prim Sch
EH48 138 C3
Blackstone Rd FK1 110 A6
Blackthorn Ct EH4 91 B2
Blackthorn Gr FK11 4 A5
Blackwood Cres EH9 121 E5
Blackwood Gdns KY11 46 F7
Blackwood Gdns KY11 46 F7
Blackwood Rd KY11 46 F6
Blackwood Rd KY11 46 F7
Blaeberry Gdns EH4 91 B2
BLAEBERRYHILL 161 C5
Blaeberryhill Rd EH47 161 C5
Blaefaulds Cres FK6 57 D8
Blair Ave EH51 63 E5
BLAIRBURN 42 C8
Blairdenon Cres FK9 59 F3
Blairdenon Dr FK10 5 B2
Blairdenon Rd FK12 4 A6
Blair Dr Dunfermline KY12 29 B6
Kelty KY4 12 D8
Blairforkie Dr FK9 1 F8
Blair Gr KY12 26 A8
BLAIRHALL 26 A7
Blairhall Prim Sch KY12 26 A8
Blairhill View EH48 138 C3
Blairlodge Ave FK2 82 C8
BLAIRLOGIE 3 B6
Blairmore Rd KY11 46 F7
Blairmuckhole & Forrestdyke
Rd ML7 158 E2
Blairmuir Terr EH52 115 F5
Blair Pl Falkirk FK2 59 F7
Kirkcaldy KY2 16 D5
Blair St Edinburgh EH1 229 A3
Blair's Cotts FK2 61 C1
Blair Terr FK5 39 A4
Blairwood Terr KY12 26 E7
Blairwood Wlk KY12 26 E7
Blake St EH29 89 C1
Blamey Cres KY4 13 B2
Blandfield EH7 93 D3
Blantyre Terr EH10 121 A4
Blawarie Rd EH48 126 D5
Blawhorn Moss National
Nature Reserve* EH48 138 B5
Bleachfield Edinburgh EH6 93 D4
Falkirk FK2 60 A5
Bleachfield Ct KY11 29 E3
Blenheim Ct Carluke ML8 215 B1
Penicuik EH26 192 A8
Stirling FK9 2 C2
Blenheim Pl FK5 38 E5
Blie Brae EH29 88 F2
Blindwell Brae EH41 131 F1
Blindwells FK12 4 F6
Blinkbonnie Terr FK1 108 A6
BLINKBONNY 148 B4
Blinkbonny Ave EH4 92 D1
Blinkbonny Cres EH4 92 C1
Blinkbonny Gdns
Edinburgh EH4 92 D1
West Calder EH55 182 E6
Blinkbonny Grove W EH4 92 D1
Blinkbonny Rd
Currie EH14 148 B4
Edinburgh EH4 120 D8
Falkirk FK1 59 E4
Blinkbonny Terr EH4 92 C1
Blink O'forth EH32 125 E8
Blinny St ML7 180 A3
Bloom Ct EH54 143 B3
Bloomfield Pl 1 EH48 141 B6
Bloom Pth EH54 143 C3
Bluebell Cl 8 FK1 60 B4
Bluebell Gdns EH54 164 C8
Blyth Rd EH52 115 C4
Blyth St KY1 17 E8
Boat Gn EH3 93 C3
Bobbin Wynd FK7 6 D6
Bogend Rd
Bannockburn FK7 19 E8
Larbert FK2 38 B8
Torwood FK5 37 F8
BOGHALL 141 E7

Boghall Dr EH48 141 E5
Boghall Farm Cotts
EH10 171 B6
Boghall Farm Steadings
EH48 141 F5
Boghall Prim Sch EH48 141 F6
Boghall Rdbt EH48 141 F5
Boghead Cres EH48 140 E5
Bogies Wynd 9 KY1 17 D6
Boglily Cotts KY3 16 D3
Boglily Rd KY2 16 D3
Bogpark Rd EH21 124 A6
Bog Rd Laurieston FK2 60 F4
Penicuik EH26 191 E5
Whitburn EH47 161 A7
Bog Rdbt FK2 60 F4
Bog Road Ind Est FK2 60 F4
Bogsmill Rd EH14 120 B1
Bog The EH51 64 A8
Bogwood Ct EH22 174 D7
Bogwood Dr KY12 28 A2
Bogwood Rd EH22 174 E6
Bohun Ct FK7 7 D4
Bolam Dr KY3 33 F2
BOLTON 129 F1
Bolton Council Hos
EH41 220 C8
Bolton Steading EH41 129 F1
Bo'mains Ind Est EH51 63 F5
Bo'mains Rd EH51 63 E6
Bomar Ave EH51 64 A8
Bon Accord Cres ML7 179 E5
BONALY 149 A5
Bonaly Ave EH13 149 B5
Bonaly Brae EH13 149 B5
Bonaly Cres EH13 149 B5
Bonaly Ctry Pk* EH13 148 F2
Bonaly Dr EH13 149 A5
Bonaly Gdns EH13 149 B5
Bonaly Gr EH13 149 B5
Bonaly Prim Sch EH13 149 A5
Bonaly Rd EH13 149 A5
Bonaly Rise EH13 149 B5
Bonaly Steading EH13 149 A5
Bonaly Terr EH13 149 B5
Bonaly Wester EH13 149 A5
Bonar Pl EH6 93 D5
Bond St FK10 4 A3
BO'NESS 63 E8
Bo'ness Acad EH51 64 A6
Bo'ness Hospl EH51 63 E7
Bo'ness & Kinneil Rly*
EH51 63 C7
Bo'ness Motor Mus*
EH51 64 C8
Bo'ness Public Sch EH51 63 F7
Bo'ness Rd
Grangemouth FK3 62 B6
Polmont FK2 61 F3
Queensferry EH30 67 F1
Bo'ness Sta* EH51 64 A8
Bonhard Ct EH51 64 B6
Bonhard Rd KY11 27 B7
Bonhard Way EH51 64 B5
Bonnar St KY12 29 A4
BONNINGTON 93 D4
Bonnington Ave EH6 93 D5
Bonnington Bsns Ctr EH6 93 F4
Bonnington Gait EH6 93 E4
Bonnington Ind Est EH6 93 E4
Bonnington Mill Bsns Ctr
EH6 93 E5
Bonnington Rd
Edinburgh EH6 93 E4
Wilkieston EH27 146 A6
Bonnington Rd La EH6 93 E4
Bonnington Terr EH6 93 D5
Bonnybank Ct EH23 195 D8
Bonnybank Rd EH23 195 D8
BONNYBRIDGE 58 B5
Bonnybridge Hospl FK4 58 C6
Bonnybridge Ind Est FK4 58 A4
Bonnybridge Prim Sch
FK4 58 B6
Bonnybridge Rd FK4 57 E5
Bonnybridge Nature Reserve*
FK4 58 A5
Bonnyfield Rd FK4 58 A5
Bonnyhaugh EH6 93 D4
Bonnyhaugh La EH6 93 D4
Bonnyhill Rd
Bonnybridge FK4 58 D3
Falkirk FK1 59 A4
Bonnymill Pl FK4 58 B5
Bonnymuir Cres FK4 57 F5
Bonnymuir Pl FK4 58 B5
BONNYRIGG AND
LASSWADE 173 D7
Bonnyrigg L Ctr EH19 173 B7
Bonnyrigg Prim Sch
EH19 173 C6
Bonnyrigg Rd EH22 152 E1
Bonnyside Rd FK4 58 B5
Bonnyton Pl KY11 29 C3
Bonnytoun Ave EH49 85 C8
Bonnytoun Terr EH49 85 C8
Bonnyvale Pl FK4 57 F5
Bonnyview Gdns FK4 58 B7
Bonthrone Pl FK4 58 B7
Boothacre La EH6 94 C4
Booth Ave KY11 46 D5
Booth Pl EH7 60 B4
Boreland Pk KY11 47 C3

Boreland Rd Dysart KY1...18 A8
Inverkeithing KY11....47 C3
BORESTONE........7 A2
Borestone Cres FK7....7 A4
Borestone Ct FK7.....7 A2
Borestone Pl FK7.....7 A2
Borestone Prim Sch FK7..7 A2
Boroughdales EH42....78 C2
Boroughloch EH8.....229 B1
Boroughloch Sq EH8...229 B1
Boroughmuir High Sch
EH10..............121 A5
Boroughmuir High Sch
Annexe EH10........121 A5
Borrowlea Rd FK7.....7 C7
Borrowmeadow Rd FK7..7 E7
Borrows Gate FK9.....1 F3
BORROWSTOUN........63 F5
Borrowstoun Cres EH51..63 F5
BORROWSTOUN MAINS...63 E5
Borrowstoun Pl EH51...63 F5
BORTHWICK.........196 B4
Borthwick Castle Pl
EH23..............195 F3
Borthwick Castle Rd
EH23..............195 F2
Borthwick Castle Terr
EH23..............195 F3
Borthwick Pl EH12....120 E7
Borthwick's Cl EH1...229 A3
Borthwick View EH7...172 A7
Boswall Ave EH5.....92 F5
Boswall Cres EH5.....92 F5
Boswall Dr EH5.......93 A5
Boswall Gdns EH5.....92 F5
Boswall Gn EH5.......93 A5
Boswall Gr EH5.......92 F6
Boswall Loan EH5.....92 F6
Boswall Parkway EH5...92 E6
Boswall Pl EH5.......92 F5
Boswall Quadrant EH5..92 F5
Boswall Rd EH5.......93 A6
Boswall Sq EH5.......92 F5
Boswall Terr EH5.....92 F5
Boswell Dr Kinghorn KY3..35 A3
Oakley KY12........66 F6
Boswell Rd KY5......14 B8
Bothkennar Prim Sch FK2 39 F3
Bothkennar Rd FK2....39 E3
Bothwell Ct KY11.....29 A2
Bothwell Gdns
Dunbar EH42........78 D1
Inverkeithing KY11, KY12..29 A2
Bothwell Ho EH7.....94 A2
Bothwell St
Dunfermline KY11.....29 B2
Edinburgh EH7.......94 A2
Boulevard East Rdbt
EH54..............143 F2
Boundary Road E EH14..147 F8
Boundary Road N EH14..147 E7
Boundary St EH51.....64 B8
Bouprie Rise KY11....48 B4
Bourtree Gr KY12.....26 D7
Bow Butts KY12......29 A2
Bowhill Ct EH31......52 B2
Bowhill Terr EH5.....93 B5
BOWHOUSE..........61 E5
Bowhousebog or Liquo
ML7...............179 A2
Bowhousebog Rd ML7...179 A2
Bowhouse Dr KY1.....35 B8
Bowhouse Gdns
Alloa FK10.........10 B5
Kirkcaldy KY1.......35 B7
Bowhouse Prim Sch FK3..61 E5
Bowhouse Rd Alloa FK10..10 B5
Bowhouse Sq FK3.....61 D5
Bowling Green Pl FK4..57 F5
Bowling Green Rd
Kirkliston EH29......89 B1
Whitburn EH47.......161 A6
Bowling Green The EH6...93 F5
Bowling Green Wynd
KY12..............26 A7
Bowling La FK6.......93 F5
Bowmont Pl EH8......229 B1
Bowmont Terr EH42....78 E2
Bowmore Wlk ML7.....180 A3
Bow St FK8..........7 A8
Bowyett EH48........111 F6
Boxton Rd California FK1..81 D7
Standburn FK1.......82 C3
Boyd La FK2.........60 B6
Boyd-Orr Dr EH26.....191 F8
Boyd Pl KY5.........14 A8
Boyd's Entry EH1.....229 B3
Boyd St Falkirk FK2...60 B6
Laurieston FK2......61 A3
Boyle Dr KY11.......46 C4
Bracken Ave FK1......60 A2
Bracken La FK9......2 B3
Brackenlees Rd FK2...40 B5
Brackensbrae EH52....115 B5
Bracklinn Brae KY12...28 E5
Bracklinn Pl FK1.....59 F1
Bradbury St FK2.....39 B2
Braeburn Dr EH14.....60 A2
Braefoot Tynninghame EH42..76 C3
Whitburn EH47.......161 B7
Braefoot Gr KY11.....48 B2
Braefoot Rd EH51.....64 A5

Braefoot Terr EH16....122 A1
BRAEHEAD..........7 C5
Braehead Alloa FK10...4 D1
Alva FK10..........5 A7
Bo'ness EH51.......63 F7
Braehead Ave
Edinburgh EH4.......91 A3
Linlithgow EH49.....84 E5
Tullibody FK10......4 C2
Braehead Bank EH4....91 A3
Braehead Bsns Units
EH49..............84 E6
Braehead Cres EH4....91 A3
Braehead Dr
Edinburgh EH4.......91 A3
Linlithgow EH49.....84 E5
Braehead Gr Bo'ness EH51..63 F7
Edinburgh EH4.......91 A3
Braehead Ho KY1.....17 D5
Braehead Loan EH4....91 A3
Brae Head Lodge KY1...17 D5
Braehead Pk
Edinburgh EH4.......91 A3
Linlithgow EH49.....84 E5
Braehead Pl EH49.....84 E5
Braehead Prim Sch FK7..7 C4
Braehead Rd
Edinburgh EH4.......91 A3
Linlithgow EH49.....84 E6
Stirling FK7........7 C3
Braehead Rdbt EH54...143 D3
Braehead Row EH4....91 A3
Brae Heads Loan EH41..103 D5
Braehead Terr EH49...84 E5
Braehead View EH4....91 A3
Braekirk Ave EH27....145 D3
Braekirk Gdns EH27...145 D3
Braemar Cres
Carluke ML8........215 A3
Falkirk FK2.........60 C6
Braemar Dr Falkirk FK2..60 C6
Halbeath KY11.......30 A4
Braemar Gdns Denny FK6..36 D3
Grangemouth FK2.....82 D8
Halbeath KY11.......30 A4
Braemar Pl FK5......13 A2
Braemount KY4.......13 A2
BRAEPARK..........91 B3
Braepark Rd EH4.....91 A4
Brae Pk EH4.........91 A4
Brae Rd FK3, EH51....62 D6
Braes High Sch FK2...82 B8
Braeside Alloa FK10...5 C1
Shieldhill FK1......81 D6
Braeside Cres EH47...181 D5
Braeside Gdns EH53...144 B3
Braeside Pk EH53.....144 B3
Braeside Pl
Grangemouth FK2.....82 B8
Laurieston FK2......61 B4
Westquarter FK2.....61 B4
Braeside Rd
Gorebridge EH23.....195 D8
Loanhead EH20......172 D8
Braeside Road N EH23..195 D8
Braeside Road S EH23..195 D7
Braes The Lochgelly KY5..14 A8
Tullibody FK10......4 D3
Braes View Denny FK6..57 D8
Shieldhill FK1......81 E7
Brae The Bannockburn FK7..7 D1
Cambusbarron FK7....6 D6
Penicuik EH26.......171 C1
Braeview East Linton EH40..103 D8
Laurieston FK2......60 F3
Stenhousemuir FK5...38 D2
Braewell Gdns EH49...84 C7
Braid Ave EH10......121 B2
Braidburn Cres EH10..121 A1
Braidburn Specl Sch
EH14..............149 D8
Braidburn Terr EH10..121 A1
Braid Cres EH10.....121 A1
Braid Farm Rd EH10...121 B1
Braid Gn EH54.......143 C7
Braid Hills App EH10..150 A8
Braid Hills Ave EH10..121 A1
Braid Hills Cres EH10..150 A8
Braid Hills Dr EH10...121 A1
Braid Hills Rd EH10...150 B8
Braidlaw Pk EH26.....191 C5
Braid Mount EH10.....150 B8
Braid Mount Crest EH10..150 B8
Braid Mount Rise EH10..150 B8
Braid Mount View EH10..150 B8
Braid Rd EH10.......150 A8
Braigh Gdns KY12....28 D6
Bramble Dr EH4......91 B2
Bramble Glade EH54...164 C8
Brambles The EH22....153 F1
Brambling Rd KY11....30 A2
Bramdean Gr EH10....150 A8
Bramdean Pl EH10....150 B8
Bramdean Rise EH10...150 B8
Bramdean View EH10...150 B8
Brand Dr EH15.......123 B7
Brandfield St EH3....228 A1
Brand Gdns EH15.....123 C7
Brandon St EH3......93 C2
Brandon Terr EH3....93 A3
Brand Pl [2] EH7.....94 A1
Brands Row KY4......30 F7
Brandyhill FK10.....5 B6
Brand Riggs KY12....27 D1
Brandy Wells KY12...27 D1
Brankholm Brae KY11..46 C4
Brankholm Cres KY11..46 D5
Brankholm La KY11....46 D2

Branning Ct [8] KY1...17 D6
BRANSHILL.........5 A1
Branshill Pk Alloa FK10..10 B8
Sauchie FK10........5 B1
Branshill Rd FK10....10 B8
Branxton Wynd KY1....35 B8
Bravo St EH51.......62 E5
Breadalbane Pl FK2...62 A2
Breadalbane St EH6...93 E4
Breadalbane Terr EH11..228 A2
Bread St EH3........228 B2
Bread Street La EH3..228 B2
Breakers Way KY11....47 F2
Brechin Dr FK2......62 A1
Breck Terr EH26.....192 A8
BREICH............182 D6
Breich Sta EH55.....182 D6
Breich Terr EH55....182 E6
Breichwater Pl EH47..182 A6
Brentham Ave FK8....7 B5
Brentham Cres FK8...7 B5
Brentwood Ct EH39...54 B6
Breslin Terr ML7....159 C5
Breton Ct FK1.......60 C3
Brewery Ct [1] EH41..10 B8
Brewery La EH42.....78 B2
Brewery Pk EH41.....130 A8
Brewhouse Ct [5] FK10..10 B6
Brewlands Ave EH5...63 D5
Brewster Pl FK6.....36 C2
Brewster Sq EH54....164 C6
Briarbank EH54......143 D4
Briarbank Terr EH11..120 E4
Briar Brae FK2......D2 D8
Briarcliff St KY1....17 F6
Briar Cotts EH47....162 C2
Briardene FK2.......61 A3
Briarhill Ave KY11...48 A3
Briar Pl KY11.......29 C3
Briar Rd FK10.......4 D6
Brickfield EH15.....95 A1
Brickworks Rd EH33..126 B7
Bridgecastle Gdns EH48..111 A2
Bridgecastle Ho EH48..111 A2
Bridgecastle Rd EH48..139 F8
Bridge Cres FK6.....36 D2
Bridge End
East Whitburn EH47..161 D7
Edinburgh EH16.....122 B3
Shotts ML7.........179 C6
Bridge End Cotts EH27..146 D6
Bridgehaugh Rd FK9...2 B2
Bridgehill FK1......110 A6
BRIDGEND..........86 C4
Bridgend Ct
Bathgate EH48......140 F6
[3] Dalkeith EH22...153 A3
Bridgend Gdns EH48..140 F6
Bridgend Pk EH48....140 F5
Bridgend Pl
Bathgate EH48......140 F6
Whitburn EH47......161 D7
Bridgend Prim Sch EH49..86 C3
Bridgend Rd FK1.....110 A6
BRIDGENESS........64 C8
Bridgeness Cres EH51..64 C7
Bridgeness La EH51...64 C7
Bridgeness Rd EH51...64 D7
BRIDGE OF ALLAN....2 A8
Bridge of Allan Prim Sch
FK9...............2 B6
Bridge of Allan Sta FK9..1 E8
Bridge Pl Broxburn EH52..115 E5
Denny FK6..........36 C2
Shotts ML7.........180 A3
Bridge Rd Balerno EH14..147 C2
Edinburgh EH13.....149 A6
Bridgeside Ave EH47..161 B5
Bridge St Bonnybridge FK4..58 A5
Cowdenbeath KY4.....13 D3
Dunfermline KY12....28 B3
East Linton EH40....103 E7
Edinburgh EH15.....95 A1
Fauldhouse EH47....181 E6
Haddington EH41....130 B8
Kincardine FK10.....23 D4
Kirkcaldy KY1.......17 B1
Musselburgh EH21....124 C6
Newbridge EH28......117 A6
Penicuik EH26.......191 F4
Tranent EH33........126 C6
Bridges The KY11.....48 A2
Bridges View KY12....29 F6
Bridge Terr [13] FK10..10 B6
Bridgeton Cotts EH48..110 F2
Bridge View KY11....68 C6
Brierbush Cres EH33..127 D5
Brierbush Rd EH33...127 D5
Briery Bank EH43....130 C7
Briery Bauks EH8....229 B2
Brighouse Park Cl EH4..91 A6
Brighouse Park Cres EH4..91 A6
Brighouse Park Ct EH4..91 A6
Brighouse Park Gait EH4..91 C6
Brighouse Park Rd EH4..91 A6
Brighouse Pk Gdns EH4..91 C6
Brighton Pl EH15....123 A8
BRIGHTONS.........82 C8
Brighton St EH1.....229 A2
Bright's Cres EH9....121 F4
Bright Terr EH11....228 A2
Brig-O-Doon Gr FK7...20 E7
Brisbane St EH54....144 F8
Bristo Pl EH1.......229 A2
Bristo Port EH1.....229 A2
Bristo Sq EH8.......229 A2
Britwell Cres FK4....94 D2

Brixwold Bank EH19...173 D6
Brixwold Dr EH19....173 D6
Brixwold Neuk EH19...173 D6
Brixwold Pk EH19....173 D6
Brixwold Rise EH19...173 D6
Brixwold View EH19...173 D6
Broadfaulds Cres EH47..161 A5
Broadgait EH31......52 B3
Broadgait Ct EH31....52 A3
Broadgait Gn EH31....52 B3
Broadhaven EH42.....78 E2
Broadhurst Rd EH22...174 C7
Broadleys Ind Pk FK7..7 D5
Broadleys Rd FK7....7 D7
Broadleys Rdbt FK7...7 D6
Broadside Pl FK6.....36 D6
Broad St Alloa FK10...10 B5
Cowdenbeath KY4....13 C2
Denny FK6..........36 F2
Stirling FK8.......7 A8
Broad Wynd Edinburgh EH6..94 A5
[7] Kirkcaldy KY1...17 D6
Brock Pl FK7........7 B2
Brock Way EH52......116 A7
Brockwood Ave FK6...191 D6
Brodick Gdns KY11....30 A4
Brodick Pl FK1......59 C4
Brodick Rd KY2......16 E7
Brodie Ave EH39.....54 D6
Brodie Ct EH39......54 D7
Brodie Rd EH42......106 D8
Brodie St FK7.......60 B8
Brodie Wlk KY11.....30 A4
Broich The FK12.....10 B8
Bronte Pl FK5.......39 A3
Brookbank Terr ML8...215 A1
Brooke La FK3.......61 C5
Brooke St FK3.......61 C5
Brookfield Pl FK12...5 A6
Brookfield Terr EH25..171 E6
Brookside FK2.......61 E1
Brook St Alva FK12...5 A6
Menstrie FK11......3 F6
Broomage Ave FK5....38 B3
Broomage Bank FK5...38 C2
Broomage Cres FK5...38 B3
Broomage Dr FK5.....38 B3
Broomage Pk FK5.....38 C1
Broombank Terr EH12..119 D4
Broomburn Gr EH12...119 E4
Broom Cres KY11.....60 A2
Broom Ct FK7........7 C3
Broomfield Cres EH11..119 E5
Broomfield Dr KY12...29 A5
Broomfield Rd KY4...13 C5
Broom Gdns KY12.....16 C8
Broom Gr KY11.......46 F8
Broomhall Ave EH12...119 D4
Broomhall Bank EH12..119 D5
Broomhall Cres EH12..119 D5
Broomhall Dr EH12...119 C5
Broomhall Gdns EH12..119 D5
Broomhall Loan EH12..119 D5
Broomhall Pk EH12...119 D5
Broomhall Pl EH12...119 D5
Broomhall Rd EH12...119 D5
Broomhall Terr EH12..119 D5
Broomhead Dr KY12...28 F5
Broomhead Pk KY12...29 A5
Broomhill KY3.......50 E8
Broomhill Ave
Burntisland KY3.....33 E1
Larbert FK5.........59 C8
Penicuik EH26.......191 E4
Broomhill Ct FK9....2 B3
Broomhill Dr FK2....152 E1
Broomhill Pk [3] EH22..152 E1
Broomhill Pl Denny FK6..36 D4
Stirling FK8.......6 E6
Broomhill Rd
Bonnybridge FK4.....58 B4
Penicuik EH26.......191 E4
Broomhills Rd EH17...150 F8
Broomhill St ML7....159 C5
BROOMHOUSE........119 E3
Broomhouse Ave EH11..119 D3
Broomhouse Bank EH11..119 E3
Broomhouse Cotts EH11..119 E4
Broomhouse Cres EH11..119 E3
Broomhouse Ct EH11..119 E3
Broomhouse Dr EH11..119 D3
Broomhouse Gardens E
EH11..............119 E4
Broomhouse Gardens W
EH11..............119 D4
Broomhouse Gr EH11..119 E3
Broomhouse Loan EH11..119 E3
Broomhouse Medway
EH11..............119 E4
Broomhouse Mkt EH11..119 E3
Broomhouse Path EH11..119 D3
Broomhouse Pk EH11..119 D3
Broomhouse Place N
EH11..............119 D3
Broomhouse Place S
EH11..............119 E3
Broomhouse Prim Sch
EH11..............119 E3
Broomhouse Rd EH12..119 D3
Broomhouse Row EH11..119 E3
Broomhouse Sq EH11..119 E3
Broomhouse Street N
EH11..............119 E4
Broomhouse Street S
EH11..............119 E3
Broomhouse Terr EH11..119 E4

Broomhouse Way EH11..119 E3
Broomhouse Wlk EH11..119 E3
Broomhouse Wynd EH11..119 E3
BROOMIEKNOWE......173 A8
Broomieknowe
Bonnyrigg and Lasswade
EH18..............173 A8
[1] Dunfermline KY11..29 C3
Tullibody FK10......4 D3
Broomieknowe Gdns
EH19..............173 B8
Broomieknowe Pk EH19..173 A8
Broomknowe Dr FK10...23 D6
Broomlea Cres EH11...119 D5
Broompark E FK11....4 A6
Broompark Gdns
Denny FK6..........36 E2
East Calder EH53....144 E3
Broompark Rd
East Calder EH53....144 E3
Edinburgh EH12.....119 E5
Broompark View EH53..144 E3
Broompark W FK11....4 A6
Broom Rd Kirkcaldy KY2..16 C7
Stirling FK7.......7 D3
BROOMRIDGE........7 D3
Broomridge Pl FK4....57 D4
Broomridge Rd FK7...7 B3
Broomside KY2.......16 C8
Broomside Pl FK5....38 C1
Broomside Terr EH12..119 E5
Broomview Ho EH11...119 C2
Broom Wlk EH54.....144 A4
Broom Wynd ML7.....179 E6
Broomyhill Pl EH49...84 D7
Broomyknowe EH14....149 B8
Broomyknowe Dr EH54..142 E6
Brora Pl KY12.......28 C1
Brosdale Ct FK1.....60 B2
Brotherstone's Way
EH33..............126 D4
Brougham Pl EH3.....228 C1
Brougham St EH3.....228 B1
BROUGHTON.........93 D3
Broughton High Sch EH4..92 F2
Broughton Market EH3..93 D2
Broughton Pl EH1....93 D2
Broughton Place La EH1..93 D2
Broughton Prim Sch EH7..93 D3
Broughton Rd EH7....93 D3
Broughton St EH1....229 A4
Brown Ave Alloa FK10..4 F1
Stirling FK9.......2 B2
Brown Cres EH48.....141 A4
Brown St FK3........61 D8
Browniebrae Pl FK2...59 F8
Brownrigg Farm Cotts
EH39..............74 C6
Brown's Cl EH8......229 C3
Brown's Ct FK11.....229 C3
Brown's Pl
East Linton EH40....103 D8
Edinburgh EH1......228 C2
Brown St Armadale EH48..139 F4
Edinburgh EH8......229 B2
Falkirk FK1........59 D5
[6] Edinburgh EH41..130 B8
Shotts ML7.........180 B3
Whitburn EH47......161 A6
BROXBURN Broxburn...115 E6
Dunbar EH42........107 A7
Broxburn Acad EH52...115 C5
Broxburn Cotts EH42..107 A7
Broxburn Prim Sch EH52 115 E5
Bruart Ave FK5......38 F3
Bruce Cres Falkirk FK2..39 B3
Plean FK7..........20 D3
Bruce Dr Fallin FK7...8 C5
Stenhousemuir FK5...38 E3
Bruce Pl FK3........61 E8
Bruce Rd Bathgate EH48..141 C5
Grangemouth FK3....61 E7
Bruce St Alloa FK10...10 C7
Bannockburn FK7....7 E1
Bathgate EH48......141 C4
Clackmannan FK10....11 A4
Dunfermline KY12....28 F4
Edinburgh EH10.....121 A2
Falkirk FK2........60 C6
Kinghorn KY3.......35 A3
Plean FK7..........20 D3
Stirling FK8.......2 B1
Bruce View FK7......7 B1
BRUNSTANE.........123 D6

Brunstane Bank EH15 . . . . .123 D6
Brunstane Cres EH15 . . . . .123 C6
Brunstane Dr EH15 . . . . .123 C6
Brunstane Gdns
  Edinburgh EH15 . . . . .123 C7
  Penicuik EH26 . . . . .191 D6
Brunstane Gdns Mews
  EH15 . . . . .123 C7
Brunstane Mill Rd EH15 . . . . . .123 F7
Brunstane Prim Sch
  EH15 . . . . .123 C6
Brunstane Rd EH15 . . . . .123 C6
Brunstane Road N EH15 . .123 C6
Brunstane Road S EH15 . . .123 C6
Brunstane Sta EH15 . . . . .123 C6
Brunswick Pl **7** EH7 . . . . .93 E2
Brunswick Rd EH7 . . . . .93 E2
Brunswick St EH7 . . . . .93 E2
Brunswick Street La EH7 . .93 E2
Brunswick Terr EH7 . . . . .93 E2
Brunt Ct EH42 . . . . .106 E8
Brunt Gr EH42 . . . . .106 D8
Brunt La EH42 . . . . .78 D1
Brunton Ct EH21 . . . . .124 C6
Brunton Pl **8** EH7 . . . . .93 F2
Brunton's Cl EH22 . . . . .153 A3
Brunton Terr EH7 . . . . .93 F2
Brunt Pl EH42 . . . . .106 E8
BRUNTSFIELD 121 B5
Bruntsfield Ave EH10 . . . . . . .121 A5
Bruntsfield Cres
  Dunbar EH42 . . . . .78 D1
  Edinburgh EH10 . . . . .121 B5
Bruntsfield Gdns EH10 . . . .121 B5
Bruntsfield Pl EH10 . . . . .121 B5
Bruntsfield Prim Sch
  EH10 . . . . .121 A5
Bruntsfield Terr EH10 . . . . . .121 B5
Bryans Ave EH22 . . . . .174 B6
Bryans Rd EH22 . . . . .174 A6
Bryce Ave Edinburgh EH7 . . .94 F2
  Falkirk FK2 . . . . .60 A8
Bryce Cres EH14 . . . . .148 A5
Bryce Gdns EH14 . . . . .148 A5
Bryce Gr EH7 . . . . .94 F2
Bryce Pl EH14 . . . . .148 A5
Bryce Rd EH14 . . . . .148 A5
Bryden Ct FK3 . . . . .61 E8
Bryony The FK10 . . . . .4 B1
Bryson Pl **1** Bathgate EH48 .141 B6
  Stenhousemuir FK5 . . . . .38 C5
Bryson Rd EH11 . . . . .120 F5
Bryson St FK2 . . . . .60 A8
Bryson Street Ind Est FK2 60 B6
Bubbles Rdbt EH54 . . . . .143 E2
Buccleuch Ct EH22 . . . . .152 F4
Buccleuch Pl EH8 . . . . .229 B1
Buccleuch Place La EH3 .229 B1
Buccleuch St
  Dalkeith EH22 . . . . .153 A3
  Edinburgh EH8 . . . . .229 B1
Buccleuch Terr EH8 . . . . .229 B1
Buchanan Cres EH54 . . . . . . .143 A5
Buchanan Ct Bo'ness EH51 .63 E5
  Falkirk FK2 . . . . .60 A8
Buchanan Dr FK9 . . . . .2 B3
Buchanan Gdns
  Cairneyhill KY12 . . . . .27 D1
  Polmont FK2 . . . . .61 D2
Buchanan's Ct EH1 . . . . .229 C3
Buchanan St
  Dunfermline KY12 . . . . .29 A3
  Edinburgh EH6 . . . . .93 F3
Buchan Ave FK2 . . . . .39 B1
Buchan Ct EH52 . . . . .115 C5
Buchan La EH52 . . . . .115 E5
Buchan Pl FK3 . . . . .61 A5
Buchan Rd Bathgate EH48 .140 F7
  Broxburn EH52 . . . . .115 C5
  Grangemouth FK3, EH51 . . . .62 D6
Buckie Rd EH22 . . . . .174 A6
Buckingham Terr EH4 . . . . . .228 A4
Buckstane Pk EH10 . . . . .150 A7
Buckstone Ave EH10 . . . . . . .150 B6
Buckstone Bank EH10 . . . . .150 B7
Buckstone Circ EH10 . . . . . . .150 C6
Buckstone Cres EH10 . . . . . . .150 B7
Buckstone Crook EH10 . . .150 C5
Buckstone Ct EH10 . . . . .150 B6
Buckstone Dell EH10 . . . . . . .150 B7
Buckstone Dr EH10 . . . . .150 B7
Buckstone Gate EH10 . . . . . .150 C6
Buckstone Gdns EH10 . . . . .150 B6
Buckstone Gn EH10 . . . . .150 B7
Buckstone Grove EH10 . . . .150 B7
Buckstone Hill EH10 . . . . . . .150 C7
Buckstone Howe EH10 . . . .150 C6
Buckstone Lea EH10 . . . . . . .150 C6
Buckstone Loan EH10 . . . . . .150 B6
Buckstone Loan E EH10 .150 C6
Buckstone Neuk EH10 . . . . .150 C7
Buckstone Pl EH10 . . . . .150 B6
Buckstone Prim Sch
  EH10 . . . . .150 B7
Buckstone Rd EH10 . . . . .150 B6
Buckstone Rise EH10 . . . . . . .150 C6
Buckstone Row EH10 . . . . . . .150 C7
Buckstone Shaw EH10 . . . . .150 C5
Buckstone Terr EH10 . . . . . . .150 B6
Buckstone View EH10 . . . . . .150 B7
Buckstone Wynd EH10 . . . .150 C6
Buckyburn Pl KY12 . . . . .29 E6
Buffies Brae KY12 . . . . .28 F4
Bughtknowes Dr EH48 . . . .141 C7

BUGHTLIN 91 A1
Bughtlin Dr EH12 . . . . .91 A1
Bughtlin Gdns EH12 . . . . .119 A8
Bughtlin Gn EH12 . . . . .91 A1
Bughtlin Loan EH12 . . . . .119 A8
Bughtlin Mkt EH12 . . . . .119 B8
Bughtlin Pk EH12 . . . . .119 B8
Bughtlin Pl EH12 . . . . .91 A1
Buie Haugh EH29 . . . . .88 F1
Buie Rigg EH29 . . . . .88 F2
Builyeon Rd EH30 . . . . .89 A8
Buller St KY5 . . . . .14 B7
Bullet Loan EH41 . . . . .130 C8
Bulloch Cres FK6 . . . . .36 D1
Bull's Cl EH1 . . . . .229 C3
Bunbrae Wlk EH19 . . . . .173 C5
Bungalows The FK5 . . . . .38 B1
Buntine Cres FK7 . . . . .7 A3
Burder Pk FK2 . . . . .39 A2
BURDIEHOUSE 151 A4
Burdiehouse Ave EH17 . . . .151 B4
Burdiehouse Burn Nature
  Reserve★ EH17 . . . . .151 C4
Burdiehouse Crossway
  EH17 . . . . .151 B4
Burdiehouse Dr EH17 . . . . . .151 A3
Burdiehouse Loan EH17 . .151 A4
Burdiehouse Medway
  EH17 . . . . .151 B4
Burdiehouse Pl EH17 . . . . . .151 B4
Burdiehouse Prim Sch
  EH17 . . . . .151 B4
Burdiehouse Rd EH17 . . . . .151 A3
Burdiehouse Sq EH17 . . . . .151 A3
Burdiehouse St EH17 . . . . . .151 A4
Burdiehouse Terr EH17 . . . .151 B4
Burgess Hill EH49 . . . . .85 A6
Burgess Rd EH30 . . . . .68 C1
Burgess St EH6 . . . . .94 A5
Burges Terr EH9 . . . . .122 A4
Burgh Ct KY5 . . . . .14 A7
Burghlee Cres EH20 . . . . .172 C7
Burghlee Terr EH20 . . . . .172 C7
Burgh Mews **1** FK10 . . . . . . .10 B6
Burgh Mills La EH49 . . . . .84 C6
Burghmuir Ct EH49 . . . . .85 D8
Burghmuir Ind Est FK8 . . . .7 B6
Burghmuir Rd FK7 . . . . .7 B6
Burgh Rd KY4 . . . . .13 C8
Burghtoft EH17 . . . . .151 E5
Burleigh Cres KY11 . . . . .47 C3
Burleigh Way FK10 . . . . .10 C6
Burlington St EH6 . . . . .93 F5
Burnbank Cairneyhill KY12 .27 D1
  Carnock EH22 . . . . .27 C7
  Livingston EH54 . . . . .143 D5
  Loanhead EH20 . . . . .172 A8
Burnbank Cres EH20 . . . . . .151 A1
Burnbank Gr EH20 . . . . .151 A1
Burnbank Rd Falkirk FK2 . .60 B7
  Grangemouth FK3 . . . . .61 D5
Burnbank Terr EH25 . . . . . . .171 E6
Burnbrae Alloa FK10 . . . . .10 C8
  Edinburgh EH12 . . . . .119 A8
  Fauldhouse EH47 . . . . .181 F5
  Sauchie FK10 . . . . .5 C1
Burnbrae Ave
  Bonnyrigg EH19 . . . . .173 C4
  5 Edinburgh EH12 . . . . . . .119 A8
Burnbrae Dr **3** EH19 . . . . . .173 C4
Burnbrae Dr Alva FK12 . . . .5 B6
  Falkirk FK1 . . . . .60 A5
Burnbrae Gr **6** EH12 . . . . . . .119 A8
Burnbrae Loan EH19 . . . . . .173 C5
Burnbrae Pend EH19 . . . . . .173 C5
Burn Brae Pk FK10 . . . . .23 F4
Burnbrae Pl **4** EH12 . . . . .119 A8
Burnbrae Rd
  Bonnyrigg EH19 . . . . .173 C4
  Falkirk FK1 . . . . .60 A5
  Harthill ML7 . . . . .160 A6
  Shotts ML7 . . . . .179 E3
  Stoneyburn EH47 . . . . .162 B1
Burnbrae Terr
  Bonnyrigg and Lasswade
  EH19 . . . . .173 C4
  Whitburn EH47 . . . . .161 C6
Burndene Dr EH20 . . . . .151 A1
Burn Dr FK7 . . . . .7 C4
Burnee FK10 . . . . .5 E3
Burnet's Cl EH1 . . . . .229 A3
Burney Pl KY11 . . . . .46 E4
Burnfield EH54 . . . . .143 A2
Burnfield Pl FK2 . . . . .60 D7
Burnfoot Ct FK3 . . . . .61 D6
Burnfoot La **1** FK1 . . . . .60 B4
Burngrange Cotts EH55 .163 C2
Burngrange Ct EH55 . . . . . . .163 C2
Burngrange Gdns EH55 .163 B2
Burngrange Pk EH55 . . . . . .163 C2
Burngrange Works EH55 163 B2
Burnhead Cres EH16 . . . . . . .151 B6
Burnhead Gr EH16 . . . . .151 B6
Burnhead La FK1 . . . . .60 C4
Burnhead Loan EH16 . . . . . .151 B6
Burnhead Path E EH16 . . .151 B6
Burnhead Path W EH16 . .151 B6
Burnhead Rd FK5 . . . . .38 C3
Burnhouse Dr
  Dechmont EH52 . . . . .114 C2
  Whitburn EH47 . . . . .160 E5
Burnhouse Farm Steadings
  EH27 . . . . .145 C4
Burnhouse Ind Est EH47 160 F5
Burnhouse Rd EH52 . . . . . . .114 C3
Burnhouse Sch EH47 . . . . . .161 A5

Burnlea Dr EH47 . . . . .162 A1
Burnlea Pl EH47 . . . . .162 A1
Burns Ave Armadale EH48 .139 F4
  Grangemouth FK3 . . . . .61 D5
  Stenhousemuir FK5 . . . . .38 B3
Burns Cres Harthill ML7 . . .159 F6
  Laurieston FK2 . . . . .60 F4
  Whitburn EH47 . . . . .161 A6
Burns Ct EH54 . . . . .144 C5
BURNSIDE 54 C7
Burnside Dechmont EH52 .114 B2
  Edinburgh EH12 . . . . .119 A8
  Haddington EH41 . . . . .129 E8
  Prestonpans EH32 . . . . .96 E1
Burnside Ave
  Armadale EH48 . . . . .139 D6
  Easthouses EH22 . . . . .174 D7
  Kinghorn KY3 . . . . .34 F3
  Polbeth EH55 . . . . .163 F5
Burnside Bsns Ct KY11 . . .47 C4
Burnside Cotts EH49 . . . . . . .86 E4
Burnside Cres
  Clackmannan KY12 . . . . .11 B5
  Easthouses EH22 . . . . .174 D7
  Fauldhouse EH47 . . . . .181 E6
  Plean FK7 . . . . .20 C4
  Polbeth EH55 . . . . .163 F5
  Rosyth KY11 . . . . .47 A5
  Shotts ML7 . . . . .179 D6
Burnside Ct Alva FK12 . . . . . .5 A7
Cairnmuir Rd EH12 . . . . .119 E8
Cairns Cres FK7 . . . . .7 F1
Cairns Wlk FK6 . . . . .36 D1
Burnside Gdns
 1 Burntisland KY3 . . . . .33 D1
  Whitecross EH49 . . . . .83 F6
Burnside La EH55 . . . . .163 F5
Burnside Pk EH14 . . . . .147 C2
Burnside Pl Falkirk FK2 . . . .39 B3
  Rosyth KY11 . . . . .47 A4
Burnside Rd
  Bathgate EH48 . . . . .140 F7
  Gorebridge EH23 . . . . .174 D1
  Menstrie FK11 . . . . .3 F6
  Polbeth EH55 . . . . .163 F5
  Ratho Station EH12 . . . . .118 A7
  Uphall EH52 . . . . .115 A4
Burnside Rdbt EH54 . . . . . . .143 F2
Burnside St Alloa FK10 . . . . . .5 A7
  Rosyth KY11 . . . . .47 A5
  Stirling FK7 . . . . .7 C6
Burnside Terr
  Addiewell EH55 . . . . .162 D1
  Cowdenbeath KY4 . . . . .13 A2
  East Calder EH53 . . . . .144 F5
  Falkirk FK1 . . . . .59 E5
  Fauldhouse EH47 . . . . .181 E6
  Oakley KY12 . . . . .27 A7
  Polbeth EH55 . . . . .163 F5
  Redding FK2 . . . . .61 C1
Burnside View EH55 . . . . . . .162 D1
Burnsknowe EH54 . . . . .142 E6
Burns Pl KY12 . . . . .28 E3
Burns St Dunfermline KY12 .28 E5
  Edinburgh EH6 . . . . .94 A4
  High Valleyfield KY12 . . . . . . .26 A2
  Kelty Cowdenbeath KY4 . . . .13 A2
  Stirling FK8 . . . . .2 A2
Burns Terr Bathgate EH48 .141 C5
  Cowie FK7 . . . . .20 D7
BURNTISLAND 33 E2
Burntisland Prim Sch KY3 33 F1
Burntisland Rd KY3 . . . . .34 F7
Burntisland Sta KY3 . . . . .33 E2
Burnvale Broxburn EH52 . . .116 A4
  Livingston EH54 . . . . .143 D5
Burnvale Ave EH48 . . . . .141 C4
Burnvale Pl EH54 . . . . .144 A3
BURNWYND 146 C5
Burt Ave KY3 . . . . .34 F3
Burt Gr KY11 . . . . .29 E1
Burt St KY12 . . . . .29 A6
Bush EH33 . . . . .124 B6
Bush St EH21 . . . . .124 B6
Bute EH54 . . . . .142 F5
Bute Cres Dunfermline KY12 29 E3
  Shotts ML7 . . . . .179 D6
Bute Pl FK3 . . . . .61 D6
Bute St FK2 . . . . .60 A8
Bute Wynd KY1 . . . . .17 B2
Butlerfield Ind Est EH22 .174 A3
Butler's Brae EH54 . . . . .143 B4
Butlers Brae★
  EH33 . . . . .128 C6
Butteries View EH48 . . . . . . .139 D5
Butts The EH41 . . . . .130 B8
Buxley Farm Steading
  EH33 . . . . .126 F3
Buxley Rd EH33 . . . . .38 C5
Byburn EH52 . . . . .114 F8
By-Pass Rd FK4 . . . . .57 E5
Byrehope Rd EH52 . . . . .115 B4
Byreside EH47 . . . . .142 A1
Byres The KY11 . . . . .46 C5
Byron Rd ML7 . . . . .179 B6

C

Cables Wynd EH6 . . . . .93 F5
Cables Wynd Ho EH6 . . . . . . .93 F5
Caddell's Row Cotts EH4 .91 B5
Cadell Dr FK2 . . . . .39 A5
Cadell Pl
  Cockenzie & Port Seton
  EH32 .97 C4
  Fauldhouse EH47 . . . . .181 E5
Cadell Reach KY11 . . . . .47 A7

Cadell Sq **4** EH33 . . . . .126 D6
Cadgers Loan FK7 . . . . .20 B2
Cadiz St EH6 . . . . .94 A5
Cadogan Rd EH16 . . . . .151 A7
Cadzow Ave EH51 . . . . .63 F6
Cadzow Cres EH51 . . . . .63 F7
Cadzow La EH51 . . . . .63 F7
Cadzow Pl EH7 . . . . .94 A1
Caerketton Cres EH13 . . . . .149 D8
Caerketton Cotts EH13 . . .149 D8
Caerlaverock Ct **1** EH12 . .119 B7
Caesar Rd EH33 . . . . .126 C6
Caesar Way EH33 . . . . .126 C6
Caird's Row EH21 . . . . .124 B7
Cairnbank Gdns EH26 . . . . .191 E4
Cairnbank Rd EH26 . . . . .191 E4
Cairncubie Rd KY12 . . . . .29 C8
CAIRNEYHILL 27 C2
Cairneyhill Prim Sch
  KY12 .27 D2
Cairneyhill Rd KY12 . . . . .28 B2
Cairneymount Ave FK2 . . .83 A6
Cairneymount Rd ML8 . . . .215 A2
Cairngorm Cres KY12 . . . . . . .16 F5
Cairngorm Rd FK3 . . . . .61 C5
Cairn Gr KY12 . . . . .28 C2
Cairnhill Ct ML8 . . . . .215 A2
Cairnie Pl EH47 . . . . .161 A5
Cairn Lea EH48 . . . . .141 C5
Cairnmuir Rd EH12 . . . . .119 E8
Cairnoch Way FK7 . . . . .7 F1
Cairnoch Wlk FK6 . . . . .36 D1
Cairnpapple Henge & Cairn★
Cairnpapple Ho **2** EH48 .141 A6
Cairns Cres FK7 . . . . .7 F1
Cairns Dr EH14 . . . . .168 B8
Cairns La EH55 . . . . .168 B8
Cairn's La EH51 . . . . .64 B7
Cairns Street E KY1 . . . . .17 E7
Cairns Street W KY1 . . . . .17 D7
Cairns The
  Charlestown KY11 . . . . .45 A4
  Menstrie FK11 . . . . .4 A6
Cairntows Cl EH16 . . . . .122 D4
Cairnwell Pl
  Cairneyhill KY12 . . . . .27 D1
  Kirkcaldy KY2 . . . . .16 F7
Caithness Ct KY11 . . . . .17 E7
Caithness Dr KY11 . . . . .30 C1
Caithness Pl Edinburgh EH5 93 B5
  Kirkcaldy KY1 . . . . .17 E7
Caiysie EH10 . . . . .150 A4
Caiystane Ave EH10 . . . . . . .150 A5
Caiystane Cres EH10 . . . . . .150 A5
Caiystane Dr EH10 . . . . .149 F5
Caiystane Gdns EH10 . . . . .150 A6
Caiystane Hill EH10 . . . . . . .150 A6
Caiystane Terr EH10 . . . . . . .150 A5
Caiystane View EH10 . . . . . .150 A5
Cakemuir Gdns EH16 . . . . . .122 F4
Cakemuir Gr EH16 . . . . .122 F4
Calaisburn Pl KY11 . . . . .29 E1
Calais View KY11 . . . . .29 F1
Calaiswood Sch KY11 . . . . . .30 B1
Calderburn Rd EH55 . . . . . . .164 A5
Calder Cres
  Armadale EH48 . . . . .140 A5
  Edinburgh EH11 . . . . .119 B1
Caldercruix Rd FK1 . . . . .108 A1
Calder Ct Edinburgh EH11 .119 C2
  Stirling FK7 . . . . .7 C5
Calder Dr Edinburgh EH11 .119 C1
  Shotts ML7 . . . . .180 B4
Calder Gdns EH11 . . . . .119 C2
Calder Gr EH11 . . . . .119 C2
CALDERHALL 144 E4
Calderhall Ave EH53 . . . . . . .144 E3
Calderhall Cres EH53 . . . . . .144 F3
Calderhall Terr EH53 . . . . . . .144 F3
CALDERHEAD 179 E4
Calderhead High Sch
  ML7 .179 F5
Calderhead Rd ML7 . . . . .179 D7
Calder House Rd EH53 . . . .144 B3
Calder Junc EH11 . . . . .119 B1
Calder Park Rd EH53 . . . . . . .144 B2
Calder Pk EH11 . . . . .119 C1
Calder Pl
  Dalgety Bay KY11 . . .48 A3
  Edinburgh EH11 . . . . .119 C1
  Falkirk FK1 . . . . .60 D1
Calder Rd
  Edinburgh, Sighthill
  EH11 . . . . .119 D2
  Edinburgh, Stenhouse
  EH11 . . . . .120 A3
  Hermiston EH14 . . . . .118 F1
  Livingston EH54 . . . . .164 C7
Calder Rd Gdns EH11 . . . . .120 A3
Calder's Lawn EH41 . . . . . . .101 A1
Calder View EH11 . . . . .119 B1
Caledon Gn FK3 . . . . .61 B7
Caledonia Ct KY11 . . . . .46 C5
Caledonia Hts KY11 . . . . .46 C3
Caledonian Brewery★
  EH11 . . . . .120 E5
Caledonian Cres EH11 . . . .228 A1
Caledonian Ct Falkirk FK2 .60 C7
  Kirknewton EH27 . . . . .145 D3
Caledonian Pl EH11 . . . . . . .228 A1
Caledonian Rd Alloa FK10 . . .10 A5
  Edinburgh EH11 . . . . .228 A1
  Fauldhouse EH47 . . . . .181 D5
Caledonian Terr EH47 . . . . .181 D5
Caledonia Rd Kirkcaldy KY2 17 A4
  Rosyth KY11 . . . . .46 C5
  Shotts ML7 . . . . .179 E5
Caledonia Terr FK4 . . . . .57 F5
Caledonia Way KY11 . . . . . . .46 A3

Bru–Cam 235

Calender Ave KY1 . . . . .17 C7
Calgary Ave EH54 . . . . .143 F4
CALIFORNIA 81 E5
California Prim Sch FK1 . . .81 E5
California Rd
  Maddiston FK2 . . . . .82 F6
  Shieldhill FK1 . . . . .81 E6
California Terr FK1 . . . . .81 F5
Callander Dr FK5 . . . . .59 C8
Callander Pl TD13 . . . . .218 F4
Callander Terr KY11 . . . . .30 A4
Callendar Ave FK1 . . . . .60 B1
Callendar Bsns Pk FK1. . . .60 E3
Callendar Bvd FK1 . . . . .60 E3
Callendar House★ FK1 . . . .60 D3
Callendar Park Dr FK1 . . . .60 D4
Callendar Park Terr FK1. . .60 D4
Callendar Park View FK1. .60 D4
Callendar Park Wlk FK1. . .60 D4
Callendar Rd FK1 . . . . .60 C4
Callendar Riggs FK1 . . . . .60 C4
Callendar Square Sh Ctr **5**
  FK1 . . . . .60 B4
Calliope Rd KY1 . . . . .46 B1
CALTON 229 C4
Calton Cres FK7 . . . . .7 B4
Caltonhill EH1 . . . . .229 B4
Calton Hill★ EH7 . . . . .229 B4
Calton Rd EH8 . . . . .229 B3
Caltrop Pl FK7 . . . . .7 E3
Calum Macdonald Ct
  KY1 . . . . .46 E3
Cambridge Ave EH6 . . . . .93 F3
Cambridge Gdns EH6 . . . . . . .93 E3
Cambridge St Day Hospl
  EH1 . . . . .228 B1
Cambridge St EH1 . . . . .228 B2
CAMBUS .9 B8
CAMBUSBARRON 6 C6
Cambusbarron Prim Sch
  FK7 . . . . .6 D5
CAMBUSKENNETH 2 D1
Cambuskenneth Abbey★
  FK9 . . . . .2 D8
Cambusnethan St **1** EH7 .94 B1
Cambus Pools Wildlife
  Reserve★ FK10 . . . . .8 F8
Camdean Cres KY11 . . . . .46 D5
Camdean La KY11 . . . . .46 D5
Camdean Prim Sch KY11. .46 D4
CAMELON 59 C5
Camelon Ed Ctr **1** FK1 . .59 E5
Camelon Rd FK1 . . . . .59 F5
Camelon Rdbt FK1 . . . . .59 D6
Camelon Sta FK1 . . . . .59 D6
Camera Obscura★ EH1 . . .228 C2
Cameron Cres
  Bonnyrigg and Lasswade
  EH19 . . . . .172 F5
  Edinburgh EH16 . . . . .122 B3
Cameron Dr KY11 . . . . .18 A8
Cameron Gr KY11 . . . . .47 B3
Cameron House Ave
  EH16 . . . . .122 B3
Cameronian Dr ML8 . . . . . . .215 A3
Cameronian St **9** FK8 . . . . . .7 B7
Cameron Knowe EH49 . . . . .86 D6
Cameron March EH16 . . . . .122 A3
Cameron Pk EH16 . . . . .122 B3
Cameron Pl FK2 . . . . .39 B2
Cameron Smaill Rd
  EH14 . . . . .147 C4
Cameron St KY12 . . . . .28 E4
Cameron Terr
  Edinburgh EH16 . . . . .122 B3
  Limerigg FK1 . . . . .108 A3
Cameron Toll EH16 . . . . .122 B3
Cameron Toll Gdns EH16 122 B3
Cameron Toll Lade EH16 122 B3
Cameron Toll Sh Ctr
  EH16 . . . . .122 A3
Cameron Way
  Livingston EH54 . . . . .143 E7
  Prestonpans EH32 . . . . .97 A2
Camilla Gr KY2 . . . . .15 C2
Camilla Rd KY2 . . . . .15 B2
CAMMO .90 F2
Cammo Bank EH4 . . . . .91 A2
Cammo Brae EH4 . . . . .91 A2
Cammo Gdns EH4 . . . . .90 F2
Cammo Gr EH4 . . . . .90 F2
Cammo Hill EH4 . . . . .90 F2
Cammo Parkway EH4 . . . . . .91 A2
Cammo Pl EH4 . . . . .91 A2
Cammo Rd EH4, EH12 . . . . . .90 F2
Cammo Wlk EH4, EH12 . . . . .90 F1
Campbell Ave EH12 . . . . . . .120 C8
Campbell Cres
  Laurieston FK2 . . . . .60 F3
  Lochgelly KY5 . . . . .14 B8
Campbell Ct
  Longniddry EH32 . . . . .98 D5
  Stirling FK7 . . . . .6 F4
Campbell Dr FK5 . . . . .38 B2
Campbell Park Cres
  EH13 . . . . .148 F6
Campbell Park Dr EH13 .148 F6
Campbell Pl FK2 . . . . .60 F3
Campbell Rd
  Edinburgh EH12 . . . . .120 C8
  Longniddry EH32 . . . . .98 D5
Campbell's Cl EH8 . . . . .229 C3
Campbell St KY12 . . . . .29 A4
Campend Cotts EH22 . . . . . .152 D5

Camperdown Rd
Inverkeithing/Dunfermline
KY11 . . . . .46 D1
Rosyth KY11 . . . . .46 C1
Campfield St FK2 . . . . .60 B6
Campie Ct EH21 . . . . .124 B6
Campie Gdns EH21 . . . . . . .124 B6
Campie La EH21 . . . . .124 B6
Campie Prim Sch EH21 . . . .124 B6
Campie Rd EH21 . . . . .124 B6
Campie Terr FK2 . . . . .39 F2
Camp Rd Crombie KY12 . . . .44 D5
Mayfield EH22 . . . . .174 E7
Campsie Cres KY2 . . . . .16 F7
Campsie Rd FK3 . . . . .61 C6
Camps Ind Est EH27 . . . . . .145 C5
Camps Rd KY12 . . . . .27 C6
Camps Rigg EH54 . . . . .143 B7
CAMPTOUN 100 F8
Campus Rdbt EH54 . . . . . . .143 C1
Campview EH22 . . . . .152 B7
Campview Ave EH22 . . . . . .152 B7
Campview Cres EH22 . . . . .152 C7
Campview Gdns EH22 . . . . .152 B7
Campview Gr EH22 . . . . . . .152 C7
Campview Rd EH19 . . . . . . .173 B6
Campview Terr EH22 . . . . . .152 B7
Camp Wood View EH22 . . .174 E5
Camus Ave EH10 . . . . .150 A6
Camus Pk EH10 . . . . .150 A6
Camuan La EH10 . . . . .121 B3
Canal Bank Ind Est FK4 . . . .58 A4
Canal Side Dr FK2 . . . . .61 A1
Canal St
Falkirk, Camelon FK1 . . . . . .59 D5
Falkirk FK2 . . . . .60 B7
Canal View Prim Sch
EH14 . . . . .148 E8
Canal Wlk FK2 . . . . .61 C1
Canalyard Ind Est FK2 . . . . .60 B1
Canavan Ct Falkirk FK2 . . . . .60 C7
Stirling FK7 . . . . .7 C3
Canavan Pk FK2 . . . . .60 C7
Canberra St EH54 . . . . .144 A5
Candie Ct FK3 . . . . .61 E6
Candie Rd FK3 . . . . .62 A8
Candimline Ct ML8 . . . . . . .215 B1
Candlemaker Row EH1 . . . .229 A2
Candlemaker's Cres
EH17 . . . . .151 F6
Candlemaker's Pk EH17 . . .151 F6
Candlergigs FK10 . . . . .10 B6
Candleriggs Ct ☑ KY12 . . . .28 E5
Caneluk Ave ML8 . . . . .215 B1
Canmore Dr FK5 . . . . .38 E4
Canmore Gr KY12 . . . . .29 B5
Canmore Prim Sch KY11 . . .29 C1
Canmore St
Dunfermline KY12 . . . . .29 A3
Kinghorn KY3 . . . . .34 F1
Queensferry EH30 . . . . .89 B8
Canmore Terr KY12 . . . . .29 A7
Canning St EH3 . . . . .228 B2
Canning Street La EH3 . . . .228 A2
Cannonmills Br EH3 . . . . . . .93 C3
Cannons Way FK2 . . . . .39 A1
Cannop Cres EH47 . . . . . . .161 F1
Canon Byrne Glebe KY12 . . . .
CANONGATE 229 C3
Canongate Edinburgh EH8 . .229 B3
Spott EH42 . . . . .106 D4
Canongate Venture EH1 . . .229 B3
Canon La EH3 . . . . .93 C2
Canon Lynch Ct KY12 . . . . . .28 F4
CANONMILLS 93 C2
Canonmills EH3 . . . . .93 C2
Canon St EH3 . . . . .93 C2
Canthill Gdns ML7 . . . . . . .179 A3
Cantlie Pl KY11 . . . . .46 E3
Cantsdam Rd KY4 . . . . .12 F7
Canty Gr EH22 . . . . .98 C3
Capelaw Rd EH13 . . . . .149 A5
Caplaw Way EH26 . . . . .191 C5
Caponflat Cres EH41 . . . . . .100 F1
Caponhall Ct ☑ EH33 . . . . .126 C5
Caponhall Dr EH33 . . . . . . .126 C5
Caponhall Rd EH33 . . . . . . .126 C5
Caponhall Way ☑ EH33 . . .126 C6
Cappers Ct EH54 . . . . .139 F4
Captain's Dr EH16 . . . . .151 B5
Captain's Loan EH16 . . . . . .151 B5
Captain's Rd EH16, EH17 . .151 B5
Captain's Rove EH16 . . . . . .151 B6
Caputhall Rd EH54 . . . . . . .142 C5
Carberry Cl EH21 . . . . .124 E3
Carberry Gr EH21 . . . . .153 E8
Carberry Gr EH21 . . . . .124 D3
Carberry Mains Cotts
EH21 . . . . .125 A1
Carberry Pl ☑ EH12 . . . . . .120 E7
Carberry Rd EH21 . . . . .124 E3
Carbrook Dr FK7 . . . . .20 C3
Carbrook Pl FK3 . . . . .61 E6
Carcraig Pl KY11 . . . . .48 B3
Cardross Ave EH52 . . . . . . .115 B5
Cardross Cres EH52 . . . . . .115 C5
Cardross Rd EH52 . . . . .115 C5
Cardrowan Rd FK7 . . . . .20 D1
Carey Ct FK7 . . . . .20 C4
Carfrae Cotts EH4 . . . . .221 D8
Carfrae Gdns EH4 . . . . .92 A2
Carfrae Gr EH4 . . . . .92 A2

Carfrae Pk EH4 . . . . .92 A2
Carfrae Rd EH4 . . . . .92 A2
Cargilfield Sch EH4 . . . . . . .91 B4
Cargilfield View EH4 . . . . . . .91 B4
Cargil Terr EH5 . . . . .93 B5
Carhowden Rd FK2 . . . . .61 B3
Carlaverock Ave EH33 . . . .126 D5
Carlaverock Cl EH33 . . . . . .126 D5
Carlaverock Cres EH33 . . . .126 D5
Carlaverock Ct EH33 . . . . . .126 C5
Carlaverock Dr EH33 . . . . . .126 D5
Carlaverock Gr EH33 . . . . . .126 D5
Carlaverock Terr EH33 . . . .126 C5
Carlaverock View EH33 . . . .126 D4
Carlaverock Wlk ☑
EH33 . . . . .126 D5
Carledubs Ave EH52 . . . . . .115 A5
Carledubs Cres EH52 . . . . .115 A6
Carlekemp EH39 . . . . .53 F8
Carlie Ave FK9 . . . . .2 A6
Carlin Craig KY3 . . . . .34 F1
Carlin Cres KY3 . . . . .34 F1
Carlingnose Ct KY11 . . . . . . .68 C6
Carlingnose Pk KY11 . . . . . .68 C6
Carlingnose Point KY11 . . . .68 C6
Carlingnose View KY11 . . . . .68 C6
Carlingnose Way KY11 . . . . .68 C6
Carlin La ML8 . . . . .215 B1
Carlisle App EH23 . . . . .195 C8
CARLOPS 206 C4
Carlops Ave EH26 . . . . .191 E6
Carlops Cres EH26 . . . . .191 E6
Carlops Rd EH26 . . . . .191 D5
Carlouk La ML8 . . . . .215 B1
Carlowrie Ave EH30 . . . . . . .89 E7
Carlowrie Cres EH30 . . . . . . .89 E7
Carlowrie Farm Cotts
EH29 . . . . .89 F4
Carlowrie Pl EH23 . . . . .174 D1
Carlton Terr EH7 . . . . .229 C4
Carlton Terrace Brae
EH7 . . . . .229 C4
Carlton Terrace La EH7 . . . .229 C4
Carlton Terrace Mews
EH7 . . . . .229 C4
CARLUKE 215 A2
Carluke High Sch ML8 . . . .215 A2
Carluke L Ctr ML8 . . . . .215 B1
Carluke Prim Sch ML8 . . . .215 A3
Carlyle Ct
Haddington EH41 . . . . .130 B8
Livingston EH54 . . . . .144 C5
Carlyle Gdns EH41 . . . . . . .101 A1
Carlyle Pl Edinburgh EH7 . . .94 A2
Musselburgh EH21 . . . . . . .124 C6
Carlyle Rd KY1 . . . . .17 B4
Carlyle St KY12 . . . . .26 B2
Carlyle Terr EH48 . . . . .141 C5
Carmel Ave EH29 . . . . .89 A2
Carmelaws EH49 . . . . .85 A5
Carmelite Rd EH30 . . . . .89 B8
Carmel Rd EH29 . . . . .89 A1
Carmichael Ct FK9 . . . . .2 A7
Carmichael Pl EH6 . . . . .93 E4
Carmondean Centre Rd
EH54 . . . . .143 A6
Carmondean Centre Rdbt
EH54 . . . . .143 B6
Carmondean Centre S
EH54 . . . . .143 A6
Carmondean Prim Sch
EH54 . . . . .143 B7
Carmuir ML11 . . . . .201 A1
Carmuirs Ave FK1 . . . . .59 B5
Carmuirs Dr FK1 . . . . .59 C5
Carmuirs Prim Sch FK1 . . . .59 D5
Carmuirs St FK1 . . . . .59 C5
Carnach FK10 . . . . .10 D6
Carnaughton Pl FK12 . . . . . . .4 F6
Carnbee Ave EH16 . . . . . . .151 C6
Carnbee Cres EH16 . . . . . . .151 C6
Carnbee Dell EH16 . . . . . . .151 C6
Carnbee End EH16 . . . . . . .151 C6
Carnbee Pk EH16 . . . . .151 C6
Carnbee Pl KY12 . . . . .29 C4
Carnegie Ave EH19 . . . . .46 E7
Carnegie Campus (Bsns Pk)
KY11 . . . . .46 E7
Carnegie Coll KY11 . . . . .30 A5
Carnegie Ct
Dunfermline KY12 . . . . .29 A4
Edinburgh EH8 . . . . .229 B2
Carnegie Dr
Dunfermline KY12 . . . . .29 A4
Falkirk FK1 . . . . .59 D6
Carnegie Drive Ret Pk
KY12 . . . . .29 A4
Carnegie L Ctr KY2 . . . . .29 A4
Carnegie Prim Sch KY11 . . .47 D3
Carnegie Rd EH54 . . . . .142 B6
Carnegie St EH8 . . . . .229 B2
Carneil Rd KY12 . . . . .27 C7
Carneil Terr KY12 . . . . .27 C7
Carnethie St EH24 . . . . .172 F2
Carnethy Ave
Edinburgh EH13 . . . . .149 B6
Penicuik EH26 . . . . .191 F6
Carnethy Cres KY2 . . . . .16 F7
Carnethy Ct EH26 . . . . .191 F5
CARNOCK 27 D6
Carnock Prim Sch KY12 . . . .27 D7
Carnock Rd
Dunfermline KY12 . . . . .26 F7
Gowkhall KY12 . . . . .27 E7

Carnock St FK7 . . . . .20 E8
Carnwaith La ML8 . . . . .215 B1
Carnwath Rd ML8 . . . . .215 A1
Caroline Cres FK12 . . . . .4 F6
Caroline Gdns
Edinburgh EH12 . . . . .119 E7
Mid Calder EH53 . . . . .144 B2
Caroline Park Ave EH5 . . . . .92 D7
Caroline Pk EH53 . . . . .144 B2
Caroline Pl EH12 . . . . .119 E7
Caroline Terr EH12 . . . . . . .119 E7
Carpenters Wynd FK10 . . . . . .9 F6
Carperstane EH39 . . . . .54 D1
Carpet La EH6 . . . . .94 A5
Carradale Ave EH54 . . . . . . .59 C4
Carribber Ave EH49 . . . . .84 A6
Carrick Cres EH22 . . . . .174 C8
Carrick Ct FK7 . . . . .7 C5
Carrick Dr KY11 . . . . .48 A3
Carrick Gdns EH54 . . . . . . .164 E6
Carrick Gr KY11 . . . . .48 A3
Carrick Knowe Ave EH12 . .119 F5
Carrick Knowe Dr EH12 . . .119 E5
Carrick Knowe Gdns
EH12 . . . . .119 F5
Carrick Knowe Gr EH12 . . .119 F5
Carrick Knowe Hill EH12 . .119 F5
Carrick Knowe Loan
EH12 . . . . .119 F5
Carrick Knowe Parkway
EH12 . . . . .119 F5
Carrick Knowe Pl EH12 . . . .119 F5
Carrick Knowe Prim Sch
EH12 . . . . .119 F5
Carrick Knowe Rd EH12 . . .119 F4
Carrick Knowe Terr
EH12 . . . . .119 F5
Carrick Pl Falkirk FK2 . . . . . .39 A3
Falkirk, Tamfourhill FK1 . . . .59 C4
CARRIDEN 64 C7
Carriden Brae EH51 . . . . .64 D6
Carriden Glade EH51 . . . . . .63 D6
Carriden Ind Est EH51 . . . . .64 E7
Carriden Pl EH51 . . . . .64 C6
Carriden View EH51 . . . . . . .64 C6
CARRINGTON 194 D6
Carrington Cres EH4 . . . . . . .92 E3
Carrington Mains Cotts
EH23 . . . . .194 D5
Carrington Rd EH4 . . . . .92 F2
CARRON 39 A2
Carronbank Ave FK2 . . . . . . .39 B2
Carronbank Cres FK6 . . . . . .36 E3
Carronbank Ct FK2 . . . . .39 B2
Carron Ct ☑ EH48 . . . . . . .141 A6
Carron Gr KY11 . . . . .29 F4
Carrongrange Ave FK5 . . . . .38 E2
Carrongrange Gdns FK5 . . . .38 E2
Carrongrange Gr FK5 . . . . . .38 E1
Carrongrange Rd FK5 . . . . . .38 E1
Carrongrange Sch FK5 . . . . .38 E2
Carrongrove Ave FK2 . . . . . .39 A2
Carrongrove Bsns Pk FK2 . .39 A2
Carrongrove Rd FK2 . . . . . . .39 A2
Carronhall Ave FK2 . . . . .39 C4
Carron La KY11 . . . . .29 F4
Carronlea Dr FK2 . . . . .39 B3
Carron Pl Edinburgh FK6 . . .94 B5
Grangemouth FK3 . . . . .61 D8
Kirkcaldy KY2 . . . . .16 D8
Stirling FK7 . . . . .7 B2
Carron Prim Sch FK2 . . . . . .39 A2
Carron Rd FK2 . . . . .39 A1
Carron Rdbt FK2 . . . . .39 A1
Carron St KY11 . . . . .29 F4
CARRONSHORE 39 C3
Carronshore Prim Sch
FK2 . . . . .39 C4
Carronshore Rd FK2 . . . . . . .39 C4
Carronside Pl FK6 . . . . .36 E3
Carronside St FK2 . . . . .60 B8
Carronvale Ave FK5 . . . . .38 D1
Carronvale Rd Larbert FK5 . .59 D8
Stenhousemuir FK5 . . . . . . .38 C1
Carronview FK5 . . . . .38 D2
Carron View FK2 . . . . .82 E7
Carron Wlk EH54 . . . . .144 A4
Carrubber's Cl EH1 . . . . . . .229 A3
Carsaig Ct FK1 . . . . .2 A5
Carsebridge Ct FK10 . . . . . .10 D8
Carsebridge Rd FK10 . . . . . .10 D8
Carsebridge Row FK10 . . . . .10 D8
Carse Cres FK2 . . . . .61 A4
Carse Knowe EH49 . . . . .85 D7
Carse Terr FK10 . . . . .10 D8
Carseview Bannockburn FK7 . .7 E2
Tullibody FK10 . . . . .4 A3
Carse View Airth FK2 . . . . . . .22 E3
Bo'ness EH51 . . . . .63 D5
Carson Pl KY11 . . . . .46 C5
Carswell Pl KY11 . . . . .28 F6
Cartmore Rd KY5 . . . . .14 A8
Cask Cres FK8 . . . . .7 C8
Casselbank St EH6 . . . . .93 F4
Cassel's La EH6 . . . . .93 F4
Castellau Cotts EH42 . . . . . .78 D2
Castings Ave FK2 . . . . .60 B7
Castings Ct Falkirk FK2 . . . . .60 B7
Castings Dr FK2 . . . . .60 B6
Castings Ho FK2 . . . . .60 C6
Castings Rd FK2 . . . . .60 B6
Castings The KY12 . . . . .12 C5
Castlandhill Farm Steadings
KY11 . . . . .46 F2
Castlandhill Rd KY11 . . . . . .47 A2
Castle Ave Airth FK2 . . . . . . .22 E3

Castle Ave continued
Cockenzie & Port Seton
EH32 . . . . .97 E4
Edinburgh EH12 . . . . .119 D5
Gorebridge EH23 . . . . .195 C8
Falkirk FK2 . . . . .39 C3
Castle Brae KY11 . . . . .46 F6
Castlebrae Bsns Ctr
EH16 . . . . .122 E3
Castlebrae Com High Sch
EH16 . . . . .122 E3
Castlebrae Glebe EH16 . . .122 D4
Castlebrae Gr EH16 . . . . . . .122 D3
Castlebrae Pl EH16 . . . . . . .122 D3
Castlebrae Rigg EH16 . . . . .122 D3
Castlebrae Wynd EH16 . . . .122 D3
Castle Bsns Pk The FK9 . . . . .1 E2
Castle Cres Denny FK6 . . . . .36 D2
East Calder EH53 . . . . .144 F2
Castledean Ct EH19 . . . . . .173 D6
Castle Dr Airth FK2 . . . . .22 E3
Dunfermline KY12 . . . . .29 A5
Falkirk FK2 . . . . .60 C7
Menstrie FK11 . . . . .3 F6
Stirling FK8 . . . . .7 A8
Castledean Ct EH19 . . . . . .173 D6
Castle Gate Dunbar EH42 . . .78 D3
Rosyth KY11 . . . . .46 E3
Castle Gogar* EH12 . . . . . .118 D7
Castle Gogar Rigg EH12 . . .118 C6
Castlehill Bo'ness EH51 . . . . .63 D6
Edinburgh EH1 . . . . .228 C3
Elphinstone EH33 . . . . .126 B1
Castlehill Ave FK1 . . . . .108 A6
Castlelaw Ind Est FK2 . . . . . .60 C7
Castlelaurie St FK2 . . . . .60 B8
Castlelaw Cres EH25 . . . . . .171 E5
Castlelaw Ct EH26 . . . . .191 F6
Castlelaw Fort & Earth
House* EH26 . . . . .170 D4
Castlelaw Rd EH13 . . . . .149 A6
CASTLELOAN 63 D7
Castle Mains EH39 . . . . .53 B5
Castle Mains Pl EH39 . . . . . .53 B5
Castle Moffat EH14 . . . . . . .222 A8
Castle Moffat Cotts
EH14 . . . . .222 A8
Castlerig St EH39 . . . . .34 F2
Castle Row KY12 . . . . .28 A2
Castle St Alloa FK10 . . . . . . .10 A5
Clackmannan FK10 . . . . .11 A4
Dunbar EH42 . . . . .78 D3
Edinburgh EH2 . . . . .228 B3
Castle Terr
Clackmannan FK10 . . . . .11 A4
Cockenzie & Port Seton
EH32 . . . . .97 E4
Denny FK6 . . . . .36 C2
Edinburgh EH1, EH2 . . . . . .228 B2
Winchburgh EH52 . . . . .88 A2
Castleton Cotts EH35 . . . . . .55 E7
Castleton Cres FK3 . . . . .61 D6
Castle Vale FK9 . . . . .2 A4
Castle View Aberdour KY3 . .49 C8
Airth FK2 . . . . .22 D2
Cockenzie & Port Seton
EH32 . . . . .97 E4
Dunfermline KY11 . . . . .46 F6
Fallin FK7 . . . . .8 D4
Gorebridge EH23 . . . . .195 C7
Pencaitland EH34 . . . . .156 D6
Castleview Dr
Bridge of Allan FK9 . . . . .2 A7
Edinburgh EH16 . . . . .122 D3
Castleview Ho EH17 . . . . . . .122 D1
Castleview La EH16 . . . . . . .164 E4
Castleview Prim Sch
EH16 . . . . .122 D4
Castleview Terr
Edinburgh EH16 . . . . .122 D4
Stirling FK9 . . . . .2 A4
Castle Wlk EH32 . . . . .97 E4
Castle Wynd Kinghorn KY3 . .34 F2
☑ Stirling FK8 . . . . .7 A8
Castle Wynd N EH1 . . . . . . .228 C2

Castle Wynd S EH1 . . . . . . .228 C2
Cast The EH4 . . . . .172 D5
Catalyst Trad Pk EH11 . . . .119 C2
CAT CRAIG 107 E7
Cathcart Pl EH11 . . . . .120 F6
Cathedral La EH1 . . . . .229 A4
Catherine St FK7 . . . . .7 C1
Catherine Wynd KY12 . . . . . .25 F2
Catherine Terr EH42 . . . . . .143 B6
Cathlaw La EH48 . . . . .112 A5
Cathrine Gr EH51 . . . . .64 A5
Catriona Terr EH26 . . . . . . .171 B1
Cattle Market KY10 . . . . .11 A4
Cauldcoats Holdings
EH49 . . . . .65 B2
Cauldhame Cres FK6 . . . . . . .6 C5
Cauldhame Farm Rd FK2 . . .59 F7
Cauldhame St FK2 . . . . .59 F8
CAUSEWAYHEAD 2 B4
Causewayhead Rd FK9 . . . . . .2 C3
Causeway La KY12 . . . . .26 E1
Causewayside EH9 . . . . .121 E5
Causeway The
Bridge of Allan FK9 . . . . .2 D5
Cockenzie & Port Seton
EH32 . . . . .97 E4
Edinburgh EH15 . . . . .122 C6
Cavalry Park Dr EH15 . . . . .122 D6
Cawder Gdns FK9 . . . . .1 F8
Cawder Rd FK9 . . . . .1 F7
Cawdor Cres KY2 . . . . .16 E6
Cecil St FK7 . . . . .7 B6
Cedar Ave Kirkcaldy KY1 . . .17 C8
Stirling FK8 . . . . .6 F5
Cedarbank EH54 . . . . .143 E5
Cedarbank Sch EH54 . . . . .143 E5
Cedar Cres
Cowdenbeath KY4 . . . . .13 D6
Westquarter KY4 . . . . .61 A2
Whitburn EH47 . . . . .161 C6
Cedar Dr EH32 . . . . .97 C3
Cedar Gr Dunfermline KY11 . .46 D8
Menstrie FK11 . . . . .3 F5
Stenhousemuir FK5 . . . . . . .38 D1
Cedar Rd EH20 . . . . .171 F7
Cedar St Dunbar EH42 . . . . .78 B2
Grangemouth FK3 . . . . .61 D7
Cedars The
Edinburgh EH13 . . . . .149 B7
Tranent EH33 . . . . .4 B2
Cedar Wynd ML7 . . . . .180 B4
Cedric Rise EH54 . . . . .144 A1
Cemetery Rd
Dalkeith EH22 . . . . .152 F2
Fauldhouse EH47 . . . . .181 D5
Prestonpans EH32 . . . . .96 F2
Shotts ML7 . . . . .180 B4
Central Ave KY4 . . . . .61 C5
Central Bvd FK5 . . . . .38 B4
Central Dock Rd FK3 . . . . . . .40 E2
Central Dr FK5 . . . . .38 F3
Central Park Ave FK5 . . . . . .38 E4
Central Park Bsns Pk FK5 . .38 B4
Central Pk (Cowdenbeath
FC) KY4 . . . . .13 C4
Central Rd KY12 . . . . .44 D7
Central Ret Pk FK1 . . . . .60 C5
Central Way KY11 . . . . .48 C5
Centre Intc EH54 . . . . .144 A3
Centre Road N EH53,
EH54 . . . . .144 A3
Centre The EH54 . . . . .143 E2
Centurion Way FK2 . . . . .59 D6
Chacefield Ave FK6 . . . . .58 A6
Chacefield Wood FK6 . . . . . .57 E7
Chalmers Bldg EH9 . . . . .84 D7
Chalmer's Bldgs EH3 . . . . .228 B1
Chalmers Cres EH9 . . . . . . .121 D5
Chalmers Ho KY12 . . . . .28 F3
Chalmers Sq EH54 . . . . . . .142 C5
Chalmers St
Dunfermline KY12 . . . . .28 F4
Edinburgh EH3 . . . . .228 C1
Chalmerston Rd FK9 . . . . .1 B2
Chalton Ct FK2 . . . . .2 B7
Chalton Rd FK9 . . . . .2 B7
Chalybeate EH41 . . . . .129 F7
Chamberfield Rd KY12 . . . . .29 C6
Chamberlain Rd EH10 . . . . .121 B4
Chambers Dr FK2 . . . . .39 B2
Chambers St EH1 . . . . .229 A2
Chamfron Gdns FK7 . . . . .7 E3
Champany Holdings EH49 . .65 A2
Champfleurie Cotts EH49 . . .86 A5
Champfleurie Mews EH49 . .86 C5
Champfleurie Stables
EH49 . . . . .86 B6
Champigny Ct EH21 . . . . . .124 C5
Chancelot Cres EH6 . . . . . . .93 C5
Chancelot Gr EH5 . . . . .93 C5
Chancelot Terr EH6 . . . . .93 C5
Chandlers Rise KY11 . . . . . . .47 F4
Chandler's Rise KY11 . . . . . .47 F4
Chandlers Wlk KY11 . . . . . . .47 F4
Channel Brae EH42 . . . . . . .134 C2
CHAPEL 16 C8
Chapel Bank EH22 . . . . .154 D5
Chapel Cres FK6 . . . . .59 B3
Chapelcroft FK7 . . . . .6 D6
Chapel Ct EH16 . . . . .122 F3
Chapel Dr FK5 . . . . .38 E3
Chapelfauld Gn KY11 . . . . . .29 F3
Chapel Gr KY12 . . . . .16 C8
Chapelhill
Clackmannan FK10 . . . . .11 A3
Dirleton EH39 . . . . .53 A4
Kirkcaldy KY2 . . . . .16 D8
Chapelhill St FK10 . . . . .23 D5
Chapel La Edinburgh EH6 . . .94 A5

Chapel La continued
Falkirk FK1 . . . . .60 B5
Chapel Level KY2 . . . . . . .16 F8
Chapel Loan EH25 . . . . .172 A3
Chapel Pl
High Valleyfield KY12 . . . .26 B2
Inverkeithing KY11 . . . . . .47 C3
Kirkcaldy KY2 . . . . .17 E6
North Queensferry KY11 . . .68 C5
Pathhead EH37 . . . . . . .176 A5
Chapel Rd KY2 . . . . .16 C8
Chapel St Cowdenbeath KY4 13 C3
7 Dunfermline KY12 . . . . .28 F4
Edinburgh EH8 . . . . .229 B1
High Valleyfield KY12 . . . .26 B2
Kincardine FK10 . . . . .23 E3
Lochgelly KY5 . . . . .14 B8
Chapelton Ave EH55 . . . .163 H4
Chapelton Ct EH55 . . . . .163 H4
Chapelton Dr EH55 . . . . .164 A4
Chapelton Gdns EH55 . . .163 H4
Chapelton Pl EH55 . . . . .163 H4
Chapelton Pl EH55 . . . . .164 A4
Chapelton Terr EH55 . . . .163 F5
Chapel Villas KY1 . . . . . .48 B2
Chapelwell Pl KY1 . . . . . .29 F3
Chapel Wynd EH1 . . . . . .228 C2
Chapman's Brae EH48 . . .140 F8
Charing Cross **1** FK3 . . . .40 D1
Chariot Dr EH28 . . . . . . .117 A5
Charles Ave FK9 . . . . .2 B6
Charles Cres
Bathgate EH48 . . . . .141 F5
Carluke ML8 . . . . .215 B1
Charles Ct KY11 . . . . .45 F3
Charles Dr FK5 . . . . .59 C8
Charlesfield EH8 . . . . . . .229 A2
Charlesfield La EH54 . . . .143 B2
Charlesfield Rd EH54 . . . .164 C8
Charles La EH48 . . . . . . .141 F6
Charles Logan Pl KY11 . . .46 F4
Charles Rodger Pl FK9 . . . .2 A6
Charles St Alloa FK10 . . . . .9 F8
Dunfermline KY11 . . . . . . .29 B2
Edinburgh EH8 . . . . .229 A2
Penicuik EH26 . . . . .191 E7
Shotts ML7 . . . . .180 B4
Stirling FK8 . . . . .7 A5
Charles Street La EH8. . . .229 A2
CHARLESTOWN 45 B4
Charles Way KY11 . . . . . .45 E3
Charles Way S KY11 . . . . .45 E3
Charlotte Dundas Ct FK3. .40 A1
Charlotte La EH2 . . . . . . .228 B3
Charlotte Sq EH2 . . . . . .228 B3
Charlotte St
Grangemouth FK2 . . . . . . .82 D8
Kirkcaldy KY1 . . . . .17 B3
Shotts ML7 . . . . .180 A3
Charlton Gr EH25 . . . . . .171 F3
Charrier The FK11 . . . . . . .3 F6
Charterhall Gr EH9 . . . . .121 D3
Charterhall Rd EH9 . . . . .121 D3
Charteris Ct EH32 . . . . . . .98 D5
Charteris Pk EH32 . . . . . .98 D5
Charteris Rd EH32 . . . . . .98 D5
CHARTERSHALL 7 A1
Chartershall Rd
Bannockburn FK7 . . . . . . .19 A6
Stirling FK7 . . . . .7 A3
Charter St FK7 . . . . .7 A3
Chattan Ave FK9 . . . . .2 B4
Chattan Ind Est FK4 . . . . .58 C4
Chatterrig EH13 . . . . . . .149 F7
Checkbar Rdbt FK5 . . . . . .58 C7
Cherry Ave EH48 . . . . . .141 E6
Cherrybank KY12 . . . . . . .29 D5
Cherry La KY22 . . . . .174 E6
Cherry Pl KY4 . . . . .13 C3
Cherry Rd EH19 . . . . . . .173 B6
Cherryton Dr FK10 . . . . . .11 A5
Cherry Tree Ave EH14 . . .147 E3
Cherry Tree Cres EH14 . .147 E3
Cherry Tree Gdns EH14 . .147 D3
Cherry Tree Gr EH14 . . . .147 D3
Cherry Tree Loan EH14 . .147 E3
Cherry Tree Pk EH14 . . . .147 D3
Cherry Tree Pl EH14 . . . .147 E3
Cherry Tree View EH14 . .147 E3
Chessel's Ct EH8 . . . . . . .229 B3
Chesser Ave EH14 . . . . . .120 C3
Chesser Cotts EH11 . . . . .120 C4
Chesser Cres EH14 . . . . . .120 C4
Chesser Gdns EH11 . . . . .120 B4
Chesser Gr EH14 . . . . . . .120 C3
Chesser Loan EH14 . . . . .120 B3
Chester Dr EH22 . . . . . . .174 D5
Chesterhall Ave EH33 . . . .127 D6
CHESTERHILL 175 C7
Chesters Ct EH19 . . . . . .173 B6
Chesters St EH19 . . . . . .173 B6
Chesters St EH3 . . . . .228 A3
Chesters The EH39. . . . . . .72 F4
Chesters View EH19 . . . . .173 B6
Chester View FK10 . . . . . .10 C4
Chestnut Ave Kirkcaldy KY1 17 C7
Whitburn EH47 . . . . .161 C6
Chestnut Cres FK6. . . . . . .36 C3
Chestnut Ct EH21 . . . . . . .124 A4
Chestnut Gr Bo'ness EH51. .63 C5
Bonnyrigg and Lasswade
EH19 . . . . .173 B6
Cockenzie & Port Seton
EH32 . . . . .97 D3
Dunfermline KY11 . . . . . . .46 B8
Livingston EH54 . . . . . . .144 B5
Stenhousemuir FK5 . . . . . .38 F3

Chestnut Gr continued
Winchburgh EH52 . . . . . . .87 F2
Chestnut La FK10 . . . . .4 A3
Chestnut St EH5 . . . . .92 E7
Cheviot Pl FK3 . . . . .61 E5
Cheviot Rd KY2 . . . . .16 F7
Cheyne St EH4 . . . . .93 A2
Chief's Cl **5** KY1 . . . . .17 D6
Chisholm Ave FK9 . . . . .2 B4
Chisholm Cres KY5 . . . . . .14 A7
Chisholm Pl FK3 . . . . .61 B6
Chisholm Pl KY11 . . . . . . .29 D8
Chisholm Terr EH26. . . . .191 F7
Chisholm St FK4 . . . . .58 A2
Chrisella Terr FK2 . . . . . . .83 A6
Christian Cres EH15. . . . .123 C7
Christian Gr EH15 . . . . . .123 B7
Christiemiller Ave EH7 . . .94 E2
Christiemiller Gr EH7 . . . .94 E1
Christiemiller Pl EH7 . . . .94 E2
Christie Pl KY1 . . . . .17 D7
Christie St KY12 . . . . .29 B5
Christie Terr FK5 . . . . .38 E3
Chuckethall Pl EH54 . . . .142 E7
Chuckethall Rd EH54. . . .142 E7
Chuckie Pend EH3 . . . . . .228 B2
Church Ct Alloa FK10 . . . . .10 A6
Church La KY1 . . . . .17 C4
Philpstoun EH49 . . . . .86 D6
Church Gdns
Longniddry EH32 . . . . .98 E5
Stoneyburn EH47. . . . . . .162 B1
Church Gr Alloa FK10 . . . . .5 C1
Burntisland KY3 . . . . .33 D1
Church Hill EH10 . . . . . . .121 B4
Churchill Dr EH10 . . . . . .121 B4
Churchill Pl EH10 . . . . . .121 B4
CHURCHILL 121 B4
Churchill Dr FK9 . . . . .2 A6
Churchill Pl Falkirk FK2 . . .60 C7
Rosyth KY11 . . . . .46 F3
Churchill St KY1 . . . . .9 F8
Churchill Way EH27 . . . . .145 E3
Church La Denny FK6 . . . . .36 D3
Kirkcaldy KY1 . . . . .17 C4
Limekilns KY11 . . . . .45 D3
Plean FK7 . . . . .20 D2
Church Pk EH48 . . . . .141 B6
Church Pl Armadale EH48 .140 A5
Bathgate EH48 . . . . .141 B6
Crossgates KY4 . . . . .30 F7
Falkirk FK2 . . . . .60 B6
Fauldhouse EH47 . . . . . . .181 E6
Inverkeithing/Dunfermline
KY11 . . . . .45 D3
Longridge EH47 . . . . .161 C1
Church Rd Bo'ness EH51 . .63 E7
Bonnyrigg and Lasswade
EH18 . . . . .151 F1
California FK1 . . . . .81 F5
North Berwick EH39 . . . . .54 C7
Church St Addiewell EH55 .162 D1
Alloa FK10 . . . . .10 A6
Bonnybridge FK4 . . . . .58 C3
Broxburn EH52 . . . . .115 E5
Burntisland KY3 . . . . .33 D1
Cowdenbeath KY4 . . . . . .13 D3
Dunbar EH42 . . . . .78 E2
Falkirk FK2 . . . . .39 C2
Haddington EH41 . . . . . .130 B8
Harthill ML7 . . . . .147 B1
Inverkeithing KY11 . . . . . .47 C3
Kingseat KY12 . . . . .12 B1
Kirkcaldy KY1 . . . . .17 E6
Limekilns KY11 . . . . .45 D3
Loanhead EH20 . . . . .172 C7
Lochgelly KY5 . . . . .14 B7
Stenhousemuir FK5 . . . . . .38 E3
Tranent EH33 . . . . .126 C7
Churchway KY3 . . . . .98 E5
Church Wlk Denny FK6. . . .36 E2
Kinghorn KY3. . . . . .35 A3
Church Wynd KY11 . . . . . .63 F7
Churchyard Ct ML7 . . . . .179 E4
Cinderhall Pl EH33. . . . . .126 B1
Circle The EH22 . . . . .152 B8
Circus Gdns EH3. . . . . . . .228 B4
Circus La EH3 . . . . .93 B2
Circus Pl EH3. . . . . .228 B4
Citadel Pl EH6 . . . . .93 F6
Citadel St EH6 . . . . .93 F6
Citron Glebe **4** KY1 . . . . .17 D6
City Art Ctr* EH1. . . . . . .229 A3
City Obsy* EH7 . . . . .229 B4
City of Edinburgh By-Pass
The
Dalkeith EH18, EH22. . . . .152 C4
Edinburgh, Dreghorn EH10,
EH13. . . . . .149 C4
Edinburgh, East Hermiston EH11,
EH12, EH14 . . . . .119 A2
Edinburgh, Fairmilehead EH10,
EH13. . . . . .149 C4
Civic Sq **1** EH33 . . . . . . .126 D6
Clackmae Gr EH16 . . . . . .150 F8
Clackmae Rd EH16. . . . . .150 F8
CLACKMANNAN 11 B3
Clackmannan Prim Sch
FK10 . . . . .11 A4
Clackmannan Rd FK10 . . . .10 D6
Clackmannanshire Com
Healthcare Ctr EH10. . . . .10 C8
Clackmannan Tower*
FK10 . . . . .10 F4
Clanranald Ave EH32 . . . . .97 B2
Clanranald Pl FK1 . . . . . . .59 F1
Clarebank Cres EH6 . . . . . .94 B4
Clare Ct EH39. . . . . .54 B7

Claremont FK10 . . . . .9 F8
Claremont Bank EH7. . . . . .93 D3
Claremont Bsns Ctr EH7 . .10 A6
Claremont Cres EH7 . . . . . .93 D3
Claremont Ct EH7 . . . . .93 D3
Claremont Dr FK9 . . . . .2 C7
Claremont Gdns EH6 . . . . .94 B4
Claremont Gr EH7. . . . . . . .93 D3
CLAREMONT PARK 94 C4
Claremont Pk EH6 . . . . . . .94 B4
Claremont Prim Sch FK10. .9 E8
Claremont Rd EH6 . . . . . . .94 B4
Claremont St FK4 . . . . .57 F6
Clarence St EH3 . . . . .93 B2
Clarendon Cres
Edinburgh EH4. . . . . .228 A4
Linlithgow EH49 . . . . .85 B6
Clarendon Pl FK8 . . . . .7 A7
Clarendon Rd
Linlithgow EH49 . . . . .85 B6
Stirling FK8 . . . . .7 A7
Claret Rd
Grangemouth, Bowhouse
FK3 . . . . .61 E6
Grangemouth, Oil Refinery
FK3 . . . . .62 C7
Clarinda Ave FK1 . . . . .59 B5
Clarinda Gdns EH22. . . . .153 D3
Clarinda Pl FK5 . . . . .38 C4
Clarinda Terr EH16 . . . . . .122 A1
Clark Ave Edinburgh EH5 . .93 C5
Clark Bldgs EH35 . . . . . . .155 E7
Clarke Sq EH54 . . . . .142 C6
Clark Pl Edinburgh EH5 . . .93 B5
Kirkcaldy KY2 . . . . .17 A5
Clark Rd Edinburgh EH5 . . .93 B5
Inverkeithing KY11 . . . . . .47 B2
Clarkson Rd EH52. . . . . . .115 D5
Clark St EH7 . . . . .7 B2
Claverhouse Dr EH16 . . . .151 B8
Clay Acres Ct **3** KY12 . . . .28 F4
Claycrofts Pl FK7 . . . . .7 B6
Clayhills Dr FK7 . . . . .6 E5
Clayhills Gr EH14 . . . . . . .147 B1
Clayhills Pk EH14 . . . . . .147 B1
Cleekim Dr EH15 . . . . . . .123 B4
Cleekim Rd EH15 . . . . . . .123 B4
Cleghorn Dr EH52. . . . . . .115 B5
CLEIKIMIN 123 B5
Cleikiminfield EH15. . . . .123 B4
Cleikiminrig EH15 . . . . . .123 B4
Cleish Gdns KY11 . . . . . . .29 F2
Cleish Pl KY11 . . . . .29 F2
Cleland St EH47 . . . . .161 B7
Clement Rise EH54. . . . . .144 B1
Clerics Hill EH29 . . . . .89 A1
Clerk Gr KY11 . . . . .29 F1
Clerkington Rd EH41. . . . .129 E8
Clerkington Wlk EH41 . . .129 E8
Clerk Rd EH26 . . . . .191 D5
Clerk St Edinburgh EH8 . .229 B1
Loanhead EH20 . . . . .172 C8
CLERMISTON 91 D1
Clermiston Ave EH4. . . . . .91 D2
Clermiston Dr EH4 . . . . . . .91 D2
Clermiston Gdns EH4 . . . .91 D2
Clermiston Gr EH4 . . . . . . .91 D2
Clermiston Hill EH4 . . . . . .91 D2
Clermiston Loan EH4 . . . . .91 D2
Clermiston Medway EH4 . .91 D2
Clermiston Pk EH4 . . . . . . .91 D2
Clermiston Pl EH4 . . . . . . .91 D2
Clermiston Prim Sch EH4 .91 C2
Clermiston Rd EH12. . . . .119 C7
Clermiston Road N EH4 . . .91 D3
Clermiston Terr EH12. . . . .91 D2
Clermiston View EH4 . . . . .91 D2
Clerwood Bank EH12 . . . .119 D8
Clerwood Gdns EH12 . . . .119 D8
Clerwood Gr EH12 . . . . . .119 D8
Clerwood Loan EH12. . . . .119 D8
Clerwood Pk EH12 . . . . . .119 D8
Clerwood Pl EH12 . . . . . .119 D8
Clerwood Row EH12 . . . . .119 D8
Clerwood Terr EH12 . . . . .119 E8
Clerwood View EH12 . . . .119 E8
Clerwood Way EH12 . . . . .119 D8
Cleuch Ave
North Middleton EH23. . . .195 F2
Tullibody KY3 . . . . .4 B2
Cleuchbrae EH55 . . . . . . .163 D3
Cleuch Dr FK12. . . . . .4 B2
Cleuch Pl FK12. . . . . .82 F7
Cleuch Rd
North Middleton EH23. . . .195 F2
Stirling FK9 . . . . .2 C3
Cleveland Dr KY11 . . . . . . .47 B2
Cliffie's Brae FK2 . . . . .83 A3
Clifford Pk
North Berwick EH39 . . . . .54 C6
Clifford Rd

Clifford Rd continued
Stirling FK8 . . . . .7 B5
Cliftonhall Rd EH28. . . . . .116 F4
Clifton Hall Sch EH28. . . .116 D2
Cliftonhall Yards EH28 . . .116 F4
Clifton Rd Livingston EH53 145 C7
Newbridge EH28 . . . . . . .116 E2
Clifton Terr **3** EH12 . . . . .120 F7
Clifton Trad Est EH28 . . .116 F4
Clifton View EH52. . . . . . .116 A6
Climpy Rd ML11 . . . . .200 D3
Clinkum Bank KY12 . . . . . .26 C3
Clinton Rd EH9 . . . . .121 B4
Clive St EH47 . . . . .179 E4
Clive St ML7 . . . . .179 E4
Cloanden Pl KY2. . . . . .17 A3
Clockluine Rd KY11 . . . . . .47 E6
Clockmill La EH7, EH8. . . .94 B1
Cloglands ML11. . . . . .217 F7
Close The KY11 . . . . .46 D1
Clova Dr EH54 . . . . .164 E5
Clovenstone Dr EH14 . . . .148 E7
Clovenstone Gdns EH14 . .148 E8
Clovenstone Prim Sch
EH14. . . . . .148 E7
Clovenstone Rd EH14 . . . .148 E8
Clovenstone Rdbt EH14 . .148 E7
Cloverbank EH54 . . . . . . .143 E5
Cloverfoot Cotts EH16. . . .123 B2
Clover Rd EH51. . . . . .63 E5
Clover Way KY12 . . . . .26 A8
Cloves The FK11 . . . . .4 B2
Cluanie Ave ML7 . . . . . . .179 E6
Clufflat EH30 . . . . .67 F2
Clufflat Brae EH30 . . . . . . .67 F2
Clune Rd KY12. . . . . .27 E7
Clunie Rd KY11 . . . . .29 E3
Clunivar St KY12 . . . . .28 D5
Cluny Ave EH10 . . . . .121 B2
Cluny Dr Edinburgh EH10 .121 B2
Stenhousemuir FK5. . . . . . .38 F4
Cluny Gdns EH10 . . . . . . .121 C2
Cluny Pl EH10 . . . . .121 C3
Cluny Terr EH10 . . . . .121 B2
Clyde Cres
Dunfermline KY11 . . . . . . .29 F2
Larbert FK5 . . . . .38 B3
Clyde Dr Livingston EH54 .144 B4
Shotts ML7 . . . . .180 B4
Clydesdale St EH51 . . . . . .63 F6
Clyde St Falkirk FK1 . . . . . .59 E5
Grangemouth FK3 . . . . . . .40 B1
Clydevale Pl EH54 . . . . . .115 A2
Clydevale Terr EH54 . . . . .115 A1
Coalgate EH10 . . . . .10 B6
Coalgate Ave EH33. . . . . .126 E7
Coalgate Rd EH33 . . . . . .126 D7
Coalhill EH6. . . . . .93 F5
Coal Neuk EH33 . . . . .126 C6
Coal Neuk Ct EH33. . . . . .126 C6
Coalpots Way KY10 . . . . . . .5 E3
Coal Rd KY12 . . . . .28 F3
Coal Wynd Bannockburn FK7 .7 D1
Kirkcaldy KY1 . . . . .17 C4
Coal Wynd Ind Est KY11 . .17 C4
Coastguard Cotts TD13. . .218 F4
COATES. 120 F7
Coates Cotts EH32 . . . . . . .99 F4
Coates Cres EH3 . . . . . . .228 A3
Coates Gdns EH12 . . . . . .120 F7
Coates Pl EH3 . . . . .228 A2
Coatfield La EH6 . . . . .94 A5
Coats Cres EH10. . . . . .4 E1
Cobblebrae Cres FK2 . . . . .39 B1
Cobden Cres EH9. . . . . . .121 F4
Cobden Ct KY4 . . . . .30 F6
Cobden Rd EH9 . . . . .121 F4
Cobden St FK12. . . . . .5 A6
Cobden Terr EH11 . . . . . .228 A2
Coblecrook Gdns FK12 . . . .4 F6
Coblecrook La FK12 . . . . . .4 F6
Coburg St EH6 . . . . .93 F6
Cochran Ave Falkirk FK1. . .60 B4
Inverkeithing KY11 . . . . . .47 D2
Cochrane Cres EH48 . . . . .94 A4
Cochrane Pl EH6 . . . . .94 A4
Cochrane Sq EH54 . . . . . . .46 B1
Cochrane Sq EH54 . . . . . .164 D6
Cochrane St
Bathgate EH48 . . . . .141 F4
Falkirk FK1 . . . . .60 B4
Cochrane Way KY11 . . . . . .48 A5
Cochrie Pl FK10 . . . . .4 C2
Cochrina Pl EH24 . . . . . . .172 D2
Cockburn Cres
Balerno EH14. . . . . .168 B7
Whitecross EH49 . . . . .84 A6
Cockburn Ct EH35 . . . . . .155 E7
Cockburn Dr EH35 . . . . . .155 D6
Cockburn Pl EH11. . . . . . . .47 A6
COCKBURNSPATH. 218 E4
Cockburnspath Prim Sch
TD13. . . . . .218 E4
Cockburn Sq EH37 . . . . . .176 B5
Cockburn St
Edinburgh EH1 . . . . .229 A3
Falkirk FK1. . . . . .60 B4
Cockburdno Farm EH14 .168 A6
Cockenzie Prim Sch EH32 97 C3
Cocklaw St KY4 . . . . .12 D8
Cockles Brae EH41. . . . . .130 E3
Cockmilane Brae EH41. . .130 D6
Cockpen Ave EH19 . . . . . .173 A5

Cockpen Cres EH19. . . . . .173 A5
Cockpen Dr EH19 . . . . . . .173 A5
Cockpen Pl EH19 . . . . . . .173 A5
Cockpen Rd EH19 . . . . . . .173 D6
Cockpen Terr EH19 . . . . . .173 A5
Cockpen View EH19. . . . . .173 A5
Coillesdene Ave EH15 . . . .123 D7
Coillesdene Cres EH15 . . .123 D7
Coillesdene Dr EH15 . . . . .123 D7
Coillesdene Gdns EH15 . . .123 D7
Coillesdene Gr EH15 . . . . .123 D7
Coillesdene Ho EH15. . . . .123 D7
Coillesdene Loan EH15. . . .123 E7
Coillesdene Terr EH15 . . . .123 D7
Coire Loan ML7. . . . . .180 B3
Coldingham Pl KY12 . . . . . .29 D4
Colegate Rd EH23, EH37 . .196 D8
Coles Pl KY4. . . . . .31 A6
Colinshiel Ave EH48. . . . . .140 E7
Colinshiel Ct EH48 . . . . . .139 F6
Colinshiel St EH48 . . . . . .140 E7
Colinshiel View EH48 . . . .139 F7
Colinswell Rd KY3 . . . . . . .33 D1
COLINTON. 149 C7
Colinton Gr EH14 . . . . . . .120 D2
Colinton Grove W EH14 . .120 D2
COLINTON MAINS 120 D1
Colinton Mains Cres
EH13. . . . . .149 E6
Colinton Mains Dr EH13 . .149 D7
Colinton Mains Gdn
EH13. . . . . .149 D8
Colinton Mains Gn EH13 . .149 D7
Colinton Mains Gr EH13 . .149 D7
Colinton Mains Loan
EH13. . . . . .149 D7
Colinton Mains Pl EH13 . .149 E7
Colinton Mains Rd EH13 . .149 D6
Colinton Mains Terr
EH13. . . . . .149 E7
Colinton Prim Sch EH13 . .149 D7
Colinton Rd
Edinburgh EH10, EH14 . . .120 E3
Edinburgh, Firr Hill EH13,
EH14. . . . . .149 D8
College Cres FK2 . . . . .60 D7
College Rdbt EH54. . . . . . .143 D2
College Wynd EH1 . . . . . .229 A2
Collier Pl EH16 . . . . .122 F4
Colliers La EH48 . . . . .139 E5
Colliers Way FK7. . . . . .8 D4
Colliery Cres EH22 . . . . . .174 A4
Colliery View EH22 . . . . . .174 B4
Collingwood Ct FK1. . . . . . .59 E5
Collins Cres KY11 . . . . .47 F2
Collins Pl EH3 . . . . .93 B2
Collinswell Dr KY3 . . . . . . .33 D1
Colliston Rd KY12 . . . . . . .28 D7
Coll Pl FK3 . . . . .61 D6
Collyland Rd EH10 . . . . . . .5 D3
Colmestone Gate EH10. . . .150 A6
Colonsay Ave FK3 . . . . .61 D2
Colonsay Terr FK1 . . . . .60 B2
Colonsay Way EH5 . . . . . . .92 C6
Colquhoun St FK7 . . . . .7 C6
Colquhoun Terr FK7 . . . . . .7 C6
Colsnaur FK11. . . . . .4 A4
Colstoun Mains Cotts
EH41. . . . . .130 E4
Coltbridge Ave EH12 . . . . .120 D7
Coltbridge Gdns EH12. . . .120 E8
Coltbridge Millside **2**
EH12. . . . . .120 E7
Coltbridge Terr EH12 . . . .120 D7
Coltbridge Vale **1** EH12. . .120 E7
Coltness Ave ML7 . . . . . . .198 A8
Colton Ct KY12 . . . . .28 E4
Columba Ave EH4. . . . . . . .92 B2
Columba Rd EH4. . . . . .92 B2
Columbia Ave EH54 . . . . .143 E3
Colville Gdns FK10 . . . . . . .10 A6
Colville Pl EH3 . . . . .93 B2
Colvin St EH42 . . . . .78 E2
Combfoot Cotts EH53 . . . .144 C4
COMELY BANK 92 F2
Comely Bank Ave EH4. . . . .93 A2
Comely Bank Gr EH4 . . . . .92 F2
Comely Bank Pl EH4 . . . . .93 A2
Comely Bank Place Mews **2**
EH4. . . . . .93 A2
Comely Bank Rd EH4 . . . . .92 F2
Comely Bank Row EH4 . . . .93 A2
Comely Bank St EH4 . . . . .92 F2
Comely Bank Terr **1** EH4 .93 A2
Comely Green Cres **6**
EH7. . . . . .94 A1
Comely Green Pl **5** EH7 . .94 A1
Comely Park Gdns **17** FK1 .60 B4
Comely Park La KY12 . . . . .29 A3
Comely Park Prim Sch
FK1. . . . . .60 B4
Comely Park Terr **14** FK1. .60 B4
Comely Pk
Dunfermline KY12 . . . . . . .29 B3
Grangemouth FK2 . . . . . . .82 B7
Comely Pl FK1 . . . . .60 B4
Comely Terr FK2. . . . . .82 E7
COMISTON 150 A4
Comiston Dr EH10 . . . . . .121 A1
Comiston Gdns EH10. . . . .121 A2
Comiston Gr EH10 . . . . . .150 A2
Comiston Pl EH10 . . . . . . .121 A2
Comiston Rd EH10 . . . . . .150 A4
Comiston Rise EH10 . . . . .150 A3

Comiston Springs Ave EH10 .... 150 A7
Comiston Terr EH10 .... 121 A2
Comiston View EH10 .... 150 A7
Commando Access Way KY11 .... 46 C1
Commercial Prim Sch KY11 .... 29 C3
Commercial Rd KY11 .... 47 C2
Commercial School La 4 KY12 .... 29 A3
Commercial St
Edinburgh EH6 .... 93 F6
Kirkcaldy KY1 .... 17 D6
Commercial Wharf EH6 .... 94 A6
Commissioner St EH51 .... 64 A8
Commodores Wlk KY11 .... 46 C1
Compass Sch The EH41 .... 129 F8
Compressor House Rd FK3 .... 62 C5
Compton Rd FK3 .... 61 C5
COMRIE 26 D7
Comrie Terr EH51 .... 63 F6
Comyn Dr FK2 .... 82 C7
Concorde Way KY11 .... 47 D3
Coneyhill Rd FK9 .... 2 B7
Coneypark FK7 .... 6 E6
Conference Sq EH3 .... 228 B2
Congalton Mains Cotts EH39 .... 74 A6
Conifer Rd EH22 .... 174 E7
Coningsby Pl FK10 .... 10 A6
Connaught Pl EH6 .... 93 D5
Connelly Ct KY12 .... 26 F7
Conner Ave FK2 .... 60 A8
Connolly Dr FK6 .... 36 C4
Connolly Pl FK6 .... 36 F1
Conroy Ct 1 FK6 .... 36 E1
Considine Gdns 4 EH8 .... 94 C1
Considine Terr 3 EH8 .... 94 C1
Constable Rd FK7 .... 7 B6
Constitution Pl EH6 .... 94 A6
Constitution St EH6 .... 94 A5
Conwaine St 2 FK8 .... 7 B8
Conway Ct FK1 .... 59 F4
Cook Cres EH22 .... 174 D5
Cookies Wynd EH32 .... 96 E1
Cook Pl KY1 .... 18 A8
Cook Sq KY5 .... 14 B8
Cook St KY1 .... 18 A8
Cooperage Quay FK8 .... 7 C8
Cooperage Way FK10 .... 10 D8
Co-operative Bldgs EH33 .... 126 E6
Cooper Bsns Pk EH52 .... 115 E5
Cooper's Cl EH8 .... 229 B3
Cooper's La FK10 .... 23 E4
Cope La EH32 .... 97 C4
Copeland Cres KY4 .... 13 B2
Copland Pl FK12 .... 4 F7
Copper Beech Wynd KY12 .... 27 D1
Corbett Pl KY11 .... 29 F1
Corbie Dr EH22 .... 153 D2
Corbiehall EH51 .... 63 E7
Corbiehill Ave EH4 .... 92 A3
Corbiehill Cres EH4 .... 91 F3
Corbiehill Gdns EH4 .... 92 A3
Corbiehill Gr EH4 .... 92 A3
Corbiehill Pk EH4 .... 92 A3
Corbiehill Pl EH4 .... 91 F3
Corbiehill Rd EH4 .... 92 A3
Corbiehill Terr EH4 .... 91 F3
Corbieshot EH15 .... 123 B5
Corbiewood Dr FK7 .... 19 E8
Corbiewynd EH15 .... 123 B5
Cordiner Cl FK8 .... 1 F2
Cordiner's Land EH1 .... 228 C2
Corentin Ct FK1 .... 60 C3
Cormailin Pl KY12 .... 26 B2
CORNBANK 191 D6
Cornbank St James' Prim Sch EH26 .... 191 D5
Corn Exchange Rd 1 FK8 .... 7 B7
Corn Exchange Village EH14 .... 120 C3
Cornfield Pl EH54 .... 143 B4
Cornhill Cres FK7 .... 7 B3
Cornhill Terr EH6 .... 94 B4
CORNTON 2 B3
Cornton Bsns Pk FK9 .... 2 B2
Cornton Cres FK9 .... 2 A5
Cornton Prim Sch FK9 .... 2 A4
Cornton Rd FK9 .... 2 A4
Cornton Vale Cotts FK9 .... 2 A4
Cornwallis Pl EH3 .... 93 D2
Cornwall St EH1 .... 228 B2
Corona Cres FK4 .... 57 F5
Coronation Pl
Easthouses EH22 .... 174 D7
Skinflats FK2 .... 39 F3
Tranent EH33 .... 126 C6
Corpach Dr KY12 .... 28 F2
Corporation St FK1 .... 60 C4
Corrennie Dr EH10 .... 121 B2
Corrennie Gdns EH10 .... 121 B1
Corrie Ave FK5 .... 38 F4
Corrie Ct EH22 .... 174 B4
Corrie Pl FK1 .... 59 C4
CORSLET 148 A6
Corslet Cres EH14 .... 148 B5
Corslet Pl EH14 .... 148 A5
Corslet Rd EH14 .... 148 A5
Corston Pk EH54 .... 144 A4
CORSTORPHINE 119 F6
Corstorphine Bank Ave EH12 .... 119 C7
Corstorphine Bank Dr EH12 .... 119 D7
Corstorphine Bank Terr EH12 .... 119 C7
Corstorphine High St EH12 .... 119 D6
Corstorphine Hill Ave EH12 .... 119 E7
Corstorphine Hill Cres EH12 .... 119 E7
Corstorphine Hill Gdns EH12 .... 119 E7
Corstorphine Hill Nature Reserve* EH4 .... 91 E2
Corstorphine Hill Rd EH12 .... 119 E7
Corstorphine Hospl EH12 .... 119 F6
Corstorphine House Ave 1 EH12 .... 119 E6
Corstorphine House Terr 2 EH12 .... 119 E6
Corstorphine Park Gdns EH12 .... 119 E6
Corstorphine Prim Sch EH12 .... 119 D6
Corstorphine Rd EH12 .... 120 B7
Cortachy Ave FK2 .... 39 A3
Cortleferry Dr EH22 .... 152 E1
Cortleferry Gr EH22 .... 152 E1
Cortleferry Pk 1 EH22 .... 152 E1
Cortleferry Terr 2 EH22 .... 152 E1
Corunna Ct ML8 .... 215 B1
Corunna Pl EH6 .... 93 F5
Corunna Terr EH26 .... 192 A8
Cossars Wynd EH42 .... 78 D2
Costkea Way EH20 .... 172 A8
Cotburn Cres KY3 .... 33 F2
Cotland Dr FK2 .... 59 F8
Cotlands Ave EH32 .... 98 D4
Cotlands Pk EH32 .... 98 D4
Cotlaws EH29 .... 89 A1
Cottage Cres FK1 .... 59 E5
Cottage Gn EH4 .... 91 B4
Cottage Homes EH13 .... 149 B7
Cottage La EH21 .... 124 E5
Cottage Pk EH4 .... 92 A1
Cottages The EH42 .... 77 F1
Cotton La FK2 .... 61 A3
Cotts The EH49 .... 86 F3
Coulport Pl KY12 .... 28 F2
Council Hos EH39 .... 101 E7
Countess Ave EH42 .... 78 D2
Countess Cres EH42 .... 78 D2
Countess of Moray Hospl KY3 .... 49 B7
Countess Rd EH42 .... 78 D2
County Houses KY4 .... 31 A6
County Rd EH32 .... 96 E1
County Sq EH32 .... 96 E1
Couper Ave EH39 .... 54 C6
Couperfield EH6 .... 93 F6
Couper Gr KY11 .... 29 F1
Couper St EH6 .... 93 F6
Courthill FK12 .... 5 A7
Court St EH41 .... 130 A8
Courtyard The Falkirk FK1 .... 60 E3
Oakley KY12 .... 26 F5
COUSLAND 154 D5
Cousland Cres EH47 .... 142 B1
Cousland Intc EH54 .... 143 F5
Cousland Rd
Dalkeith EH22 .... 153 D4
Livingston, Craigshill EH54 .... 144 A6
Livingston, Livingston Village EH54 .... 143 C4
Cousland Terr EH47 .... 142 B1
Couston Dr KY11 .... 48 B4
Couston Pl KY11 .... 48 B4
Couston Rd KY11 .... 48 B4
Couston St KY12 .... 29 B4
COVE 219 A4
Cove Cres ML7 .... 179 E6
Covenanter Rd ML7 .... 159 D4
Covenanters La EH30 .... 68 B1
Covenanters Rise KY11 .... 46 E6
Cowal Pl KY11 .... 30 C1
Cowane St FK8 .... 2 B1
Cowan Rd EH11 .... 120 E4
Cowan's Cl EH8 .... 229 B1
Cowan St Bathgate EH48 .... 141 E5
Bonnybridge FK4 .... 58 A6
Cowan Terr EH26 .... 191 F7
COWDENBEATH 13 E4
Cowdenbeath Bsns Ctr KY4 .... 13 D3
Cowdenbeath L Ctr KY4 .... 13 C4
Cowdenbeath Prim Sch KY4 .... 13 D3
Cowdenbeath Rd KY3 .... 33 E2
Cowdenbeath Sta KY4 .... 13 D4
Cowden Cres EH22 .... 153 D3
Cowden Gr EH22 .... 153 D3
Cowden Hill Gdns FK4 .... 58 B6
Cowdenhill Rd EH51 .... 64 B7
Cowden La EH22 .... 153 D3
Cowden Pk EH22 .... 153 D3
Cowden Terr EH22 .... 153 D3
Cowden View EH22 .... 153 D3
Cowgate EH1 .... 229 A2
Cowgatehead EH1 .... 229 A2
COWIE 20 D7
Cowiehall Rd FK7 .... 20 D8
Cowie Prim Sch FK7 .... 20 D7
Cowie Rd Bannockburn FK7 .... 7 E1
Cowie FK7 .... 20 A8
Cowpits Ford Rd EH21 .... 124 C3
Cowpits Rd EH21 .... 124 D2
Cow Wynd FK1 .... 60 B4
COXET HILL 6 F4
Coxfield EH11 .... 120 C4
Coxithill Rd FK7 .... 7 A3
Cragganmore FK10 .... 4 A2
Crags Sp Ctr EH3 .... 229 B2
Craigallan Pk EH51 .... 64 B7
Craig Ave
Haddington EH41 .... 101 B1
Whitburn EH47 .... 160 F6
Craigbank Alloa FK10 .... 5 C1
Crossford KY12 .... 28 C2
Craigbank Prim Sch FK10 .... 5 C1
Craigbank Rd FK1 .... 110 A5
Craigbeath Ct KY4 .... 13 B5
Craigburn Ct 4 FK1 .... 59 F2
Craig Cres FK9 .... 2 D3
Craigcrook Ave EH4 .... 92 A2
Craigcrook Gdns EH4 .... 92 B1
Craigcrook Gr EH4 .... 92 A1
Craigcrook Pk EH4 .... 92 A1
Craigcrook Pl 6 EH4 .... 92 C2
Craigcrook Rd EH4 .... 91 F3
Craigcrook Sq EH4 .... 92 A2
Craigcrook Terr 5 EH4 .... 92 C2
Craig Ct Bridge of Allan FK9 .... 2 A5
Burntisland KY3 .... 33 D2
Craigdimas Gr KY11 .... 48 A2
Craigearn Ave KY2 .... 16 B7
Craigearn Pl KY2 .... 16 C7
Craigend Dr FK2 .... 83 A6
Craigend Pk EH16 .... 122 C1
Craigend Rd FK7 .... 7 A3
Craigengar Ave EH52 .... 115 A4
Craigengar Pk EH54 .... 144 A4
CRAIGENTINNY 94 E2
Craigentinny Ave EH7 .... 94 E2
Craigentinny Avenue N EH6 .... 94 D4
Craigentinny Cres EH7 .... 94 E2
Craigentinny Gr EH7 .... 94 E1
Craigentinny Pl EH7 .... 94 E1
Craigentinny Prim Sch EH7 .... 94 D2
Craigentinny Rd EH7 .... 94 D2
Craigflower Ct KY12 .... 26 E1
Craigflower Gdns KY12 .... 26 E1
Craigflower Ho KY12 .... 26 E1
Craigflower View KY12 .... 43 E8
Craigfoot Ct KY1 .... 35 B6
Craigfoot Pl KY1 .... 35 B7
Craigfoot Wlk KY1 .... 35 B7
Craigford Dr FK7 .... 7 D1
Craigforth Cres FK8 .... 1 F1
Craighall Ave EH6 .... 93 C6
Craighall Bank EH6 .... 93 C6
Craighall Cres EH6 .... 93 C6
Craighall Gdns EH6 .... 93 C5
Craighall Rd EH6 .... 93 C6
Craighall St FK8 .... 1 E1
Craighall Terr
Edinburgh EH6 .... 93 C5
Musselburgh EH21 .... 124 F6
Craighill Gdns EH10 .... 120 F1
Craighill View EH48 .... 138 E3
Craigholm La KY3 .... 33 F1
Craighorn FK11 .... 4 A5
Craighorn Dr FK1 .... 59 E2
Craighorn Rd FK12 .... 4 E6
Craighouse Ave EH10 .... 120 F2
Craighouse Gdns EH10 .... 120 F2
Craighouse Pk EH10 .... 120 F2
Craighouse Rd EH10 .... 120 F2
Craighouse Terr EH10 .... 120 F2
Craigiebield Cres EH26 .... 191 E4
Craigie Ct FK5 .... 38 B2
CRAIGIELAW 71 A4
Craigielaw Farm Cotts EH32 .... 71 B4
Craigielaw Pk EH32 .... 71 A4
Craigievar Ave FK2 .... 39 A3
Craigievar Cl KY12 .... 29 E5
Craigievar Gdns KY2 .... 16 E5
Craigievar Sq EH12 .... 119 B7
Craigievar Wynd EH12 .... 119 A7
Craiginn Ct EH48 .... 138 D3
Craiginn Terr EH48 .... 138 D3
Craigkennochie Terr KY3 .... 33 F1
Craiglaw EH52 .... 114 C2
Craiglaw Pl EH52 .... 114 C2
Craiglaw Terr 3 FK2 .... 82 D8
Craiglea FK9 .... 2 C3
Craiglea Ct EH48 .... 138 D3
Craiglea Dr EH10 .... 121 A2
Craiglea Pl EH10 .... 120 F1
CRAIGLEITH 92 D2
Craigleith FK10 .... 5 E3
Craigleith Ave Falkirk FK1 .... 59 E2
North Berwick EH39 .... 54 D6
Craigleith Avenue N EH4 .... 120 C8
Craigleith Avenue S EH4 .... 120 C8
Craigleith Bank EH4 .... 92 C1
Craigleith Cres EH4 .... 92 C1
Craigleith Dr EH4 .... 92 D1
Craigleith Gdns EH4 .... 92 C1
Craigleith Gr EH4 .... 92 C1
Craigleith Hill EH4 .... 92 D1
Craigleith Hill Ave EH4 .... 92 D2
Craigleith Hill Cres EH4 .... 92 D2
Craigleith Hill Gdns EH4 .... 92 E2
Craigleith Hill Gn EH4 .... 92 D2
Craigleith Hill Gr EH4 .... 92 D2
Craigleith Hill Loan EH4 .... 92 D2
Craigleith Hill Pk EH4 .... 92 D2
Craigleith Hill Row EH4 .... 92 D2
Craigleith Rd
Edinburgh EH4 .... 92 E1
Grangemouth FK3 .... 61 D6
Craig Leith Rd FK7 .... 7 D6
Craigleith Ret Pk EH4 .... 92 D2
Craigleith Rise EH4 .... 120 C8
Craigleith Terr FK12 .... 5 A7
Craigleith View
Edinburgh EH4 .... 120 D8
1 North Berwick EH39 .... 54 B7
Tullibody FK10 .... 4 D3
CRAIGLOCKHART 120 D1
Craiglockhart Ave EH14 .... 120 C2
Craiglockhart Bank EH14 .... 120 C1
Craiglockhart Cres EH14 .... 120 C1
Craiglockhart Dell Rd EH14 .... 120 C2
Craiglockhart Drive N EH14 .... 120 D2
Craiglockhart Drive S EH14 .... 120 C1
Craiglockhart Gdns EH14 .... 120 C2
Craiglockhart Gr EH14 .... 149 C8
Craiglockhart L Ctr EH14 .... 120 D2
Craiglockhart Loan EH14 .... 120 C2
Craiglockhart Pk EH14 .... 120 C1
Craiglockhart Pl EH14 .... 120 D2
Craiglockhart Prim Sch EH11 .... 120 E4
Craiglockhart Quadrant EH14 .... 120 C1
Craiglockhart Rd EH14 .... 120 C1
Craiglockhart Road N EH14 .... 120 D2
Craiglockhart Terr EH14 .... 120 E3
Craiglockhart View EH14 .... 120 D2
Craigluscar Ct KY12 .... 28 B7
Craigluscar La KY12 .... 28 A6
Craigluscar Rd KY12 .... 28 B7
CRAIGMILLAR 122 D3
Craigmillar Castle* EH16 .... 122 D2
Craigmillar Castle Ave
Edinburgh, Craigmillar EH16 .... 122 D3
Edinburgh, Niddrie Mains EH16 .... 122 E3
Craigmillar Castle Gdns EH16 .... 122 D3
Craigmillar Castle Loan EH16 .... 122 E4
Craigmillar Castle Rd EH16 .... 122 D2
Craigmillar Pk EH16 .... 122 A3
Craigmillar Pl FK5 .... 38 F4
Craigmore Gdns KY12 .... 26 E1
Craigmount KY2 .... 16 D7
Craigmount App EH12 .... 119 C7
Craigmount Ave EH12 .... 119 C7
Craigmount Avenue N EH4 .... 91 B1
Craigmount Bank EH4 .... 91 B1
Craigmount Bank W EH4 .... 91 B1
Craigmount Brae EH12 .... 91 B1
Craigmount Cres EH12 .... 119 C8
Craigmount Ct EH4 .... 91 B2
Craigmount Dr EH12 .... 119 B8
Craigmount Gdns EH12 .... 119 C7
Craigmount Gr EH12 .... 119 B7
Craigmount Grove N EH12 .... 119 B8
Craigmount High Sch EH12 .... 119 B7
Craigmount Hill EH4 .... 91 B1
Craigmount Loan EH12 .... 119 B8
Craigmount Pk EH12 .... 119 C7
Craigmount Pl EH12 .... 119 C8
Craigmount Terr EH12 .... 119 C7
Craigmount View EH12 .... 119 B8
Craigmount Way EH12 .... 91 C1
Craigmuir Pl EH4 .... 92 C5
Craigmyle St KY12 .... 29 C5
Craigomus Cres FK11 .... 3 F6
Craigour Ave EH17 .... 151 D8
Craigour Cres EH17 .... 151 E8
Craigour Dr EH17 .... 151 E8
Craigour Gdns EH17 .... 151 E8
Craigour Gn EH17 .... 151 D8
Craigour Gr EH17 .... 151 E8
Craigour Loan EH17 .... 151 E8
Craigour Park Prim Sch EH17 .... 151 E7
Craigour Pl EH17 .... 122 D1
Craigour Terr EH17 .... 151 E8
Craigpark EH48 .... 111 F5
Craigpark Ave EH28 .... 117 C2
Craigpark Cres EH28 .... 117 C2
Craigridge Pl KY11 .... 48 C5
Craigrie Rd FK10 .... 10 F4
Craigrie Terr FK10 .... 11 A4
Craigrigg Cotts EH48 .... 110 F3
Craigrigg Terr EH48 .... 110 E3
Craigroyston Gr EH4 .... 92 A4
Craigroyston High Sch EH4 .... 92 B4
Craigroyston Pl EH4 .... 92 A5
Craigroyston Prim Sch EH4 .... 92 B4
Craigs Ave EH12 .... 119 C6
Craigs Bank EH12 .... 119 B7
Craigs Chalet Pk EH49 .... 84 B4
Craigs Cres
Edinburgh EH12 .... 119 C7
Craigs Cres *continued*
Grangemouth FK2 .... 82 F7
Craigs Ct EH48 .... 111 F5
Craigs Dr EH12 .... 119 B7
Craigseaton EH52 .... 115 B6
Craigs Gdns EH12 .... 119 B7
Craigs Gr EH12 .... 119 C6
CRAIGSHILL 144 B5
Craigshill East Rd EH54 .... 144 A5
Craigshill Rd EH54 .... 144 A5
Craigshill St EH54 .... 144 A5
Craigs Loan EH12 .... 119 C7
Craigs Pk EH12 .... 119 B7
Craigs Rd Edinburgh EH12 .... 119 B7
West Craigs EH12 .... 118 E8
Craigs Rdbt FK7 .... 7 B7
Craig St Blackridge EH48 .... 138 E3
Rosyth KY11 .... 47 A4
Craigs Terr FK2 .... 82 E7
Craigston Dr KY12 .... 29 D5
Craigston Pk KY12 .... 29 D5
Craigs Way FK2 .... 82 F7
Craigswood EH54 .... 144 A6
Craig The KY11 .... 46 D3
Craigton Cres FK12 .... 4 F6
Craigton Ct EH52 .... 87 F2
Craigton Pl
Cowdenbeath KY4 .... 13 C2
Winchburgh EH52 .... 87 F2
Craigview Alloa FK10 .... 5 D2
Bo'ness EH51 .... 64 C7
Craigward FK10 .... 10 A6
Craigwell Path KY12 .... 44 D7
Crame Terr EH22 .... 152 E2
CRAMOND 91 C5
Cramond Ave EH4 .... 91 C5
Cramond Bank EH4 .... 91 B5
CRAMOND BRIDGE 90 F3
Cramond Bridge Cotts EH4 .... 90 F3
Cramond Brig Toll EH4 .... 90 F4
Cramond Cres EH4 .... 91 B5
Cramond Ct FK1 .... 60 B2
Cramond Gdns
Edinburgh EH4 .... 91 B5
Kirkcaldy KY2 .... 16 F7
Cramond Glebe Gdns EH4 .... 91 C6
Cramond Glebe Rd EH4 .... 91 B6
Cramond Glebe Terr EH4 .... 91 B6
Cramond Gn EH4 .... 91 B6
Cramond Gr EH4 .... 91 B5
Cramond Pk EH4 .... 91 B5
Cramond Pl
Dalgety Bay KY11 .... 48 C4
Edinburgh EH4 .... 91 C5
Cramond Prim Sch EH4 .... 91 B5
Cramond Regis EH4 .... 91 B4
Cramond Road N EH4 .... 91 C5
Cramond Road S EH4 .... 91 E4
Cramond Roman Fort* EH4 .... 91 C6
Cramond Terr EH4 .... 91 B5
Cramond Vale EH4 .... 91 A5
Cramond Village EH4 .... 91 B7
CRANSHAWS 223 C1
Cranshaws Dr FK2 .... 61 C2
Cranston Dr EH22 .... 154 D5
Cranston St
Edinburgh EH8 .... 229 B3
Penicuik EH26 .... 191 E5
Crarae Ave EH12 .... 120 D8
Crathes Ave FK5 .... 39 A4
Crathes Gdns EH54 .... 164 E6
Crathie Dr FK6 .... 36 D3
Crathie Way KY11 .... 30 A4
Craufurdland EH4 .... 91 A3
Crawfield Ave EH51 .... 63 D6
Crawfield La EH51 .... 63 F5
Crawfield Rd EH51 .... 63 E4
Crawford Dr FK2 .... 82 B7
Crawford Pl KY12 .... 29 C7
Crawford Sq FK2 .... 22 D4
Crawfurd Rd EH16 .... 122 A3
Crawhall Pl 2 FK5 .... 38 B2
Crawlees Cres EH22 .... 174 E6
Craws Knowe ML11 .... 201 A1
Creel Ct EH39 .... 54 C7
Creran Dr FK6 .... 57 D6
Crescent The
Edinburgh EH10 .... 121 A2
Gorebridge EH23 .... 174 C3
Rosyth KY11 .... 46 B1
Crest Bsns Ctr FK7 .... 7 D5
Creteil Ct FK1 .... 60 C3
Creteil Pl FK3 .... 61 D8
Crewe Bank EH5 .... 92 E5
Crewe Cres EH5 .... 92 E5
Crewe Gr EH5 .... 92 E5
Crewe Loan EH5 .... 92 D5
Crewe Pl EH5 .... 92 D5
Crewe Road Gdns EH5 .... 92 D5
Crewe Road N EH5 .... 92 D5
Crewe Road S EH4 .... 92 E3
Crewe Road W EH5 .... 92 D5
Crewe Terr EH5 .... 92 E5
Crewe Toll EH4 .... 92 D4
CRICHTON 196 F8
Crichton Ave EH37 .... 176 A5
Crichton Castle* EH37 .... 196 E7
Crichton Dr
Grangemouth FK3 .... 61 E8
Pathhead EH37 .... 176 A5
Crichton Mains Steedings EH37 .... 175 F1
Crichton Rd EH37 .... 176 A5
Crichton St EH8 .... 229 A2
Crichton Terr EH37 .... 176 A5
Cricketfield Pl EH48 .... 140 A5

Cricket Pl FK2 61 C1
Crighton Pl 2 EH6 93 F3
Crimond Pl FK1 81 E7
Crinan Pl KY11 30 A4
Cringate Gdns FK7 7 F1
Croall St 6 EH7 93 E2
Crockers Hedges EH41 102 C4
Crockett Gdns EH26 191 D5
Crockett Pl FK2 60 B8
Croft-An-Righ EH8 229 C4
Croft An Righ KY3 35 A4
Croften Righ KY11 47 C3
Crofters Gate EH47 161 E6
Crofters Way EH47 161 E6
Croft Est FK4 57 B3
Croftfoot Dr EH47 182 A6
Croftfoot Pl FK6 36 D4
Croft Gdns KY12 27 C7
Crofthead Ct FK8 2 A1
Crofthead Ctr EH54 164 D8
Crofthead Intc EH54 164 F8
Crofthead Rd Stirling FK8 2 A1
Stoneyburn EH47 162 A1
Crofthead St FK2 59 F8
CROFTMALLOCH 161 B5
Croftmalloch Prim Sch EH47 161 B5
Croftmalloch Rd EH47 161 B5
Croft Pl EH54 143 C5
Croftsacre TD13 218 F3
Croftshaw Rd FK12 5 A7
Croftside Ct FK3 61 E6
Crofts Rd TD13 218 F3
Croft's Rd FK10 4 B3
Croft St Dalkeith EH22 153 A3
Penicuik EH26 191 E4
Crofts The EH42 104 E1
Cromar Dr KY11 47 C8
Cromarty Campus KY11 46 C1
Cromarty Ct EH54 144 C4
Cromarty Pl KY1 17 E7
CROMBIE 44 D7
Crombie Prim Sch KY12 44 D7
Cromwell Anchorage EH42 78 E3
Cromwell Ct EH42 78 E3
Cromwell Dr FK1 60 D4
Cromwell Pl EH6 93 E6
Cromwell Quay EH42 78 E3
Cromwell Rd
Burntisland KY3 33 F1
Falkirk FK1 60 D4
North Berwick EH39 54 A7
Rosyth KY11 46 F5
Cromwell Road W FK1 60 D4
Crookston Ct EH21 124 E4
Crookston Rd EH21 124 E4
Crophill FK10 5 C2
Crosbies Ct FK8 7 B7
Cross Brae FK1 81 D6
CROSSBURN 108 E6
Cross Cotts EH32 97 A1
Crossen La ML8 215 B1
CROSSFORD 28 B1
Crossford Prim Sch KY12 28 A2
Crossgatehead Rd FK2 82 D8
CROSSGATES 30 F6
Crossgates Prim Sch KY4 30 E6
Crossgreen Dr EH52 115 A5
Crossgreen Pl EH52 115 A5
Crosshall Pl FK1 81 D6
Crosshill Dr
Bathgate EH48 141 C6
Bo'ness EH51 63 F5
Cross Loan EH35 155 F7
Crossroads KY11 30 B5
Crossroads Pl KY11 46 F4
Cross Row KY11 45 B4
Cross St Dysart KY1 18 A7
Falkirk FK2 39 B1
Cross The 8 Alloa FK10 10 B6
Linlithgow EH49 85 A7
Lochgelly KY5 14 B7
Pencaitland EH34 156 E6
Cross Way KY11 48 C5
Crosswood Ave EH14 168 B8
Crosswood Cres EH14 168 B8
Crosswood Terr EH55 203 F3
Cross Wynd KY12 29 A4
Crowhill Rd KY11 48 D4
Crown Ct 3 EH33 126 D6
Crownest Loan FK5 38 E2
Crown Gdns FK10 9 F8
Crown Pl EH6 93 F4
Crown St EH6 93 F4
Crozier Cres FK5 38 B2
Cruachan Ave FK9 2 B3
Cruachan Ct Falkirk FK1 60 C2
Penicuik EH26 192 A6
Cruachan Pl FK3 61 F5
Cruckburn Wynd FK7 6 F4
Cruden Rd EH51 62 D5
Cruickness Rd KY11 68 C8
Cruickshank Dr FK1 81 D6
Cruikshank's Ct 3 FK6 36 E1
Crum Cres FK7 7 C2
Crusader Ct EH54 144 A1
Crusader Dr EH25 171 F3
Crusader Rise EH54 144 A1
Crystalmount EH22 153 A4
Cuddies La EH13 149 B7
Cuddyhouse Rd KY4, KY12 12 D3
Cuddy La EH10 121 A3
Cuffabouts EH51 64 D7
Cuguen Pl EH18 152 B1
CUIKEN 191 E6
Cuiken Ave EH26 191 E6
Cuiken Bank EH26 191 D6
Cuikenburn EH26 191 E7
Cuiken Prim Sch EH26 191 D6
Cuiken Terr EH26 191 E6
Cuil Gr KY12 28 D5
Cuillin Ct FK1 60 C1
Cuillin Pl FK3 61 E5
Culduie Circ FK2 62 A1
Cullalo Cres KY3 49 C8
Cullaloe Ct KY11 48 C4
Cullaloe Nature Reserve* KY3 32 B4
Cullaloe View KY4 13 C2
Cullen Cres KY2 16 E7
Cullen Sq EH54 142 D6
Culloch Rd FK1 108 B6
Culmore Pl FK1 60 E1
CULROSS 42 C8
Culross Abbey* KY12 25 D1
Culross Palace* KY12 42 C8
Culross Prim Sch KY12 42 D8
Cultenhove Cres
Grangemouth FK3 61 E6
Stirling FK7 7 A3
Cultenhove Pl FK7 7 A3
Cultenhove Rd
Stirling, Coxet Hill FK7 7 A3
Stirling FK7 7 A4
Cultins Rd EH11 119 B3
Cult Ness KY11 46 D3
Cultrig Dr EH47 161 A5
Culvain Pl FK1 60 C2
Culzean Cres KY2 16 C7
Culzean Pl FK5 38 F4
Cumberland St EH3 93 C2
Cumbernauld Rd FK4 57 A3
Cumbrae Ct KY2 17 A8
Cumbrae Dr FK1 59 C4
Cumbrae Terr KY2 17 A8
Cumin Pl EH9 121 E4
Cumlodden Ave EH12 120 C8
Cumnor Cres EH16 122 B1
Cunnigar Gdns EH53 144 C4
Cunnigar Hill View EH53 144 C4
Cunnigar Ho EH53 144 C4
Cunningham Cres EH52 115 D6
Cunningham Ct
Longniddry EH32 98 D4
North Berwick EH39 54 A6
Cunningham Dr ML7 159 D5
Cunningham Gdns FK2 60 F5
Cunningham Rd
Rosyth KY11 46 D2
Stenhousemuir FK5 39 A3
Stirling FK7 7 D7
Cunningham St FK3 61 C6
Curlew Brae EH54 143 D5
Curlew Gdns KY11 30 A2
Curling Knowe KY4 30 F6
Curling Pk KY4 30 F6
Curling Pond La EH47 161 B1
Curran Cres EH52 115 F5
CURRIE 147 F3
Currie High Sch EH14 147 F4
Curriehill Castle Dr EH14 147 D4
Curriehill Rd EH14 147 F5
Curriehill Sta EH14 147 F5
Currie Prim Sch EH14 147 F4
Currieside Ave ML7 179 E4
Currieside Pl ML7 179 D4
Currievale Dr EH14 147 E4
Currievale Farm EH14 147 E5
Currievale Park Gr EH14 147 E4
Currievale Pk EH14 147 E4
Cursiter Ct FK5 38 B2
Cushenquarter Dr FK7 20 D3
Custom House Sq EH42 78 E3
Customs Rdbt FK8 2 B1
Customs Wharf EH6 94 A6
Custonhall Pl FK6 36 D2
CUTHILL 96 E1
Cuthill Brae EH55 162 E3
Cuthill Cres EH47 162 C2
Cuthill Terr EH47 162 C2
Cuttyfield Pl FK2 39 C3
Cypress Glade EH54 164 D7
Cypress Gr KY11 46 C8

D

Daiches Braes EH15 123 D6
Daintree Terr FK1 59 E5
Dairy Cotts EH39 53 A1
Daisyhill Ct EH47 162 D7
Daisyhill Rd EH47 162 D7
Daisy Terr EH11 120 E4
Dalbeath Cres KY4 13 A2
Dalbeath Gdns KY4 12 F1
Dalbeath Marsh Nature Reserve* KY4 12 F4
Dalcross Way KY12 29 E5
Dalderse Ave FK2 60 B6
Dalgety Ave EH7 94 B2
DALGETY BAY 48 C3
Dalgety Bay Prim Sch KY11 48 B4
Dalgety Bay Sports & L Ctr KY11 48 A4
Dalgety Bay Sta KY11 47 F5
Dalgety Gdns KY11 48 D5
Dalgety House View KY11 48 D4
Dalgety Rd EH7 94 B2
Dalgety St EH7 94 B1
Dalgleish Ct FK8 7 B8
Dalgrain Ind Est FK3 40 C1
Dalgrain Rd FK3 40 B1
Dalhousie Ave EH19 173 A6
Dalhousie Avenue W EH19 173 A6
Dalhousie Bank EH22 152 F2
Dalhousie Bsns Pk EH19 173 D4
Dalhousie Cres EH22 152 F1
Dalhousie Dr EH19 173 A6
Dalhousie Gdns EH19 173 A6
Dalhousie Pl EH19 173 A6
Dalhousie Rd EH22 152 E1
Dalhousie Road E EH19 173 A6
Dalhousie Road W EH19 173 A6
Dalhousie Terr EH10 121 A2
DALKEITH 153 A2
Dalkeith Ctry Pk* EH22 153 A5
Dalkeith High Sch EH22 153 D5
Dalkeith Rd
Edinburgh, Prestonfield EH16 122 A4
Edinburgh, St Leonard's EH16 229 C1
Dalkeith St EH15 123 C7
Dallas Ave KY3 33 F1
Dallas Dr KY2 16 E7
Dalling Ave EH48 140 F5
Dalling Rd EH48 140 F5
Dalmahoy Cres EH14 147 C3
Dalmahoy Rd EH28 117 D2
DALMENY 89 F7
Dalmeny House* EH30 69 D1
Dalmeny Prim Sch EH30 89 E7
Dalmeny Rd EH6 93 D5
Dalmeny St EH6 93 F3
Dalmeny Sta EH30 89 D8
Dalmeny View KY11 48 C4
Dalmore Dr FK12 4 E6
Dalmorglen Pk FK7 6 F6
Dalratho Rd FK3 61 E8
DALRY 120 F6
Dalry Gait EH12 120 F7
Dalrymple Cres
Edinburgh EH9 121 E4
Musselburgh EH21 124 A6
Dalrymple Gdns EH22 154 D5
Dalrymple Loan EH21 124 C5
Dalry Pl EH11 228 A2
Dalry Prim Sch 5 EH11 120 F6
Dalry Swim Ctr EH11 228 A1
Dalton Ct EH22 174 E5
Dalum Ct EH20 172 A8
Dalum Dr EH20 172 A8
Dalum Gr EH20 172 A8
Dalum Loan EH20 172 A8
Dalyell Pl EH48 140 A5
Daly Gdns KY12 25 F2
Dalziel Ct EH47 162 C2
Dalziel Pl EH7 94 B1
Damhead Holdings Scheme
Bilston EH10 171 C8
Edinburgh EH10 150 D1
Damside EH4 228 A3
Dancebase* EH3 228 C2
DANDERHALL 152 C7
Danderhall Cres EH22 152 B7
Danderhall Prim Sch EH22 152 B8
Dania Ct EH11 119 F4
Daniel Pl KY11 46 C5
Danube St EH4 228 A4
D'arcy Cres EH22 174 F7
D'arcy Rd EH22 174 E6
D'arcy Terr EH22 174 E7
Dargai Pl EH52 115 A5
Darian La EH51 63 F7
Darmeid Pl ML7 198 B8
Darnaway St EH3 228 B4
Darnell Rd EH5 93 B5
Darney Terr KY3 34 F2
Darnley St FK8 7 A8
Darrach Dr FK6 36 A2
Darroch Ct EH8 229 B3
Darwin St EH54 144 A5
Davaar Dr KY2 16 E8
Davaar Pl FK1 59 C4
Davenport Pl KY11 46 F3
David Ave FK8 7 A5
David Cres KY11 47 A8
David Henderson Ct KY12 29 A4
David Lloyd Edinburgh Newhaven Harbour Ctr EH6 93 D7
David Millar Pl 5 KY12 28 E5
David Scott Ave EH22 174 E7
David's Loan FK2 39 D1
Davidson Gdns EH4 92 A3
Davidson La ML8 215 B1
Davidson Pk EH4 92 E3
Davidson Pl EH41 100 F1
Davidson Rd EH4 92 E3
DAVIDSONS MAINS 91 E3
Davidson's Mains Prim Sch EH4 91 F3
Davidson St FK7 7 C1
Davidson Terr EH41 100 F1
Davidson Way EH54 143 E7
David St Dunfermline KY12 29 A5
Kirkcaldy KY1 17 B3
Lochgelly KY5 14 B8
David The First St KY3 34 F2
Davies Row EH12 119 D6
Davie St EH8 229 B2
Daviot Rd KY12 29 E5
Dawson Ave Alloa FK10 9 F8
Livingston EH54 143 F5
Dawson Pl EH51 63 E5
Dawson St FK2 60 B8
Deacons Ct EH49 85 A5
DEAN 92 F1
Dean Acres KY12 26 D7
Dean Bank La EH3 93 B2
Deanbank Pl EH23 195 D7
Dean Br EH4 228 A4
DEANBURN 191 E7
Deanburn EH26 191 E7
Deanburn Gdns EH47 142 B1
Deanburn Gr EH51 63 D6
Deanburn Pk EH49 84 F5
Deanburn Prim Sch EH51 63 D5
Deanburn Rd EH49 84 F5
Deanburn Wlk EH51 63 D6
Dean Cres FK8 2 C1
Dean Ct EH32 98 C4
Dean Dr KY12 28 A2
Deanery Cl EH7 94 C1
DEANFIELD 63 D7
Deanfield Cres EH51 63 E7
Deanfield Dr EH51 63 E6
Deanfield Pl EH51 63 E7
Deanfield Rd EH51 63 E7
Deanfield Terr EH51 63 E6
Dean Gallery* EH4 120 F8
Deangate Gdns EH51 63 D6
Dean Gr KY12 28 B2
Deanhaugh St EH3 93 B2
Deanpark Ave EH14 147 C1
Deanpark Bank EH14 147 C1
Deanpark Brae EH14 147 C1
Deanpark Cres EH14 147 C1
Dean Park Cres EH4 228 A4
Deanpark Ct EH14 147 B1
Deanpark Gdns EH14 147 C1
Deanpark Gr EH14 147 C1
Dean Park Mews EH4 93 A2
Deanpark Pl EH14 147 C1
Dean Park Pl EH22 174 A5
Dean Park Prim Sch EH14 168 C8
Deanpark Sq EH14 147 C1
Dean Path EH4 92 F1
Dean Path Bldgs EH4 228 A3
Dean Pk Gowkhall KY12 27 E7
Longniddry EH32 98 C4
Newtongrange EH22 174 A5
Dean Pl Penicuik EH26 191 D6
Seafield EH47 142 B1
Dean Rd Bo'ness EH51 63 E6
Kirkcaldy KY2 17 A4
Longniddry EH32 98 C4
Penicuik EH26 191 D6
Dean Ridge KY12 27 E7
DEANS 142 F6
Deans East Rd
Livingston, Deans EH54 142 F7
Livingston, Nether Dechmont EH54 143 B6
Deans High Sch EH54 143 A7
Deans Ind Est EH54 142 C6
Deans North Rd
Livingston, Deans EH54 142 E6
Livingston, Nether Dechmont EH54 143 A6
Deans Prim Sch EH54 142 E5
Deans Rd EH54 142 D6
Deans Rdbt EH54 142 D5
Deans S EH54 142 E5
Deans Service Units EH54 142 E6
Dean St Edinburgh EH4 93 A2
Whitburn EH47 161 A6
Deanswood Pk EH54 142 E6
Dean Terr Edinburgh EH4 228 A4
Rosewell EH24 172 D1
Dean The EH40 75 E1
Deantown Ave EH21 153 E8
Deantown Dr EH21 124 E1
Deantown Path EH21 124 E1
Deas Rd Inverkeithing KY11 47 B2
Shotts ML7 179 C5
Deas Wharf KY1 17 C4
DECHMONT 114 C2
Dechmont Inf Sch EH52 114 B2
Dechmont Rd EH12 119 A6
Dechmont Rdbt EH52 114 D2
DEDRIDGE 143 E1
Dedridge East Ind Est EH54 144 A1
Dedridge East Rd EH54 144 A1
Dedridge North Rd EH54 164 D8
Dedridge Prim Sch EH54 144 A2
Dedridge West Rd EH54 164 E8
Dee Dr EH54 144 B5
Dee Pl KY11 29 F2
Deep Sea World (Scotland's National Aquarium)* KY11 68 C5
Deerhill EH52 114 C2
Deerpark FK10 5 E1
Deer Park Dr EH54 114 D1
Deerpark Prim Sch FK10 5 F1
Deer Park Rd
Abercorn EH30 66 F2
Dechmont EH54 114 D1
Deer Path ML7 159 E5
Deeside Dr ML8 215 A3
Deeside Pl KY11 30 C1
Dee St ML7 179 D5
Delaney Ct FK10 10 A6
Delisle St EH42 78 D2
Dell Ave EH48 139 E6
Dell Rd EH13 149 B7
Delph Rd FK10 4 C2
Delphwood Cres FK10 4 D2
Delph Wynd FK10 4 C2
Delta Ave EH21 125 A5
Delta Cres EH21 125 A6
Delta Ct 2 EH21 125 A6
Delta Dr EH21 125 A6
Delta Gdns EH21 125 A5
Delta Pl EH21 124 D4
Delta Rd EH21 125 A5
Delta View EH21 125 A6
De Moray Ct FK9 2 A4
Demoreham Ave FK6 36 F1
Dempster Pl KY12 28 F5
Denbecan FK10 10 D5
Denburn Pl KY2 17 C6
Denburn Rd KY1 17 D7
Denend Cres KY2 17 B6
Denham Green Ave EH5 93 B5
Denham Green Pl EH5 93 B5
Denham Green Terr EH5 93 B5
Denholm Ave EH21 123 F4
Denholm Dr EH21 124 A4
Denholm Gr EH48 139 E7
Denholm Rd EH21 123 F5
Denholm Way EH21 123 F4
Den La ML7 179 D6
DENNY 36 F1
Denny High Sch FK6 57 E8
DENNYLOANHEAD 57 D5
Denny Prim Sch FK6 36 D2
Denny Rd Denny FK4 57 E6
Larbert FK5 38 A1
Denovan Rd FK6 36 E4
Den Rd KY2, KY1 17 C6
De Quincey Path EH18 172 E6
De Quincey Rd EH18 172 E6
Dequincey Wlk 6 EH33 126 C5
Derby St EH6 93 D6
Deroran Pl FK8 6 F5
Derwent Ave FK1 59 F4
Devlin Ct FK7 7 B2
Devonbank FK10 5 E3
Devon Ct FK10 4 B2
Devon Dr FK10 4 E4
Devon Pl Cambus FK10 4 A1
Edinburgh EH12 120 F7
Devon Rd FK10 10 C6
Devon St FK3 40 A1
Devon Terr KY11 29 E2
Devon Valley Dr FK10 5 D2
Devon Village FK10 5 E4
Devonway FK10 10 F5
Dewar Ave FK10 23 E4
Dewar Pl EH3 228 A2
Dewar Place La EH3 228 A2
Dewar Sq EH54 142 D5
Dewar St Dunfermline KY12 28 F4
Lochgelly KY5 14 A7
DEWARTOWN 175 D5
Dewshill Cotts ML7 158 B4
Dew Way KY11 46 D1
Dickburn Cres FK4 57 F5
Dick Cres KY3 33 E1
Dick Gdns EH47 160 F6
Dickies Wells FK12 5 C7
Dick Pl Edinburgh EH9 121 D4
Rosyth KY11 46 E5
Stoneyburn EH47 162 C2
Dickson Ct
Dunfermline KY12 29 A2
Lochgelly KY5 14 A7
Dicksonfield EH7 93 E2
Dickson Gr EH19 173 B7
Dickson St
Dunfermline KY12 29 A1
Edinburgh EH6 93 F3
West Calder EH55 163 D2
Dick St KY12 29 C5
Dick Terr EH26 191 F6
Dinmont Dr EH16 122 B2
DIRLETON 53 B4
Dirleton Ave EH39 54 A7
Dirleton Castle* EH39 53 B4
Dirleton Ct EH39 53 F7
Dirleton Gdns FK10 9 F7
Dirleton La FK10 9 F6
Dirleton Prim Sch EH39 53 A4
Dirleton Rd Dirleton EH39 53 B5
North Berwick EH39 53 E6
Distillery La EH11 120 F7
Distillery Wynd EH40 103 E7
Diverswell FK10 5 D2
Dixon Ct EH47 160 F5
Dixon Terr EH47 161 A5
Dobbie Ave Larbert FK5 59 C8
Stenhousemuir FK5 38 C1
DOBBIE'S KNOWE 173 A7
Dobbie's Rd EH18 173 A7
Dobson's Pl EH41 129 F8
Dobson's View EH41 129 F8
Dobson's Wlk EH41 129 F7
Dochart Cres FK2 61 F2
Dochart Dr EH4 91 C1
Dochart Path FK3 61 D5
Dochart Pl FK1 60 D2
Dock Pl EH6 93 F6
Dock Rd FK3 40 D1
Dock St Bo'ness EH51 64 A8
Edinburgh EH6 93 F6
Falkirk FK2 39 C2
Doctor's Pk FK10 23 E3
Dog Well Wynd EH49 85 A7
Dollar Ave FK2 60 A7
Dollar Cres KY2 16 D7
Dollar Ct 2 KY12 28 E5
Dollar Gdns FK2 60 A7
Dollar Gr KY3 33 E1
Dollar Ind Est FK1, FK2 60 A5
Dollar Rd KY3 33 E1
Dolphin Ave EH14 147 F4
Dolphin Gardens E EH14 147 F4

Dolphin Gardens W
EH14 . . . . 147 E4
DOLPHINGSTONE 125 F7
Dolphingstone View
EH32 . . . . 125 F8
Dolphingstone Way
EH32 . . . . 125 F8
Dolphin Rd EH14. . . . . 147 F4
Donaldson Ave FK10 . . . . 4 E1
Donaldson Ct FK10 . . . . 23 E3
Donaldson Pl FK7. . . . . 6 D6
Donaldson Rd FK2 . . . . 61 A1
Donaldson's EH49 . . . . 84 F5
Donald St KY12. . . . . 29 C6
Don Dr EH54. . . . . 144 B5
Donibristle Gdns KY11 . . . . 48 B2
Donibristle Ho KY11 . . . . . . 48 B2
Donibristle Ind Est KY11 . . 48 B5
Donibristle Ind Pk KY11. . . 48 A4
Donibristle Prim Sch
KY11. . . . . 48 B2
Donnelly Ho FK9 . . . . 2 D6
Don Rd KY11 . . . . 29 F1
Don St FK3 . . . . 40 A1
Doocot Brae EH51 . . . . 64 B7
Doo'cot Brae FK10. . . . . 10 A8
Doo'cot Hill FK10. . . . . 5 D2
Doocot Pl EH32. . . . . 126 A8
Doo Dells La KY3 . . . . 34 F2
Doon Ave EH42. . . . . 78 C2
Doon Hill Hall★ EH42. . . . 106 F4
Doon Wlk EH54. . . . . 144 A4
Dora Ct KY4 . . . . 13 D6
Dornie Wynd ML7. . . . . 180 B3
Dornoch Pl KY11. . . . . 47 C8
Dorrator Ct FK1 . . . . 59 E5
Dorrator Rd FK1 . . . . 59 E6
Dorset Pl EH10 . . . . 121 A5
Double Dykes EH21 . . . . . . 124 D4
Double Hedges Pk EH16 . 122 A1
Double Hedges Rd EH16 . 122 A1
Double Row KY11. . . . . 45 B4
Dougall Ct EH22 . . . . 174 D5
Dougall Pl EH22 . . . . 174 D5
Dougall Rd EH22. . . . . 174 D5
Dougans Sq EH48. . . . . 139 F6
Douglas Ave Airth FK2. . . . . . 22 D3
Grangemouth, Bowhouse
FK3. 61 E6
Grangemouth, Brightons
FK2. 82 D8
Linlithgow EH49 . . . . 84 E6
Douglas Cres
Bonnyrigg and Lasswade
EH19. . . . . 173 B7
Edinburgh EH12. . . . . 120 F8
Longniddry EH32. . . . . 98 E6
Douglas Dr Bo'ness EH51. . . 63 E6
Crossford KY12. . . . . 28 A2
Dunfermline KY12. . . . . 28 E5
Stirling FK7 . . . . 7 C4
Douglas Gardens Mews 5
EH4 . . . . 120 F8
Douglas Gdns EH4 . . . . 120 F8
Douglas Pk KY12. . . . . 28 E6
Douglas Pl Bo'ness EH51. . . 63 F6
Linlithgow EH49 . . . . 84 E6
Stenhousemuir FK5. . . . . 38 F4
Douglas Rd Bo'ness EH51 . . 63 F6
Longniddry EH32. . . . . 98 E6
Rosyth KY11 . . . . 46 C2
Douglas Rise EH54. . . . . . . 144 A2
Douglas St Bannockburn FK7 . 7 E1
Dunfermline KY12. . . . . 29 A4
Kirkcaldy KY1 . . . . 17 B3
Stirling FK8 . . . . 2 B1
Douglas Terr Bo'ness EH51. 63 F6
Edinburgh EH11. . . . . 228 A2
Stirling FK7 . . . . 6 E6
Douglas Wynd EH52 . . . . . 115 B6
Doune Cres FK5 . . . . 39 A4
Doune Pk KY11 . . . . 48 C4
Doune Terr EH3 . . . . 228 B4
Dovecot Brae EH33 . . . . . . 126 C7
Dovecot Cres KY1. . . . . 18 B8
Dovecote Pl EH54. . . . . 143 C4
Dovecot Gr EH14. . . . . 120 B1
Dovecot Loan EH14 . . . . . . 120 A1
Dovecot Pk Aberdour KY3 . . 49 B6
Edinburgh EH14. . . . . 149 A8
Linlithgow EH49 . . . . 85 D8
Pencaitland EH34 . . . . 156 E6
Dovecot Pl
Dunfermline KY11. . . . . 47 A7
Tullibody FK10. . . . . 4 B3
Dovecot Rd
Edinburgh EH12. . . . . 119 D5
Tullibody FK10. . . . . 4 B3
Westquarter FK2. . . . . 61 A2
Dovecot Way
Dunfermline KY11. . . . . 47 A7
Pencaitland EH34 . . . . 156 E7
Dovecot Wynd KY11 . . . . . . 46 F7
Dovehill FK10. . . . . 10 B8
Dover Dr KY11. . . . . 47 A8
Dover Hts KY11. . . . . 47 A8
Dover Pk KY11. . . . . 47 A8
Dover Way KY11. . . . . 47 A8
Dowan Pl FK7 . . . . 6 E6
Dower Cres EH51. . . . . 64 B8
Dower Pl FK2. . . . . 22 D4
Dowie's Mill Cotts EH4. . . . 90 F4
Dowie's Mill La EH4. . . . . . . 90 F4
Dowlaw Rd TD13, TD14 . . . 219 F2
Downfield KY4. . . . . 13 C6
Downfield Pl EH11 . . . . 120 F6
Downie Gr EH12 . . . . 119 F6
Downie Pl EH21 . . . . 124 C6
Downie Terr EH12 . . . . 119 F6
Downing Ct EH25 . . . . 172 A4
Downing Point KY11 . . . . . . 48 B2
Downs Cres FK10 . . . . 9 F6
Dr Campbell Ave FK7 . . . . . 20 D8
DREGHORN. 149 D5
Dreghorn Ave EH13 . . . . . . 149 E5
Dreghorn Dr EH13 . . . . 149 E5
Dreghorn Gdns EH13. . . . . 149 E6
Dreghorn Gr EH13 . . . . 149 F5
Dreghorn Junc EH10,
EH13 . . . . 149 E5
Dreghorn Link EH13 . . . . . 149 E5
Dreghorn Loan EH13. . . . . 149 B6
Dreghorn Pk EH13 . . . . 149 D6
Dreghorn Pl EH13. . . . . 149 E5
DREM. 73 A4
Drem Farm Cotts EH39. . . . 73 A4
Drem Sta EH39 . . . . 73 A3
Drip Rd FK9 . . . . 1 F2
Dronachy Rd KY2 . . . . 16 F4
Drossie Rd FK1 . . . . 60 A3
Drove Loan FK6 . . . . 57 F6
Drove Loan Cres FK6. . . . . . 57 E7
Drove Rd EH48 . . . . 139 F7
Droverhall Ave KY4 . . . . 31 A6
Droverhall Pl KY4. . . . . 31 A6
Drover Pl FK5 . . . . 38 C4
Drover Round FK5 . . . . 38 C4
Drovers Rd EH52. . . . . 116 A6
Dr Porter Gdns FK7 . . . . 8 D4
DRUM 94 A2
Drumacre Rd EH51. . . . . 64 B6
Drum Ave EH17 . . . . 151 E6
Drumbowie Prim Sch FK1 82 D2
DRUMBRAE. 91 C2
Drum Brae Ave EH12. . . . . 119 C8
Drum Brae Cres EH4. . . . . . . 91 C2
Drum Brae Dr EH4 . . . . 91 D1
Drum Brae Gdns EH12 . . . 119 C8
Drum Brae Gr EH4. . . . . 91 C1
Drumbrae L Ctr EH4. . . . . . . 91 C1
Drum Brae N EH4. . . . . 91 B2
Drum Brae Neuk EH12 . . . 119 C8
Drum Brae Park App
EH12 . . . . 119 C8
Drum Brae Pk EH12. . . . . . 119 C8
Drum Brae Pl EH12 . . . . . . 119 C8
Drumbrae Prim Sch EH4 119 C8
Drumbrae Rdbt EH12 . . . . 119 C6
Drum Brae S EH12. . . . . . . 119 C8
Drum Brae Terr EH4 . . . . . . 91 C1
Drum Brae Wlk EH4. . . . . . . 91 B1
Drumclair Ave FK1. . . . . . . 108 A6
Drum Cotts Bo'ness EH51 . . 64 C6
Edinburgh EH17. . . . . 151 F5
Drum Cres EH17 . . . . 151 F6
Drumcross Rd EH48. . . . . . 141 B7
Drumdryan St EH3. . . . . . . 228 B1
Drum Farm La EH51. . . . . . . 64 C6
Drumlanrig Pl FK5. . . . . 38 F4
Drummohr Ave EH21. . . . . 125 B5
Drummohr Gdns EH21 . . . 125 B5
Drummond Com High Sch 10
EH7. . . . . 93 D2
Drummond La FK8. . . . . 7 A6
Drummond Pk FK3. . . . . 61 E6
Drummond Pl
Blackridge EH48 . . . . 138 C3
Bonnybridge FK4. . . . . 58 A7
Dunfermline KY12. . . . . 29 D5
Edinburgh EH3. . . . . 93 D2
Falkirk FK1 . . . . 59 F2
Grangemouth FK3 . . . . 61 E8
Stirling FK8 . . . . 7 A6
Drummond Place La FK8. . . 7 A6
Drummond Sq
Livingston EH54. . . . . 164 C6
Lochgelly KY5 . . . . 14 B8
Drummond St EH8. . . . . . . 229 B2
Drummore Dr EH32. . . . . . 125 E8
Drummormie Rd KY12 . . . . 27 C1
Drumpark Ave EH51 . . . . . . 64 B6
Drumpark St FK7 . . . . 7 B3
Drum Pl
East Whitburn EH47 . . . . . . 161 E7
Edinburgh EH17. . . . . 151 F6
Drum Rd Bo'ness EH51. . . . . 64 C6
Dunfermline KY11. . . . . 29 F2
Drumsheugh Gdns EH3 . . 228 A3
Drumsheugh Pl EH3 . . . . . 228 A2
Drumshoreland Ave
EH53 . . . . 144 B7
Drumshoreland Cres
EH53 . . . . 144 B7
Drumshoreland Pl EH53. . 144 B8
Drumshoreland Rd EH53 . 144 B7
Drumside Terr EH51 . . . . . . 64 C7
Drum St EH17 . . . . 151 F5
Drum Terr EH7 . . . . 94 A2
Drum View Ave EH22. . . . . 152 B8
Drumview Gdns EH51 . . . . . 64 A5
Drunmmohr Terr EH21. . . 125 A5
Drybrough Cres EH16. . . . 122 D4
Dryburgh Ave FK6 . . . . 36 D2
Dryburgh Way FK3. . . . . 61 F6
Dryden Ave EH20 . . . . 172 A7
Dryden Cotts EH34. . . . . . . 157 F4
Dryden Cres EH20 . . . . 172 A7
Dryden Gait EH7. . . . . 93 E3
Dryden Gdns EH7. . . . . 93 E3
Dryden Glen EH20 . . . . 171 F7
Dryden Gr EH25 . . . . 172 A4
Dryden Loan EH20. . . . . 171 F7
Dryden Pk EH20 . . . . 171 F7
Dryden Pl Edinburgh EH9 . . 121 F5
Loanhead EH20. . . . . 171 F7
Dryden Rd EH20 . . . . 171 F7
Dryden St EH7. . . . . 93 E3
Dryden Terr Edinburgh EH7 93 E3
Loanhead EH20. . . . . 172 A7
Dryden Vale EH20. . . . . 171 F7
Dryden View EH20. . . . . . . 172 A7
DRYLAW 92 C3
Drylaw Ave EH4 . . . . 92 C2
Drylaw Cres EH4. . . . . 92 B3
Drylaw Gdns
East Linton EH40. . . . . 103 D8
Edinburgh EH4. . . . . 92 B3
Drylaw Gn EH4 . . . . 92 B2
Drylaw Gr EH4. . . . . 92 B2
Drylawhill EH40. . . . . 75 D1
Drylaw House Gdns EH4 . . 92 B3
Drylaw House Paddock
EH4 . . . . 92 B3
Drylaw Terr EH40. . . . . 103 D8
Drylie Ct KY4 . . . . 13 B4
Drylie St KY4 . . . . 13 B4
Drysdale Ave EH47. . . . . . . 161 B7
Drysdale St FK10 . . . . 10 B6
Duart Cres EH4. . . . . 91 C1
Dublin Meuse EH3 . . . . 93 C1
Dublin St EH1 . . . . 229 A4
Dublin Street Lane N 2
EH3 . . . . 93 D2
Dublin Street Lane S
EH1 . . . . 229 A4
Duchess Anne Cotts EH51 63 C6
DUDDINGSTON 122 E6
Duddingston Ave EH15. . . 122 E7
Duddingston Cres
Edinburgh EH15. . . . . 123 B6
Newton EH52. . . . . 88 A8
Duddingston Terr EH52. . 88 A8
Duddingston Gardens N
EH15 . . . . 122 F7
Duddingston Gardens S
EH15 . . . . 122 F6
Duddingston Grove E
EH15 . . . . 122 F7
Duddingston Grove W
EH15 . . . . 122 F6
Duddingston House Ctyd
EH15 . . . . 122 E5
Duddingston Loan EH15. . 122 E6
Duddingston Mains Cotts
EH15 . . . . 123 B6
Duddingston Mills EH8. . . 122 E7
Duddingston Park S
EH15 . . . . 123 A5
Duddingston Pk EH15. . . . 123 A7
Duddingston Prim Sch
EH15. . . . . 122 E7
Duddingston Rd EH15. . . . 122 F7
Duddingston Rise EH15 . . 122 F6
Duddingston Road W
EH16 . . . . 122 D5
Duddingston Row EH15 . . 122 F5
Duddingston Square E
EH15 . . . . 122 F7
Duddingston Square W
EH15 . . . . 122 F6
Duddingston View EH15. . 122 F6
Duddingston Yds EH15. . . 123 A5
Dudgeon Pl EH29. . . . . 89 B2
Dudley Ave EH6 . . . . 93 D6
Dudley Avenue S EH6 . . . . . 93 E5
Dudley Bank EH6 . . . . 93 D6
Dudley Cres EH6. . . . . 93 D6
Dudley Gdns EH6 . . . . 93 D6
Dudley Gr EH6. . . . . 93 D6
Dudley Terr EH6. . . . . 93 D6
Duff Cres FK8 . . . . 1 F1
Duff Ct EH39. . . . . 54 A7
Duff Rd EH11 . . . . 120 F6
Duff St EH11. . . . . 120 F6
Duff Street La EH11 . . . . . . 120 F6
Duffy Pl KY11. . . . . 46 E3
Dugald Stewart Ave EH51 . 64 A7
Duke Pl EH6. . . . . 94 A4
Duke St Alva FK12 . . . . 5 A7
Bannockburn FK7 . . . . 7 C1
Clackmannan FK10 . . . . 11 B4
Dalkeith EH22 . . . . 153 A3
Denny FK6. . . . . 36 C2
Dunbar EH42. . . . . 78 A2
Edinburgh EH6. . . . . 94 A4
Grangemouth FK3. . . . . 61 F8
Rosewell EH24 . . . . 172 D1
West Barns EH42 . . . . 77 F1
Duke's Wlk EH8 . . . . 94 B1
Duloch Park Prim Sch
KY11. . . . . 30 B1
Dumbarton Rd
Cambusbarron FK8 . . . . 6 E8
Stirling FK8. . . . . 7 B7
Dumbeg Pk EH14 . . . . 148 D8
DUMBIEDYKES. 229 B2
Dumbiedykes Rd EH8 . . . . 229 C2
Dumbryden Dr EH14 . . . . . 119 F1
Dumbryden Gdns EH14. . . 119 F2
Dumbryden Gr EH14 . . . . . 119 E1
Dumbryden Ind Est EH14 119 F1
Dumbryden Rd EH14. . . . . 119 F1
Dumyat Ave FK10. . . . . 4 B2
Dumyat Dr FK1 . . . . 59 E3
Dumyat L Ctr FK11. . . . . 4 A7
Dumyat Rd Alva FK12. . . . . . 4 E6
Menstrie FK11. . . . . 3 F6
Stirling FK9 . . . . 2 C3
Dumyat Rise FK5 . . . . 38 C5
Dumyat St FK10. . . . . 4 F1
Dunard Gdn EH9. . . . . 121 D3
Dunavon Gdns FK6 . . . . 36 D4
DUNBAR 78 D1
Dunbar Ave FK5 . . . . 38 F4
Dunbar Gate FK6 . . . . 36 E3
Dunbar Gram Sch EH42. . . 78 B2
Dunbar L Pool EH42 . . . . . . 78 D3
Dunbar Pl KY2. . . . . 16 E5
Dunbar Prim Sch EH42 . . . 78 C2
Dunbar Rd
Haddington EH41 . . . . 101 B1
North Berwick EH39 . . . . . . 54 E6
Dunbar's Cl EH1 . . . . 229 B3
Dunbar St EH3. . . . . 228 B1
Dunbar Sta EH42 . . . . 78 E1
Dunbar Town House Mus★
EH42. . . . . 78 D2
Duncairn Ave FK4. . . . . 57 F6
Duncan Ave FK2. . . . . 39 B3
Duncan Buchanan Ct FK8 . . 2 A2
Duncan Cres KY11 . . . . 29 E2
Duncan Ct EH39 . . . . 54 A6
Duncan Gdns EH33 . . . . . . 126 C7
Duncan Gn EH54. . . . . 143 B7
Duncan Pl EH6 . . . . 94 A4
Duncanson Ave FK10. . . . . . 10 A8
Duncanson Dr KY3. . . . . 34 A1
Duncan St Bonnybridge FK4. 57 F5
Edinburgh EH9. . . . . 121 F4
Kirkcaldy KY2 . . . . 17 A4
Duncarron Ind Est FK6. . . . 36 F1
Duncarron Pl FK6. . . . . 36 E2
Duncrahill Cotts EH34. . . . 178 B8
Duncur Rd EH31 . . . . 52 C3
Dundaff Ct FK6 . . . . 36 D1
Dundarroch St FK5 . . . . 38 B1
Dundas Ave
North Berwick EH39 . . . . . . 54 C6
Queensferry EH30. . . . . 89 C8
Dundas Cotts FK4. . . . . 57 A2
Dundas Cres
Clackmannan FK10 . . . . 11 A4
Dalkeith EH22. . . . . 152 E2
Laurieston FK2 . . . . 61 A3
Dundas Gdns EH23. . . . . . . 174 B1
Dundas Gr EH22 . . . . 152 E2
Dundas Pk EH19 . . . . 173 C7
Dundas Pl EH29. . . . . 89 B2
Dundas Rd Dalkeith EH22. . 152 E2
Laurieston FK2 . . . . 61 A4
North Berwick EH39 . . . . . . 54 D6
Rosyth KY11 . . . . 67 D8
Stirling FK9 . . . . 2 B4
Dundas St Bathgate EH48. . 141 A8
Bo'ness EH51 . . . . 63 F7
Bonnyrigg and Lasswade
EH19. . . . . 173 C7
Edinburgh EH3. . . . . 228 C4
Grangemouth FK3 . . . . 61 C8
Lochgelly KY5 . . . . 14 B7
Townhill KY12 . . . . 29 C7
Dundee Ct 5 FK2. . . . . 60 A8
Dundee Pl FK2 . . . . 60 A8
Dundee St EH11 . . . . 228 A1
Dundee Terr EH11 . . . . 120 F5
Dundonald Rd KY11. . . . . . . 46 C3
Dundonald St EH3 . . . . 93 C2
Dundonnell Way KY11 . . . . 30 A1
Dundrennan Cotts EH16. . 122 C2
Dunearn Bank KY3. . . . . 33 D1
Dunearn Dr KY2 . . . . 16 F6
Dunearn Prim Sch KY2 . . . 16 E7
Dunedin Sch EH16. . . . . . . 122 A2
Dunedin St EH7. . . . . 93 D3
Dunelm Pk EH19. . . . . 173 C6
DUNFERMLINE. 29 C5
Dunfermline Abbey★
KY12. . . . . 28 F3
Dunfermline Bsns Ctr
KY11. . . . . 29 B1
Dunfermline Bsns Pk
KY11. . . . . 46 D5
Dunfermline High Sch
KY11. . . . . 29 B1
Dunfermline Mus★ KY12. . 29 B3
Dunfermline Queen Margaret
Sta KY12 . . . . 29 F5
Dunfermline Rd
Crossgates KY4. . . . . 30 E6
Limekilns KY11 . . . . 45 E4
Dunfermline Support Ctr 5
KY12. . . . . 29 A3
Dunfermline Town Sta
KY12. . . . . 29 B3
Dunfermline Wynd KY11 . . 47 A2
Dungavel La ML8 . . . . 215 B1
Dunglass Church★ TD13 . 218 E4
Dunimarle St KY12. . . . . 26 A2
DUNIPACE. 36 D4
Dunipace Cres KY12 . . . . . . 29 E5
Dunipace Prim Sch FK6. . . 36 D3
Dunkeld Pl FK2. . . . . 39 C1
Dunlaw Wynd EH16 . . . . . . 151 B6
Dunlin Brae EH54. . . . . 143 C5
Dunlin Dr KY11 . . . . 30 B4
Dunlop Ct EH54. . . . . 142 C5
Dunlop's Ct EH1 . . . . 228 C2
Dunlop Sq EH54 . . . . 142 D5
Dunlop Terr EH26. . . . . 192 A5
Dunmar Cres FK10. . . . . 4 E1
Dunmar Dr FK10. . . . . 4 E1
DUNMORE. 22 C7
Dunn Cres KY11 . . . . 29 E3
Dunnet Way EH52. . . . . 116 A6
Dunnikier Prim Sch KY2 . . 17 B5
Dunnikier Rd KY1. . . . . 17 C5
Dunnikier Way KY1 . . . . 17 B8
Dunning Pl FK2. . . . . 39 C1
Dunnottar Dr FK5. . . . . 38 F4
Dunnottar Pl KY2. . . . . 16 E4
Dunn Pl EH52. . . . . 87 E2
Dunn St EH52. . . . . 115 B5
Dunn Terr ML7 . . . . 159 F6
Dunollie Ct 2 EH12. . . . . . 119 B7
Dunollie Gdns EH41. . . . . . 130 C8
Dunpender Dr EH41. . . . . . 100 F1
Dunpender Rd EH40 . . . . . 103 C8
Dunrobin Ave FK5 . . . . 38 F5
Dunrobin Pl EH3. . . . . 93 B2
Dunrobin Rd KY2 . . . . 16 E4
Dunsapie Ct EH15. . . . . 122 D6
Dunsire St KY1 . . . . 17 E8
Dunsmuir Ct EH12 . . . . 119 D6
Duns Rd EH41 . . . . 220 F7
Dunster Rd FK9. . . . . 2 C3
Dunure Cres FK4 . . . . 58 A5
Dunure Pl KY2. . . . . 16 E4
Dunure St FK4. . . . . 58 A5
Dunvegan Ave
Kirkcaldy KY2 . . . . 16 D5
Stenhousemuir FK5. . . . . 38 F4
Dunvegan Ct Alloa FK10. . . . 10 B6
Crossford KY12 . . . . 28 B1
Edinburgh EH4. . . . . 91 B4
Dunvegan Dr Falkirk FK2. . . 39 C1
Stirling FK9 . . . . 2 B3
Dunvegan Gdns EH54 . . . . 164 E6
Dunvegan Pl
Bonnybridge FK4. . . . . 57 F6
Polmont FK2 . . . . 62 A1
Dura Rd ML2, ML7 . . . . 198 C5
Durar Dr EH4. . . . . 91 C1
Durham Ave
Bathgate EH48 . . . . 140 E6
Edinburgh EH15. . . . . 122 F7
Durham Bank EH19 . . . . . . 173 C6
Durham Dr Bathgate EH48 140 E6
Edinburgh EH15. . . . . 123 A6
Durham Gardens N EH15 123 A7
Durham Gardens S EH15 . 123 A6
Durham Gr
Bonnyrigg and Lasswade
EH19. . . . . 173 C6
Edinburgh EH15. . . . . 123 A7
Durham Pl EH19 . . . . 173 C6
Durham Place E EH15. . . . 123 A7
Durham Place La EH15. . . 123 A7
Durham Place W EH15 . . . 122 F7
Durham Rd EH15 . . . . 123 A7
Durham Road S EH15 . . . . 123 A6
Durham Sq EH15. . . . . 123 A7
Durham Terr
Edinburgh EH15. . . . . 122 F7
Newmills KY12 . . . . 26 C1
Durie Pk KY3 . . . . 50 D8
Durie Pl KY11. . . . . 29 F4
Durie's Pk EH33 . . . . 126 B1
Durwood Gr EH16. . . . . 122 B2
Dury Way EH21 . . . . 125 A5
Dyfrig St ML7. . . . . 179 E5
Dyke Brow ML7. . . . . 160 A6
Dyke Ct ML7. . . . . 160 A6
DYKEHEAD 179 D5
Dykehead Prim Sch ML7 179 E5
Dyke Rd ML7 . . . . 160 A6
Dykeside Rd EH48 . . . . 140 F8
Dykes Rd EH26 . . . . 191 E7
Dymond Gr KY11. . . . . 46 F8
DYSART. 18 B7
Dysart Prim Sch KY1 . . . . . 18 A7
Dysart Rd KY1 . . . . 17 F6
Dysart View KY1 . . . . 18 B8

E

Eagle Brae EH54. . . . . 143 D4
Eagle Rock★ EH4. . . . . 91 A7
Eagles View EH54. . . . . 114 C1
Eardley Cres KY11 . . . . 47 A7
Eardley Pl 1 FK5 . . . . 38 B2
Earl Grey St EH3. . . . . 228 B2
Earl Haig Gdns EH5 . . . . 93 B5
Earl of Mar Ct FK10 . . . . 10 B6
Earlsburn Ave FK7 . . . . 7 A3
Earls Ct FK10 . . . . 10 B5
Earl's Gate Rdbt FK3. . . . . . 61 A7
Earlshill Dr FK7. . . . . 7 F1
Earls Pl EH47 . . . . 181 E6
Earl's Rd FK3 . . . . 61 B8
Earlston Pl 3 EH7 . . . . 94 A1
Earn Ct Alloa FK10. . . . . 10 C6
Grangemouth FK3. . . . . 61 D5
Earn Gr KY11 . . . . 29 F4
Earn Pl FK6. . . . . 57 D6
Earn Rd KY11. . . . . 17 D8
Earn Terr ML7 . . . . 179 E6
Earthship Fife & Ecology
Ctr★ KY3. . . . . 34 D4
East Adam St EH8. . . . . 229 B2
East Albert Rd KY1. . . . . 17 C5
East Ave KY12 . . . . 26 A7
East Baldridge Dr KY12 . . . 28 E5
East Bankton Pl EH54 . . . . 164 F7
East Barnton Ave EH4. . . . . . 91 E3
East Barnton Gdns EH4 . . . 91 E3
East Bay KY11 . . . . 68 C5
East Boreland Pl FK6 . . . . . . 36 D3
East Bridge St FK1. . . . . 60 C4
East Brighton Cres EH15 . 123 A8
East Broomhill Rd KY3 . . . . 50 E8
East Broughton Pl 8 EH3 93 D2
East Burn Ct KY1 . . . . 17 D7
Eastburn Dr FK1. . . . . 60 C4
Eastburn Twr FK1. . . . . 60 C4
East Caiystane Pl EH10. . . 150 A5
East Caiystane Rd EH10 . . 150 B5

EAST CALDER............144 F3
East Calder Prim Sch
  EH53..................144 F4
East Campbell Ct EH32...98 D5
East Camus Pl EH10.....150 A6
East Camus Rd EH10....150 A6
East Castle Rd EH10.....121 A5
East Castle St FK10......10 B5
East Champanyie EH16..121 E3
East Clapperfield EH16..122 A1
East Claremont St EH7...93 D3
East Comiston EH10.....150 A6
EAST CRAIGS............119 A7
East Craigs Prim Sch
  EH12..................119 B8
East Craigs Rigg EH12..119 A7
East Craigs Wynd EH12.119 A7
East Croft EH28.........117 E2
Eastcroft EH54.........142 F3
Eastcroft Dr FK2.........62 A2
Eastcroft St FK5.........38 B1
East Cromwell St........93 F6
East Crosscauseway EH8 229 B1
East Ct
  Edinburgh, Greendykes
  EH16.................122 C3
  [1] Edinburgh, Ravelston
  EH4..................92 C1
East Dr Dunfermline KY12.29 B3
  Stenhousemuir FK5......38 C1
East End EH55...........163 D3
East End Park (Dunfermline
  Athletic FC) KY12.....229 C4
EASTER ABERDOUR.......49 C8
Easter Bankton EH54....165 A8
Easter Belmont Rd EH12 120 B8
Easter Broomhouse Cotts
  EH42.................106 D7
Easter Carmuirs Prim Sch
  FK1...................59 B6
Easter Cornton Rd FK9...2 B4
Easter Craiglockhart Hill
  Nature Reserve★ EH10 120 E1
Easter Currie Cres EH14.148 A5
Easter Currie Ct EH14...148 A5
Easter Currie Pl EH14...148 A5
Easter Currie Terr EH14.148 A5
Easter Dalry Dr [2] EH11.120 F6
Easter Dalry Pl [3] EH11.120 F6
Easter Dalry Rd EH11...120 F6
Easter Dalry Rigg [1]
  EH11.................120 F6
Easter Dalry Wynd EH11.120 F7
Easter Drylaw Ave EH4...92 C3
Easter Drylaw Bank EH4.92 C3
Easter Drylaw Dr EH4....92 C3
Easter Drylaw Gdns EH4.92 C3
Easter Drylaw Gr EH4....92 C3
Easter Drylaw Loan EH4.92 C3
Easter Drylaw Pl EH4....92 C3
Easter Drylaw View EH4.92 C4
Easter Drylaw Way EH4..92 C3
Easter Ferrygate Pk EH39 53 E7
Easterfield Ct EH54......143 C3
Easter Haugh EH13.....149 E7
Easter Hermitage EH6....94 B3
EASTER HOWGATE.......171 A5
Easter Inch Moss & Seafield
  Law Nature Reserve★
  EH47.................142 A2
Easter Inch Rd EH48....141 D2
Easter Inch Steadings
  EH48.................141 D1
Easter Langside Ave
  EH22.................153 D3
Easter Langside Pl EH22 153 D3
Easter Livilands EH7.......7 C4
EASTER MILLERHILL.....152 E8
Eastern Ind Est EH15...123 C4
Easter Park Dr EH4.......91 E4
EASTER PENCAITLAND...156 F5
Easter Rd Broxburn EH52 115 F5
  Edinburgh, Hillside EH7..93 E2
  Edinburgh, South Leith EH7 94 A4
  Shotts ML7...........179 D5
Easter Road Stadium
  (Hibernian FC)★ EH7..94 A2
Easter Steil EH10........120 F1
Easterton Cres FK7......20 E7
Easterton Dr FK7........20 E7
Easterton Gr FK7........20 E7
Easterton Gdns EH48...139 E6
Eastertoun Prim Sch
  EH48.................139 E6
Easter Warriston EH7....93 C4
East Farm of Gilmerton
  EH17.................151 E6
East Fenton Farm Cotts
  EH39..................73 C8
East Fergus Pl KY1.......17 B3
East Fettes Ave EH4......92 F3
EASTFIELD Harthill.....159 C4
  Penicuik.............191 F6
Eastfield EH15..........123 F7
Eastfield Cotts
  Penicuik EH26........191 F7
  Stenton EH41.........104 B1
Eastfield Farm Rd EH26.191 F7
Eastfield Gdns EH15....123 F7
Eastfield Ind Est EH26..191 F6
Eastfield Loan EH33....152 B1
Eastfield Park Rd EH26..191 F6
Eastfield Pl EH15.......123 F7
Eastfield Rd Carluke ML8..215 A1
  Fauldhouse EH47......181 F7
  North Berwick EH39....54 D6
  Ratho Station EH28...118 A6

Eastfield View EH47.....181 F7
EAST FORTUNE..........74 B3
East Fountainbridge EH3 228 B2
East Garleton Cotts
  EH39.................100 F6
Eastgate KY3............34 F3
East Glen Ave EH54.....142 E6
East Harbour Rd KY11....45 B3
EAST HERMISTON.......119 A1
East Hermitage Pl EH6....94 A4
EASTHOUSES...........174 C7
Easthouses Ct EH22....174 C8
Easthouses Ind Est EH22 174 D8
Easthouses Pl EH22.....153 C1
Easthouses Rd
  Dalkeith EH22........153 C1
  Easthouses EH22......174 C7
Easthouses Way EH22...153 C1
East Kilngate Pl EH17...151 D5
East Kilngate Rigg EH17.151 D5
East Kilngate Wynd
  EH17.................151 D5
East Leven St KY3.......50 E8
East Lillyput EH5........93 B5
East Link Rd FK9........2 D5
East Links Family Pk★
  EH42..................77 D2
East Links Rd Dunbar EH42 78 E2
  Gullane EH31..........52 A2
EAST LINTON..........103 C7
East Linton Prim Sch
  EH40.................103 D7
East Linton Station Ind Site
  EH40.................103 D7
East Loan EH33..........97 A1
East London St EH7......93 D2
East Lorimer Pl EH32....97 C4
East Mains FK11..........4 A6
East Mains Ind Est FK2 116 B6
East Mains of Ingliston
  EH28.................118 A6
East Main St
  Armadale EH48.......140 A6
  Blackburn EH47.......162 D7
  Broxburn EH52........115 F5
  Harthill ML7..........159 F5
  Uphall EH52...........115 A4
  Whitburn EH47........161 B7
East March St KY1........17 E7
East Market St EH8.....229 B3
East Mayfield EH9.......121 F4
East Meikle Pinkerton Cotts
  EH42.................107 C4
East Mill Rd EH49........84 D7
East Montgomery Pl [3]
  EH7...................93 F2
East Murrayfield EH12....7 E1
East Newington Pl EH9..121 F5
East Norton Pl EH7.......93 F1
Easton Ct FK8............2 B2
Easton Dr FK1...........81 D7
Easton Rd EH48.........140 F7
East Parkside EH16.....229 C1
East Pier St EH51........63 E5
East Pilton Farm Ave EH5 92 E5
East Pilton Farm Rigg
  EH5...................92 E5
East Pilton Farm Wynd
  EH5...................92 F5
East Plean Prim Sch FK7 20 C3
East Port KY12...........29 A4
East Port Ave EH41.....130 B6
East Preston St EH8....121 F5
East Preston Street La [6]
  EH8.................121 E5
East Quality St KY1......18 A7
East Queensway EH26..191 F7
East Rd Grangemouth FK3..62 C5
  North Berwick EH39....54 D7
East Restalrig Terr EH6...94 A4
EAST SALTOUN.........157 E4
East Savile Rd EH16....121 F3
East Sciennes St [3] EH9 121 E5
East Scotland Street La [1]
  EH3...................93 D2
East Seaside EH32.......96 F2
East Stirling St FK12.....5 B7
East Suffolk Rd EH16...122 A3
East Telferton EH7........94 F1
East Terr EH30...........68 C1
East Toll KY3............33 E1
East Trinity Rd EH5......93 C6
East Vennel FK10........10 B6
East Vows Wlk KY1.......35 B7
East Way KY1............48 C5
East Werberside EH4......92 E4
East Werberside Pl EH4..92 E4
East Whitefield KY12.....29 F6
Eastwood Pk
  Fauldhouse EH47.....181 F7
  Livingston EH54.......143 A7
Ebenezer Pl FK1.........81 F5
Eccles Ct FK7.............7 A4
ECCLESMACHAN.........113 E4
Ecclesmachan Rd EH52 114 F5
Eccles Pl FK3............83 A5
Echline EH30............88 F8
Echline Ave EH30........89 A8
Echline Dr EH30.........67 F1
Echline Gdns EH30......67 F1
Echline Gn EH30.........67 F1
Echline Gr EH30.........68 A1
Echline Pk EH30.........88 F8
Echline Pl EH30..........68 A1
Echline Prim Sch [1] EH30 68 A1
Echline Rigg EH30........68 A1
Echline Terr EH30........89 A8

Echline View EH30........89 A8
Echobank KY11..........47 B2
Eden Dr EH54...........144 B4
Edenhall Bank EH21....124 C5
Edenhall Cres EH21....124 C4
Edenhall Ct EH21.......124 C4
Edenhall Hospl EH21...124 C4
Edenhall Rd EH21......124 C4
Eden La EH10...........121 B3
Eden Rd Alloa FK10.......9 F8
  Dunfermline KY11......29 E2
Edgar St KY12............29 A3
Edgefield Pl EH20.......172 C8
Edgefield Rd EH20......151 C1
Edgefield Road Ind Est
  EH20.................172 C8
EDGEHEAD..............175 C7
Edgehead Rd EH37.....175 C7
Edina Pl EH7............94 A2
Edina St EH7.............93 F2
EDINBURGH............228 C3
Edinburgh Acad (Prep Sch)
  EH3...................93 A4
Edinburgh Acad The EH3 93 B2
Edinburgh Airport EH12 118 B8
Edinburgh Butterfly & Insect
  World★ EH18........152 C2
Edinburgh Castle★ EH1.228 C3
Edinburgh Coll of Art
  EH3.................228 C2
Edinburgh Int Climbing
  Arena EH28..........117 B2
Edinburgh Napier Univ
  (Comely Bank Campus)
  EH4...................92 F2
Edinburgh Napier Univ
  (Craighouse Campus)
  EH11.................120 C2
Edinburgh Napier Univ
  (Craiglockhart Campus)
  EH14.................120 D1
Edinburgh Napier Univ
  (Marchmont Campus)
  EH9..................121 D5
Edinburgh Napier Univ
  (Merchiston Campus)
  EH10.................121 A4
Edinburgh Park Sta
  EH11.................119 A3
Edinburgh Pk EH12....118 F5
Edinburgh Pk EH12....119 A4
Edinburgh Playhouse The★
  EH1.................229 B4
Edinburgh Quay EH3...228 B1
Edinburgh Rd
  Bathgate EH48.......141 C5
  Carlops EH46.........206 B1
  Cockenzie & Port Seton
  EH32..................97 B3
  Dalkeith EH22........153 A3
  Harthill ML7..........159 C5
  Linlithgow EH49.......85 B7
  Musselburgh EH21....124 A6
  Newbridge EH28......112 A6
  Penicuik EH26........192 A8
  South Queensferry EH30 68 C1
  Tranent EH33.........126 B6
  West Barns EH42.......77 F1
Edinburgh Rudolf Steiner
  Sch EH10............120 F4
Edinburgh Sch of Agriculture
  EH9...................92 C6
Edinburgh's Telford Coll
  EH5...................92 C6
Edinburgh Technopole
  EH26.................171 B4
Edinburgh Waverley Sta
  EH1.................229 A3
Edinburgh West Off Pk
  EH12.................119 A4
Edinburgh Zoo (Royal
  Zoological Society of
  Scotland)★ EH12....119 F7
Edington Cottage Hospl
  EH39..................54 C7
Edington Pl KY1.........18 B8
EDMONSTONE..........152 B8
Edmonstone Ave EH22.152 B8
Edmonstone Dr EH22..152 B8
Edmonstone Rd EH22..152 B8
Edmonstone Terr EH22.152 B8
Edmonton Ave EH54...143 F4
Edward Ave
  Stenhousemuir FK5....38 C4
  Stirling FK8...........2 C1
Edward Pl FK2............39 F3
Edward Rd FK8...........32 B3
Edwards Ct EH41.......129 F8
Edward St
  Dunfermline KY12......29 B5
  Kirkcaldy KY2.........17 B7
Edzell Way KY11.........30 A1
Eglingtoun Dr KY12.....28 F6
Eglinton Cres EH12....120 F7
Eglinton Pl KY11.........47 D2
Egypt Mews KY11.......121 C3
Eighth St EH22.........174 B5
Eildon St EH3............93 C3
Eildon Terr EH3.........93 C4
Eilean La KY12..........26 E1
Eildon Terr EH51........63 E7
Elbe St EH6.............94 A5
Elcho Ct EH32..........98 F3
Elcho Pl EH32..........97 C4
Elcho Rd EH32..........98 E5
Elcho Terr Aberlady EH32.71 C4
  Edinburgh EH15.......123 C8

Elcho Terr continued
  Longniddry EH32......98 E5
Elder Ct [6] EH33......126 C6
Elder Pl KY11...........46 E5
Elderslie Dr FK2.........82 B7
Elder St Dunbar EH42...78 B1
  Edinburgh EH1........229 A4
  Tranent EH33.........126 C7
Elder Street E EH1.....229 A4
ELDINDEAN............173 C8
Eldindean Ct KY12......28 D6
Eldindean Pl EH19.....173 B8
Eldindean Rd EH19....173 C8
Eldindean Terr EH19...173 C8
Eldin Ind Est EH20.....151 C2
Eldin Pl FK2............93 F2
Eldrick Ave EH47.......181 E5
Eldrick Cres EH47......181 D5
Eldrick La EH47........181 D6
Eldrick View EH47......181 E5
Electra Pl EH15..........95 A1
Elgin Ct KY12...........29 A2
Elgin Pl FK7.............7 C3
Elgin Pl FK1............60 C8
Elgin St Dunfermline KY12.29 A2
  Edinburgh EH7........93 F2
  Kirkcaldy KY2.........17 B6
Elgin Street N EH7......93 F2
Elgin Terr EH7..........93 F2
Elgol Path ML7.........180 B3
ELIBURN...............143 A5
Eliburn North Rdbt EH54 143 B6
Eliburn Rd EH54.......143 B4
Eliburn South Rd EH54.143 C4
Elie Ave EH54..........142 F5
Elim Dr FK1.............81 C6
Elizabeth Ave
  Grangemouth FK3......61 E8
  Stenhousemuir FK5....38 C2
Elizabeth Cres FK5......59 B6
Elizabeth Ct EH47......141 F6
Elizabeth Gdns EH47...162 B2
Elizabeth La EH48......141 F6
Elizabeth St
  Dunfermline KY11......29 D2
  Stirling FK8............7 A5
Elizabeth Wlk KY12......23 B4
Ellaleon Gr KY12.........28 B1
Ellangowan Terr EH16..122 C1
Ellen's Glen Loan EH17.151 C7
Ellen's Glen Rd EH17...151 C6
Ellen St EH41...........161 B7
Ellersly Rd EH12.......120 C7
Elliot Gdns EH14......149 C8
Elliothill St KY11........29 B2
Elliot Pk EH14.........149 C8
Elliot Pl Edinburgh EH14.149 C8
  [5] Larbert FK5........38 B2
Elliot Rd EH14.........149 C8
Elliot St Dunfermline KY11..29 B2
  Edinburgh EH7........93 F2
Elliot Terr FK2..........60 A8
Ellis Pl EH52...........115 B5
Ellon Pl KY12...........29 D6
Ellon Rd KY2............16 C7
Elmbank FK11............4 A6
Elmbank Cres FK4.......57 D6
Elmbank Rd FK3..........7 A3
Elmbank St FK3.........61 C6
Elm Ct EH47............162 B8
Elm Dr FK2..............61 A2
Elmfield Ct EH22.......153 A3
Elmfield Pk EH22......153 A3
Elmfield Rd EH22......153 A3
Elm Gr Blackburn EH47..162 E8
  Dunfermline KY11......46 C8
  Livingston EH54......144 B5
  Stenhousemuir FK5....38 D1
Elm Pk EH47...........162 B8
Elm Pl Edinburgh EH6....94 B4
  Kirkcaldy KY2.........16 F5
  Mayfield EH22.........174 D6
Elm Rd EH48............141 E6
Elm Row
  Bonnyrigg and Lasswade
  EH18.................152 B1
  Edinburgh EH7.........93 E2
Elm Sq EH47............161 C6
Elm St Dunbar EH42......78 B1
  Stirling FK8............1 E1
Elm Terr EH47..........162 B8
Elmwood Pk EH54......142 F7
Elmwood Rd ML7.......180 B2
Elmwood Terr EH6......94 B3
ELPHINSTONE..........126 B1
Elphinstone Cres FK2...22 E4
Elphinstone Ct [2] EH33 126 C6
Elphinstone Prim Sch
  EH33.................126 B1
Elphinstone Rd EH33...126 B5
Elphinstone Sq EH54...142 C6
Elphinstone St FK10.....23 E4
Elphinstone Tower Farm
  Cotts EH33...........125 F1
Elphinstone Wlk [8]
  EH33.................126 C6
Elpin FK10..............10 D5
Eltringham Gdns EH14..120 C4
Eltringham Gr EH14....120 C4
Eltringham Terr EH14..120 C4
Emily Ct EH23..........174 C2
Emily Pl EH23..........174 D1
Emma's Way FK4........57 F5
Empire Gate ML7......179 F4
Empire St EH6..........94 A5
Endrick Ct FK5..........38 C5

EAS-Ett 241

Endrick Dr FK6..........57 E6
Endrick Pl FK7...........7 A4
Engelen Dr FK10.........10 B5
Engine Gn The FK10......5 D3
Engine La EH48.........141 B6
Engine Pl [3] EH48.....141 A6
Engine Rd
  Gorebridge EH23......174 B1
  Loanhead EH20.......172 C8
Ennis Ct EH55..........163 E4
Ennis Pk EH55..........163 E5
Enterprise Ctr EH20...172 A7
Enterprise Way KY11....46 E6
Entryfoot EH48.........137 F2
ENTRY HEAD...........146 E7
Eppiestane Rd EH47...161 C6
Epworth Gdns FK2......82 B8
Erbach Ave FK2.........61 B4
Ercall Rd FK2...........82 E8
Erica Gr KY11...........46 E8
Ericht Pl ML7...........179 E6
Eriskay Ct FK1..........60 C2
Erngath Rd EH51........64 A7

Erskine Beveridge Ct
  KY11.................29 B2
Erskine Brae KY12.......25 F3
Erskine Gdns ML7......179 D5
Erskine Hill FK2.........61 E1
Erskine Loan EH31.......52 A3
Erskine Pl
  Clackmannan FK10.....10 F5
  Mid Calder EH53......144 C6
Erskine Rd Broxburn EH52 115 C6
  Gullane EH31...........52 A3
Erskine Sq KY11.........29 C2
Erskine St Alloa FK10....10 D7
  Alva FK12..............5 A7
  Lochgelly KY5.........14 A6
Erskine Way
  Livingston EH54.......143 D8
  Shotts ML7............179 E4
Erskine Wynd KY12......27 A7
Esdaile Bank EH9.......121 D4
Esdaile Pk EH9.........121 D4
ESKBANK..............152 F2
Eskbank Ct EH22.......152 E2
Eskbank Rdbt
  Bonnyrigg and Lasswade
  EH22.................173 D8
  Dalkeith EH22.........152 F2
Eskbank Terr EH22.....152 F2
Eskdaill Ct [1] EH22...153 A3
Eskdaill St EH22.......153 A3
Eskdale Ct EH19........173 A7
Eskdale Dr EH19........173 A7
Eskdale Mews EH21....124 C6
Eskdale Terr EH19......173 A7
Esk Dr EH54...........144 B4
Eskfield Gr EH22.......152 D2
Esk Glades EH22.......153 B4
ESKGROVE............172 F8
Eskgrove Dr EH25......171 E6
Eskhill EH26...........191 F5
Eskmill Rd EH26.......191 F5
Eskmills EH21..........124 B5
Esk Pl EH22............152 F3
Eskside Ct EH22........152 F4
Eskside E EH21.........124 C6
Eskside W EH21........124 C6
Eskvale Cres EH26.....192 A5
Eskvale Ct EH26........192 A5
Eskvale Dr EH26........192 A5
Eskvale View EH26.....192 A6
Eskview Ave FK2.........38 D1
Eskview Cres EH21.....124 B5
Eskview Cres FK2.......38 D1
Eskview Gr Dalkeith EH22 152 F3
  Musselburgh EH21....124 B5
Eskview Rd Mayfield EH22 174 D6
  Musselburgh EH21....124 B5
Eskview Terr EH21.....124 B5
Eskview Villas FK2......152 F2
Esmonde Ct KY11.......46 E2
Esplanade Edinburgh EH1.228 C3
  Kirkcaldy KY1..........17 C2
  [1] Stirling FK8........7 A8
Esplanade Terr EH15...123 D8
Essendean Pl EH4......91 D1
Essendean Terr EH4....91 A4
Essex Brae EH4..........91 A4
Essex Pk EH4............91 A4
Essex Rd EH4...........91 A4
Esslemont Rd EH16....122 A2
Estate Ave FK1...........60 C4
Ethel Terr EH10........121 A2
Etive Ct Dalgety Bay KY11..48 A2
  Stirling FK8............2 B3
Etive Way FK2............2 A2
Etive Wlk Livingston EH54.144 A4
  Shotts ML7............179 E4
Etna Ct EH48...........140 B5
Etna Ct FK2............60 D7
Etna Rd FK2............60 D7
Etna Road Rdbt FK2.....60 E7
Eton Terr EH4..........228 A4
Ettrick Cres KY11.......48 A4
Ettrick Ct Falkirk FK1....60 C1
  Grangemouth FK3......61 F6
Ettrickdale Pl EH3.......93 B3
Ettrick Dr EH54.........144 B4
Ettrick Gr EH11.........121 A5
Ettrick Loan EH10......120 F4
Ettrick Rd EH10........120 F4

Evans Gdns EH19 .... 173 D8
Evans St FK5 .... 38 C3
Eva Pl EH9 .... 121 E2
Evelyn Terr EH10 .... 171 C1
Everard Rise EH54 .... 144 A2
Evergreen Trailer Ct FK6 .. 37 A2
Evershed Ct KY11 .... 29 E1
Evershed Dr KY11 .... 29 E1
Ewart Ave EH48 .... 140 A5
Ewart Gr EH51 .... 63 F5
Eweford Cotts EH42 .. 106 B8
Ewerland EH4 .... 91 A4
Ewing Ave FK2 .... 60 B7
Ewing Ct FK7 .... 7 C3
Ewing Dr FK2 .... 60 B7
Ewing Pl FK2 .... 60 B7
Ewing St Cowdenbeath KY4 . 13 B2
Lochgelly KY5 .... 14 A6
Penicuik EH26 .... 191 F7
Ewingston Mill Steading
EH36 .... 220 B3
Ewington Pl EH47 .... 162 B2
Excise La KY11 .... 23 E3
Excise St FK10 .... 23 E4
Exmouth St EH54 .... 144 A5
Eyre Cres EH3 .... 93 C2
Eyre Pl EH3 .... 93 C2
Eyre Place La EH3 .... 93 C2
Eyre Terr EH3 .... 93 C2

F

FACTOR'S PARK 120 C5
Factory Rd Bathgate EH48 140 F4
Cowdenbeath KY4 .... 13 D4
Kirkcaldy KY1 .... 17 D6
Fair-A-Far EH4 .... 91 B5
Fair-A-Far Cotts EH4 .. 91 B5
Fair-A-Far Shot EH4 .. 91 B5
Fairbairn Pl EH54 .... 143 C3
Fairbairn Rd EH54 .... 143 C3
Fairbrae EH11 .... 119 F3
Fairfax Ct KY3 .... 33 F1
FAIRFIELD 5 B2
Fairfield Alloa FK10 .... 5 C1
Livingston EH54 .... 143 A3
Fairfield Rd FK4 .... 58 A6
Fairfield Pl FK2 .... 60 C5
Fairfields FK2 .... 21 E5
Fairfield Sch FK10 .... 5 B1
Fairford Gdns EH16 .. 122 B1
Fairgreen Pl FK7 .... 19 E8
Fairhaven Terr FK2 .... 62 A8
Fairhill Rd FK7 .... 7 B1
Fairinsfell EH52 .... 115 B5
Fair Isle Prim Sch KY2 .. 16 E8
Fair Isle Rd KY2 .... 16 E8
Fairley Ct KY12 .... 27 D1
Fairley Dr FK5 .... 38 A3
Fairlie Dr FK1 .... 59 D5
Fairlie Gdns FK1 .... 59 D5
Fairlie St FK1 .... 59 C5
Fairmile Ave EH10 .. 150 B5
FAIRMILEHEAD 150 B5
Fairmont Pk EH47 .... 160 F6
Fairmount Dr FK10 .... 5 B2
Fair Pl KY11 .... 47 B3
Fairspark Terr EH51 .... 63 E5
Fairview Rd EH12, EH28.. 117 F7
Fairway EH41 .... 129 E8
Fairways KY12 .... 29 B6
Fairways Ave FK2 .... 82 F6
Fairways Bsns Pk EH54 . 114 D1
Fairways Pl FK4 .... 58 B7
Fairway The KY1 .... 17 F8
Fairyburn Rd KY10 .... 9 F8
Fairy Fa' Cres KY4 .... 30 F6
Fairykirk Rd KY11 .... 47 A3
Faith Mission Coll The ■
EH17 .... 151 E6
FALA 224 C7
Falahill Cotts EH38 .. 214 B4
Falcon Ave EH10 .... 121 B3
Falcon Brae EH54 .. 143 D5
Falcon Ct EH10 .... 121 B3
Falcon Dr FK5 .... 38 B3
Falconer Ct FK7 .... 7 C3
Falconer Rise EH54 .. 144 A2
Falcon Gdns EH10 .... 121 B3
Falcon Rd EH10 .... 121 B3
Falcon Road W EH10.. 121 B3
Falcons The EH31 .... 52 B3
FALKIRK 60 D6
Falkirk & District Royal Infmy
FK1 .... 60 A4
Falkirk Grahamston Sta
FK1 .... 60 B5
Falkirk High Sch FK1 .. 59 E4
Falkirk High Sta FK1 .. 60 A3
Falkirk Rd Bannockburn FK7. 19 F8
Bonnybridge FK4 .... 58 C2
Cowie FK7 .... 20 A6
Falkirk FK2, FK3 .... 60 F6
Falkirk, Glen Village FK1.. 60 B1
Larbert FK5 .... 38 B1
Linlithgow EH49 .... 84 E7
Falkland Gdns EH10 .. 93 E1
Falkland Pl FK5 .... 38 E4
Falla Hill EH47 .... 181 D6
Falla Hill Prim Sch EH47 181 D6
Fallas Pl EH47 .... 181 D5

Fallhills Ct EH26 .... 192 C1
FALLIN 8 C4
Fallin Prim Sch FK7 .. 8 C5
Fallodon Cres KY2 .... 17 A3
FALSIDE 140 E5
Falside Cres EH48 .... 140 E5
Falside Dr EH48 .... 140 E5
Falside Terr EH48 .... 140 E5
Faraday Pl EH55 .... 162 E2
Farm Ave EH18 .... 172 F6
Farm Cotts EH21 .... 125 C5
Farmer's Bldgs EH37 .. 176 B5
Farm Pl EH54 .... 143 A3
Farm Rd Cowdenbeath KY4.. 13 B3
Cowie FK7 .... 20 D8
Crombie KY12 .... 44 D6
Fallin FK7 .... 8 D4
Roslin EH25 .... 192 F6
Farm Row KY12 .... 30 B6
Farm St FK2 .... 39 A1
Farmstead Rd KY11 .... 47 F4
Farmstead Way EH51 .... 64 C6
Farne Ct KY2 .... 16 F8
Farnell Way KY12 .... 29 D6
Farquharson Way FK1 .. 59 F1
Farquhar Sq EH48 .. 138 C3
Farquhar Terr EH30.. 68 A1
Farrer Gr EH7 .... 94 E1
Farrer Terr EH7 .... 94 F1
Farrier Ct EH47 .... 94 F2
Fa'side Ave ⁑ EH33.. 126 D5
Fa'side Avenue Ct EH21.. 125 B4
Fa'side Avenue N EH21.. 125 B4
Fa'side Avenue S EH21.. 125 B4
Fa'side Bldgs EH21 .. 125 B4
Fa'side Cres
⁑ Tranent EH33 .... 126 D5
Wallyford EH21 .... 125 B4
Fa'side Dr EH21 .... 125 B4
Fa'side Gdns EH21 .. 125 B4
Fa'side Rd EH33 .... 126 D5
Fa'side Terr EH21 .... 125 B4
Fa'side View EH33 .. 126 B4
FAUCHELDEAN 87 F1
Fauldburn EH12 .... 91 B1
Fauldburn Pk EH12 .. 91 B1
FAULDHOUSE 181 E5
Fauldhouse Bsns Ctr
EH47 .... 181 D4
Fauldhouse Rd EH47.. 161 B2
Fauldhouse Sta EH47.. 181 C5
Featherhall Ave EH12 .. 119 D6
Featherhall Crescent N
EH12 .... 119 D6
Featherhall Crescent S
EH12 .... 119 D6
Featherhall Gr EH12.. 119 D6
Featherhall Pl EH12.. 119 D6
Featherhall Rd EH12.. 119 D6
Featherhall Terr EH12.. 119 D6
Fell's Rd EH55 .... 163 F5
Fells Rigg EH54 .... 143 A7
Fendoch Rd FK3 .... 61 F7
FENTON BARNS 73 B8
Fenton Barns Farm Cotts
EH39 .... 73 A8
Fenton Barns Ret Village
EH39 .... 53 A1
Fenton St FK10 .... 10 A7
Fentoun Gait EH31.. 52 C2
Fereglan FK10 .... 23 E4
Fergus Ave EH54 .... 143 F4
Ferguson Ct EH21.. 124 C3
Ferguson Dr Denny FK6.. 36 D1
Falkirk FK2 .... 39 A5
Musselburgh EH21 .. 124 B3
Ferguson Gdns EH21.. 124 C3
Ferguson Gn EH21.. 124 B3
Ferguson Gr FK4 .... 58 B6
Ferguson Pl KY3 .... 33 F1
Ferguson Rd KY11 .... 47 A7
Ferguson St FK8 .... 1 F2
Ferguson View EH21.. 124 B3
Ferguson Way
Livingston EH54 .... 143 D8
Newtongrange EH22.. 174 B4
Fergus Pl KY11 .... 29 D1
Fergusson Rd EH52.. 115 E5
Fergus Wynd KY1 .... 17 B1
Fernbank Cornton FK9.. 2 B3
Livingston EH54 .... 143 E5
FERNIEHILL 151 E7
Ferniehill Ave EH17.. 151 E6
Ferniehill Dr EH17 .. 151 E6
Ferniehill Gdns EH17.. 151 F7
Ferniehill Gr EH17 .. 151 F7
Ferniehill Pl EH17 .. 151 E6
Ferniehill Rd EH17 .. 151 E6
Ferniehill Sq EH17.. 151 E6
Ferniehill Terr EH17.. 151 E6
Ferniehill Way EH17.. 151 F7
Fernielaw Ave EH13.. 149 A5
Fernie Pl KY12 .... 28 E5
Fernieside Ave EH17.. 151 E8
Fernieside Cres EH17.. 151 F8
Fernieside Dr EH17.. 151 E8
Fernieside Gdns EH17.. 151 E8
Fernieside Gr EH17.. 151 E8
Fernieside Pl EH17.. 151 E8
Fernlea EH52 .... 114 F5
Fern Lea Gr FK2 .... 39 C3
Ferrard Rd KY12 .... 17 A4
Ferrier Cres EH48.. 140 A6
Ferris Way KY11 .... 48 B4
Ferrybarns Ct KY11.. 68 B6
Ferryburn Gn EH30.. 89 C8
Ferry Ct FK9 .... 2 A3

Ferryfield EH5 .... 93 A4
Ferry Gait Cres EH4.. 92 A4
Ferry Gait Dr EH4.. 92 A4
Ferry Gait Gdns ⁑ EH4 .. 92 A4
Ferry Gait Pl EH4 .. 92 A4
Ferry Gait Wlk ⁑ EH4.. 92 A4
Ferrygate Cottages EH39.. 53 C6
Ferryhill Prim Sch EH4.. 92 C3
Ferryhill Rd
Inverkeithing KY11 .... 47 B1
North Queensferry KY11.. 68 B7
Ferry La KY11 .... 68 B6
Ferry Muir EH30 .... 89 B7
Ferrymuir Gait EH30.. 89 B8
Ferrymuir La EH30.. 89 B8
Ferrymuir Rd EH30.. 89 B8
Ferry Orch FK9 .... 2 D1
Ferry Rd
Edinburgh, Drylaw EH4,
EH5.. .... 92 D4
Edinburgh, Trinity EH5.. 93 C5
North Queensferry KY11.. 68 B6
South Alloa FK7.. .... 9 F4
Stirling FK9 .... 2 D1
Ferry Road Ave EH4.. 92 C4
Ferry Road Dr EH4.. 92 D5
Ferry Road Gdns EH4.. 92 C4
Ferry Road Gr EH4.. 92 C4
Ferry Road Pl EH4.. 92 C4
Ferry Toll Pl KY11.. 46 E1
Ferry Toll Rd KY11.. 46 E1
Festival Sq EH3 .... 228 B2
Festival Theatre * EH8.. 229 A2
Fetteresk Cotts EH26.. 191 E4
Fettes Ave EH4 .... 92 F2
Fettes Coll EH4.. .... 92 F3
Fettes Rise EH4 .... 92 E2
Fettes Row EH3 .... 93 C2
Fiddich Dr EH4.. .... 164 E5
Fidra Ave Burntisland KY3 .. 33 D1
Dirleton EH39 .... 53 B5
Fidra Ct EH39.. .... 53 F7
Fidra Rd EH39 .... 54 A7
Fieldfare View KY11.. 30 A3
Fife Coll (Priory Campus)
KY11 .... 17 C5
Fife Leisure Pk KY11.. 30 C5
Fife Pl KY11 .... 46 B2
Fifth St EH22 .... 174 B5
Figgate Bank EH15.. 95 B1
Figgate La EH15 .... 95 B1
Figgate St EH15 .... 95 A1
Fillyside Ave EH7 .. 94 E2
Fillyside Rd EH7, EH5.. 94 E3
Fillyside Terr EH7.. 94 E3
Fincastle Pl FK2 .... 20 D8
Finches The EH31.. 52 B3
Findhorn Pl
Edinburgh EH9.. .... 121 E4
Falkirk FK1 .... 60 D2
Kirkcaldy KY2 .... 16 E8
Findlay Ave EH7 .... 94 C3
Findlay Cotts EH7 .. 94 C3
Findlay Cres EH7 .. 94 C3
Findlay Gdns EH7.. 94 C3
Findlay Gr EH7 .... 94 C3
Findlay Medway EH7.. 94 C3
Findlay St KY11 .... 46 E4
Fingal Pl EH9.. .... 229 A1
Finglen Cres FK10 .. 4 D4
Fingzies Pl EH6 .... 94 B4
Finistere Ave FK1 .. 60 B3
Finlaggan Ct ⁑ EH22.. 119 A8
Finlarig Ct FK5 .... 38 F4
Finlay Ave EH53 .... 144 F3
Finlay Pl EH22 .... 174 F6
Finlayson Pl FK5 .. 38 C5
Fintry Ave EH54 .... 144 B5
Finbark Rd FK3 .... 61 E5
Finbark Rd EH3 .... 144 E3
Fire Mus * EH3 .... 228 C2
Fir Gr Dunfermline KY11.. 46 E8
Livingston EH54 .... 144 B5
Westquarter FK2 .... 61 B2
Fir La FK5 .... 38 D1
Firpark Terr FK7 .... 6 E5
FIRTH HILL 149 D8
Firrhill Cres EH13 .. 149 E8
Firrhill Dr EH13 .... 149 E7
Firrhill High Sch EH14.. 149 D8
Firrhill Loan EH13 .. 149 E7
Firrhill Pk EH13.. .... 149 F7
Firs Cres FK7 .... 7 D2
Firs Entry FK7 .... 7 D2
Firs Rd FK10 .... 4 D2
Firs St FK2 .... 60 C6
First Gait EH14 .... 147 E8
Firs The Bannockburn FK7.. 7 D2
Dalgety Bay KY11 .... 48 B2
First St EH22 .... 174 B4
Firth Cres EH26 .... 171 D1
Firth Rd Livingston EH54.. 143 F7
Penicuik EH26 .... 171 D1
Roslin EH25 .... 192 F6
Fir View EH20 .... 171 F7
Firwood Dr EH51 .. 63 D5
FISHCROSS 5 D3
Fischcross Prim Sch FK10.. 5 D3
Fishergate Rd EH32 .. 97 E3
Fishermans Wlk FK9 .. 2 A3
FISHERROW 124 C3
Fisherrow Ind Est EH21.. 124 A6
Fishers Rd EH32 .... 97 D4
Fishers' Rd EH49 .. 63 D3
Fishers Wynd EH21.. 124 B6
Fishmarket Sq EH6.. 93 D7
Fishwives' Cswy EH15.. 95 A1

Fitzallan Pl EH48.. .... 141 B3
Fitzgerald Pl EH48.. 111 F5
Fitzroy Sq KY1 .... 18 A7
Fitzroy St KY1 .... 18 A7
Five Gates EH42.. 76 B5
Fivestanks Ct EH52.. 115 A5
Fivestanks Pl EH52.. 115 B5
Flare Rd FK3 .... 62 B5
Flax Mill Rd ML7.. 159 F5
Fleets Gr EH33 .... 126 D4
Fleets Ind Est EH33 .. 126 C3
Fleets Rd EH33 .... 126 C5
Fleets View EH33 .. 126 D4
Fleming Dr FK5.. .... 57 D8
Fleming Gdns FK1.. 59 E6
Fleming Pl EH48 .... 138 E3
Fleming Rd EH54 .. 142 F2
Fleming St FK6.. .... 36 E1
Flemington Gdns EH47.. 160 F6
Fleming Way KY3 .. 33 E2
Fleshmarket Cl EH1.. 229 A3
Flesh Wynd ⁑ KY1.. 17 D6
Fletcher Gr EH26 .. 191 F8
Fleurs Pk FK9.. .... 1 F3
Flint Cres FK7.. .... 20 D8
Floors Pl KY2.. .... 16 D5
Floors Terr KY2 .... 16 D5
Florabank Rd EH41.. 101 A1
Flora Stevenson Prim Sch ⁑
EH4 .... 92 F2
Flotterstone Visitor Ctr *
EH26.. .... 170 E3
Flower Pl KY4.. .... 12 F8
Flying Scotsman Way The
EH32.. .... 125 F8
Fodbank View KY11.. 29 E4
Fod St KY11.. .... 30 B5
Follyburn Pl EH54.. 143 B4
Foote St KY5 .... 14 A6
Foot Pl KY11 .... 46 E3
Forbes Cres FK5.. .... 38 D1
Forbeslea Gdns KY12.. 27 E7
Forbes Rd Edinburgh EH10 121 B5
Falkirk FK1 .... 60 D4
Rosyth KY11 .... 46 C2
Forbes St Alloa FK10.. 9 F6
Edinburgh EH8.. .... 229 B1
Forbes Terr KY2.. .... 17 B5
FORDELL.. .... 31 B6
Fordell Bank KY11.. 48 C4
Fordell Gdns
Dalgety Bay KY11 .... 47 E2
Kirkcaldy KY2.. .... 16 D5
Fordell Ind Est KY4.. 13 B1
Fordell Way KY11 .. 47 D2
Fordel Mains Cotts EH22 154 D2
Ford Rd Bonnybridge FK4.. 58 A5
Haddington EH41.. 130 C8
Ford's Rd EH11 .... 120 B4
Ford View KY12 .... 27 E5
Foregate Gdns FK1.. 59 E4
Forebraes EH54 .... 10 B7
Foredale Terr EH15.. 64 D7
Foreshore Way EH51.. 64 D7
Foreshot Terr EH39.. 53 B5
Forestbank EH54 .. 143 E5
Forester Gr FK10 .. 4 E1
Forester's Lea Cres KY12.. 29 E4
Forester's View EH33.. 126 D6
Forest Kirk ML8 .... 215 B1
Forest Pl KY12 .... 27 D7
Forest Rd KY12.. .... 29 D7
Forest View FK2 .... 61 F1
Forfar Pl KY2 .... 62 A1
Forge The KY12.. .... 28 C6
Forgie Cres FK2 .... 83 A5
Forglen Cres FK9 .... 2 A6
Forglen Rd FK9.. .... 2 B6
Forkenford EH16.. 122 D5
Forker Ave KY11 .... 46 D4
Forkneuk Rd EH52.. 114 E4
Forkneuk Steadings
EH52 .... 114 C4
Forman Gr KY11 .... 29 E1
Forres Dr KY7 .... 16 C7
Forres St EH3.. .... 228 B4
Forrester Ct KY5 .... 14 B7
Forrester Gait FK5.. 37 E6
Forrester High Sch EH12 119 D4
Forrester Park Ave EH12.. 119 D4
Forrester Park Dr EH12.. 119 D4
Forrester Park Gdns
EH12 .... 119 D4
Forrester Park Gn EH11.. 119 D4
Forrester Park Gr EH12.. 119 D4
Forrester Park Loan
EH12 .... 119 D4
Forrester Pl FK2 .... 22 D3
Forrester Rd
Armadale EH48 .... 139 F7
Edinburgh EH12.. 119 D7
Falkirk FK2 .... 22 D3
Forrester St FK2.. .... 61 A1
FORRESTFIELD 137 A3
Forrestfield Rd ML6.. 137 A5
Forrest Hill EH1 .... 229 A2
Forrest Pl Armadale EH48 140 A4
Harthill ML7 .... 159 E5
Forrest Rd Edinburgh EH1 229 A2
Stirling FK8 .... 2 B1
Forrest St ML7 .... 179 D5
Forrest Wlk EH52 .. 114 F3
Forsyth La FK7 .... 7 C1
Forteviot Ho EH17.. 151 D8
FORTH 201 A1

Forth Ave Kirkcaldy KY2 .... 17 A5
Larbert FK5.. .... 38 B3
Forth Ave Ind Est KY2.. 17 A5
Forthbank Ind Est FK10.. 10 B4
Forthbank Stadium (Stirling
Albion FC) FK7.. .... 7 E7
Forth Bridge Visitor Ctr *
KY11.. .... 68 A6
Forthclyde Way FK3.. 40 B1
Forth Cres Alloa FK10.. 10 C5
Dalgety Bay KY11 .... 48 B4
High Valleyfield KY12.. 26 B2
Stirling FK8 .... 7 B8
Forth Ct
Cockenzie & Port Seton
EH32 .... 97 E4
Dalgety Bay KY11 .... 48 B4
Dunfermline KY12.. 29 A2
Stirling FK8 .... 2 B1
Forth Dr EH54 .... 144 B5
Forth Gdns
Cockenzie & Port Seton
EH32 .... 97 E4
Oakley KY12 .... 26 E7
Forth Grange FK3.. 97 E4
Forth Ho EH6.. .... 93 E6
Forth Ind Est EH5.. 92 E7
Fort Ho EH6 .... 93 E6
Forth Park Dr KY2.. 17 A5
Forth Park Maternity Hospl
KY2.. .... 17 A5
Forth Pk Bridge of Allan FK9.. 2 A5
Queensferry EH30.. 89 E8
Stirling FK9.. .... 1 F5
Forth Pl Burntisland KY3.. 50 E8
Queensferry EH30.. 67 F1
Stirling FK8 .... 7 B8
Forth Prim Sch ML11.. 201 A1
Forth Rd KY11 .... 46 B2
Forth Reach KY11 .. 47 F2
Forthside Terr KY11.. 68 C5
Forthside Way FK7.. 7 B8
Forth St Cambus FK10.. 9 A8
Dunfermline KY12.. 29 A2
Edinburgh EH1 .... 93 D2
Fallin FK7 .... 8 D4
Grangemouth FK3.. 61 D8
Kincardine FK10.. 23 D3
North Berwick EH39.. 54 C7
Stirling FK8 .... 2 B1
Forth Street La EH39.. 54 C7
Forth Terr
Grangemouth FK3.. 61 D8
Stirling FK8 .... 7 B8
Forthvale Ct FK9 .. 2 B2
Forth Valley Coll
Clackmannan FK10.. 10 D8
Forth Valley Coll Falkirk
FK2.. .... 60 E6
Forth Valley Coll Raploch
Campus FK8.. .... 2 A2
Forth Valley Coll Stirling
FK7.. .... 7 C6
Forth Valley Royal Hospl
FK5.. .... 37 F3
Forthview FK7.. .... 7 E1
Forth View
Dalgety Bay KY11 .... 48 B4
Inverkeithing KY11.. 47 B2
Kincardine FK10.. 23 D3
Kirknewton EH27.. 145 E3
Stirling FK8 .... 2 B1
West Barns EH42.. 77 F1
Forthview Ave EH21.. 125 A4
Forth View Ave EH14.. 147 F4
Forth View Cotts KY12.. 26 A1
Forthview Cres
Bo'ness EH51 .... 63 D6
Musselburgh EH21.. 125 A5
Forth View Cres
Currie EH14.. .... 147 F4
Danderhall EH22.. 152 B7
Edinburgh EH14.. 147 F5
Forthview Ct EH33.. 126 D7
Forthview Dr EH33.. 59 F2
⁑ Tranent EH33 .... 126 D7
Forthview Dr EH21.. 125 B5
Forthview Gdns FK2.. 82 C8
Forth View Ind Est KY12.. 26 B1
Forth View Loan EH22.. 153 D2
Forthview Pl EH22.. 153 D2
Forthview Prim Sch EH4.. 92 D4
Forthview Rd
Edinburgh EH4.. .... 92 C2
Longniddry EH32.. 98 E6
Forth View Rd EH14.. 147 F4
Forthview Terr
Edinburgh EH4.. .... 92 B2
Falkirk FK1 .... 60 C4
Grangemouth FK2.. 82 B8
Wallyford EH21.. .... 125 B4
Forthview Wlk EH33.. 126 D7
Forth Wynd EH32.. 97 E4
Forties Campus KY11.. 46 D1
Forties Rd FK3, EH51.. 62 D5
Fortingall Cres KY2.. 62 A2
Fortissat Ave ML7.. 179 D6
Fort Kinnaird Sh Ctr
EH15.. .... 123 C4
Fort Prim Sch
Edinburgh EH6.. .... 93 E6
Edinburgh EH6.. .... 93 E6
Fortuna Ct FK1 .... 60 C4
Fortune Ave EH41.. 101 A1
Foulden Pl KY12 .... 29 D3

Foulford Pl KY4. . . . . .13 B4
Foulford Prim Sch KY4 . . . 13 B5
Foulford Rd KY4. . . . . .13 B4
Foulford St K4. . . . . .13 C4
Foulis Cres EH14. . . . . .148 E6
Foulshiels Rd EH47 . . . . . .162 C2
Foundry La EH20. . . . . .151 D1
Foundry Loan FK5. . . . . .38 B2
Foundry Rd
  Bonnybridge FK4. . . . . .58 B5
  Shotts ML7 . . . . .179 F4
Foundry St
  Dunfermline KY12. . . . . .29 A4
  Falkirk FK2 . . . . .60 A8
FOUNTAINBRIDGE 228 A1
Fountainbridge EH3. . . . . .228 A1
Fountain Cl EH1. . . . . .229 B3
Fountainhall Rd EH9 . . . . .121 E4
Fountainhead Rd EH48. . . .141 E7
Fountainpark EH11 . . . . . .229 A1
Fountainpark Cres EH51 . .64 C7
Fountain Pl
  Cowdenbeath KY4. . . . . .13 D3
  Loanhead EH20 . . . . .172 C8
  Pathhead EH37. . . . . .176 A5
Fountain Rd FK9. . . . . .2 A7
Fourth Gait EH14 . . . . .147 E7
Fourth St EH22 . . . . .174 D6
Fowler Cres Denny FK6 . . . .36 E1
  Loanhead EH20 . . . . .172 D8
  Maddiston FK2 . . . . .83 A5
Fowler Pl FK2 . . . . .61 E3
Fowlers Ct EH32 . . . . .96 F2
Fowler Sq EH20. . . . . .172 D8
Fowler St EH33 . . . . .126 C7
Fowler Terr EH11. . . . . .120 F5
Fox Covert Ave EH12 . . . . . .91 E1
Fox Covert Gr EH12 . . . . . . .91 E1
Fox Covert RC Prim Schs
  EH12. . . . . .91 E2
Foxdale Ave FK4. . . . . .58 A4
Foxdale Ct FK4 . . . . .58 A4
Foxdale Dr FK4 . . . . .58 A4
Foxdale Pl FK4 . . . . .58 A4
Foxglove Neuk KY12 . . . . . .29 A5
Foxknowe Pl EH54. . . . . . .143 B4
Fox Spring Cres EH10 . . . .150 A7
Fox Spring Rise EH10 . . . .150 A7
Fox St EH6 . . . . .94 B5
Frances Ind Pk KY1. . . . . . . .18 B8
Frances View KY1 . . . . .18 A8
Franchi St FK5 . . . . .38 F5
Francis Ct KY12. . . . . .28 D5
Francis St KY5. . . . . .14 B7
FRANKERTON. 36 A2
Frankfield Cres KY1. . . . . . .48 C4
Frankfield Pl KY11 . . . . .48 C4
Frankfield Rd KY11 . . . . .48 C4
Fraser Ave Edinburgh EH5 .93 A5
  Inverkeithing KY11. . . . . . . .47 D2
Fraser Cres EH5. . . . . .93 A5
Fraser Dr KY5 . . . . .14 B7
Fraser Gdns EH5. . . . . .93 A5
Fraser Gr EH5 . . . . .93 A5
Fraser La EH26 . . . . .171 B2
Fraser of Allander Ho FK9 .2 D6
Fraser Pl Dysart KY1. . . . . . .18 A8
  Grangemouth FK3. . . . . .61 B2
  Stirling FK9 . . . . .2 B4
Fraser Rd EH54 . . . . .142 F2
Frederick Cres KY11 . . . . . .28 E7
Frederick St EH2 . . . . .228 C4
Frederick Wilson Pk KY2 . .17 A7
Freeland Ave EH52. . . . . . .115 B5
Freelands Rd EH28. . . . . . .117 E3
Freeland Terr EH52 . . . . . .115 B5
Freeport Village EH55. . . .163 A4
Fremantle St EH54. . . . . . .144 A5
Freskyn Pl EH52. . . . . .116 A6
Frew Ct KY11. . . . . .29 C1
Frew Pl KY12 . . . . .12 A1
Friar's Bank Terr EH42. . . . .78 D2
Friars Brae EH49. . . . . .85 A6
Friar's Croft EH42. . . . . .78 D2
Friars Loan EH49 . . . . .85 A6
Friars St FK8 . . . . .7 B8
Friars Way EH49 . . . . .85 A5
Friarton Gdns EH26 . . . . . .191 C5
Friary Ct KY11. . . . . .47 C2
Friendship Gdns FK2 . . . . . .39 C3
Frobisher Ave FK1. . . . . .59 F4
Frogston Ave EH10. . . . . . .150 B5
Frogston Brae EH17. . . . . .150 B4
Frogston Gdns EH10 . . . . .150 C5
Frogston Road E EH17 . . . .150 C5
Frogston Road W EH10. . . .150 C4
Frogston Terr EH10. . . . . . .150 C5
Fruitmarket Gall The*
  EH3. . . . . .229 A3
Fulfordlees Cotts TD13. . . .218 D1
Fullerton Dr FK2. . . . . .61 E3
Fulmar Brae EH54 . . . . . . .143 C5
Fulmar Cres EH54 . . . . .44 D5
Fulmar Dr KY11. . . . . .30 A2
Fulmar Way KY11 . . . . .48 B4
Furcheons Pk EH8 . . . . . . .122 E8
Furnace Pl KY1. . . . . .13 E6
Furniss Ave KY11 . . . . .46 D5
Fyne La ML7. . . . . .179 E6

G

Gaberston Ave FK10 . . . . . .10 C7
Gabriel's Rd EH2 . . . . .229 A4
Gagarin Way KY4 . . . . .13 E6
Gair Cres ML8 . . . . .215 A3

Gairdoch Dr FK2. . . . . .39 C3
Gairdoch St FK2 . . . . .60 B8
Gairloch Cres FK2 . . . . .61 C2
Gair Rd ML8 . . . . .215 B5
Gair Wynd ML7 . . . . .180 B3
Galabraes Cres EH48. . . . .141 C7
Galachlawshot EH10 . . . . .150 C6
Galachlawside EH10 . . . . .150 C5
Galadale EH22. . . . . .174 A6
Galadale Cres EH22. . . . . .174 A6
Galadale Dr EH22 . . . . .174 A6
Gala Gn EH42 . . . . .78 B2
Galbraith Cres FK5. . . . . . . .38 C4
Gallacher Gn EH54. . . . . . .143 C8
Gallacher Pl KY4. . . . . .13 E5
Gallamuir Dr FK7 . . . . .20 D3
Gallamuir Rd FK7. . . . . .20 D5
GALLATOWN. 17 E8
Gallolee The EH13. . . . . . . .149 D5
Galloway Cres EH52. . . . . .115 C6
Galloway Ct FK1, FK2. . . . . .60 B6
Galloways Entry EH8. . . . . .229 C3
Gallows Knowe EH4. . . . . . .92 A2
Gallowsknowe EH40 . . . . . .84 D7
Gallows Loan KY12. . . . . . . .25 D2
Galloway St FK1. . . . . .60 B6
Gallowswood Rd EH49 . . .141 A3
Galmeilen EH52 . . . . .115 C6
Galt Ave EH21 . . . . .125 A5
Galt Cres EH21. . . . . .125 A5
Galt Dr EH21 . . . . .125 A5
Galt Rd EH21 . . . . .125 B5
Galt Terr EH21. . . . . .125 A5
Gambeson Cres FK7 . . . . . . .7 D3
Gamekeeper's Loan EH4 . . .91 B5
Gamekeeper's Pk EH4 . . . . .91 B5
Gamekeeper's Rd EH4 . . . . .91 B5
Gannel Hill View FK10 . . . . .5 E4
Garbett Pl FK2. . . . . .60 A7
Garbett Rd EH54. . . . . .143 C1
Garden City EH47. . . . . . . .162 A2
Garden Ct KY12 . . . . .29 D7
Gardeners Ct KY12. . . . . . . .29 B4
Gardeners Ct EH51. . . . . . . .64 A6
GARDENERS' LAND 29 B4
Gardeners' St KY12. . . . . . . .29 B4
Gardener St EH42. . . . . .78 C3
Gardeners well Villas [3]
  EH48. . . . . .141 B7
Gardener's Wlk EH26 . . . . .191 C6
Gardenhead FK2. . . . . .61 F2
Garden Pl Cairneyhill KY12 .27 C1
  Clackmannan FK10. . . . . . . .11 A4
  Livingston EH54 . . . . .143 C4
  Townhill KY12 . . . . .29 D7
Garden St FK1. . . . . .60 C5
Gardens The
  Aberlady EH32. . . . . .71 D5
  Dirleton EH39 . . . . .53 B5
Garden Terr
  Clackmannan FK10 . . . . . . .11 A4
  Edinburgh EH4. . . . . .91 E4
  Falkirk FK1 . . . . .60 C5
  Westquarter FK2. . . . . .61 A2
Gardiner Ct EH32. . . . . .97 B1
Gardiner Gr EH4. . . . . .92 B2
Gardiner Pl
  Cowdenbeath KY4. . . . . .13 B2
  Newtongrange EH22. . . . . .174 B6
Gardiner Rd
  Edinburgh EH4. . . . . .13 C2
  Prestonpans EH32 . . . . .97 A1
Gardiner's Cl EH32 . . . . .97 C4
Gardiner's Pl EH33. . . . . . .126 C7
Gardner St KY5 . . . . .14 B7
Gardner Terr
  Edinburgh EH4. . . . . .92 B2
  Prestonpans EH32. . . . . . . .26 A8
Gardner Cres EH47 . . . . . .160 F6
Gardner Cres EH35 . . . . . .228 B2
Gardner La EH48. . . . . .141 A6
Gardner Terr EH47 . . . . . . .162 A1
Gardrum Gdns FK1. . . . . . . .81 D7
Gardrum Pl FK2 . . . . .82 F7
Gardrum Terr FK1 . . . . .81 F5
Gareloch Way EH47 . . . . . .161 D7
Garleton Ct EH31. . . . . .52 B2
Garleton Dr EH41. . . . . . . .100 F1
GARLETON HILLS. 101 A5
Garleton Pk EH32. . . . . .71 C4
Garngrew Rd FK4. . . . . .57 A3
Garrison Pl FK1. . . . . .60 B5
Garry Pl Falkirk FK1. . . . . . . .60 D2
  Grangemouth FK3 . . . . .61 E5
Garry St KY5. . . . . .14 B8
Garry Way FK7 . . . . .7 D5
Garry Wlk EH54 . . . . .144 B4
Garscube Terr EH12 . . . . . .120 D8
Gartclush Gdns FK7. . . . . . .19 E8
Gartcows Ave FK1. . . . . .60 A4
Gartcows Cres FK1 . . . . .60 A3
Gartcows Dr FK1. . . . . .60 A4
Gartcows Gdns [5] FK1. . . .59 F4
Gartcows Pl FK1. . . . . .60 A3
Gartcows Rd FK1 . . . . .60 A3
Garten Dr ML7 . . . . .180 B3
Garthill Gdns FK1. . . . . .60 A4
Garthill La FK1 . . . . .60 A4
Gartmorn Dam Ctry Pk*
  FK10. . . . . .11 B8
Gartmorn Rd FK10. . . . . .5 D1
GARVALD. 132 D2
Garvald La FK6. . . . . .36 C1
Garvock Bank KY11. . . . . . .29 F4
Garvock Cres FK10. . . . . . . .10 A8
GARVOCK HILL 29 C4
Garvock Hill KY11 . . . . .29 D4

Garvock Terr KY12. . . . . . . .29 D4
Gascoigne Ct [8] FK2. . . . . .60 A8
Gasworks La
  North Berwick EH39 . . . . . . .53 F6
  Whitburn EH47 . . . . .161 B7
Gas Wynd KY1 . . . . .17 B2
Gateside Ave
  Bonnybridge FK4 . . . . .58 C6
  Haddington EH41. . . . . . . .100 D1
Gateside Commerce Pk
  EH41. . . . . .129 D8
Gateside Ct KY4 . . . . .13 A3
Gateside Ind Est KY4 . . . . . .13 A3
Gateside Rd
  Haddington EH41 . . . . .129 D8
  Kirkliston EH29 . . . . .89 A1
  Stirling FK7 . . . . .7 A3
  Whitburn EH47 . . . . .160 F6
Gateway Bsns Pk FK3. . . . . .45 C1
Gauger's Bush EH42 . . . . . .76 B7
Gauze Ct EH51. . . . . .64 A6
Gauze Pl EH51. . . . . .64 A6
Gavald Grange Steading
  EH41. . . . . .132 D3
Gavin Pl EH54 . . . . .143 B5
Gavins Lee EH33 . . . . .126 C4
Gavins Rd FK10. . . . . .4 F1
GAYFIELD. 93 E3
Gayfield Cl [4] EH1. . . . . . . .93 E2
Gayfield Pl [8] EH7. . . . . . . .93 E2
Gayfield Place La EH1. . . . . .93 E2
Gayfield Sq EH1 . . . . .93 E2
Gayfield St EH1. . . . . .93 E2
Gayfield Street La [6] EH1 .93 E2
Gaynor Ave EH20 . . . . .172 B8
Gean Rd FK10 . . . . .9 F8
Geatons Rd KY5 . . . . .14 C8
Geddes' Entry EH1. . . . . . . .229 A3
Gelder Dr EH54. . . . . .144 A5
Gellatly Rd KY11 . . . . .29 D2
Gentle's Entry EH8. . . . . . .229 C3
George Ave EH20 . . . . .172 B8
George Burn Wynd KY1 . . .17 C3
George Cres
  Loanhead EH20 . . . . .172 C8
  Ormiston EH35 . . . . .155 D7
George Dr EH20 . . . . .172 C8
George Grieve Way
  EH33 . . . . .126 D4
George Heriot's Sch EH3 . .228 C1
George IV Bridge EH1. . . . .229 A2
George Laing Ct FK5 . . . . . .38 E2
George Pl EH48. . . . . .141 A6
George Sq EH8 . . . . .229 A1
George Square La EH8. . . .229 A1
George Square Theatre*
  EH8. . . . . .229 A1
George St Alva FK12. . . . . . . .5 A6
  Armadale EH48 . . . . .139 F6
  Bathgate EH48 . . . . .141 A6
  Bo'ness EH51 . . . . .63 F6
  Cowdenbeath KY4 . . . . .13 B4
  Dunfermline KY12. . . . . .29 B2
  Edinburgh EH2. . . . . .228 B3
  Falkirk FK2 . . . . .60 B5
  Grangemouth FK3 . . . . .61 F8
  Kincardine FK10 . . . . .23 E3
  Kirkcaldy KY1 . . . . .17 B3
  Laurieston FK2 . . . . .60 F3
  Ormiston EH35 . . . . .155 C7
  Stenhousemuir FK5. . . . . . . .38 C3
George Terr EH20. . . . . . . .172 C8
George Watson's Coll
  EH10. . . . . .120 F3
George Watson's Coll Lower
  Prim Sch EH10 . . . . .120 F3
George Watson's Coll Upper
  Prim Sch EH10 . . . . .120 F3
George Way [5] EH33. . . . .126 C6
George Wlk [5] EH33 . . . . .126 C6
Georgian House* FK2. . . . .228 B3
Gerald Terr FK5 . . . . .38 E3
Gibbdun Pl FK6. . . . . .57 E7
Gibb's Entry EH8. . . . . .229 B2
Gibbshill Pl ML7 . . . . .159 D5
Gib Gr KY11 . . . . .29 E1
Gibraltar Ct EH22 . . . . .153 B3
Gibraltar Gdns EH22 . . . . .153 B3
Gibraltar Rd EH22 . . . . .153 A3
Gibraltar Terr EH22. . . . . . .153 B3
Gibson Dr EH22. . . . . .153 C4
Gibsongray St FK2 . . . . .60 A7
Gibson St Denny FK6. . . . . .36 E1
  Edinburgh EH7. . . . . .93 E4
Gibson Terr EH11 . . . . .228 A1
Gideon Ct EH40 . . . . .103 B6
Gideon St EH48. . . . . .141 B7
GIFFORD 220 F6
Giffordgate EH41 . . . . .130 B8
Gifford Pk EH8 . . . . .229 B1
Gifford Rd EH41. . . . . .130 C7
Gilberstoun EH15 . . . . .123 D5
Gilberstoun Brig EH15. . . .123 D5
Gilberstoun Loan EH15 . . .123 D5
Gilberstoun Pl EH15 . . . . . .123 D6
Gilberstoun Wynd EH15 . .123 D5
Gilbert Ave EH39. . . . . .54 C6
Gilburn Pl Bo'ness EH51. . . .63 E4
  Shotts ML7 . . . . .179 F4
Gilchrist Cres EH47. . . . . . .161 B6
Gilchrist Dr FK1 . . . . .59 E4
GILCHRISTON 220 A4
Gilchriston Rd EH36 . . . . . .93 H5
Gilfillan Pl FK2 . . . . .39 C2
Gilfillan Rd KY11 . . . . .29 E4
Gillespie Cres EH10 . . . . . .228 B1
Gillespie Gr KY12 . . . . .26 E7

Gillespie Pl
  Armadale EH48. . . . . .139 F4
  Edinburgh EH11. . . . . .228 B1
  Stirling FK7 . . . . .7 B1
Gillespie St EH3 . . . . .228 B1
Gillespie Terr FK7 . . . . .20 C2
Gillie-burn Gdns ML7 . . . .179 E4
Gillie Ct KY11 . . . . .29 C2
Gillies Dr FK7. . . . . .7 C4
Gillies Hill FK7 . . . . .6 D5
Gill Pk FK6 . . . . .36 E2
Gillsland Rd EH10. . . . . . . .120 F4
Gill Way KY11 . . . . .46 C5
GILMERTON. 151 F6
Gilmerton Dykes Ave
  EH17. . . . . .151 D5
Gilmerton Dykes Cres
  EH17. . . . . .151 C6
Gilmerton Dykes Dr
  EH17. . . . . .151 D5
Gilmerton Dykes Gdns
  EH17. . . . . .151 C6
Gilmerton Dykes Gr
  EH17. . . . . .151 C6
Gilmerton Dykes Loan
  EH17. . . . . .151 D5
Gilmerton Dykes Pl
  EH17. . . . . .151 C6
Gilmerton Dykes Rd
  EH17. . . . . .151 C5
Gilmerton Dykes St
  EH17. . . . . .151 D5
Gilmerton Dykes Terr
  EH17. . . . . .151 D5
Gilmerton Dykes View
  EH17. . . . . .151 D5
Gilmerton Pl EH17 . . . . . . .151 D5
Gilmerton Prim Sch
  EH17. . . . . .151 D6
Gilmerton Rd
  Bonnyrigg and Lasswade
    EH18. . . . . .152 C4
  Dalkeith EH22 . . . . .152 E3
  Edinburgh EH17. . . . . .151 D7
Gilmerton Road Rdbt
  EH22. . . . . .152 D3
Gilmerton Station Rd
  EH17. . . . . .151 E4
Gilmore Pk EH11. . . . . .228 A1
Gilmore Place La EH3. . . . .228 B1
Gilmour Rd EH16 . . . . .121 F3
Gilmour St
  Cowdenbeath KY4. . . . . .13 D6
  Edinburgh EH8. . . . . .229 B2
Gilsay Ct FK1. . . . . .60 D2
Gilston Cres FK2. . . . . .62 A1
Gipsy La KY11. . . . . .29 F3
Gladney Sq KY1. . . . . .17 B2
GLADSMUIR. 128 B7
Gladsmuir ML11 . . . . .201 A1
Gladsmuir Junc EH33 . . . .128 A7
Gladstone Pl
  Dunfermline KY12. . . . . .29 B2
  Edinburgh EH6. . . . . .94 B4
  Stirling FK8 . . . . .7 A6
Gladstone Rd FK5 . . . . .38 D3
Gladstone's Gait EH19 . . . .173 D7
Gladstone Terr EH9 . . . . . .121 E5
Glaive Ave FK7 . . . . .7 D3
Glamaig Way KY11. . . . . . . .30 B1
Glamis Gdns
  Dalgety Bay KY11 . . . . .48 B3
  Polmont FK2 . . . . .61 F1
Glamis Pl KY11 . . . . .48 B3
Glamis Rd KY2. . . . . .16 D7
Glamis Terr KY3 . . . . .34 F3
Glanville Pl [7] EH3. . . . . . . .93 B2
Glasclune Ct EH39 . . . . .54 D7
Glasclune Gdns EH39 . . . . .54 D7
Glasgow Rd
  Bathgate EH48 . . . . .140 F6
  Denny FK6. . . . . .36 E1
  Edinburgh EH12. . . . . .119 B6
  Falkirk FK1 . . . . .59 C6
  Gogar EH12 . . . . .118 C5
  Longcroft FK4 . . . . .57 C4
  Stirling FK7 . . . . .7 B2
Glaskhill Terr EH26 . . . . . . .191 E6
Glass Cres EH52 . . . . .87 F2
Glassel Park Rd EH32 . . . . .98 C4
Glasshouse Loan FK10 . . . .10 A6
Glass Pl EH52. . . . . .87 F2
Glass Rd EH52 . . . . .87 F1
Glasswork St KY1. . . . . .17 B3
Glebe Ave Stirling FK8 . . . . .7 A7
  Uphall EH52. . . . . .15 B7
Glebe Cres Alva FK12 . . . . . .5 B7
  Athelstaneford EH39 . . . . .101 F7
  Stirling FK8 . . . . .7 A7
Glebe Ct EH47 . . . . .181 D6
Glebe Gdns
  Edinburgh EH12. . . . . .119 E6
  [3] Prestonpans EH32 . . . . .96 F1
Glebe Gr EH12 . . . . .119 E6
Glebe Pk Inverkeithing KY11 47 B1
  Kirkcaldy KY1 . . . . .17 C5
Glebe Pl
  Bonnyrigg and Lasswade
    EH18. . . . . .151 F1
  Burntisland KY3. . . . . .33 E1
  Kinghorn KY3. . . . . .34 E2
Glebe Rd Bathgate EH48 . .141 C6
  Edinburgh EH12 . . . . .119 D6
  Kincardine FK10 . . . . .23 E5
  Uphall EH52. . . . . .115 A4
  West Calder EH55 . . . . . . .163 D2

Fou-Gle 243

Glebe Rd continued
  Whitburn EH47 . . . . .161 A6
Glebe St Dalkeith EH22. . . .153 A3
  Denny FK6 . . . . .36 E2
  Falkirk FK1. . . . . .60 B5
Glebe Terr Alloa FK10 . . . . .10 A6
  Edinburgh EH12. . . . . .119 D6
  Haddington EH41 . . . . .101 A1
  Inverkeithing KY11 . . . . .47 B1
  Uphall EH52. . . . . .115 A5
Glebe The Aberdour KY3. . .49 C8
  Alva FK12 . . . . .5 B7
  Clackmannan FK10 . . . . . . .11 A4
  Dalmeny EH30. . . . . .89 F2
  East Linton EH40. . . . . . . .103 C8
  East Saltoun EH34 . . . . . . .157 F4
  Edinburgh EH4. . . . . .91 B6
  Kirkliston EH29 . . . . .89 A1
  Linlithgow EH49 . . . . .85 A5
  North Berwick EH39. . . . . . .53 A5
  Pencaitland EH34 . . . . .156 F7
  West Calder EH55 . . . . . . .163 D2
Gledhill Ave EH51. . . . . .64 D5
Glenafeoch Rd ML8. . . . . . .215 A1
Glen Albyn Dr KY2 . . . . .16 B8
Glenallan Dr EH16 . . . . . . .122 B2
Glenallan Loan EH16 . . . . .122 B2
Glenalmond EH47. . . . . . . .161 C5
Glenalmond Ct
  Broxburn EH52 . . . . .115 B5
  Whitburn EH47 . . . . .161 C5
Glenalmond Terr EH48 . . . .141 B8
Glenard View EH51 . . . . . . .64 D6
Glen Artney Gr KY11 . . . . . .29 D1
Glenavon Dr KY12 . . . . .27 C1
Glen Avon Pl FK2. . . . . .82 F7
Glenbank Terr FK48. . . . . . .141 B8
Glenbank FK1 . . . . .60 B1
Glenbare Ct EH48. . . . . . . .141 C6
Glen Beasdale Ct KY11. . . .29 D1
Glenbervie FK5 . . . . .38 A4
Glenbervie Ave EH54 . . . . . .38 A3
Glenbervie Bsns Pk FK5 . . .38 A3
Glenbervie Cres EH55 . . . . .38 B3
Glenbervie Dr FK5. . . . . .38 A3
Glenbervie Gr KY11. . . . . . .29 D1
Glenbervie Rd FK3 . . . . .61 F6
Glenbo Dr FK5 . . . . .57 E7
Glen Brae FK1 . . . . .60 B3
Glenbrae Ct FK1 . . . . .60 B3
Glen Bridge KY12 . . . . .28 F4
Glenbridge Ct KY12 . . . . . . .28 F4
Glenbrook EH14 . . . . .167 E8
Glenburn Ave EH14 . . . . . .147 A1
Glen Bruar Pl KY2 . . . . .16 B8
Glenburn Gdns EH47 . . . . .161 D6
Glenburn Gr KY12. . . . . .28 C5
Glenburn Rd Falkirk FK1 . . .60 D1
  North Berwick EH39 . . . . . . .54 D6
Glenburn Way EH51. . . . . . .63 D5
Glencairn Cres EH12. . . . . .120 F7
Glencairn St Falkirk FK1. . . .59 F5
  Stirling FK7 . . . . .7 B3
Glencairn Terr EH48. . . . . .141 C8
Glencoe EH47 . . . . .161 D6
Glencoe Path EH32. . . . . . . .97 A2
Glencoe Rd Carluke ML8 . .215 A1
  Stirling FK8 . . . . .2 A1
Glencorse Pk EH26 . . . . . .192 C8
Glencorse Prim Sch
  EH26. . . . . .171 B1
Glencoul Ave KY11. . . . . . . .48 A3
Glen Cres Falkirk FK1 . . . . . .60 B3
  Livingston EH54 . . . . .142 E6
Glencross Gdns EH26 . . . . .191 C5
Glen Ct EH54. . . . . .142 E6
Glendevon Ave EH12 . . . . .120 B6
Glendevon Cotts EH52 . . . .87 D2
Glendevon Ct EH52 . . . . . . .87 F2
Glendevon Dr Falkirk FK2 . .82 F7
  Stirling FK8 . . . . .1 F2
Glendevon Gdns EH12 . . . .120 B6
Glendevon Gr EH12 . . . . . .120 B6
Glendevon Pk
  Edinburgh EH12. . . . . .120 B6
  Winchburgh EH52 . . . . .87 E2
Glendevon Pl EH12. . . . . . .120 B6
Glendevon Rd EH12 . . . . . .120 B6
Glendevon Terr EH12 . . . . .120 B6
Glendinning Cres EH16. . . .151 B8
Glendinning Dr EH29. . . . . .88 F2
Glendinning Pl EH29 . . . . . .88 F2
Glendinning Rd EH29. . . . . .89 A2
Glendinning Way EH29 . . . .89 A2
Gleneagles Ct EH47. . . . . .142 E5
Gleneagles Way EH54 . . . .142 E5
Glenesk Cres EH22. . . . . . .152 F2
Glenfarg Cres KY4 . . . . .13 D5
Glenfield Carnock KY12. . . .27 C6
  Livingston EH54 . . . . .143 A3
Glenfield Ave KY4 . . . . .13 C6
Glenfield Cres KY4. . . . . . . .13 C5
Glenfield Ct KY4 . . . . .13 C5
Glenfield Gr KY4 . . . . .13 C5
Glenfield Ind Est KY4. . . . . .13 C5
Glenfield Rd KY4 . . . . .13 C6
Glenfinlas St EH3 . . . . .228 B3
Glen Fruin Gr KY11 . . . . . . .29 D1
Glenfuir Ct FK1. . . . . .59 D4
Glenfuir Rd FK1. . . . . .59 E5
Glenfuir St FK1 . . . . .59 F5
Glengairn Wlk KY11 . . . . . . .29 D1
Glengarry Cres KY11 . . . . . .59 F2
Glengarry Terr EH32. . . . . . .97 A2

Glen Gdns FK1 . . . . .60 A3
Glengyle Terr EH3 . . . . .228 C1
Glenisla Ct EH47 . . . . .161 D5
Glenisla Gardens La EH9 121 D3
Glenisla Gdns EH9 . . . . .121 D3
Glenisla Gr KY11 . . . . .29 D1
Glen Isla Rd KY2 . . . . .16 C8
Glen Kinchie FK10 . . . . .4 A2
Glenkinchie Distillery★
EH34 .156 E2
Glenkinchie Hos EH34 . . .156 E2
Glenlee Ave EH8 . . . . .122 C8
Glenlee Gdns EH8 . . . . .122 C8
Glenlockhart Bank EH14 120 D1
Glenlockhart Rd EH11 . . .120 C1
Glenlockhart Valley
EH14 .120 D2
Glen Lyon Ct FK2 . . . . .62 A2
GLENMAVIS 141 D7
Glenmavis Cres ML8 . . . .215 A1
Glenmavis Ct ML8 . . . . . . .215 A1
Glenmavis Dr EH48 . . . . . . .141 B7
Glenmore EH47 . . . . .161 C6
Glenmore Dr FK4 . . . . .57 F6
Glen More Gdns KY2 . . . . . .16 B8
Glen Moriston Dr KY12 . . .27 C1
Glen Nevis Dr KY11 . . . . .29 D1
Glennie Gdns EH33 . . . . . . .126 D6
Glenochil Pk FK10 . . . . .4 E4
Glenochil Rd FK1 . . . . .60 A3
Glenochil Terr FK10 . . . . .4 E4
Glenogle Ct EH3 . . . . .93 B2
Glenogle Ho █ EH3 . . . . .93 B2
Glenogle Pl █ EH3 . . . . .93 B2
Glenogle Rd EH3 . . . . .93 B2
Glenogle Swim Ctr EH30 . .93 B2
Glenogle Terr EH3 . . . . .93 B2
Glenorchy Rd EH39 . . . . .54 B6
Glenorchy Terr EH9 . . . . . . .121 F4
Glenpeffer Ave EH32 . . . . . .71 D4
Glen Pl EH26 . . . . .191 E6
Glen Rd Armadale EH48 . .139 F6
Livingston EH54 . . . . .142 E6
Shotts ML7 . . . . .179 F4
Torwood FK5 . . . . .37 D7
GLENSBURGH 40 A1
Glensburgh Rd FK3 . . . . .61 A8
Glenshee EH47 . . . . .161 C5
Glenshiel Gr KY11 . . . . .29 D1
Glenside Ct
Armadale EH48 . . . . .139 E6
Grangemouth FK3 . . . . .61 E6
Glenside Gdns EH48 . . . . .139 E6
Glen St EH3 . . . . .228 C1
Glen Terr Denny FK6 . . . . . . .36 D1
Livingston EH54 . . . . .142 E6
Glen The Bathgate EH48 . .141 B8
Tullibody FK10 . . . . .4 C3
Glentye Dr FK10 . . . . .4 E4
Glenview Gdns FK1 . . . . .59 E2
Glen Tye Rd FK7 . . . . .7 D5
Glenure Loan EH4 . . . . .91 D1
Glenvarloch Cres █
EH16 .151 B8
Glenview Frankerton FK6 . .36 A3
Menstrie FK11 . . . . .4 A4
Penicuik EH26 . . . . .191 E6
Glen View Bo'ness EH51 . . . .63 D4
Bonnybridge FK4 . . . . .57 D5
Glenview Cres EH47 . . . . . .162 B2
Glen View Cres EH23 . . . . .195 C8
Glenview Dr FK1 . . . . .59 F2
Glen View Pl EH23 . . . . .195 C7
Glen View Rd EH23 . . . . . . .174 C1
Glen View Wlk EH23 . . . . . .195 D7
GLEN VILLAGE 60 B1
Glen Way █ EH48 . . . . .141 B7
Glenwinnel Rd FK12 . . . . .4 E7
Glenwood Dr EH48 . . . . . . .139 D6
Glenyards Rd FK4 . . . . .57 F2
Gloag Pl EH55 . . . . .163 D3
Globe Pk EH52 . . . . .115 C8
Globe Rd KY11 . . . . .46 D2
Glomach Gr KY12 . . . . .28 E5
Gloucester La EH3 . . . . .228 B4
Gloucester Pl EH3 . . . . .228 B4
Gloucester Sq EH3 . . . . . . .228 B4
Gloucester St EH3 . . . . .228 B4
Glover's Ct KY3 . . . . .35 A3
Glowroram Dr FK6 . . . . .57 E7
Glynwed Ct FK2 . . . . .62 C7
Godfrey Ave FK6 . . . . .36 D1
Godfrey Cres FK5 . . . . .38 C1
Goff Ave EH7 . . . . .94 F1
GOGAR .118 D5
Gogarbank Farm EH12 . .118 C2
Gogar Bridge Rd EH12 . .118 A7
Gogar Loan FK9 . . . . .2 C5
Gogarloch Bank EH12 . . .119 B5
Gogarloch Haugh EH12 . .119 B5
Gogarloch Muir EH12 . . . .119 B5
Gogarloch Rd EH12 . . . . . .119 B5
Gogarloch Syke EH12 . . . .119 B5
Gogar Mains Farm Cotts
EH12 .118 C7
Gogar Pl FK7 . . . . .7 C2
Gogar Rbdt EH12 . . . . .118 E5
Gogar Sta Rd EH11 . . . . . . .119 A2
Gogar Station Rd EH12 . .118 E3
Gogarstone Rd EH12,
EH28 .118 B5

GOLDENACRE 93 B4
Goldenacre Terr EH3 . . . . . .93 B4
Goldenstones Ave EH42 . . .78 E1
Goldpark Pl EH54 . . . . .143 A3
Golf Course Rd
Bonnyrigg and Lasswade
EH19 .173 B8
Cowdenbeath KY4 . . . . .13 C6
Linlithgow EH49 . . . . .84 E5
Livingston EH54 . . . . .143 B8
Golf Ct EH32 . . . . .71 C4
Golf Dr EH32 . . . . .97 E4
Golfdrum St KY12 . . . . .28 E4
Golf House Rd EH42 . . . . . . .78 F1
Gollet Way KY12 . . . . .43 F8
Goodall Cres EH52 . . . . .114 B2
Goodall Pl EH52 . . . . .114 B2
Goodman Pl FK2 . . . . .82 E7
Goodtrees Gdns EH17 . . . .151 D8
Goodtrees Terr EH17 . . . . .151 D8
Goosecroft Rd FK8 . . . . .7 B8
Goosedubs Pl FK2 . . . . .59 F8
Goose Gn Ct EH21 . . . . .124 D7
Goose Green Ave EH21 . .124 D7
Goose Green Cres EH21 .124 D7
Goose Green Pl EH21 . . . .124 D7
Goose Green Rd
Gullane EH31 . . . . .52 A2
Musselburgh EH21 . . . . .124 D7
Gordon Ave
Bathgate EH48 . . . . .141 B5
Bonnyrigg and Lasswade
EH19 .172 F6
Gordon Cres FK9 . . . . .2 A8
Gordon Ct Broxburn EH52 .115 F5
Edinburgh EH6 . . . . .94 A4
Gordon Dr FK10 . . . . .10 C7
Gordon Loan EH12 . . . . . . .119 E7
Gordon Pl FK1 . . . . .59 E5
Gordon Rd
Edinburgh EH12 . . . . .119 E7
Rosyth KY11 . . . . .46 B2
Gordon St
Cowdenbeath KY4 . . . . .13 D6
Easthouses EH22 . . . . .174 C7
Edinburgh EH6 . . . . .94 A4
Lochgelly KY5 . . . . .14 A8
Gordon Terr
Dunfermline KY11 . . . . .29 B1
Edinburgh EH16 . . . . .122 A2
Gordon Way EH54 . . . . .143 D7
Gore Ave EH23 . . . . .195 D8
GOREBRIDGE 195 B8
Gorebridge L Ctr EH23 . .174 C1
Gorebridge Prim Sch
EH23 .174 C1
Goremire Rd ML8 . . . . .215 C1
GORGIE .120 D5
Gorgie Mills Sch EH11 . . .120 D5
Gorgie Park Cl EH14 . . . . . .120 D4
Gorgie Park Rd EH14 . . . . .120 D4
Gorgie Pk Cl EH14 . . . . .120 D4
Gorgie Rd EH14 . . . . .120 C4
Gorrie St Denny FK6 . . . . . . .36 D2
Dunfermline KY11 . . . . .29 C2
Gorsebank EH54 . . . . .143 F5
Gorton Loan EH24 . . . . .172 D2
Gorton Pl EH24 . . . . .172 D2
Gorton Rd EH24 . . . . .172 D2
Gort FK3 .61 C5
Goschen Pl EH52 . . . . .115 B5
Goschen Terr EH52 . . . . . . .115 B5
Gosford House★ EH32 . . . .71 A2
Gosford Pl EH6 . . . . .93 D5
Gosford Rd
Cockenzie & Port Seton
EH32 . . . . .97 C4
Kirkcaldy KY2 . . . . .16 C7
Longniddry EH32 . . . . .98 E6
Goshen Pl FK5 . . . . .38 E2
Goshen Rd FK5 . . . . .38 E2
Goth La EH30 . . . . .68 B1
Goulden Pl KY12 . . . . .28 D6
Gourlaybank EH41 . . . . .101 A1
Gourlay St KY2 . . . . .17 A4
Gowan Ave FK2 . . . . .60 B6
Gowanbank EH54 . . . . .143 D5
Gowanbrae Dr KY12 . . . . . . .29 D4
Gowanbrae Pl KY12 . . . . . . .29 C4
Gowanbrae Terr KY12 . . . .29 D4
Gowanhill Farm Rd
EH14 .147 C5
Gowanhill Gdns FK8 . . . . . . .1 F1
Gowan La EH52 . . . . .60 B6
Gowanlea Dr FK1 . . . . .108 B6
Gow Cres KY1 . . . . .17 B4
GOWKHALL 27 F7
GOWKSHILL 174 B3
Gowl Cl █ EH41 . . . . .130 B8
Gracefield Ct EH21 . . . . . . .124 B6
GRACEMOUNT 151 B8
Gracemount Ave EH16 . .151 B7
Gracemount Bsns Pav
EH16 .151 C5
Gracemount Dr EH16 . . . .151 B6
Gracemount High Sch
EH16 .151 C6
Gracemount House Dr
EH16 .151 B6
Gracemount L Ctr EH16 . .151 B8
Gracemount Pl EH16 . . . . .151 B6
Gracemount Prim Sch
EH16 .151 B6
Gracemount Rd EH16 . . . .151 A5
Gracemount Sq EH16 . . . .151 A5
Grace St KY5 . . . . .14 C8
Gracie Cres FK7 . . . . .8 D4

Gracie's Wynd EH48 . . . . . .140 B5
Gradlon Pl FK1 . . . . .60 B3
Graeme High Sch FK1 . . . . .60 E4
Graeme Pl FK1 . . . . .59 E1
Graham Ave Larbert FK5 . .38 B3
Stirling FK9 . . . . .2 C4
Graham Cres EH51 . . . . .64 A7
Graham Ct EH47 . . . . .162 E8
Grahamsdyke Ave EH51 . . .64 A7
Grahamsdyke Cres FK4 . .58 A3
Grahamsdyke La EH51 . . . .64 A7
Grahamsdyke Pl EH51 . . . .64 B6
Grahamsdyke Rd
Bo'ness EH51 . . . . .64 A7
Bonnybridge FK4 . . . . .58 A4
Grahamsdyke St FK2 . . . . . .60 F4
Grahamsdyke Terr EH51 . .64 B7
Grahams Rd FK1 . . . . .60 B6
Graham's Rd EH26 . . . . .171 B1
Grahams Road Rdbt FK1 . .60 B5
Graham St
Bridge of Allan FK9 . . . . .2 B7
Edinburgh EH6 . . . . .93 E5
GRAHAMSTON 60 C6
Graham Terr FK2 . . . . .22 D4
Graham Way EH54 . . . . .143 D8
Grainger St KY5 . . . . .14 B8
Grampian Cres FK3 . . . . .61 E5
Grampian Ct KY11 . . . . .46 E2
Grampian Gdns KY2 . . . . . .16 F5
Grampian Pl KY11 . . . . .46 E1
Grampian Rd Rosyth KY11 . .46 E2
Stirling FK7 . . . . .6 E6
Grampion Ct EH54 . . . . .143 E1
Granary Rd FK2 . . . . .60 A8
Granary Sq FK2 . . . . .60 B7
Granary The FK42 . . . . .78 E3
Granby Ave EH54 . . . . .143 F4
Granby Rd EH16 . . . . .121 F3
Grandfield EH6 . . . . .93 C5
Grandville EH6 . . . . .93 C6
Grange Ave FK2 . . . . .60 D6
Grangeburn Rd FK3 . . . . .40 E1
Grange Cotts KY2 . . . . .34 F5
Grange Cres EH9 . . . . .121 D4
Grange Crescent E EH32 . .96 F1
Grange Crescent W
EH32 .125 F8
Grange Ct
█ Edinburgh EH9 . . . . .121 E5
North Berwick EH39 . . . . .54 C6
Grange Dr
Dunfermline KY11 . . . . .46 C8
Falkirk FK2 . . . . .60 D6
Grange Gdns FK9 . . . . .2 C7
Grange Knowe EH49 . . . . . .85 B8
Grange La FK3 . . . . .40 C1
Grangelea Ct FK3 . . . . .61 E8
Grange Loan Bo'ness EH51 .64 B7
Edinburgh EH9 . . . . .121 D4
Grange Loan Gdns EH9 . .121 D4
GRANGEMOUTH 61 B7
Grangemouth Ent Ctr FK3 61 A7
Grangemouth High Sch
FK3 . . . . .61 E5
Grangemouth Mus★ FK3 . .40 D1
Grangemouth Rd
Bo'ness EH51 . . . . .63 B6
Falkirk FK2 . . . . .60 E5
Grangemouth FK51 . . . . .62 D5
GRANGEPANS 64 A7
Grangepans EH51 . . . . .64 B8
Grange pans Ind Est EH51 .64 B8
Grange Pk KY11 . . . . .29 C1
Grange Pl
Grangemouth FK3 . . . . .61 D8
Redding FK2 . . . . .60 E3
Grange Prim Sch EH51 . . . .64 B7
Grange Rd Alloa FK9 . . . . .9 F6
Broxburn EH52 . . . . .115 F4
Burntisland KY3 . . . . .33 D1
Dunfermline KY11 . . . . .46 C6
Edinburgh EH9 . . . . .121 D5
Livingston EH54 . . . . .144 A3
North Berwick EH39 . . . . .54 B6
Polmont FK3 . . . . .61 D8
Prestonpans EH32 . . . . .96 F1
Grange Terr Bo'ness EH51 . .64 B7
Edinburgh EH9 . . . . .121 D3
Grange The FK2 . . . . .82 E8
Grange View
Linlithgow EH49 . . . . .85 C8
Stenhousemuir FK5 . . . . .38 E1
Grange Wynd KY11 . . . . .46 C8
Grannies Park Ind Est
EH22 .153 A4
Grannus Mews EH21 . . . . .124 D5
Grant Ave EH13 . . . . .149 A6
GRANTON 92 E6
Granton Cres EH5 . . . . .92 F6
Granton Gdns EH5 . . . . .92 F5
Granton Gr EH5 . . . . .92 F6
Granton Harbour★ EH5 . . .92 F8
Granton Mains Ave EH4 . . .92 C6
Granton Mains Bank EH4 .92 C6
Granton Mains Brae EH4 . .92 C6
Granton Mains E EH4 . . . . .92 C6
Granton Mains Gait EH4 . .92 C6
Granton Mains Vale EH4 . .92 C6
Granton Mains Wynd EH4 .92 C6
Granton Medway EH5 . . . . .92 E6
Granton Mill Cres EH4 . . . .92 B5
Granton Mill Dr EH4 . . . . . . .92 C6
Granton Mill March EH4 . .92 B5
Granton Mill Pk EH4 . . . . . . .92 B5

Granton Mill Pl EH4 . . . . . . .92 C6
Granton Mill Rd EH4 . . . . . .92 B5
Granton Mill W EH4 . . . . . . .92 B5
Granton Park Ave EH5 . . . .92 E7
Granton Pl EH5 . . . . .92 F6
Granton Prim Sch EH5 . . . .92 F6
Granton Rd EH5 . . . . .93 A6
Granton Sq EH5 . . . . .92 F7
Granton Terr EH5 . . . . .92 F6
Granton View
Dalgety Bay KY11 . . . . .47 F2
Edinburgh EH5 . . . . .92 F6
Grant Pl FK9 . . . . .2 B4
Grant Rd EH32 . . . . .97 A2
Grant's Bank KY12 . . . . .29 A4
Grant St Alloa FK10 . . . . .9 F6
West Calder EH55 . . . . .163 D3
Grantully Pl EH9 . . . . .121 F4
Granville Terr EH10 . . . . . . .121 A5
Granville Way KY11 . . . . .46 E3
Grassmarket EH1 . . . . .228 C2
Gray Buchanan Ct FK2 . . .61 D2
Gray Pl KY4 . . . . .13 C6
Gray Pl KY11 . . . . .29 D1
Gray's Ct EH8 . . . . .229 B2
Gray's Loan EH10 . . . . .120 F4
Gray St ML7 . . . . .180 A4
Graystale Rd FK7 . . . . .7 A3
Graystonelee Rd ML7 . . . .179 D6
Great Cannon Bank EH15 .95 A1
Great Carleton Pl EH16 . .123 A3
Great Carleton Sq EH16 .123 A3
Great Junction St EH6 . . . . .93 F5
Great King St EH3 . . . . .93 C2
Great Michael Cl EH6 . . . . .93 C7
Great Michael Rd EH6 . . . . .93 C6
Great Michael Rise EH6 . . .93 D6
Great Michael Sq EH6 . . . . .93 D7
Great Stuart St EH3 . . . . . .228 A3
Grebe Gdns KY11 . . . . .30 A1
Greenacre EH14 . . . . .148 E7
Greenacre Ct FK7 . . . . .7 E1
Greenacre Dr FK4 . . . . .58 A3
Greenacre Pl
Bannockburn FK7 . . . . .7 E1
Bonnybridge FK4 . . . . .58 A3
Greenacres KY12 . . . . .12 B1
Green Apron Pk EH39 . . . . .54 B6
GREENBANK Edinburgh . .149 F8
Falkirk 59 C3
Greenbank Ave EH10 . . . . .121 A1
Greenbank Cres EH10 . . . .150 A8
Greenbank Ct EH41 . . . . . . .72 B6
Greenbank Dr
Cowdenbeath KY4 . . . . .13 A2
Edinburgh EH10 . . . . .120 F1
Greenbank Gdns EH10 . . .149 F8
Greenbank Gr EH10 . . . . . .149 F8
Greenbank La EH10 . . . . . . .121 A1
Greenbank Loan EH10 . . .149 F8
Greenbank Pk EH10 . . . . . .149 F8
Greenbank Pl
Edinburgh EH10 . . . . .121 A1
Falkirk FK1 . . . . .59 D4
Greenbank Rd
Edinburgh EH10 . . . . .120 F1
Falkirk, Greenbank FK1 . . . .59 D3
Falkirk, Summerford FK2 . . .59 D3
Greenbank Rise EH10 . . . .149 F8
Greenbank Row EH10 . . . .149 F8
Greenbank Terr EH10 . . . .121 A1
GREENBURN 181 E6
Greenburn Rd EH47 . . . . . .181 E5
Greencornhills Rdbt FK7 . .19 F8
Greencraig Ave FK1 . . . . .81 C6
Greendale Pk EH4 . . . . .92 A4
GREENDYKES 122 F3
Greendykes Ave EH16 . . . .122 F3
Greendykes Cotts EH33 . .127 C8
Greendykes Dr EH16 . . . . .122 F3
Greendykes Gdns EH16 . .122 F3
Greendykes Ho EH16 . . . . .122 F3
Greendykes Ind Est
EH52 .115 D6
Greendykes Loan EH16 . .122 F3
Greendykes Rd
Broxburn EH52 . . . . .115 E6
Edinburgh EH16 . . . . .122 F3
Tranent EH33 . . . . .127 D6
Greendykes Steadings
EH52 .115 E7
Greenend Dr EH17 . . . . .151 C8
Greenend Gdns EH17 . . . .151 C7
Greenend Gr EH17 . . . . .151 C8
Greenfield Cres EH14 . . . .168 C8
Greenfield Pk EH21 . . . . . .124 B3
Greenfield Rd EH14 . . . . . . .168 C8
Greenfield St Alloa FK10 . .10 B7
Bonnybridge FK4 . . . . .58 B6
Greenhall Rd EH23 . . . . . . .174 C1
Greenhead FK12 . . . . .5 B6
Greenheads Rd EH39 . . . . .54 E6
GREENHILL 58 A2
Greenhill Ct
Edinburgh EH10 . . . . .121 B5
Fauldhouse EH47 . . . . .181 E6
Greenhill Gdns EH10 . . . . .121 B5
Greenhill Pk
Edinburgh EH10 . . . . .121 B4
Penicuik EH26 . . . . .191 D5
Greenhill Pl EH10 . . . . .121 B4
Greenhill Rd
Blackridge EH48 . . . . .138 E3
Bonnybridge FK4 . . . . .58 A3

Greenhithe Terr FK2 . . . . .82 E7
Greenhorn's Well Ave █
FK1 . . . . .59 F3
Greenhorn's Well Cres █
FK1 . . . . .59 F3
Greenhorn's Well Dr █
FK1 . . . . .59 F3
Green La
Bonnyrigg and Lasswade
EH18 .172 F8
Grangemouth FK3 . . . . .61 E8
Greenlaw Gr EH26 . . . . .171 A1
Greenlaw Hedge EH13 . . .149 E8
GREENLAW MAINS 192 A8
Greenlaw Rig EH13 . . . . . . .149 E8
Greenloanings KY2 . . . . .16 D8
Greenmantle Loan █
EH16 .122 B1
Greenmount KY4 . . . . .13 A2
Greenmount Dr
Burntisland KY3 . . . . .33 F1
Shieldhill FK1 . . . . .81 C6
Greenmount Road N KY3 .33 F2
Greenmount Road S KY3 .34 A1
Greenpark FK17 . . . . .151 C8
Greenpark Dr FK2 . . . . .61 E2
Greenrigg Cotts ML7 . . . . .159 F5
Greenrigg Prim Sch ML7 159 F4
Greenshank Dr KY11 . . . . . .30 A2
GREENSIDE 229 B4
Great Cannon Bank EH15 .111 F6
Greenside La EH1 . . . . .229 B4
Greenside Pl
Edinburgh EH1 . . . . .229 B4
Rosewell EH24 . . . . .172 D2
Greenside Row EH1 . . . . . .229 B4
Greenside St FK10 . . . . .10 B6
Green St Edinburgh EH7 . .93 D2
Townhill KY12 . . . . .28 E7
Greens The FK2 . . . . .82 E6
Green The Alva FK12 . . . . .5 A7
Balerno EH14 . . . . .168 D8
Bathgate EH48 . . . . .141 C7
Edinburgh EH4 . . . . .91 F4
Loanhead EH20 . . . . .151 C1
Pencaitland EH34 . . . . .156 F6
West Barns EH42 . . . . .77 F1
Greendale Dr Fa EH51 . . . . .63 D5
Greenvale Dr FK2 . . . . .82 E8
Greenwells Dr FK2 . . . . .82 F8
Greenwell St EH47 . . . . . . .181 F6
Greenwell Terr FK2 . . . . .82 E7
Greenwood Ave FK8 . . . . .7 A8
Greenwood Dr EH54 . . . . . .143 D6
Greenwood St ML7 . . . . . . .179 E5
Gregory Rd EH54 . . . . .143 D6
Greig Cres EH48 . . . . .140 A5
Greig Ct KY11 . . . . .47 B2
Greig Pl KY5 . . . . .14 A7
Greig Rd KY11 . . . . .46 B2
Grendon Ct FK8 . . . . .7 A6
Grendon Gdns FK8 . . . . .7 A6
Grenville The FK7 . . . . .59 F4
Greville St KY12 . . . . .27 D2
Greyfriars FK1 . . . . .229 A2
Greyfriars Bobby Meml★
EH1 . . . . .229 A2
Greyfriars Wlk KY11 . . . . . . .47 C3
Greygoran FK10 . . . . .5 C2
Grey School Cnr EH21 . . . .96 F1
Grierson Ave EH5 . . . . .93 A6
Grierson Cres
Cambusbarron FK7 . . . . .6 D1
Edinburgh EH5 . . . . .93 A6
Grierson Gdns EH5 . . . . .93 A6
Grierson Rd EH5 . . . . .92 F6
Grierson Sq EH5 . . . . .93 A6
Grierson Villas EH5 . . . . .93 A6
Grieve Ct EH26 . . . . .191 F8
Grieve St Dunfermline KY12 .28 E4
Kirkcaldy KY2 . . . . .17 A1
Griffith Dr EH47 . . . . .161 A6
Griffiths St FK1 . . . . .60 B4
Grigor Ave EH4 . . . . .92 D3
Grigor Dr EH4 . . . . .92 D3
Grigor Gdns EH4 . . . . .92 E3
Grigor Terr EH4 . . . . .92 D3
Grindlay St EH3 . . . . .228 B2
Grindlay Street Ct EH3 . . .228 B2
Groathill Ave EH4 . . . . .92 C2
Groathill Gardens E █
EH4 . . . . .92 C2
Groathill Gardens W █
EH4 . . . . .92 C2
Groathill Loan EH4 . . . . .92 C3
Groathill Road N EH4 . . . . .92 C3
Groathill Road S EH4 . . . . .92 C2
Grodwell Dr FK12 . . . . .4 E7
Grosvenor Cres EH12 . . . .120 F7
Grosvenor Gdns EH12 . . .120 F7
Grosvenor St EH12 . . . . . . .228 A2
Grove Cres FK2 . . . . .39 A2
Grove End EH18 . . . . .173 B8
Grove St Denny FK6 . . . . .36 C2
Edinburgh EH3 . . . . .228 A2
Musselburgh EH21 . . . . .124 D5
Grove Terr EH3 . . . . .228 A2
Grove The EH21 . . . . .124 E5
Grundie's Well Rd EH17 . .151 E6
Guardians Wood EH12 . . .120 C7
Guardwell Cres EH17 . . . .151 C7
Guardwell Loan EH17 . . . .151 D7
Guildhall St KY12 . . . . .29 A3
GUILDIEHAUGH 141 C4
Guildiehaugh Rdbt EH48 .141 D5
Guildie Howes Rd EH23 . .195 F2
Guildry Gr KY12 . . . . .29 E4
Guildry The EH49 . . . . .65 E5

GULLANE 52 A1
GULLANE HILL 51 E2
Gullane Prim Sch EH31 ..52 B2
Gullan's Cl EH1 ....229 B3
Gunner Rd FK3, EH51 ....62 C8
Gunn Rd FK3 ....61 C5
Guthrie Cres FK5 ....38 B2
Guthrie St EH1 ....229 A2
Guttergates Rd KY11 ....30 B5
Gyle Ave EH12 ....118 F5
Gylemuir Prim Sch EH12 119 C5
Gylemuir Rd EH12 ......119 C6
Gyle Park Gdns EH12 ..119 A6
Gyle Rbdt EH12 ....118 F5
Gylers Rd EH39 ....53 A4
Gyle Sh Ctr EH12 ......119 A5

H

HADDINGTON 130 D7
Haddington Inf Sch
EH41 ....130 A8
Haddington Pl
Aberlady EH32 ....71 D4
Edinburgh EH7 ....93 E2
Haddington Rd
East Linton EH40 ......103 D7
Musselburgh EH21 .....125 B6
North Berwick EH39 ....54 C5
Tranent EH33 ....126 E6
Haddington Station Ind Est
EH41 ....129 B8
Haddon's Ct EH8 ......229 B2
Haddow Gr KY3 ....50 D8
Hadfast Rd EH22 ......154 D5
Hadrian Way EH51 ......64 B6
HAGGS 57 A3
Haig Ave Kirkcaldy KY1 .17 D7
Stirling FK8 ....2 A2
Haig Cres Bathgate EH48 141 C5
Dunfermline KY12 ......29 C5
Haig Homes EH11 .....120 A4
Haig St FK3 ....61 C6
Hailes App EH13 ......149 A7
Hailes Ave EH13 ......149 A7
Hailes Bank EH13 .....149 A7
Hailes Castle* EH41 ..103 A4
Hailes Cres EH13 .....149 A7
Hailes Gdns EH13 .....149 A7
Hailes Gr EH13 ....149 A7
Hailesland Gdns EH14 119 E1
Hailesland Gr EH14 ...119 E1
Hailesland Pk EH14 ...119 F1
Hailesland Pl EH14 ...119 E1
Hailes Loan EH41 .....103 B4
Hailes Pk EH13 ....148 F7
Hailes Pl Dunfermline KY12 29 E4
[2] Inverkeithing/Dunfermline
KY11 ....29 C3
Hailes St EH3 ....228 B1
Hailes Terr EH13 .....149 A7
Hailstonegreen ML11 ..201 A1
Hailstones Cres EH48 139 F6
Hainburn Pk EH10 ....149 F5
Haining Gr FK2 ....83 B5
Haining Pl
Grangemouth FK3 ......61 F8
Livingston EH54 ......143 B5
Haining Rd EH49 ....83 F6
Haining Terr EH49 .....83 F6
Haining Valley Steadings
EH49 ....83 E6
HALBEATH 30 A5
Halbeath Dr KY11 .....29 F5
Halbeath Intc Bsns Pk
KY11 ....30 B6
Halbeath Pl KY11 .....29 E5
Halbeath Rd
Dunfermline KY11 .....29 D5
Halbeath KY11 ....30 A5
Halbeath Ret Pk KY11 .30 A6
Halberts Cres FK7 ......7 B2
Haldane Ave
Bridge of Allan FK9 ....2 A6
Haddington EH41 .....100 E1
Haldane Gr KY12 ......26 D7
Haldane Sq EH54 .....164 C5
Halket Cres FK2 ....39 C2
Halketshall KY11 ......45 C4
Halkett Cres KY11 .....29 D2
Hallam Rd FK5 ....38 D2
Hallcraigs EH27 ......145 E3
Hall Cres EH31 ....52 A2
Hallcroft Cl EH28 ....117 C2
Hallcroft Cres EH28 ..117 C2
Hallcroft Gdns EH28 ..117 C2
Hallcroft Grn EH28 ...117 C2
Hallcroft Neuk EH28 ..117 C2
Hallcroft Pk EH28 ....117 C2
Hallcroft Rise EH28 ..117 C2
Halley's Ct KY1 ....17 B2
HALLGLEN 60 D1
Hallglen Prim Sch FK1 .60 E1
Hallglen Rd FK1 ....60 B1
Hallglen Sh Ctr FK1 ...60 C1
Hallglen Terr FK1 .....60 B1
Hallhead Rd EH16 .....122 A2
Hallhill EH47 ....54 F5
Halliburton Terr EH39 .53 A4
Hallows The KY1 ....17 F8
Hallpark FK10 ....10 C8
Hall Rd EH52 ....115 B5
Hall Row KY11 ....54 A5
Hall St Cowdenbeath KY4 13 C4
Lochgelly KY5 ....14 B8
Hall Terr EH48 ....111 F5

Hallyards Cotts EH29 ..117 B8
Hallyards Rd
Newbridge EH29 ......117 B8
Ratho Station EH28 ...117 D6
Halmyre St EH6 ....93 F4
Halyard Rise KY11 .....47 F2
Halyard Terr KY2 ......15 B2
Hamburgh Pl EH6 ......93 E6
Hamilton Ave
Linlithgow EH49 ......84 E6
Stenhousemuir FK5 ....38 E4
Hamilton Cres
Grangemouth FK2 ......82 E6
Gullane EH31 ....52 A2
Newtongrange EH22 ..174 B6
Hamilton Ct EH39 .....54 A7
Hamilton Dr
Edinburgh EH15 ......122 F8
Falkirk FK1 ....60 A4
Stirling FK9 ....2 C4
Hamilton Drive W EH15 122 F7
Hamilton Gdns
Armadale EH48 ....139 F4
Edinburgh EH15 ......122 F7
Hamilton La
Bathgate EH48 ....140 E7
Bo'ness EH51 ....63 F8
Hamilton Pk
Edinburgh EH15 ......122 F8
Linlithgow EH49 ......84 F6
Hamilton Pl Edinburgh EH3 .93 B2
Linlithgow EH49 ......84 E6
Rosyth KY11 ....46 E4
Hamilton Rd
Bathgate EH48 ....140 F7
Grangemouth FK3 .....61 E6
Gullane EH31 ....52 B2
North Berwick EH39 ...54 A7
Stenhousemuir FK5 ....38 D6
Hamiltons Cl EH30 ....68 C1
Hamilton's Folly Mews
EH8 ....229 B1
Hamilton Sq Bo'ness EH51 63 D5
Livingston EH54 .....164 F7
Hamilton St Falkirk FK1 ..59 D6
Lochgelly KY5 ....14 B6
Hamilton Terr
Edinburgh EH15 ......123 A7
High Valleyfield KY12 .26 B2
Inverkeithing KY11 ...47 C2
Hamilton Way EH47 ..161 E6
Hamilton Wynd EH6 ...93 E6
Hammermen's Entry EH8 229 B3
Hampton Pl [5] EH12 ..120 E7
Hampton Terr [4] EH12 120 E7
Handax ML11 ....201 A1
Haney's Way EH51 .....64 B8
Hanlon Gdns FK2 ......62 A1
Hannah Pk (Shotts Bon
Accord FC) ML7 ......179 D6
Hanover Cl [4] EH48 ..141 A7
Hanover Ct
Broxburn EH52 ....115 E5
Livingston EH54 .....143 B2
Edinburgh EH2 ....2 D4
Hanover Grange FK3 ...61 D8
Hanover Ho EH54 .....143 B2
Hanover St EH2 ......228 C4
Happy Valley Rd EH47 162 E7
Harbour Ct EH42 ......78 D3
Harbour Dr KY11 ......47 F3
Harbour La EH30 ......68 B1
Harbour Pl Burntisland KY3 50 B8
Dalgety Bay KY11 .....47 F2
Edinburgh EH15 ....95 A1
Inverkeithing KY11 ...47 C2
Harbour Rd Bo'ness EH51 64 C7
Kinghorn KY3 ....35 A2
Musselburgh EH21 ...124 A6
Harbour View EH21 ..124 B6
Harbour Way KY11 ....48 A4
HARBURN 185 C8
Harburn EH55 ....185 C8
Harburn Ave EH54 ....142 F6
Harburn Avenue W EH54 142 F7
Harburn Dr EH55 .....163 E3
Harburn La EH55 .....163 E3
Harburn Rd EH55 ....163 E3
Harcourt Rd KY2 ......17 B5
Hardengreen Bsns Ctr
EH22 ....152 E1
Hardengreen Ind Est
EH22 ....152 E1
Hardengreen Junc EH22 173 E7
Hardengreen La EH22 .152 E1
Harden Pl EH11 ....120 F5
Hardgate EH41 ....101 B1
Hardgate Ct EH41 ....101 B1
Hardhill Dr EH48 .....140 E6
Hardhill Pl EH48 .....140 B5
Hardhill Rd EH48 ....140 D6
Hardhill Road Travelling
Peoples Site EH48 ...140 C5
Hardhill Terr EH48 ..140 C5
Hardie Cres FK7 ....8 C4
Hardie Ct KY1 ....7 C3
Hardie Rd EH54 .....142 D7
Hardie Terr EH40 ....103 D8
Hardwell Cl EH8 .....229 B2
Hardy Gdns EH48 ....141 F5
Hareburn Ave FK1 ....110 A5
Harelaw EH22 ....152 D8
Harelaw Rd EH13 ....149 B6
Hares Cl EH32 ....97 C4
Hareside ML11 ....217 F8
Harestanes Rd EH48 .139 F3
Harewood Cres EH16 .122 E4

Harewood Dr EH16 ....122 E4
Harewood Rd EH16 ...122 E4
Harkenburn Gdns EH26 191 C6
Harkness Cres EH33 ..126 D6
Harlands The FK10 .....9 E2
Harlaw Bank EH14 ....168 C8
Harlaw Gait EH14 ....147 D1
Harlaw Gr EH26 ......191 D5
Harlaw Hill EH32 .....96 F2
Harlawhill Gdns EH32 .97 A2
Harlaw March EH14 ..168 D8
Harlaw Ranger & Visitor
Ctr* EH14 ....169 A7
Harlaw Rd Balerno EH14 168 E8
Currie EH14 ....148 A2
Harley Ct FK2 ....60 B8
Harley Gdns FK4 ......58 B5
Harley St KY11 ....47 A4
Harlington EH42 ....82 E7
Harlow Ave FK2 ....61 D1
Harmeny Sch EH14 ...168 D8
Harmony Cres EH19 ..173 D7
Harmony Ct EH19 ....173 D7
Harmony St EH19 ....173 D7
Harmony Wlk EH19 ..173 D7
Harness Ct EH20 .....172 C7
Harpenside Cres EH39 .53 C5
Harperdean Cotts EH41 101 A3
Harperdean Terr EH41 100 F1
Harperrig Way EH13 ..149 F7
Harper's Brae EH26 ..192 B6
Harriebrae Pk KY12 ...28 F4
Harrier Ct KY11 ....30 A2
Harriet St KY1 ....12 A7
Harris Ct FK10 ....10 B5
Harris Dr KY2 ....16 F8
Harrismith Pl EH7 .....94 A2
Harrison Gdns EH11 ..120 E4
Harrison La EH11 .....120 F5
Harrison Pl
Edinburgh EH11 ......120 E4
Falkirk FK1 ....59 F5
Harrison Rd EH11 ....120 E5
Harris Pl Dunfermline KY11 29 C1
Grangemouth FK3 .....61 C5
Harrysmuir Cres EH53 144 A7
Harrysmuir Gdns EH53 144 A7
Harrysmuir N EH53 ..144 A7
Harrysmuir Prim Sch
EH54 ....143 E5
Harrysmuir Rd EH53 .144 A7
Harrysmuir S EH53 ..144 A7
Harrysmuir Terr EH53 144 A7
Hartfield Terr ML7 ...198 B8
HARTHILL 159 F5
Harthill Rd
Blackridge EH48 .....138 D2
Fauldhouse EH47 ....185 B1
Hartington Gdns EH10 121 A5
Hartington Pl EH10 ..121 A5
Hartley Pl FK2 ....61 B6
Hart St EH1 ....93 D2
Hart Street La EH1 ....93 D2
HARTWOOD 179 A3
Hartwood Gdns ML7 ..179 A2
Hartwoodhill Hospl ML7 179 C4
Hartwood Rd Shotts ML7 179 A3
West Calder EH55 ....163 D2
Hart Wynd FK7 ....7 F1
Harvest Dr EH28 .....117 B5
Harvesters Pl EH14 ..148 E8
Harvesters Sq EH14 ..148 E8
Harvesters Way EH14 148 D8
Harvest Rd EH28 .....117 B5
Harvest St FK9 ....2 A4
Harvey Ave FK2 ....61 F2
Harvey Wynd FK8 ......2 A1
Harvie Gdns EH48 ....140 D7
Harvieston Villas EH23 195 D7
Hastie's Cl EH1 ......229 A2
Hatfield Pl [8] EH48 ..140 A7
Hatton Pl EH9 ....121 D5
Haugh Gdns FK2 ....39 B1
Haugh Park EH14 ....120 A2
Haugh Rd Burntisland KY3 50 D8
North Berwick EH39 ...54 F7
Stirling FK8 ....2 B2
Haugh St Edinburgh EH3 .93 B2
Falkirk FK2 ....39 B1
Haughs Way FK6 ....36 E2
Haven's Edge KY11 ...45 E3
Haven The
Dalgety Bay KY11 .....47 F2
South Alloa FK7 ....9 F7
Hawes Brae EH30 .....68 D1
Hawk Brae EH54 .....143 C5
Hawkcraig Rd KY3 ....49 D7
Hawkhead Cres EH16 .153 E2
Hawkhead Cres EH16 .151 A8
Hawkhead Gr [8] EH16 151 A8
Hawkhill EH7 ....94 B3
Hawkhill Ave EH7 .....94 A3
Hawkhill Rd Alloa FK10 ..10 C6
Kincardine FK10 ......23 D5
Hawkill Cl EH7 ....94 A3
Hawkins Terr EH26 ..192 B8
Hawksmuir [8] KY1 ...12 A6
Hawkwood Terr ML11 201 A1
Hawley Rd FK1 ....60 D1
Hawthorn Bank
Carnock KY12 ....27 C6
Cockenzie & Port Seton
EH32 ....97 B4
Seafield EH47 ....66 A6
South Queensferry EH30 68 B1
Hawthornbank La EH4 228 A3
Hawthornbank Pl EH6 .93 C5
Hawthornbank Rd EH41 100 F1

Hawthornbank Terr EH6 ..93 E6
Hawthorn Cres
Cowdenbeath KY4 .....12 F1
Easthouses EH22 ....174 D8
Fallin FK7 ....8 D4
Stirling FK8 ....1 F2
Hawthorn Ct EH47 ...163 A8
Hawthornden Ave EH19 173 B7
Hawthornden Gdns
EH19 ....173 A7
Hawthornden Pl EH7 ..93 E3
Hawthornden Prim Sch
EH19 ....172 F6
Hawthorn Dr Denny FK6 .36 D3
Falkirk FK1 ....59 E4
Fallin FK7 ....8 D4
Harthill ML7 ....159 E6
Shotts ML7 ....180 C4
Hawthorn Gdns EH20 .151 B1
Hawthorn Pl Allanton ML7 198 A8
Edinburgh EH17 ......151 E5
Ormiston EH35 ......159 D7
Uphall EH52 ....114 F4
Hawthorn Rd EH32 ....97 B1
Hawthorn St FK3 ......61 C6
Hawthorns The EH31 ..52 B3
Hawthorn Terr EH32 ..97 B3
Hawthornvale EH6 ....93 D6
Hay Ave EH16 ....122 F4
Hay Dr EH16 ....123 A4
HAYFIELD 17 B6
Hayfield Edinburgh EH12 119 A8
Falkirk FK2 ....60 C7
Hayfield Ind Est KY2 ..17 A7
Hayfield Pl KY2 ....17 A7
Hayfield Rd Falkirk FK2 .60 C7
Kirkcaldy KY1, KY2 ...17 C7
Hayford Mills FK7 .....6 D6
Hayford Pl FK7 ....6 D6
Haygate Ave FK2 ......82 E8
Hay Gdns EH16 ......122 F5
Hay Gr KY11 ....29 F1
Haymarket EH12 .....228 A2
Haymarket Cres EH54 143 A5
Haymarket Sta EH12 228 A2
Haymarket Terr EH12 120 F7
Haymarket Yds EH12 .120 F7
Haypark Bsns Ctr FK2 .61 E2
Haypark Rd FK6 ......57 D6
Hay Pl EH16 ....122 F4
Hay Rd EH16 ....122 F4
Hays Com Bsns Ctr EH16 122 F4
HAYWOOD 202 A2
Hayworth Ave FK2 .....61 A8
Hazel Ave Kirkcaldy KY7 17 B6
Menstrie FK11 ....3 F6
Hazelbank Gdns FK8 ...2 A2
Hazelbank Terr EH11 .120 E4
Hazel Cres EH47 ......36 D3
Hazel Ct EH42 ....78 B1
Hazeldean Ave EH51 ..63 D5
Hazeldean Terr EH16 122 B2
Hazel Dr EH19 ....173 B6
Hazel Gr Dunfermline KY11 46 E8
Falkirk FK2 ....60 D7
Livingston EH54 .....144 B6
Shotts ML7 ....180 B4
Hazelhurst EH52 ......82 E8
Hazel La EH20 ....171 E7
Hazel Pl EH42 ....61 C6
Hazel Rd FK3 ....61 C6
Hazelwood Gr EH16 .122 C2
Headlesscross Rd EH47 180 F2
HEAD OF MUIR 57 E6
Head of Muir Prim Sch
FK6 ....57 D6
Headrigg Row EH16 ..122 B1
Headrig Rd EH30 .....88 D8
Heaghs Rd KY11 ......29 E5
HEADWELL 29 E5
Headwell Ave KY12 ...29 E5
Headwell Ct KY12 ....29 E5
Headwell Rd KY12 ....29 E5
Headwell Sch KY12 ...29 E5
Heaney Ave EH53 ....144 B7
Heather Ave FK5 ......81 C6
Heatherbank EH54 ...143 D5
Heatherbell Ct ML7 ..159 D5
Heatherdale Gdns FK6 .57 E7
Heatherfield Glade EH54 164 C8
Heather Gr
Dunfermline KY11 .....46 F8
Maddiston FK2 ....83 A5
Heather Pk EH47 ....142 B1
Heathervale Wlk EH48 140 B5
Heatherwood Croft ..142 F1
Heatherwood Pk EH53 144 B7
Heath Pk KY11 ....46 F7
Heath Rd KY11 ....46 A6
Hedge Row EH20 .....171 E7
Hedges Loan FK7 ......7 E1
Hedges The Falkirk FK1 .59 E5
Tranent EH33 ....126 C5
Heggie's Wynd KY1 ...17 E7
Heights Rd EH48 .....138 D3
Heinsberg Rd EH26 ..191 E5
Helen La KY11 ....68 C6
HELENSFIELD 41 B6
Helenslea Cotts [4] EH48 141 B6
Helmsdale Pk KY12 ...28 F2
Henderland Rd EH12 .120 D7
Henderson Ave FK10 ..10 A8
Henderson Cres EH52 115 B5
Henderson Ct EH53 ..144 F3
Henderson Gdns
Edinburgh EH6 ....93 F5

Henderson Gdns continued
Tranent EH33 ....126 D6
Henderson Pl Alva FK12 ..5 A7
Broxburn EH52 ......115 B5
Edinburgh EH3 ....93 C2
Stirling FK7 ....20 C4
Henderson Place La EH3 93 B2
Henderson Row EH3 ...93 B2
Henderson St
Bridge of Allan FK9 ...2 B7
Edinburgh EH6 ....93 F5
Kingseat KY12 ....12 B1
Lochgelly KY5 ....14 A6
Henderson Terr EH11 .120 F5
Hendry Cres KY2 ......17 A6
Hendry Rd KY2 ....17 A6
Hendry St FK2 ....60 B7
Hendry's Wynd KY1 ...17 B2
Hennings The FK10 ....5 C1
Henry Ross Pl EH30 ..68 B1
Henryson Cres FK5 ...38 B2
Henryson Rd KY11 ..109 D4
Henry St Alva FK12 ....5 A6
Bo'ness EH51 ....64 A5
Grangemouth FK3 .....61 E8
Hens Nest Rd EH47 ..161 E6
Hepburn Dr EH22 ....153 C2
Hepburn Rd [3] EH41 101 A1
Herald Rise EH54 ....143 F2
Herbertshire St FK6 ..36 E2
Herbison Cres ML7 ..180 A4
Hercus Loan EH21 ..124 B6
Herd Gn EH54 ....143 B7
Herdmanflatt ML11 ..201 A1
Herdmanflatt Hospl
EH41 ....101 A1
Hershdill Ave FK1 .....81 C6
Herschel Terr EH20 ..172 A7
HERIOT 214 C2
Heriot Bridge EH1 ...228 C2
Heriot Gdns Burntisland FK2 61 D1
Burntisland KY3 ....33 F1
Heriothill Terr EH7 ...93 C3
Heriot Pl EH3 ....228 C2
Heriot Row EH3 .....228 B4
Heriot-Watt Univ EH14 147 E8
Heriot Way EH38 ....214 C1
Heritage Pk FK2 ......39 A3
Hermand Cres EH11 ..120 E4
Hermand Gdns EH55 .163 E3
Hermand Ho EH55 ...163 F3
Hermand St EH11 ....120 D4
Hermand Terr EH11 ..120 D4
HERMISTON 118 F1
Hermiston Gait Ret Pk
EH11 ....119 A3
Hermiston House Rd EH12,
EH14 ....118 E1
Hermiston Junc EH11,
EH12 ....119 A2
HERMITAGE 94 B3
Hermitage Dr EH10 ..121 B1
Hermitage Gdns EH10 121 B2
Hermitage of Braid Nature
Reserve* EH10 ......121 C1
Hermitage Park Gr EH6 94 B3
Hermitage Park Lea EH6 94 B3
Hermitage Park Prim Sch
EH6 ....94 B3
Hermitage Park S EH6 94 B3
Hermitage Pl EH6 .....94 B3
Hermitage Pl EH6 .....94 A4
Hermitage Rd EH6 .....2 E6
Hermitage Terr EH10 .121 B2
Hermits Croft EH8 ..229 C1
Heron Ind Complex
EH54 ....142 D7
Heron Pl EH5 ....92 F7
Heron Sq EH54 ......142 D7
Hervey St FK10 ....10 A8
Hesperus Crossway FK5 92 F7
Hetherington Dr FK10 11 B4
HEUGH 54 F5
Heugh Brae EH39 ....54 E5
Heugh Rd EH39 ......54 E5
Heugh St FK1 ....60 A3
Heugh Study EH39 ...54 E5
Heugh The
North Berwick EH39 ...54 E5
Tranent EH33 ....126 C7
Hewitt Pl KY3 ....49 C7
Hie Dyke ML11 ......217 E8
Higginson Loan EH22 174 E5
High Academy Gr EH48 139 E5
High Academy St EH48 139 E5
High Beveridgewell KY12 28 F5
HIGH BONNYBRIDGE ...58 C3
High Brae EH48 ....55 E3
High Buckstone EH10 150 C6
Highfield Livingston EH54 143 A3
North Berwick EH39 ...54 B7
Highfield Cres EH49 ..84 E7
Highfield Rd EH39 ....54 A6
Highland Dr FK5 ......39 A3
Highland Dykes Cres FK4 58 A6
Highland Dykes Dr FK4 58 B6
Highlander Way FK10 ..4 D2
Highlea Circ EH14 ...168 B7
Highlea Gr EH14 ....168 B8
High Mdw ML8 ....215 A2
High Mill Rd ML8 ....215 A2
High Park Rise EH26 191 F4
High Port EH49 ....85 B7

High Rd Maddiston FK2....83 A5
Roslin EH25............192 F6
Spott EH42............106 C3
High Riggs EH3..........228 B2
High School Wynd EH1...229 B2
High School Yds EH1....229 B2
High St Aberdour KY3.....49 B7
  Aberlady EH32.........71 C4
  Airth FK2.............22 D3
  Alloa FK10............10 B6
  Bathgate EH48.......141 B7
  Bonnybridge FK4.......58 A5
  Bonnyrigg and Lasswade,
  Broomieknowe EH19...173 B7
  Bonnyrigg and Lasswade
  EH18.................152 A1
  Burntisland KY3........50 E8
  Clackmannan FK10.....10 F4
  Cockenzie & Port Seton
  EH32.................97 C4
  Cowdenbeath KY4.......13 D4
  Dalkeith EH22........153 A3
  Dunbar, Belhaven EH42..78 A2
  Dunbar EH42...........78 D2
  Dunfermline KY12......29 A3
  Dysart KY1............18 A7
  East Linton EH40.....103 D8
  Edinburgh EH1........229 A3
  Falkirk FK1...........60 B4
  Gifford EH41.........220 F6
  Haddington EH41......130 B8
  Inverkeithing KY11.....47 B2
  Kincardine FK10.......23 E4
  Kinghorn KY3..........34 F2
  Kirkcaldy KY1.........17 C3
  Kirkliston EH29.......89 B1
  Linlithgow EH49.......85 A7
  Loanhead EH20........172 C8
  Lochgelly KY5.........14 B7
  Musselburgh EH21.....124 D6
  North Berwick EH39....54 C7
  Ormiston EH35........155 E7
  Penicuik EH26........191 F4
  Prestonpans EH32......96 E1
  Shotts ML7...........179 F4
  Slamannan FK1........108 B7
  South Queensferry EH30..68 C1
  Tranent EH33.........126 D6
High Station Ct FK1.....60 A3
High Station Rd FK1.....60 A3
HIGH VALLEYFIELD......26 A2
High View Gr FK1........81 D6
Hillary Rd FK5..........38 E1
Hillbank KY11.........229 B2
Hillcoat Loan EH15......95 A1
Hillcoat Pl EH15........95 A1
Hill Cres EH48.........141 B7
Hillcrest Bo'ness EH51...63 F5
  Cowdenbeath KY4.......13 B3
Hillcrest Ave KY2.......16 E6
Hillcrest Dr FK10.......10 C6
Hillcrest Pl FK6........57 D7
Hillcrest Sq FK2........81 F7
Hill Ct Dunfermline KY12..29 D5
  South Queensferry EH30..68 B1
HILLEND...............47 E4
Hillend Ind Pk KY11.....48 C5
Hillend Rd KY11........47 B3
Hillfield Rd KY11.......47 B2
Hillfoots Rd Menstrie FK9..3 C6
  Stirling FK9...........2 E4
Hillfoot Terr ML8......215 A1
Hill Gr KY2............26 D7
Hillhead EH19.........173 B8
Hillhead Ave ML8......215 A2
Hillhead Dr FK1........59 F2
Hillhouse Wynd EH27...145 F3
Hillhouse Ave EH48....140 F8
Hillhouse Cres EH27...145 F3
Hillhouse Farm Steadings
  EH49.................85 B3
Hillhouse Rd Denny FK6..57 E7
  Edinburgh EH4.........92 B2
Hillhouseridge Rd ML7..179 D5
Hillhouse Terr EH27...145 F3
Hillock Ave FK2........61 C2
HILL OF BEATH.........13 A1
Hill of Beath Prim Sch
  KY4..................12 F1
Hill of Kinnaird FK2....38 E7
Hill of St Margaret KY12..29 F5
Hillpark Ave EH4.......91 F3
Hillpark Brae EH4.......91 F1
Hillpark Cres
  Bannockburn FK7.......7 C2
  Edinburgh EH4.........91 F2
Hillpark Ct EH4........91 F3
Hillpark Dr Bannockburn FK7.7 D2
  Edinburgh EH4.........91 F1
Hillpark Gdns EH4.......91 F2
Hillpark Gn EH4........91 F2
Hillpark Gr EH4........91 F2
Hillpark Loan EH4......92 A2
Hillpark Rd EH4........91 F2
Hillpark Terr EH4.......91 F2
Hillpark Way EH4.......92 A2
Hillpark Wood EH4......92 A2
Hill Pk FK10...........10 B7
Hill Pl Alloa FK10......10 A8
  Edinburgh EH8........229 B2
  Kirkcaldy KY1.........17 C4
  Mayfield EH22........174 E5
  Shotts ML7...........179 E5

Hill Rd Gullane EH31.....51 F2
  Harthill ML7.........159 D5
  Pathhead EH37........176 A5
HILLSIDE..............93 F2
Hillside FK10...........5 C2
Hillside Ave KY11.......48 A3
Hillside Camp Rd KY11...46 E1
Hillside Cotts
  Cousland EH22........154 D5
  Linlithgow EH49.......85 C7
Hillside Cres EH7.......93 F2
  EH23.................195 D8
Hillside Crescent N
  EH23.................195 D8
Hillside Crescent S EH23 195 D8
Hillside Dr EH48......138 D3
Hillside Gr EH51.......64 C6
Hillside Pl
  Blackridge EH48......138 D3
  Longridge EH47......161 C1
Hillside Rd EH30.......90 D4
Hillside Sch KY3........49 C8
Hillside St EH7........93 F2
Hillside Terr Alloa FK10..10 B7
  Edinburgh EH30........90 D5
  Westquarter FK2.......61 B3
Hill Sq EH8...........229 B2
Hill St Alloa FK10......10 B7
  Cowdenbeath KY4.......13 C4
  Dunfermline KY12......29 A4
  Dysart KY1............18 A7
  Edinburgh EH2........228 C4
  Inverkeithing KY11.....47 B2
  Kirkcaldy KY1.........17 B3
  Stirling FK7...........7 B3
Hill Street North La EH2 228 C4
Hill Street South La EH2 228 C4
Hilltop EH49...........84 D7
Hilltown Terr EH22....123 C1
Hillview Cowdenbeath KY4..13 B3
  Edinburgh EH4.........92 B2
  Oakley KY12...........26 F7
Hillview Ave EH52......115 F6
Hillview Cotts EH28...117 D2
Hillview Cres
  Crossgates KY4........30 E6
  Edinburgh EH12.......119 D7
Hillview Ct KY12........30 A6
Hillview Dr
  Bridge of Allan FK9.....2 A6
  Edinburgh EH12.......119 C7
Hillview Gdns EH35....155 F7
Hillview La EH54......164 F4
Hillview Pl Broxburn EH52.115 F5
  Crossgates KY4........30 E6
  Fallin FK2............8 C4
Hillview Rd
  Bonnybridge FK4.......58 C3
  Edinburgh EH12.......119 C7
  Grangemouth FK2......82 D8
  Ormiston EH35........155 E7
  Stenhousemuir FK5.....38 C3
Hillview Terr Alloa FK10..10 C6
  Edinburgh EH12.......119 D7
Hillwood Ave EH28....117 C5
Hillwood Cres EH28...117 C5
Hillwood Gdns EH28...117 C6
Hillwood Pl EH30......68 B1
Hillwood Prim Sch EH28 117 C5
Hillwood Rd EH28.....117 C5
Hillwood Rise EH28...117 C5
Hillwood Terr
  Ratho Station EH28...117 C5
  Rosyth KY11..........47 A3
Hilton Rd FK7..........20 E8
Hilton Cres FK10......10 D7
Hilton Ct EH41........130 A8
Hilton Farm Steadings
  KY11.................46 B3
Hilton Rd Alloa FK10....10 D7
  Cairneyhill KY12.......27 E1
  Rosyth KY11..........46 C2
Hilton Terr FK7........8 C4
Hilton View KY4........13 C6
Hirst Cres FK7.........8 D4
Hirst Ct FK7...........8 D4
Hirst Gdns ML7........179 C5
Hirst Rd ML7..........158 D3
Hoban Sq EH52........115 F6
Hobart St EH54.........143 E3
Hochsauerland Brea
  EH54.................143 E3
Hodge St FK1...........60 B4
Hogan Pl FK4...........57 E5
Hogarth Ave EH23.....174 C2
Hoggan Cres KY11......29 C2
Hoggan Way Alva FK12....4 F6
  Loanhead EH20........172 C7
Hoghill Ct EH53.......144 E3
Hoghill Pl EH53.......144 E3
Holborn Pl KY11........46 F5
Holbourne Pl FK11......4 A7
Holden Way KY11.......48 B5
Holly Ave FK5..........38 F3
Holly Bank EH22.......174 E7
Hollybank Pl EH53....144 F2
Hollybank Terr EH11...120 C4
Holly Cres KY11........46 E8
Holly Gr Livingston EH54.144 B6
  Menstrie FK11..........3 F6
Hollyhock Glade EH54..144 C7
Holly Pl KY1...........17 C7
Holly Terr EH19.......173 B6
Holly Wlk EH20.......171 E7
Holmes Cl EH52.......115 B4
Holmes Farm La EH52...115 B5
Holmes Gdns EH52....115 B4
Holmes Holdings EH52..115 C4
Holmes Rd EH52.......115 B4

Holmlea Ave 2 FK2.....82 D8
Holton Cotts FK10......5 C1
Holton Cres FK10.......5 C1
Holton Ct 1 FK10.......5 C1
Holton Sq FK10.........5 C1
Holy Cross RC Prim Sch
  EH6..................93 C5
Holy Family RC Prim Sch
  EH52.................87 E2
HOLYGATE.............115 D6
Holygate Pl EH52......115 D5
Holy Name RC Prim Sch
  EH32.................26 E7
HOLYROOD.............122 A7
Holyrood Bsns Pk EH16.122 D4
Holyrood Gait EH8.....229 C3
Holy Rood High Sch
  EH15.................122 D6
Holyrood Park Rd EH16 229 C1
Holyrood Pk★ EH8, EH15,
  EH16.................122 B7
Holyrood Pl
  Dunfermline KY12......29 B4
  Stenhousemuir FK5.....38 E4
Holyrood Rd EH8......229 C3
Home Farm Cotts
  Bonnybridge FK6.......57 F6
  Edinburgh EH30........90 E7
Home Farm Rd FK7......6 E5
Home Pk KY3...........49 C7
Home St EH3..........228 B1
Homesteads The FK8.....6 D7
Honeybank Cres ML8...215 A3
Honeyman St EH4......139 E7
Hood Pl KY11..........46 E2
Hookney Terr FK6......36 C2
Hope Cotts EH51........64 D5
HOPEFIELD...........173 B6
Hopefield Dr EH47.....162 C8
Hopefield Pk EH19....173 A6
Hopefield Pl
  Blackburn EH47.......162 C8
  Bonnyrigg and Lasswade
  EH19.................173 A6
Hopefield Prim Sch
  EH19.................173 A6
Hopefield Rd EH47....162 C8
Hopefield Terr
  Bonnyrigg and Lasswade
  EH19.................173 A6
  Edinburgh EH6.........93 E6
Hope La EH15.........123 B7
Hopelands Rd EH26....190 E5
Hope Lane N EH15......123 B8
Hopepark EH48.........140 E6
Hope Park Cres
  Edinburgh EH8.......229 B1
  2 Haddington EH41....101 A1
Hope Park Gdns EH48..140 E6
Hope Park Sq EH8.....229 B1
Hope Park Terr FK4.....57 F6
Hope Park Terr EH8....229 B1
Hope Pk EH41.........101 A1
Hope Pl Musselburgh EH21 124 F6
  Tranent EH33.........126 C7
Hope St Bo'ness EH51...63 F8
  Carluke ML8.........215 A2
  Cowdenbeath KY4.......13 C6
  Edinburgh EH2........228 B3
  Falkirk FK1...........60 B5
  Inverkeithing KY11.....47 B1
  Queensferry EH30......89 B8
  Stirling FK8...........1 F1
Hope Street La EH2....228 B3
Hope Terr EH9.........121 C4
Hopetoun Cres EH7......93 E2
Hopetoun Dr
  Bridge of Allan FK9.....2 A8
  Haddington EH41......100 F1
Hopetoun Fishery★ EH52 88 F5
Hopetoun House★ EH30..66 F2
Hopetoun La EH48......140 A3
Hopetoun Mews 1 EH41 100 F1
Hopetoun Mon★ EH39..100 E5
Hopetoun Pk EH31......52 A3
Hopetoun Pl KY2.......16 C6
Hopetoun Rd EH30......68 A1
Hopetoun St
  Bathgate EH48.......141 B6
  Edinburgh EH7.........93 E3
Hopetoun Terr
  Gullane EH31..........52 A3
  Ormiston EH35........155 E7
Hopetoun View KY11....48 C4
Hopeward Ct KY11......48 C3
Hopeward Mews KY11...48 C3
Hoprig EH53...........99 A1
Hoprig Pk TD13........218 F3
Hoprig Rd TD13........218 F3
Hopronbeam Cres FK2....61 A3
Hornel Pl FK5..........38 B2
Horne Terr EH11.......228 A1
Horsburgh Bank EH14..147 C3
Horsburgh Gdns EH14..147 C3
Horsburgh Gr EH14....147 C3
Horse Wynd EH8......229 C3
Hoseason Gdns EH4.....91 D1
Hosie Rigg EH15.......123 B5
Hospital Cross Head KY11 29 C1
Hospital Hill KY11......29 B1
Hospital Intc EH54....143 D4
Hospital Rd EH41......100 F1
Hot Pot Wynd KY1......18 A6
Houldsworth Cres ML7..198 A8
Houldsworth St KY12....26 A7
Houliston Ave KY11.....47 B3
House O'Hill Ave EH4....92 A3
House O'Hill Brae EH4...92 A3

House O'Hill Cres EH4....92 A3
House O'Hill Gdns EH4...92 B3
House O'Hill Gn EH4.....92 A3
House O'Hill Gr EH4.....92 A3
House O'Hill Pl EH4.....92 A3
House O'Hill Row EH4...92 B3
House O'Hill Terr EH4...92 B2
House O' Muir EH26....170 E2
House O' Muir Rd ML7...158 B3
Housepark Pl EH54....143 B3
Houston Ct 1 KY12......28 F4
Houston Ind Est EH54..144 A8
Houston Rd EH54......115 A1
Houston Terr EH54....115 A1
Houstoun Gdns EH52...114 F3
Houstoun Ind Est
  Dechmont EH54.......114 C1
  Livingston EH54......143 F8
Houstoun Intc EH54...143 E7
Houstoun Mains Holdings
  EH52.................114 E2
Houstoun Rd
  Livingston, Eliburn EH54..143 B5
  Livingston, Ladywell EH54 143 D6
  Houstoun Road W EH54..142 E5
Howard Cres KY11......29 C2
Howard Pl Dysart KY1...18 A7
  Edinburgh EH3.........93 C3
Howard St Edinburgh EH3 93 C3
  Falkirk FK1...........59 F4
Howburn Cres ML7.....159 E6
Howburn Rd ML7......159 D6
HOWDEN...............143 E4
Howden East Rd EH54...143 F4
Howden Hall Cres EH16.150 F6
Howden Hall Ct EH16..150 F6
Howden Hall Dr EH16..150 F6
Howden Hall Gdns EH16.151 A6
Howden Hall Loan EH16..150 F6
Howden Hall Pk EH16...150 F5
Howden Hall Rd EH16..151 A5
Howden Hall Way EH16.151 A5
Howden St Andrew's RC Prim
  Sch EH54.............143 F4
Howden South Rd EH54.143 E3
Howden St EH8........229 B1
Howden West Rd EH54..143 D4
Howe Ness KY11........46 D3
Howe Pk EH10.........149 F5
Howe St EH3..........228 C4
Howetown FK10.........5 D4
Howieson Ave EH51.....63 F5
Howieson Gn EH52.....114 F4
Howie's Pl FK7.........59 B4
Howlands Rd FK7........7 A4
Howley Ave EH54.......143 E4
Howpark Rd TD13, TD14..219 E1
Hudson Rd KY11........46 F3
Hugh Ave KY5..........14 B8
Hughes Cres EH22.....174 F6
Hugh Miller Pl EH3......93 B2
Hugh Pl KY5...........14 B8
Hugh Russell Pl EH30...89 B8
Huly Hill Rd EH28.....117 A5
HUMBIE...............178 B2
Humbie Cotts EH29......88 F4
Humbie Prim Sch EH36..178 B2
Humbie Rd EH29........89 A2
Humbie Smallholdings
  EH27.................145 F4
Humbie Terr KY3........49 C8
Humbug Cres FK9........2 A6
Hume Ct FK9...........2 A6
Hummel Rd EH31........52 A3
Hungerage Sq EH33....126 D5
Hunthurn Ave EH49......85 C7
Hunt Cl EH22.........153 A4
Hunter Ave EH20......172 D8
Hunter Ct EH20........172 D8
HUNTERFIELD..........174 D2
Hunterfield Ct EH23...195 C8
Hunterfield Pk EH23...174 C1
Hunterfield Rd EH23...195 B8
Hunterfield Terr EH23..174 B1
Hunter Gdns
  Bonnybridge FK4.......58 A5
  Broxburn EH52........116 A5
  Denny FK6............36 D2
Hunter Gr Bathgate EH48 141 E5
  Whitburn EH47.......160 F5
Hunter Pl Dunfermline KY12 28 E5
  Falkirk FK2...........39 A4
  Kirkcaldy KY1.........17 B3
  Shotts ML7...........179 E5
Hunter Rd EH54.......143 C2
Hunter's Cl EH41......228 C2
Hunters Ct EH21......124 D7
Hunters Hill EH26.....191 C6
Hunter's La EH47......161 A4
Hunter Sq Edinburgh EH1 229 A3
  Gorebridge EH23......195 D8
Hunter St Kirkcaldy KY1..17 B4
  Shotts ML7...........179 D5
Hunter Terr
  Bonnyrigg and Lasswade
  EH19.................173 B7
  Loanhead EH20........172 D8
Huntingdon Pl EH7......93 E2
Hunting Pk EH54......144 E1
HUNTINGTON..........100 B1
Huntlaw Rd EH34......156 E6
Huntly Ave EH54......144 B6
Huntly Cres Kirkcaldy KY2 16 C8
  Stirling FK8...........1 F2
Huntly Rd EH39.........93 A3
Huntly Terr ML7......180 B3

Hunt Pl KY12..........28 B1
Huron Ave EH54.......143 F3
Hursted Ave EH22.....174 D7
Hurworth St FK1........59 F3
Husband Pl KY1.........29 F1
Hutchison Ave EH14...120 C3
Hutchison Cotts EH14..120 C3
Hutchison Crossway
  EH14.................120 C4
Hutchison Gdns EH14..120 C3
Hutchison Gn KY11.....29 B1
Hutchison Gr EH14....120 D3
Hutchison Ho EH14....120 D3
Hutchison Loan EH14..120 C3
Hutchison Medway EH14 120 C3
Hutchison Pk EH14....120 C4
Hutchison Pl EH14....120 C4
Hutchison Rd EH14....120 C4
Hutchison Terr EH14...120 C3
Hutchison View EH14...120 C4
Hutton Pk FK10........10 C7
Hutton Rd EH8........229 C3
Hutton Sq EH54........164 C6
Hyndford Ho EH39......54 A7
Hyndfords Ct EH1......229 B3
Hyvot Ave EH17.......151 D6
Hyvot Bank Ave EH17..151 E6
Hyvot Ct EH17........151 D5
Hyvot Gdns EH17......151 D6
Hyvot Gn EH17........151 D6
Hyvot Gr EH17........151 D6
Hyvot Loan EH17......151 D6
Hyvot Mill Dr EH17....151 D6
Hyvot Pk EH17........151 D5
Hyvot Rd EH17........151 D6
Hyvot Terr EH17......151 D6
Hyvot View EH17......151 D5

I

Ibris Pl EH39...........54 A7
Icehouse Brae N FK2....61 B4
Icehouse Brae S FK2....61 B4
Imex Ctr EH20........172 A7
Implement Rd EH42......77 E1
Imrie Pl EH26........191 F5
Inch Ave KY3..........49 B6
Inch Colm Ave FK5......38 C4
Inch Colm Pl KY11......68 B6
Inchcolm Rd KY11......29 E3
Inchcolm Terr EH30.....89 B8
Inchcorse Pl EH48.....141 C1
Inch Cres EH48.......141 D5
Inchcross EH48.......140 F3
Inchcross Dr EH48....140 F2
Inchcross Ind Est EH48..140 F3
Inchcross Rk EH48....140 F2
Inchcross Steadings
  EH48.................140 F2
Inches Rdbt FK5........38 C4
Inches The
  Dalgety Bay KY11......48 B2
  Grangemouth FK3......61 E8
Inchgarvie Ave KY3.....33 D1
Inchgarvie Cres KY11...29 E3
Inchgarvie Pk EH30.....68 A1
Inch Garvie Terr FK5...38 C4
Inchkeith Ave EH30.....89 C8
Inchkeith Cres KY11.....35 B6
Inchkeith Ct KY11......29 F3
Inchkeith Dr KY11......29 E3
Inchkeith 1 Gr KY3 EH23 126 D7
Inchkeith Pl FK1.......60 B2
Inchmickery Ave KY11...48 D5
Inchmickery Rd KY11...48 C5
Inchmuir Rd EH48......141 B2
Inchna FK11............4 A6
INCH THE.............122 B2
Inchview EH21.........124 D6
Inch View Kinghorn KY3..34 F1
  Kirkcaldy KY1.........35 B7
Inchview Cres EH21....125 C5
Inchview Gdns KY11.....48 B3
Inchview N EH32........96 E1
Inchview Rd EH21.....125 C5
Inchview Terr EH7......94 F1
Inch Wood Ave EH48...141 D4
Inchyra Pl FK3.........61 E5
Inchyra Rd FK3........61 E5
India Pl EH3..........228 B4
India St EH3..........228 B4
Industrial Rd EH6......94 B4
Industry Homes EH6.....93 E5
Industry La EH6........93 E5
Infirmary St EH1......229 B2
Ingleston Ave FK6......36 D4
Inglewood Gdns FK10....10 A8
Inglewood Ho FK10......4 F1
Inglewood Pl 3 EH16..151 B8
Inglewood Rd FK10......9 F8
Inglewood St EH54....143 F5
Inglis Ave EH32........97 C4
Inglis Cres KY3........34 F3
Inglis' Ct EH1........228 C2
Inglis Dr FK2..........39 D2
Inglis Farm EH32.......97 C3
Inglis Green Gait 3
  EH14.................120 B2
Inglis Green Rd EH14..120 B2
Inglis Green Rigg 2
  EH14.................120 B2
Inglis La KY12..........28 F5
Inglis Pl FK2..........82 E8
Inglis Pl KY12..........29 A4
Ingliston Rd EH28.....117 F6
Ingram Pl FK2.........82 E6

Inkerman Ct EH26 . . . . .192 A8
Innellan Cres ML7 . . . . .179 E6
Innerpeffray Dr FK2 . . . . .39 A3
INNERWICK 218 A7
Innerwick Prim Sch
  EH42 . . . . .218 A7
Innes Bldgs **1** EH33 . . . .126 C6
Innova Way KY11 . . . . .46 D1
Inn Pl EH54 . . . . .143 B2
Institution St KY1 . . . . .17 E7
Inverallan Ct FK9 . . . . .1 F8
Inverallan Dr FK9 . . . . .1 F7
Inverallan Rd FK9 . . . . .1 F7
Inveralmond Com High Sch
  EH54 . . . . .143 D5
Inveralmond Dr EH4 . . . .91 A5
Inveralmond Gdns EH4 . .91 A5
Inveralmond Gr EH4 . . . .91 A5
Inverary Dr FK5 . . . . .38 F5
Inveravon Rd EH20 . . . . . .151 B1
Inveravon Rdbt EH51 . . . .62 D5
INVERESK 124 E5
Inveresk Brae EH21 . . . . .124 D5
Inveresk Est The EH21 . .124 D4
Inveresk Gate EH21 . . . . .124 D5
Inveresk Ind Est EH21 . . .124 C5
Inveresk Lodge Gdn★
  EH21 . . . . .124 D4
Inveresk Mill Est EH21 . .124 D4
Inveresk Rd EH21 . . . . . . .124 C5
Inveresk Village Rd
  EH21 . . . . .124 D4
Inverewe Pl KY11 . . . . .30 A1
INVERKEITHING 47 B1
Inverkeithing Her Ctr★
  KY11 . . . . .47 B2
Inverkeithing High Sch
  KY11 . . . . .47 D3
Inverkeithing Prim Sch
  KY11 . . . . .47 D3
Inverkeithing Rd
  Aberdour KY3 . . . . .49 B7
  Crossgates KY4 . . . . .30 E6
Inverkeithing Sta KY11 . .47 C3
Inverkip Dr ML7 . . . . .179 E5
INVERLEITH 93 A4
Inverleith Ave EH3 . . . . . .93 B4
Inverleith Avenue S EH3 .93 B4
Inverleith Gdns EH3 . . . .93 A4
Inverleith Pl EH3 . . . . .92 F3
Inverleith Pl EH3 . . . . .93 A4
Inverleith Place La EH3 . .93 B4
Inverleith Row EH3 . . . . . .93 A3
Inverleith Terr EH3 . . . . . .93 B3
Inverleith Terrace La EH3 .93 C3
Invertiel Bank KY1 . . . . . . .17 B1
Invertiel Rd KY1 . . . . .35 A8
Invertiel Terr KY1 . . . . .17 B1
Inzievar Ho KY12 . . . . .26 F4
Inzievar Terr KY12 . . . . . . .27 A6
Iona Pl FK1 . . . . .60 B2
Iona Rd KY11 . . . . .29 E3
Iona St EH6 . . . . .93 F3
Iona Street La FK6 . . . . . . .93 F3
Ireland Ave EH47 . . . . . . .160 F6
Irene Terr KY1 . . . . .82 E2
Ironmills Rd EH22 . . . . . . .152 F3
Irvine Cres EH48 . . . . .140 F6
Irvine Pl FK8 . . . . .7 A8
Irving Ct FK1 . . . . .59 E5
Islands Cres FK10 . . . . . . .60 B2
Islay Ct FK3 . . . . .61 D5
Islay Rd KY11 . . . . .29 E2
Ivanhoe Cres EH16 . . . . . .122 B1
Ivanhoe Pl FK8 . . . . .2 A2
Ivanhoe Rise EH54 . . . . . .144 A2
Ivybank Ct FK2 . . . . .61 E2
Ivy Gr KY11 . . . . .46 A8
Ivy La KY1 . . . . .18 A7
Ivy Terr EH11 . . . . .120 E5
Izatt Ave KY11 . . . . .29 B1
Izatt Terr FK10 . . . . .11 A4

J

Jack Kane Sports Ctr
  EH15 . . . . .123 A4
Jacklin Gn EH54 . . . . .143 B7
Jackson Ave FK3 . . . . .61 D7
Jackson Pl EH54 . . . . .143 C4
Jackson's Cl EH1 . . . . .229 A3
Jackson's Entry EH8 . . . .229 C3
Jackson St EH26 . . . . .191 E5
Jacobite Way EH32 . . . . . .97 B1
Jacob Pl FK1 . . . . .2 A2
Jacobs Way EH23 . . . . . . .195 C8
Jamaica Mews EH3 . . . . .228 B4
Jamaica St EH3 . . . . .228 B4
Jamaica Street North La
  EH3 . . . . .228 B4
Jamaica Street South La
  EH3 . . . . .228 B4
James Bank KY12 . . . . . . .29 A4
James Cornwall Ct FK3 . .61 F6
James Craig Wk EH2 . . . .229 B4
James Croft Terr FK1 . . . .59 F1
James Ct KY4 . . . . .13 C2
James' Ct EH1 . . . . .229 A3
James Gillespie's High Sch
  EH9 . . . . .121 C5
James Gillespie's Prim Sch
  EH9 . . . . .121 C5
James Gr KY1 . . . . .17 B2
James Hog Cres KY12 . . .26 F6
James Lean Ave EH22 . . .153 B3

James Leary Way EH19. . .173 C8
James Miller Rd KY11 . . . .46 E2
Jameson Pl EH6 . . . . .93 F3
James' Park La KY3. . . . . . .33 F1
James' Pk KY3. . . . . .33 F1
James Short Pk FK1 . . . . .60 B3
James Smith Ave FK2 . . . .82 E6
James St Alva FK12. . . . . . . .5 A6
  Armadale EH48 . . . . .139 F5
  Bannockburn FK7 . . . . .7 C1
  Cowdenbeath KY4 . . . . . .13 C2
  Dunfermline KY12 . . . . . . .29 A4
  Edinburgh EH15. . . . . . . .123 C8
  Falkirk FK2 . . . . .60 B6
  Laurieston FK2 . . . . .61 A3
  Longcroft FK4 . . . . .57 A3
  Musselburgh EH21 . . . . .124 D6
  Stenhousemuir FK5. . . . . .38 D2
  Stirling FK8 . . . . .2 B1
James Street La EH15. . .123 C8
James Watt Ave EH51. . . .64 A7
James Wilson Dr FK2 . . . .83 A5
James Wylie Pl FK10. . . . .23 F4
James Young High Sch The
  EH54. . . . . .143 E1
James Young Rd EH48 . .141 B3
Jamieson Ave
  Bo'ness EH51 . . . . .63 E6
  Stenhousemuir FK5. . . . . .38 E3
Jamieson Gdns ML7 . . . .179 E5
Janefield EH17 . . . . .151 A4
Jane St EH6 . . . . .93 F4
Jardine Pl EH48 . . . . .140 E7
Jarnac Ct **7** EH22 . . . . .153 A3
Jarvey St EH48 . . . . .141 B7
Jarvie Pl **6** FK2 . . . . . . .60 A8
Jarvie Rd FK2 . . . . .61 A1
Jasper Ave FK2. . . . . .61 A4
Jawbanes Rd KY2 . . . . . . .35 A8
Jean Armour Ave **1**
  EH16 . . . . .122 A1
Jean Armour Dr EH22 . . .153 D2
Jean Armour Gdns KY12 . .17 A7
Jeanette Stewart Dr
  EH22 . . . . .173 F4
Jeffrey Ave EH4 . . . . .92 B1
Jeffrey Bank EH51 . . . . . .63 F7
Jeffrey St EH1 . . . . .229 B3
Jeffrey Terr FK2 . . . . .61 F2
Jellyholm Rd FK10 . . . . . . .10 E8
Jenks Loan EH22 . . . . . . .174 A5
Jennie Rennie's Rd KY11. .29 B1
Jessfield Pl EH51 . . . . .63 F5
Jessfield Terr EH6 . . . . . . .93 D6
Jewel & Esk Coll
  Dalkeith EH22 . . . . .152 F1
  Edinburgh EH15. . . . . . . .123 D6
Jewel The EH15 . . . . .123 B5
Jim Bush Dr EH32 . . . . . .125 E7
Jock's Hill Cres EH49 . . . .84 E7
JOCK'S LODGE 94 D1
Jock's Lodge **8** EH46. . .94 C1
John Bernard Way EH23 .195 C6
John Brown Ct EH41 . . . . .101 B3
John Connelly Ct **5** KY12 .28 E5
John Cotton Bsns Ctr EH7 .94 A2
John Cowane Row FK49. . .2 A4
John Cres EH33. . . . . .126 C6
John Davidson Dr FK6 . . .36 C4
John Humble St EH42 . . .174 E5
John Hunter Ct KY1 . . . . . .17 B4
John Knox Ho★ EH1. . . . .229 B3
John Knox Pl EH26 . . . . . .191 F5
John Knox Rd EH32 . . . . .98 E5
John McDouall Stuart Mus★
  KY1. . . . . .18 A7
John Mason Ct EH30. . . . .89 C8
John Muir Birthplace★
  EH42. . . . . .78 D2
John Muir Dr EH42 . . . . .106 D8
John Muir Dry Pk★ EH42 .77 D4
John Muir Gdns EH42. . .106 D8
John Muir Pl EH42 . . . . . .106 D8
John Muir Way EH42. . . .106 D8
John Murray Dr FK9 . . . . . . .2 A4
Johnnie Cope's Rd EH33 .126 A7
Johnny Moat Pl EH32 . . . .96 F1
John O'Hara Ct EH14 . . . .59 D5
John Row Pl KY12 . . . . . . .27 A7
John Rushforth Pl FK8 . . . .1 F3
Johnsburn Gn EH14 . . . .147 B1
Johnsburn Haugh EH14 .147 B1
Johnsburn Pk EH14 . . . .168 B8
Johnsburn Rd EH14. . . . .147 B1
John's La EH6 . . . . .94 A5
John Smith Way ML7 . . .179 D5
John's Pl EH6 . . . . .94 A5
John St Dunfermline KY12 .29 B2
  Edinburgh EH15. . . . . . . .123 C8
  Falkirk FK2 . . . . .60 B7
  Kincardine FK10 . . . . .23 D3
  Kirkcaldy KY2 . . . . .17 B5
  Longcroft FK4 . . . . .57 A3
  Penicuik EH26 . . . . .191 F6
Johnston Ave
  Stenhousemuir FK5. . . . . .38 F3
  Stirling FK9 . . . . .2 B3
  Uphall EH52. . . . . .114 F3
Johnston Cres
  Dunfermline KY11 . . . . . . .29 B1
  Lochgelly KY5 . . . . .14 B7
Johnston Ct **7** Falkirk FK2 .60 A8
  Uphall EH52. . . . . .114 F3
Johnstone Ct FK12 . . . . . . .5 A6
Johnstone La ML8 . . . . . .215 B1
Johnstone St Alva FK12. . . .5 A6
  Menstrie FK11. . . . . .3 F6

Johnston Pk
  Cowdenbeath KY4 . . . . . .13 C5
  Inverkeithing KY11 . . . . . .47 B2
Johnston Pl Denny FK6 . .36 C1
  Penicuik EH26 . . . . .191 F8
Johnston St FK7 . . . . .7 C1
Johnston Terr
  Cockenzie & Port Seton
    EH32. . . . . .97 D4
  Edinburgh EH1. . . . . .228 C2
  Penicuik EH26 . . . . .191 E5
John Street Lane E EH15 .123 C8
John Street Lane W
  EH15 . . . . .123 C8
John Stuart Gait KY12. . . .26 F6
John Wood Pl KY4 . . . . . . .30 F7
Jones Ave FK5. . . . . .59 C8
Jones Gn EH54 . . . . .143 A7
Jones St KY12 . . . . .12 A1
JOPPA 123 D7
Joppa Gdns EH15 . . . . . .123 C7
Joppa Gr EH15. . . . . .123 C7
Joppa Pk EH15 . . . . .123 D7
Joppa Rd EH15 . . . . .123 C7
Joppa Station Pl EH15 . .123 C7
Joppa Terr EH15 . . . . .123 C7
Jordan La EH10 . . . . .121 B3
Joseph Cumming Gdns
  EH52 . . . . .115 B4
Joseph Scott Gdns EH52 .115 E4
Jubilee Ave EH54 . . . . . . .142 F6
Jubilee Cres EH23 . . . . . .174 C1
Jubilee Ct KY11 . . . . .29 A3
Jubilee Dr KY11 . . . . .46 B1
Jubilee Rd Denny FK6. . . .36 B3
  Ratho Station EH28 . . . . .118 A7
  Whitburn EH47 . . . . .161 A6
Jubilee Way FK4. . . . . .57 F5
Junction Pl **8** Alloa FK10 . .10 B6
  Edinburgh EH6. . . . . .93 F5
Junction Rd KY11 . . . . . . .17 D7
Juner Pl EH23 . . . . .174 C1
Juniper Ave EH14 . . . . . . .148 C5
Juniper Gdns EH14 . . . . .148 C6
Juniper Gr
  Dunfermline KY11 . . . . . . .46 D8
  Edinburgh EH14. . . . . . . .148 C6
  Livingston EH54. . . . . . . .144 B6
JUNIPER GREEN 148 C6
Juniper Green Prim Sch
  EH14. . . . . .148 D6
Juniper La EH14 . . . . .148 C6
Juniperlee EH14 . . . . .148 D6
Juniper Park Rd EH14. . . .148 D6
Juniper Pl EH14 . . . . .148 C5
Juniper Terr EH14 . . . . . .148 C6
Jura EH54 . . . . .142 F5
Jura Pl FK3 . . . . .61 D5
Justinhaugh Dr EH49 . . . .84 D7
Jute Pl KY1 . . . . .18 A7
Jutland St KY11 . . . . .46 D6

K

Kaemuir Ct EH48. . . . . . . .110 F5
Kaim Cres EH48 . . . . .141 D5
KAIMES 151 A5
Kaimes Ave EH27 . . . . . . .145 E3
Kaimes Cres EH27 . . . . . .145 E3
Kaimes Ct EH12. . . . . .119 F6
Kaimes Gr EH27 . . . . .145 F3
Kaimes Pl EH27 . . . . .119 F7
Kaimes Specl Sch EH16 .151 C6
Kaimes View EH22 . . . . .152 B7
Kaims Brae EH54 . . . . . . .143 C2
Kaims Ct EH54 . . . . .143 B2
Kaims Dr EH54 . . . . .143 B2
Kaims Gdns EH54 . . . . . .143 C2
Kaims Gr EH54 . . . . .143 C2
Kaims Pl EH54 . . . . .143 B2
Kaims Terr EH54. . . . . . . .143 B2
Kaims Wlk EH54 . . . . .143 C2
Kames Pl KY12 . . . . .29 C1
Kason Rd ML7. . . . . .179 E6
Kerries Ct EH6 . . . . .57 B8
Katesmill Rd EH14 . . . . . .149 B8
Katherine St Kirkcaldy KY2 .17 E3
  Livingston EH54. . . . . . . .144 A5
Katrine Cres EH12 . . . . . . .29 B1
Katrine Ct FK10. . . . . .10 C5
Katrine Dr KY12 . . . . .29 B1
Katrine Pl FK6 . . . . .57 D6
Katrine Rd Shotts ML7 . .179 E6
  Whitburn EH47 . . . . .161 D7
Kay Gdns EH32 . . . . .97 C4
Kay Rd KY12 . . . . .43 F8
Keavil Farm Steadings
  KY12 . . . . .45 B8
Keavil Pl KY12 . . . . .28 B1
Kedslie Pl EH16. . . . . .150 F7
Kedslie Rd EH16 . . . . .150 F8
KEILARSBRAE. 10 C8
Keir Ave FK8 . . . . .2 A2
Keir Ct FK9 . . . . .2 A7
Keirfold Ave FK10. . . . . .4 A7
Keir Gdns FK9 . . . . .2 A7
Keir Hardie Ave FK2 . . . . .61 A3
Keir Hardie Dr FK2 . . . . . .174 E5
Keir Hardie Rd EH49. . . . .84 D7
Keir Hardie Terr KY11 . . . .29 B1
Keirsbeath Ct KY12 . . . . . .12 B2
Keirsbeath Rise KY12 . . .12 B1

Keir St Bridge of Allan FK9. . . .2 A7
  Cowdenbeath KY4. . . . . . .13 B4
  Edinburgh EH3. . . . . .228 C2
Keith Ave FK7 . . . . .7 C4
Keith Cres EH4 . . . . .92 B1
Keith Gdns EH52. . . . . . . .115 C6
Keith Marischal EH36 . . .177 F5
Keith Pl Dunfermline KY12 .29 D4
  Inverkeithing KY11 . . . . . .47 C3
Keith Row EH4 . . . . .92 C1
Keith St FK10 . . . . .23 D3
Keith Terr EH4. . . . . .92 B1
Kekewich Ave EH7 . . . . . .94 F2
Kelliebank EH7 . . . . .9 E6
Kelliebank Ind Est FK10. . . .9 E5
Kellie Pl Alloa FK10 . . . . . .10 A7
  Dunbar EH42. . . . . .106 E8
Kellie Rd EH42. . . . . .106 D8
Kelly Ct FK8 . . . . .7 A8
Kelly Dr FK6. . . . . .36 E3
Kelly's La ML8 . . . . .215 B1
Kellywood Cres FK10 . . . .23 F3
Kelso Dr ML8 . . . . .215 C1
Kelso Pl KY12 . . . . .29 A4
Kelso St EH52. . . . . .115 B5
Kelt Rd FK6. . . . . .57 A6
KELTY 12 D8
Kelty Ave EH51. . . . . .64 A7
Kelvin Dr ML7 . . . . .180 B4
Kelvin Sq EH54 . . . . .144 B8
Kelvin St FK3 . . . . .40 A1
Kemper Ave FK1. . . . . .60 C3
Kemp Pl EH3. . . . . .93 B2
Kemp's Cnr EH7 . . . . .94 C2
Kemp's End EH33 . . . . . .126 C4
Kempston Pl EH30 . . . . . .89 C8
Kendieshill Ave EH2. . . . . .83 A5
Kenilworth Ct FK9 . . . . .2 B7
Kenilworth Dr
  Edinburgh EH16. . . . . . . .151 B8
  Laurieston FK2 . . . . .60 F4
Kenilworth Gate FK9. . . . . .2 C7
Kenilworth La FK3 . . . . . . .61 C5
Kenilworth Rd FK9. . . . . . . .2 B7
Kenilworth Rise EH54 . . .143 F1
Kenilworth St EH3 . . . . . .61 D5
Kenmore Ave
  Livingston EH54. . . . . . . .142 F6
  Polmont FK2 . . . . .62 A2
Kenmore Terr KY2 . . . . . . .16 E7
Kenmuir St FK1 . . . . .59 A5
Kenmure Ave EH8 . . . . . .122 C8
Kenmure Pl
  Dunfermline KY12 . . . . . . .29 C5
  Stenhousemuir FK5. . . . . .38 F4
Kennard Rd FK2 . . . . .82 C8
Kennard St Falkirk FK2 . . .60 C6
  Lochgelly KY5 . . . . .14 B8
Kennedie Pk EH53 . . . . . .144 C3
Kennedy Cres
  Dunfermline KY12 . . . . . . .29 B5
  Kirkcaldy KY2 . . . . .17 B6
  Tranent EH33. . . . . .126 D7
Kennedy Ct EH41 . . . . . . .129 F8
Kennedy Way FK2 . . . . . . .22 E3
Kenneil Mus & Roman
  Fortlet★ EH51. . . . . .63 C6
KENNET. 11 C2
Kennet Village FK10 . . . . .11 D3
Kenningknowes Rd FK7. . . .6 E5
Kennington Ave EH20. . . .172 B8
Kennington Terr EH20 . . .172 B8
Kentigern Mall EH16. . . . .191 F5
Kent Rd Alloa FK10 . . . . . . .9 F8
  Stirling FK7 . . . . .7 B5
Kent St KY12 . . . . .29 C6
Keppel Rd EH39 . . . . .54 A6
Keppock Cres EH32 . . . . .97 B2
Keppock Pl FK1. . . . . .59 F1
Kepscaith Cres EH47. . . .161 B5
Kepscaith Gr EH47 . . . . . .161 B5
Kepscaith Rd EH47. . . . . .161 B5
Kerr Ave EH22 . . . . .152 E2
Kerr Cres FK4 . . . . .57 A3
Kerr Ct KY3. . . . . .33 E1
Kerrisk Dr KY11. . . . . .29 F1
Kerr Pl Denny FK6 . . . . . . .36 D2
  Dunfermline KY11 . . . . . . .29 F1
Kerr Rd EH33 . . . . .126 C6
Kerr St EH3. . . . . .93 B2
Kerr's Wynd EH21 . . . . . .124 D6
Kerr Way **1** EH33. . . . . . .126 C5
Kersebonny Rd FK7. . . . . . .6 C7
Kerse Gdns FK2 . . . . .60 E5
Kersegreen Rd FK10 . . . .10 F5
Kershill Circ FK2 . . . . .60 C7
Kershill Cres FK2 . . . . .60 C7
Kerse La FK1. . . . . .60 C4
Kerse Pl FK1. . . . . .60 C5
Kerse Rd Grangemouth FK3 .61 D8
  Stirling, Loanhead FK7 . . . .7 C7
Kersiebank Ave FK3 . . . . .61 E6
Kersie Rd FK9. . . . . .9 A3
Kersie Terr FK7. . . . . .9 A3
Kestrel La EH11 . . . . .30 B3
Kestrel Brae EH54. . . . . . .143 C5
Kestrel Dr FK2 . . . . .82 E7
Kestrel Way EH47 . . . . . . .30 A2
Kettil'stoun Cres EH49 . . .84 D5
Kettil'stoun Gr EH49 . . . . .84 D5
Kettil'stoun Grn EH49 . . .84 D5
Kettil'stoun Mains EH49 .84 D5
Kettlestoun Rd EH49. . . . .84 D7
Keverkae FK10. . . . . .9 F6
Kevock Rd EH18 . . . . .172 F8
Kew Gdns **2** EH48 . . . . .141 B6
Kew Terr **3** EH12. . . . . . .120 E7

Kidd St KY1 . . . . .17 D7
Kidlaw Cres FK10 . . . . .4 D3
Kier Ct FK9. . . . . .2 B7
KILBAGIE. 11 D1
Kilbagie St FK10 . . . . .23 D4
Kilbean Dr FK1 . . . . .59 E2
Kilbirnie Terr FK6 . . . . .36 D3
Kilbrennan Dr FK1 . . . . . . .59 B4
Kilburn Rd KY12 . . . . .28 A2
Kilchurn Ct **1** EH12. . . . .119 A7
Kilcruik Rd KY3. . . . . .34 F3
Kildean Hospl FK8. . . . . . . .1 F2
Kildimmery EH49 . . . . .85 E6
Kildonan Pk KY12 . . . . . . .28 F2
Kildrummy Ave FK5. . . . . .38 F4
KILDUFF 101 C8
Kilduthie Pl FK10 . . . . .23 D6
Kilfinan Rd ML7 . . . . .179 D6
Kilgour Ave KY1 . . . . .17 D7
Kilgraston Rd EH9 . . . . . .121 D4
Killin Ct KY12. . . . . .28 F2
Killin Pl FK2. . . . . .82 A2
Kilnacre EH14 . . . . .148 C6
Kilnburn FK2 . . . . .60 B5
Kilrie FK2. . . . . .59 C4
Kilmory Gdns ML8 . . . . . .215 A3
Kilmory Dr FK9 . . . . .33 D1
Kilmun Rd KY2 . . . . .16 D7
Kilncadzow Rd ML8. . . . .215 C1
Kilncraigs Ct FK10 . . . . . . .10 C5
Kilncraigs Rd FK10 . . . . . .10 C6
Kilncroftside EH14 . . . . . .120 B2
Kilne Pl EH14 . . . . .143 A4
Kilngate Brae EH14 . . . . .151 D5
Kilns Pl FK2 . . . . .59 F6
Kilns Rd FK1 . . . . .60 A5
Kilpair St **5** EH41. . . . . . .130 B8
Kilpunt Gdns EH52 . . . . . .116 A5
Kilpunt Rdbt EH52 . . . . . .116 A5
Kilpunt View EH52 . . . . . .116 A5
Kilrie Cotts KY2 . . . . .33 F7
Kilrymont ML11 . . . . .201 A1
Kilsland Terr EH51 . . . . . . .63 D7
Kilspindie Ct EH32 . . . . . . .71 D4
Kilsyth Rd FK4 . . . . .57 A3
Kilwinning Pl EH21 . . . . .124 C6
Kilwinning St EH21 . . . . .124 D6
Kilwinning Terr EH21 . . . .124 D6
Kimmerghame Dr EH4 . . .92 E3
Kimmerghame Loan EH4 .92 E4
Kimmerghame Pl EH4 . . .92 E4
Kimmerghame View EH4 .92 E3
Kinacres Gr EH51 . . . . . . .64 D7
Kincaids Ct EH3 . . . . .229 A2
Kincairne Ct FK10. . . . . . . .23 E4
KINCARDINE 23 F4
Kincardine Rd FK2 . . . . . . .39 C3
Kincraig Pl KY12 . . . . .29 F2
Kinellan Gdns EH12. . . . .120 C8
Kinellan Rd EH12 . . . . . . .120 C7
King Cres EH55 . . . . .163 D3
King Edwards Way EH29 .89 A1
Kingfisher Brae EH54 . . .143 C5
Kingfisher Pl KY11. . . . . . .35 A3
KINGHORN 35 A2
Kinghorn Pl EH6 . . . . .93 D5
Kinghorn Prim Sch KY3. . .34 F2
Kinghorn Rd
  Burntisland KY3. . . . . .34 A1
  Kirkcaldy KY1, KY2 . . . . . .33 B7
Kinghorn Sta KY3. . . . . . . .34 F2
King James Dr FK10 . . . . . .4 C2
King James IV Rd KY11. . .46 C1
Kinglass Ave FK3 . . . . .64 A7
Kinglass Ct EH51. . . . . . . .64 A6
Kinglass Dr EH51 . . . . .64 A5
Kinglass Pk EH51 . . . . . . .64 A5
King Malcolm Cl FK10 . . .150 D5
King O' Muirs Ave FK10 . . .4 E4
King O' Muirs Dr FK10 . . . .4 E4
King O' Muirs Farm Steading
  FK10. . . . . .4 F4
King O' Muirs Rd FK10 . . . .4 E4
King Robert Ct FK8 . . . . . . .2 B1
King's Ave EH32 . . . . .98 D4
Kingsburgh Cres EH5. . . .92 E7
Kingsburgh Ct EH4 . . . . .103 D8
Kingsburgh Gdns EH40. .103 D8
Kingsburgh Rd EH12. . . .120 C7
King's Cramond EH4 . . . . .91 B4
King's Cres Carluke ML8 .215 A2
  Rosyth KY11. . . . . .46 C2
King's Ct **1** Falkirk FK1 . . .60 B4
  Stenhousemuir FK5. . . . . .38 D2
King's Ct Alloa FK10 . . . . . .10 A7
  Longniddry EH32 . . . . .98 D4
Kings Dr KY11 . . . . .47 A8
King's Dr KY3. . . . . .34 F3
KINGSEAT 12 B1
KINGSETHILL 29 C6
Kingseat Pl FK1 . . . . .60 C2
Kingseat Rd
  Dunfermline KY12. . . . . . .29 D6
  Halbeath KY11, KY12 . . . .30 B6
Kingsfield EH49. . . . . .85 D8
Kingsgate Sh Ctr KY12. . .29 A4
Kings Gn EH11. . . . . .120 E5
King's Gr EH32 . . . . .98 D4
Kings Haugh EH16 . . . . . .122 C4
Kingshill Rd ML7 . . . . .198 A8
Kingshill View ML11 . . . .217 F8
King's Knoll EH39 . . . . . . .54 B7

King's Knoll Gdns EH39 . . . .54 C7
King's Knot★ FK8 . . . . 6 F8
KINGSKNOWE 120 B1
Kingsknowe Ave EH14 . . . .120 A1
Kingsknowe Cres EH14. . .120 A1
Kingsknowe Ct EH14. . . . .119 F1
Kingsknowe Dr EH14. . . . .120 A1
Kingsknowe Gdns EH14. . .120 A1
Kingsknowe Gr EH14. . . . .149 A8
Kingsknowe Pl EH14 . . . . .149 A8
Kingsknowe Rd EH14 . . . .119 F1
Kingsknowe Road N
  EH14 . . . . .120 A2
Kingsknowe Road S
  EH14 . . . . .120 A1
Kingsknowe Sta EH14. . . .120 A1
Kingsknowe Terr EH14. . .120 A1
Kingslaw Ct 1 EH33 . . . .126 D5
Kingslaw Farm Cotts
  EH33 . . . . .126 F6
Kingsley Ave FK5 . . . . . . .38 F3
King's Mdw EH16 . . . . . . .122 B4
King's Meadow Prim Sch
  EH41. . . . . .130 A8
King's Park Prim Sch
  EH22. . . . . .153 A2
King's Park Rd FK8 . . . . . 7 A7
King's Pk EH22 . . . . .98 D5
King's Pl KY11 . . . . .46 C4
Kingsport Ave EH54. . . . .143 F4
King Sq EH55 . . . . .163 D3
Kings Rd FK3 . . . . .61 F8
King's Rd Edinburgh EH15 . .95 A1
  Longniddry EH32 . . . . . . .98 D5
  Rosyth KY11 . . . . .46 E5
  Tranent EH33. . . . . .126 C5
  Whitburn EH47 . . . . .161 A6
King's Road Prim Sch
  KY11 . . . . .46 E4
King's Stables La 3 EH1 . .228 C2
King's Stables Rd EH1 . . .228 C2
King St Alloa FK10 . . . . . . .10 B7
  Armadale EH48 . . . . .140 A6
  Bathgate EH48 . . . . .141 B6
  Cowdenbeath KY4. . . . . . .13 B4
  Edinburgh EH6. . . . . .93 F5
  Falkirk FK2 . . . . .60 C6
  Fallin FK7. . . . . .8 C4
  Inverkeithing KY11 . . . . . .47 C2
  Kirkcaldy KY2 . . . . .17 B6
  Musselburgh EH21 . . . . .124 D5
  Shotts ML7 . . . . .179 E4
  Stenhousemuir, Antonshill
    FK5. . . . . .38 F3
  Stirling FK8 . . . . 7 B7
Kingstables La 3 EH1 . . . .7 A8
King's Terr FK15 . . . . . . .94 F1
King's Theatre★ EH3 . . . .228 B1
Kingsthorne Pk EH54 . . . .114 F1
KINGSTON 54 A1
Kingston Ave EH16 . . . . .122 C1
Kingston Cotts EH39 . . . . .53 E1
Kingswell Pk EH10 . . . . . .10 C7
Kinleith Ind Est EH14 . . .148 B4
Kinloch Pl FK3. . . . . .61 E5
Kinloss Ct KY12 . . . . .26 A2
Kinnaird Ave FK2 . . . . . . .39 B3
Kinnaird Dr FK5 . . . . .38 E3
Kinnaird Pl
  Dunfermline KY12. . . . . . .29 D6
  Kirkcaldy KY2 . . . . .17 D6
Kinnaird Prim Sch FK5 . . .38 D5
Kinnear Rd EH3. . . . . .93 A4
KINNEIL. 63 D5
Kinneil Dr EH51. . . . . .63 D6
Kinneil Prim Sch EH51 . . . .63 F6
Kinneil Rd EH51. . . . . .63 D7
Kinneil Sta★ EH51 . . . . . . .63 D7
Kinninmonth St KY1 . . . . .17 B2
Kinnis Ct KY11 . . . . .29 F1
Kinnonmonth Ave 5 KY3 . .33 D1
Kintail Pl KY11. . . . . .30 A4
Kintyre Pl FK1. . . . . .59 C4
Kippielaw Dr EH22. . . . . .153 C2
Kippielaw Gdns EH22. . . .153 C1
Kippielaw Medway EH22 .153 C1
Kippielaw Pk EH22 . . . . .174 D8
Kippielaw Rd EH22. . . . . .153 C1
Kippielaw Steading EH22 .153 D1
Kippithill EH36 . . . . .178 B2
Kirk Ave FK5 . . . . .38 E2
Kirkbank Rd KY3. . . . . . . .33 F1
Kirkbrae Clackmannan KY10 .10 D4
  Garvald EH41 . . . . .132 D2
Kirk Brae Edinburgh EH16 .151 A8
  Innerwick EH42. . . . . . . .218 A7
  Kincardine FK10 . . . . .23 E5
  Longridge EH47. . . . . . . .161 C1
Kirkbride Terr FK7. . . . . . .20 C3
Kirkburn FK1. . . . . .108 B7
KIRKCALDY 17 C3
Kirkcaldy High Sch KY1. . .17 B8
Kirkcaldy Mus & Art Gallery★
  KY1. . . . . .17 B7
Kirkcaldy North Prim Sch
  KY2. . . . . .17 B6
Kirkcaldy Rd
  Burntisland KY3. . . . . . . .33 F2
  Crossgates KY4. . . . . . . .31 A6
  Kinghorn KY3. . . . . .33 F6
Kirkcaldy Sta★ KY1 . . . . . .17 A4
Kirkcaldy West Prim Sch
  KY1. . . . . .17 B2

Kirk Cramond EH4 . . . . . . .91 C6
Kirkfield E EH54 . . . . .143 B3
Kirkfield View EH54. . . . .143 C3
Kirkflat EH52 . . . . .115 A5
Kirkford Ct KY4. . . . . .13 A4
Kirkgate Alloa FK10. . . . . .10 B6
  Burntisland KY3. . . . . . . .50 E8
  Currie EH14 . . . . .148 A3
  Dunfermline KY12 . . . . . . .28 F3
  Edinburgh EH16. . . . . . . .151 A7
  Inverkeithing KY11 . . . . . .47 B4
  Linlithgow EH49 . . . . .85 A7
  West Calder EH55 . . . . . .163 D3
Kirkgate Ho EH6. . . . . . . .94 A4
Kirkhall Pl FK6 . . . . .36 E2
KIRKHILL. 192 A5
  Broxburn 115 C5
Kirkhill Ct Broxburn EH52 .115 C5
  Fauldhouse EH47 . . . . . . .181 E6
  Gorebridge EH23. . . . . . .195 C8
Kirkhill Dr EH16 . . . . .122 A4
Kirkhill Gdns
  Edinburgh EH16. . . . . . . .122 A5
  Penicuik EH26 . . . . .191 F5
Kirkhill Pk EH52. . . . . . . .115 C5
Kirkhill Pl EH52. . . . . . . .115 D5
Kirkhill Prim Sch EH52 . . .115 D5
Kirkhill Rd Broxburn EH52 .115 D5
  Edinburgh EH16. . . . . . . .122 A4
  Penicuik EH26 . . . . .191 F5
Kirkhill Terr
  Broxburn EH52 . . . . .115 C5
  Edinburgh EH16. . . . . . . .122 A5
  Gorebridge EH23. . . . . . .174 A1
Kirkhill Way EH26. . . . . . .191 F5
Kirk La EH54 . . . . .143 B2
Kirkland Dr FK6 . . . . .36 B2
Kirklands Dunfermline KY12 .29 A2
  Edinburgh EH11. . . . . . . .119 D4
  Penicuik EH26 . . . . .191 E5
Kirklands Park Cres EH29 .88 F2
Kirklands Park Gdns EH29 .88 F2
Kirklands Park Gr EH29 . . .88 F2
Kirklands Park Rigg EH29 .88 F2
Kirklands Park St EH29. . .88 F2
Kirklands The FK7 . . . . 6 F3
KIRKLISTON 89 B1
Kirkliston L Ctr EH29 . . . . .88 F2
Kirkliston Prim Sch EH29 .89 A2
Kirkliston Rd EH30. . . . . . .89 B8
Kirk Loan EH12 . . . . .119 E6
KIRKNEWTON. 145 F2
Kirknewton Ct EH27 . . . . .145 C3
Kirknewton Prim Sch
  EH27. . . . . .145 D2
Kirknewton Sta EH27 . . . .145 C3
Kirk Pk Dunbar EH42 . . . . .78 B2
  Edinburgh EH16. . . . . . . .151 B8
Kirk Pl EH51. . . . . .64 D7
Kirk Ports EH39. . . . . .54 C7
Kirk Rd Aberlady EH32. . . . .71 C4
  Bathgate EH48 . . . . .141 C5
  Shotts ML7 . . . . .179 F4
Kirkside Cres FK7. . . . . 7 B5
Kirkslap FK6. . . . . .36 E2
Kirk St Culross KY12. . . . . .25 D1
  Edinburgh EH6. . . . . .93 F4
  Kincardine FK10 . . . . .23 E4
  Prestonpans EH32. . . . . . .96 F2
Kirkstyle Gdns EH29 . . . . .89 B1
KIRKTON Burntisland 33 D1
  Livingston 143 A1
Kirkton Ave EH48 . . . . . .141 D5
Kirkton Bank EH26. . . . . .191 D5
Kirkton Bsns Ctr EH54 . . .143 B3
Kirkton Ct EH48. . . . . . . .141 D6
Kirkton Dr KY3 . . . . .33 D1
Kirkton North Rd EH54 . . .143 C3
Kirkton Pl Bathgate EH48 .141 D5
  Cowdenbeath KY4. . . . . . .13 B5
  Falkirk FK2 . . . . .39 C3
Kirkton Rd KY3 . . . . .33 E1
Kirkton South Rd EH54. . .143 C3
Kirkview EH41. . . . . .130 C8
Kirkway FK2. . . . . .22 D4
Kirkwood Ave FK2 . . . . . . .61 C2
Kirkwood Cres KY12 . . . . .28 B7
Kirk Wynd
  Clackmannan FK10 . . . . . .11 A5
  2 Falkirk FK1. . . . . .60 B4
  Kirkcaldy KY1 . . . . .17 C4
  Stirling FK7 . . . . 7 B4
Kisimul Ct 3 EH12. . . . . .119 D6
Kitchener Cres EH32. . . . . .98 E5
Kittle Yds EH9 . . . . .121 E4
Klondyke St EH21. . . . . . .123 E4
Knapphill KY11 . . . . .46 F7
Knightsbridge Ho EH54 . .143 C8
Knightslaw Pl EH26. . . . . .191 D5
KNIGHTSRIDGE 143 C7
Knightsridge Ct EH52. . . .114 C2
Knightsridge East Rd
  EH54. . . . . .143 D8
Knightsridge Ind Est
  EH54. . . . . .143 C7
Knightsridge Prim Sch
  EH54. . . . . .143 D7
Knightsridge Rd EH52. . . .114 C2
Knightsridge Rdbt EH54 . .143 D7
Knightsridge West Rd
  EH54. . . . . .143 B7
Knights Way FK6 . . . . .36 C2
Knockenhair Rd EH42. . . . .78 B2
Knockhill Cl KY5. . . . . .14 B7

Knockhouse Farm Cotts
  KY12 . . . . .28 B4
Knockhouse Gdns KY12 . . .28 B2
Knockhouse Rd KY12 . . . . .28 B2
Knockhouse Terr KY12. . . .28 B2
Knoll Croft Rd ML7. . . . . .180 A3
Knowehead Rd
  Crossford KY12. . . . . .28 A2
  Redding FK2 . . . . .61 C2
Knowepark Ct EH47. . . . .162 A2
Knowepark Rd EH47 . . . . .162 A1
Knowesley Pk EH41. . . . .129 D8
Knowes Rd EH41. . . . . . .129 E8
Knowe The Alloa FK10 . . . . 5 C2
  Dalgety Bay KY11 . . . . . . .48 C3
Knowetop EH54. . . . . . . .164 C1
Knowetop Pl EH25. . . . . .171 F3
Knowfaulds Rd FK10. . . . . 4 B3
Knox Acad EH41. . . . . . . .129 F8
Knox Ct EH41. . . . . .130 A8
Knox Pl EH41. . . . . .130 A8
Komarom Pl EH22. . . . . . .153 D3
Kyle Ave FK7 . . . . .20 E7
Kyle Cres KY11 . . . . .30 C1
Kyle Pl EH7. . . . . .229 C4
Kyles The KY1 . . . . .17 E6

L

Labrador Ave EH54 . . . . .143 F4
Laburnum Arch Ct 4
  EH32 . . . . .96 F1
Laburnum Ave EH54 . . . . .97 E3
Laburnum Dr KY1. . . . . . . .17 C8
Laburnum Gr
  Burntisland KY3. . . . . . . .33 F2
  Stirling FK8 . . . . 6 F5
Laburnum Pl EH22 . . . . . .174 E6
Laburnum Rd
  Dunfermline KY11. . . . . . .29 C1
  Whitburn EH47 . . . . .161 C6
Lade Braes KY11 . . . . .48 B3
Lade Ct EH49 . . . . .84 E7
Lade Dr FK5 . . . . .59 C8
Lade Gn KY11. . . . . .48 B3
Lade Mill FK7. . . . . 7 C1
Lade Rd FK4 . . . . .58 A5
Ladeside Ave EH47. . . . . .162 C8
Ladeside Cres EH47. . . . . .38 E1
Ladeside Dr EH47. . . . . . .162 C8
Ladeside Gdns EH47 . . . .162 B8
Ladeside Prim Sch FK5 . . .59 C8
Lade The EH14. . . . . .108 B8
Ladiesbeuchan EH12 . . . .119 E5
Lady Anne Ct KY4. . . . . . .30 E6
Lady Brae EH23 . . . . .195 D7
Lady Brae Pl EH23 . . . . . .195 E8
Lady Burn Pl KY3 . . . . . . .35 A3
Lady Campbell's Wlk
  EH52 . . . . .29 A4
Ladycroft EH14. . . . . . . .147 C2
Lady Ct EH47 . . . . .161 E7
Lady Emily Way EH23 . . . .195 C8
Lady Hall Rd TD13 . . . . . .218 F4
Lady Helen Cotts KY5. . . .15 B8
Lady Helen St KY1 . . . . . .17 B2
Lady Jane Gdns EH39 . . . .54 C6
Lady Jane Rd EH39 . . . . . .54 D6
Lady Lawson St EH3 . . . .228 C2
Lady Menzies Pl 4 EH7. . .94 A2
Lady Nairn Ave KY1. . . . . . 17 E8
Lady Nairn Cres EH8 . . . .122 D7
Lady Nairn Gr EH8. . . . . .122 D7
Lady Nairn Loan EH8 . . . .122 D7
Lady Nairn Pl EH8 . . . . . .122 D7
Lady Nairn Rd KY12. . . . . .28 E6
Lady Pl EH54 . . . . .143 B5
Lady Rd EH16. . . . . .122 C3
Lady Road Pl EH22 . . . . . .174 B6
Ladysgate Ct FK2 . . . . . . .39 B3
Ladysmill FK2 . . . . .60 D5
Ladysmill Ct EH6. . . . . . . .93 C7
Ladysmith Ind Est EH47 . .161 C5
Ladysmith Rd EH9 . . . . . .121 E2
Ladysneuk Rd FK9 . . . . 2 D2
Lady Victoria Bsns Ctr
  EH22. . . . . .174 A4
LADYWELL 143 D6
Ladywell EH21. . . . . .124 C6
Ladywell Ave EH12. . . . . .119 D5
Ladywell
  Edinburgh EH12. . . . . . . .119 D6
  Larbert FK5. . . . . .38 A3
Ladywell Dr FK10 . . . . 4 B3
Ladywell East Rd EH54 . . .143 D6
Ladywell Gdns EH12 . . . . .119 D5
Ladywell Gr FK10 . . . . . . .11 A4
Ladywell Pl FK10 . . . . 4 B3
Ladywell Rd EH12. . . . . . .119 D6
Ladywell View EH51. . . . . .63 D5
Ladywell Way EH12 . . . . .124 C6
Ladywell West Rd EH54 . .143 C6
LADYWOOD 192 A6
Ladywood EH10. . . . . .11 C4
Ladywood Pl EH54 . . . . . .143 B5
Lady Wynd EH1 . . . . .228 C2
Lafferty Pl FK6 . . . . .36 F1
Lagan Rd ML8 . . . . .215 A1
Laggan Ave ML7. . . . . . . .180 B3
Laggan Path ML7. . . . . . .179 C6
Laichpark Pl EH14. . . . . .120 B3
Laichpark Rd EH14. . . . . .120 B3
Laidlaw Gdns EH33 . . . . .126 C4
Laing Gdns EH52. . . . . . .115 C6

Laing Terr
  Edinburgh EH15. . . . . . . .123 C8
  Penicuik EH26 . . . . .191 F7
Laird's Dr FK10 . . . . .11 B3
Laird's Entry EH37 . . . . . .176 C3
Laird Terr EH19. . . . . . . .173 D6
Laira Terr FK6 . . . . .36 D3
Lakeside Rd KY2. . . . . . . .16 F4
Lamb Ct EH39 . . . . .54 A7
Lambert Dr KY12 . . . . .29 D4
Lamberton Ave FK7. . . . . . 7 C3
Lamberton Ct EH34 . . . . .156 E6
Lambert Terr FK10. . . . . . .10 C7
Lambie St EH47 . . . . .161 B7
Lamb's CI EH8 . . . . .229 B1
Lambs Ct EH6. . . . . .93 C7
Lamb's Pend EH26. . . . . .191 F4
Lamer Ct EH42. . . . . .78 E3
Lamer St EH42. . . . . .78 E3
Lamington Rd EH33. . . . .128 C2
Lammerlaws Rd KY3 . . . . .50 F8
Lammermoor Gdns EH33 .126 B6
Lammermoor Terr
  Edinburgh EH16. . . . . . . .122 C1
  Tranent EH33. . . . . .126 B6
Lammermuir Cres
  Dunbar EH42. . . . . .78 C2
  Haddington EH41. . . . . . .130 C8
Lammermuir Ct EH31 . . . .52 B2
Lammermuir Pl KY2 . . . . . .16 F5
Lammerview
  Gladsmuir EH33 . . . . . . .128 C2
  7 Tranent EH33 . . . . . . .126 C5
Lammerview Terr EH31 . . .52 A2
Lamond View FK5 . . . . . . .38 D1
Lamont Cres FK7. . . . . 8 D5
Lamont Way EH54 . . . . . .143 D8
Lanark Ave EH54. . . . . . .143 A6
Lanark Rd
  Edinburgh, Kingsknowe
    EH14. . . . . .120 B1
  Edinburgh, Wester Hailes
    EH14. . . . . .147 D3
Lanark Road W EH14. . . .147 D3
Landale Gdns KY3 . . . . . . .33 E2
Landale Pl KY3 . . . . .33 E2
Landale St KY5 . . . . .14 B8
Lane The EH21. . . . . .124 E1
Langfauld Gdns EH48 . . . .140 E5
Langhill Farm Cotts
  EH25. . . . . .171 F6
Langhill Pl FK6 . . . . .36 C1
Langlaw Rd EH22 . . . . . . .174 D8
LANGLEES. 39 D1
Langlees Prim Sch FK2 . . .60 B8
Langlees St FK2 . . . . .39 C1
Lang Loan
  Edinburgh EH17, EH20 . . .151 C3
  Loanhead EH20 . . . . .151 B2
Lang Rigg EH30. . . . . .68 A1
Langriggs EH41. . . . . . . .130 B8
Langside EH40. . . . . .103 D8
Langside Cres EH55. . . . .164 A5
Langside Ct EH48. . . . . . .138 B3
Langside Gdns EH55 . . . .164 A6
LANGTON 144 F3
Langton Ave EH53 . . . . . .144 E4
Langton Gdns EH53 . . . . .144 F3
LANGTON PK 144 F3
Langton Rd
  East Calder EH53 . . . . . .144 F3
  Edinburgh EH9 . . . . .121 E3
  Westquarter FK2 . . . . . . .61 A3
Langton Steadings EH53 .144 F2
Langton Terr EH53. . . . . .144 E4
Langton View EH53. . . . . .144 F4
Lanrigg Ave EH47 . . . . . .181 E7
Lanrigg Ct EH47 . . . . . . .181 F7
Lanrigg Rd EH47 . . . . . . .181 F7
Lansbury Ct 2 EH22. . . . .153 A3
Lansbury St KY1. . . . . . . .17 E7
Lansdowne Cres
  Edinburgh EH12. . . . . . . .228 A2
  Kincardine FK10 . . . . .23 E4
  Shotts ML7 . . . . .180 B3
Lapicide Pl EH6. . . . . .93 D5
La Porte Prec 5 FK3. . . . .40 D1
Lapwing Dr KY11 . . . . .47 B7
Larach Ct KY2 . . . . .16 C8
Larbert FK4 . . . . .58 B6
Larbert High Sch FK5. . . . .38 E1
Larbert Rd FK4 . . . . .58 B6
Larbert Sta FK5 . . . . .38 C2
Larbert Village Prim Sch
  FK5 . . . . .38 B1
Larbourfield EH11 . . . . . .119 D1
Larchbank EH54 . . . . . . .143 E5
Larch Cres EH22 . . . . . . .174 F6
Larch Dr EH47 . . . . .161 C6
Larchfield EH14. . . . . . . .147 C2
Larchfield Neuk EH14. . . .147 C2
Larchfield Path ML7 . . . . .180 B2
Larch Gr Dunfermline KY11. . .46 D8
  Livingston EH54. . . . . . . .144 B6
  Stenhousemuir FK5 . . . . . .38 F3
Larch St KY3. . . . . .61 C6
Largo Pl EH6. . . . . .93 E6
Larkfield Dr EH22. . . . . . .152 E1
Larkfield Rd EH22. . . . . . .152 E2
Lasswade Bank EH17. . . .151 C5
Lasswade Ct EH18 . . . . . .152 A1
Lasswade Gr EH17 . . . . . .151 C5
Lasswade High Sch Ctr
  EH19. . . . . .173 A7
Lasswade Prim Sch
  EH19. . . . . .173 C8

Lasswade Rd
  Bonnyrigg and Lasswade EH17,
    EH20. . . . . .151 F2
  Dalkeith EH22 . . . . .152 E2
  Edinburgh EH16, EH17 . . .151 C6
  Loanhead EH20 . . . . .172 D8
Latchburn View EH47 . . . .162 C7
Latch Pk EH13 . . . . .121 A6
Latch Rd EH42 . . . . .78 E1
Latch The KY12 . . . . .27 C1
Lathallan Dr FK2. . . . . . . .61 E2
Lauderdale Cres EH42 . . . .78 C2
Lauderdale St EH9 . . . . . .121 C5
Lauder Loan EH9 . . . . . . .121 E4
Lauder Lodge 14 EH22. . . .153 A3
Lauder Pl EH40 . . . . .103 E6
Lauder Rd Dalkeith EH22 . .153 C2
  Edinburgh EH9. . . . . .121 D4
  Kirkcaldy KY2 . . . . .17 C6
Lauder St KY12 . . . . .29 C6
Laura Fergusson Ct EH12 .91 B1
Laurel Bank EH22. . . . . . .153 C2
Laurelbank Ave FK4. . . . . .58 A3
Laurelbank Ct EH53. . . . . .144 F2
Laurel Bank Pl EH22 . . . .174 E6
Laurel Bank Rd EH22 . . . .174 E6
Laurel Cres KY2 . . . . .17 B7
Laurel Ct Denny FK6 . . . . .36 D3
  Falkirk FK1 . . . . .59 C6
Laurel Gr Bonnybridge FK4 . .57 F3
  Westquarter FK2 . . . . . . .61 A2
Laurelhill Bsns Pk FK7. . . . 6 F6
Laurelhill Gdns FK8. . . . . . .6 F5
Laurelhill Pl FK8. . . . . 7 A5
Laurel Pl FK4. . . . . .57 F3
Laurel Rd KY11 . . . . .46 C2
Laurels The FK10 . . . . 4 B1
Laurel Terr EH11. . . . . . .120 E5
Laurencecroft Rd FK8. . . . 2 B2
Laurie Gdns FK2. . . . . . . .82 B8
Laurie St EH6. . . . . .94 A4
LAURIESTON 61 B4
Laurieston Ind Est FK2. . . .60 F3
Laurieston Prim Sch FK2 .61 A3
Laurieston Rd FK3 . . . . . . .61 A6
Laurieston Building EH3 . .228 C2
Lauriston Castle★ EH4. . . . .91 E5
Lauriston Dr KY12 . . . . . . .29 D5
Lauriston Farm Rd EH4 . . .91 F4
Lauriston Gdns EH3. . . . .228 C1
Lauriston Pk EH3. . . . . . .228 C2
Lauriston Pl EH3. . . . . . .228 C2
Lauriston St EH3. . . . . . .228 C2
Lauriston Terr FK12 . . . . . . 5 A3
Laurmont Ct FK2 . . . . .61 A3
Laverockbank Ave EH5 . . .93 C6
Laverockbank Cres EH5. . .93 C6
Laverockbank Gdns EH5 . .93 C6
Laverockbank Gr EH5 . . . .93 C6
Laverockbank Rd EH5 . . . .93 C6
Laverockdale Cres EH13 .149 B6
Laverockdale Loan EH13 .149 B5
Laverockdale Pk EH13 . . .149 B5
Laverock Dr EH26 . . . . . .191 D6
Laverock Pk EH49. . . . . . .85 A5
Lavery Ave FK5 . . . . .38 E1
Lawers Cres FK2. . . . . . . .62 A1
Lawers Pl FK3 . . . . .61 E5
Lawers Sq EH26. . . . . . . .192 A7
Lawfield Prim Sch EH22 . .174 D7
Lawfield Rd EH22 . . . . . . .174 D7
Lawhead Cotts EH40 . . . . .75 F3
Lawhead Pl EH26 . . . . . . .191 C6
Lawhouse Toll EH15 . . . . .123 B4
Lawnmarket EH1 . . . . . . .229 A3
Law Pl Denny FK6. . . . . . . .36 E1
  Edinburgh EH15. . . . . .95 A1
Law Prim Sch EH29 . . . . . .54 C6
Law Rd Dunfermline KY11. . .29 F4
  North Berwick EH39 . . . . . .54 C7
Lawrence Ct FK5 . . . . .38 B5
Lawrie Dr EH26 . . . . .191 E7
Lawrie Terr EH20 . . . . . . .172 B7
Lawson Cres EH30 . . . . . . .89 C8
Lawson Ct EH42 . . . . .78 D2
Lawson Gdns KY1. . . . . . .17 E8
Lawson Glade EH54 . . . . .164 C7
Lawson Pl Dunbar EH42 . . .78 D2
  Maddiston FK2 . . . . .83 A5
Lawson St KY1. . . . . .17 E8
Lawson Way EH33 . . . . . .126 C5
Lawswell FK10. . . . . 5 E3
Laxdale Dr FK6. . . . . .57 D7
Laxford Cres KY11 . . . . . . .48 A3
LEADBURN 208 E3
Leadburn Ave KY12 . . . . . .29 A7
Leadervale Rd EH16. . . . .150 F8
Leadervale Terr EH16 . . . .150 F8
Leadside Cres KY12 . . . . . .29 A7
Leamington Dr EH10 . . . .228 B1
Leamington Rd EH3. . . . .228 A1
Leamington Terr EH10 . . .121 B5
Leamington Wharf EH3. . .228 A1
Leapark Dr FK4 . . . . .57 F3
Lea Rig ML11. . . . . .217 F7
Learmonth Ave EH4. . . . . .92 F2
Learmonth Cres
  Edinburgh EH4. . . . . .92 F2
  West Calder EH55. . . . . .163 D3
Learmonth Ct EH4 . . . . . .92 F1
Learmonth Gardens La 1
  EH4 . . . . .92 F1
Learmonth Gdns EH4. . . . .92 F1
Learmonth Gr EH4. . . . . . .92 F2
Learmonth Pk 2 EH4 . . . . .92 F2
Learmonth Pl EH4 . . . . . .228 A4

Learmonth St FK1 . . . . 60 B4
Learmonth Terr EH4 . . . . 228 A4
Learmonth Terrace La
EH4 . . . . 228 A4
Learmonth Garden Mews ④
EH4 . . . . 93 A2
Leaston Farm Cotts
EH36 . . . . 220 A2
Lec Ct FK2 . . . . 60 F4
Ledi Ave FK10 . . . . 4 B2
Ledi Pl FK1 . . . . 81 E7
Ledi Terr EH26 . . . . 192 A7
Ledi View FK9 . . . . 2 B3
Ledmore Pl FK1 . . . . 60 E1
Lee Cres EH15 . . . . 123 B8
Legion Ct KY2 . . . . 17 A5
Leighton Cres EH22 . . . . 174 D7
Leighton St KY12 . . . . 26 B2
Leishman Ct EH48 . . . . 138 D2
Leishman Dr KY11 . . . . 29 C1
Leishman Twr FK1 . . . . 60 E1
Leisure Bowl The FK10 . . . . . 10 B7
LEITH 94 C6
Leith Acad EH6 . . . . 94 A3
Leith Dock KY3 . . . . 33 F2
Leithhead EH27 . . . . 166 E4
Leith Pl FK6 . . . . 57 D7
Leith Prim Sch EH6 . . . . 94 A4
Leith St EH1 . . . . 229 A4
Leith Victoria Swim Ctr
EH6 . . . . 93 F5
Leith Walk Prim Sch EH7 . 93 E2
Leith Waterworld EH6 . . . . 94 A4
Leith Wlk EH7 . . . . 93 F3
Lempockwells EH34 . . . . . . 156 D6
Lempockwells Rd EH34 . 156 E6
Lendrick Ave FK1 . . . . 59 F2
Lennel Ave EH12 . . . . 120 C8
Lennie Cotts EH12 . . . . 118 D8
Lennox Ave FK7 . . . . 7 A4
Lennox Gdns EH49 . . . . 84 D7
Lennoxlove Acredales Cotts
EH41 . . . . 130 B7
Lennoxlove House*
EH41 . . . . 130 B5
Lennox Milne Ct EH41 . . . 130 B8
Lennox Rd EH41 . . . . 130 C8
Lennox Row EH5 . . . . 93 B6
Lennox St EH4 . . . . 228 A4
Lennox Street La EH4 . . . . 228 A4
Lennox Terr FK3 . . . . 61 F5
Lennymuir EH12 . . . . 90 B1
Leny Cres FK1 . . . . 60 A1
Lenzie Ave EH54 . . . . 143 A6
Leopold Pl EH7 ① 93 E2
Leslie Pl EH3 . . . . 93 B2
Leslie Rd KY11 . . . . 46 F5
Leslie St KY1 . . . . 35 B8
Leslie Way EH47 . . . . 78 D1
Lesslie's Bldgs KY3 . . . . 33 E1
Lestrange Ave FK12 . . . . 5 B7
LETHAM 39 C8
Letham Ave EH53 . . . . 144 B7
Letham Cotts FK2 . . . . 39 D8
Letham Cres EH53 . . . . 144 B7
Letham Dr FK1 . . . . 129 F8
Letham Gait KY11 . . . . 47 F3
Letham Gdns Dunbar EH42 . . 78 D2
  Pumpherston EH53 . . . . 144 B7
Letham Hill Ave KY11 . . . . . . 47 E4
Letham Holdings EH53 . 144 C6
Letham Mains Smallholdings
EH41 . . . . 129 C7
Letham Pk Dunbar EH42 . . . . 78 D2
  Pumpherston EH53 . . . . 144 B7
Letham Pl Dunbar EH42 . . . . 78 C3
  Pumpherston EH53 . . . . 144 B7
Letham Prim Sch EH54 . 144 B5
Letham Rd Dunbar EH42 . . . 78 C2
  Pumpherston EH54 . . . . 144 A8
Letham Rise KY11 . . . . 47 F3
Letham Terr EH53 . . . . 144 B7
Letham Terrs FK2 . . . . 22 C1
Letham Way KY11 . . . . 47 F3
Lethen View FK10 . . . . 4 C3
Leuchatsbeath Dr KY4 . . . . 13 B6
Leven Cl EH3 . . . . 228 B1
Leven Ct FK10 . . . . 10 C5
LEVENHALL 125 A6
Leven Pl ML7 . . . . 179 E6
LEVEN SEAT 182 A4
Levenseat Ind Est EH47 . 181 F4
Leven St Edinburgh EH3 . . 228 B1
  Falkirk FK2 . . . . 60 B8
Leven Terr EH3 . . . . 228 C1
Leven Wlk EH54 . . . . 144 A4
Lewis Ct Alloa FK10 . . . . 10 B5
  Falkirk FK1 . . . . 60 B2
Lewis Rd FK2 . . . . 61 F1
Lewis Terr EH11 . . . . 228 A2
Lewisvale Ave EH21 . . . . . . 124 E5
Lewisvale Ct EH21 . . . . 124 E5
Leyden Pk EH19 . . . . 173 B8
Leyden Pl EH19 . . . . 173 B7
Leyland Rd EH48 . . . . 141 C3
Leys Park Rd KY12 . . . . 29 B4
LIBERTON 150 F7
Liberton Brae EH16 . . . . 151 A8
Liberton Dr EH16 . . . . 150 E7
Liberton Gdns EH16 . . . . . . 151 A6
Liberton High Sch EH17 . 151 C8
Liberton Hospl EH16 . . . . . 151 B7
Liberton Pl EH16 . . . . 151 A6
Liberton Prim Sch EH16 . 122 A2

Liberton Rd EH16 . . . . 122 A1
Library La ⑦ FK3 . . . . 40 D1
Liddesdale Pl EH3 . . . . 93 B2
Liddle Dr EH51 . . . . 63 E5
Lidgate Shot EH28 . . . . 117 E2
Liggar's Pl KY12 . . . . 28 F1
Liggat Pl EH52 . . . . 115 F5
Liggat Syke EH52 . . . . 115 B5
Liggat Syke Pl EH52 . . . . . . 116 A5
Lighton Terr EH47 . . . . 162 B1
Lilac Ave EH22 . . . . 174 F6
Lilac Cres KY1 . . . . 17 C8
Lilac Gr KY11 . . . . 46 D8
Lillies La EH41 . . . . 220 F7
Lilly's La KY11 . . . . 29 B1
Lilybank Ct FK10 . . . . 5 D1
Lilyhill Terr EH8 . . . . 94 C1
Lily Terr EH11 . . . . 120 E4
Lime Ave EH30 . . . . 66 F2
Limebank Pk EH53 . . . . 144 F2
Limefield EH47 . . . . 151 E5
Limefield Ave EH55 . . . . 164 A5
Limefield Cres EH48 . . . . . . 141 D7
Limefield Gdns EH55 . . . . . 164 A5
Limefield House Bsns Ctr
EH55 . . . . 164 B5
Limefield La EH48 . . . . 141 D6
Limefield Pl EH48 . . . . 141 D6
Limefield Rd
  Bathgate EH48 . . . . 141 D7
  Polbeth EH55 . . . . 164 A5
  West Calder EH55 . . . . 163 E3
Lime Gr Dunfermline KY11 . . 29 E1
  Livingston EH54 . . . . 144 B6
  Mayfield EH22 . . . . 174 D8
  North Berwick EH39 . . . . 54 F6
  Polmont FK2 . . . . 61 E2
  Stenhousemuir FK5 . . . . 38 D1
LIMEKILNS 45 E3
Limekilns EH34 . . . . 157 A6
Limekilns Prim Sch EH13 145 A3
Limekilns Prim Sch KY11 . 45 E3
Limekilns Rd KY12 . . . . 28 F1
Lime Pl EH19 . . . . 173 B6
Lime Rd FK1 . . . . 59 B4
LIMERIGG 108 B2
Limerigg Prim Sch FK1 . 108 C1
Lime St FK3 . . . . 61 C5
Limes The EH10 . . . . 121 A4
Limetree Wlk EH42 . . . . 76 D5
Lime Tree Wlk FK10 . . . . 10 A5
Limeylands Cres EH35 . . . 155 E6
Limeylands Ct EH35 . . . . . . 155 D7
Limeylands Rd EH35 . . . . . 155 D7
Limpet Ness KY11 . . . . 46 D3
Linburn Gr KY11 . . . . 29 F4
Linburn Pk EH27 . . . . 146 A5
Linburn Pl KY11 . . . . 29 F3
Linburn Rd
  Dunfermline KY11 . . . . 29 F3
  Wilkieston EH27 . . . . 146 B5
Lindean Pl EH6 . . . . 94 B4
Lindean Terr EH27 . . . . 145 E4
Linden Ave Denny FK6 . . . . . 36 C3
  Stirling FK7 . . . . 7 C6
Linden Gr EH54 . . . . 144 B6
Linden Pl EH20 . . . . 172 D8
Lindores Dr Kirkcaldy KY2 . 16 E8
  Tranent EH33 . . . . 126 D6
Lind Rd FK4 . . . . 57 C4
Lindsay Dr FK9 . . . . 2 B4
Lindsay Gdns EH48 . . . . 141 C5
Lindsay Pl Edinburgh EH6 . . 93 E5
  Lochgelly KY5 . . . . 14 A8
Lindsay Rd EH6 . . . . 93 E6
Lindsay Row EH24 . . . . 172 D1
Lindsay Sq EH54 . . . . 142 D5
Lindsay St EH6 . . . . 93 E6
Lindsay's Wynd KY12 . . . . . . 26 F6
Lindsay Way EH54 . . . . 143 D8
Lindsey Cir EH24 . . . . 172 D1
Lingerwood Farm Cotts
EH22 . . . . 174 A4
Lingerwood Rd EH22 . . . . . 174 A4
Lingerwood Wlk EH22 . . . . 174 A4
Linhouse Dr EH53 . . . . 144 E3
Linhouse Rd EH53 . . . . 144 E3
Linkfield Rd EH21 . . . . 124 E6
Link Rd Crombie KY12 . . . . . 44 D6
  Dalgety Bay KY11 . . . . 47 F3
  Oakley KY12 . . . . 26 F7
Links Ave EH21 . . . . 124 B7
Links Ct Bo'ness EH51 . . . . . 64 A8
  Cockenzie & Port Seton
  EH32 . . . . 97 D4
Links Dr KY12 . . . . 28 A2
Links Gardens La EH6 . . . . . 94 B5
Links Gdns EH6 . . . . 94 B4
Links Pl Bo'ness EH51 . . . . . . 64 B7
  Burntisland KY3 . . . . 50 E8
  Cockenzie & Port Seton
  EH32 . . . . 97 E4
  Edinburgh EH6 . . . . 94 A5
Links Rd Bo'ness EH51 . . . . . 64 A8
  Cockenzie & Port Seton
  EH32 . . . . 97 E4
  Longniddry EH32 . . . . 98 E5
  North Berwick EH39 . . . . 54 B7
Links St Kirkcaldy KY1 . . . . . . 17 B2
  Musselburgh EH21 . . . . 124 C6
Links View
  Cockenzie & Port Seton
  EH32 . . . . 97 E4
  Edinburgh EH6 . . . . 94 A5
Links Wlk Bo'ness EH51 . . . . 64 A8
  Cockenzie & Port Seton
  EH32 . . . . 97 E4
Links Wlk EH32 . . . . 97 E4
LINKTOWN 17 B2
LINLITHGOW 85 C6

Linlithgow Acad EH49 . . . . 84 E5
LINLITHGOW BRIDGE 84 D8
Linlithgow Bridge Prim Sch
EH49 . . . . 84 D7
Linlithgow Canal Ctr*
EH49 . . . . 85 A6
Linlithgow L Ctr EH49 . . . . . 84 D5
Linlithgow Palace* EH49 . 85 A7
Linlithgow Pl FK5 . . . . 38 C4
Linlithgow Prim Sch EH49 84 F6
Linlithgow Rd EH51 . . . . 63 F6
Linlithgow Sta EH49 . . . . 85 A6
Linlithgow Story Mus The
EH49 . . . . 85 A7
Linlithgow Terr EH35 . . . . . 155 E7
Linmill Rd FK1 . . . . 110 A5
Linn Dean Wildlife Reserve*
EH36 . . . . 224 E6
Linnet Brae EH54 . . . . 143 C5
Linnet Way KY11 . . . . 30 A2
Linn Mill Clackmannan FK10 11 D6
  Queensferry EH30 . . . . 67 E2
Linn Pl Airth FK2 . . . . 22 E3
  Broxburn EH52 . . . . 115 E4
Linsay Macdonald Ct
KY12 . . . . 29 D3
Linties Nest KY3 . . . . 34 F2
Linton Ct KY2 . . . . 16 E6
Linton Pl KY11 . . . . 46 E3
Lint Riggs FK1 . . . . 60 B5
Lintview EH51 . . . . 108 B5
Linty La EH26 . . . . 191 D6
Linum Gr KY1 . . . . 17 C7
Linview La EH54 . . . . 164 F4
Linwell Ct KY3 . . . . 34 B1
Lionthorn Rd FK1 . . . . 59 F1
Lion Well Wynd EH49 . . . . . . 84 F7
Lipney FK11 . . . . 4 A6
Lismore Ave
  ⑬ Edinburgh EH8 . . . . 94 C1
  Kirkcaldy KY2 . . . . 16 F8
Lismore Cres EH8 . . . . 94 C1
Lismore Ct FK1 . . . . 60 B2
Lismore Pl KY2 . . . . 16 F7
Lister Ct FK9 . . . . 2 A6
Lister Rd EH54 . . . . 143 B1
Listloaning Pl EH30 . . . . 84 D7
Listloaning Rd EH49 . . . . 84 D7
Liston Dr EH29 . . . . 89 A2
Liston Pl EH29 . . . . 89 A2
Liston Rd EH29 . . . . 89 A1
Lithgow Pl FK6 . . . . 57 C8
Little Acre EH22 . . . . 174 D8
Little Carriden EH51 . . . . 64 E7
Little Craigs View ⑬ KY3 . 33 D1
Little Denny Rd FK6 . . . . 36 D1
Little Foothorn KY12 . . . . 44 E6
Little France Cres EH16 . 122 E1
Little France Dr EH16 . . . . 122 E1
Little France Ho EH17 . . . . 151 D8
Little France Mills EH16 . 122 D1
Littlejohn Ave EH10 . . . . . . 149 F8
Littlejohn Rd EH10 . . . . 149 E8
Littlejohn Wynd EH10 . . . . 149 F8
Little King St EH1 . . . . 229 A4
Little Mill Bsns Pk EH4 . . 84 C8
Little Pinkerton Cotts
EH42 . . . . 107 A5
Little Rd EH16 . . . . 151 B7
Little Sales Ave KY11 . . . . . . 47 F3
Little Sandhaven KY12 . . . . 42 D8
Little Spott Cotts EH42 . . . 105 F2
Little Wood Gr EH19 . . . . . . 173 B5
Livery St EH48 . . . . 141 A7
Livesay Rd KY11 . . . . 46 D1
Livesey Terr EH26 . . . . 192 A8
Livilands Ct FK8 . . . . 7 B5
Livilands Gate FK8 . . . . 7 B5
Livilands La FK8 . . . . 7 B5
LIVINGSTON 143 D6
Livingston Designer Outlet
EH54 . . . . 143 E5
Livingstone Cres FK2 . . . . . . 60 E5
Livingstone Dr
  Bo'ness EH51 . . . . 63 D6
  Burntisland KY3 . . . . 33 F2
  Laurieston FK2 . . . . 60 F2
Livingstone E Rdbt EH54 114 D1
Livingstone Pl EH9 . . . . 121 D5
Livingstone Quadrant
ML7 . . . . 159 D4
Livingston North Sta
EH54 . . . . 143 B6
Livingston Rd
  Dechmont EH52, EH54 . . . 114 D1
  Livingston EH54 . . . . 143 C5
Livingston South Sta
EH54 . . . . 165 A7
LIVINGSTON VILLAGE . . . 143 C2
Livingston Village Prim Sch
EH54 . . . . 143 B3
Lixmount Ave EH5 . . . . 93 C4
Lixmount Gdns EH5 . . . . 93 C4
Lizzie Brice's Rdbt EH54 . 144 B1
Llynallan Rd ML7 . . . . 158 F4
LOAN 89 F1
LOANBURN 191 E5
Loanburn EH26 . . . . 191 E5
Loanburn Ave EH26 . . . . . . 191 F6
Loanfoot Cres EH52 . . . . . . 115 A5
Loanfoot Gdns FK7 . . . . 20 C4

Loanfoot Rd EH52 . . . . 115 A4
LOANHEAD Roslin 172 B7
  Stirling 7 E6
Loanhead Ave Denny FK4 . 57 D6
  Grangemouth FK3 . . . . 61 E6
Loanhead Cotts EH29 . . . . . 89 B2
Loanhead L Ctr EH20 . . . . 172 B8
Loanhead Pl KY2 . . . . 17 A5
Loanhead Prim Sch
EH20 . . . . 172 C8
Loanhead Rd EH20 . . . . 151 A2
Loaning Cres EH7 . . . . 94 D2
Loaning Mills EH7 . . . . 94 D2
Loaninghill Pk EH52 . . . . . . 115 B4
Loaninghill Rd EH52 . . . . . . 115 B4
Loaning Rd EH7 . . . . 94 D2
Loan Pl ML7 . . . . 159 E6
LOANSTONE 192 B5
Loan The Bo'ness EH51 . . . . 63 D6
  Loanhead EH20 . . . . 172 B7
  Pathhead EH37 . . . . 175 C7
  South Queensferry EH30 . . 68 B1
  Torphichen EH48 . . . . 111 F6
  Wallyford EH21 . . . . 125 B6
Lobachber Cres ML7 . . . . . . 180 B3
Lochaber Dr FK5 . . . . 38 E3
Loch Awe Way EH47 . . . . . 161 B7
Lochbank EH54 . . . . 143 E5
Lochbrae FK10 . . . . 5 D2
Lochbridge Rd EH39 . . . . 54 D6
Loch Ctr EH33 . . . . 126 D6
Loch Earn Way EH47 . . . . . 161 C7
LOCHEND 94 B2
Lochend Ave Dunbar EH42 . 78 E1
  Edinburgh EH7 . . . . 94 B3
Lochend Castle Barns
EH7 . . . . 94 B2
Lochend Cl EH8 . . . . 229 C3
Lochend Cres
  Dunbar EH42 . . . . 78 D1
  Edinburgh EH7 . . . . 94 C2
Lochend Dr EH7 . . . . 94 C2
Lochend Gdns
  Dunbar EH42 . . . . 78 D1
  Edinburgh EH7 . . . . 94 B2
Lochend Gr EH7 . . . . 94 C2
Lochend Ho EH7 . . . . 94 C2
Lochend Ind Est EH28 . . . . 117 B5
Lochend Pk EH7 . . . . 94 B3
Lochend Quadrant EH7 . . . 94 C2
Lochend Rd Dunbar EH42 . . 78 E1
  Edinburgh EH7 . . . . 94 B3
  Ratho Station EH28, EH29 . 117 A7
Lochend Road N EH21 . . . . 124 B6
Lochend Road S
  Edinburgh EH7 . . . . 94 B2
  Musselburgh EH21 . . . . 124 B6
Lochend Sq EH7 . . . . 94 B3
Loch Fyne Way EH47 . . . . . 161 C7
LOCHGELLY 14 C7
Lochgelly Ind Pk KY5 . . . . . . 14 D7
Lochgelly North Specl Sch
KY5 . . . . 14 B8
Lochgelly Rd KY4 . . . . 13 D5
Lochgelly South Prim Sch
KY5 . . . . 14 A7
Lochgelly West Prim Sch
KY5 . . . . 14 A7
Lochgreen Rd FK1 . . . . 59 E2
Lochgreen Rdbt FK1 . . . . 59 F2
Lochhead Ave FK6 . . . . 36 E1
Lochhead Ct KY12 . . . . 29 A6
Lochhill Cotts EH32 . . . . 99 C7
Lochies Rd Burntisland KY3 34 A1
  Clackmannan FK10 . . . . 11 A4
Lochies Sch FK10 . . . . 5 F1
Lochinvar Pl FK4 . . . . 58 C3
Lochinvar Rd KY11 . . . . 46 C1
Lochlands Ave FK5 . . . . 59 B8
Lochlands Bsns Pk FK5 . . . . 59 B8
Lochlands Ind Est FK5 . . . . . 59 A8
Lochlands Loan FK5 . . . . 59 B7
Lochlea Gr KY2 . . . . 17 A7
Lochlea Terr KY2 . . . . 17 A7
Loch Linnhe Ct EH47 . . . . . 161 C7
Lochmaben Dr FK5 . . . . 38 F4
Loch Maree Way EH47 . . . 161 B7
Lochpark Pl FK6 . . . . 36 D1
Lochrin Bldgs EH3 . . . . 68 B1
Loch Rd Edinburgh EH4 . . . . 92 A2
  South Queensferry EH30 . . 68 B1
  Tranent EH33 . . . . 126 D6
Lochridge Pl FK6 . . . . 36 D1
LOCHRIN 228 A1
Lochrin Bldgs EH3 . . . . 228 B1
Lochrin Pl EH3 . . . . 228 B1
Lochrin Terr EH3 . . . . 228 B1
Lochshot Pl EH54 . . . . 143 A3
Lochside Ave EH12 . . . . 118 F4
Lochside Cotts FK2 . . . . 61 B2
Lochside Cres
  Edinburgh EH12 . . . . 118 F4
  Redding FK2 . . . . 61 B2
Lochside Ct EH12 . . . . 119 A4
Lochside Pl EH12 . . . . 118 F4
Lochside Rd FK1 . . . . 108 C1
Lochside View EH12 . . . . . . 118 F5
Lochside Way EH12 . . . . . . 119 A4
Loch Sq EH33 . . . . 126 D6
Loch St KY12 . . . . 29 A3
Loch Trool Way EH47 . . . . . 161 B7
Lochview Ct EH8 . . . . 229 C3
Lockerby Cotts EH16 . . . . . 151 C6
Lockerby Cres EH16 . . . . . . 151 C6
Lockerby Gr EH16 . . . . 151 C6
Lockharton Ave EH14 . . . . 120 E2
Lockharton Cres EH14 . . . 120 F2
Lockharton Gdns EH14 . . 120 E3

Lockhart Terr EH25 . . . . 171 F3
Lock Rd KY11 . . . . 67 B8
Lock Sixteen FK1 . . . . 59 D5
Lodemeia Pk EH22 . . . . 153 D4
Lodge Dr FK5 . . . . 38 F2
Lodge St EH41 . . . . 130 A8
LOGANLEA 162 C1
Loganlea Ave EH7 . . . . 94 D1
Loganlea Cres EH55 . . . . . . 162 C1
Loganlea Dr EH7 . . . . 94 D2
Loganlea Gdns EH7 . . . . 94 C2
Loganlea Loan EH7 . . . . 94 D1
Loganlea Pl
  Addiewell EH55 . . . . 162 D1
  Edinburgh EH7 . . . . 94 D1
Loganlea Rd
  Addiewell EH55 . . . . 162 C1
  Edinburgh EH7 . . . . 94 D2
Loganlea Terr
  Addiewell EH55 . . . . 162 C1
  Edinburgh EH7 . . . . 94 D2
Logan Rd KY12 . . . . 43 F8
Logan St EH3 . . . . 93 C2
Logan Way EH54 . . . . 143 D8
Logie Dr FK5 . . . . 38 A3
Logie Green Gdns EH7 . . . . 93 C3
Logie Green Loan EH7 . . . . 93 C3
Logie Green Rd EH7 . . . . 93 C3
Logie La Bridge of Allan FK9 2 C7
  Stirling FK9 . . . . 2 D4
Logie Mill EH7 . . . . 93 D3
Logie Pl KY12 . . . . 28 D5
Logie Rd FK9 . . . . 2 D4
Lomond Cres
  Dunfermline KY11 . . . . 29 F2
  Stenhousemuir FK5 . . . . 38 F3
  Stirling FK9 . . . . 2 B4
  Whitburn EH47 . . . . 161 A6
Lomond Ct FK10 . . . . 10 C5
Lomond Dr Bannockburn FK7 . 7 E1
  Falkirk FK2 . . . . 39 C1
Lomond Gdns KY2 . . . . 16 F5
Lomond Rd Edinburgh EH5 . 93 A6
  Grangemouth FK3 . . . . 61 E5
  Shotts ML7 . . . . 179 E6
Lomond St FK10 . . . . 4 E1
Lomond Vale EH26 . . . . 192 A7
Lomond View EH48 . . . . 110 F4
Lomond Way FK6 . . . . 57 D6
Lomond Wlk EH20 . . . . 151 A1
London Rd Dalkeith EH22 . 153 A3
  Edinburgh EH7, EH8 . . . . 94 B1
London St EH3 . . . . 93 D2
Loney Cres FK6 . . . . 57 E8
Longannet Cotts FK10 . . . . . 24 B1
Longannet Power Sta
FK10 . . . . 41 D7
Longannet Rdbt FK10 . . . . . . 24 A2
Longbraes Gdns KY2 . . . . . . 16 D6
Long Byres EH52 . . . . 115 E5
Long Craig Rigg EH5 . . . . . . 92 C7
Long Craigs EH32 . . . . 97 E4
Long Craigs Terr KY3 . . . . 35 A3
Long Craig Wlk KY1 . . . . 35 B8
Long Cram EH41 . . . . 129 F7
LONGCROFT 57 B3
Longcroft Gdns EH49 . . . . . . 84 E7
Longcroft Holdings FK7 . . . 57 B3
Long Crook EH30 . . . . 89 A8
Longdales EH52 . . . . 217 F7
Longdales Ave FK2 . . . . 60 A8
Longdales Ct FK2 . . . . 60 A8
Longdales Pl FK2 . . . . 60 A8
Longdales Rd FK2 . . . . 60 A8
LONG DALMAHOY 146 E4
Long Dalmahoy Rd
  Currie EH14 . . . . 147 C5
  Ratho EH27 . . . . 146 E4
Longdyke Pl FK2 . . . . 39 C4
Longdykes Rd EH32 . . . . 97 D5
Longford ML11 . . . . 201 A1
Longformacus Rd EH16 . 151 B7
Longhill Gdns EH11 . . . . 48 B3
Longnewton Cotts EH41 . 220 D3
LONGNIDDRY 98 F5
Longniddry Farm Cotts
EH32 . . . . 98 E5
Longniddry Prim Sch
EH32 . . . . 98 E5
Longniddry Sta EH32 . . . . . . 98 F5
Longpark Pl EH54 . . . . 143 A4
LONGRIDGE 161 C1
Longridge Prim Sch
EH47 . . . . 161 C2
Longridge Rd EH47 . . . . 161 A5
Long Row Halbeath KY12 . . 30 A7
  Menstrie FK11 . . . . 4 A7
  Tyninghame EH42 . . . . 76 C3
LONGSTONE 120 B2
Longstone Ave
  East Linton EH40 . . . . 103 D7
  Edinburgh EH14 . . . . 120 A2
Longstone Cotts EH14 . . . 120 A2
Longstone Cres EH14 . . . . 120 A3
Longstone Gdns EH11 . . . 119 F3
Longstone Gr EH14 . . . . 120 A2
Longstone Pl EH14 . . . . 120 A2
Longstone Prim Sch
EH14 . . . . 120 A1
Longstone Rd EH14 . . . . . . 120 A2
Longstone St EH14 . . . . 120 A2
Longstone Terr EH11 . . . . . 119 F3
Longstone View EH11 . . . . 119 F3

Longyester Farm Cotts
EH41 . . . . .221 A4
Lonsdale Cres KY3 . . . . .33 E1
Lonsdale Terr EH3 . . . . . . .228 C1
Lookaboutye Brae FK10 . . .11 A3
Loom Rd KY2 . . . . .17 B6
Lord Gambier Wharf KY1 . .17 D5
Lord President Rd EH39 . . .54 A7
Loretto Ct EH21 . . . . .124 B4
Loretto Jun Sch EH21 . . .124 C6
Loretto RC Prim Sch
EH21 . . . . .124 D6
Loretto Schs EH21 . . . . . .124 D6
Lorimar Pl FK2 . . . . .39 B2
Lorimer Gdns KY12 . . . . . . .29 D6
Lorimer View EH14 . . . . . .148 E6
Lorne Gdns FK2 . . . . .60 F3
Lorne Gr EH20 . . . . .151 A1
Lorne Ho KY12 . . . . .29 A4
Lorne La EH39 . . . . .54 C7
Lorne Pl EH6 . . . . .93 F3
Lorne Prim Sch EH6 . . . . . .93 F3
Lorne Rd FK5 . . . . .38 C2
Lorne Sq EH6 . . . . .93 F3
Lorne St Bridge of EH6 . . .93 F3
Kirkcaldy KY1 . . . . .17 E7
Lorn Pl KY11 . . . . .30 C1
Lornshall Acad FK10 . . . . . .4 E2
Lornshill Cres FK10 . . . . . . .9 F8
Losshill FK11 . . . . .4 A6
Lothian Bank EH22 . . . . . .152 F1
LOTHIANBRIDGE 173 F6
Lothianburn Junc EH10 . .150 B4
Lothian Cres Bo'ness EH51 . .64 A6
Stirling FK9 . . . . .2 C3
Lothian Ct KY11 . . . . .47 A2
Lothian Dr EH22 . . . . .174 C8
Lothian Rd Dalkeith EH22 . .153 A2
Edinburgh EH1 . . . . .228 B2
Lothian St Bathgate EH48 . .141 A7
Bo'ness EH51 . . . . .64 A6
Bonnyrigg and Lasswade
EH19 . . . . .173 C7
Burntisland KY3 . . . . .50 E8
Dalkeith EH22 . . . . .153 A3
Edinburgh EH1 . . . . .229 A2
Rosewell EH24 . . . . .172 D2
Lothians View KY11 . . . . . . .47 A2
Lothian Terr Kirkcaldy KY2 . .17 A7
Newtongrange EH22 . . . . .174 B4
Louburn EH48 . . . . .138 D3
Loudens Wlk FK6 . . . . .36 D5
Loughborough Rd KY1 . . . .17 F7
Loughrigg KY11 . . . . .47 A7
Louisa Sq EH24 . . . . .172 D2
Louise St KY11 . . . . .29 D2
Louvain Gdns EH48 . . . . . .139 F4
Lovedale Ave EH14 . . . . . .147 B1
Lovedale Cres EH14 . . . . .147 B1
Lovedale Gdns EH14 . . . . .147 C1
Lovedale Gr EH14 . . . . . . .147 B1
Lovedale Rd EH14 . . . . . . .147 C1
Lovells Glen EH49 . . . . .84 C8
Lovers La EH30 . . . . .89 C8
Lovers Loan Alva FK12 . . . . .5 B7
Dunfermline KY12 . . . . .28 F2
Lovers Wlk FK8 . . . . .2 B1
Low Brae EH48 . . . . .111 F5
Low Causewayside
Culross KY12 . . . . .42 D8
Newmills KY12 . . . . .26 C1
LOW TORRY 26 D1
Low Cswy Culross KY12 . . . .25 E1
Torryburn KY12 . . . . .26 E1
Low Doors The EH27 . . . .145 E2
Lower Alderston Rd
EH41 . . . . .100 E1
Lower Bathville EH48 . . . .140 A5
Lower Bridge St FK8 . . . . . . .2 A1
Lower Broomieknowe
EH18 . . . . .173 A8
Lower Castlehill FK8 . . . . . .2 A1
Lower Gilmore Pl EH3 . . .228 B1
Lower Glebe KY3 . . . . .49 C8
Lower Granton Rd EH5 . . .93 A7
Lower Joppa EH15 . . . . . . .123 C2
Lower London Rd EH7 . . . .94 A1
Lower Ridge Ct EH47 . . . .161 B2
LOWER SALTOUN 157 F5
Lower Valleyfield View
EH26 . . . . .191 F4
Low Port Prim Sch EH49 . .85 A7
Lowrie Ave EH26 . . . . .191 C5
Lowrie Vale FK11 . . . . .46 F4
LOW TORRY 26 D1
LOW VALLEYFIELD 26 A1
Ludgate FK10 . . . . .10 A6
Luffness Ct EH32 . . . . .71 D4
Luffness Gdns EH32 . . . . .71 D4
Luffness Mains Cotts
EH32 . . . . .72 B4
Lufra Bank EH5 . . . . .93 A6
Lugton Brae EH22 . . . . . . .152 F4
Lulach Ct KY12 . . . . .47 A8
Lumley Ct FK3 . . . . .61 D8
Lumley Pl FK3 . . . . .61 D8
Lumley St FK3 . . . . .61 D8
LUMPHINNANS 13 D5
Lumphinnans Prim Com Sch
KY4 . . . . .13 D5
Lumphinnans Rd KY5 . . . .14 A7
Lumsdaine Dr KY11 . . . . . .48 A1
Lumsden Ct
Broxburn EH52 . . . . .115 C5
Ratho EH28 . . . . .117 D2
Lundin Rd KY12 . . . . .28 A4

Lussielaw Rd EH9 . . . . . . .121 F3
Lutton Court Bsns Ctr
EH8 . . . . .229 B1
Lutton Pl EH8 . . . . .229 B1
Lyall Cres FK2 . . . . .61 E2
Lyars Rd EH32 . . . . .98 E6
Lyarthall EH52 . . . . .115 C5
Lychgate La EH52 . . . . . . .115 D5
Lychgate Rd FK10 . . . . .4 B2
Lydgait EH41 . . . . .101 A1
Lydgait Gdns EH41 . . . . . .101 A1
Lyefield Pl EH54 . . . . .143 B4
Lygon Rd EH16 . . . . .121 F2
Lyle Gn EH54 . . . . .143 B4
Lynburn Prim Sch KY11 . . .29 F2
Lynbank Hospl KY11 . . . . . .30 A5
Lynburn Cres KY11 . . . . . . .30 B5
Lynedoch Pl EH3 . . . . .228 A3
Lynedoch Place La EH3 . .228 A3
Lyne Gr KY12 . . . . .28 C2
Lyness St EH7 . . . . .61 E2
Lyne St EH7 . . . . .94 A1
Lynn Lea Ave EH41 . . . . . .130 C8
Lyon Cres FK9 . . . . .2 A6
Lyoncross FK4 . . . . .57 D4
Lyon Ct EH51 . . . . .63 D6
Lyon Dr EH54 . . . . .164 E6

M

MacAdam Pl FK1 . . . . .59 D6
McAdam Sq EH54 . . . . . . .164 D6
McAffee Gdns EH48 . . . . .139 F3
McAllister Ct FK7 . . . . .7 D1
MacAlpine Ct FK10 . . . . .4 D3
MacArthur Cres FK2 . . . . . .82 E6
McAulay Brae FK7 . . . . .20 C3
Macbeth Moir Rd EH21 . .125 A6
Macbeth Rd KY11 . . . . .29 E3
Mccafferty Way KY5 . . . . . .40 C1
McCall Gdns EH40 . . . . . .103 D7
McCallum Ct EH48 . . . . . . .139 F4
McCambridge Pl FK5 . . . . .38 C5
McCann Ave EH52 . . . . . . .115 B5
McCann Ct FK7 . . . . .7 A4
McCartney Rd FK5 . . . . .38 C4
McCathie Dr EH22 . . . . . . .174 B6
McClelland Cres KY11 . . . .29 B1
McCormack Pl FK5 . . . . . . .38 B5
Mac Cormick Terr EH26 . .191 F8
Mccraken Ct FK1 . . . . .81 F5
McDiarmid Gr EH22 . . . . .174 B4
MacDonald Ave EH48 . . .139 F6
McDonald Cres FK2 . . . . . .60 C7
McDonald Ct KY12 . . . . . . .27 D1
MacDonald Ct FK5 . . . . . . .38 B5
McDonald Dr FK7 . . . . .7 A4
MacDonald Gdns EH47 . .162 E8
MacDonald Pl KY3 . . . . . . .34 A2
MacDonald Rd EH7 . . . . . . .93 E3
MacDonald Sq KY11 . . . . . .30 B5
McDonald St
Edinburgh EH7 . . . . .93 E3
Inverkeithing/Dunfermline
KY11 . . . . .47 B7
McDouall Stuart Pl KY1 . . .18 A7
McDowall Rd EH9 . . . . . . .121 F3
Macduff Cres KY3 . . . . .34 F2
Mace Ct FK7 . . . . .7 D3
McEwan Sq EH3 . . . . .228 A1
Macfarlane Cres FK1 . . . . . .60 B5
Macfarlane Ct EH33 . . . . .126 B1
Macfarlane Pl EH52 . . . . .114 F3
McGahey Ct EH52 . . . . . . .174 B4
McGhee Pl FK1 . . . . .59 F2
McGinley Way EH49 . . . . . .84 D5
McGowan Rd FK2 . . . . .60 C7
McGregor Ave KY5 . . . . . . .14 A8
McGregor Pend EH32 . . . . .97 B2
McGregor Rd Rosyth KY11 . .46 D2
Stirling FK7 . . . . .7 C1
Machrie Ct KY1 . . . . .59 C4
Mcinally Cres FK2 . . . . .59 F8
Macindoe Cres KY1 . . . . . .17 D7
McIntosh Ct EH52 . . . . . . .115 C5
Macintosh Pl FK1 . . . . .60 A1
Macintosh Rd
Livingston EH54 . . . . .142 F1
Livingston EH54 . . . . .163 F8
McIntyre La EH33 . . . . . . .127 D6
McKane Pl KY12 . . . . .28 F1
McKay Dr KY11 . . . . .29 F1
McKell Ct FK1 . . . . .60 A3
McKenzie Cres KY15 . . . . .14 C7
McKenzie Pl FK7 . . . . .59 F2
Mackenzie Pl EH3 . . . . . .228 B4
Mackenzie St KY1 . . . . .17 E7
Mackenzie Terr FK3 . . . . . .61 C6
Mackie Pl KY1 . . . . .29 F2
McKinlay Cres FK10 . . . . . .10 C7
McKinlay Terr EH20 . . . . .172 A7
McKinnon Dr EH22 . . . . . .174 D5
McKinnon Rd EH47 . . . . . .161 F7
McLachlan Ave FK6 . . . . . . .36 C1
McLachlan Gdns EH32 . . . .97 B2
McLachlan St FK5 . . . . .38 C2
McLardy Ct EH52 . . . . .114 F3
McLaren Ave EH49 . . . . . . .84 A6
McLaren Ct FK5 . . . . .38 D2
McLaren Rd EH9 . . . . .122 A4
McLaren Terr
Edinburgh EH11 . . . . .228 A2
Stirling FK7 . . . . .7 B3
MacLaren Terr FK2 . . . . . . .39 A2

McLauchlan Rise KY3 . . . .49 B7
McLauchlan View ML7 . . .159 F6
Maclean Cres FK12 . . . . . . .5 C7
Maclean Ct FK7 . . . . .7 C3
Maclean Gate KY11 . . . . . .46 F7
Maclean Gdns KY11 . . . . . .46 E7
McLean Pl
Bonnyrigg and Lasswade
EH18 . . . . .172 C6
Gorebridge EH23 . . . . . . .174 D1
Maclean Pl KY11 . . . . .46 E7
McLean Prim Sch KY12 . . .28 E5
Maclean Terr EH48 . . . . . .138 C3
Maclean Wlk KY11 . . . . . . .46 F7
McLeod Cres EH32 . . . . . . .96 F1
McLeod St Broxburn EH52 . .115 C6
Edinburgh EH11 . . . . .120 E6
McMartin Ct EH47 . . . . . .161 D7
MACMERRY 127 E6
Macmerry Bsns Pk EH33 . .127 D6
Macmerry Ind Est EH33 . .127 E6
Macmerry Prim Sch
EH33 . . . . .127 D6
Macmillan Rd EH54 . . . . .143 C1
McNab Gdns EH5 . . . . .59 F2
Macnair Ave EH39 . . . . . . .54 C6
McNeil Cres EH48 . . . . . . .140 A6
McNeill Ave EH20 . . . . . . .172 B8
McNeill Path EH33 . . . . . .126 C6
McNeill Pl EH20 . . . . .172 B8
McNeill Terr EH20 . . . . . .172 A8
McNeill Wlk ❷ EH33 . . . .126 C5
McNeill Wlk ❷ EH33 . . . .126 C5
McPhail Sq EH33 . . . . . . .126 D6
Macpherson Dr FK8 . . . . . . .2 A2
Macpherson Pl ❻ FK1 . . .59 F2
McQuade St EH19 . . . . . . .173 D8
McRae Cres KY3 . . . . .33 F2
McRobert Ctr FK9 . . . . .2 D5
McTaggart Ave FK6 . . . . . . .36 E2
MacTaggart Loan EH22 . .174 B4
McVean Pl FK4 . . . . .57 B4
Madderfield Mews EH47 . .85 B7
MADDISTON 83 B6
Maddiston Prim Sch FK2 . .82 F7
Maddiston Rd FK2 . . . . .82 E8
Madeira Pl EH6 . . . . .93 E5
Madeira St EH6 . . . . .93 E6
Madelvic Sq EH5 . . . . .92 E7
Madill Pl FK5 . . . . .38 F3
Madison Pl FK3 . . . . .61 D8
Maesterton Pl EH22 . . . . .174 B4
Magdala Cres EH12 . . . . . .120 F7
Magdala Mews EH12 . . . . .120 F7
MAGDALENE 123 B6
Magdalene Ave EH15 . . . .123 B6
Magdalene Dr EH15 . . . . .123 B6
Magdalene Gdns EH15 . .123 B6
Magdalene Loan EH15 . . .123 B6
Magdalene Medway
EH15 . . . . .123 B6
Magdalene Pl EH15 . . . . .123 B6
Maggie Wood's Loan FK1 . .59 F4
Magnus Rd EH51 . . . . .62 D5
Magpie Gdns EH22 . . . . . .153 D2
Mag's Bank FK1 . . . . .131 B1
Maidencraig Cres EH4 . . . .92 C2
Maidencraig Gr EH4 . . . . . .92 C2
MAIDENPARK 63 E6
Maidenpark Pl EH51 . . . . . .63 E6
Maidlands EH52 . . . . .85 C7
Maid of the Forth ✱ EH30 . .68 D1
Main Point EH3 . . . . .228 C2
Main Rd Charlestown KY11 . .45 B4
Crombie KY12 . . . . .44 E7
Grangemouth FK3 . . . . .62 B8
Macmerry EH33 . . . . .127 C5
North Queensferry KY11 . . .68 B6
Mains Farm Pl EH47 . . . . .161 E6
Mains Gdns EH33 . . . . . . .126 D2
Mains of Craigmillar
EH16 . . . . .122 D2
Mains Rd Harthill ML7 . . . .159 E5
Linlithgow EH49 . . . . .84 F6
Main St Aberdour KY3 . . . .49 C8
Airth FK2 . . . . .22 D4
Alloa FK10 . . . . .5 D1
Auchtertool KY2 . . . . .15 B2
Avonbridge FK1 . . . . .110 A6
Balerno EH14 . . . . .147 C1
Bannockburn FK7 . . . . .7 D1
Blackridge EH48 . . . . .138 C3
Bo'ness EH51 . . . . .64 A8
Bonnybridge FK4 . . . . .58 B5
Cairneyhill KY12 . . . . .27 D1
California FK1 . . . . .81 F5
Cambusbarron FK7 . . . . . . .6 D5
Camelon FK1 . . . . .60 A4
Carnock KY12 . . . . .27 C7
Carrington EH23 . . . . .194 D5
Clackmannan FK10 . . . . . .11 A4
Comrie KY12 . . . . .26 D7
Cowdenbeath, Hill of Beath
KY4 . . . . .13 A1
Cowdenbeath, Lumphinnans
KY4 . . . . .13 E6
Cowie FK7 . . . . .20 D7
Crossford KY12 . . . . .28 A3
Crossgates KY4 . . . . .30 F6
Dalgety Bay KY11 . . . . .47 F4
Dalmeny EH30 . . . . .89 E7
Dechmont EH52 . . . . .114 C2
East Calder EH53 . . . . . . .144 E4

Main St continued
East Saltoun EH34 . . . . . .157 E4
East Whitburn EH47 . . . . .161 D7
Edinburgh EH4 . . . . .91 F3
Elphinstone EH33 . . . . . . .126 B1
Falkirk, Bainsford FK2 . . . . .60 B7
Falkirk, Camelon FK1 . . . . . .59 E5
Falkirk, Carronshore FK2 . .39 C3
Fallin FK7 . . . . .8 E3
Fauldhouse EH47 . . . . . . .181 D6
Forth ML11 . . . . .201 B1
Gifford EH41 . . . . .220 F7
Gorebridge EH23 . . . . . . .195 C7
Grangemouth, Brightons
FK2 . . . . .82 D8
Grangemouth, Rumford FK2 . .82 F7
Gullane EH31 . . . . .52 B2
Halbeath KY11 . . . . .30 B5
High Valleyfield KY12 . . . . .25 F1
Hill of Beath KY4 . . . . .30 F8
Kingseat KY12 . . . . .12 B1
Kirkliston EH29 . . . . .89 A2
Kirknewton EH27 . . . . . . .145 E2
Limekilns KY11 . . . . .45 D3
Linlithgow EH49 . . . . .84 D7
Livingston, Deans EH54 . .142 E6
Livingston, Livingston Village
EH54 . . . . .143 C2
Loanhead EH20 . . . . .171 F7
Lochgelly KY5 . . . . .14 B7
Longniddry EH32 . . . . .98 E5
Longridge EH47 . . . . .161 C1
Mid Calder EH53 . . . . .144 C3
Newton EH52 . . . . .88 A8
Newtongrange EH22 . . . . .174 B4
North Queensferry KY11 . . .68 C5
Ormiston EH35 . . . . .155 E7
Pathhead, Dewartown
EH23 . . . . .175 D5
Pathhead EH37 . . . . .176 B5
Philpstoun EH49 . . . . .86 D7
Plean FK7 . . . . .20 D3
Polmont FK2 . . . . .61 E2
Ratho EH28 . . . . .117 D2
Redding FK2 . . . . .61 C2
Roslin EH25 . . . . .172 A3
Shieldhill FK1 . . . . .81 D6
Shotts ML7 . . . . .180 A3
Slamannan FK1 . . . . .108 B7
Stenhousemuir FK5 . . . . . .38 E2
Stenhousemuir, Larbert FK5 . .38 C2
Stirling FK7 . . . . .7 B4
Stoneyburn, Bents EH47 . .162 A1
Stoneyburn EH47 . . . . . . .162 B2
Torryburn KY12 . . . . .26 D1
Townhill KY12 . . . . .29 D8
Tullibody FK10 . . . . .4 B2
Tyninghame EH42 . . . . .76 C3
West Calder EH55 . . . . . . .163 D3
Westfield EH48 . . . . .110 F5
Winchburgh EH52 . . . . .88 A3
Main Street E FK11 . . . . .4 A6
Main Street W
Dalgety Bay KY11 . . . . .47 E4
Menstrie FK11 . . . . .3 F6
Main End EH52 . . . . .71 C4
Maitland Ave
Bannockburn FK7 . . . . .7 D1
Musselburgh EH21 . . . . . .124 A6
Maitland Cres FK7 . . . . .7 B3
Maitland Hog La EH29 . . . .89 A1
Maitland Park Rd EH21 . .124 A6
Maitland Rd
Kirkliston EH29 . . . . .89 A2
Rosyth KY11 . . . . .67 B8
Maitland St
Dunfermline KY12 . . . . .28 F4
Musselburgh EH21 . . . . . .124 A6
Majors Loan FK1 . . . . .60 A4
Majors Pl FK1 . . . . .60 A3
Malbet Pk EH16 . . . . .151 B7
Malbet Wynd EH16 . . . . . .151 C7
Malcolm Ct
Bathgate EH48 . . . . .140 F5
Dunfermline KY11 . . . . .29 B1
Malcolm Dr FK5 . . . . .38 E4
Malcolm St
Dunfermline KY11 . . . . .29 B2
Dunfermline KY11 . . . . .29 C2
Malcolm's Wynd KY1 . . . . .17 C5
Mallace Ave EH48 . . . . . . .140 B5
Mallard Brae EH54 . . . . . .143 C5
Mallard Gr KY11 . . . . .30 A1
Mallard Wlk EH32 . . . . . . .125 E8
Mall Ave EH14 . . . . .124 C6
Mallens Brae EH48 . . . . . .112 A5
Mallens Terr EH14 . . . . . . .147 C1
Malleny Gdn ✱ EH14 . . . .147 D2
Malleny Millgate EH14 . . .168 D8
Mall Sh Ctr The ❻ FK1 . . . .60 B4
Mall The EH54 . . . . .143 C6
Malplaquet Ct ML8 . . . . . .215 B1
Malta Gn EH3 . . . . .93 B2
Malta Terr EH3 . . . . .93 B2
Maltings The
Auchtertool KY2 . . . . .15 B2
Falkirk FK1 . . . . .59 F5
Haddington EH41 . . . . . . .130 A7
Linlithgow EH49 . . . . .84 D6
North Berwick EH39 . . . . .101 F8
Mamre Dr FK1 . . . . .81 F5
Mandela Ave FK2 . . . . .60 C7
Manderston St EH6 . . . . . .93 F4
Mandora St ML8 . . . . .215 B1
Manitoba Ave EH54 . . . . . .143 C4
Mannafields Christian Sch ❺
EH7 . . . . .93 E3

Mannan Dr FK10 . . . . .11 B4
Mannering Pl ❺ EH16 . . .151 B8
Mannerston Holdings
EH49 . . . . .65 D3
Mannfield Ave FK4 . . . . . . .57 F4
Manor Cres FK10 . . . . .4 B2
Manor Gdns Dunbar EH42 . .78 A2
Inverkeithing/Dunfermline
KY11 . . . . .30 A2
Manor Loan FK9 . . . . .3 B5
Manor Pl EH3 . . . . .228 A3
MANOR POWIS 3 B3
Manor Powis Cotts FK9 . . .3 B3
Manor St FK1 . . . . .60 B4
Manor Steps FK9 . . . . .3 C3
Manor Wynd FK2 . . . . .83 A5
Man O' War Way FK10 . . . .64 B8
Manse Ave
Armadale EH48 . . . . .139 E6
Whitburn EH47 . . . . .161 A6
Manse Cres FK7 . . . . .7 B4
Manse Ct EH53 . . . . .144 F4
Manse Gdns
Athelstaneford EH39 . . . .101 F7
East Calder EH53 . . . . . . .144 F4
Mansefield Ct
❸ Bathgate EH48 . . . . . .141 A7
Livingston EH54 . . . . .143 C3
Mansefield Gr EH48 . . . . .141 A6
Mansefield St EH48 . . . . .141 A7
Manse Gr EH47 . . . . .162 C2
Manse La ❷ Burntisland KY3 . .50 F8
Cockenzie & Port Seton
EH32 . . . . .97 C4
Musselburgh EH21 . . . . . .124 D6
Manse Pk EH52 . . . . .114 F5
Manse Rd Aberdour KY3 . .49 B7
Bannockburn FK7 . . . . .7 E1
Bathgate EH48 . . . . .141 E6
Falkirk FK1 . . . . .60 B4
Inverkeithing KY11 . . . . . . .47 B2
Slamannan FK1 . . . . .108 B7
Manse Rd
Carrington EH23 . . . . .194 D5
Crossgates KY4 . . . . .30 E7
Dirleton EH39 . . . . .53 A5
Edinburgh EH12 . . . . .119 D6
Inverkeithing KY11 . . . . . .201 B1
Inverkeithing KY11 . . . . . . .47 B2
Kincardine FK10 . . . . .23 E5
Kinghorn KY3 . . . . .34 F3
Kirkliston EH29 . . . . .89 A1
Linlithgow EH49 . . . . .85 A6
Roslin EH25 . . . . .172 A3
Shotts ML7 . . . . .180 A3
Torpichen EH48 . . . . .111 F5
Whitburn EH47 . . . . .161 B6
Manse St Aberdour KY3 . . .49 C7
Edinburgh EH12 . . . . .119 D6
Manse Terr FK10 . . . . .11 A4
Manse View
Armadale EH48 . . . . .139 E5
Innerwick EH42 . . . . .107 F1
Philpstoun EH49 . . . . .86 D7
Masewood Cres EH47 . . . .161 B6
Mansfield Ave Alloa FK10 . . .5 D1
Musselburgh EH21 . . . . . .124 C5
Newtongrange EH22 . . . . .174 C6
Mansfield Ct EH21 . . . . . . .124 D5
Mansfield Pl
Edinburgh EH3 . . . . .93 D2
Musselburgh EH21 . . . . . .124 C5
Newtongrange EH22 . . . . .174 B6
Mansfield Rd
Balerno EH14 . . . . .168 C8
Musselburgh EH21 . . . . . .124 C6
Newtongrange EH22 . . . . .174 B6
Mansionhouse Rd
Edinburgh EH9 . . . . .121 D5
Falkirk FK1 . . . . .59 D5
Manson Sq EH54 . . . . .142 C6
Manuel Rigg FK2 . . . . .82 E6
Manuel Sta❋ EH49 . . . . . . .84 A7
Maple Ave FK5 . . . . .38 F3
Maple Ct FK❿ EH54 . . . . . .10 B6
Maple Pl FK6 . . . . .36 C3
Maple St KY2 . . . . .16 C2
Maplewood Pk EH54 . . . . .142 E7
Maranatha Cres FK2 . . . . . .82 C8
Marchbank Dr EH14 . . . . .168 C8
Marchbank Gdns EH14 . . .168 C8
Marchbank Gr EH14 . . . . .168 C8
Marchbank Way EH14 . . . .147 C1
Marchbank Pl EH14 . . . . .168 C8
Marches Dr EH14 . . . . .191 C5
Marches The
Armadale EH48 . . . . .140 A5
❻ Stirling FK8 . . . . .7 B7
Marchfield Gr EH4 . . . . .92 A3
Marchfield Park La EH4 . . .91 F3
Marchfield Pl EH4 . . . . .91 F3
Marchfield Terr EH4 . . . . . .92 A3
March Gait EH4 . . . . .91 F3
Marchglen FK13 . . . . .5 F5
March Gr EH4 . . . . .92 A2
Marchhall Cres EH16 . . . .122 A5
Marchhall Pl EH16 . . . . . .122 A5
Marchhall Rd EH16 . . . . . .122 A5
Marchlands La EH51 . . . . . .64 A7
Marchlands Terr EH51 . . . .63 F7
MARCHMONT 121 C5
Marchmont Ave FK2 . . . . . .61 E2
Marchmont Cres EH9 . . . .121 D5
Marchmont Rd EH9 . . . . . .61 F2

Marchmont Mews FK2 . . . . 61 F2
Marchmont Rd EH9 . . . . . 121 C5
Marchmont St EH9 . . . . . 121 C5
March Pines EH4 . . . . 91 F2
March Rd EH4 . . . . 92 A2
Marchside Ct FK10 . . . . 5 C1
Marchwood Ave EH48 . . . 141 C6
Marchwood Cres EH48 . . 141 C6
Marchwood Ct EH33 . . . . 126 B1
Mardale Cres EH10 . . . . . 121 A4
Maree Ct FK10 . . . . 10 C6
Maree Pl Crossford KY12 . . 28 B1
 Kirkcaldy KY2 . . . . 16 E8
Maree Wlk EH54 . . . . 144 A4
Margaret Ave
 Bathgate EH48 . . . . 141 F6
 Longcroft FK4 . . . . 57 A3
Margaret Ct FK6 . . . . 36 E1
Margaret Dr FK4 . . . . 58 A6
Margaret Rd FK7 . . . . 7 C2
Margaret Rose Ave EH10 150 C5
Margaret Rose Cres
 EH10 . . . . 150 C5
Margaret Rose Dr EH10 . 150 C5
Margaret Rose Loan
 EH10 . . . . 150 C5
Margaret Rose Way
 EH10 . . . . 150 C5
Margaret Rose Wlk
 EH10 . . . . 150 C5
Margaret Terr FK5 . . . . 38 E4
Maria St KY1 . . . . 17 C5
Marina Ave EH48 . . . . 141 F6
Marina Rd EH48 . . . . 141 E6
Marine Dr EH4 . . . . 92 A6
Marine Espl EH6 . . . . 94 C5
Marine Par EH39 . . . . 54 D7
Mariner Ave FK1 . . . . 59 B5
Marine Rd Dunbar EH42 . . 78 C3
 Gullane EH31 . . . . 52 A3
Mariner Dr FK1 . . . . 59 B5
Mariner Gdns FK1 . . . . 59 C6
Mariner Rd FK1 . . . . 59 C5
Mariners St KY2 . . . . 17 B6
Mariners Wlk KY11 . . . . . . 47 F3
Marine Terr EH31 . . . . 52 A3
Marion St KY1 . . . . 17 B2
Marionville Ave EH7 . . . . . 94 C1
Marionville Cres EH7 . . . . 94 C2
Marionville Dr EH7 . . . . . . 94 C2
Marionville Gr EH7 . . . . . . 94 C2
Marionville Meadway EH7 94 C2
Marionville Pk EH7 . . . . . . 94 B1
Marionville Rd EH7 . . . . . . 94 B2
Marion Wilson View FK5 . 38 C3
Marischal Pl [7] EH4 . . . . . 92 C2
Maritime La EH6 . . . . 94 A5
Maritime St EH6 . . . . 94 A5
Marjoribanks St EH48 . . . 141 B6
Marjory Ct EH48 . . . . 141 C5
Marjory Pl EH48 . . . . 141 C4
Market Ct [5] EH41 . . . . . 101 A1
Marketgate EH35 . . . . 155 E7
Market La EH49 . . . . 85 A7
Market Loan EH33 . . . . . . 126 C7
Market Pl
 North Berwick EH39 . . . . 54 C7
 Whitburn EH47 . . . . 161 A7
Market St Bo'ness EH51 . . 63 F8
 Dunfermline KY12 . . . . . . 29 A4
 Edinburgh EH1 . . . . 229 A3
 Haddington EH41 . . . . . . 130 B8
 Mid Calder EH53 . . . . . . 144 C4
 Musselburgh EH21 . . . . . 124 B6
Market View EH33 . . . . . . 126 C7
Market Way EH33 . . . . 126 C7
Markfield Rd KY11 . . . . . . 48 C4
Mark La [4] EH41 . . . . 130 B8
Markle Steading EH40 . . . 103 A8
Marlborough Dr FK9 . . . . . 2 C3
Marlborough St EH15 . . . 123 B8
Marly Gn EH39 . . . . 54 B6
Marly Rise EH39 . . . . 54 B6
Marmion Ave EH25 . . . . . 171 F3
Marmion Cres
 Edinburgh EH16 . . . . 122 B1
 North Berwick EH39 . . . . 54 B7
Marmion Ct [4] EH39 . . . . 54 B7
Marmion Rd
 Bathgate EH48 . . . . 141 A7
 Grangemouth FK3 . . . . . 61 D5
 North Berwick EH39 . . . . 54 C7
Marmion St FK2 . . . . 60 B8
Mar Pl Alloa FK10 . . . . 10 A7
 Alloa, Sauchie FK10 . . . . . 5 C1
 Stirling FK8 . . . . 7 A8
Marquis Dr FK10 . . . . 11 B4
Marrfield Rd EH54 . . . . . . 115 A1
Marrfield Terr EH54 . . . . . 115 A1
Marschal Ct FK7 . . . . 7 D3
Marsden Ct FK9 . . . . 2 C2
Marshal Dr FK1 . . . . 81 F5
Marshall Pl KY11 . . . . 29 B1
Marshall Rd EH29 . . . . 89 A1
Marshall's Ct EH1 . . . . . . 229 B4
Marshall St
 Cockenzie & Port Seton
 EH32 . . . . 97 B4
 Cowdenbeath KY4 . . . . . . 13 D3
 Edinburgh EH8 . . . . 229 A2
 Grangemouth FK3 . . . . . . 61 D8
Marshall Terr FK3 . . . . 61 D8
Marshall Twr FK1 . . . . 60 D4
Marshall Way FK10 . . . . . . 4 C4
Marshill FK10 . . . . 10 A6
Mar St FK10 . . . . 10 B6
Mar Terr FK10 . . . . 11 A4

Martin Brae EH54 . . . . 143 C5
Martin Gr EH19 . . . . 173 D8
Martin Pl EH22 . . . . 152 E2
Maryburn Rd EH22 . . . . . . 174 C8
Mary Erskine Sch The
 EH4 . . . . 92 B1
Mary Erskine & Stewart's
 Melville Jun Sch The [1]
 EH4 . . . . 92 C1
Maryfield
 [2] Edinburgh, Drum EH7 . 93 F2
 Edinburgh, Portobello EH15 . 95 B1
Maryfield Dr EH51 . . . . 64 D6
Maryfield Pl EH53 . . . . . . 144 C2
Maryfield Pl
 Bonnyrigg and Lasswade
 EH19 . . . . 173 C7
 [2] Edinburgh EH7 . . . . . 94 A2
 Falkirk FK1 . . . . 59 B4
Maryflats Pl FK3 . . . . 61 E7
Maryhall St KY1 . . . . 17 C5
Mary Pl Clackmannan FK10 . 11 A5
 Dunfermline KY11 . . . . . . 29 B2
Mary Reid Int Spa Acad
 EH11 . . . . 228 B2
Mary's EH11 . . . . 93 A2
Mary Sq FK2 . . . . 61 A4
Mary St FK7 . . . . 6 B4
Mary Stevenson Dr FK10 . 10 A8
Mary Street Rdbt FK2 . . . . 60 F3
Marytree Ho EH17 . . . . . . 151 D8
Marywell KY1 . . . . 17 C5
Masefield Way EH12 . . . . . 90 B1
Mason Pl EH18 . . . . 172 F6
Massereene Rd KY2 . . . . . 16 F5
Masterton Prim Sch KY11 47 B8
Masterton Rd KY11 . . . . . 47 A7
Mathers Ave EH47 . . . . . . 160 F6
Mather Terr FK2 . . . . 60 F4
Mathew Ct FK3 . . . . 61 D8
Mathieson Pl KY11 . . . . . . 29 F1
Mathews Crofts EH48 . . . 138 C3
Matthews Dr EH22 . . . . . . 173 F4
Matthew St
 Edinburgh EH16 . . . . 122 F3
 Kirkcaldy KY2 . . . . 17 B6
Mauchline Gr KY2 . . . . 17 A8
Maukeshill Ct EH54 . . . . . 143 C2
Mauldeth Rd EH52 . . . . . 115 C5
Maule Terr EH31 . . . . 52 A2
Maulsford Ave EH22 . . . . 152 B7
Maurice Ave FK7 . . . . 7 D4
Maurice Pl EH9 . . . . 121 D2
MAURICEWOOD 191 E7
Mauricewood Ave EH26 . 191 F7
Mauricewood Bank EH26 191 F7
Mauricewood Gr EH26 . . 191 F7
Mauricewood Pk EH26 . . 191 F7
Mauricewood Prim Sch
 EH26 . . . . 192 A8
Mauricewood Rd EH26 . . 191 F8
Mauricewood Rise EH26 . 191 F7
Mavisbank EH20 . . . . 172 C7
Mavis Bank EH48 . . . . 141 B8
Mavisbank Ave FK1 . . . . . . 81 C6
Mavisbank Gdns EH48 . . 141 B8
Mavisbank Pl EH18 . . . . . 172 E6
Mavishall EH37 . . . . 224 D8
Maxton Cres FK12 . . . . 5 C7
Maxton Ct EH22 . . . . 153 A3
Maxton Pl KY11 . . . . 46 E3
Maxwell Cres KY4 . . . . 13 A2
Maxwell Ct EH21 . . . . 124 B6
Maxwell Pl [6] FK8 . . . . 7 B8
Maxwell Rd EH39 . . . . 53 A4
Maxwell Sq EH54 . . . . . . 164 C6
Maxwell St EH10 . . . . 121 A3
Maxwell Twr FK1 . . . . 60 D3
Maybank Villas EH12 . . . 119 D7
Mayburn Ave EH20 . . . . . 151 B1
Mayburn Bank EH20 . . . . 172 B8
Mayburn Cres EH20 . . . . . 151 B1
Mayburn Ct EH20 . . . . . . 172 B8
Mayburn Dr EH20 . . . . . . 151 B1
Mayburn Gr EH20 . . . . . . 172 B8
Mayburn Hill EH20 . . . . . 172 B8
Mayburn Loan EH20 . . . . 151 B1
Mayburn Terr EH20 . . . . . 151 B1
Mayburn Vale EH20 . . . . . 172 B8
Mayburn Wlk EH20 . . . . . 172 B8
Mayburn Pl EH20 . . . . . . 119 A8
Maybury Rd
 Edinburgh, Bughtlin EH4,
 EH12 . . . . 91 A1
 Edinburgh, East Craigs
 EH12 . . . . 119 A7
MAYFIELD Armadale 140 A5
 Dalkeith 174 F5
 Edinburgh 121 F4
Mayfield Ave EH21 . . . . . 124 B3
Mayfield Cres
 Clackmannan FK10 . . . . . 11 A5
 Loanhead EH20 . . . . 172 C7
 Musselburgh EH21 . . . . . 124 B4
Mayfield Ct
 Armadale EH48 . . . . 139 F4
 Loanhead EH20 . . . . 172 C8
 Stirling FK7 . . . . 7 B3
Mayfield Dr
 Armadale EH48 . . . . 139 F5
 Longcroft FK4 . . . . 57 B3
Mayfield Gardens La
 EH9 . . . . 121 F4
Mayfield Gdns EH9 . . . . . 121 F4
Mayfield Gdns La EH9 . . . 121 F4
Mayfield Ind Est EH22 . . 174 C5
Mayfield L Ctr EH22 . . . . 174 D6
Mayfield Mews [2] FK1 . . . 59 F4

Mayfield Pk EH21 . . . . 124 B3
Mayfield Pl
 Edinburgh EH12 . . . . 119 D6
 Mayfield EH22 . . . . 174 D6
 Musselburgh EH21 . . . . . 124 B3
Mayfield Prim Sch EH22 174 D5
Mayfield Rd
 Easthouses EH22 . . . . . . 174 D8
 Edinburgh EH9 . . . . 121 F3
 Redding FK2 . . . . 61 C2
Mayfield St FK7 . . . . 7 B4
Mayfield Terr EH9 . . . . . . 121 F4
Mayflower St KY12 . . . . . . 29 C7
Maygate [8] KY12 . . . . 29 A3
Mayne Ave FK9 . . . . 2 B6
Mayshade Rd EH20 . . . . . 151 B1
May Terr EH39 . . . . 54 A7
Mayville Bank EH21 . . . . . 125 A6
Mayville Gardens E EH5 . . 93 C6
Mayville Gdns EH5 . . . . . . 93 C6
Mayville Pk EH42 . . . . 78 C3
MEADOWBANK 94 B2
Meadowbank
 Edinburgh EH8 . . . . 94 B1
 Livingston EH54 . . . . 143 E5
 Ormiston EH35 . . . . 155 E6
Meadowbank Ave [6] EH8 94 B1
Meadowbank Cres
 Edinburgh EH8 . . . . 94 B1
 Ormiston EH35 . . . . 155 D7
Meadowbank Pl [1] EH8 . . 94 C1
Meadowbank Rd
 Kirknewton EH27 . . . . . . 145 C1
 Ormiston EH35 . . . . 155 E7
Meadowbank Sh Pk EH8 . 94 A2
Meadowbank Sports Ctr
 EH7 . . . . 94 B1
Meadowbank St FK2 . . . . . 61 C1
Meadowbank Terr [5] EH8 94 B1
Meadowbank View EH7 . 145 F3
Meadow Cres EH47 . . . . . 181 E5
Meadow Ct Burntisland KY3 . 33 E1
 Carluke ML8 . . . . 215 C1
 Denny FK6 . . . . 36 D4
Meadow Dr EH47 . . . . 162 A1
Meadowend KY12 . . . . 28 C2
Meadowfield
 Burntisland KY3 . . . . 33 E2
 Cowdenbeath KY4 . . . . . . 13 A8
 Dalgety Bay KY11 . . . . . . 48 B4
Meadowfield Ave EH8 . . . 122 E7
Meadowfield Ct EH8 . . . . 122 D7
Meadowfield Dr EH8 . . . . 122 E7
Meadowfield Gdns EH8 . 122 D6
Meadowfield Ind Est KY3 . 33 E1
Meadowfield Rd FK7 . . . . . 7 C7
Meadow Gn FK10 . . . . 5 B1
Meadow Gr FK10 . . . . 11 D3
Meadowhead Ave EH55 . 162 E1
Meadowhead Cres EH55 162 E1
Meadowhead Gdns EH55 162 E1
Meadowhead Loan EH55 162 E1
Meadowhead Pl EH55 . . . 162 E1
Meadowhead Terr EH55 . 162 D1
Meadowhouse Rd EH12 . 119 D6
Meadow La EH8 . . . . 229 A1
Meadowland Rd FK9 . . . . . 2 A6
Meadowmill Loan EH33 . 126 D7
Meadowmill Sports Ctr
 EH33 . . . . 126 C8
Meadowpark
 Haddington EH41 . . . . . . 130 A8
 Seafield EH47 . . . . 163 A8
Meadowpark Ave EH48 . . 140 F5
Meadowpark Cres EH48 . 140 F5
Meadowpark Rd EH48 . . . 140 F5
Meadow Park Sch EH41 . 130 A8
Meadow Pk FK12 . . . . 5 A6
Meadow Pl Bilston EH25 . 171 E6
 Dunfermline KY11 . . . . . . 29 F3
 Edinburgh EH9 . . . . 121 E1
 Stirling FK8 . . . . 2 C1
 Stoneyburn EH47 . . . . . . 162 A1
Meadow Place La EH47 . . 162 A1
Meadow Place Rd EH12 . 119 C5
Meadow Rd
 Riccarton EH14 . . . . 147 F7
 Stoneyburn EH47 . . . . . . 162 A1
Meadowside Rd KY11 . . . 48 A7
Meadow St FK1 . . . . 60 C4
Meadows Tennis Complex
 EH8 . . . . 121 D1
Meadows The
 Falkirk, Carronshore FK2 . 39 B2
 Falkirk FK1 . . . . 60 C4
 Stirling FK9 . . . . 2 B3
Meadows Yard Nature
 Reserve ★ EH7 . . . . 94 E3
Meadow View
 Crossford KY12 . . . . 28 B2
 Halbeath KY12 . . . . 30 A5
Mearenside EH12 . . . . 119 A8
Medwyn Pl KY11 . . . . 9 F6
Meeks Rd FK2 . . . . 60 B5
Meetinghouse Dr EH33 . . 126 C7
Meggat Pl EH26 . . . . 192 A7
Meggetgate EH14 . . . . . . 120 D3
Meggetland Sq EH14 . . . 120 D3
Meggetland Terr EH14 . . 120 D3
Meggetland View EH14 . 120 D3
Meggetland Wynd EH14 . 120 D3
Meikle Inch La EH48 . . . . 141 C3
Meikle Rd EH54 . . . . 143 C5
Meiklerig Cotts EH22 . . . 105 A1

Meikle Sq KY1 . . . . 18 A7
Melbourne Pl EH39 . . . . . 54 D7
Melbourne Rd
 Broxburn EH52 . . . . 115 F5
 North Berwick EH39 . . . . 54 D7
Melbourne St EH54 . . . . . 144 A5
Meldrum Cres KY3 . . . . . . 33 D1
Meldrum Ct KY11 . . . . 29 F1
Meldrum Rd Kirkcaldy KY1 . 17 D6
 Kirkcaldy KY2 . . . . 17 C8
Meldrum Rd KY7 . . . . 7 C4
Melford Ave ML7 . . . . 180 B3
Melfort Dr FK7 . . . . 7 C4
Melgund Pl KY5 . . . . 14 B8
Melgund Terr FK7 . . . . 93 D2
Mellerstain Rd KY2 . . . . . . 16 C6
Mellock Gdns FK1 . . . . 59 E2
Mellor Ct KY11 . . . . 46 E4
Melrose Cres KY2 . . . . 17 C6
Melrose Dr FK3 . . . . 61 F6
Melrose Pl [9] FK1 . . . . 60 B4
Melville Cotts EH18 . . . . . 152 C4
Melville Cres EH3 . . . . . . 228 A3
Melville Dr EH9 . . . . 229 A1
Melville Dykes Rd EH18 . 152 C1
Melville Dykes Road Rdbt
 EH22 . . . . 152 D2
Melville Gate EH22 . . . . . 152 D3
Melville Gate Rd EH22 . . 152 E4
Melville Gdns KY3 . . . . 50 D8
Melville Grange Cotts
 EH18 . . . . 152 B4
Melville La [3] FK1 . . . . 60 B5
Melville Pl
 Bridge of Allan FK9 . . . . . 2 A7
 Dunfermline KY12 . . . . . . 29 B4
 Edinburgh EH3 . . . . 228 A3
 Kirkcaldy KY2 . . . . 16 D5
Melville Rd EH22 . . . . 152 E2
Melville St Edinburgh EH3 228 A3
 [2] Falkirk FK1 . . . . 60 B5
 Lochgelly KY5 . . . . 14 B8
Melville Street La EH3 . . 228 A3
Melville Terr
 [7] Dalkeith EH22 . . . . . 152 E1
 Edinburgh EH9 . . . . 229 B1
 Stirling FK8 . . . . 7 B6
Melville View EH18 . . . . . 173 A8
MENSTRIE 3 E6
Menstrie Bsns Ctr FK11 . . . 3 E6
Menstrie Castle ★ 3 E6
Menstrie Pl FK10 . . . . 4 A6
Menstrie Prim Sch FK11 . . 3 E6
Menstrie Rd FK10 . . . . 4 C3
Menteith Ct FK10 . . . . 10 C6
Menteith Dr KY11 . . . . 29 F1
Menteith Rd FK9 . . . . 2 A3
Mentone Ave EH15 . . . . . . 95 B1
Mentone Gdns EH9 . . . . . 121 F4
Mentone Terr EH9 . . . . . . 121 F4
Menzies Cres KY2 . . . . 16 F5
Menzies Dr FK8 . . . . 2 A1
Menzies Rd EH48 . . . . 141 A6
Mercat Gait Ctr EH32 . . . . 97 A1
Mercat Pl FK10 . . . . 11 B4
Mercat Sh Ctr KY1 . . . . . . 17 C3
Mercat Wynd [2] FK10 . . . 10 B6
Mercer Pl KY11 . . . . 47 F3
Mercer Row EH10 . . . . 23 E3
Merchant St EH1 . . . . 229 A2
Merchants Way KY1 . . . . . 47 C2
MERCHISTON 120 F4
Merchiston Ave
 Edinburgh EH10 . . . . 121 A5
 Falkirk FK2 . . . . 60 A7
Merchiston Bank Ave
 EH10 . . . . 121 A4
Merchiston Bank Gdns
 EH10 . . . . 121 A4
Merchiston Castle Sch
 EH14 . . . . 149 B7
Merchiston Cres EH10 . . 121 A4
Merchiston Gdns
 Edinburgh EH10 . . . . 120 F3
 Falkirk FK2 . . . . 60 A6
Merchiston Gr EH11 . . . . 120 F4
Merchiston Ind Est FK2 . . 60 C8
Merchiston Mews EH10 . 121 A5
Merchiston Pk EH10 . . . . 121 A5
Merchiston Pl EH10 . . . . . 121 A5
Merchiston Rd FK2 . . . . . . 60 A6
Merchiston Terr EH10 . . . 120 F4
Merchiston Terr FK2 . . . . . 60 A7
Meredith Dr FK5 . . . . 38 F3
Merker Terr EH54 . . . . 84 E6
Merkland Cres KY11 . . . . . 48 A3
Merkland Rd EH25 . . . . . . 171 E6
Merlin Dr KY11 . . . . 47 A7
Merlin Way KY11 . . . . 48 B5
Merrick Rd FK3 . . . . 61 F5
Merrick Way FK3 . . . . 61 F5
Merryfield Ave EH33 . . . . 127 D5
Merrylees EH14 . . . . 65 D1
Mertoun Pl EH11 . . . . 120 F5
Merville Cres FK1 . . . . 81 F5
Merville Terr FK1 . . . . 81 E5
Methven Dr KY11 . . . . 29 B5
Methven Pl KY11 . . . . 17 B2
Methven Terr EH18 . . . . . 172 F6
Meuse La EH2 . . . . 229 A3
Meylea St EH48 . . . . 141 D4
Michaelson Sq EH54 . . . . 143 E3
Mid Beveridgewell KY12 . 28 F5
Mid Brae [1] KY12 . . . . 28 F5
MID CALDER 144 C4

Mid Calder Prim Sch
 EH53 . . . . 144 C2
Mid Cswy KY12 . . . . 42 D8
Middlebank Ave [1] KY1 . . 47 C8
Middlebank Cres [2] KY11 47 C8
Middlebank Holdings
 KY11 . . . . 47 B6
Middlebank Rise KY11 . . . 47 C8
Middlebank St KY11 . . . . . 47 A4
Middlebank Wildlife Ctr
 (SSPCA) ★ KY11 . . . . 47 B6
Middleby St EH9 . . . . 121 F4
MIDDLEFIELD 60 D6
Middlefield EH7 . . . . 93 E3
Middlefield Ind Est FK2 . . 60 E7
Middlefield Rd FK2 . . . . . . 60 D6
Middle Jetty Rd KY11 . . . . 67 B8
Middleknowe EH14 . . . . . 148 C8
Middlemas Rd EH42 . . . . 106 D8
Middlemass Ct EH14 . . . . 60 B6
Middle Meadow Wlk
 EH8 . . . . 229 A1
Middlemuir Rd FK7 . . . . . . 7 C6
Middle Norton EH28 . . . . 117 F5
Middlepark EH14 . . . . 148 C8
Middleshot Rd EH31 . . . . . 52 A3
Middleshot Sq EH32 . . . . . 97 B2
Middle Street La FK3 . . . . 40 C1
MIDDLETON 196 A1
Middleton FK11 . . . . 4 A5
Middleton Ave EH52 . . . . 115 A4
Middleton Rd EH52 . . . . . 115 A4
Middle Wlk KY12 . . . . 29 B3
Middlewood Pk EH54 . . . 142 E7
Midfield Ho EH18 . . . . . . 172 E5
Mid Gogarloch Syke
 EH12 . . . . 119 A5
Midhope Pl EH52 . . . . 87 F2
Mid Liberton EH16 . . . . . 122 D5
Midlothian Community Hospl
 EH19 . . . . 229 B1
Midlothian Snowsports Ctr ★
 EH10 . . . . 150 A2
Midmar Ave EH10 . . . . . . 121 C2
Midmar Dr EH10 . . . . 121 C2
Midmar Gdns EH10 . . . . . 121 B2
Mid New Cultins EH11 . . 119 B2
Mid Rd KY3 . . . . 34 F3
Mid Road Ind Est EH32 . . 125 F8
Mid St Bathgate EH48 . . . 141 B6
 Kirkcaldy KY1 . . . . 17 D6
 Livingston EH54 . . . . 142 D6
 Lochgelly KY5 . . . . 14 B7
Mid Steil EH11 . . . . 120 E1
Midthorn Cres FK2 . . . . . . 60 E5
Midtown FK11 . . . . 3 F6
MILESMARK 28 D6
Milesmark Prim Sch KY12 28 D5
Millar Cres EH10 . . . . 121 A3
Millar Pl Bonnybridge FK4 . 58 E6
 Edinburgh EH10 . . . . 121 A3
 Falkirk FK2 . . . . 39 A5
 Stirling FK8 . . . . 2 C1
Millar Place La EH10 . . . . 121 A3
Millar Rd EH33 . . . . 126 C5
Millars Wynd EH10 . . . . . . 5 C2
Millbank EH14 . . . . 147 E7
Millbank Cres FK10 . . . . . 11 A5
Millbank Gr EH23 . . . . 195 C7
Millbank Pl EH52 . . . . 114 F4
Millbank Sq EH47 . . . . . . 161 B7
Millbank Terr FK2 . . . . 82 F7
Millbrae EH53 . . . . 144 C4
Millbrae Wynd [1] EH14 . 120 B2
Millbrook Pl FK11 . . . . 3 F6
Millburn Cres EH48 . . . . . 139 D6
Millburn Rd
 Bathgate EH48 . . . . 140 F6
 Westfield EH48 . . . . 110 F5
Millburn St FK2 . . . . 60 D5
Mill Ct Bathgate EH48 . . . 141 A7
 Falkirk FK2 . . . . 39 B3
Milldean Gr KY12 . . . . 29 D5
Milledge ML8 . . . . 215 A2
Millennium Wheel Dr FK1 59 A5
Miller Ave EH54 . . . . 28 B2
Miller Cres EH51 . . . . 64 D5
Millerfield EH49 . . . . 84 D7
Millerfield Pl EH9 . . . . . . 121 D5
Millerhill Rd EH22 . . . . . . 152 D7
Miller Pk FK2 . . . . 61 F1
Miller Pl Airth FK2 . . . . 22 E4
 Harthill ML7 . . . . 159 F6
Miller Rd Dunfermline KY12 28 E5
 Grangemouth EH51 . . . . 62 E5
Miller Row EH4 . . . . 228 A3
Millers Ct EH33 . . . . 126 B5
Miller St Carluke ML8 . . . 215 A2
 Harthill ML7 . . . . 159 E6
Mill Farm Rd KY3 . . . . 49 F8
Millfield Haddington EH41 130 A7
 Livingston EH54 . . . . 143 A2
Millfield Dr FK2 . . . . 61 E2
Millflats St FK2 . . . . 39 A1
Millgate EH52 . . . . 87 F2
Millhall Gdns FK2 . . . . 61 F1
Millhall Rd FK7 . . . . 7 D5
Millhaugh La EH48 . . . . . 141 A7
Millhill EH21 . . . . 124 D6
Mill Hill FK7 . . . . 6 D6

Millhill La EH21...........124 D6
Millhill St KY11...........29 B2
Millhill Wynd EH21........124 D6
Millhouse 9 EH3..........93 B2
Millie St KY1.............17 D6
Mill La Edinburgh EH6.....93 F5
Kincardine FK10..........23 E3
Stenton EH42.............104 C2
Mill Lade EH49...........84 E7
Mill of Airthrey Ct FK9...1 F8
Mill Pl EH49.............84 C8
Mill Rd Alloa FK10........10 B6
Armadale EH48...........139 E6
Bathgate EH48...........141 A7
Blackburn EH47..........162 C7
Cambusbarron FK7........6 D6
Clackmannan FK10........11 A5
Dunfermline KY11........29 B2
Falkirk FK2..............39 B3
Harthill ML7............159 F5
Linlithgow EH49..........84 C7
Mill Rdbt EH54..........143 A3
Mill Road Ind Est EH49...84 D8
Millside EH12............120 D7
Mill St Alloa FK10........10 B6
Dunfermline KY12.........28 F4
Kirkcaldy KY1............17 B1
Mill Walk Bsns Pk EH39...54 E6
Millway EH34.............157 A6
Mill Wynd
East Linton EH40.........103 E7
Haddington EH41.........130 A7
Prestonpans EH32........96 F2
Miln-Acre EH6...........93 D4
Milne Cres KY4...........13 C3
Milne Park Rd FK7........19 E8
Milne Rd Dunfermline KY11.47 A7
Rosyth KY11..............46 E1
Milnquarter Rd FK4.......58 A3
Milrig Smallholdings
EH27....................145 C3
Milsey Ct EH39...........54 D7
Milton FK7...............7 C1
Milton Brae FK7..........7 B2
MILTON BRIDGE..........171 B2
Milton Cl FK6............36 D3
Milton Cres
Bannockburn FK7.........7 C1
Edinburgh EH15..........123 A6
Milton Dr EH15...........123 D7
Milton Gardens N EH15...123 A6
Milton Gardens S EH15...123 A6
Milton Gdns FK7..........7 B1
Milton Glen EH15.........123 E7
Milton Gn KY12...........29 A2
Milton Gr Bannockburn FK7.7 C1
Edinburgh EH15..........123 E7
Milton Link EH15.........123 C6
Milton Mill EH26.........171 C2
Milton Pk KY2............15 B2
Milton Pl FK6............36 D3
Milton Rd Bannockburn FK7..7 C1
Edinburgh EH15..........123 B6
Milton Road E EH15......123 D7
Milton Road W EH15......122 F6
Milton Row FK6...........36 E3
Milton St EH8............94 A1
Milton Terr
Edinburgh EH15..........123 E7
Stirling FK7.............7 B1
Mineral Rd ML7..........179 D6
Mine Rd FK9.............2 A8
Miner's Terr EH21........125 B5
Miners Wlk EH22.........153 D4
MINGLE..................64 A6
Mingle Pl EH51...........64 A6
Minstrel Ct EH25.........172 A3
Minthill Pl ML7..........159 D5
Minto Ct FK12............126 D7
Minto Gdns FK12..........5 B6
Minto Pl KY2.............16 F4
Minto St Edinburgh EH9...121 F4
Lochgelly KY5............14 B8
Mission La 8 FK1.........60 B4
Mitchell Cres Alloa FK10..9 F7
Cowdenbeath KY4.........13 A1
Mitchell Brae EH41.......130 E5
Mitchell Pl Falkirk FK1...59 E1
2 Kirkcaldy KY1..........17 D6
Mitchell Rd KY11.........46 C1
Mitchell's Cl 1 EH41.....130 B8
Mitchell St Dalkeith EH22..152 F3
Edinburgh EH6...........94 A5
Kirkcaldy KY1............17 C4
Mitchell Way EH33........126 D7
Mitchell Wlk KY11........46 F3
Moat Dr EH14............120 D4
Moat Ho EH14............120 D4
Moat Pl EH14............120 D4
Moat St EH14............120 D4
Moat Terr EH14..........120 D4
Moat View EH25..........171 F3
Mochray Ct FK4..........57 E5
Mochrum Dr KY12.........45 B8
Modan Rd FK7............7 A3
Moffat Ave
Bonnyrigg and Lasswade
EH19....................173 B6
Falkirk FK2..............39 C3
Moffat Cres KY5..........14 A7
Moffat Pl FK4............64 A8
Moffat Rd EH35..........155 D6
Moffat Wlk EH33.........126 C4
Moidart Rd EH47.........161 D7

Moira Pk EH7.............94 E1
Moira Terr EH7...........94 E1
Moira Terrace La EH7.....94 E1
Moir Ave EH21...........125 A6
Moir Cres EH21..........125 A6
Moir Ct KY4.............12 E8
Moir Dr EH21............125 B6
Moir Pl EH21............125 A6
Moir St FK10............10 A8
Moir Terr EH21..........125 A6
Mollison Ave ML7........159 E6
Monar Ct KY11...........48 A3
Monastery St KY12.......29 A3
Moncks Rd FK1...........60 D4
Moncrieffe Ho EH17......151 D8
Moncrieff Terr EH9......121 E5
Moncreiff Way EH54......143 D8
Moncur St KY12..........29 C7
Monkbarns Gdns 4
EH16....................151 B8
Monkland Rd EH41........140 F6
Monkmains Rd EH41......130 C7
Monkrigg Ct EH41.........130 C7
Monkrigg Pl EH41........130 C7
Monkrigg Steading
EH41....................130 D6
Monksrig Rd EH26........191 C5
MONKSWOOD.............174 B5
Monkswood Rd EH22.....174 B4
MONKTONHALL...........122 A1
Monktonhall Farm Cotts
EH21....................124 B3
Monktonhall Pl EH21.....124 B3
Monktonhall Terr EH21...124 B4
Monkwood Ct EH49.......121 D4
Monmouth Terr EH3.......93 B4
Montague St EH8.........229 B1
Montagu Terr EH3........93 B4
Monteith Wlk ML7........179 E6
Montfort Pl FK1..........60 B3
Montgomery Cres FK2.....39 B2
Montgomery Dr FK2.......39 B2
Montgomery Pl FK2.......39 B2
Montgomery St
Edinburgh EH7...........93 F2
Falkirk FK2..............60 E5
Grangemouth FK3........61 C6
Kirkcaldy KY2............17 B5
Montgomery Street La
EH7....................93 E2
Montgomery Way FK9.....2 B3
Montgomery Well FK2.....39 B2
Montpelier EH10.........121 B5
Montpelier Pk EH10......121 A5
Montpelier Terr EH10.....121 A5
Montrose Rd Polmont FK2..62 A1
Stirling FK9.............2 C4
Montrose Terr EH7........229 C4
Montrose Way FK4.......57 D5
Monument View FK8......2 B2
Moodie St KY12..........29 A3
Moore Cotts EH52........115 D5
Moore House Sch EH48...141 E5
Mooreland Gdns EH55....162 C1
Moorelands EH55.........162 C1
Moorelands Pl EH55......162 C2
Moorfield Cotts EH22.....152 C8
Moorfoot Ct EH14........173 B7
Moorfoot Pl
Bonnyrigg and Lasswade
EH19....................173 B6
Penicuik EH26...........191 E6
Moorfoot Prim Sch
EH23....................196 A3
Moorfoot View
Bilston EH25............171 C5
Bonnyrigg and Lasswade
EH19....................173 B6
Gorebridge EH23.........195 C7
Moorings The KY11.......47 F2
Moor Rd Fala EH37.......224 B7
Pathhead EH37..........176 D4
Pencaitland EH35, EH37..177 B6
Moorside St ML8.........215 A2
Morar Ct FK3............61 D5
Morar Dr FK2............39 C1
Morar Pl FK3............61 D5
Morar Rd KY12...........28 B1
Moray Way N KY11........180 B3
Moray Way S KY11........48 B2
MOREDUN...............151 D7
Moredun Dell 2 EH17.....151 E7
Moredun Dykes Rd EH17..151 D6
Moredun Ho EH17.........151 E7
Moredun Park Ct EH17....151 D7
Moredun Park Dr EH17....151 D7
Moredun Park Gdns
EH17....................151 D7
Moredun Park Gn EH17...151 E7
Moredun Park Grn EH17...151 E7
Moredun Park Loan
EH17....................151 D7
Moredun Park Rd EH17...151 E8
Moredun Park St EH17....151 E7

Moredun Park View
EH17....................151 E7
Moredun Park Way
EH17....................151 D7
Moredun Park Wlk 1
EH17....................151 E7
Moredunvale Bank EH17.151 D8
Moredunvale Gn EH17....151 D8
Moredunvale Gr EH17....151 D8
Moredunvale Loan EH17..151 D8
Moredunvale Pk EH17....151 D8
Moredunvale Pl EH17.....151 D8
Moredunvale Rd EH17....151 D8
Moredunvale Way EH17...151 D8
Morgan Ct FK7...........7 C3
Morgan Way EH48.........140 A4
Morham Gait EH10........149 E8
Morham Gdns EH10.......149 E8
Morham Lea EH10........149 E8
Morham Pk EH10.........149 E8
Morham Village Houses
EH41....................131 D5
Morison Gdns EH30.......68 B1
Moriston Ct FK3..........61 E4
Moriston Dr FK4.........164 F6
Morley Cres FK7..........7 A3
Morlich Cres KY11.......48 A2
Morlich Gr KY11.........48 A2
Morlich Pl KY11..........48 A2
Morlich Rd KY11.........48 A2
Morlich Wlk EH54........144 A4
Mornay Way ML7..........179 D5
MORNINGSIDE...........121 A2
Morningside Dr EH10.....121 A2
Morningside Gdns EH10..120 F2
Morningside Gr EH10.....120 F1
Morningside Pk EH10.....121 A3
Morningside Pl EH10.....121 A3
Morningside Rd EH10.....121 A3
Morningside Terr EH10...121 A3
Morris Ct KY11...........47 C2
Morrison Ave
Bonnybridge FK4.........57 F6
Tranent EH33............126 E5
Morrison Cir EH3........228 A2
Morrison Cres EH3.......228 A2
Morrison Dr
Bannockburn FK7.........7 C2
Dunfermline KY11........46 F8
Morrison Link EH3.......228 A2
Morrison St EH3.........228 A2
Morrison Way EH54......143 D8
Morris Rd EH22..........174 C6
Morris Sq EH54..........143 F2
Morris Terr FK8..........7 A8
Mortimer Ct KY11........48 B2
MORTONHALL.............150 E5
Mortonhall Gate EH16...150 E5
Mortonhall Park Ave
EH17....................150 F5
Mortonhall Park Bank
EH17....................151 A5
Mortonhall Park Cres
EH17....................151 A5
Mortonhall Park Dr
EH17....................151 A5
Mortonhall Park Gdns
EH17....................150 F5
Mortonhall Park Gr EH17.150 F5
Mortonhall Park Loan
EH17....................150 F5
Mortonhall Park Pl EH17.151 A5
Mortonhall Park Terr
EH17....................151 A5
Mortonhall Park Way
EH17....................150 F5
Mortonhall Rd EH9.......121 D3
Morton St EH15..........123 C7
Morven Ct FK1...........60 C2
Morven Dr FK2...........61 D2
Morven Gr KY2...........16 F7
Morven Pl KY11..........48 A3
Morvenside EH14.........148 C8
Morvenside Cl EH14......148 C8
Morven St EH4...........91 C1
Mossband La ML7.........179 E6
Mossbank
Cowdenbeath KY4.........13 B2
Livingston EH54.........143 E5
Rosyth KY11.............46 F5
Mossburn Ave ML7.......159 D5
Mossburn Ind Est ML7...159 D5
Mosscastle Rd FK1........108 A7
MOSSEND................163 C3
Mossend EH55...........163 D3
Mossend Terr KY4........13 B2
Mossgiel Ave Cowie FK7...20 D7
Stirling FK8.............2 A2
Mossgiel Cotts EH54.....142 D7
Mossgiel St KY1..........59 B5
Mossgiel Terr FK2........61 A3
Mossgiel Wlk 3 EH16.....122 A1
MOSSGREEN.............31 A6
Mosshat Ind Est EH47....162 B7
Mosshat Rd EH55........202 F3
Mosshouse FK7..........6 F4
Mosside Ct EH47.........162 D8
Mosside Dr EH47.........141 D1
Mosside Rd EH47.........162 D8
Mosside Terr
Bathgate EH48...........141 B3
Blackburn EH47..........141 D1
Moss Intc EH54..........143 D6
Moss Rd Airth FK2........21 E7
Fallin FK7...............8 C4

Moss-Side Rd KY4........13 B3
Moss Way KY11..........48 B5
Moston Terr EH9.........121 F4
Motion St KY5...........14 A7
Moubray Gdns FK10......4 B1
Moubray Gr EH30.........89 C8
Moubray Rd KY11........48 C5
Moulin Way KY12.........29 E5
Mound PI EH1............228 C3
Mound The EH2...........228 C3
Mount Alvernia EH16....151 B7
Mount Bartholomew FK4.58 A5
Mountbatten PI KY11.....46 E3
Mountbatten St FK3......61 B5
Mountcastle Bank EH8....122 F8
Mountcastle Cres EH8....122 F8
Mountcastle Drive N
EH8.....................122 F8
Mountcastle Drive S
EH15....................123 A6
Mountcastle Gdns EH8...122 F8
Mountcastle Gn 1 EH8...94 E1
Mountcastle Gr EH8......122 E8
Mountcastle Loan EH8....122 E8
Mountcastle Pk 8 EH8....94 E1
Mountcastle Pl 2 EH8....94 E1
Mountcastle Terr EH8....122 E8
Mountfair Gdns EH33....127 C5
Mountfair Pl EH33.......127 C5
Mount Grange EH9.......121 D3
Mount Hooly Cres KY11..68 C6
Mounthooly Loan EH10...150 D5
Mount Hope FK9.........2 B7
Mountjoy Ct EH21........124 C7
Mountjoy Terr EH21.....124 C7
Mount Lodge Pl EH15....123 B8
Mount Oliphant FK7.....20 D7
Mount Pleasant EH48....139 F5
Mount Vernon Rd EH16..151 B8
Mount William FK10.....5 E1
Mowbray Gdns KY4......30 E6
Mowbray Rise EH54......143 F1
Mowbray Ct FK7..........7 D4
Moy Ct FK3..............61 D5
Mucklehill Pk KY11......47 A2
Mucklets Ave EH21......124 A4
Mucklets Cres EH21......124 A3
Mucklets Ct EH21........124 A3
Mucklets Dr EH21.......124 A4
Mucklets Pl EH21........124 A4
Mudale Ct FK1...........60 D1
MUIRALEHOUSE...........19 E8
Muiralehouse Rd FK7....19 E8
Muir Ct KY4.............30 E6
Muirdale Terr EH4.......92 B2
Muirdyke Ave FK2.......39 C3
Muiredge and Jersy Rd
ML7....................179 A8
Muirend Ave EH14.......148 E2
Muirend Ct EH51.........64 B6
Muirend Rd FK7..........7 B5
Muirepark Ct EH51......64 A6
MUIRFIELD..............52 C3
Muirfield Apartments
EH31....................52 B2
Muirfield Ct EH31........52 B2
Muirfield Ct EH40........103 E7
Muirfield Dr Gullane EH31.52 B2
Uphall EH52.............114 E4
Muirfield Gdns
Gullane EH31............52 B2
Loanhead EH20..........172 C7
Muirfield Gr EH31........52 C2
Muirfield Ho EH31........52 B3
Muirfield Pk EH31........52 B3
Muirfield Rd
Dunbar EH42............106 D7
Stenhousemuir FK5......38 E2
Muirfield Station EH31...52 B2
Muirfield Steading EH31..52 C3
Muirfield Terr EH31......52 B2
Muirfield Way EH54......142 E6
Muirhall Pl FK5..........38 C3
Muirhall Rd FK5.........38 C3
Muirhead Ave EH22......60 A8
Muirhead Pl Falkirk FK2..82 A8
Harthill ML7............159 D4
Penicuik EH26...........191 F8
Muirhead Rd FK5........38 F4
MUIRHOUSE.............92 B6
Muirhouse Ave EH4......92 B4
Muirhouse Avenue N EH4.92 B4
Muirhouse Bank EH4.....92 B4
Muirhouse Cl EH4.......92 A4
Muirhouse Cres EH4.....92 A5
Muirhouse Dr EH4.......92 A5
Muirhouse Gdns EH4.....92 A5
Muirhouse Gn EH4.......92 B4
Muirhouse Gr EH4.......92 A5
Muirhouse Loan EH4.....92 B5
Muirhouse Medway EH4..92 B5
Muirhouse Parkway EH4.92 A5
Muirhouse Pk EH4.......92 B4
Muirhouse Place E EH4..92 B4
Muirhouse Place W EH4..92 B4
MUIRHOUSES............64 D5
Muirhouses Ave EH51....64 C6
Muirhouses Cres EH51...64 C6
Muirhouses Sq EH51.....64 C6
Muirhouse Terr EH4.....92 A4
Muirhouse View EH4.....92 A4
Muirhouse Way EH4......92 B4
Muirlaun ML11...........201 A1
Muirlee Rd ML8..........215 B1
Muirpark EH22...........152 E1

Moss-Side Rd KY4........13 B3
Muirpark Ct EH33........126 E5
Muirpark Dr Shieldhill FK1..81 D6
Tranent EH33............126 E5
Muirpark Gdns
Tranent EH33............126 E5
Tullibody FK10..........4 E4
Muirpark Gr EH33........126 E5
Muirpark Pl EH33........126 E5
Muirpark Rd EH33........126 E5
Muirpark Terr EH33......126 E5
Muirpark Wynd EH33.....126 E5
Muir Pl Dunfermline KY12..29 D7
Lochgelly KY5...........14 C8
Muir Rd Bathgate EH48...140 F7
Lochgelly KY5...........14 C8
Pumpherston EH54......144 A8
Townhill KY12...........29 D7
Muir's Ct EH52..........114 F4
Muirside Ave FK10.......4 C3
Muirside Ct KY12........27 C1
Muirside Dr EH33........126 C5
Muirside Gr KY12........27 C1
Muirside Gr KY12........27 C1
Muirside La KY12........44 C8
Muirside Rd
Cairneyhill KY12........27 C1
Tullibody FK10..........4 C3
Muir St FK5.............38 D2
Muirs The FK10..........4 C4
MUIRTON................7 E6
Muirton Rd FK7..........7 E6
Muirton Rdbt FK7........7 F7
Muirton Way KY11........48 B5
Muir Wood Cres EH14....148 B5
Muir Wood Dr EH14......148 B5
Muir Wood Gr EH14.....148 B5
Muir Wood Pl EH14.....148 B5
Muir Wood Rd EH14.....148 B6
Mulberry Dr KY11........29 E1
Mulberry Pl EH6.........93 D5
Muldron Terr ML7........180 B2
Mulberry Rd FK10........10 B5
Grangemouth FK3........61 D6
Mulloch Ave 1 FK2.......60 A8
Multiplex Rdbt EH54....143 E1
Multres Wk EH1..........229 A4
Multres Wlk Sh EH22....229 A4
Mumrills Rd EH22........61 C4
MUNGAL.................60 A8
Mungalend Ct FK2........60 B7
Mungalhead Rd FK2......60 A7
Mungal Mill Ct FK2......59 F8
Mungal Pl FK2...........60 B8
Mungle 1 EH55...........163 D3
Mungle St EH55..........163 D3
Mungoswells Cotts EH39..72 C2
Munnoch Way FK7........2 B4
Munro Ave EH13.........149 A5
Munro Dr EH13..........149 A5
Munro Gate FK9.........2 A5
Munro Gdns FK2.........60 F3
Munro Pl FK10...........9 F6
Munro Rd FK7............7 E6
Munro St Kirkcaldy KY1..17 B2
Lochgelly KY5...........14 B8
Munro Way EH14.........143 C8
Murano Pl EH7...........93 F2
Murderdean Rd EH22.....174 A5
Murdoch Terr EH11......228 A1
Murdostoun Cres ML7....159 F6
Murieston Cres EH11....120 E6
Murieston Crescent La
EH11....................120 F6
Murieston Dr EH54.......165 A6
Murieston Dr EH54.......165 D6
Murieston East Rd EH54.165 B8
Murieston Gdns EH54....165 A7
Murieston Gr EH54......165 A6
Murieston La EH11......120 E6
Murieston Mews EH54...164 F6
Murieston Pk EH54......164 F5
Murieston Pl EH11......120 E6
Murieston Rd
Edinburgh EH11.........120 E6
Livingston EH54.........164 E4
Murieston Terr EH11....120 E6
Murieston Vale EH54....164 F4
Murieston Valley EH54...164 F4
Murieston Way EH54.....165 A7
Murieston West Rd EH54.164 F7
Murieston Wlk EH54.....164 E4
Murieston Wood EH54....164 F5
Murnin Ct FK7...........7 C3
Murnin Rd FK4..........58 A4
Murnin Road Ind Est FK4.58 A4
Murrayburn App EH11....119 D1
Murrayburn Dr EH14.....119 E1
Murrayburn Gate EH14..148 D8
Murrayburn Gdns EH14..119 E1
Murrayburn Gr EH14.....119 E1
Murrayburn Junc EH14..148 D8
Murrayburn Pk EH14....119 E1
Murrayburn Pl EH14.....119 D1
Murrayburn Prim Sch
EH11....................119 E2
Murrayburn Rd EH14....119 E2
Murray Cotts EH12......119 C6
Murray Cres FK2........83 A4
Murray St Armadale EH48.139 F4
Dunbar EH42............106 D8
MURRAYFIELD...........120 B7
Murrayfield Ave EH12...120 C7
Murrayfield Dr
Blackburn EH47.........162 D8
Edinburgh EH12.........120 C7

Murrayfield Gdns EH12. . . . .120 D7
Murrayfield Hospl (Private)
   EH12. . . . . .120 A7
Murrayfield Pl
   Bannockburn FK7 . . . . .7 D1
   Edinburgh EH12. . . . . .120 D7
Murrayfield Prim Sch
   EH47. . . . . .141 D1
Murrayfield Rd EH12. . . . . . .120 C7
Murrayfield Stadium
   (Scottish Rugby) EH12. . .120 C6
Murrayfield Terr
   Bannockburn FK7 . . . . .7 D1
   Blackburn EH47. . . . . .162 D8
Murray Pl Aberdour KY3. . . . .49 C8
   Cambusbarron FK7 . . . . .6 D5
   Stirling FK8 . . . . .7 B7
Murrays Brae The EH17. . . . .151 C4
Murraysgate Cres EH47. . . . .160 F6
Murraysgate Ind Est
   EH47. . . . . .160 F6
Murrays The EH17. . . . . .151 C4
Murray Terr KY2. . . . . .17 B5
Murray Way EH54. . . . . .143 D8
Murray Wlk KY1. . . . . .29 E4
Murrell Rd KY3. . . . . .49 C8
Murrel Terr KY3 . . . . .49 C8
Museum of Childhood*
   EH1. . . . . .229 B3
Museum of Communication*
   KY3. . . . . .50 E8
Museum of Edinburgh*
   EH8. . . . . .229 B3
Museum of Fire* EH3 . . . . . .228 C2
Music Hall La 2 KY12. . . . . . .29 A3
MUSSELBURGH 124 C7
Musselburgh Bsns Pk
   EH21. . . . . .124 D5
Musselburgh Grammar Sch
   EH21. . . . . .124 C5
Musselburgh Gram Sch
   EH21. . . . . .124 C5
Musselburgh Mus*
   EH21. . . . . .124 C6
Musselburgh Prim Sch
   EH21. . . . . .124 C6
Musselburgh Rd
   Dalkeith EH22. . . . . .153 B4
   Edinburgh EH15. . . . . .123 E7
Musselburgh Sports Ctr
   EH21. . . . . .124 D5
Musselburgh Sta EH21. . . . .124 A4
Myers Ct KY12. . . . . .29 D3
Myles Farm Cotts EH33 . . . .126 A4
Myles Ho FK2. . . . . .7 A8
Mylneburn Gdns KY11. . . . . .45 D3
Mylne Pl FK2. . . . . .39 B2
Myothill Rd FK6 . . . . .57 D7
Myot View FK6 . . . . .36 A3
Myre Cres KY3. . . . . .35 A3
Myre Dale EH19 . . . . .173 C6
MYRESIDE. 120 E3
Myreside Gr EH10 . . . . .120 F2
Myreside Ct EH10. . . . . .120 F2
Myreside Rd EH10 . . . . .120 F3
Myreside View EH14. . . . . . .120 E3
Myreton KY11. . . . . .4 A6
Myreton Dr FK7. . . . . .19 E8
Myreton Motor Mus*
   EH32. . . . . .72 B3
Myreton Rd FK3. . . . . .61 D6
Myreton Way FK1. . . . . .59 F3
Myretoungate FK12. . . . . .4 E6
Myrtle Cres Bilston EH25. . . .171 E6
   Kirkcaldy KY2. . . . . .17 B7
Myrtle Gr EH22 . . . . .174 C1
Myrtle Terr EH11 . . . . .120 E5
Myrtle Wynd KY12. . . . . .28 F5

N

Nagle Rd KY12. . . . . .12 A1
Nailer Rd Falkirk FK1 . . . . . . .59 E6
   Stirling FK7 . . . . .7 B2
Nairn Ct FK1. . . . . .60 D1
Nairn Rd EH54. . . . . .143 F8
Nairn St KY1. . . . . .17 D6
Naismith Ct FK3 . . . . .40 E1
Namayo Ave FK2. . . . . .61 A4
Namur Rd EH26. . . . . .192 A8
Nantwich Dr EH7 . . . . .94 E3
Napier Ave EH48. . . . . .141 C6
Napier Cres FK2. . . . . .60 A7
Napier Loan EH10. . . . . .120 F4
Napier Pl FK2 . . . . .60 A7
Napier Rd EH10. . . . . .121 A4
Napier Sq EH54. . . . . .144 A8
Napier St KY1. . . . . .17 E8
Nasmyth Ct EH54 . . . . .144 B6
Nasmyth Rd KY11. . . . . .46 B1
Nasmyth Sq EH54. . . . . .144 A6
Natal Pl KY4 . . . . .13 D3
National Gallery of
   Scotland* EH2. . . . . .228 C3
National Liby of Scotland*
   EH1. . . . . .229 A2
National Monument*
   EH7. . . . . .229 B4
National Museum of Flight*
   EH39. . . . . .75 D5
National Museum of
   Scotland* EH1. . . . . .229 A2
National Museums Collection
   Ctr* EH5 . . . . .92 D6
National Portrait Gall*
   EH2. . . . . .229 A4

National War Museum of
   Scotland* EH1. . . . . .228 C3
Navar Ct ML7. . . . . .180 A3
Nebit The FK12. . . . . .4 E6
Neidpath Ct
   2 Edinburgh EH12. . . . . . .119 A7
   Longniddry EH32. . . . . .98 E5
Neidpath Dr FK5. . . . . .39 A4
Neidpath Pl KY12. . . . . .29 D6
Neilson Ct EH47. . . . . .162 B8
Neilson Gr KY3 . . . . .33 E1
Neilson Park Rd EH41. . . . . .130 A8
Neilson Sq EH54. . . . . .142 C5
Neilson St FK1. . . . . .60 B4
Neilburn EH54. . . . . .142 F6
Nellfield EH14 . . . . .151 B8
Nelson Ave EH54. . . . . .143 F3
Nelson Gdns FK3. . . . . .40 E1
Nelson Monument* EH7 229 B4
Nelson Pl EH3. . . . . .229 A4
Nelson St EH51. . . . . .62 E6
Nelson St Edinburgh EH3 . . .228 C4
   Grangemouth FK3. . . . . .61 E8
   Kirkcaldy KY2 . . . . .17 D4
   Rosyth KY11. . . . . .46 C5
Ness Ct EH33 . . . . .126 C4
Ness The KY12. . . . . .26 E1
Nether Bakehouse EH8 . . . . .229 C3
Netherbank EH16. . . . . .150 F6
Netherbank View EH16. . . . .150 F6
Netherbeath Rd KY4 . . . . .30 F8
Netherby Rd Airth FK2 . . . . . .22 C4
   Edinburgh EH5. . . . . .93 A6
Nether Craigour EH17. . . . . .122 D1
Nether Craigwell EH8 . . . . . .229 C3
Nether Currie Cres EH14. . . .148 B5
Nether Currie Pl EH14 . . . . .148 B5
Nether Currie Prim Sch
   EH14. . . . . .148 B5
Nether Currie Rd EH14. . . . .148 B5
NETHER DECHMONT. 143 B7
Nether Dechmont Cotts
   EH54. . . . . .143 B7
Nether Dechmont Pl
   EH54. . . . . .143 B7
Netherfaulds Dr FK6. . . . . . . .36 D1
Netherfield Rd FK2 . . . . .61 D1
Nethergate KY3. . . . . .35 A3
Nethergate The FK12 . . . . .4 E6
Netherlaw EH39. . . . . .54 B6
Nether Liberton EH16. . . . . .122 A2
Nether Liberton Ct EH16 .122 A2
Nethermains Prim Sch
   FK6. . . . . .36 D1
Nethermains Rd FK6. . . . . . . .36 C2
Nethershot Rd EH32 . . . . .97 A2
Nether St Dysart KY1. . . . . . .17 D6
   Kirkcaldy KY1 . . . . .17 D6
Netherton Gr EH47. . . . . .161 B4
Netherton Pl EH47. . . . . .161 B4
Netherton Rd KY4 . . . . .13 C6
Netherton St ML7. . . . . .159 D5
Nethertown Broad St
   KY12. . . . . .29 A2
Netherwood Pk EH54 . . . . . .143 A7
Nettlehill Dr EH54 . . . . .115 A1
Nettlehill Rd
   Livingston EH54. . . . . .143 F8
   Uphall Station EH54 . . . . . . .115 A1
Nevis Cres FK10 . . . . .10 B8
Nevis Dr EH54 . . . . .144 A6
Nevis Gdns EH26. . . . . .192 A7
Nevis Pl Falkirk FK1. . . . . .60 C2
   Grangemouth FK3. . . . . .61 E5
   Shotts ML7 . . . . .180 B3
New Arthur Pl EH8. . . . . .229 B2
New Assembly Cl EH1. . . . . .229 A3
Newbattle Abbey Coll
   EH22. . . . . .153 A1
Newbattle Abbey Cres
   EH22. . . . . .173 B8
Newbattle Com High Sch
   EH22. . . . . .174 C7
Newbattle Gdns EH22 . . . . . .153 A1
Newbattle Rd
   Dalkeith EH22. . . . . .152 F2
   Newtongrange EH22. . . . . . .174 A7
Newbattle Terr EH10. . . . . . .121 B4
New Bell's Ct EH6 . . . . .94 A5
Newbiggin Cres FK10 . . . . .4 C2
NEWBIGGING 15 C2
Newbigging
   Auchtertool KY2. . . . . .15 C2
   Musselburgh KY2. . . . . .124 D5
Newbigging Rd KY12. . . . . . . .27 F7
Newbigging Terr KY2. . . . . . .15 C2
Newbigging Rd FK3. . . . . .61 E6
NEWBRIDGE. 117 A6
Newbridge Ind Est EH28 .116 F5
Newbridge Junc EH28 . . . . . .117 A6
Newbridge Rd EH28. . . . . . . .117 A5
New Broompark EH5. . . . . . . .92 E7
New Broughton 4 EH3 . . . . .229 A4
Newburn Pl KY12. . . . . .29 D3
Newbyres Ave EH23. . . . . . . .174 C1
Newbyres Cres EH23. . . . . . .195 C8
Newbyres Gdns EH23 . . . . . .195 C8
Newbyth Stables EH40. . . . . .75 D5
Newbyth Steading EH40. . . . .75 D5
Newcarron Ct 3 EH42 . . . . . .75 D5
New Carron Rd FK5. . . . . .39 A3
New Century Rd ML7. . . . . . .179 E4
New Coll EH1. . . . . .228 C3
New Cove Farm Cotts
   TD13. . . . . .219 A4
NEWCRAIGHALL. 123 E4

Newcraighall Bsns Pk
   EH15. . . . . .123 B4
Newcraighall Dr EH21. . . . . .123 D4
Newcraighall Prim Sch
   EH21. . . . . .123 E4
Newcraighall Rd EH15. . . . . .123 C4
Newcraighall Sta EH21 . .123 D4
New Cut Rigg EH6. . . . . .93 D5
NEWHAILES 124 A6
Newhailes Ave EH21. . . . . . .124 A6
Newhailes Cres EH21. . . . . . .124 A6
Newhailes Ind Est EH21. . . .123 F5
Newhailes Rd EH21. . . . . . . .123 F5
Newhall (Gdn)* EH26 . . . . . .206 F6
New Hallglen Rd FK1. . . . . . . .60 D2
Newhalls Rd EH30 . . . . .68 C1
NEWHAVEN 93 D6
Newhaven Main St EH6 . . . . . .93 D7
Newhaven Pl EH6 . . . . .93 D5
Newhaven Rd EH6. . . . . .93 D5
New Holygate EH52. . . . . . . .115 D5
New Hos Drem EH39. . . . . . . .73 A4
   East Fortune EH39. . . . . .74 D3
   Garnet EH41 . . . . .132 D2
Newhouse FK8 . . . . .7 A5
Newhouse Ave EH42. . . . . . . .78 E1
Newhouse Bsns Pk FK3 . . . . .61 C7
Newhouse Dr FK1 . . . . .59 E2
Newhouse Pl EH42. . . . . .78 F1
Newhouse Rd FK3 . . . . .61 D7
Newhouses Rd EH52. . . . . . . .116 A4
Newhouse Terr EH42. . . . . . . .78 E1
New Hunterfield EH23 . . . . . .174 B2
NEWINGTON 121 E4
Newington La FK5 . . . . .37 D6
Newington Rd EH9. . . . . .121 E5
New John's Pl EH8. . . . . .229 B1
New La EH6 . . . . .93 D6
New Lairdship Pl EH11 . . . . .119 D3
New Lairdship Yards
   EH11. . . . . .119 D3
Newland Ave EH48. . . . . .141 B6
Newlandrig EH23 . . . . .175 D3
Newlands EH27 . . . . .166 F7
Newlands Ct
   Bathgate EH48. . . . . .140 F6
   Stirling FK7 . . . . .20 D2
Newlands Pk
   Dunfermline KY12. . . . . .29 B5
   Edinburgh EH9. . . . . .121 F4
Newlands Pl EH10. . . . . .4 C3
Newlands Rd
   Bannockburn FK7 . . . . .19 D8
   Grangemouth FK3. . . . . .61 C6
   Polmont FK2 . . . . .82 C8
Newlands Road Rdbt 5
   FK2 .82 C8
New Line Rd FK7 . . . . .19 A7
NEWLISTON 116 C6
Newliston Dr KY2. . . . . .16 C7
New Liston Rd EH29 . . . . .89 A1
Newmains Rd EH29 . . . . .89 A2
Newmarket FK7 . . . . .7 E1
New Market Rd EH14 . . . . . . .120 C3
Newmarket St 7 FK1. . . . . . . .60 B5
New Mart Gdns EH14 . . . . . .120 B3
New Mart Pl EH14 . . . . .120 C3
New Mart Rd EH14. . . . . .120 B3
New Mart Sq EH14 . . . . .120 B3
New Meadowspot EH22 .153 A2
Newmill and Canthill Rd
   ML7. . . . . .179 B6
NEWMILLS. 26 D1
Newmills FK10. . . . . .4 B3
Newmills Ave EH14 . . . . .147 D3
Newmills Cres EH14. . . . . . . .147 D3
Newmills Gr EH14. . . . . .147 D3
Newmills Rd Currie EH14. . . .147 C4
   Dalkeith EH22. . . . . .153 B3
Newmills Terr EH22. . . . . . . .153 B3
New Orchardfield EH6 . . . . . . .93 F4
Newpark Cres EH7. . . . . .7 A2
Newpark Rd
   Livingston EH54. . . . . .164 D6
   Stirling FK7 . . . . .7 B2
Newpark Rdbt EH54. . . . . . . .164 D7
NEW PENTLAND 171 F7
New Row
   Dunfermline KY12 . . . . .29 A3
   East Fortune EH39. . . . . .74 B3
   Kincardine FK10 . . . . .24 A3
   Tranent EH33. . . . . .126 C6
New Skinners Cl EH1 . . . . . .229 B3
New St Bridge of Allan FK9 . . .1 F8
   Cockenzie & Port Seton
      EH32. . . . . .97 C4
   Edinburgh EH8. . . . . .229 B3
   Musselburgh EH21. . . . . . . .124 B6
   Prestonpans EH32. . . . . .96 F1
   Slamannan FK1 . . . . .108 A7
   Tranent EH33. . . . . .126 C6
New Star Bank EH22 . . . . . . .174 A5
New Struan Sch FK10. . . . . . . .9 F7
New Swanston EH10 . . . . . . .149 F5
Newtoft St EH17 . . . . .151 E6
NEWTON 88 A8
Newton Ave FK2. . . . . .40 A3
Newton Church Rd EH22 .152 C7
Newton Cotts EH22. . . . . . . .153 A8
Newton Cres KY11. . . . . .47 A4
NEWTONGRANGE 174 A6
Newtongrange L Ctr
   EH19. . . . . .174 A5
Newtongrange Pl EH22 . . . . .174 A4
Newtongrange Prim Sch
   EH22. . . . . .174 B5
Newtonlees Cotts EH42. . . . .106 F7
Newton Loan Ct EH23 . . . . . .174 B2

Newtonmore Dr KY2. . . . . . . .16 F8
Newton Pl KY11. . . . . .46 F1
Newton Port EH41. . . . . .101 B1
Newton Rd FK2. . . . . .40 A2
Newtonshaw FK10. . . . . .5 C1
Newton St
   Easthouses EH22. . . . . .174 C8
   Edinburgh EH11. . . . . .120 E5
Newton St
   New Tower Pl EH15 . . . . .95 B1
   EH6 .63 F4
NEWTOWN 127 E1
NEW TOWN. 63 F6
Newtown Cotts EH51. . . . . . . .63 F6
Newtown St EH51. . . . . .63 F6
New Well Wynd EH49 . . . . . . .84 F6
NEW WINTON. 127 B3
Newyearfield Bsns Pk
   FK5. . . . . .38 A3
Newyearfield Rdbt EH54 .143 C5
Ney Ct KY11 . . . . .30 A1
Nicholfield EH6 . . . . .93 D6
Nicholson Pl FK1. . . . . .59 F2
Nicholson Way EH54. . . . . . .143 D7
Nicklaus Gn EH54. . . . . .143 B8
Nicol Dr KY3. . . . . .34 A2
Nicol Pl EH52. . . . . .115 D5
Nicol Rd EH52. . . . . .115 D6
Nicolson Sq EH8. . . . . .229 B2
Nicolson St EH8 . . . . .229 B2
Nicol St KY1. . . . . .17 B3
Nicolton Ave FK2. . . . . .82 E7
Nicolton Ct 2 FK2. . . . . .82 F7
Nicolton Rd FK2 . . . . .83 B8
NIDDRIE 123 A3
Niddrie Cotts EH15. . . . . .123 A4
Niddrie Farm Gr EH16. . . . . .123 A5
Niddrie House Ave EH16 .122 F3
Niddrie House Dr EH16. . .123 A3
Niddrie House Gdns
   EH16. . . . . .122 F3
Niddrie House Pk EH16 . .122 F3
Niddrie House Sq EH16 . .122 F3
NIDDRIE MAINS 122 E4
Niddrie Mains Ct EH16. . .123 A4
Niddrie Mains Dr EH16. . .123 A4
Niddrie Mains Rd EH15. . . . . .122 F4
Niddrie Mains Terr
   EH16. . . . . .122 F4
Niddrie Marischal Cres
   EH16. . . . . .122 F4
Niddrie Marischal Dr
   EH16. . . . . .123 A4
Niddrie Marischal Gn
   EH16. . . . . .122 F3
Niddrie Marischal Gr
   EH16. . . . . .123 A4
Niddrie Marischal Loan 2
   EH16. . . . . .122 F4
Niddrie Marischal Pl
   EH16. . . . . .122 F4
Niddrie Marischal Rd
   EH16. . . . . .123 A4
Niddrie Marischal St 3
   EH16. . . . . .122 F4
NIDDRIE MILL. 123 A4
Niddrie Mill Ave EH15. . . . . .123 A4
Niddrie Mill Cres EH15. . . . . .123 A5
Niddrie Mill Dr EH15 . . . . . . .123 A4
Niddrie Mill Gr EH15 . . . . . . .123 A4
Niddrie Mill Pl EH15 . . . . . . .123 A4
Niddrie Mill Prim Sch
   EH16. . . . . .122 F4
Niddrie Mill Terr EH15. . . . . .123 A4
Niddry St EH1 . . . . .229 A3
Niddry St S EH1. . . . . .229 B2
Nidry St EH52. . . . . .87 F1
Nidry View EH52. . . . . .87 F2
Nigel Loan EH16. . . . . .151 B8
Nigel Ross Ave EH54 . . . . . . .143 F1
Nightingale Way EH3 . . . . . .228 C2
Nile Gr EH10. . . . . .121 B3
Nile St KY2. . . . . .17 B6
Nimmo Ave EH32 . . . . .97 A1
Ninian Rd EH51. . . . . .62 E6
Ninth St EH22 . . . . .174 B6
Nisbet Dr FK6. . . . . .36 D2
Nisbet Rd EH31 . . . . .51 F2
Nithsdale Pl KY11. . . . . .30 C1
Nith St KY11 . . . . .29 F2
Niven Ct KY11. . . . . .47 C3
Niven's Knowe Rd EH20. . . . .171 F7
No 1 Dock Road E KY11. . . . .46 B1
No 2 Dock Road W KY11. . . . .46 B1
No 2 Dock Road W KY11. . . . .46 B1
No 3 Dock Road W KY11. . . . .46 B1
No 7 Pit Rd KY4. . . . . .13 C4
Nobel Pl EH25. . . . . .171 F3
Nobel View FK2 . . . . .82 B8
Noble Pl EH6 . . . . .94 B4
Normand Brae KY1. . . . . .18 A7
Normand Rd KY1. . . . . .18 A8
Normandy Pl KY11. . . . . .46 E2
Norman Rise EH54 . . . . .143 F1
North Approach Rd FK10 . .23 E3
North Ave FK2. . . . . .83 B7
Northbank Cotts EH48 . . . . .141 B7
Northbank Ct EH51 . . . . .64 A5
Northbank Dr EH51 . . . . .64 A5
Northbank Pk EH51. . . . . .63 F5
Northbank Rd KY12. . . . . .27 D1
North Bank Rd FK32. . . . . .96 E1

North Bank St EH1. . . . . .229 A3
North Belton Cotts EH42 .105 B7
NORTH BERWICK 54 D8
North Berwick High Sch
   EH39. . . . . .54 C6
North Berwick Sports Ctr
   EH39. . . . . .54 C6
North Berwick Sta EH39 . . . . .54 B7
North Bridge EH1. . . . . .229 A3
North Bridge St
   Bathgate EH48 . . . . .141 A6
   Grangemouth FK3. . . . . .40 C1
NORTH BROOMAGE 38 A3
North Broomage Rdbt
   FK5. . . . . .38 A3
North Bughtlin Bank EH12 91 B1
North Bughtlin Brae EH12 91 B1
North Bughtlinfield EH12. .91 A1
North Bughtlin Gate EH12. .91 B1
North Bughtlin Neuk
   EH12 . . . . .91 B1
North Bughtlin Pl EH12. . .91 B1
North Bughtlin Rd EH12. . .91 B1
North Bughtlinrig EH12. . .91 A1
North Bughtlinside EH12. .91 A1
North Cairntow EH16 . . . . . .122 D5
North Castle St Alloa FK10 .10 A5
   Edinburgh EH2. . . . . .228 B4
North Charlotte St EH2. . . . .228 B3
Northcliff KY11. . . . . .68 B6
North Clyde Street La
   EH1 . . . . .229 A4
Northcote St EH11. . . . . .120 F6
North Cres EH32 . . . . .97 A1
North East Circus Pl 6
   EH3 . . . . .228 B4
North East Cumberland
   Street La EH3. . . . . .93 C2
North Elphinstone Farm
   Cotts EH33 . . . . .126 B2
North End FK7 . . . . .6 D6
Northern Research Station
   (Forestry Commission)
   EH25. . . . . .171 B4
North Esk Rd KY11. . . . . .46 C2
NORTHFIELD 122 D8
Northfield
   Cowdenbeath KY4. . . . . .13 C6
   Tranent EH33. . . . . .126 E6
Northfield Ave
   Edinburgh EH8. . . . . .122 D8
   Shotts ML7 . . . . .180 B2
Northfield Broadway
   EH8 . . . . .122 E8
Northfield Cir EH8. . . . . .122 D8
Northfield Cotts EH55. . . . . .163 C3
Northfield Cres
   Edinburgh EH8. . . . . .122 E8
   Longridge EH47. . . . . .161 C1
Northfield Ct
   Prestonpans EH32. . . . . . . .125 F8
   West Calder EH55. . . . . . . .163 C3
Northfield Dr EH8. . . . . .122 E7
Northfield E EH33. . . . . .126 E6
Northfield Farm Ave
   EH8 . . . . .122 E8
Northfield Farm Rd EH8. .122 E8
Northfield Gdns
   Clackmannan FK10 . . . . .11 B4
   Prestonpans EH32. . . . . . . .125 F8
Northfield Gr EH8. . . . . .122 E7
Northfield Mdws EH47. . . . . .161 B1
Northfield Park Gr EH8 . . . . .122 E8
Northfield Pk EH8. . . . . .122 E8
Northfield Rd Denny FK6 . . . .36 C4
   Edinburgh EH8. . . . . .122 D8
Northfield Terr
   Edinburgh EH8. . . . . .122 D8
   Longridge EH47. . . . . .161 C1
Northflat Pl ML8. . . . . .215 C1
North Fort St EH6. . . . . .93 E6
North Gate EH48. . . . . .111 F6
North Grange Ave EH32. . . . . .96 F1
North Grange Gr EH32. . . . . . .96 F1
North Green Dr FK2. . . . . .22 D4
North Greendykes Rd
   EH52. . . . . .115 E7
North Greens EH15. . . . . . . .123 B5
North Gyle Ave EH12. . . . . . .119 B6
North Gyle Dr EH12. . . . . . . .119 B7
North Gyle Farm Ct
   EH12 . . . . .119 A6
North Gyle Farm La
   EH12 . . . . .119 A6
North Gyle Gr EH12. . . . . . . .119 A6
North Gyle Loan EH12. . . . . .119 A7
North Gyle Pk EH12. . . . . . . .119 A7
North Gyle Rd EH12. . . . . . . .119 B7
North Gyle Terr EH12. . . . . . .119 A6
North High St EH21. . . . . .19 A7
North Hillhousefield EH6. .93 E6
North Junction St EH6. . . . . . .93 E6
North Larches KY11. . . . . .29 F4
Northlawn Ct EH4. . . . . .91 E4
Northlawn Terr EH4. . . . . .91 E4
NORTH LEITH. 93 F5
North Leith Mill EH6. . . . . . . .93 E6
North Leith Mill EH6. . . . . . . .93 F6
North Leith Sands EH6. . . . . .93 F6
North Loanhead KY11. . . . . . .45 E3
North Lorimer Pl EH32. . . . . . .97 B4
North Main St FK2 . . . . .39 C3

North Meggetland EH14 120 E3
NORTH MERCHISTON 120 E5
NORTH MIDDLETON 195 F3
North Muir Ave FK2 82 A8
North Overgate KY3 34 F3
Northpark Pl EH54 143 B5
North Park Terr EH4 93 A2
North Peffer Pl EH16 122 D4
North Pilrig Hts EH7 93 D4
NORTH QUEENSFERRY 68 D6
North Queensferry Prim Sch KY11 68 C6
North Queensferry Sta KY11 68 C6
North Rd Dunbar EH42 78 C3
Fauldhouse EH47 181 E7
Inverkeithing KY11 47 C6
North Reeves Pl EH47 161 B5
North Richmond St EH8 229 B2
Northrig Cotts EH41 131 B7
North Roundall KY11 45 E3
North Row KY11 45 B4
North St Andrew La EH2 229 A4
North St Andrew St EH2 229 A4
North St David St EH2 229 A4
North Seton Pk EH32 97 D4
North Shore Rd FK3 40 E2
North St Alloa FK10 10 A7
Armadale EH48 139 F6
Bo'ness EH51 63 F8
Clackmannan FK10 11 A4
Dunbar EH42 78 A2
Falkirk FK2 60 B8
Lochgelly KY5 14 A7
Ratho EH28 117 D2
Stirling FK9 2 D1
Northumberland Place La EH3 228 C4
Northumberland St EH3 228 C4
Northumberland Street NW La EH3 228 C4
Northumberland Street SE La EH3 228 C4
Northumberland Street SW La EH3 228 C4
North View Burntisland KY3 50 F8
West Calder EH55 163 D3
North View Cotts KY4 31 A8
North Way KY11 48 C5
North Werber Pk EH4 92 E3
North Werber Pl EH4 92 E4
North West Cumberland Street La EH3 93 C2
Northwood Pk EH54 142 E7
Northwood Rd FK10 4 D2
North Wynd EH22 153 A3
Norton Pk EH7 94 A2
Norton Pl KY11 29 E1
Norton St FK12 5 B7
Norval Pl KY11 46 F4
Norvell Lodge EH48 141 E6
Norway Gdns KY11 30 A2
Norwood Ave Alloa FK10 9 F7
Bonnybridge FK4 58 B7
Whitburn EH47 161 B5
Norwood Cres FK10 9 F7
Norwood Ct
Bonnybridge FK4 58 B7
Whitburn EH47 161 A5
Norwood Gr FK10 9 F7
Norwood Ind Est EH47 161 A5
Norwood Pl FK4 58 B7
Nosirrom Terr EH49 65 E5
Novar Cres KY1 17 B2
NUNGATE 130 C8
Nungate Gdns EH41 130 C7
Nungate Rd EH39 54 B7
Nursery Rd FK1 59 E4
Nursery The EH18 172 F7

O

Oak Ave EH20 171 F7
Oakbank FK2 61 A2
Oakbank Ave EH53 144 E2
Oakbank Cotts EH55 163 D6
Oakbank Park Dr EH53 165 C7
Oakbank Park Rd EH53 165 C8
Oakbank Parkway EH53 165 C8
Oakbank Park Way EH53 165 C8
Oakbank Pk EH54 165 B8
Oakbank Pl EH52 88 A2
Oakbank Rd EH53 144 E2
Oakbank Rdbt EH53 165 C8
Oak Cres Mayfield EH22 174 E6
Plean FK7 20 C3
Oak Dr Fallin FK7 8 D4
Stenhousemuir FK5 38 D1
Oakfield Pl EH8 229 B2
Oakfield St KY4 12 F8
Oak Gr Dunfermline KY11 46 E8
Livingston EH54 144 B6
Oakhill View FK2 83 B6
Oak La EH12 91 E1
Oaklands Sch EH4 92 B4
OAKLEY 26 F7
Oakley Ind Est KY12 26 F7
Oak Pl EH22 174 F6
Oak St FK8 1 F1
Oaktree Ct KY1 17 C8
Oaktree Junc EH41 129 B8
Oaktree Sq KY1 17 C8
Oakum Bay KY12 26 C1
Oakville Terr EH6 94 B3
Oak Way EH26 171 A1
Oakwood Pk EH54 142 E7
Oakwood Sch FK2 60 F4
Oatlands Pk EH49 85 B5
Oatridge Agricultural Coll EH52 114 F8
Oberon FK10 9 F8
Observatory Gn EH9 121 E2
Observatory Rd EH9 121 E2
Ocean Dr EH6 93 E7
Ocean Terminal Sh Ctr EH6 93 F7
Ocean Way EH6 94 A6
Ochil Ave KY2 16 F5
Ochil Cres FK8 2 B2
Ochil Ct Queensferry EH30 89 C8
Tullibody FK10 4 C3
Ochil Dr Maddiston FK2 83 A5
Stenhousemuir FK5 38 E3
Ochil Gdns FK4 57 F2
Ochil Hills Woodland Pk★ FK12 5 E8
Ochil La EH47 160 F6
Ochilmount FK7 7 F1
Ochil Rd Alva FK12 5 B7
Menstrie FK11 4 A7
Stirling FK9 2 C4
Ochil St Alloa FK10 10 A7
Fallin FK7 8 C4
Grangemouth FK3 61 D7
Tullibody FK10 4 B3
Ochil Terr
Dunfermline KY11 29 E2
Falkirk FK2 39 A2
Ochiltree Cres EH53 144 B2
Ochiltree Ct EH53 144 B2
Ochiltree Dr EH53 144 B2
Ochiltree Gdns EH16 122 C1
Ochiltree Terr FK1 59 B5
Ochilvale Terr FK10 5 D3
Ochilview Alva FK12 5 A7
Cowie FK7 20 E6
Ochil View
Cowdenbeath KY4 13 E6
Denny FK6 57 D8
Kincardine FK10 23 D4
Shieldhill FK1 81 D7
Ochil View Ct FK5 38 C5
Ochilview Dr KY12 26 B2
Ochilview Pk (Stenhousemuir FC & E Stirlingshire FC) FK5 38 D3
Ochilview Pl EH51 63 E6
Ochilview Rd EH51 63 E6
Ochilview Sq EH48 139 F5
Ochilview Terr EH51 63 E6
Ochre Cres FK7 20 C8
Octavia St KY2 17 B5
Ogilface Cres EH48 138 C2
Ogilvie Pl FK9 2 A6
Ogilvie Rd FK8 7 A5
Ogilvie Sch Campus EH54 143 D7
Ogilvie Terr EH11 120 E4
Ogilvie Way EH54 143 D7
Ogilvy Cres EH47 181 F6
O'Hanlon Way FK8 1 F2
Old Abbey Rd EH39 54 B7
Old Assembly Cl EH1 229 A3
Old Bellsdyke Rd FK5 38 A3
Old Brewery La FK10 10 B7
Old Bridge St 11 FK10 10 B6
Old Bridge Wynd FK9 2 A4
Old Broughton 3 EH3 93 D2
Old Burdiehouse Rd EH17 151 A3
OLD CAMBUS 219 C2
Old Church La EH15 122 C6
Old College EH1 229 A2
Old Course Gate EH21 124 D7
OLD CRAIGHALL 124 A2
Old Craighall Junc EH21 124 B2
Old Craighall Rd EH22 152 F8
Old Dalkeith Colliery EH22 153 E6
Old Dalkeith Rd
Danderhall EH16 152 C6
Edinburgh EH16 122 C2
Old Dean Rd EH32 98 D4
Old Deans Rd EH48 142 A5
Old Denny Rd FK5 38 A3
Old Drove Rd
Cambusbarron FK7 6 C5
Carlops EH46 205 B4
Old Eastfield St ML7 159 D5
Old Edinburgh Rd EH22 152 F3
Old Farm Ave EH13 149 C7
Old Farm Ct EH34 156 E6
Old Farm Pl EH13 149 B7
Old Fishmarket Cl EH1 229 A3
Old Forge Gr KY12 26 E7
Old Glendevon Farm Cotts EH52 87 D1
Old Golf Course Rd EH48 140 B4
Old Granary EH39 54 C8
Old Hall Knowe Pl EH48 141 C4
Old Hall Knowe Terr EH48 141 C4
OLDHAMSTOCKS 218 C3
Old Hillview Pl KY4 30 E6
Old Kirk Pl KY12 29 D4
Old Kirk Rd
Dunfermline KY12 29 D4
Edinburgh EH12 119 E7
North Queensferry KY11 68 C6
Old Linburn Rd KY11 29 F4
Old Liston Rd EH28 117 A6
Old Mill Ct
Dunfermline KY11 29 B2
East Whitburn EH47 161 F7
Old Mill Gr EH47 161 F7
Old Mill La
Edinburgh EH16 122 A2
Gifford EH41 220 F6
Oakley KY12 26 E6
Old Mill Rd
Broxburn EH52 115 F5
Hartwood ML7 179 B1
Old Mill Way FK6 36 B2
Old Newmills Rd EH14 147 D3
Old Orch The KY11 45 D3
OLD PENTLAND 150 F1
Old Perth Rd KY4 13 A4
OLD PHILPSTOUN 86 F7
Old Redding Rd FK2 60 F3
Old Refinery Rd FK3 62 A8
Old St Mary's La EH51 64 A8
Old Sch Ct 1 EH49 84 E6
Old School Ct FK10 4 B2
Old Schoolhouse The KY4 31 A6
Old Sheriffmuir Rd FK9 2 C6
Old Star Rd EH22 174 A5
Old Tolbooth Wynd EH8 229 B3
Old Toll Cottages EH41 130 C8
OLD TOWN 228 B2
Old Town Bannockburn FK7 7 D1
Broxburn EH52 115 F5
Old Town Jail Mus★ 7 FK8 7 A8
Oldwalls Pl FK3 61 E7
Oldwalls Rd FK3, EH51 62 C8
Old Well Ct EH48 141 D3
Old Well Rd EH48 141 D3
Oldwood Pl EH54 143 B4
Oliphant Ct FK8 2 B1
Oliphant Gdns EH21 125 C5
Olive Bank Rd EH21 124 B5
Olivebank Ret Pk EH21 124 A6
Oliver Rd FK1 60 D4
Ollerton Ct KY1 17 B5
Olympia Arc KY1 17 B5
Onich Pl ML7 180 B3
Onslow St EH54 144 A5
Orchard Bank EH4 92 E1
ORCHARD BRAE 92 E1
Orchard Brae EH4 92 F1
Orchard Brae Ave EH4 92 E1
Orchard Brae Gardens W EH4 92 E1
Orchard Brae Gdns EH4 92 F1
Orchard Brae W 1 EH4 92 F2
Orchard Cres
Edinburgh EH4 92 D1
Prestonpans EH32 96 F1
Orchardcroft 5 FK8 7 B7
Orchard Ct
East Linton EH40 103 E6
Kinghorn KY3 35 A4
Longniddry EH32 98 D4
Orchard Dr EH4 92 D1
Orchardfield EH40 103 D7
Orchardfield Ave EH12 119 D6
Orchardfield Terr EH27 146 A6
Orchard Gdns KY3 35 A4
Orchard Gr Crombie KY12 44 D6
Edinburgh EH4 92 F2
Falkirk FK2 83 B5
Haddington EH41 101 A1
Kincardine FK10 23 E3
Polmont FK2 61 F2
Orchardhead Loan EH16 151 A8
Orchardhead Rd EH16 151 A8
Orchardhead Way KY11 46 D2
Orchard House Day Hospl FK8 2 A1
Orchard La
Dunfermline KY11 29 D1
Dysart KY1 18 A7
Orchard Pk EH33 126 C7
Orchard Pl Dysart KY1 18 A7
Edinburgh EH4 92 E1
Livingston EH54 143 B5
Orchard Rd
Bridge of Allan FK9 2 A6
Edinburgh EH4 92 E1
Grangemouth FK3 62 C8
Kinghorn KY3 34 F3
Orchard Road S EH4 92 D1
Orchardson Rd FK5 38 B2
Orchard Sq KY11 45 D3
Orchard St Falkirk FK1 60 B5
Grangemouth FK3 61 D7
Orchard Terr
Edinburgh EH4 92 E1
Kinghorn KY3 34 F4
Torryburn KY12 26 F1
Orchard The
Crossford KY12 28 B2
Grangemouth FK2 82 D8
Musselburgh EH21 124 B5
Ormiston EH35 155 E7
Tranent EH33 126 C7
Tullibody FK10 4 B2
Orchard Toll EH4 92 E1
Orchard View EH22 152 E2
Ordnance Rd KY12 44 D6
Oriel Cres KY2 17 A4
Oriel Rd KY2 16 E5
Orkney Ct FK10 10 B5
Orkney Pl Falkirk FK1 60 B2
Kirkcaldy KY1 17 E7
Orlit Cotts EH39 74 D3
Ormelie Terr EH15 123 C8
Ormidale Terr EH12 120 D7
ORMISTON 155 F7
Ormiston Ave EH33 126 E6
Ormiston Crescent E EH33 126 E6
Ormiston Crescent W EH33 126 E6
Ormiston Cross★ EH35 155 E7
Ormiston Dr Alloa FK10 4 E2
East Calder EH53 145 A3
Ormiston Farm Steadings EH27 145 C2
Ormiston Pk KY12 29 C6
Ormiston Pl EH32 96 E1
Ormiston Prim Sch EH35 155 E7
Ormiston Rd
Pathhead EH37 176 A5
Tranent EH33 126 E5
Ormiston Terr EH12 119 D6
Ormond Ct FK5 38 A3
Oronsay Ave FK2 83 A6
Orrin Gr KY11 48 A3
Orrock Dr KY3 33 E2
Orrok La EH16 122 A1
Orrok Pk EH16 122 A2
Orr Terr ML7 159 C4
Orwell Pl Dunfermline KY12 29 C4
Edinburgh EH11 120 F6
Orwell Terr EH11 120 F6
Osborne Ct EH32 97 C4
Osborne Dr FK10 23 F4
Osborne Gdns FK1 59 F3
Osborne House Sch KY1 18 A7
Osborne St FK1 59 F3
Osborne Terr
Cockenzie & Port Seton EH32 97 C4
Edinburgh EH12 120 E7
Osprey Cres KY11 30 A3
Ossian Dr EH54 164 F6
Ostlere Rd KY2 17 A4
Oswald Ave FK3 61 F8
Oswald Ct EH9 121 D3
Oswald Rd EH9 121 D3
Oswald St FK1 60 B4
Oswalds Wynd KY1 17 C4
Oswald Terr EH12 119 D6
Otterburn Pk EH14 149 B8
Otterston Gr KY11 48 B4
Otterston Pl KY2 16 E8
Oudenarde Ct ML8 215 B1
Our Dynamic Earth★ EH8 229 C3
Our Lady of Lourdes RC Prim Sch EH47 162 C8
Our Lady's Prim Sch 1 FK8 1 F2
Our Lady's RC Prim Sch EH47 162 B2
Overhailes Farm Cotts HE41 103 A5
Overhaven KY11 45 E3
Overshiel Farm Cotts EH53 145 B6
Overton Cres Denny FK6 36 D1
East Calder EH53 145 A3
Redding FK2 61 B1
Overton Ct
Dunfermline KY11 46 F7
Kirkcaldy KY1 17 E8
Overton Mains KY1 17 E8
Overton Rd
Grangemouth, Bowhouse FK3 61 E6
Grangemouth, Oil Refinery FK3 62 B8
Kirkcaldy KY1 17 D8
Overton Terr FK6 36 C2
Owen Sq EH54 143 F1
Owen Stone St EH48 141 D3
Oxcars Dr KY11 48 B3
Oxcraig St EH5 92 F7
Oxenfoord Ave EH37 176 B5
Oxenfoord Dr EH37 176 A5
Oxford St EH8 229 C1
Oxford Terr EH4 228 A4
Oxgang Rd FK3 61 E7
OXGANGS 149 F6
Oxgangs Ave EH13 149 F7
Oxgangs Bank EH13 149 F6
Oxgangs Brae EH13 149 F6
Oxgangs Broadway EH13 149 F6
Oxgang Sch FK3 61 E7
Oxgangs Cres EH13 149 F7
Oxgangs Dr EH13 149 E7
Oxgangs Farm Ave EH13 149 E6
Oxgangs Farm Dr EH13 149 E6
Oxgangs Farm Gdns EH13 149 E6
Oxgangs Farm Gr EH13 149 E6
Oxgangs Farm Loan EH13 149 E6
Oxgangs Farm Terr EH13 149 E6
Oxgangs Gdns EH13 149 E7
Oxgangs Gn EH13 149 F7
Oxgangs Gr EH13 149 F7
Oxgangs Hill EH13 149 F7
Oxgangs Ho EH13 149 F7
Oxgangs Loan EH13 149 F7
Oxgangs Medway EH13 149 F6
Oxgangs Path EH13 149 F6
Oxgangs Path E EH13 149 F6
Oxgangs Pk EH13 149 F6
Oxgangs Pl EH13 149 E7
Oxgangs Prim Sch EH13 149 D7
Oxgangs Rd EH13 150 A5
Oxgangs Rise EH13 149 F7
Oxgangs Road N EH13 149 E6
Oxgangs Row EH13 149 F6
Oxgangs St EH13 149 F6
Oxgangs Terr EH13 149 E6
Oxgangs View EH13 149 F6

P

Paddockhall Cotts EH49 65 C1
Paddockholm The EH12 119 E6
Paddock The Dirleton EH39 53 B5
Gullane EH31 52 A2
Longniddry EH32 98 B3
Musselburgh EH21 124 D7
North Berwick EH39 54 C6
Whitekirk EH42 75 E8
Page St KY5 14 B8
Paisley Ave EH8 122 D7
Paisley Cl EH1 229 B3
Paisley Cres EH8 122 C8
Paisley Dr EH8 122 D7
Paisley Gdns EH8 122 C8
Paisley Gr EH8 122 D7
Paisley Terr EH8 122 C8
Palmer Ct FK3 61 D8
Palmer Pl Currie EH14 147 F4
Kingseat KY12 12 A1
Palmer Rd EH14 147 F4
Palmer Rise EH54 143 E1
Palmerston Pl EH12 228 A3
Palmerston Place La EH12 228 A2
Palmerston Rd EH9 121 D5
Panbrae Rd EH51 63 E7
Pan Ha' KY1 18 A6
PANHALL 18 A6
Pankhurst Loan EH22 153 D3
Panmure Pl EH3 228 C1
Pannie Rd KY1 17 D7
Panstead St FK3 61 E7
Panton Gn EH54 143 B8
Papana Cotts EH41 132 D2
Papermill Wynd EH7 93 E3
Papple Farm Cotts EH41 132 D5
Paradise La FK10 23 E3
Paradykes Ave EH20 172 B8
Paradykes Prim Sch EH20 172 B8
Pardovan Cres EH49 86 D7
Pardovan Holdings EH49 86 C7
Pardovan Pl FK1 59 F6
Paris Ave FK6 36 E1
Paris St FK3 61 E8
Parkandarroch Cres ML8 215 A1
Park Ave Bilston EH25 171 E6
Cowdenbeath KY4 13 C3
Denny FK4 57 E6
Dunbar EH42 78 C2
Dunfermline KY12 29 A3
East Calder EH53 144 F4
Edinburgh EH15 123 A7
Gorebridge EH23 174 C1
Grangemouth FK2 82 D8
Laurieston FK2 60 F4
Loanhead EH20 172 B7
Musselburgh EH21 124 E5
Stenhousemuir FK5 38 D1
Stirling FK8 7 A6
Park Cres Alloa FK10 5 C1
Bannockburn FK7 7 D2
Bonnyrigg and Lasswade EH19 173 B7
Easthouses EH22 174 C8
Edinburgh EH16 151 B8
Falkirk FK2 39 A2
Gifford EH41 220 F6
Loanhead EH20 172 B7
Westquarter FK2 61 A3
Park Ct Broxburn EH52 115 B5
Musselburgh EH21 124 E5
Shotts ML7 179 F4
Park Dr Bannockburn FK7 7 D2
Grangemouth FK2 82 D8
Musselburgh EH21 125 A4
Stenhousemuir FK5 38 D2
West Calder EH55 164 A5
Parkdyke FK7 6 E6
Parkend Haddington EH41 129 F3
Penicuik EH26 191 F4
Parkend Cres FK1 81 C6
Parker Ave EH7 94 E1
Parker Rd EH7 94 F1
Parker Terr EH7 94 F1
PARKFOOT 57 C4
Parkfoot Ct FK1 60 B3
Parkgate Alva FK12 4 F6
Rosyth KY11 46 F4
Park Gdns Bannockburn FK7 7 D2
Edinburgh EH16 151 B8
4 Grangemouth FK2 82 D8
Musselburgh EH21 124 E5
Park Gr EH16 151 B7
Parkgrove Ave EH4 91 C2
Parkgrove Bank EH4 91 C2
Parkgrove Cres EH4 91 C2
Parkgrove Dr EH4 91 C2
Parkgrove Gdns EH4 91 C2
Parkgrove Gn EH4 91 C2
Parkgrove Loan EH4 91 C2
Parkgrove Neuk EH4 91 C2
Parkgrove Path EH4 91 D2
Parkgrove Pl EH4 91 D2
Park Grove Pl EH21 124 E5
Parkgrove Rd EH4 91 C2
Parkgrove Row EH4 91 C2
Parkgrove St EH4 91 D2
Parkgrove Terr EH4 91 C2
Park Grove Terr EH21 124 E5
Parkgrove View EH4 91 C2
Parkhall Dr FK2 83 A6

PARKHEAD.....119 F2
Parkhead Ave EH11....119 E2
Parkhead Cotts EH55...163 E2
Parkhead Cres
 Edinburgh EH11....119 E2
 West Calder EH55...163 E3
Parkhead Ct FK10....10 C8
Parkhead Dr EH11....119 E2
Parkhead Gdns
 Edinburgh EH11....119 E2
 West Calder EH55...163 E3
Parkhead Gr EH11....119 E2
Parkhead Loan EH11...119 F2
Parkhead Pk EH22....174 C8
Parkhead Pl
 Easthouses EH22....174 C8
 Edinburgh EH11....119 E2
Parkhead Prim Sch
 EH55.....119 E2
Parkhead Rd Alloa FK10...10 C8
 Falkirk FK1....60 B1
 Linlithgow EH49....84 F8
Parkhead Smallholdings
 EH49.....64 A1
Parkhead St EH11...119 E2
Parkhead Terr EH11...119 E2
Parkhead View EH11...119 E2
Park Hill EH23....174 F6
Park La Aberdour KY3...49 C7
 Bo'ness EH51....64 B7
 🟦 Dunfermline KY12....28 F4
 Edinburgh EH15....123 A7
 Haddington EH41....129 E8
 Musselburgh EH21....124 E5
 Stirling FK8....2 A6
Parkland Gr Comrie KY12..26 D7
 Stoneyburn EH47....161 F1
Parklands EH52....115 D4
Parklands Cres KY11...48 A3
 Park La KY11....47 A5
PARKNEUK.....28 D6
Parkneuk KY12....28 D6
Parkneuk Rd KY12....28 D5
Park Par EH47....181 E6
Park Pl Alloa FK10...10 C7
 Clackmannan FK10....11 B4
 Cowdenbeath KY4....30 F8
 Dunfermline KY12....29 B4
 Edinburgh EH6....93 C6
 Kinghorn KY3....34 F2
 Kirkcaldy KY1....17 B3
 Livingston EH54....143 B5
 Stirling FK7....6 F6
Park Prim Sch FK10...10 B5
Park Rd Blackridge EH48...138 E3
 Bonnyrigg and Lasswade
  EH19....173 B7
 Broxburn EH52....115 E5
 Cockenzie & Port Seton
  EH32....97 D4
 Cowdenbeath KY4....13 B3
 Dalkeith EH22....152 F2
 Edinburgh EH6....93 C6
 Falkirk FK2....39 A1
 Gifford EH41....220 F6
 Gorebridge EH23....174 C1
 Grangemouth FK3....61 D8
 Harthill ML7....160 A6
 Kirkcaldy KY1....17 E8
 Menstrie FK11....4 A6
 Newtongrange EH22....174 B5
 Ormiston EH35....155 D6
 Rosyth KY11....46 F5
 Shotts ML7....179 D5
Park Road Prim Sch KY11 47 A4
Park Road W KY11....46 D5
Parkside EH28....117 A6
Parkside Ct
 🟦 Dalkeith EH22....153 A3
 Plean FK7....20 C3
Parkside Pl EH22....153 A3
Parkside Rd ML7....179 D4
Parkside Sq KY11....47 A4
Park St
 Edinburgh EH8....229 C1
 Rosyth KY11....46 F1
Parkside Terr EH16....229 C1
Park St Alva FK12....5 A7
 Bonnybridge FK4....58 C4
 Cowdenbeath KY4....13 C3
 Cowie FK7....20 E8
 Falkirk FK1....60 B5
 Lochgelly KY5....14 B7
Park Terr Broxburn EH52..115 B5
 Grangemouth FK2....82 D8
 Kirknewton EH27....145 E2
 Stirling FK8....7 A6
 Tullibody FK10....4 B1
Parkvale Pl EH6....94 B4
Park View Broxburn EH52..115 B5
 Fauldhouse EH47....181 E7
 Grangemouth FK2....82 E8
 Kirkcaldy KY2....16 F6
 Loanhead EH20....172 B7
Park-View EH32....98 E5
Park View
 Musselburgh EH21....124 E5
 Newcraighall EH21....123 E4
 Pencaitland EH34....156 F7
 Prestonpans EH32....97 B1
 Stoneyburn EH47....162 C2
 Westfield EH48....110 F4
 Whitburn EH47....161 A7
Parkview Ave FK1....59 F2
Park View Ct FK1....59 E5
Park View E EH32....97 D4
Park View Terr EH32...47 B2

Park View W EH32....97 D4
Parkville Ct EH48...138 E3
Parkway FK10....10 B7
Parkway Ct FK10....10 A7
Parkwood Cres EH52...115 D4
Parkwood Gdns EH52...115 D5
Parliament Sq EH1...229 A3
Parliament St EH6...93 F5
Parrot La EH23....195 C8
Parrotshot EH15....123 B5
Parsonage The EH21...124 D6
PARSONS GREEN.....94 B1
Parsons Green Prim Sch
 EH8....122 D7
Parsons Green Terr 🟦
 EH8....94 C1
Parsonspool
 Bonnyrigg and Lasswade
  EH19....173 C5
 Dunbar EH42....78 D2
Paterson Dr FK1....81 C6
Paterson La KY4....13 D3
Paterson Pl
 Bonnybridge FK4....58 C5
 Bridge of Allan FK9....2 A6
Paterson's Ct KY12...115 F5
Paterson Twr FK1....60 D4
Paterson Way KY11...29 B1
Path Brae EH29....89 A1
Pathfoot Ave FK9....2 C7
Pathfoot Dr FK9....2 C7
Pathfoot Rd FK9....2 C6
PATHHEAD Kirkcaldy....17 D6
 Mayfield....176 B5
Pathhead Ct 🟦 KY1...17 D6
Pathhead Prim Sch KY1..17 D7
Path The Airth FK2....22 D4
 Bannockburn FK7....7 D2
 Kirkcaldy KY1....17 D5
Patie's Rd EH14....149 C8
Pat Kelly Ave FK7....6 F4
Paton Ct FK10....10 B7
Paton St Alloa FK10...10 A7
 Dunfermline KY12....29 C6
Patrick Dr FK1....81 E7
Patriothall 🟦 EH3...93 B2
Patterson Pl KY2....17 B6
Patterson St KY2....17 B6
PATTIESMUIR.....46 B4
Pattison St EH6....94 A5
Pattle Ct EH39....54 A7
PAULVILLE.....141 A5
Pavilions Bsns Pk FK10...9 E7
Pavilions The FK10....9 E7
Pavilion View FK10....9 F8
Paxstone Cres ML7....159 E5
Paxstone Dr ML7....159 E5
Paxton Cres KY5....14 A8
Paxton Pl KY5....14 B8
Peachdales EH41....129 F8
Peacock Ave EH19...173 E7
Peacock Ct EH6....93 D7
Peacock Parkway EH19..173 E6
Peacock Pl EH19....173 D6
Peacocktail Cl EH15...123 B4
Pearce Ave EH12....119 C7
Pearce Gr EH12....119 C7
Pearce Rd EH12....119 C7
Pearson Ave FK4....57 D5
Pearson Pl FK4....57 D5
Pearson View FK10....10 C8
Peasehill Brae KY11...46 D3
Peasehill Fauld KY11...46 D2
Peasehill Gait KY11...46 D3
Peasehill Rd KY11....46 E3
Peathill Brae KY11...58 A6
Peathill Terr FK4....58 A5
Peatville Gdns EH14...120 A1
Peatville Terr EH14...120 A1
Peddie Pl FK3....61 E8
Peden St ML7....159 E5
Peebles Rd Penicuik EH26..191 F3
 West Linton EH46....208 F3
Peebles St KY1....93 D5
Peel Pentland Ctr EH20..151 A1
Peel Prim Sch EH54...143 C4
Peel Rdbt EH54....143 C4
Peel Terr EH9....121 F4
Peffer Bank EH16....122 D4
Peffer Ind Est EH16...122 C4
Peffermill Ind Est EH16..122 C4
Peffermill Rd EH16...122 C4
Peffer Pl EH16....122 D4
Peffer's Pl EH41....130 A8
Peffer St EH16....122 D4
Peggy's Mill Rd EH4...91 A4
Peirson Rd KY11....29 F4
Pelstream Ave FK7....7 B4
Pembroke Pl 🟦 EH12...120 E7
Pembroke St FK5....38 C3
PENCAITLAND.....156 D7
Pencaitland Prim Sch
 EH34....156 E6
Pencraig Brae EH40...103 D6
Pender Gdns FK2....82 E7
Penders La FK1....60 A5
Pendreich Ave EH19...173 D6
Pendreich Dr EH19...173 C8
Pendreich Gr EH19...173 C8
Pendreich Terr EH19...173 C8
Pendreich View EH19...173 C8
Pendreich Way FK9....2 D6
PENICUIK.....191 D4
Penicuik Ctr The EH26..191 E5

Penicuik High Sch EH26..191 E5
Penicuik Rd EH25, EH26...171 E3
Pennelton Pl EH51....63 E5
Pennyschool Pl FK10....11 A5
Pennywell Ct EH4....92 B5
Pennywell Gdns EH4....92 B5
Pennywell Gr EH4....92 B5
Pennywell Medway EH4...92 B5
Pennywell Pl EH4....92 B5
Pennywell Rd EH4....92 B5
Pennywell Villas EH4....92 B6
PENSTON.....127 F5
Penston Farm Cotts
 EH33....127 F5
Pentland Ave
 Bathgate EH48....141 F5
 Currie EH14....147 F4
 Edinburgh EH13....149 A7
 Gorebridge EH23....174 B3
 Penicuik EH26....191 E6
Pentland Cres
 Edinburgh EH10....150 A7
 Rosewell EH24....172 D3
Pentland Ct Bilston EH25..171 E6
 Dalgety Bay KY11....48 C4
Pentland Dr
 Edinburgh EH10....149 F6
 Whitburn EH47....161 C6
Pentlandfield Bsns Pk
 EH25....171 C5
Pentland Gait Office Pk
 EH11....119 B1
Pentland Gr EH10....149 A7
Pentland Hills Regional Pk★
 EH14, EH26....189 D7
Pentland Ind Est EH20..172 A7
Pentland Pk
 Livingston EH54....144 B4
 Loanhead EH20....171 F8
Pentland Pl
 Cairneyhill KY12....27 E1
 Currie EH14....147 F4
 Kirkcaldy KY2....16 F6
Pentland Prim Sch EH13 149 F6
Pentland Rd
 Bonnyrigg and Lasswade
  EH19....173 A7
 Edinburgh EH13....149 A7
 Edinburgh, Old Pentland
  EH10, EH20....150 D1
 Loanhead EH20....172 A8
Pentland Rise KY11...48 C5
Pentlands Gdns EH10...149 A7
Pentlands Science Pk
 EH26....171 C3
Pentland Terr
 Dunfermline KY11....29 E2
 Edinburgh EH10....150 A8
 High Valleyfield KY12...26 A1
 Penicuik EH26....191 E6
Pentland View
 Currie EH14....147 F4
 Dalkeith EH22....153 C2
 East Whitburn EH47....161 E7
 Edinburgh EH10....150 A6
 Uphall EH52....115 A5
Pentland View Cres
 EH25....171 F3
Pentland View Ct
 Currie EH14....148 A4
 Livingston EH54....143 A6
Pentland View Pl EH25...171 F3
Pentland View Rd
 Kirkliston EH29....89 A2
 Roslin EH25....171 F3
Pentland View Terr EH25 171 F3
Pentland Way FK3....61 E5
Pentland Wlk EH47...161 C6
People's Story The★
 EH8....229 B3
Peploe Ave 🟦 FK5...38 B2
Peploe Rise KY11....47 A7
Peppercraig Quarry Ind Site
 EH41....100 F2
Percival St KY1....17 A5
Perdieus Mount KY12...29 A4
Perdrixknowe EH14...120 D3
Persevere Ct EH6....93 F6
Perth Rd KY4....13 D6
Perth's Gr EH32....97 A2
Perth St Edinburgh EH3...93 B2
 Livingston EH54....144 A6
Petershill Gdns EH48...141 C7
Petershill Wildlife Reserve★
 EH48....141 C8
Peterswell Brae FK7....7 E1
Petrel Way KY11....30 A2
Pettigrew's Cl 🟦 EH22...153 A3
PETTYCUR.....34 F1
Pettycur Bay KY3....34 E1
Pettycur Ho KY3....34 F1
Pettycur Rd KY3....34 F1
Peveril Rise EH54....164 E8
Peveril Terr EH16....151 B8
Phantassie Cotts EH40...103 F7
Phantassie Doocot★
 EH40....103 F7
Pheasantry The FK10...10 D5
Philip Ave Bathgate EH48..141 E5
 Linlithgow EH49....84 E7
Philip Dr FK5....38 D2
Philip Pl FK2....62 B7
Philip St FK2....60 B7
Philpingstone La EH51...64 C7
Philpingstone Rd EH51...64 D8
PHILPSTOUN.....86 D7
Phoenix Ind Est FK7....7 C7
Phoenix La KY12....28 F4

Picardy Pl EH1....229 A4
Pierhead Bldgs KY11...68 C5
Pier Pl EH6....93 D7
Pier Rd EH51....64 C8
Piersfield Gr EH8....94 D1
Piersfield Gro EH8....94 D1
Piersfield Terr EH8....94 D1
PIERSHILL.....94 E1
Piershill La 🟦 EH8...94 C1
Piershill Pl EH8....94 C1
Piershill Sq E EH8....94 D1
Piershill Square W EH8..94 C1
Piershill Terr 🟦 EH8...94 D1
Pike Rd FK7....7 D4
Pilgrims Hill EH49....85 D8
Pilkham Ct KY4....13 C3
Pilmuir St KY12....29 A5
PILRIG.....93 E4
Pilrig Gdns EH6....93 E3
Pilrig Glebe 🟦 EH6...93 F3
Pilrig House Cl EH6....93 E4
Pilrig Hts EH6....93 E3
Pilrig Ind Est EH6....93 E4
Pilrig Park Sch EH6....93 E4
Pilrig St EH6....93 E3
PILTON.....92 E5
Pilton Ave EH5....92 E5
Pilton Cres EH5....92 F5
Pilton Dr EH5....92 F5
Pilton Drive N EH5....92 E6
Pilton Gdns EH5....92 F5
Pilton Loan EH5....92 F5
Pilton Pk EH5....92 F5
Pilton Pl EH5....92 F5
Pineapple The★ FK2...22 B6
Pinebank EH54....143 E5
Pine Cres FK11....3 F6
Pinefield Glade EH54...164 C8
Pine Gn EH51....63 C6
Pine Gr Alloa FK10...10 C6
 Dunfermline KY11....46 E8
 Livingston EH54....144 B5
 Penicuik EH26....171 A1
 Westquarter FK2....62 B2
Pinegrove Gdns EH4....91 B2
Pine St EH42....78 B1
Pines The EH31....52 B3
Pine Wlk FK5....38 D1
Pinewood Dr KY11...48 B3
Pinewood Pk EH54....142 E7
Pinewood Pl
 Blackburn EH47....162 E8
 Mayfield EH22....174 E6
Pinewood Rd EH22....174 E6
Pinewood Sch EH47...162 E8
Pinewood View EH22...174 E6
Pinkerton Ave 🟦 KY11...47 C7
Pinkerton Cresent KY11...47 C7
Pinkerton Gr KY11....47 C8
Pinkerton Pl KY11....46 F5
Pinkerton St 🟦 KY11...47 C8
Pinkhill EH12....120 A6
Pinkie Ave EH21....124 E5
PINKIE BRAES.....124 E5
Pinkie Dr EH21....124 E5
Pinkie Hill Cres EH21...124 E5
Pinkie Rd EH21....124 E6
Pinkie St Peter's Prim Sch
 EH21....124 E6
Pinkie Terr EH21....124 F5
Pinkie Wlk 🟦 EH33...126 D5
Pinnel Pl KY11....48 C4
Pipe La EH15....95 A1
Piper Cres KY3....33 D2
Pipe St EH15....95 A1
Pirig Cotts EH6....93 F3
Pirleyhill Dr FK1....81 D6
Pirleyhill Gdns FK1....60 A2
Pirnhall Rd
 Bannockburn, Chartershall
  FK7....19 A8
 Bannockburn FK7....19 D7
Pirniefield Bank EH6....94 C4
Pirniefield Gdns EH6....94 C4
Pirniefield Gr EH6....94 C4
Pirniefield Pl EH6....94 C4
Pirniefield Terr EH6....94 C4
Pirnhall Prim Sch 🟦
 EH4....92 C5
Pirrie St EH6....93 F4
Pitbauchlie Bank KY11...29 C1
Pitcairn Gr EH10....149 F8
Pitcairn St KY11....29 C2
Pitcaple Gdns EH54....164 C8
PITCORTHIE.....29 E1
Pitcorthie Dr KY11....46 E8
Pitcorthie Prim Sch EH11 29 E1
Pitcorthie Rd KY11....29 C1
PITCOX.....105 C3
Pitcox Cotts EH42....105 C3
Pitdinnie Pl KY12....27 D1
Pitdinnie Rd KY12....27 D2
Pitfairn Rd FK10....5 E3
Pitfirane Pk KY12....28 B1
Pitfour Pl KY2....16 C7
Pitlochry Pl 🟦 EH7...94 A2
Pitmedden Rd KY11...30 A1
Pit Rd KY4....13 C6
Pitreavie Bsns Pk KY11...46 C7
Pitreavie Ct KY11....46 C8
Pitreavie Dr KY11....46 D6
Pitreavie Ind Est KY11...46 D6
Pitreavie Prim Sch KY11..46 D8
Pitsligo Rd EH10....121 B4
Pittencrieff Ct EH21...124 F6

Pittencrieff House Mus★
 KY12....28 F3
Pittencrieff Pk★ KY12...28 F3
Pittencrieff Prim Sch
 KY12....28 F4
Pittencrieff St KY12...28 F4
Pittsburgh Rd KY11...30 B5
Pitt St EH6....93 E5
Pitt Terr FK8....7 B6
Pittville St EH15....123 C8
Pittville Street La EH15..123 B8
Place Charente EH22...153 C2
Plane Gr KY11....46 F8
Plane St EH42....78 B1
Plantation St KY5....14 B7
Player Dr KY12....12 A1
Player Gn EH54....143 B8
Players Rd FK7....7 C7
PLEAN.....20 C3
Pleanbank Cotts FK7...20 B3
Plean Ctry Pk★ FK7...20 B1
Plean Ind Est FK7....20 D1
Pleasance Edinburgh EH8..229 B2
 Falkirk FK1....60 B4
Pleasance Brae KY12...27 D1
Pleasance Ct
 🟦 Falkirk FK2....60 B4
 Halbeath KY12....30 B7
Pleasance Gdns FK1....60 B4
Pleasance Rd
 Dunfermline KY12....29 F6
 Falkirk FK1....60 B3
 Halbeath KY12....30 A6
Pleasance Row ML11...201 B3
Pleasance Sq 🟦 FK1...60 B4
Pleasance The FK32...71 C4
Pleasures The FK10....9 E7
Plewlandcroft EH30...68 B1
Plewlands Ave EH10...120 F2
Plewlands Gdns EH10...120 F2
Plewlands Ho EH10....68 B1
Plewlands Pl EH30....89 B8
Plewlands Terr EH10...120 F2
Pleydell Pl 🟦 EH16...151 B8
Plough La 🟦 EH33...126 D6
Plover Brae EH54....143 D5
Plover Cres KY11....30 B1
Plummer Ct EH22....153 A4
Pointgarry Rd EH39...54 B7
POLBETH.....163 F5
Polbeth Ave EH55....163 F5
Polbeth Cres EH55....163 F5
Polbeth Gdns EH55....163 F5
Polbeth Ind Est EH55...163 E4
Polbeth Pl EH55....163 F5
Polbeth Rd EH55....163 F5
Polbeth West Calder Ind Est
 EH55....163 E4
Poldrate EH41....130 B8
Polkemmet Bsns Ctr
 EH47....160 F5
Polkemmet Ctry Pk★
 EH47....160 C7
Polkemmet Dr ML7....160 A6
Polkemmet La ML7....159 F5
Polkemmet Prim Sch
 EH47....161 A5
Polkemmet Rd
 Harthill ML7....159 F6
 Whitburn EH47....160 C5
Pollard Gdns EH11....120 A4
Pollock Wlk KY12....28 E5
Polmaise Ave FK7....7 B3
Polmaise Cres FK7....8 C5
Polmaise Ct FK7....7 B3
Polmaise Rd
 Cambusbarron FK7....6 E3
 Stirling FK7....6 F5
POLMONT.....61 F2
Polmont House Gdns FK2..61 E1
Polmont Pk FK2....61 E3
Polmont Rd FK2....61 B3
Polmont Sports Ctr FK2..61 D1
Polmont Sta FK2....61 E1
POLMONT STATION.....61 E1
Polson Gdns EH33....126 B6
POLTON.....172 D6
Polton Avenue Rd EH19..173 A6
Polton Bank EH18....172 E6
Polton Bank Terr EH18...172 E6
Polton Cotts EH18....172 D6
Polton Ct EH19....173 B7
Polton Dr EH19....173 A7
Polton Gdns EH18....173 A7
POLTONHALL.....172 F6
Poltonhall Ind Est EH18..172 F7
Polton Pl EH19....173 B7
Polton Rd
 Bonnyrigg and Lasswade
  EH18....173 A8
 Loanhead EH20....172 C7
Polton Road W EH18,
 EH19....172 F6
Polton St EH19....173 B6
Polton Terr EH18....173 A7
Polton Vale EH20....172 C7
Polwarth Ave FK2....82 C8
Polwarth Cres
 Edinburgh EH11....121 A5
 Prestonpans EH32....97 A1
Polwarth Gdns EH11...120 F5
Polwarth Gr EH11....120 F5
Polwarth Ho KY9....2 D6
Polwarth Pk EH11....120 F5
Polwarth Pl EH11....120 F5

Polwarth Terr
Edinburgh EH10 . . . .**120** F4
Prestonpans EH32 . . . .**97** A1
Pomathorn Bank EH26 . . . . .**191** F4
Pomathorn Rd EH26 . . . .**191** F4
Pompee Rd FK10 . . . .**5** B1
Ponton St EH3 . . . .**228** B1
Poolewe Dr FK2 . . . .**61** C2
Poplar Cres KY2 . . . .**17** B7
Poplar Gdns KY2 . . . .**17** A7
Poplar Gr Dunfermline KY11 .**46** E8
Livingston EH54 . . . .**144** B6
Poplar La EH6 . . . .**94** B5
Poplar Pk EH7 . . . .**97** D3
Poplar St Dunbar EH42 . . . .**78** B1
Grangemouth FK3 . . . .**61** C7
Mayfield EH22 . . . .**174** E6
Poplars The FK10 . . . .**4** B1
Poplar Terr EH19 . . . .**173** B6
Portal Rd FK3 . . . .**61** C5
PORT BRAE **17** C4
Port Buchan EH52 . . . .**115** D5
Port Downie FK1 . . . .**59** D5
PORT EDGAR **67** F1
Port Edgar Marina & Sailing
Sch EH30 . . . .**67** F2
Porteous' Pend EH1 . . . .**228** C2
Porter Ave FK9 . . . .**2** B3
Porterfield KY12 . . . .**26** E7
Porterfield Rd EH4 . . . .**92** E3
Portgower Pl EH4 . . . .**93** A2
Port Hamilton EH3 . . . .**228** B2
Port Laing Wynd KY11 . . . . . .**68** C7
Portland Gdns EH6 . . . .**93** E6
Portland Pl Edinburgh EH6 . . .**93** E6
Fauldhouse EH47 . . . .**181** C5
Portland Row EH6 . . . .**93** E6
Portland St EH6 . . . .**93** E6
Portland Terr EH6 . . . .**93** E6
PORTOBELLO **123** B8
Portobello High Sch
EH15 . . . .**122** F7
Portobello L Ctr EH15 . . . . . .**95** A1
Portobello Rd EH7, EH8 . . . . .**94** E1
Portobello Swim Ctr
EH15 . . . .**123** C8
PORT OF LEITH **93** E8
Portree Cres FK2 . . . .**62** A1
Portsburgh Sq EH1 . . . .**228** C2
Port St Clackmannan FK10 . . . .**11** A4
Inverkeithing KY11 . . . .**47** C2
Stirling FK8 . . . .**7** B7
Posthill FK10 . . . .**5** D1
Postings The KY1 . . . .**17** C3
Post Office La KY11 . . . .**68** C6
Potter Pl FK2 . . . .**39** F3
Potterrow EH8 . . . .**229** A2
Potter's Path EH33 . . . .**126** C6
Pottery St KY1 . . . .**17** E8
Pottery The
Edinburgh EH15 . . . .**95** A1
Prestonpans EH32 . . . .**96** E1
Pottishaw Cotts EH47 . . . . . .**161** C7
Pottishaw Pl EH48 . . . .**141** C1
Pottishaw Rd EH48 . . . .**140** F1
Pottis Rd FK7 . . . .**7** B3
Povert Rd EH19, EH23 . . . . . .**173** F2
Powderhall Brae EH7 . . . .**93** D4
Powderhall Rd EH7 . . . .**93** D3
Powderhall Rigg EH7 . . . .**93** D4
Powdermill Brae EH23 . . . . .**195** D6
Powdrake Rd FK3 . . . .**61** F8
Powie's Path EH53 . . . .**144** D4
Pratt St KY1 . . . .**17** A1
President Kennedy Dr
FK7 . . . .**20** C3
Pressmennan Wood Forest
Trail★ EH42 . . . .**133** E6
PRESTON **97** A2
Preston Ave
Linlithgow EH49 . . . .**84** F6
Prestonpans EH32 . . . .**97** B1
Preston Cres
Inverkeithing KY11 . . . .**47** D1
Linlithgow EH49 . . . .**84** F6
Prestonpans EH32 . . . .**97** B1
Preston Cross Cotts EH32 .**97** A1
Preston Ct Linlithgow EH49 . .**84** F6
Prestonpans EH32 . . . .**97** B1
PRESTONFIELD **122** B4
Prestonfield Ave EH16 . . . . .**122** B4
Prestonfield Bank EH16 . . . .**122** A4
Prestonfield Cres EH16 . . . .**122** A4
Prestonfield Gdns
Edinburgh EH16 . . . .**122** A4
② Linlithgow EH49 . . . .**84** F6
Prestonfield Pk EH16 . . . . . .**122** D4
Prestonfield Prim Sch
EH16 . . . .**122** B3
Prestonfield Rd EH16 . . . . . .**122** B4
Prestonfield Terr EH16 . . . . .**122** A4
Preston Gdns EH32 . . . .**125** F8
Prestongrange (Ind Mus)
EH32 . . . .**125** C8
Prestongrange Rd EH32 . . . .**125** E8
Prestongrange Terr EH32 . . .**96** E1
Prestonhall Cres EH24 . . . . .**172** D2
Prestonhall Rd EH24 . . . .**172** D2
Preston House Gdns EH9 . . .**84** E4
Prestonkirk Gdns EH40 . . . .**103** E8
Preston Lodge High Sch
EH32 . . . .**97** A1

Preston Market Cross★
EH32 . . . .**97** A1
Preston Mill★ EH40 . . . .**103** F8
PRESTONPANS **96** E2
Prestonpans Ind Est
EH32 . . . .**126** A8
Prestonpans Inf Sch ⑤
EH32 . . . .**96** F1
Prestonpans Prim Sch
EH32 . . . .**126** A8
Prestonpans Sta EH32 . . . . .**126** A8
Preston Pk EH4 . . . .**84** F6
Preston Pl EH37 . . . .**176** A4
Preston Rd
East Linton EH40 . . . .**103** E8
Linlithgow EH49 . . . .**84** F6
Prestonpans, Cuthill EH32 . . . . .**97** B1
Prestonpans, Preston EH32 .**97** A1
Preston St
High Valleyfield KY12 . . . .**26** A2
Rosewell EH24 . . . .**172** D2
Preston Street Prim Sch
EH8 . . . .**229** C1
Preston Terr
Inverkeithing KY11 . . . .**47** D1
Linlithgow EH49 . . . .**84** F6
Prestonpans EH32 . . . .**97** B1
Sauchie EH35 . . . .**5** B2
Preston Tower★ EH32 . . . . . .**97** A1
Preston Twr EH32 . . . .**97** A1
Pretoria Pl
Edinburgh EH4 . . . .**91** F3
North Berwick EH39 . . . .**54** D7
Quality Street Junc EH4 . .**91** F3
Quality Street La EH4 . . . . .**91** F3
Quarrolhall Cres FK2 . . . . . .**39** B3
Quarrybank
Cousland EH22 . . . .**154** C5
Edinburgh EH14 . . . .**148** C8
Quarry Bank EH14 . . . .**148** C8
Quarrybank Cl EH14 . . . .**148** C8
Quarrybank Ct EH14 . . . .**148** C8
Quarrybank End EH14 . . . . .**148** C8
Quarry Brae
Grangemouth FK2 . . . .**82** E8
Kirkcaldy KY1 . . . .**17** F8
Quarry Cl EH8 . . . .**229** B1
Quarry Cotts
Blackridge EH48 . . . .**138** C3
Edinburgh EH15 . . . .**123** B4
Quarry Ct KY4 . . . .**13** B3
Quarryfoot Gdns EH19 . . . .**173** B7
Quarryfoot Gn EH19 . . . .**173** C7
Quarryfoot Pl EH19 . . . .**173** B7
Quarryford Farm Cotts
EH41 . . . .**221** C4
QUARRYHEADS **173** B8
QUARRYHOLES **94** B3
Quarry Howe EH14 . . . .**147** C1
Quarry Knowe FK7 . . . .**6** E3
Quarryknowes The EH51 . .**63** E6
Quarry Pl Alloa FK10 . . . .**10** C8
Shotts ML7 . . . .**179** D5
Quarry Rd
Cambusbarron FK7 . . . .**6** C5
Fauldhouse EH47 . . . .**181** F6
Shotts ML7 . . . .**179** D5
Quarryside Cl KY12 . . . .**28** C6
Quarry St ML7 . . . .**179** D5
Quarryview EH14 . . . .**148** C8
Quarrywood Ct EH54 . . . . . .**143** D3
Quartermile EH3 . . . .**229** A2
Quayside Mills EH6 . . . .**93** F5
Quayside St EH6 . . . .**93** F6
Quebec Ave EH54 . . . .**143** E4
Queen Anne Dr EH28 . . . . . .**117** B5
Queen Anne High Sch
KY11 . . . .**28** F6
Queen Anne Pk EH28 . . . . . .**117** B5
Queen Anne St KY11 . . . .**29** A4
Queen Charlotte La EH6 . . .**94** A5
Queen Charlotte St EH6 . . .**94** A5
Queen Margaret Ct EH10 .**150** D5
Queen Margaret Dr
Musselburgh EH21 . . . .**123** F3
South Queensferry EH30 . . . . . .**68** C1
Queen Margaret Fauld
KY12 . . . .**29** F6
Queen Margaret Gdns
KY12 . . . .**29** F6
Queen Margaret Hospl
KY12 . . . .**28** F6
Queen Margaret Pk KY12 . . .**29** F6
Queen Margaret's Pl KY3 . .**34** F1
Queen Margaret Univ
EH21 . . . .**124** A3
Queen Margaret Univ Way
EH21 . . . .**124** A3
Queen Mary Terr KY11 . . . . . .**47** B2
Queens Ave
Broxburn EH52 . . . .**115** E4
Haddington EH41 . . . .**100** F1
Queen's Ave
Bridge of Allan FK9 . . . .**2** B6
Edinburgh EH4 . . . .**92** B2
Queen's Avenue S ③ EH4 .**92** C2
Queen's Bay Cres EH15 . . . .**123** D7
Queens Cres Kinghorn KY3 .**34** F1
Livingston EH54 . . . .**143** B6
Queen's Cres Carluke ML8 .**215** A4
Edinburgh EH9 . . . .**121** A4
Falkirk FK1 . . . .**59** F5
Stenhousemuir FK5 . . . .**38** D3
Queen's Ct
Bridge of Allan FK9 . . . .**1** F7
Dunfermline KY12 . . . .**29** A3
Stirling FK8 . . . .**2** A2
Queen's Dr Denny FK6 . . . . . .**36** E3
Falkirk FK1 . . . .**59** F5

Queens Dr continued
Stenhousemuir FK5 . . . .**38** C3
Queen's Dr California FK1 . .**81** F5
Edinburgh, Canongate EH8 **229** C2
Edinburgh, Willowbrae
EH8 . . . .**122** C6
Pencaitland EH34 . . . .**156** E6
Stenhousemuir FK5 . . . .**38** C2
QUEENSFERRY **89** A7
Queensferry High Sch
EH30 . . . .**89** D8
Queensferry Mus★ EH30 .**68** C1
Queensferry Prim Sch ①
EH30 . . . .**68** C1
Queensferry Rd
Dunfermline KY11 . . . .**46** D7
Edinburgh EH4 . . . .**91** C2
Edinburgh, Orchard Brae
EH4 . . . .**92** D1
Kirkliston EH29 . . . .**89** A2
Rosyth KY11 . . . .**46** E5
Queensferry Recn Ctr
EH30 . . . .**89** D8
Queensferry Street La
EH2 . . . .**228** B3
Queensferry Terr EH4 . . . . . .**92** E1
Queen's Gallery★ EH8 . .**229** C3
Queen's Gall The★ EH8 .**229** C3
Queens Gdns
Bridge of Allan FK9 . . . .**1** F7
East Calder EH53 . . . .**144** E4
Queen's Gdns EH4 . . . .**92** C2
Queenshaugh KY12 . . . .**27** C7
Queenshaugh Dr FK8 . . . .**2** C1
Queen's La FK9 . . . .**2** A7
Queen's Park Ave EH8 . . . . .**94** B1
Queen's Park Ct EH8 . . . . . .**122** C8
Queen's Pl EH42 . . . .**78** F1
Queen's Rd
Broxburn EH52 . . . .**115** E4
Dunbar EH42 . . . .**78** E2
Edinburgh EH4 . . . .**92** C2
Stirling FK8 . . . .**6** F7
Queen St Alloa FK10 . . . .**10** B7
Alva FK12 . . . .**5** A7
Bannockburn FK7 . . . .**7** C2
Edinburgh EH2 . . . .**228** C4
Falkirk FK1 . . . .**60** C5
Grangemouth FK3 . . . .**61** F8
Inverkeithing KY11 . . . .**47** B2
Stirling FK8 . . . .**7** A8
Queens Terr EH53 . . . .**144** E4
Queen's Terr FK3 . . . .**2** A7
Queenstonbank EH39 . . . . . .**52** E3
Queen Street Gardens E
EH3 . . . .**228** C4
Queen Street Gardens W
EH3 . . . .**228** C4
Queensway EH26 . . . .**191** E7
Queens Way KY11 . . . .**46** B2
Queen's Wlk EH16 . . . .**122** E3
Quentin Ct EH54 . . . .**143** E1
Quentin Rise EH54 . . . .**143** E1
Quidenham Ct EH30 . . . .**54** A6
Quilts The EH6 . . . .**93** F5
Quilts Wynd EH6 . . . .**93** E5
Quoiters Ct EH47 . . . .**162** C7

Race Rd EH48 . . . .**140** E7
Raeburn Cres
Kirkcaldy KY2 . . . .**17** A4
Whitburn EH47 . . . .**161** B5
Raeburn Mews EH4 . . . .**93** A2
Raeburn Pl EH4 . . . .**93** A2
Raeburn Rd EH4 . . . .**38** B2
Raeburn Rigg EH54 . . . .**143** B6
Raeburn St EH4 . . . .**93** A2
Rae Ct FK2 . . . .**39** C3
Rae's Ct EH54 . . . .**151** A5
Raes Gdns EH19 . . . .**173** A5
Rae St Cowdenbeath KY4 . . . . .**13** C2
Stenhousemuir FK5 . . . .**38** D3
Rainhill Cl ① FK2 . . . .**82** F7
Raith Ave KY4 . . . .**13** C3
Raith Cres KY2 . . . .**17** A4
Raith Ctr KY4 . . . .**13** B3
Raith Dr KY2 . . . .**17** A3
Raith Gdns KY2 . . . .**17** A3
RAITH PARK **16** D5
Raleigh Ct FK1 . . . .**59** E5
Ramillies Ct Carluke ML8 . .**215** A1
Penicuik EH26 . . . .**192** A8
Ramsay Ave FK2 . . . .**61** A3
Ramsay Colliery EH20 . . . . .**172** C8
Ramsay Cotts EH19 . . . .**173** F3
Ramsay Cres
Bathgate EH48 . . . .**141** C6
Burntisland KY3 . . . .**34** A2
Mayfield EH22 . . . .**174** E5
Ramsay Ct Kincardine FK10 .**23** E4
Livingston EH54 . . . .**144** C5
Ramsay Gdn EH1 . . . .**228** C3
Ramsay La Edinburgh EH1 .**228** C3
Kincardine FK10 . . . .**23** E4
Limekilns KY11 . . . .**45** D3
Ramsay Pl Edinburgh EH15 . .**95** B1
Penicuik EH26 . . . .**191** C6
Stirling FK8 . . . .**2** B2
Ramsay Rd KY1 . . . .**17** B1
Ramsay Terr EH18 . . . .**172** F6

Ramsay Wlk EH22 . . . .**174** E5
Ramsey Pl KY11 . . . .**46** F3
Ramsey Tullis Dr FK10 . . . .**4** C1
Randolph Cliff EH3 . . . .**228** A3
Randolph Cres
Bannockburn FK7 . . . .**7** C1
Dunbar EH42 . . . .**106** D8
Edinburgh EH3 . . . .**228** A3
Grangemouth FK2 . . . .**82** D8
Randolph Ct Kirkcaldy KY1 . .**18** A8
Stirling FK8 . . . .**7** A5
Randolph Gdns FK6 . . . .**36** D1
Randolph Ind Est KY1 . . . . . .**18** A8
Randolph La EH3 . . . .**228** B3
Randolph Pl
Bannockburn FK7 . . . .**7** C2
Edinburgh EH3 . . . .**228** B3
Kirkcaldy KY1 . . . .**17** F8
Randolph Rd FK8 . . . .**7** B4
Randolph St
Cowdenbeath KY4 . . . .**13** D3
Dunfermline KY12 . . . .**29** A4
Randolph Terr FK7 . . . .**7** A4
Randyford Rd FK2 . . . .**60** D5
Randyford St FK2 . . . .**60** E5
Rankeillor St EH8 . . . .**229** B1
Rankin Ave EH9 . . . .**121** F2
Rankin Cres FK4 . . . .**57** D5
Rankin Dr EH9 . . . .**121** E2
Rankine Sq EH54 . . . .**142** C5
Rankine Wynd FK10 . . . .**4** C2
Rankin Rd EH9 . . . .**121** F3
Rannoch Ct FK10 . . . .**10** C5
Rannoch Dr Crossford KY12 .**28** B1
Whitburn EH47 . . . .**161** C7
Rannoch Gr EH4 . . . .**91** D1
Rannoch Pl Edinburgh EH4 .**91** D1
Shieldhill FK1 . . . .**81** E7
Shotts ML7 . . . .**179** E6
Stenhousemuir FK5 . . . .**38** F4
Rannoch Rd Edinburgh EH4 **91** D1
Grangemouth FK3 . . . .**61** D4
Kirkcaldy KY2 . . . .**16** E8
Rosyth KY11 . . . .**46** E2
Whitburn EH47 . . . .**161** C7
Rannoch Wlk
Livingston EH54 . . . .**144** A4
Whitburn EH47 . . . .**161** C7
Ransome Gdns EH4 . . . .**91** D1
RAPLOCH **1** F2
Raploch Prim Sch ③ FK8 . .**1** F2
Raploch Rd FK8 . . . .**1** F1
Rashiehill ML11 . . . .**201** A1
Rashiehill Cres EH55 . . . . . .**182** F6
Rashiehill Rd FK1 . . . .**108** A6
Rashiehill Terr EH55 . . . . . .**182** F6
Rashierigg EH52 . . . .**115** B5
Rashierigg Pl EH47 . . . .**161** B2
Ratcliffe Terr EH9 . . . .**121** C4
Rathbone Pl EH15 . . . .**95** B1
RATHO **117** D1
Ratho Park Rd EH28 . . . .**117** E2
Ratho Pk EH28 . . . .**117** D1
Ratho Pl EH47 . . . .**29** C3
Ratho Prim Sch EH28 . . . . . .**117** D2
RATHO STATION **117** D5
Rattray Cres EH10 . . . .**149** E8
Rattray Dr EH10 . . . .**149** E8
Rattray Gdns EH47 . . . .**162** F7
Rattray Gn EH10 . . . .**149** E8
Rattray Loan EH10 . . . .**149** E8
Rattray St EH51 . . . .**64** B8
Rattray Terr KY5 . . . .**14** A7
Rattray Way EH10 . . . .**149** F8
Raveling Dr EH14 . . . .**147** B2
Raveling Gait EH14 . . . .**147** B2
Raveling Hill EH14 . . . .**147** B2
Raveling Pk EH14 . . . .**147** B2
Raveling Rd EH14 . . . .**147** B2
Raveling Wynd EH14 . . . .**147** C2
RAVELSTON **120** B8
Ravelston Dykes EH12 . . . . .**120** D8
Ravelston Dykes La EH4 .**120** A8
Ravelston Dykes Rd EH4 .**120** A8
Ravelston Heights EH4 . . . .**92** C5
Ravelston House Gr ③
EH4 . . . .**92** C4
Ravelston House Loan
EH4 . . . .**92** C4
Ravelston House Pk EH4 . .**92** C4
Ravelston House Rd EH4 . .**92** C4
Ravelston Pk EH4 . . . .**120** E8
Ravelston Pl EH4 . . . .**120** F8
Ravelston Rise EH4 . . . .**120** C8
Ravelston Terr EH4 . . . .**120** F8
Ravelston Woods Nature
Reserve★ EH4 . . . .**92** B1
Ravelsykes Rd EH26 . . . .**191** C5
Ravendean Gdns EH26 . . . .**191** C5
Ravens Craig ⑩ KY1 . . . .**17** E5
Ravenscraig Castle★ KY1 .**17** E5
Ravenscraig St KY1 . . . .**17** F6
Ravenscraig View KY1 . . . . .**17** E6
Ravenscroft Gdns EH17 . . . .**151** E5
Ravenscroft Pl EH17 . . . .**151** E5
Ravenscroft St EH17 . . . .**151** E5
Ravenshaugh Cres EH21 . .**125** A6
Ravenshaugh Rd EH21 . . . .**125** A7
Ravenswood Pl ML11 . . . . . .**217** F8
Ravenswood Rd EH16 . . . . .**122** B4
Ravenswood Rise EH54 . . . .**164** E8
Raw Holdings EH53 . . . .**145** B5
Recreation Pk (Alloa Athletic
FC) FK10 . . . .**10** C6
Rectory La KY1 . . . .**18** A7

Redbrae Ave EH51 . . . . .64 A5
Redbrae Rd FK1 . . . . .59 D6
Redbraes Gr EH7 . . . . .93 D4
Redbraes Pl EH7 . . . . .93 D4
Redburn Rd
  Blackridge EH48 . . . . .138 B2
  Prestonpans EH32 . . . . .96 E1
Redburn Road N EH32 . . . . . .96 E1
Redburn Wynd KY1 . . . . .17 C4
Redcraig Rd EH53 . . . . .144 E7
Redcrays KY2 . . . . .16 C7
Redcroft Pl EH47 . . . . .162 A1
Redcroft St EH22 . . . . .152 A8
Redcroft Terr EH47 . . . . .162 A1
REDDING 61 C1
Redding Ind Est FK2 . . . . .61 A1
REDDINGMUIRHEAD 82 A8
Redding Rd
  Grangemouth FK2 . . . . .82 D8
  Laurieston FK2 . . . . .60 F2
  Redding FK2 . . . . .61 B1
Reddingrig Ct FK2 . . . . .82 A8
Reddingrig Pl FK2 . . . . .82 A8
Redding Road Rdbt FK2 . . . . .60 F2
Reddoch Rd FK3 . . . . .61 F5
Redford Ave EH13 . . . . .149 C6
Redford Bank EH13 . . . . . . .149 D6
Redford Cres EH13 . . . . .149 C6
Redford Dr EH13. . . . . .149 B6
Redford Gdns EH13 . . . . . . .149 D6
Redford Gr EH13. . . . . .149 D6
Redford Loan EH13 . . . . . . .149 C6
Redford Neuk EH13 . . . . . . .149 D6
Redford Pl EH13 . . . . .149 D6
Redford Rd EH13 . . . . .149 B6
Redford Terr EH13 . . . . .149 C6
Redford Wlk EH13 . . . . .149 C6
Redgauntlet Terr EH16 . . . . .122 C1
Redhall FK7 . . . . .8 A4
Redhall Bank Rd EH14 . . . . .120 B1
Redhall Cres EH14 . . . . .120 B2
Redhall Dr EH14 . . . . .120 A2
Redhall Gdns EH14 . . . . .120 A2
Redhall Gr EH14 . . . . .120 A2
Redhall House Ave EH14 . . .120 C1
Redhall House Dr EH14 . . . .120 B1
Redhall Pl EH14 . . . . .120 A2
Redhall Rd EH14 . . . . .120 A2
Redhall Sch EH14 . . . . .120 A1
Redhall View EH14 . . . . .120 B1
Redhaws Rd ML7 . . . . .180 A3
Redheugh Cotts TD13 . . . . .219 E3
Redheugh Loan EH23 . . . . . .174 C1
Redheughs Ave EH12 . . . . . .119 A4
Redheughs Rigg EH12 . . . . .119 A4
Redholm EH39 . . . . .54 E6
Redholm Pk EH39 . . . . .54 E6
Redhouse Cotts EH49 . . . . . .86 F3
Redhouse Ct EH47 . . . . .162 E7
Redhouse Ind Est FK2 . . . . . .82 B8
Redhouse Rd EH47 . . . . .141 D1
Redhouse Rd EH47 . . . . .163 A8
Redlands Ct EH47 . . . . .161 E7
Redlands Rd FK10 . . . . .4 A3
Redmill Cotts EH47 . . . . .161 E7
Redmill Ct EH47 . . . . .161 E7
Redmill Ind Est EH47 . . . . . .161 E6
Redmill View EH47 . . . . .161 E7
Redmire Cres ML7 . . . . .198 B8
Red Moss Wildlife Reserve*
  EH14. . . . . .168 C4
Redpath Dr FK2 . . . . .39 A4
Red Row Aberlady EH32 . . . .71 C4
  Limekilns KY11 . . . . .45 D3
  Pathhead EH37 . . . . .176 C8
Redside EH39 . . . . .55 B1
Redwell Pl FK10 . . . . .9 F7
Redwing Brae EH54 . . . . . . .143 D6
Redwood Gr EH22 . . . . .173 F5
Redwood Wlk EH47 . . . . . . .174 A5
Reed Dr EH22. . . . . .174 A6
Reedlands Dr FK6 . . . . .57 D7
Regal Gr ML7 . . . . .179 E4
Regal Lodge EH19 . . . . .173 B7
Regent Pl EH7 . . . . .94 A2
Regent Rd EH7, EH8 . . . . . .229 B4
Regent Sq EH49 . . . . .85 B7
Regent St Edinburgh EH15 .123 B8
  Kincardine FK10 . . . . .23 E3
Regent Street La EH15 . . . . .123 B8
Regents Way KY11 . . . . .48 B3
Regent Terr EH7 . . . . .229 C4
Regent Terrace Mews
  EH7 . . . . .229 C4
Regis Ct EH4 . . . . .91 B4
Register Pl EH2 . . . . .229 A4
Register St EH51. . . . . .63 E8
Reid Ave KY4 . . . . .30 C6
Reid Pl FK5. . . . . .38 B2
Reid Rd EH48. . . . . .141 C4
Reid's Cl EH8. . . . . .229 C3
Reid St Dunfermline KY12 . . .29 A3
  Lochgelly KY5 . . . . .14 B8
Reid Terr EH3 . . . . .93 B2
Reilly Gdns FK4. . . . . .58 B3
Reilly Rd FK4 . . . . .58 B3
Relugas Gdns EH9 . . . . .121 E3
Relugas Pl EH9 . . . . .121 E3
Relugas Rd EH9 . . . . .121 E3
Rendall Gdns EH52. . . . . . . .115 F5
Rennie Pl EH40 . . . . .103 C8
Rennie's Isle EH6 . . . . .93 F6
Rennie Sq EH54. . . . . .164 C6
Rennie St FK1 . . . . .60 A3
Research Avenue 1 EH14 147 F8

Research Avenue N
  Hermiston EH14 . . . . .118 F1
  Riccarton EH14 . . . . .147 E8
Research Avenue S EH14 147 F8
RESTALRIG 94 D2
Restalrig Ave EH7 . . . . .94 D1
Restalrig Cir EH7 . . . . .94 C3
Restalrig Cres EH7 . . . . .94 C3
Restalrig Dr EH7 . . . . .94 C2
Restalrig Gdns EH7 . . . . .94 C2
Restalrig Ho EH7 . . . . .94 C2
Restalrig Pk EH7 . . . . .94 B3
Restalrig Rd EH7 . . . . .94 B3
Restalrig Road S EH7 . . . . . .94 C1
Restalrig Sq EH7 . . . . .94 C3
Restalrig Terr EH6 . . . . .94 A4
Restondene EH34 . . . . .142 E5
Retail Pk Rdbt EH54. . . . . . .143 E1
Retreat Cres EH42 . . . . .78 D1
Retreat Gdns EH42. . . . . .78 D1
Reveston La EH47 . . . . .161 B5
Reynard Gdns EH49 . . . . .84 A6
Rhodders Gr FK12 . . . . .5 B7
Rhodes Cotts EH39. . . . . .54 F7
Rhodes Pk EH39 . . . . .54 F6
Rhodes Smallholdings
  EH39 . . . . .55 A6
Rhodes St KY11. . . . . .29 B2
RICCARTON 147 E7
  Clackmannan. 11 B5
Riccarton Ave EH14 . . . . . . .148 A5
Riccarton Cres EH14 . . . . . .148 A4
Riccarton Dr EH14 . . . . .148 A5
Riccarton Gr EH14 . . . . .148 A5
Riccarton Mains Rd
  EH14 . . . . .148 A6
Riccarton Rd EH49. . . . . .84 F5
Richard Quinn St FK7 . . . . . .20 D8
Richmond Dr FK2 . . . . .82 C8
Richmond La EH8. . . . . .229 B2
Richmond Pl
  Edinburgh EH8. . . . . .229 B2
  Lochgelly KY5 . . . . .14 B7
Richmond Terr
  Bo'ness EH51 . . . . .63 F7
  Edinburgh EH11. . . . . .228 A2
Riddochhill Cres EH47 . . . . .162 C7
Riddochhill Ct EH47 . . . . . . .162 B8
Riddochhill Dr EH47 . . . . . . .162 C7
Riddochhill Rd EH47 . . . . . .162 C8
Riddochhill View EH47 . . . . .162 B8
Ridge Ct EH47 . . . . .161 B2
Ridge Way KY11 . . . . .48 B5
Riding Pk EH4 . . . . .91 B4
Ridley Dr KY11. . . . . .46 F3
Riego St EH3 . . . . .228 B2
Rifle Rd EH51 . . . . .62 D8
Riggonhead Ct [4] EH33 .126 D7
Riggonhead Gdns [5]
  EH33 . . . . .126 D7
Rigg Pk EH42 . . . . .78 C2
Riggs View KY12 . . . . .27 D1
Rigley Terr EH32. . . . . .125 E8
Rig Pl EH32. . . . . .71 C4
Rig St EH32. . . . . .71 C4
Rillbank Cres EH9 . . . . .229 A1
Rillbank Terr EH9 . . . . .121 D5
Rimmon Cres ML7 . . . . .179 E6
Ringans La FK7 . . . . .6 F3
Ring Rd FK10. . . . . .10 B7
Ringwood Pl [2] EH16 . . . .151 B8
Rintoul Ave EH23 . . . . .26 A8
Rintoul Pl Blairhall KY12. . . . .26 A8
  Edinburgh EH3. . . . . .93 B2
Riselaw Cres EH10. . . . . .150 A8
Riselaw Pl EH10 . . . . .150 A8
Riselaw Rd EH10. . . . . .150 A8
Riselaw Terr EH10 . . . . .150 A8
Ritchie Ct KY12 . . . . .29 A7
Ritchie Pl Bo'ness EH51 . . . . .64 A5
  Edinburgh EH11. . . . . .120 F5
  Grangemouth FK3 . . . . .61 C5
Inverkeithing/Dunfermline
  KY11 . . . . .29 F3
Rivaldsgreen Cres EH49 . . . .85 A6
River Almond Wlk EH4 . . . . . .90 F4
Riverbank View FK8 . . . . .2 C1
Riverbank Ct EH47 . . . . .161 F7
Riverbank View FK8 . . . . .7 C8
River Gore Gr EH23 . . . . . . .195 C8
River Gore Rd EH23 . . . . . . .195 C8
River Gore View EH23. . . . . .195 C8
Riversdale Cres EH12 . . . . . .120 C7
Riversdale Gr EH12 . . . . .120 C7
Riversdale Rd EH12. . . . . . . .120 C7
RIVERSIDE 2 B1
Riverside Edinburgh EH4. . . . .91 B7
  Newbridge EH28. . . . . .116 F6
Riverside Ct
  Linlithgow EH49 . . . . .84 C7
  Livingston EH54. . . . . .143 C3
Riverside Dr
  Haddington EH41 . . . . .101 B1
  Stirling FK8 . . . . .2 C1
Riverside Gdns EH41. . . . . . .124 B5
Riverside Lea Crofts
  EH44 . . . . .162 F7
Riverside Pl EH41. . . . . .101 C1
Riverside Prim Sch
  Livingston EH54. . . . . .144 A4
  Stirling FK8 . . . . .2 B1
Riverside Rd
  Edinburgh EH30. . . . . .90 E3
  Grangemouth FK3 . . . . .62 B5
Riverside Terr FK10. . . . . .23 F3
Riverside View FK10 . . . . . . .10 B4
River St FK2 . . . . .39 A1
Riverview FK10 . . . . .10 A7

River View KY11 . . . . .48 B2
River Wlk KY11 . . . . .48 B2
River Wynd FK9 . . . . .2 A4
R L Stevenson's Birthplace*
  EH3. . . . . .93 C3
Road 3a FK3. . . . . .62 C7
Road 4b FK3. . . . . .62 C7
Road 5a FK3. . . . . .62 C7
Road 30b FK3 . . . . .62 B6
Road 30c FK3 . . . . .62 B6
Road 4 FK3. . . . . .62 C6
Road 6 FK3. . . . . .62 C7
Road 7 FK3. . . . . .62 C7
Road 8 FK3. . . . . .62 C7
Road 9 FK3. . . . . .62 C7
Road 10 FK3. . . . . .62 C7
Road 11 FK3. . . . . .62 C6
Road 13 FK3. . . . . .62 C6
Road 15 FK3. . . . . .62 C6
Road 17 FK3. . . . . .62 C6
Road 21 FK3. . . . . .62 A6
Road 24 FK3. . . . . .62 A6
Road 25 FK3. . . . . .62 B6
Road 26 FK3. . . . . .62 B6
Road 27 FK3. . . . . .62 B6
Road 28 FK3. . . . . .62 B6
Road 29 FK3. . . . . .62 B6
Road 30 FK3. . . . . .62 A6
Road 31 FK3. . . . . .62 B6
Road 32 FK3. . . . . .62 B6
Road 33 FK2, FK3. . . . . .62 B6
Roanhead Terr FK10 . . . . . . .23 E4
Roanshead Rd EH22 . . . . . .174 C8
Robb's Loan EH14 . . . . .120 C4
Robb's Loan Gr EH14. . . . . .120 C4
Robert Bruce Ct FK5. . . . . . . .38 A2
Robert Burns Dr EH16. . . . . .122 A1
Robert Burns Mews
  EH22 . . . . .173 D3
Robert De Quincy Pl
  EH32 . . . . .125 F8
Robert Dick Ct FK10 . . . . . . .4 C2
Robert Dow Ct KY5 . . . . .14 B8
Robert Hardie Ct FK5 . . . . . .38 C2
Robert Kay Pl FK5. . . . . .38 B5
Robert Kinmond Ave FK10. . .4 C2
Robert Knox Ave FK10 . . . . . .4 C2
Roberts Ave FK2 . . . . .61 D2
Robert Smillie Ave EH22 .174 E5
Robert Smith Ct KY4 . . . . . . .13 E6
Robert Smith Pl EH22 . . . . .152 F4
Robertson Ave
  Bathgate EH48 . . . . .140 E5
  Bonnybridge FK4. . . . . .58 B6
  Edinburgh EH11. . . . . .120 D5
  Prestonpans EH32. . . . . .97 A2
  Tranent EH33. . . . . .126 D6
Robertson Ct
  Armadale EH48. . . . . .139 F4
  Stenhousemuir FK5. . . . . . . .38 D2
Robertson Dr EH33 . . . . . . .126 D7
Robertson Gait EH11 . . . . . .120 D6
Robertson Gdns EH48. . . . . .140 A4
Robertson Pl FK7 . . . . .7 B3
Robertson Rd KY12 . . . . .29 D5
Robertsons Bank EH23 . . . .195 D7
Robertson's Cl
  [3] Dalkeith EH22. . . . . . . .153 A3
  Edinburgh EH1. . . . . .229 B2
Robertson's Ct EH8. . . . . . . .229 C4
Robertson St FK12. . . . . .5 B7
Robertson Way EH54. . . . . .143 D7
Roberts St KY11. . . . . .17 E8
Robert St ML7 . . . . .179 E4
Robert Wilson Gr KY12 . . . .29 D8
Robins Neuk EH33. . . . . .127 C5
Rocheid Pk EH4 . . . . .92 F4
Rochester Terr EH10. . . . . . .121 A4
Rocks Rd KY11. . . . . .45 A4
Rockville Gr EH49. . . . . .85 A6
Rockville Terr EH19 . . . . . . .173 B8
Roddinglaw Cotts EH12 . . . .118 C3
Roddinglaw Rd EH12,
  EH28 . . . . .118 C3
Rodel Dr FK2. . . . . .61 F1
Rodgers St FK6. . . . . .36 E1
Rodney St Edinburgh EH7. . .93 C2
  Grangemouth FK3 . . . . .61 C6
Roebuck Pk FK5. . . . . .38 E2
Roebuck Pl EH51 . . . . .63 D5
Rolland St KY12 . . . . .29 A3
Rollock St FK8 . . . . .7 A5
Roman Bldgs FK2. . . . . .59 D5
Roman Camp EH37 . . . . . . .176 B4
Roman Camp Cotts
  EH52. . . . . .115 C2
Roman Camp Way EH37 .176 B4
Roman Ct EH37. . . . . .176 B4
Roman Dr FK1. . . . . .59 D5
Roman Pk EH22. . . . . .153 D2
Roman Rd Bonnybridge FK4 .58 A4
  Inverkeithing KY11 . . . . .47 B2
Roman St EH22 . . . . .153 D2
Roman Terr EH22 . . . . .153 D2
Roman View EH22 . . . . .153 D2
Roman Way EH51. . . . . .63 D5
Romero Pl EH16 . . . . .121 F5
Romyn Rd KY11 . . . . .46 C1
Ronades Rd FK2. . . . . .60 A8
Ronald Cres FK5. . . . . .38 B1
Ronald Pl FK8 . . . . .7 B8
Ronaldshay Cres FK3 . . . . . .61 E8
Ronaldson Gr KY12 . . . . .29 D5
Roodlands Bsns Pk EH41 100 F1
Roodlands Ct EH41 . . . . . . .100 E1
Roodlands Hospl EH41 . . . .100 E1
Roods Cres KY11 . . . . .47 B3
Roods Rd KY11. . . . . .47 B2

Roods Sq KY11 . . . . .47 C3
Rood Well Cotts EH42. . . . .104 E1
Roomlin Gdns KY1. . . . . .17 F7
Roosevelt Rd EH27 . . . . .145 E3
Rope Wlk EH32 . . . . .96 E1
Rosabelle Rd EH25. . . . . . . .171 F3
Rosabelle St KY1 . . . . .17 E7
Rose Ave EH19. . . . . .173 D6
ROSEBANK 36 D4
Rosebank Alloa FK10 . . . . .5 D1
  Bridgend EH49 . . . . .86 F4
  Cowdenbeath KY4 . . . . .13 D4
  Dunfermline KY11 . . . . .29 C2
Rosebank Ave KY4 . . . . .59 F5
Rosebank Cotts EH3 . . . . . . .228 A2
Rosebank Gdns Alloa FK10 10 C8
  Dunfermline KY12. . . . . .28 D6
  Edinburgh EH5. . . . . .93 A5
Rosebank Gr EH5. . . . . .93 A5
  Grangemouth FK2. . . . . .82 B7
  Kincardine FK10 . . . . .23 F3
Rosebank Gr EH5 . . . . .93 A5
Rosebank Pk EH54. . . . . . . .164 A8
Rosebank Rd
  Edinburgh EH5. . . . . .93 A5
  Livingston EH54. . . . . .164 A8
Rosebank Rdbt Falkirk FK1 .59 F5
  Livingston EH54. . . . . .164 B8
Rosebank Way EH54 . . . . . .164 A8
Rosebay Glade EH54 . . . . . .164 C7
Roseberry Ct EH30. . . . . .89 C8
Roseberry Pk EH54 . . . . . . .142 E5
Rosebery Ave EH30 . . . . .89 C8
Rosebery Cres
  Bathgate EH48 . . . . .141 B5
  Edinburgh EH12. . . . . .120 F7
  Gorebridge EH23. . . . . .195 C6
Rosebery Crescent La
  EH12 . . . . .120 F7
Rosebery Ct
  Dalgety Bay KY11 . . . . .47 F2
  Kirkcaldy KY1 . . . . .17 B5
Rosebery Gr KY11. . . . . .47 F2
Rosebery Pl
  Dalgety Bay KY11 . . . . .47 F2
  Gullane EH31. . . . . .52 A2
  Livingston EH54. . . . . .143 B5
  Stirling FK8 . . . . .2 C2
ROSEBURN 120 D7
Roseburn Ave EH12 . . . . . . .120 D7
Roseburn Cliff EH12 . . . . . .120 D7
Roseburn Dr EH12. . . . . .120 D7
Roseburn Gdns EH12. . . . . .120 D7
Roseburn Maltings EH12.120 E7
Roseburn Pl EH12 . . . . .120 D7
Roseburn Prim Sch
  EH12. . . . . .120 D6
Roseburn St EH12 . . . . .120 D6
Roseburn Terr EH12 . . . . . . .120 E7
Rosebush Cres KY11 . . . . . . .29 C3
Rose Cotts EH19 . . . . .173 D6
Rose Cres KY12 . . . . .29 A4
Rose Ct EH4 . . . . .91 E4
Rosedale Ct EH24 . . . . .193 D8
Rosedale Gr EH24 . . . . .172 D1
Rosedale Neuk EH24 . . . . . .172 D1
Rosefield Ave EH15 . . . . . . .123 A8
Rose Gdns
  Bonnyrigg and Lasswade
    EH19 . . . . .173 D6
  Cairneyhill KY12 . . . . .27 D2
Rose Gr EH19 . . . . .173 D6
Rosehall EH41. . . . . .129 F8
Rosehall Ct EH41 . . . . .129 F8
Rosehall Pl EH41 . . . . .129 F8
Rosehall Rd ML7 . . . . .179 C3
Rosehall Terr FK1 . . . . .60 B4
Rosehall Wlk EH41. . . . . . . .129 F8
Rosehill Cres KY4 . . . . .13 B3
Rosehill Pl EH54 . . . . .143 B3
Rose La
  South Queensferry EH30 . . .68 B1
  Torryburn KY12 . . . . .26 E1
Roseland Hall FK3 . . . . .61 B7
Roselea Dr FK2 . . . . .82 E8
Rosemary Ct FK6 . . . . .36 D2
Rosemead Terr FK6 . . . . .81 F5
Rosemill Ct KY12 . . . . .26 C1
Rosemount Dr EH22 . . . . . . .96 F2
Rosemount Ave KY2 . . . . . . .17 A8
Rosemount Bldgs EH3 . . . .228 A2
Rosemount Ct
  Bathgate EH48 . . . . .141 B6
  Carluke ML8 . . . . .215 A2
Rosemount Gdns FK1. . . . . . .81 D6
Rosemount Mews EH32 . . . .96 F2
Roseneath EH9 . . . . .121 D5
Roseneath St EH9. . . . . .121 D5
Roseneath Terr EH9 . . . . . . .121 D5
Rose Neuk EH19 . . . . .173 D6
Rose Path EH19. . . . . .173 D6
Rose Pk
  Bonnyrigg and Lasswade
    EH19 . . . . .173 D6
  Edinburgh EH5. . . . . .93 B5
Rose Pl EH19 . . . . .173 D6
Rose St Alloa FK10. . . . . .4 E1

Rose St continued
  Bonnybridge FK4. . . . . .58 B6
  Burntisland KY3. . . . . .50 E8
  Cowdenbeath KY4 . . . . .13 C3
  Dunfermline KY12 . . . . .29 B4
  Edinburgh EH2. . . . . .228 C3
  Tullibody FK10. . . . . .4 D4
Rose Street North La
  EH2 . . . . .228 C3
Rose Street South La
  EH2 . . . . .228 C3
Rose's Wlk EH52. . . . . .114 F4
Rosetay Ct KY12 . . . . .29 C4
Rose Terr
  Bonnyrigg and Lasswade
    EH19. . . . . .173 D6
  Denny FK6. . . . . .36 D1
  Stenhousemuir FK5. . . . . . . .38 F3
Rosethorn Wynd KY12 . . . . .29 C3
Rosevale Pl EH6 . . . . .94 B4
Rosevale Terr EH6 . . . . .94 B4
Roseville Gdns EH5 . . . . .93 C6
Rose Way EH19 . . . . .173 D6
ROSEWELL 172 D2
Rosewell Prim Sch EH24 172 E2
Rosewell Rd EH18, EH19,
  EH24 . . . . .172 F4
Rose Wynd KY2 . . . . .17 B3
Rosin Ct KY1 . . . . .17 C7
ROSLIN 171 F3
Roslin Bio Ctr EH25. . . . . . . .171 E3
Roslin Glen Ctry Pk*
  EH25. . . . . .171 F1
Roslin Prim Sch EH25 . . . . .171 F3
Roslin Prim Sch (Bilston
  Annexe) EH25 . . . . .171 E6
Ross Ave EH14. . . . . .48 A2
Ross Cres Falkirk FK1 . . . . . .59 C5
  Tranent EH33. . . . . .126 D5
Ross Ct Addiewell EH55. . . .183 C8
  Stirling FK7 . . . . .7 B3
Rossend Terr KY3. . . . . .50 D8
Ross Gdns Edinburgh EH9. .121 F3
  Kirkcaldy KY1 . . . . .17 E7
Rossglen Ct EH25. . . . . .172 A3
Ross High Sch EH33. . . . . . .126 C6
Rosshill Terr EH30. . . . . .89 D8
Rossie Pl EH7 . . . . .94 A2
Ross La KY12 . . . . .28 F4
Rossland Pl KY3 . . . . .34 F2
Rosslyn Chapel* EH25 .172 A3
Rosslyn Cres EH6. . . . . .93 E3
Rosslyn Sch EH7 . . . . .17 F8
Rosslyn St KY1 . . . . .17 F8
Rosslyn Terr EH6 . . . . .93 E3
Rossness Dr KY3. . . . . .34 F1
Ross Pl Edinburgh EH9. . . . .121 F3
  Kinghorn KY3. . . . . .34 F1
  Newtongrange EH22. . . . . . .174 B6
Ross Rd EH16. . . . . .122 A2
Ross's Cl [2] EH41 . . . . . . .130 B8
Ross's St EH32. . . . . .29 B5
Ross Way KY11 . . . . .143 C7
ROSYTH 46 F4
Rosyth Europarc KY11 . . . . .46 D1
Rosyth Sta KY11. . . . . .46 E6
Rothesay Mews EH4 . . . . . .120 F8
Rothesay Pl
  Edinburgh EH3. . . . . .228 A3
  Musselburgh EH21 . . . . .124 D5
Rothesay Terr EH3 . . . . .228 A3
Rothes Dr EH54. . . . . .164 F6
Roughburn Rd FK9. . . . . .2 A6
Roughlands Cres FK2 . . . . . . .39 B3
Roughlands Dr FK2 . . . . .39 A3
Roull Gr EH12. . . . . .119 D5
Roull Pl EH12. . . . . .119 D5
Roull Rd EH12 . . . . .119 D5
Roundel The FK2 . . . . .60 D7
Roundelwood FK10 . . . . .5 B1
Roundhouse FK7 . . . . .20 D8
Round The KY12 . . . . .29 C3
Rowallan Ct [4] EH22 . . . . .153 A3
Rowallan Dr ML7 . . . . .179 E4
Rowan Cres Falkirk FK1 . . . . .59 A4
  Menstrie FK11. . . . . .3 F6
  Shotts ML7. . . . . .180 A4
Rowan Ct FK7 . . . . .7 E1
Rowan Dr EH47 . . . . .141 E1
Rowanfield Sch EH4 . . . . .92 C3
Rowan Gdns EH19. . . . . . . .173 B6
Rowan Gr
  Dunfermline KY11 . . . . .29 D1
  Livingston EH54. . . . . .144 B5
Rowanhill Cl EH32 . . . . .97 D3
Rowanhill Dr EH32. . . . . .97 D3
Rowanhill Pk EH32. . . . . .97 C3
Rowanhill Way EH32 . . . . . . .97 D3
Rowan La EH47 . . . . .141 D1
Rowan Pl EH47 . . . . .141 D1
Rowan St Blackburn EH47 .141 D1
  Dunbar EH42. . . . . .78 B1
Rowans The Alloa FK10. . . . . .5 C2
  Gullane EH31. . . . . .52 B3
Rowan Terr
  Blackburn EH47. . . . . .162 D8
  Cowdenbeath KY4 . . . . .13 C3
Rowantree Ave EH14. . . . . .147 E4
Rowantree Gr EH14 . . . . . . .147 E4
Rowantree Rd EH22. . . . . . .174 E7
Rowantree Wlk FK5. . . . . . . .38 B4
Roxburghe Lodge Wynd
  EH42. . . . . .78 F1
Roxburghe Pk EH42. . . . . . . .78 F1

Roxburghe Terr EH42 . . . . . .78 F1
Roxburgh Pl
Edinburgh EH8 . . . . .229 B2
Stenhousemuir FK5 . . . . . . .38 F4
Roxburgh St
Edinburgh EH8 . . . . .229 B2
Grangemouth FK3 . . . . .61 F8
Royal Blind Sch The
Edinburgh EH10 . . . . .121 B3
Edinburgh EH16 . . . . .121 F3
Royal Botanic Garden★
EH3 .93 B3
Royal Cir EH3 . . . . .228 B4
Royal Coll of Physicians
EH2 . . . . .228 C4
Royal Commonwealth Pool★
EH16 . . . . .121 A5
Royal Commonwealth Pool
EH16 . . . . .121 F6
Royal Cres EH3 . . . . .93 A2
Royal Ct EH26 . . . . .191 D7
Royal (Dick) Veterinary Coll
EH8 . . . . .229 B1
Royal Edinburgh Hospl
EH10 . . . . .121 A3
Royal Garden Apartments
EH1 . . . . .229 A3
*Royal Highland Ctr (Royal
Highland Showground)*★
EH28 . . . . .117 E6
Royal High Prim Sch The
EH8 . . . . .122 D8
Royal High Sch The EH4 . .91 D3
Royal Hospl for Sick Children
EH9 . . . . .121 D5
Royal Infirmary of Edinburgh
EH16 . . . . .122 E1
Royal Lyceum Theatre The★
EH3 . . . . .228 B2
Royal Mile Prim Sch
EH8 . . . . .229 C3
Royal Observatory★ EH9 121 D2
Royal Park Pl █ EH8 . . . . .94 B1
Royal Park Terr EH8 . . . . .94 B1
Royal Scot Ct EH48 . . . .141 B6
Royal Scots Medway
EH19 . . . . .172 F5
Royal Scots Pl EH19 . . . .172 F6
Royal Scottish Acad★
EH2 . . . . .228 C3
Royal Scot Way KY12 . . . .29 A5
Royal Stuart Way FK7 . . . .7 E7
Royal Terr Edinburgh EH7 .229 C4
Linlithgow EH49 . . . . .84 F6
Royal Victoria Hospl EH4 . .92 C3
Royal Yacht Britannia The★
EH6 .93 F7
Roy Dr EH54 . . . . .164 F5
Royston Mains Ave EH5 . .92 E6
Royston Mains Cl EH5 . . . .92 D6
Royston Mains Cres EH5 . .92 D6
Royston Mains Gdns EH5 . .92 E6
Royston Mains Gn EH5 . . . .92 E6
Royston Mains Pl EH5 . . . .92 E6
Royston Mains Rd EH5 . . . .92 E6
Royston Mains St EH5 . . . .92 D6
Royston Prim Sch EH5 . . . .92 E6
Royston Rd EH54 . . . . . . .142 E7
Royston Rdbt EH54 . . . . . .142 D7
Royston Terr EH3 . . . . .93 B4
Rulley View FK6 . . . . .36 C4
Rullion Green Ave EH26 .191 D7
Rullion Green Cres EH26 191 D7
Rullion Green Gr EH26 . . .191 D7
Rullion Rd EH26 . . . . .191 C6
RUMBLINGWELL 28 D5
Rumblingwell KY12 . . . . . .28 D5
RUMFORD 82 E7
Rumlie The FK1 . . . . .108 A6
Run The EH51 . . . . .64 C7
Rushbank EH54 . . . . .143 E6
Ruskie Rd FK9 . . . . .2 B3
Ruskin Pl EH22 . . . . .174 E5
Russel Ct KY5 . . . . .14 B8
Russell Ave EH48 . . . . . . .139 F7
Russell Ct KY11 . . . . .29 F1
Russell Gdns EH12 . . . . . .120 E7
Russell Gr KY5 . . . . .33 F2
Russell Hill Ct KY5 . . . . . . .38 B1
Russell Pl Bathgate EH48 .141 A3
Bonnybridge FK4 . . . . .57 D5
Edinburgh EH5 . . . . .93 B6
█ Kirkcaldy KY1 . . . . .17 C5
Oakley KY12 . . . . .26 E2
Russell Rd Bathgate EH48 .141 A3
Edinburgh EH11 . . . . .120 E6
Russell St
Cowdenbeath KY4 . . . . .13 B4
Lochgelly KY5 . . . . .14 B8
Russell Way EH48 . . . . . .141 A3
Russel St FK2 . . . . .60 B6
Rutherford Ct
Bridge of Allan FK9 . . . . .2 A8
Kirkcaldy KY1 . . . . .17 E2
Rutherford Dr EH16 . . . . .122 B1
Rutherford Gdns EH46 . . .206 B1
Rutherford Sq EH54 . . . . .164 C6
Ruthven Pl EH16 . . . . .122 C1
Ruthven Rd EH39 . . . . .53 A4
Rutland Court La EH3 . . . .228 B2
Rutland Pl EH3 . . . . .228 B3
Rutland Sq EH1 . . . . .228 B3
Rutland St EH1 . . . . .228 B3
Ryebank EH54 . . . . .143 E6

Ryehill Ave EH6 . . . . .94 B3
Ryehill Gdns EH6 . . . . .94 B3
Ryehill Gr EH6 . . . . .94 B3
Ryehill Pl EH6 . . . . .94 B4
Ryehill Terr EH6 . . . . .94 B4
Rymalton KY1 . . . . .17 D6

S

Sacred Heart RC Prim Sch
█ Grangemouth FK3 . . . . . .61 E6
Penicuik EH26 . . . . .191 E5
Saddletree Loan EH16 . . .122 C2
Sailors' Wlk KY3 . . . . .50 D8
Sainford Cres FK2 . . . . .39 A1
St Alban's Rd EH9 . . . . . . .121 E3
St Andrew Pl EH6 . . . . .94 A4
St Andrew's Ct FK5 . . . . . . .38 B3
St Andrew's Dr north FK2 . .22 B7
Armadale EH48 . . . . .139 F7
Uphall EH52 . . . . .114 F4
St Andrew's RC High Sch
KY2 .17 D8
St Andrew's Rd Dunfermline
Falkirk FK1 . . . . .60 E4
Gorebridge EH23 . . . . .174 C2
St Andrew St
Dalkeith EH22 . . . . .153 A3
Dunfermline KY11 . . . . .29 C2
North Berwick EH39 . . . . . . .54 C7
St Andrew's Way EH54 . . .142 E6
St Andrews Way Bsns Units
EH54 . . . . .142 E5
St Anne's Ave EH18 . . . . .172 E6
St Anne's Cres FK7 . . . . . . .7 E1
St Anne's Ct EH22 . . . . . . .174 A5
St Ann's Path EH18 . . . . .172 E6
St Ann's Pl █ EH41 . . . . .130 B8
St Anthony La EH6 . . . . . . .93 F5
St Anthony Pl EH6 . . . . . . .93 F5
St Anthony's RC Prim Sch █
EH48 . . . . .139 F5
St Anthony St EH6 . . . . . . .93 F5
St Augustine's High Sch
EH12 . . . . .119 C4
St Baldred's Cres EH39 . . .54 D7
St Baldred's Ct EH39 . . . . .54 D7
St Baldred's Rd EH39 . . . . .54 D6
St Bernadette's RC Prim Sch
FK10 .4 A2
St Bernard's Cres EH4 . . . .93 A2
St Bernard's Row █ EH4 . .93 B2
St Bride's RC Prim Sch
KY4 .13 C3
St Bridgets Brae KY11 . . . .48 C4
St Brycedale Ave KY1 . . . . .17 B4
St Brycedale Ct KY1 . . . . . .17 B4
St Brycedale Rd KY1 . . . . . .17 B4
St Catherine Pl EH22 . . . . .82 F7
St Catherines Cres ML7 . .179 D6
St Catherine's Gdns
EH12 . . . . .120 A6
St Catherine's Manor
EH16 . . . . .120 A6
St Catherine's Pl EH9 . . . .121 E5
St Catherine's RC Prim Sch
EH16 . . . . .151 B5
St Catherine's Wynd KY12 .28 F3
St Clair Ave EH6 . . . . .94 A3
St Clair Cres EH25 . . . . . .171 A2
St Clair Pl EH6 . . . . .94 A3
St Clair Rd EH6 . . . . .94 A4
St Clair St KY3 . . . . .35 A2
St Clairs Entry KY3 . . . . . . .35 A2
St Clair St Edinburgh EH6 . .94 A3
Kirkcaldy KY1 . . . . .17 E2
St Clair Terr EH10 . . . . . . .120 F1
St Clement's Cres EH21 . .125 B4
St Clement's Gdns N
EH21 . . . . .125 B4
St Clement's Gdns S
EH21 . . . . .125 B4
St Clement's Terr EH21 . .125 B4
St Colme Ave KY3 . . . . .49 A5
St Colme Cres KY3 . . . . . . .49 B7
St Colme Dr KY11 . . . . .48 D5
St Colme Rd KY11 . . . . .48 D4
St Colme St EH3 . . . . .228 B4
St Colm's Abbey★ KY11 . . . .49 B2
St Colm's Ed Ctr & Coll
EH3 .93 B3
St Columba's RC High Sch
KY11 . . . . .29 F3
St Columba's RC Prim Sch
EH48 . . . . .141 E6
St Crispin's Pl FK1 . . . . . . .60 B4
St Crispin's Specl Sch
EH16 . . . . .121 E3
St Cuthbert's RC Prim Sch
EH14 . . . . .120 D4
St Davids EH22 . . . . .174 A5
St Davids Ave EH22 . . . . .153 A2
St David's Bsns Pk KY11 . .48 A4
St David's Ct
Dalgety Bay KY11 . . . . .48 A3
Larbert FK5 . . . . .38 B1
St David's Dr KY11 . . . . . . .48 A4
St Davids Gdns EH22 . . . .153 A1
St David's Pl EH3 . . . . .228 A2
St David's RC High Sch
EH22 . . . . .153 D5
St David's RC Prim Sch █
EH14 . . . . .92 C5
St David's RC Prim Sch
EH22 . . . . .153 C2

St Davids Terr EH22 . . . . .153 A2
St David's Terr EH3 . . . . .228 A2
St Enoch Cres EH54 . . . . .143 B6
St Fillans Cres KY3 . . . . . . .49 C8
St Fillans Gr KY3 . . . . .49 C8
St Fillans Pl KY2 . . . . .16 D7
St Fillans Rd KY2 . . . . .16 D7
St Fillan's Terr EH10 . . . .121 A1
St Francis RC Prim Sch
FK2 .60 A6
St Francis' RC Prim Sch
EH16 . . . . .122 E4
St Gabriel's RC Prim Sch █
EH32 . . . . .96 F1
St George's Ct FK5 . . . . . . .38 B1
St George's Sch EH12 . . . .120 E8
St Georges Sch for Girls
EH12 . . . . .120 D7
St Germains EH32 . . . . . . .98 B2
St Germains Cnr EH33 . . .126 D7
St Germains Terr EH33 . . .126 D7
St Giles Cathedral★ EH1 229 A3
St Giles Sq FK1 . . . . .59 B6
St Giles St EH1 . . . . .229 A3
St Giles Way FK1 . . . . .59 B6
St Helen's Pl EH48 . . . . . .139 F5
Sainthill Ct EH39 . . . . .54 C7
St James' Orch FK9 . . . . . . .2 B2
St James Pl Bridgend EH49 .86 F4
Kinghorn KY3 . . . . .35 A2
St James' Pl EH1 . . . . .229 A4
St James's Gdns EH26 . . .191 E4
St James Sh Ctr EH1 . . . .229 A4
St James's Pl EH1 . . . . . . .229 A4
St James's View EH26 . . .191 E4
St John Ogilvie RC Prim Sch
EH54 . . . . .142 F6
St John's Ave
Edinburgh EH12 . . . . .119 E6
Falkirk FK2 . . . . .60 C6
St John's Cres EH12 . . . . .119 E6
St John's Ct EH54 . . . . . . .143 E4
St John's Ct Falkirk FK2 . . .60 C6
Inverkeithing KY11 . . . . .47 D3
St John's Dr KY12 . . . . .29 C3
St John's Gate FK6 . . . . . . .36 C2
St John's Gdns Denny FK6 . .36 C2
St John's Gr FK6 . . . . .36 C2
St John's Hill EH8 . . . . . . .229 B2
St John's Hospl EH54 . . . .143 D4
St John's Pl
Dunfermline KY12 . . . . .29 D3
Torphichen EH48 . . . . .111 F5
St John's Prim Sch
Edinburgh EH15 . . . . .123 A7
Rosyth KY11 . . . . .46 F3
St John's Rd
Broxburn EH52 . . . . .115 E4
Edinburgh EH12 . . . . .119 E6
St John's Terr EH12 . . . . .119 E6
St John's Way EH51 . . . . . .63 F5
**St John the Baptist RC Prim
Sch** EH47 . . . . .181 E6
St John Vianney Prim Sch █
EH16 . . . . .122 B1
St Joseph's Cotts EH33 . . .126 D8
St Josephs RC Prim Sch
EH47 . . . . .160 F5
St Joseph's RC Prim Sch
Bonnybridge FK4 . . . . .58 B4
Edinburgh EH11 . . . . .119 F3
Linlithgow EH49 . . . . .84 F6
St Katharine's Brae EH16 151 A4
St Katharine's Cres EH16 151 A4
St Katharine's Loan
EH16 . . . . .151 B5
St Kentigern Rd EH26 . . .191 D6
St Kilda Cres KY2 . . . . .16 F8
St Laurence Cres FK1 . . . .108 B6
St Lawrence EH41 . . . . . . .129 E8
St Lawrence St KY11 . . . . . .29 C1
St Leonard's 229 C1
St Leonard's Bank EH8 . . .229 C1
St Leonard's Crag EH8 . . .229 C1
St Leonard's Ct KY3 . . . . . .35 A3
St Leonard's Hill EH8 . . . .229 B1
St Leonard's La EH8 . . . . .229 C1
St Leonard's Pl
Dunfermline KY11 . . . . .29 B2
Kinghorn KY3 . . . . .34 F3
St Leonard's Prim Sch
KY11 . . . . .29 B1
St Leonard's St
Dunfermline KY11 . . . . .29 B2
Edinburgh EH8 . . . . .229 B1
St Lukes RC Prim Sch
EH22 . . . . .174 D5
St Magaret Wynd KY12 . . .29 F6
St Magdalenes EH49 . . . . . .85 B7
St Margaret's Acad EH54 143 D3
St Margaret's Cave Mus★
KY12 . . . . .28 F4
St Margaret's Cres FK2 . . .61 E2
St Margarets Ct EH39 . . . . .54 C7
St Margarets Dr KY12 . . . . .29 B7
St Margaret's Dr EH49 . . .139 E5
St Margarets Gdns FK2 . . .61 E2
St Margaret's Pl EH9 . . . .121 C4

St Margaret's Prim Sch
Dunfermline KY11 . . . . .29 C3
Redding FK2 . . . . .61 D1
South Queensferry EH30 . . . .68 C1
St Margaret's RC Prim Sch
Cowie FK7 . . . . .20 D7
Loanhead EH20 . . . . .172 C8
St Margaret's Rd
Edinburgh EH9 . . . . .121 B4
North Berwick EH39 . . . . . . .54 C7
St Margaret's Sch EH16 . .122 A3
St Margaret St KY12 . . . . . .29 A3
St Margarets Well KY12 . . .29 B5
St Marie's RC Prim Sch
KY2 .17 D8
St Mark's La EH15 . . . . . . .123 B8
St Mark's Pl EH15 . . . . . . .123 B8
St Mark's RC Prim Sch
EH14 . . . . .149 E7
St Martin's Ct EH41 . . . . .130 B8
St Martin's Gate EH41 . . .130 B8
St Martins La EH33 . . . . . .126 E6
St Martin's RC Prim Sch
EH33 . . . . .126 D6
St Mary's Cathedral★
EH2 . . . . .228 A3
St Mary's Church★ EH41 130 B8
St Mary's Glebe KY1 . . . . . .17 C5
St Mary's (Leith) Prim Sch
EH6 .94 B5
St Mary's Music Sch
EH12 . . . . .120 F7
St Mary's Pl FK3 . . . . .61 F8
St Mary's Pl
Bathgate EH48 . . . . .141 C5
Edinburgh EH15 . . . . .123 C8
Kirkcaldy KY1 . . . . .17 C5
St Mary's Place La EH15 . .123 C8
*St Mary's Pleasance & Lady
Kitty's Garden*★ EH41 . . .130 B8
St Mary's RC Cath★ EH41 229 A4
St Mary's RC Prim Sch
Bannockburn FK7 . . . . .7 D2
Bathgate EH48 . . . . .141 A6
Bo'ness EH51 . . . . .64 A7
Bonnyrigg and Lasswade
EH19 . . . . .173 B6
█ Edinburgh EH7 . . . . .93 D2
Haddington EH41 . . . . .130 A8
Polbeth EH55 . . . . .163 F5
St Mary's Rd KY1 . . . . .17 C5
St Mary's St EH1 . . . . .229 B3
St Mary's Wynd █ FK8 . . . .7 A8
St Matthew's Prim Sch
EH24 . . . . .172 E2
St Michael's Ave EH21 . . .124 B5
St Michael's Hospl EH49 . .85 C6
St Michaels La EH49 . . . . . .85 B7
St Michael's Wynd EH49 . .85 A7
St Modans Ct █ FK1 . . . . . .60 B4
St Modan's High Sch FK7 . .7 F8
St Mungo's High Sch FK2 60 A6
St Mungo's RC Prim Sch
FK10 . . . . .10 C5
St Mungo's View EH26 . . .191 F5
St Mungo's Wynd FK10 . . .10 A6
St Nicholas RC Prim Sch
EH52 . . . . .115 C4
ST NINIANS 7 B4
St Ninian's Dr EH12 . . . . .119 D7
St Ninian's Prim Sch FK7 . .7 A4
St Ninian's Prim Sch EH7 94 C2
St Ninian's RC Prim Sch
EH54 . . . . .144 A1
St Ninians Rd
Cambusbarron FK7 . . . . .6 E5
Stirling FK7 . . . . .7 B6
St Ninian's Rd
Edinburgh EH12 . . . . .119 D7
Linlithgow EH49 . . . . .84 F7
St Ninian's Row EH1 . . . .229 A4
St Ninian's Terr EH10 . . . .120 F1
St Ninians Way
Blackness EH49 . . . . .65 E4
█ Musselburgh EH21 . . . . .125 A6
St Ninian's Way EH49 . . . .84 F7
St Patrick's Prim Sch
ML7 . . . . .179 F4
St Patrick's Sq EH8 . . . . . .229 B1
St Patrick's RC Prim Sch
FK6 .36 E3
St Patrick St EH8 . . . . .229 B1
St Paul's Dr EH48 . . . . . . .140 A5
St Paul's RC Prim Sch
EH53 . . . . .144 F4
St Peter's Bldgs EH11 . . .228 A1
St Peter's Ct KY11 . . . . .47 D2
St Peter's Pl EH11 . . . . . .228 A1
St Peter's RC Prim Sch EH10 121 B3
St Ronan's Terr EH10 . . . .121 A2
St Sarf's Pl KY11 . . . . .18 A7
St Serfs Gr FK10 . . . . .11 B4
St Serf's Pl FK10 . . . . .11 B4
St Serf's Prim Sch FK10 . . .4 B3
St Serf's Terr
EH22 . . . . .26 A2
St Serf's Rd FK10 . . . . .4 B3
St Serf's Wlk FK10 . . . . .4 E6
St Stephen Pl EH3 . . . . . . .93 B2
St Stephen's Ct EH11 . . . .119 C2
St Stephen St EH3 . . . . .93 B2
St Teresa Pl EH10 . . . . . . .120 F4
**St Thomas of Aquin's RC
High Sch** EH3 . . . . .228 C1
St Thomas Rd EH9 . . . . . .121 E3
St Thomas's Pl FK7 . . . . . . .6 E5

St Thomas's Well FK7 . . . . .6 D7
St Triduana's Chapel★
EH7 .94 C1
St Triduana's Rest EH7 . . .94 C2
St Valery Ct FK7 . . . . .7 A4
St Valery Dr FK7 . . . . .7 A4
St Vincent St EH3 . . . . .93 B2
Salamanca Cres EH26 . . .192 A8
Salamander Pl EH6 . . . . . . .94 B5
Salamander St EH6 . . . . . . .94 B5
Salamander Yds EH6 . . . . . .94 C5
Salen Loan ML7 . . . . .180 B3
Salisbury Mews EH9 . . . . .121 F5
Salisbury Pl EH9 . . . . .121 E5
Salisbury Rd EH16 . . . . . .121 F5
Salisbury St KY2 . . . . .17 B5
Salisbury View EH22 . . . .174 D6
Salisbury Wlk EH42 . . . . . .78 E1
Salmond Pl █ EH7 . . . . . . .94 A1
Salmon Dr FK1 . . . . .59 E1
Salmon Inn Pk FK2 . . . . . . .61 C2
Salmon Inn Rd FK2 . . . . . . .61 D2
Saltcoats Dr FK3 . . . . .61 E7
Saltcoats Farm Cotts
EH31 . . . . .52 B1
Saltcoats Gdns EH54 . . . .164 E6
Saltcoats Rd
Grangemouth FK3 . . . . .62 B8
Gullane EH31 . . . . .52 A2
Saltersgate Sch EH22 . . . .153 D5
Salters' Gr EH22 . . . . .153 C4
Salter's Rd EH22 . . . . .153 D6
Salters' Rd
Dalkeith, Woodburn
EH22 . . . . .153 C3
Pathhead EH37 . . . . .177 A2
Salter's Terr EH22 . . . . . .153 C3
Saltire Gdns EH39 . . . . . . .101 F7
Saltire Rd EH22 . . . . .153 C4
Saltire St EH5 . . . . .92 D7
Saltoun Hall EH41 . . . . . . .157 C5
Saltoun Prim Sch EH41 . .157 E5
Saltpans KY11 . . . . .45 B4
Salt Preston Pl EH32 . . . . .96 F1
Salvage Rd KY11 . . . . .46 C1
Salvesen Cres EH4 . . . . . . .92 A5
Salvesen Gdns EH4 . . . . . . .92 B5
Salvesen Gr EH4 . . . . .92 B6
Salvesen Terr EH4 . . . . . . .92 B6
Samoa Terr EH26 . . . . .192 A8
SAMUELSTON 129 A2
Samuelston East Mains Cotts
EH41 . . . . .129 A2
Sancta Maria Abbey★
EH41 . . . . .132 E1
Sandeman Ct EH3 . . . . .23 E4
Sanderling Way KY11 . . . . .30 B5
Sanderson's Gr █ EH23 . .126 D7
Sanderson's Wynd █
EH33 . . . . .126 D7
Sandersons Wynd Prim Sch
EH33 . . . . .126 D7
Sanderson Terr KY2 . . . . . .15 B2
Sandford Gate KY1 . . . . . . .17 E3
Sandford Gdns EH15 . . . .123 A8
Sandiland Dr EH53 . . . . . .144 B2
Sandilands KY11 . . . . .45 D3
Sandpiper Dr
Dunfermline KY11 . . . . .30 C2
Edinburgh EH6 . . . . .93 D7
Sandpiper Gdns KY11 . . . . .30 B1
Sandpiper Mdw FK10 . . . . .10 D5
Sandpiper Rd EH6 . . . . .93 D7
Sandport Pl EH6 . . . . .94 A6
Sandport Pl EH6 . . . . .93 F5
Sandport St EH6 . . . . .93 F6
Sandport Trad Est EH6 . . . .93 F6
Sands The EH41 . . . . .130 B8
Sandwell Cres KY1 . . . . . . .35 B6
Sandyford Ave EH49 . . . . . .84 A6
Sandyhill Ave ML7 . . . . . . .180 A3
Sandy La EH51 . . . . .51 F2
Sandyloan FK2 . . . . .61 B4
Sandy Loan Cres FK2 . . . . .61 B3
Sandy Rd KY3 . . . . .32 C5
Sandyvale Pl ML7 . . . . .180 A3
Sang Pl KY1 . . . . .17 B4
Sang Rd KY1 . . . . .17 B4
Sarazen Ct EH54 . . . . .143 B8
Sarazen Gn EH54 . . . . .143 B8
Sarti Terr FK5 . . . . .38 C3
Sauchenbush Rd KY2 . . . . .16 F5
Sauchenford Smallholdings
FK7 .20 A5
SAUCHIE 5 E1
Sauchiebank EH11 . . . . . . .120 C6
Sauchie Ct FK10 . . . . .5 B2
Sauchie St FK7 . . . . .7 A2
Saughbank EH52 . . . . .115 B5
Saughland Cotts EH37 . . .197 F7
Saughs The EH22 . . . . .174 A4
Saughton Ave EH11 . . . . .120 B6
Saughton Cres EH12 . . . . .120 B6
Saughton Gdns EH12 . . . .120 B6
Saughton Gn EH12 . . . . . .120 B6
Saughton Mains EH11 . . .120 A5
SAUGHTONHALL 120 C6
Saughtonhall Ave EH12 . .120 C6
Saughtonhall Avenue W
EH12 . . . . .120 B6
Saughtonhall Cir EH12 . . .120 C6
Saughtonhall Cres EH12 . .120 B6
Saughtonhall Dr EH12 . . . .120 B6
Saughtonhall Gdns EH12 .120 C6
Saughtonhall Gr EH12 . . . .120 C6
Saughtonhall Pl EH12 . . . .120 C6
Saughtonhall Terr EH12 . .120 C6

Saughton Loan EH12.....120 B6
Saughton Mains Ave
  EH11.....119 F3
Saughton Mains Bank
  EH11.....119 F4
Saughton Mains Dr EH11 119 F3
Saughton Mains Gdns
  EH11.....119 F4
Saughton Mains Gr
  EH11.....120 A3
Saughton Mains Loan
  EH11.....119 F4
Saughton Mains Pk
  EH11.....119 F4
Saughton Mains Pl EH11 .119 F3
Saughton Mains St EH11 .120 A4
Saughton Mains Terr
  EH11.....119 F4
Saughton Pk EH12.....120 B6
Saughton Rd EH11.....119 F3
Saughton Road N EH12 ..119 E5
Saughton Sports Complex
  EH11.....120 B4
Saunders Ct KY1.....17 B2
Saunders St
  Edinburgh EH3.....228 A4
  Kirkcaldy KY1.....17 B2
Savile Pl EH9.....121 F3
Savile Terr EH9.....121 F3
Sawers Ave FK6.....36 D1
Saw Mill Gdns EH19.....173 C5
Saw Mill Medway EH19 ..173 C5
Saxe Coburg Pl EH3.....93 B2
Saxe Coburg St EH3.....93 B2
Scarlett Pk EH21.....125 B5
Schaw Ct FK10.....5 D1
Schawpark Ave FK10.....5 D1
Schaw Rd EH32.....97 B1
Schiltron Way FK7.....7 D3
Scholars' Brae KY3.....50 E8
School Brae Bo'ness EH51. .63 F8
  Bonnyrigg and Lasswade
  EH18.....152 A1
  Dysart KY1.....18 A7
  Edinburgh EH4.....91 B6
  West Barns EH42.....105 F8
School Gn
  Bonnyrigg and Lasswade
  EH18.....152 A1
  Longniddry EH32.....98 E5
Schoolhouse Ct ML11...201 B3
Schoolhouse Ind Est
  EH55.....162 E2
School House Rd EH54. .142 E5
School La Allanton ML7 ..198 B8
  Bathgate EH48.....141 B6
  Cockenzie & Port Seton
  EH32.....97 C4
  Dalgety Bay KY11.....47 F4
  Menstrie FK11.....4 A7
  Mid Calder EH53.....144 D4
  South Queensferry EH30 ..68 B1
School Mews FK11.....4 A7
School Pl EH54.....114 F4
School Rd Aberlady EH32..71 C4
  Broxburn EH52.....115 D5
  East Linton EH40.....103 E7
  Laurieston FK2.....61 A3
  Longridge EH47.....161 C2
  North Berwick EH39.....54 D7
  Redding FK2.....61 B2
  Tullibody FK10.....4 B2
School Row KY12.....28 C6
School St
  Cowdenbeath KY4.....13 D3
  Shotts ML7.....179 E5
School View Bo'ness EH51. .64 A7
  Redding FK2.....61 C1
School Wlk FK5.....38 D3
School Wynd KY1.....17 B2
Schoolyard Ct EH25...172 A3
Sciennes EH9.....121 E5
Sciennes Gdns EH9.....121 F4
Sciennes Hill Pl ◪ EH9 ..121 E5
Sciennes House Pl ◪
  EH9.....121 E5
Sciennes Pl ◪ EH9.....121 E5
Sciennes Prim Sch EH9. 121 D5
Scion Ho FK9.....2 C5
Sclanderston Rd FK6.....57 C8
Scobie Pl KY12.....29 D4
Scollon Ave EH19.....173 C8
Scone Gdns EH8.....94 C1
Scotch Whisky Experience*
  EH1.....228 C2
Scotia Pl FK2.....60 C5
Scotland Dr KY12.....29 E4
Scotland St EH3.....93 C2
Scotmill Way KY11.....47 C3
Scots Mill Pl KY11.....47 E4
Scotstoun Ave EH30.....89 C7
Scotstoun Gn EH30.....89 B8
Scotstoun Pk EH30.....89 C7
Scotstoun Rd FK2.....20 E7
Scott Ave FK2.....61 E2
Scott Cres FK10.....10 B5
Scott Ct Alva FK12.....5 B6
  Kelty/Cowdenbeath KY4.....30 F6
  Livingston EH54.....144 C5
Scottish Agricultural Science
  Agency EH11.....119 A8
Scottish Fire Service Coll
  EH31.....52 B3
Scottish Korean War
  Memorial* EH48.....112 D6
Scottish Mining Mus The*
  EH22.....174 A4

Scottish Nat Gall of Modern
  Art* EH4.....120 E8
Scottish National Water Ski
  & Wakeboard Ctr The*
  KY12.....29 C7
Scottish Parliament The
  EH8.....229 C3
Scottish Pol Coll FK10....23 F5
Scottish Prison Service Coll
  ◪ FK2.....82 C8
Scottish Railway Exhibition*
  EH51.....64 A8
Scottish Seabird Ctr*
  EH39.....54 C8
Scott Mon* EH2.....229 A3
Scott Pl EH47.....181 F6
Scott Rd EH26.....5 D5
Scott St Dunfermline KY12 ..28 E5
  Grangemouth FK3.....61 D5
  Stirling FK8.....2 A2
Scott Terr Bathgate EH48..141 C5
  Falkirk FK2.....39 B1
SCOUGHALL.....56 C3
Scoughall Cotts EH39.....56 D3
Seabegs Cres FK4.....58 A4
Seabegs Pl FK4.....57 F4
Seabegs Rd FK4.....57 F4
Seabegs Wood Antonine
  Wall* EH57.....57 E3
SEACLIFF.....56 B5
Seacliff EH39.....56 A5
Sea Eagle Cres ◪ KY11...94 C4
SEAFIELD Edinburgh.....94 D4
  Livingston.....142 C1
  Loanhead.....171 D6
Seafield Ave EH6.....94 C4
Seafield Cl EH25.....171 E6
Seafield Cres
  Bilston EH25.....171 E6
  Dunbar EH42.....78 A1
  Kirkcaldy KY1.....35 B8
Seafield Ct ◪ FK1.....59 F2
Seafield Ind Est EH15.....94 F2
Seafield Moor Rd EH10,
  EH25.....171 C6
Seafield Pl
  Dalgety Bay KY11.....48 A2
  Edinburgh EH6.....94 C4
Seafield Prim Sch EH47. .142 B1
  Blackburn EH47.....162 F8
  Edinburgh EH6.....94 D4
  Kirkcaldy KY1.....35 B8
Seafield Rd Bilston EH25 .171 E6
Seafield Rows EH47.....142 B1
Seafield St EH6.....94 D4
Seafield Twrs ◪ KY1.....35 B8
Seafield View
  Kinghorn KY3.....35 A3
  Kirkcaldy KY1.....35 B8
Seafield Way EH15.....94 E3
Seaforth Dr EH4.....92 C2
Seaforth Pl Burntisland KY3 50 D8
  Kirkcaldy KY1.....17 F8
  ◪ Stirling FK8.....7 B8
Seaforth Rd FK2.....39 C1
Seaforth Terr
  Bonnyrigg and Lasswade
  EH19.....172 F6
  ◪ Edinburgh EH4.....92 C2
Sealcar St EH5.....92 E7
Seals Craig View ◪ KY3 ..33 D1
Sealstrand KY11.....48 C4
Seamill Gdns ◪ KY3.....33 D1
Seaport St EH6.....94 A5
Sea Rd EH42.....77 F1
Seaside Pl KY3.....49 C7
Seaton Pl FK1.....60 D4
Seaview Cres EH15.....123 E7
Seaview Pl EH15.....63 F8
Seaview Terr
  Edinburgh EH15.....123 E7
  Maddiston FK2.....82 F6
Sea Wynd EH32.....71 D5
Second Gait EH14.....147 E8
Second St EH22.....174 B5
Seco Pl KY4.....13 D4
Sedgebank EH54.....143 E6
Segal Pl KY12.....28 F4
Seggarsdean Cres EH41. 130 C7
Seggarsdean Ct EH41.....130 C8
Seggarsdean Pk EH41...130 D8
Selkirk Ave KY4.....13 C2
Selkirk Pl KY1.....67 B8
Selm Pk EH54.....144 A3
Selvage Pl KY11.....47 A3
Selvage St KY11.....47 A3
Semple St EH3.....228 B2
SETON.....97 E2
Seton Chapel* EH32 ....97 F3
Seton Ct
  Cockenzie & Port Seton
  EH32.....97 D4
  ◪ Tranent EH33.....126 C5
Seton Dr KY2.....16 D7
Seton Mains Cotts EH32..98 B3
Seton Pl
  Cockenzie & Port Seton
  EH32.....97 D4
  Dalgety Bay KY11.....48 D5
  Edinburgh EH9.....121 E5
  Kirkcaldy KY2.....16 D7
Seton Rd EH32.....98 E5
Seton Steading EH32.....98 B3
Seton Terr EH51.....64 B7

Seton View EH32.....97 E3
Seton Wynd EH32.....97 E4
Seventh St EH22.....174 B5
Shadepark Cres EH22.....153 B4
Shadepark Dr EH22.....153 B4
Shadepark Gdns EH22...153 B4
Shaftesbury Pk FK10.....10 A7
Shaftesbury St FK10.....10 A7
Shafto Pl EH51.....63 F5
Shamrock St KY12.....29 B5
Shandon Cres EH11.....120 E4
Shandon Pl EH11.....120 E4
Shandon Rd EH11.....120 E4
Shandon St EH11.....120 E4
Shandon Terr EH11.....120 E4
Shandwick Pl EH2.....228 A3
Shanks Ave FK6.....57 E8
Shanks Rd EH47.....161 B7
Shannon Dr FK1.....59 F4
Shanter Way ◪ EH16 ...122 A1
Sharpdale Loan EH16 ...122 B2
Sharp Terr FK3.....61 C6
Shaw Ave EH48.....139 F6
Shaw Cres KY5.....14 B7
Shaw Pl Armadale EH48 ..139 F6
  Grangemouth FK3.....61 C5
  Mayfield EH22.....174 D8
Shaw's Cres EH26.....171 A1
Shaws Ct EH26.....171 B1
Shaw's Pl EH7.....93 E3
Shaw's St EH7.....93 E3
Shaw St KY11.....29 D2
Shaw's Terr EH7.....93 E3
Shearer Sq KY11.....29 B1
Shearwater Cres KY11 ..30 A2
Sheephousehill EH47.....181 F6
Sheilings The FK10.....4 B1
Sheiling The KY12.....27 E1
Shepherd Cres EH48.....50 B8
Shepherdlands Gr KY12 ..26 D7
Sherbrooke Rd KY11.....46 D3
Sheriff Bank EH6.....93 F5
Sheriff Brae EH6.....93 F5
Sheriffhall Junc EH22. .152 D5
Sheriffhall Mains Cotts
  EH22.....152 E6
Sheriffmuirlands FK9.....2 C3
Sheriffmuir Rd FK9.....2 D7
Sheriff Pk EH6.....93 F5
Sheriffs Pk EH49.....85 E8
Sheriff Hall Cotts EH39 ..74 E8
Sheriff La EH54.....38 F3
Sherwood Ave EH19.....173 C6
Sherwood Cres EH19.....173 C6
Sherwood Ct EH19.....173 C6
Sherwood Dr EH19.....173 C6
Sherwood Gr EH19.....173 C6
Sherwood Ind Est EH19 .173 C7
Sherwood Loan EH19 ....173 C7
Sherwood Pk EH19.....173 C6
Sherwood Pl EH19.....173 C6
Sherwood Terr EH19.....173 C6
Sherwood View EH19 ....173 C6
Sherwood Wlk EH19.....173 D5
Shetland Ct FK10.....10 B5
Shetland Pl KY1.....17 E7
Shiel Ct FK3.....61 D4
SHIELDHILL.....81 D6
Shieldhill Prim Sch FK1. .81 D6
Shieldhill Rd FK2.....82 A8
Shields Ct EH52.....115 E5
Shields Rd KY11.....29 E3
Shiel Gdns Falkirk FK2.....39 C1
  Shotts ML7.....180 A3
Shiel Ho EH54.....144 A5
Shiel Wlk EH54.....144 A5
Shierlaw Gdns FK2.....22 D4
Shillinghill Alloa FK10.....10 B6
  Humbie EH36.....178 C1
Shinwell Pl KY11.....46 E3
Shiphaugh Pl FK8.....2 C1
Shire Way KY10.....9 F6
Shirra's Brae Rd FK7.....7 A4
Shoestanes Rd EH38 ....214 C2
Shoestanes Terr EH38 ..214 C2
SHORE.....7 C8
Shore EH6.....93 F5
Shore Pl EH6.....94 A5
Shore Rd Aberdour KY3 ..49 C7
  Airth FK2.....22 D4
  Dysart KY1.....18 B7
  South Queensferry EH30 ..68 B1
  Stirling FK8.....7 C8
Shore St EH42.....78 E3
Shore The FK10.....10 C5
Shorthope St EH21.....124 C6
SHOTTS.....179 F5
Shottsburn Rd ML7.....158 A3
Shottskirk Rd ML7.....179 C6
Shotts Rd
  Fauldhouse EH47.....181 C4
  Harthill ML7.....158 E2
  Shotts Sta ML7.....179 E4
Shrub Mount EH15.....95 A1
Shrub Place La EH7.....93 E3
Sibbald Pl EH54.....143 B5
Sibbalds Brae EH48.....140 D5
Sibbald View EH48.....140 A5
Sidegate EH41.....130 B8
Sidegate Mews EH41. .130 B8
Sidehead Rd ML7.....159 E5
Sidlaw Pl FK3.....61 C6
Sidlaw St KY2.....16 F7
Sienna Gdns EH9.....121 E5
SIGHTHILL.....119 D3

Sighthill Ave EH11.....119 E2
Sighthill Bank EH11.....119 D2
Sighthill Cres EH11.....119 D1
Sighthill Ct EH11.....119 D1
Sighthill Dr EH11.....119 D1
Sighthill Gdns EH11.....119 D1
Sighthill Gn EH11.....119 D2
Sighthill Gr EH11.....119 E2
Sighthill Ind Est EH11...119 B3
Sighthill Loan EH11.....119 D2
Sighthill Pk EH11.....119 E2
Sighthill Pl EH11.....119 D2
Sighthill Prim Sch EH11 .119 C1
Sighthill Rd EH11.....119 D2
Sighthill Rise EH11.....119 D1
Sighthill Sh Ctr EH11 ...119 D2
Sighthill St EH11.....119 D2
Sighthill Terr EH11.....119 D2
Sighthill View EH11.....119 D1
Sighthill Wynd EH11.....119 D2
Signal Station KY11.....68 C5
Silk Ho KY1.....60 B5
Silverbarton Terr KY3.....33 D1
Silverburch Glade EH54. .164 C7
SILVERBURN.....190 E5
Silverburn Dr EH26.....191 C6
Silverburn Gdns FK12.....5 C7
Silverdale Rd FK2.....82 E8
SILVERKNOWES.....91 E5
Silverknowes Ave EH4 ...91 F4
Silverknowes Bank EH4 ..91 F4
Silverknowes Brae EH4 ..92 A4
Silverknowes Cres EH4 ..91 F4
Silverknowes Ct EH4.....91 F4
Silverknowes Dell EH4 ...91 F4
Silverknowes Dr EH4.....91 F4
Silverknowes Eastway
  EH4.....91 F4
Silverknowes Gdns EH4 ..92 A4
Silverknowes Gn EH4.....91 F4
Silverknowes Gr EH4.....91 F5
Silverknowes Hill EH4 ...91 F4
Silverknowes Loan EH4 ..91 F4
Silverknowes Midway
  EH4.....92 A4
Silverknowes Neuk EH4 ..92 A3
Silverknowes Parkway
  EH4.....91 F5
Silverknowes Pl EH4.....91 F5
Silverknowes Rd EH4.....91 F5
Silverknowes Road E EH4 92 A4
Silverknowes Road S EH4. 91 F3
Silverknowes Southway
  EH4.....92 A4
Silverknowes Terr EH4 ...91 F4
Silverknowes View EH4 ..92 A4
Silver St Dunbar EH42.....78 D2
  Kincardine FK10.....23 E3
  ◪ Kirkcaldy KY1.....17 F7
Simon Sq EH8.....229 B2
Simpson Cres EH48.....141 C5
Simpson Dr FK2.....83 A6
Simpson Parkway EH54. .143 B2
Simpson Prim Sch EH48 .141 B3
Simpson Rd EH52.....116 B6
Simpson St EH3.....228 B1
Simpson Wlk KY11.....29 B1
Sinclair Cl EH11.....120 E4
Sinclair Cres FK6.....36 D1
Sinclair Ct Aberlady EH32...71 C4
  Bannockburn FK7.....7 E1
Sinclair Dr
  Cowdenbeath KY4.....13 B2
  Fallin FK7.....8 D4
Sinclair Pl
  Dunfermline KY12.....29 B4
  Edinburgh EH11.....120 E5
Sinclair Rd
  Edinburgh EH11.....120 D5
  Falkirk FK2.....39 A1
SINCLAIRTOWN.....17 F7
Sinclairtown Prim Sch
  KY1.....17 F7
Sinclair Way EH54.....143 D6
Singers Pl FK4.....57 E5
Sir George Bruce Rd KY12. 26 F7
Sir Harry Lauder Rd
  EH15.....123 B8
Sir James Black Gait KY5 .14 A8
Sir John Brown Pl KY11 ..46 F7
Sir John Graham Ct FK5 ..38 B1
Sirling Arcade ◪ FK8.....7 B7
Sir Robert Maule Pl EH7 ..23 E4
Sir Walter Scott Pend
  EH32.....96 F2
Sir William Fraser Homes
  EH13.....149 A7
Sir William Wallace Ct
  FK5.....38 B3
Sivewright Ct FK10.....23 E4
Sixth St EH22.....174 B5
Skaithmuir Ave FK2.....39 B3
Skaithmuir Cres FK2.....39 B3
Skedsbush Cotts EH41. .220 D5
Skelmorlie Pl FK5.....38 F4
Skeltiemuir Ave EH19 ...173 A5
Skeltiemuir Ct EH19.....173 B5
Skeltiemuir Gr EH19.....173 B5
Skene St FK4.....58 A6
Skibo Ct KY12.....29 A3
Skibo Pl KY11.....16 D5
SKINFLATS.....39 F3
Skivo Wynd EH54.....164 E4
Skye Ct FK3.....61 D6
Skye Cres FK2.....61 D6
Skye Rd KY11.....29 E2
Skylark Rd KY11.....47 A7
Skylaw Terr ML11.....201 A1

Skython Way FK1.....59 E2
Slaeside EH14.....147 C1
SLAMANNAN.....108 A6
Slamannan Prim Sch
  FK1.....108 A7
Slamannan Rd
  Avonbridge FK1.....109 F6
  Falkirk FK1.....60 A2
  Limerigg FK1.....108 B2
SLATEFORD.....120 C2
Slateford Gn EH14.....120 D4
Slateford Rd EH14.....120 D4
Slateford Sta EH14.....120 C3
Sleigh Dr EH7.....94 C2
Sleigh Gdns EH7.....94 C2
Sligo St KY12.....26 F7
Sloan St EH6.....93 F3
Smallburn Pl FK3.....61 E6
Small St KY1.....14 A6
Smart Village Bsns Campus
  KY10.....9 E7
SMEATON.....153 E8
Smeaton Farm Cotts
  EH22.....153 E8
Smeaton Gdns KY7.....17 C6
Smeaton Gr EH21.....124 D3
Smeaton Ind Site KY1 ...17 C7
Smeaton Rd KY1.....17 D6
Smiddy Brae FK2.....61 F4
Smiddy View FK7.....6 D6
Smiddy Wynd Alva FK12 ..5 A6
  East Linton EH40.....103 E7
  Newmills KY12.....26 C1
Smileyknowes Ct EH39 ...54 A6
Smillie Terr FK9.....2 B3
Smith Art Gallery & Mus*
  FK8.....7 A8
Smith Ave KY4.....13 B3
Smithfield Loan FK10 ....9 E6
Smithfield Mdws FK10 ...9 E6
Smithfield St EH11.....120 D5
Smith Pl FK6.....36 D1
Smith's Pl EH6.....94 A5
Smith's Terr ◪ KY1.....17 C5
Smithy Brae FK10.....145 E2
Smithy Green Ave EH22 .152 B7
Smithy Row EH39.....74 E3
Snab Brae EH51.....63 D6
Snab La EH51.....63 D7
Sneddon Pl FK2.....22 E3
Snowdon Pl FK8.....7 A6
Snowdon Place La FK7 ...7 A6
Society La EH55.....163 D3
Society Pl EH55.....163 D3
Society Rd EH30.....63 F2
Solway Dr FK6.....57 D7
Somerset Pl EH6.....94 A4
Somers Pk ◪ EH29.....28 E4
Somerville Rd KY11.....46 C2
Somerville Sq KY3.....50 E8
Somerville St KY3.....50 E8
Sommers Pk EH55.....144 C2
Sommerville Gdns EH30...89 D7
Somnerfield Ave EH41 ..129 E8
Somnerfield Cres EH41 .129 F8
Somnerfield Ct EH41.....129 F8
Somnerfield Gr EH41.....129 E8
Somnerfield Pk EH41 ...129 F8
Souillac Dr FK6.....36 C1
South Approach Rd FK2. .23 B2
South Ave Blairhall KY12 ..26 A7
  Maddiston FK2.....83 B7
Southbank EH4.....91 E4
Southbank Ct EH4.....91 E4
South Bantaskine Dr FK1. .60 A3
South Bantaskine Rd FK1. .60 A3
South Barnton Ave FK1 ..91 E3
South Beechwood EH12. .120 A6
South Belton Farm Cotts
  EH42.....105 E7
South Brae FK2.....83 A5
South Bridge EH1.....229 A3
South Bridge St
  Bathgate EH48.....141 A6
  Grangemouth FK3.....40 C1
SOUTH BROOMAGE.....38 D1
South Broomage Ave FK5 .38 C1
South Castle Dr KY11 ...46 F6
South Charlotte St EH2 .228 B3
South Clerk St EH8.....229 B1
South College St EH1 ...229 A2
South Doors EH32.....97 C4
South East Circus Pl
  EH3.....228 B4
South East Cumberland
  Street La EH3.....93 C2
South East Longridge Crofts
  EH47.....161 E2
South Elixa Pl EH8.....122 D8
Southend EH22.....174 B7
Southerton Cres KY2 ....16 F3
Southerton Gdns KY2 ...16 F3
Southerton Rd KY2.....16 F3
South Ettrick Rd EH10 ..120 F4

South Fergus Pl KY1 . . . . . . 17 B3
Southfield KY4 . . . . 13 C5
Southfield Ave ML7 . . . . . . 180 B4
Southfield Bank EH15 . . . . 122 F6
Southfield Cres
  Shotts ML7 . . . . 180 B4
  Stirling FK8 . . . . 7 A6
Southfield Ct EH42 . . . . 78 B2
Southfield Dr FKL 108 A6
Southfield Farm Gr EH15 122 E7
Southfield Gardens E
  EH15 . . . . 122 F7
Southfield Gardens W
  EH15 . . . . 122 F6
Southfield Loan EH15 . . . . 122 F6
Southfield Pl EH15 . . . . . . 123 A8
Southfield Rd
  Cousland EH22 . . . . 154 D5
  Shotts ML7 . . . . 180 B4
Southfield Road E EH15 . 122 F6
Southfield Road W EH15 122 F6
Southfield Sq EH15 . . . . . . 122 F6
Southfield Terr EH15 . . . . . 122 F6
South Fort St EH6 . . . . 93 E5
South Gait EH39 . . . . 53 F7
South Gayfield La **3** EH7 . 93 E2
South Gillsland Rd EH10 . 120 F3
South Grange Ave EH32 . . 96 F1
South Gray's Cl EH1 . . . . . 229 B3
South Gray St EH9 . . . . . . 121 F4
South Green Dr FK2 . . . . . 22 E3
South Groathill Ave EH4 . 92 C2
SOUTH GYLE 119 B4
South Gyle Access EH12 . 119 C4
South Gyle Broadway
  EH12 . . . . 119 B4
South Gyle Cres EH12 . . . 119 B4
South Gyle Crescent La
  EH12 . . . . 119 B4
South Gyle Gdns EH12 . . . 119 B5
South Gyle Ind Est EH12 119 B4
South Gyle Loan EH12 . . . 119 B5
South Gyle Mains EH12 . . 119 C5
South Gyle Pk EH12 . . . . . 119 B5
South Gyle Rd EH12 . . . . . 119 B5
South Gyle Sta EH12 . . . . 119 B5
South Gyle Wynd EH12 . . 119 C4
South Hamilton Rd **1**
  EH39 . . . . 54 A7
South Hill St KY3 . . . . 50 E8
South Hirst Rd ML7 . . . . . 158 D3
SOUTHHOUSE 151 C5
Southhouse Ave EH17 . . . 151 B5
Southhouse Brae EH17 . . 151 C5
Southhouse Broadway
  EH17 . . . . 151 B4
Southhouse Cres EH17 . . 151 C4
Southhouse Dr EH17 . . . . 151 B5
Southhouse Gdns EH17 . . 151 B4
Southhouse Gr EH17 . . . . 151 B4
Southhouse Medway
  EH17 . . . . 151 B4
Southhouse Pl EH17 . . . . 151 B5
Southhouse Rd EH17 . . . . 151 B4
Southhouse Sq EH17 . . . . 151 B5
Southhouse Terr EH17 . . . 151 C4
Southhouse Wlk EH17 . . . 151 B5
South Kersebonny Steading
  FK8 . . . . 6 C7
South Knowe KY4 . . . . 30 E5
South Larch Rd KY11 . . . . 29 F4
South Lauder Rd EH9 . . . 121 E4
South Laverockbank Ave
  EH5 . . . . 93 C6
Southlawn Ct EH4 . . . . 91 E4
South Learmonth Ave **4**
  EH4 . . . . 92 F1
South Learmonth Gdns **2**
  EH4 . . . . 92 F1
SOUTH LEITH 94 A5
South Loanhead KY11 . . . 45 E3
South Loch Pk EH48 . . . . 141 A6
South Lodge Ave EH53 . . 144 C2
South Lorimer Pl EH32 . . . 97 C3
South Lorne Pl **1** EH6 . . . 93 F3
South Lumley St FK3 . . . . 61 D8
South Mains FK7 . . . . 9 B1
South Marshall St FK1 . . . 60 D7
South Maybury EH12 . . . . 119 A6
South Mellis Pk EH8 . . . . 122 E8
South Melville La **4** FK1 . 60 B5
South Middleton EH52 . . . 115 A3
South Mid St EH48 . . . . . . 141 B6
South Morningside Prim Sch
  EH10 . . . . 121 A1
South Morton St EH15 . . . 123 C7
South Oswald Rd EH9 . . . 121 D3
Southouse Cl EH17 . . . . . 151 B4
Southouse Crossway
  EH17 . . . . 151 B4
South Overgate KY3 . . . . . 35 A3
South Oxford St EH8 . . . . 121 F5
Southpark Pl EH54 . . . . . 143 B4
South Parrotshot EH15 . . 123 B8
South Philipingstone La
  EH51 . . . . 64 C7
South Pilmuir Rd FK10 . . . 11 A4
South Pk Armadale EH48 . 139 F4
  Edinburgh EH6 . . . . 93 E5
South Pleasance Ave FK1 . 60 B4
SOUTH QUEENSFERRY . . 68 B2
South Rd
  Fauldhouse EH47 . . . . . 181 E7
  Grangemouth FK3 . . . . . 62 B5
South Roundall KY11 . . . . 45 E3

South Row
  Charlestown KY11 . . . . . . 45 B4
  Kirkcaldy KY1 . . . . 17 E8
South St Andrew St EH2 229 A4
South St David St EH2 . . 229 A3
South Scotstoun EH30 . . . 89 C7
South Seton Pk EH32 . . . . 97 D4
South Shore Rd FK3 . . . . . 41 B2
SOUTH SIDE 229 A1
South Sloan St EH6 . . . . . 93 F3
South St Armadale EH48 . 139 F5
  Bo'ness EH51 . . . . 63 F8
  Cambus FK10 . . . . 9 B8
  Cowdenbeath KY4 . . . . . 13 C2
  Dalkeith EH22 . . . . 153 A3
  Dunbar EH42 . . . . 78 B2
  Lochgelly KY5 . . . . 14 B6
  Musselburgh EH21 . . . . 124 B6
  Stirling FK9 . . . . 2 D1
South Steil EH11 . . . . 120 E1
South Trinity Rd EH5 . . . . . 93 B5
South View Burntisland KY3. 50 F8
  Prestonpans EH32 . . . . . 97 A1
  Stenhousemuir FK5 . . . . 38 D1
South Village EH51 . . . . 64 C5
South West Cumberland
  Street La EH3 . . . . 93 C2
  Soutra Aisle* EH37 . . . 224 D5
Sovereign Ct EH48 . . . . . . 140 B5
Spalding Cres EH22 . . . . 153 B3
Spa Pl EH15 . . . . 95 B1
Speedwell Ave EH22 . . . . 152 A8
Spence Ave KY3 . . . . 33 F2
Spencerfield Rd KY11 . . . . 47 D2
Spencerfield Steadings
  KY11 . . . . 47 E3
Spencer Pl Edinburgh EH5 . 93 B6
  Kirkcaldy KY1 . . . . 17 F6
Spence St Bonnybridge FK4 . 58 A6
  Edinburgh EH16 . . . . . . 121 F5
Spens La KY11 . . . . 46 C1
Spey Ct Grangemouth FK3. . 61 D5
  Stirling FK7 . . . . 7 C5
Spey Dr EH54 . . . . 144 B4
Spey St EH7 . . . . 93 E3
Spey Street La EH7 . . . . . . 93 E3
Spey Terr EH7 . . . . 93 E3
Spier's Pl EH6 . . . . 93 F5
Spilmersford View EH34 .157 A6
Spinkhill KY2 . . . . 16 C1
Spinnaker Way KY11 . . . . . 47 F2
Spinner's Ct KY12 . . . . 27 D1
Spinneys The KY11 . . . . . . 48 C3
Spinney The EH17 . . . . . . 151 D6
Spitfire Way FK3 . . . . 61 F5
SPITTAL 99 D7
Spittalfield Cres
  Edinburgh EH8 . . . . 229 B1
  Inverkeithing KY11 . . . . . 47 C2
Spittalfield Rd KY11 . . . . . . 47 C2
Spittal Hill FK9 . . . . 2 C4
Spittal St Edinburgh EH3 . 228 B2
  Stirling FK8 . . . . 7 A8
SPOTT 106 C4
Spott Ave EH42 . . . . 106 D3
Spottiswoode Gdns
  EH53 . . . . 144 C2
Spottiswoode Rd EH9 . . 121 C5
Spottiswoode St EH9 . . . 121 C5
Spott Loan EH42 . . . . 106 C3
Spott Rd EH42 . . . . 78 E1
Spott Road Ind Est EH42 . 78 E1
Sprig Way ML7 . . . . 159 E5
Springbank Gdns FK2 . . . . 60 C5
Springbank Rd
  Shotts ML7 . . . . 179 D6
  Stirling FK7 . . . . 7 C6
Springbank Terr KY12 . . . . 29 A6
Springfield EH6 . . . . 93 F4
Springfield Cres
  3 North Berwick EH39 . . 54 A7
  Queensferry EH30 . . . . . . 68 B8
Springfield Ct EH49 . . . . . . 85 D8
Springfield Dr FK1 . . . . 59 F5
Springfield Gdns **3** EH39 . 54 A7
Springfield La **3** EH6 . . . . 93 F4
Springfield Lea EH30 . . . . . 67 F1
Springfield Pl
  Gorebridge EH23 . . . . . . 195 D7
  Queensferry EH30 . . . . . . 67 F1
  Roslin EH25 . . . . 172 A4
Springfield Prim Sch
  EH49 . . . . 85 D8
Springfield Rd Alloa FK10 . 10 C7
  Denny FK6 . . . . 36 F2
  Linlithgow EH49 . . . . 85 D7
  Penicuik EH26 . . . . 208 E6
  Queensferry EH30 . . . . . . 67 F1
  Stirling FK7 . . . . 7 C5
Springfield St EH6 . . . . 93 F4
Springfield Terr
  Queensferry EH30 . . . . . . 67 F1
  West Barns EH42 . . . . . . 77 F1
Springfield View EH30 . . . . 68 A1
Spring Gdns EH8 . . . . 94 A1
Springhead Rd ML7 . . . . . 198 A8
SPRINGHILL 180 B2
Springhill Brae KY4 . . . . . . 30 F6
Springhill & Leadloch Rd ML7,
  EH47 . . . . 180 E2
Springhill Rd ML7 . . . . . . 180 B3
Springhill View ML7 . . . . . 180 B3
Springkerse Bsns Pk FK7 . 7 E7
Springkerse Ind FK7 . . . . . . 7 D7
Springkerse Rd FK7 . . . . . . 7 D6
Springkerse Rdbt FK7 . . . . 7 C7
Springkerse Ret Pk FK7 . . 7 E6
Springvalley Gdns EH10. .121 A3

Springvalley Terr EH10. . .121 A3
Springwell Pl EH11 . . . . . 120 F6
Springwood
  Dunfermline KY11 . . . . . . 47 A7
  Stirling FK7 . . . . 6 F5
Springwood Ave FK8. . . . . . 6 F5
Springwood Pk EH16. . . . 151 B8
Sprinty Ave EH35 . . . . 155 D7
Sprinty Dr EH35 . . . . 155 D7
Sprotwell Terr FK10 . . . . . . 5 D1
Spruce Dr EH47 . . . . 161 C6
Spruce Gr
  Dunfermline KY11 . . . . . . 46 D8
  Livingston EH54 . . . . . . 144 B5
Spylaw Ave EH13 . . . . 148 F7
Spylaw Bank Rd EH13 . . 149 A7
Spylaw Pk EH13 . . . . 148 F7
Spylaw Pk EH13 . . . . 148 F7
Spylaw Rd EH10 . . . . 120 F4
Spylaw St EH13 . . . . 149 B7
Square The
  Cockburnspath TD13 . . . 218 F4
  Danderhall EH22 . . . . . . 152 B8
  East Linton EH40 . . . . . . 103 E7
  Fallin FK7 . . . . 8 C3
  Gifford EH41 . . . . 220 F7
  Kirkliston EH29 . . . . 89 B1
  Newtongrange EH22 . . . 174 B5
  Penicuik EH26 . . . . 191 F4
  Spott EH42 . . . . 106 C3
  Torphichen EH48 . . . . . . 111 F5
Sraehouse Wynd ML8 . . 215 B1
Stable Ct EH42 . . . . 78 E2
Stable La Edinburgh EH10. 121 A4
  West Calder EH55 . . . . . 164 A5
Stable Rd ML7 . . . . 180 A4
Stables Rd KY11 . . . . 46 C1
Stables The
  Newtongrange EH22 . . . 174 A8
  Pathhead EH37 . . . . 175 E8
Stadium House Bsns Ctr
  EH54 . . . . 143 D2
Staffa EH54 . . . . 142 E5
Staffa Pl FK1 . . . . 60 B2
Stafford St EH3 . . . . 228 A3
Stair Pk Edinburgh EH12 . 120 C7
  North Berwick EH39 . . . . 54 B6
  Tranent EH33 . . . . 126 B7
Stance Pl FK5 . . . . 38 A3
Standalane FK10 . . . . 23 E3
STANDBURN 82 D2
Standhill Ct EH48 . . . . . . 140 F4
Standhill Rd EH48 . . . . . . 140 F4
Standingstane Rd EH30 . . 89 E5
Standing Stone Wlk KY11 . 29 E1
Standrigg Ave FK2 . . . . 82 C7
Standrigg Gdns FK2 . . . . . 82 D7
Standrigg Rd FK2 . . . . 82 B6
STANE 180 A3
Stanedykehead EH16 . . . 150 F6
Stane Gr ML7 . . . . 180 A3
Stane Prim Sch ML7 . . . . 180 A4
Stane Rd ML7 . . . . 180 A2
Stanhope Pl EH12 . . . . . . 120 E7
Stanhope St EH12 . . . . . . 120 E7
Stanistone Rd ML8 . . . . . 215 A2
Stankards Rd EH27 . . . . . 114 F3
Stanley Ave EH25 . . . . . . 171 E6
Stanley Dr
  Bridge of Allan FK9 . . . . . 2 B7
  Harthill ML7 . . . . 160 A6
Stanley Gdns FK2 . . . . 82 F6
Stanley Pk KY1 . . . . 17 B5
Stanley Pl Dunbar EH42 . . 78 C3
  Edinburgh EH7 . . . . 94 A1
  Ormiston EH35 . . . . 155 E7
Stanley Rd Edinburgh EH6 . 93 D6
  Gullane EH31 . . . . 52 A2
  Harthill ML7 . . . . 160 A6
Stanley St EH15 . . . . 95 A1
Stanley Terr Alva FK12 . . . . 5 A6
  Oakley KY12 . . . . 27 A6
Stanton Ave FK10 . . . . 9 F6
Stanwell St EH6 . . . . 93 E4
Stapeley Ave EH7 . . . . 94 E2
Starbank Rd EH5 . . . . 93 C6
Starch Mill EH41 . . . . 130 C8
Stark Ave FK1 . . . . 59 D5
Stark's Brae EH51 . . . . 64 A7
Stark's Park (Raith Rovers)
  KY1 . . . . 17 A1
Starlaw Ave EH48 . . . . 141 E5
Starlaw Bsns Pk EH54 . . 142 D4
Starlaw Cres EH48 . . . . . . 141 F5
Starlaw Gdns EH48 . . . . . 141 F5
Starlaw Rd EH47 . . . . 142 C3
Starlaw Terr EH48 . . . . . . 141 E5
Starlaw West Rdbt EH47 . 142 A3
Starlaw Wlk EH48 . . . . . . 141 F5
Starley Hall Sch KY3 . . . . . 50 B5
Starryshaw Rd ML7 . . . . . 179 E6
Station Ave EH41 . . . . 129 F8
Station Brae
  Edinburgh EH15 . . . . . . 123 A7
  Kinghorn KY3 . . . . 34 F2
Station Ct Addiewell EH55 162 E2
  Haddington EH41 . . . . . 129 F8
  North Berwick EH39 . . . . 54 B7
Station Hill EH39 . . . . 54 B7
Station Loan EH14 . . . . . . 147 C3
Station Mews EH27 . . . . . 145 D3
Station Pl KY3 . . . . 50 E8
Station Rd Addiewell EH55 162 E2
  Armadale EH48 . . . . 139 F3
  Bannockburn FK7 . . . . 7 F7
  Blackridge EH48 . . . . . . 138 D2
  Bridge of Allan FK9 . . . . . 1 F8
  Brightons FK2 . . . . 61 E1

Station Rd *continued*
  Broxburn EH52 . . . . 115 E5
  Cambus FK10 . . . . 4 B1
  Cowdenbeath KY4 . . . . . . 13 D1
  Cowie FK7 . . . . 20 D6
  Dalkeith EH22 . . . . 152 E2
  Dirleton EH39 . . . . 53 D3
  Dunbar EH42 . . . . 78 E2
  Dunfermline KY11 . . . . . . 18 A7
  East Linton EH40 . . . . . . 103 E7
  Edinburgh EH11 . . . . 119 E6
  Gifford EH41 . . . . 220 F7
  Gorebridge EH23 . . . . . . 195 C7
  Grangemouth FK3 . . . . . . 40 D1
  Gullane EH31 . . . . 52 B2
  Haddington EH41 . . . . . 130 A8
  Kincardine FK10 . . . . 23 D4
  Kirkliston EH29 . . . . 89 B1
  Kirknewton EH27 . . . . . . 145 D3
  Linlithgow EH49 . . . . 85 A7
  Loanhead EH20 . . . . 172 C8
  Lochgelly KY5 . . . . 14 B8
  Longcroft FK4 . . . . 57 B4
  Musselburgh EH21 . . . . 124 B5
  Newtongrange EH22 . . . 174 A5
  North Berwick EH39 . . . . 54 B7
  Oakley KY12 . . . . 26 F6
  Prestonpans EH32 . . . . . 96 E6
  Ratho Station EH28 . . . . 117 C5
  Roslin EH25 . . . . 172 A3
  Shotts ML7 . . . . 179 E4
  Slamannan FK1 . . . . 108 B6
  South Queensferry EH30 . 68 C1
  Stirling FK8 . . . . 7 B8
  Uphall EH52, EH54 . . . . 114 F3
  West Calder EH55 . . . . . 163 D3
  Whitecross EH49 . . . . 83 F6
  Winchburgh EH52 . . . . . . 88 A3
Station Row
  Macmerry EH33 . . . . 127 C5
  Slamannan FK1 . . . . 108 B5
Station Terr EH29 . . . . 89 B1
Station View EH30 . . . . 89 D8
Station Yd KY3 . . . . 35 A2
Staunton Rise EH54 . . . . 164 D8
Steadings Cres EH42 . . . 106 D8
Steadings The Airth FK2 . . 21 E5
  Fallin FK7 . . . . 8 A4
  Whitecross EH49 . . . . 84 B8
Steading The
  Longniddry EH32 . . . . . . 98 C2
  Mid Calder EH53 . . . . . . 144 B3
Steads' Pl EH6 . . . . 93 F4
Steel Cres FK6 . . . . 36 F1
Steele Ave EH22 . . . . 174 F6
Steel Gr KY12 . . . . 26 D7
Steel's Pl EH10 . . . . 121 B3
Steelyard The **4** EH48 . . 141 A6
Steeple Cres KY11 . . . . 48 A3
Steil Gr EH33 . . . . 126 D5
Steils The EH11 . . . . 120 E1
Stein's Pl KY4 . . . . 13 C3
Stein Sq FK7 . . . . 7 F1
STENHOUSE 120 B4
Stenhouse Ave EH11 . . . 120 B4
Stenhouse Ave W EH11 . 120 A4
Stenhouse Cotts EH11 . . 120 A3
Stenhouse Cres EH11 . . . 120 B4
Stenhouse Cross EH11 . . 120 A4
Stenhouse Dr
  Burntisland KY3 . . . . 33 C1
  Edinburgh EH11 . . . . 120 A4
Stenhouse Gdns EH11 . . 120 A4
Stenhouse Gdns N EH11 . 120 A4
Stenhouse Gr EH11 . . . . . 120 A4
Stenhouse Mill Cres
  EH11 . . . . 120 B3
Stenhouse Mill La EH11 . 120 B3
Stenhouse Mill Wynd
  EH11 . . . . 120 B3
STENHOUSEMUIR 38 D3
Stenhousemuir Prim Sch
  FK5 . . . . 38 D3
Stenhouse Pl E EH11 . . . 120 A4
Stenhouse Pl W EH11 . . . 120 A4
Stenhouse Prim Sch **1**
  EH11 . . . . 120 A4
Stenhouse Rd
  Edinburgh EH11 . . . . 120 A3
  Stenhousemuir FK2 . . . . 38 F2
Stenhouse St E EH11 . . . 120 A4
Stenhouse St W
  Burntisland KY4 . . . . 13 B4
  Edinburgh EH11 . . . . 119 F4
Stenhouse Terr EH11 . . . 120 B4
Stennis Gdns EH17 . . . . . 151 B5
STENTON 104 C1
Stenton Loan EH14 . . . . . 133 E8
Stenton Prim Sch EH42 . 104 C1
Stenton Rd EH42 . . . . 105 F8
Stephen Pl KY5 . . . . 14 B8
Stephens Croft FK2 . . . . . . 59 F8
Stephen's Dr KY11 . . . . . . 47 C3
Steps St FK5 . . . . 38 E3
Steuart Rd FK9 . . . . 1 F7
Stevenslaw's Cl EH22 . . . 220 C3
Stevenson Ave
  Edinburgh EH11 . . . . 120 C5
  Polmont FK2 . . . . 61 D1
Stevenson Coll EH11 . . . 119 C3
Stevenson Ct
  Bridge of Allan FK9 . . . . . 2 A5
  Haddington EH41 . . . . . . 39 B1
  Livingston EH54 . . . . . . 144 C5
  Longniddry EH32 . . . . 98 D4
Stevenson Dr EH11 . . . . . 120 B4
Stevenson Gr EH11 . . . . . 120 C5

Stevenson La EH22 . . . . . 174 B4
Stevenson Pk EH32 . . . . . . 98 D4
Stevenson Pl EH18. . . . . . 172 D6
Stevenson Rd
  Edinburgh EH11 . . . . 120 C5
  Penicuik EH26 . . . . 171 B1
Stevenson St FK3 . . . . 61 D5
Stevenson Terr
  Bathgate EH48 . . . . 141 C5
  Edinburgh EH11 . . . . 120 C5
Stevenson Way EH32. . . . . 98 D4
Stewart Ave Bo'ness EH51. . 63 F8
  Currie EH14. . . . . 147 E3
  Linlithgow EH49 . . . . 84 E6
Stenhousemuir FK2. . . . . . 39 A2
Stewart Clark Ave EH39 . . 89 C8
Stewart Cres Currie EH14 . 147 E4
  Lochgelly KY5 . . . . 14 A8
Stewart Ct EH55 . . . . 163 D2
Stewart Dr EH47 . . . . 160 F7
Stewartfield EH6 . . . . 93 D4
Stewartfield Cres EH52 . . 115 F5
Stewartfield Rd EH52 . . . . 115 F6
Stewart Gdns EH14 . . . . . 147 E4
Stewart Gr
  Danderhall EH22 . . . . . . 152 A8
  Harthill ML7. . . . . 159 F5
Stewart Pk EH22 . . . . 154 D5
Stewart Pl Currie EH14 . . 147 E3
  Kirkliston EH29 . . . . 89 B1
Stewart Rd Currie EH14 . . 147 E3
  Falkirk FK2 . . . . 60 C5
Stewart's Melville Coll
  EH4 . . . . 92 F1
Stewart Sq FK8 . . . . 2 A2
Stewart St Bonnybridge FK4. 57 F5
  Cambusbarron FK7 . . . . . 6 D6
  Dysart KY1. . . . . 18 B8
  Townhill KY12 . . . . 29 C7
  West Calder EH55. . . . . . 163 D3
Stirling EH11 . . . . 120 E5
  South Queensferry EH30 . 68 B1
Stewart Way EH54 . . . . . . 143 C6
STIRLING. 7 C8
Stirling Bridge* FK8 . . . . . 2 B2
Stirling Bsns Ctr FK8 . . . . . 7 B6
Stirling Castle* FK8. . . . . . 7 A8
Stirling Ind Pk FK7 . . . . 7 C7
Stirling High Sch FK8 . . . . 7 A4
Stirling Pl FK7 . . . . 20 C3
Stirling Rd Alloa FK10. . . . . . 9 F8
  Alva FK12 . . . . 4 F7
  Edinburgh EH5 . . . . 93 B6
  Fallin FK7 . . . . 8 C4
  Kirkliston EH29 . . . . 89 A2
  Larbert, North Broomage
  FK5 . . . . 38 A3
  Larbert, South Broomage FK2,
  FK5 . . . . 59 C8
  Torwood FK5 . . . . 37 E5
  Tullibody FK10 . . . . 4 B3
Stirling Royal Infmy FK8 . . 7 B5
Stirling St Alva FK12 . . . . . . 5 A6
  Denny, Dunipace FK6. . . . 36 D4
  Denny FK6 . . . . 36 E2
Stirling Sta FK8 . . . . 7 B8
Stobhill Prim Sch EH23 . 195 D8
Stobhill Rd EH23 . . . . 174 B3
Stobie Pl KY12 . . . . 26 F7
Stobs Pl KY2 . . . . 16 C7
STOCKBRIDGE 93 A2
Stockbridge Prim sch
  EH3 . . . . 93 B2
Stockbridge Ret Pk EH9 .84 D6
Stone Ave EH22 . . . . 174 D6
Stonebank EH54 . . . . 143 E6
Stone Cres EH22 . . . . 174 D6
Stonedyke Rd ML8 . . . . . 215 B3
Stonehap Crofts EH47 . .182 E8
Stonelaws Cotts EH40 . . . 75 A6
Stone Pl EH22 . . . . 174 D6
STONEYBANK 124 B6
Stoneybank Ave EH21 . . 124 B4
Stoneybank Cres EH21 . . 124 B4
Stoneybank Ct EH21 . . . . 124 A5
Stoneybank Dr EH21 . . . . 124 A5
Stoneybank Gardens N
  EH21 . . . . 124 B5
Stoneybank Gardens S
  EH21 . . . . 124 B5
Stoneybank Gdns EH21 . 124 A5
Stoneybank Gr EH21 . . . . 124 B4
Stoneybank Pl EH21 . . . . 124 B4
Stoneybank Rd EH21 . . . 124 B4
Stoneybank Terr EH21 . . 124 B4
STONEYBURN 162 C2
Stoneyburn Prim Sch
  EH47 . . . . 162 C3
Stoneycroft Rd EH30 . . . . 68 C1
Stoneyflatts EH30. . . . . 89 A8
Stoneyflatts Cres EH30. . . 89 A8
Stoneyflatts Pk EH30 . . . . 89 A8
Stoneyhill Ct EH21. . . . . . 124 A5
Stoneyhill Cres EH21. . . . 124 A5
Stoneyhill Dr EH21 . . . . . . 124 A5
Stoneyhill Farm Rd EH21 124 B5
Stoneyhill Gdns **3** EH21 124 A5
Stoneyhill Gr EH21. . . . . . 124 A5
Stoneyhill Pl EH21 . . . . . . 124 A5
Stoneyhill Prim Sch
  EH21. . . . . 124 A5
Stoneyhill Rd EH21 . . . . . 124 A5
Stoneyhill Rise EH21. . . . 124 A5
Stoneyhill Steading
  EH21 . . . . 124 B5

Stoneyhill Terr EH21....124 A5
Stoneyhill Wynd **1**
  EH21................124 A5
Stoneypath Cotts EH42..133 C3
STONEYWOOD.........36 C2
Stoneywood Pk FK6....36 B2
Stony Brae FK10........24 C2
Stories Pk EH40.......103 E7
Strachan Ct EH51.......63 D7
Strachan Gdns EH4.....92 A2
Strachan Rd EH4........92 A2
Strachan St FK1........59 E4
STRAITON.............151 A2
Straiton Mains EH20...151 A1
Straiton Park Cvn Site
  EH20................150 F1
Straiton Park Way EH20..151 A2
Straiton Pk EH20......151 A1
Straiton Pl EH15......123 B8
Straiton Pond Nature
  Reserve* EH20......151 C2
Straiton Rd
  Loanhead EH20.......171 F8
  Straiton EH20........151 A2
Strand Dr EH48........140 F1
Strang Pl FK5..........38 B2
Strang's Pl FK1........81 F5
Strathallan Ct FK9......2 A6
Strathallan Dr KY2....16 E5
Strathallan Prim Sch KY2 16 E4
Strathallan Rd FK9.....2 A6
Strathalmond Ct EH4...90 F3
Strathalmond Gn EH4...90 F3
Strathalmond Pk EH4...90 F3
Strathalmond Rd EH4...90 F3
Strathavon Terr EH48..110 F5
Strathbeg Dr KY11.....47 F3
Strathbrock Pl
  Broxburn EH52.......115 E5
  Uphall EH52.........114 F4
Strathearn Ct
  Grangemouth FK3.....61 E8
  West Barns EH42......77 F1
Strathearn Pl EH9.....121 B4
Strathearn Rd
  Edinburgh EH9.......121 C4
  North Berwick EH39....53 F7
Strathesk Gr EH26....192 A6
Strathesk Pl EH26....192 A6
Strathesk Prim Sch
  EH26...............192 A6
Strathesk Rd EH26....192 A6
Strathfillan Rd EH9...121 C4
Strathkinnes Rd KY2...17 A4
Strathlachlan Ave ML8..215 A1
Strathlogie EH48......110 F5
Strathmiglo Pl FK5.....38 F4
Strathmore Cres FK9....2 A3
Strathmore Dr
  Dunfermline KY12.....29 D5
  Stirling FK9..........2 A3
Strathmore St KY3......34 F3
Strathyre Dr EH47....162 C2
Strathyre Pl Falkirk FK1..60 A1
  Stoneyburn EH47......162 C2
Strawberry Bank
  Dalkeith EH22.......152 E1
  Linlithgow EH49......85 A6
Streets Pl KY12........29 D7
Stripehead **3** FK10....10 B6
Striven Dr FK2.........39 C1
Striven Pl KY2........16 E8
Stromness Gdns EH54..164 D4
Strowan Rd FK3........61 F7
Strowan Sq FK3........61 F7
Struan Dr KY11........47 B3
Struan Pl KY11........47 B3
Struan Wynd EH32.....97 B2
Strude Howe FK12......5 B7
Strude Mill FK12.......5 B7
Strude St FK12.........5 B7
Stuart Cres EH12......119 B8
Stuart Ct Bathgate EH48..141 C5
  Edinburgh EH12......119 B8
Stuart Gr EH12........119 B8
Stuart Gr FK3..........61 B6
Stuart Pk EH12........119 B8
Stuart Pl KY4..........13 D5
Stuart Rd KY11.........46 C2
Stuart Sq EH12........119 B8
Stuart Terr EH48......141 B5
Stuart Wynd EH12.....119 B8
Styles Pl FK1..........59 F2
Succoth Ave EH12......120 D8
Succoth Ct EH12.......120 D8
Succoth Gdns EH12....120 D8
Succoth Pk EH12.......120 D8
Succoth Pl EH12.......120 D8
Suffolk Rd EH16.......121 F3
Suffolk Rd La EH16....122 A3
Suffolk Road La EH16..121 F3
Sugarhouse Cl EH8....229 B3
Suilven Hts EH7.......61 A3
Sultery Bldg KY11.....45 B4
Summer Bank EH3......93 C2
Summerfield Gdns EH6..94 B4
Summerfield Pl EH6....78 B2
Summerfield Pl EH6....94 B4
Summerfield Rd EH42...78 C1
SUMMERFORD..........59 D4
Summerford FK1.......59 D4
Summerford Gdns FK1..59 D4
Summerford Rd FK1....59 D4
Summerhall EH8.......229 B1
Summerhall Cres EH9..229 B1
Summerhall Pl EH9....229 B1
Summerhall Sq EH9....229 B1
Summerlee EH32........96 E1

Summer Pl EH3.........93 C3
Summerside Pl EH6.....93 D5
Summerside St EH6.....93 D5
Summertrees Ct EH16..122 B1
Summerville Ct EH54..144 A8
Suna Path ML7.........180 B3
Sunart Pl FK3..........61 D5
Sunbury Mews **4** EH4..120 F8
Sunbury Pl EH4.......120 F8
Sunbury St EH4.......120 F8
Sundew Glade EH54....164 C8
Sunningdale La KY12....28 D6
Sunnybank ML7........179 F6
Sunnybank Pl **3** EH7..94 B1
Sunnybank Rd FK7......7 B3
Sunnybank Terr **2** EH7..94 B1
Sunnybrae ML11.......201 A1
Sunnybrae Terr FK2....82 C6
Sunnydale Dr EH48....138 E3
Sunnydale Rd EH48....138 E3
Sunnylaw Pl FK1........59 F3
Sunnylaw Rd FK9.......2 A8
Sunnyside Edinburgh EH7..94 A2
  Stirling FK7...........7 A4
  Stoneyburn EH47.....162 B2
Sunnyside Ave
  Bathgate EH48......141 C7
  Grangemouth FK2.....82 C7
Sunnyside Cotts
  East Linton HE41.....103 E4
  Grangemouth FK2.....82 D7
Sunnyside Ct Alloa FK10..10 B7
  Cowdenbeath KY4......13 D4
  Grangemouth FK2.....82 C7
Sunnyside Dr FK2......82 C7
Sunnyside Pl Lochgelly KY5 14 A6
  Stirling FK9..........2 A4
Sunnyside Prim Sch FK10 10 B7
Sunnyside Rd Alloa FK10..10 B7
  Falkirk FK1..........59 F5
  Grangemouth FK2.....82 D7
Sunnyside St FK1.......59 E6
Surcoat Loan FK7.......7 E3
Surgeon's Hall Mus*
  EH1................229 B2
Sutherland Ave Alloa FK10 .10 C7
  Stirling FK8...........2 C1
Sutherland Cres EH48..141 B5
Sutherland Dr FK6.....57 D8
Sutherland Ho **4** EH3..3 A2
Sutherland Pl KY1.....17 F7
Sutherland St EH12...120 F7
Sutherland Way EH54..143 C6
Suthren Yett EH32....125 E7
Suttieslea Cres EH22..174 C6
Suttieslea Dr EH22...174 C6
Suttieslea Pl EH22....174 C6
Suttieslea Rd EH22...174 C6
Suttieslea Terr EH22..174 C6
Suttieslea Wlk EH22..174 C6
Suttie Way FK9........1 F8
Sutton Park Cres FK5..38 E3
Sutton Pl FK2..........60 D5
Swallow Brae EH54....143 D6
Swallow Craig KY11....48 B1
Swallowdrum Rd KY12..28 C6
Swallow La FK10.......153 D3
Swan Cres EH23.......195 D8
Swanfield EH6..........93 F5
Swan Pl FK3...........61 D5
Swan Rd Kirkcaldy KY1..17 B3
  Tranent EH33.........126 C5
Swan Spring Ave EH10..150 A7
SWANSTON.............149 F5
Swanston Ave EH10....150 A5
Swanston Cres EH10...150 A5
Swanston Dr EH10.....150 A4
Swanston Gdns EH10..150 A5
Swanston Gn EH10....150 A5
Swanston Gr EH10.....150 B4
Swanston Loan EH10...150 A5
Swanston Muir EH10...149 F5
Swanston Pk EH10.....150 A5
Swanston Pl EH10.....150 A5
Swanston Rd EH10.....150 A4
Swanston Row EH10...150 A4
Swanston Terr EH10...150 A5
Swanston View EH10...150 A5
Swift Brae EH54.......143 D6
Swinburne Dr FK10.....5 B2
Swintons Pl KY4.......12 F1
Sword's Way FK2.......39 A1
Sycamore Ave
  Bo'ness EH51.........63 D5
  Cockenzie & Port Seton
  EH32................97 D3
Sycamore Cres KY4....13 C6
Sycamore Ct EH54....161 C6
Sycamore Gdns EH22..119 E6
Sycamore Glade EH54..164 D8
Sycamore Gr
  Dunfermline KY11.....46 C8
  Winchburgh EH52......87 F2
Sycamore Pl FK8........6 F5
Sycamore Rd EH22....119 E6
Sycamore St KY4......29 B4
Sycamores The FK10....4 B1
Sycamore Terr **3** EH12 119 E6
Sycamore Wlk EH47...162 D8
Sydney Pk EH7.........94 E2
Sydney Pl EH7.........94 E2
Sydney St EH54........144 A5
Sydney Terr EH7.......94 E2
Sylvan Gr EH51........63 C5
Sylvan Pl EH9.........121 D5
Sylvan Way EH48......140 F5

T

Tailend Ct EH54.......142 D3
Tailend Ind Pk EH54...142 D4
Tailend Rdbt EH54....142 D3
Tait Dr Larbert FK5.....59 C8
  Penicuik EH26.......191 F5
Tait St **3** EH22.......153 A3
Talbot St FK3...........61 D8
Talisker FK10...........4 B2
Talisman Pl EH16......122 B1
Talisman Rise EH54....164 D8
Talman Gdns FK2......61 E3
TAMFOURHILL..........59 C4
Tamfourhill Ave FK1...59 C4
Tamfourhill Ind Est FK1..59 C4
Tamfourhill Rd FK1....59 C4
Tam O'Shanter Dr FK7..20 D7
Tanderlane Cotts EH41..132 C3
Tanera Ct FK1..........60 B2
Tanfield EH3...........93 C3
Tanhouse Brae KY12....42 B8
Tanners Rd FK1........60 A4
Tannery La
  8 Haddington EH41..130 B8
  Stirling FK6...........2 A4
Tantallon Castle* EH39..55 F7
Tantallon Dr FK2.......39 A3
Tantallon Gdns EH54..164 E6
Tantallon Pl EH9......121 D5
Tantallon Rd EH39.....54 F4
Tantallon Terr EH39...54 E7
Tapitlaw Gr KY12......26 D7
Tappoch Pl FK5........38 A3
Taransay Dr FK2.......61 F1
Tarbert Dr EH54.......164 F7
Tarbert Pl Carluke ML8..215 A1
  Polmont FK2..........61 F1
Tarbert Terr FK10......23 F3
Tarbolton Ct KY2.......17 A7
Tarvit St EH3.........228 C1
Tashieburn Rd ML11...201 E2
Tavern Cotts KY4.......30 F8
Ta-Verne La KY11......29 D1
Taxi Way KY11.........48 C5
Tay Ct FK10............10 C6
Taylor Ave KY4........13 C4
Taylor Ct Falkirk FK2...60 C7
Taylor Gdns EH6.......93 F5
Taylor Pl Dalkeith EH22..153 C2
  8 Edinburgh EH7....94 A1
Taylor Rd EH47.......160 F6
Taylor's Rd FK5.........38 C1
Taymouth Rd FK2......62 A1
Tay Pl ML7............179 E6
Tay St Edinburgh EH11..120 F5
  Falkirk FK2...........39 C1
Tay Terr KY11..........29 E2
Teal Pl KY11...........30 A1
Tedder St FK3..........61 C5
Telferton EH7..........94 F1
Telford Ct KY7.........7 D1
Telford Dr EH4.........92 D3
Telford Gdns EH4......92 D3
Telford Gr EH4.........92 D2
Telford Pl Edinburgh EH4..92 D3
  Linlithgow EH49......84 C7
Telford Rd EH4........92 D3
Telford Sq Falkirk FK1..59 E6
Telford View EH49.....84 C6
Telny Pl KY3...........49 C7
Templar La EH31.......52 A2
Templar Pl EH31.......52 A2
Templar Rise EH54....164 D8
Templar's Cramond EH4..91 A4
Templars Cres KY3.....34 F3
TEMPLE...............194 D2
Temple Ave EH48......140 A5
Templedean Pk EH41..101 A1
Temple Denny Rd FK6..36 D2
TEMPLEHALL...........16 F7
Templehall Ave KY2....16 F7
Templeland Gr EH12...119 D7
Templeland Rd EH12...119 D7
Temple Mains Steading
  EH42................136 F8
Temple Park Cres EH11..120 F5
Temple Pk EH31.......52 A2
Ten Acres EH10........5 B1
Tenacres Pl FK3........61 E6
Tenacres Rd FK3.......61 E6
Tenant's March EH55..163 C3
Tennant St EH6........93 F4

Tennent Pk EH53......144 C2
Tenterfield Dr EH41...101 B1
Tenterfield Ho EH41...101 B1
Tenth St EH22.........174 B6
Tern Brae EH54.......143 C6
Tern Rd KY11..........30 A1
Terrace Rdbt EH54....143 E1
Terrace St KY1.........18 A7
Terrars Croft EH8.....229 C1
Terregles EH26.......191 D6
Terris Pl KY4..........13 D3
Tevidale Dr EH3........93 B2
Teviot Dr EH54........165 A7
Teviot Gr EH26........191 F7
Teviot Pl EH1.........229 A2
Teviot St FK1..........59 F4
Thane Pl KY11.........29 F1
The GYLE.............119 B6
The NEW TOWN........228 C4
Thimblehall Dr KY12...29 D4
Thimblehall Pl KY12...29 D4
Thimblehall Rd KY12...29 E4
Third Gait EH14.......147 E7
Third St EH22.........174 B5
Thirlestane EH51......64 B8
Thirlestane La EH9....121 C4
Thirlestane Pl EH51...64 B8
Thirlestane Rd EH9...121 C5
Thirlfield Wynd EH54..142 F2
Thistle Ave Denny FK6..36 D3
  Grangemouth FK3......61 B5
Thistle Chambers **4** FK8..7 B7
Thistle Ind Est
  Broxburn EH52.......116 A5
  Cowdenbeath KY4......13 E4
  Stirling FK7...........7 B7
Thistle Pl Edinburgh EH11..228 A1
  Stirling FK8...........8 A2
Thistle Sh Ctr The FK8...7 B7
Thistle St Alloa FK10....10 C6
  Burntisland KY3.......50 E8
  Cowdenbeath KY4......13 E4
  Dunfermline KY12.....29 B5
  Edinburgh EH2.......228 C4
  Falkirk FK2...........60 C6
  Kirkcaldy KY1.........17 C3
Thistles The FK8........7 B7
Thistly Cross EH42....105 E2
Thistly Cross Rdbt EH42..105 E2
Thompson's Ct EH1....228 C2
Thomson Cres
  Cockenzie & Port Seton
  EH32................97 D4
  Currie EH14.........148 B5
  Falkirk FK1...........59 E3
Thomson Ct EH52.....114 F4
Thomson Dr EH14.....148 C5
Thomson Gn EH54....143 B8
Thomson Gr Currie EH14..148 B5
  Uphall EH52.........114 F4
Thomson Pl
  Cambusbarron FK7....6 D5
  Limerigg FK1.........108 B3
  Rosyth KY11..........46 F3
Thomson Rd EH14.....148 B5
Thomson Terr ML7....179 D6
Thorburn Gr EH13.....149 C6
Thorburn Rd EH13.....149 B6
Thorburn Terr EH26...191 F4
Thornbridge FK2.......60 E4
Thornbridge Rd FK2....60 E5
Thornbridge Sq FK2....60 E5
Thorndale Gdns FK4....57 B2
Thorndene Ct **3** FK1..59 F2
Thorndene Terr FK1...108 B7
Thorne Dr EH39........54 A7
Thorne Rd FK10.........4 E1
Thorn Gr KY11.........46 F8
Thornhill Ct FK2......60 C6
Thornhill Pl KY2......17 B6
Thornhill Rd Falkirk FK2..60 C6
  Kirkcaldy KY2........17 B6
Thorn Rd ML8.........215 E3
THORNTON............218 C6
Thornton Ave FK4......58 B6
Thornton Gdns FK4....58 B6
Thorntonloch Cvn Site
  EH42................218 D7
Thorntonloch Holdings
  EH42................218 B6
Thornton Pl EH47....181 D5
Thornton Rd EH24....172 D1
Thorntree Cres EH32...97 B1
Thorn Tree Pl KY12....26 F6
Thorntreeside Ind Est
  EH6.................94 A3
Thorntree St EH6......94 A4
Thornville Terr EH6....94 A4
Thorny Bank EH22....153 D4
Thornybank Ind Est
  EH22................153 D4
Thornybauk EH3.......228 B1
Thornycroft Terr FK7...20 C3
Thornyhall EH22......153 C4
Threave Loan KY11.....30 A1
Three Bridges Rdbt FK1..59 A6
THREEMILETOWN.......86 F4
Three Sisters Ct EH1..229 B3
Threipmuir Ave EH14..168 C8

Threipmuir Gdns EH14..168 C8
Threipmuir Pl EH14...168 C8
THROSK...............9 A3
Thrums The FK2........61 A4
Thurston Rd EH14.....143 B5
Thymebank EH54......143 E6
Tibbies Loan FK7......20 D8
Timber Bush EH6......94 A6
Timmeryetts EH52....115 C6
Timmons Pk KY5......14 A8
Timmons Pl FK6........36 D1
Tinian Cres KY12......26 D1
Tinto Dr FK3...........61 E5
Tinto Pl Dunfermline KY11..29 F2
  Edinburgh EH6........93 E4
Tinto View ML11......217 F8
Tipperary Pl FK5......38 E2
Tipperlinn Rd EH10...121 A4
Tipperwell Way EH26..192 B1
Tippethill Hospl EH48..140 B1
Tippet Knowes Ct EH52..87 E3
Tippet Knowes Pk EH52..87 E3
Tippet Knowes Rd EH52..87 E2
Tiree Cres FK2.........61 D6
Tiree Pl Falkirk FK1....60 B1
  Kirkcaldy KY2........16 F8
Tirran Dr KY11.........30 B1
Titania FK10...........10 A8
Toddricks Wynd EH1...229 B3
Toddshill Rd EH29.....89 A1
Todd Sq EH54.........124 A1
Tolbooth St **3** Falkirk FK1.60 A4
  Kirkcaldy KY1.........17 C3
Tolbooth Wynd EH6....94 A5
Tollbraes Rd EH48....141 D4
TOLLCROSS...........228 B1
Tollcross EH3.........228 B1
Tollcross Prim Sch EH3..228 B1
Tollgate KY11.........29 B2
Toll House Gdns EH33..126 D4
Toll House Gr EH33...126 D5
Toll House Neuk EH33..126 D4
Toll Rd FK10...........23 F3
Toll Rdbt EH54........142 E3
Toll View TD13........218 F4
Tolmount Cres KY12....29 C3
Tolmount Dr KY12......29 C3
Tolsta Cres FK2........61 F1
Tophill Entry FK1......59 F6
Toravon Dr FK2........83 A6
Torbain KY2...........16 D8
Torbain Prim Sch KY2..16 D8
Torbain Rd KY2........16 B6
Torbane Ave EH47.....161 E7
Torbane Dr EH47......161 E7
Torbeith Gdns
  Cowdenbeath KY4......12 F1
  Hill Of Beath KY4....13 A1
TORBOTHIE............180 B4
Torbothie Rd ML7.....180 B4
TORBREX..............6 F5
Torbrex Farm FK7......7 A4
Torbrex La FK7, FK8....7 A5
Torbrex Rd FK7.........6 F4
Torburn Ave FK2.......20 D3
Torduff Rd EH13......148 F4
Torlea Pl FK5..........38 B3
Toronto Ave EH54.....143 E4
Toronto Prim Sch EH54..143 E4
Torosay Ave FK2........82 F6
TORPHICHEN..........111 E6
Torphichen Ave EH53..144 B2
Torphichen Pl EH3....228 A2
Torphichen Place La
  EH3.................228 A2
Torphichen Preceptory*
  EH48................111 F6
Torphichen Prim Sch
  Bathgate EH48.......141 B7
  Edinburgh EH3.......228 A2
TORPHIN..............148 E4
Torphin Bank EH13...148 F5
Torphin Rd EH13......148 F5
Torrance Pk EH4.......91 C1
Torrance Medway EH26..171 A1
Torridon Ave FK2......39 C1
Torridon Ct FK10......10 C5
Torridon Dr KY11......46 E2
Torridon La KY11......46 E2
Torridon Pl Kirkcaldy KY2..16 E8
  Rosyth KY11..........46 E2
Torridon Rd EH47.....161 C7
Torridon Wlk EH54....144 B4
Torrin Loan ML7......179 D6
Torry Bay Nature Reserve*
  KY12................43 D8
TORRYBURN...........26 E1
Torryburn Prim Sch KY12 26 E1
Torry Dr FK12.........4 F1
Torsonce Rd EH22....152 F2
Torvean Pl KY11.......29 C2
TORWOOD.............37 E6
Torwood Ave
  Grangemouth FK3.....61 E6
  Larbert FK5..........38 B2
Torwood Pl KY12......29 D5
Tory Bay Ct KY12......26 C1
Toscana Ct EH22......152 A8
TOUCH...............29 E5
Touchhill Cres FK7....20 C3
Touch Prim Sch KY11..29 E4
Touch Rd FK7, FK8......6 B6

Touch Wards KY12.....29 E4
Tovey Rd KY11.....46 D2
Toward Ct **3** EH12.....119 A7
Towerbank Prim Sch EH15.....95 B1
Tower Gdns The EH51.....64 C7
Tower PI Clackmannan FK10. 10 F5
  Edinburgh EH6.....94 A6
Towers Ct FK2.....60 B6
Towers PI FK9.....2 D4
Tower Sq FK10.....10 B5
Tower St Alloa FK10.....10 A7
  Edinburgh EH6.....94 A6
Tower Terr KY1.....17 F8
Tower View FK10.....5 E1
Tower Wynd EH6.....94 A6
Town Burn FK7.....6 E4
Townhall St KY11.....47 C2
Townhead Dysart KY1.....18 A7
  Kinghorn KY3.....34 F3
Townhead Apartments **9** FK10.....10 B6
Townhead Gdns EH47.. 161 C6
TOWNHILL.....29 C8
Townhill Ctry Pk* KY12.. 29 D8
Townhill Prim Sch KY12 .29 D8
Townhill Rd KY12.....29 B5
Town House St FK6.....36 E2
Townsend Cres KY1.....17 C4
Townsend PI KY1.....17 C4
Town Sq EH54.....143 E2
Trafalgar La EH6.....93 E5
Trafalgar St EH6.....93 E5
Trainers Brae EH39.....54 B6
Train Terr KY11.....46 C5
TRANENT.....126 E7
Tranent Rd EH33.....126 B1
Transy Gr KY12.....29 C4
Transy PI KY12.....29 C4
Tranter Cres EH32.....71 C4
Tranter Rd EH32.....71 C4
Traprain Cotts HE41 .103 E4
Traprain Cres EH48..140 F7
Traprain Terr
  Haddington EH41.....101 B1
  Loanhead EH20.....172 C7
Traquair Park E EH12..119 F6
Traquair Park W EH12 .119 F6
Traverse Theatre* EH3 .228 B2
Trelawney Terr EH26..192 A8
Tremayne PI KY12.....28 F6
Trenchard PI KY12.....28 F5
Trench Knowe EH10...150 A5
Tressilian Gdns **1** EH16..122 B1
Trevelyan Cres EH34..156 E6
Trevelyan PI EH34.....156 E6
Trinity.....93 C5
Trinity Acad EH6.....93 C6
Trinity Cres EH5.....93 B6
Trinity Gr EH5.....93 B6
Trinity Mains EH5.....93 B5
Trinity Prim Sch EH6 ..93 D6
Trinity Rd EH5.....93 B6
Trinity Way EH5.....93 B5
Tron Ct FK10.....4 B2
Trondheim Parkway KY11 .29 F2
Trondheim PI KY11.....29 F2
Trongate KY3.....35 A3
Tron Sq EH1.....229 A3
Trotter Haugh EH9....121 D3
Troup Ct FK3.....61 D8
Tryst Pk Edinburgh EH10 .149 F5
  Stenhousemuir FK5.....38 C3
Tryst Rd FK5.....38 D3
Tudor Ct FK2.....61 C2
Tuke St KY12.....29 A5
Tulliallan PI FK5.....39 A4
Tulliallan Prim Sch FK10 .23 E4
Tulliallan Terr FK10...23 E5
TULLIBODY.....4 C3
Tullibody Rd FK10....119 F8
Tulligarth Pk FK10....10 A7
Tulloch Ct KY4.....13 C5
Tulloch Rd ML7.....180 B3
Tummel Ct FK10.....10 C5
Tummel Dr KY2.....16 D8
Tummel PI
  Grangemouth FK3.....61 E4
  Stenhousemuir FK5.....38 E3
Turf PI EH47.....162 D7
Turnbull Gr KY1.....29 F1
Turnbull Way EH54....143 D6
Turner Ave EH14.....147 C3
Turner Pk EH14.....147 C3
Turner St EH48.....141 A7
Turnhigh Rd EH47.....161 A4
Turnhouse Farm Rd EH12 .90 C1
Turnhouse Rd EH12...118 D8
Turnstone Rd KY11.....30 B1
Turpie Dr **6** EH5.....38 B2
Turret Ct FK10.....10 C6
Turret Dr FK2.....62 A2
Turret Gdns EH32.....125 F8
Turret Rd FK3.....61 D5
Turriff PI KY1.....1 F6
Twain Ave FK5.....39 A3
Tweed Ave KY1.....17 E8
Tweeddale Ave EH41..220 F7
Tweeddale Cres EH41 .220 F7
Tweeddale Ct EH1.....229 B3
Tweeddale Dr KY11.....29 E1
Tweeddale Gr EH41...220 F6
Tweed Dr EH54.....144 B4
Tweed St Dunfermline KY11. 29 F2

Tweed St continued
  Grangemouth FK3.....40 A1
Tygetshaugh Ct FK6....36 D4
Tyler's Acre Ave EH12 .119 E5
Tyler's Acre Gdns EH12 .119 E5
Tyler's Acre Rd EH12...119 E5
Tyndrum PI KY2.....16 E7
Tynebank Rd EH41.....130 A7
Tynecastle High Sch EH11.....120 E6
Tynecastle La EH11....120 E6
Tynecastle Pk (Heart of Midlothian FC) EH11 .120 E5
Tynecastle Terr EH11 .120 E5
Tyne Cl East Linton EH40. 103 E7
  Haddington EH41.....130 B8
Tyne Ct EH41.....130 B8
Tynefield Cotts EH41...45 A4
Tyne Ho EH41.....130 B8
Tyneholm Cotts EH34 .156 E6
Tynemount Ave EH35 .155 D6
Tynemount Rd EH35...155 D7
Tyne Pk EH34.....157 A6
Tyneview EH35.....155 E7
Tynewater Prim Sch EH37.....176 A4
TYNINGHAME.....76 B3
Tyrie Ave KY1.....35 B7
Tyrie Ct KY1.....35 B7
Tyrie Gr KY1.....35 B7
Tyrie PI KY1.....35 B7
Tyrwhitt PI KY11.....46 F3
Tytler Ct EH8.....94 A1
Tytler Gdns EH8.....94 A1

U
Ugston Cotts EH41....100 C2
Uig Way ML7.....180 A3
Ulster Cres EH8.....122 D8
Ulster Dr EH8.....122 D8
Ulster Gdns EH8.....122 D7
Ulster Gr EH8.....122 D7
Ulster Terr EH8.....122 D7
Underwood Cotts FK7....6 D5
Underwood Rd FK7.....6 D5
Union Ct EH51.....64 A8
Union Dr EH47.....161 B6
Union Gdns FK1.....59 D5
Union Pk EH19.....173 B6
Union PI Brightons FK2 .82 D8
  Edinburgh EH1.....229 B4
  Larbert FK5.....38 B1
Union Rd Bathgate EH48..141 B6
  Broxburn EH52.....115 D5
  Falkirk FK1.....59 D5
  Grangemouth FK3.....40 D1
  Linlithgow EH49.....84 F6
  Whitburn EH47.....161 B6
Union St Alloa FK10...10 B6
  Bo'ness EH51.....64 A8
  Bridge of Allan FK9.....2 A7
  Burntisland KY3.....50 E8
  Cowdenbeath KY4.....13 D4
  Edinburgh EH1.....93 E2
  Falkirk FK2.....60 B7
  Kirkcaldy KY1.....17 F7
  Lochgelly KY5.....14 B8
  Shotts ML7.....179 D5
  Stenhousemuir FK5.....38 E3
  Stirling FK8.....2 A1
Unity PI ML7.....179 D4
Universal Rd FK2.....60 E7
University of Edinburgh EH8.....229 B2
University of Stirling FK9 ..2 D6
University Road W FK9..2 C6
Univ of Dundee Sch of Nursing & Midwifery Fife Campus **1** KY2.....17 A4
Univ of Edinburgh EH8 .229 A1
Univ of Edinburgh (King's Buildings Campus) EH9.....121 F2
UPHALL.....114 F4
Uphall Prim Sch EH52 .115 A5
Uphall Sta EH54.....115 A2
UPHALL STATION.....115 A1
Uphall Station Rd EH53 .144 B7
Upper Bathville EH48 .139 F4
Upper Bow EH1.....229 A3
Upper Bridge St FK8.....2 A1
Upper Broomieknowe EH18.....173 A8
Upper Castlehill **2** FK8. 7 A8
Upper Coltbridge Terr EH12.....120 E8
Upper Craigour EH17..151 E8
Upper Craigour Way EH17.....122 D1
Upper Craigs FK8.....7 B7
Upper Cramond Ct EH4..91 B4
Upper Dalhousie Cotts EH19.....173 C3
Upper Damside **1** EH4 .228 A1
Upper Dean Terr EH4 .228 A4
Upper Gilmore PI EH3 .228 B1
Upper Gilmore Terr EH3 .228 B1
Upper Gray St EH9....121 E5
Upper Grove PI EH3...228 A1
Upper Hermitage EH6...94 A4
Upper Keith EH36.....178 B2
Upper Millhill St KY11..29 B3
Upper Newmarket St **6** FK1.....60 B5

UPPER TOWN OF SALTOUN.....157 E4
Upper Wellheads KY11 .45 E3
Ure Cres FK4.....58 A6
Ure Ct FK3.....61 D8
URQUHART.....28 D2
Urquhart Cres KY2.....28 E3
Urquhart Ct KY2.....16 D5
Urquhart Cut KY12.....28 E3
Urquhart Farm Cotts KY12.....28 D2
Usher Hall* EH3.....228 B2

V
Vale Gr FK9.....1 F5
Vale of Bonny View FK4 ..57 F5
Vale PI FK6.....36 E3
Valeview FK5.....38 D2
Valleyfield Ave KY12....26 B2
Valleyfield PI
  Cowdenbeath KY4.....13 D5
  Stirling FK7.....7 C6
Valleyfield Rd EH3....228 C1
Valleyfield St EH3....228 C1
Valleyfield View EH26..191 F4
Valleyfield Woodland Pk* KY12.....26 B3
Valley Gdns N KY2.....16 F6
Valley Gdns S KY2.....16 F6
Valley Prim Sch KY2...17 A7
Valley View KY2.....16 F6
Valleyview Dr FK2.....60 A8
Valleyview PI FK2.....60 A7
Vanburgh PI EH6.....94 A4
Vancouver Ave EH7...143 F4
Vandeleur Ave EH7.....94 E2
Vandeleur Gr EH7.....94 F1
Vandeleur PI EH7.....94 F2
Vardon Gn EH54.....143 C8
Vardon Rd EH31.....52 B3
Vaucluse PI EH26.....191 E4
Veere Pk KY12.....25 E1
Veitch's Sq EH4.....93 B2
Vellore Rd FK2.....83 A6
Venachar PI KY12.....28 B1
Venachar Rd FK1.....60 A1
Vennachar St ML7....179 E6
Vennel The Denny FK6...36 E2
  Dunbar EH42.....78 E2
  Linlithgow EH49.....85 A7
  South Queensferry EH30 .68 C1
Ventnor PI EH9.....122 A4
Ventnor Terr EH9.....121 F4
Venturefair Ave KY12...29 A6
Veronica Cres KY1.....17 C8
Vetch Pk EH41.....101 A1
Veterane Cotts EH48 .141 C6
Vexhim Pk EH15.....123 B5
Vicar St FK1.....60 B5
Viceroy St KY2.....17 B6
Victoria Gdns
  Kirkcaldy KY1.....17 B4
  Newtongrange EH22..173 F6
Victoria Hospl KY2.....17 B7
Victoria Mills Ind Est EH51.....64 C8
Victoria Park Neuk EH6..93 D5
Victoria Pk
  Fauldhouse EH47.....181 E7
  Haddington EH41.....101 A1
Victoria PI Bo'ness EH51 ..64 B7
  Brightons FK2.....61 D1
  Dunbar EH42.....78 D3
  Stirling FK8.....7 A7
Victoria Prim Sch
  Edinburgh EH6.....93 D7
  Falkirk FK1.....60 D6
Victoria Rd Falkirk FK2..60 C6
  Fauldhouse EH47.....181 F7
  Grangemouth FK3.....61 E8
  Haddington EH41.....130 A8
  Harthill ML7.....159 E5
  Kirkcaldy KY1.....17 F7
  Larbert FK5.....38 B1
  Newtongrange EH22..173 F5
  North Berwick EH39....54 C7
  Stirling FK8.....7 A8
Victoria Sq FK8.....7 A7
Victoria St Alloa FK10...10 A7
  Dunbar EH42.....78 D3
  Kincardine FK10.....23 E3
  Dysart KY1.....18 A7
  Edinburgh EH1.....229 A3
  Gorebridge EH23.....174 B1
  Harthill ML7.....159 E5
  Livingston EH54.....144 A4
  Rosewell EH24.....172 D2
Victoria Terr
  Dunfermline KY12.....29 A5
  Edinburgh EH1.....229 A2
  Haddington EH41.....130 B8
  Menstrie FK11.....4 B7
  Musselburgh EH21.....124 E6
Victor Park Terr EH12..119 D7
Viewbank Dr EH19....173 C8
Viewbank Rd EH19....173 B8
Viewbank View EH19..173 C8
Viewcraig Gdns EH8..229 B2
Viewcraig St EH8.....229 B2
Viewfield EH19.....173 D8
Viewfield Ave EH19...173 D8
Viewfield Dr FK2.....4 F6
Viewfield Ho KY12.....29 B3
Viewfield PI Harthill ML7 .159 F6
  3 Stirling FK8.....7 B8

Viewfield Rd
  Edinburgh EH14.....148 E7
  Tarbrax EH55.....203 F3
Viewfield St Harthill ML7 .159 F6
  4 Stirling FK8.....7 B8
Viewfield Terr
  Cowdenbeath KY4.....13 F6
  Dunfermline KY12.....29 B3
VIEWFORTH.....228 A1
Viewforth Bo'ness EH51...64 A7
  Cockenzie & Port Seton EH32.....97 D4
  Dunbar EH42.....78 C3
  Edinburgh EH10.....228 A1
  North Berwick EH39....54 C7
  Stirling FK8.....7 B6
Viewforth Ave KY1.....17 F7
Viewforth Ct KY3.....34 F2
Viewforth Dr FK2.....61 B4
Viewforth Gdns
  Edinburgh EH10.....121 B5
  Kirkcaldy KY1.....17 F8
  Tranent EH33.....126 C6
Viewforth High Sch KY1 .17 F7
Viewforth PI Kinghorn KY3 .34 F2
  Queensferry EH30.....89 B8
Viewforth Rd EH30.....89 B8
Viewforth St EH10....121 A5
Viewforth St KY1.....17 F7
Viewforth Terr
  Edinburgh EH10.....121 B5
  Kirkcaldy KY1.....17 F8
  Tranent EH33.....126 C6
Viewpark Gdns EH19..173 B8
Viking Way KY11.....46 D2
Villabank FK6.....36 E2
Villa Dean EH24.....172 C1
Villa Dean Pk EH24...172 D1
Village La EH54.....143 B3
Villa PI FK10.....11 A5
Villa Rd EH30.....68 B1
Vinefields EH34.....156 F6
Vineyard Bsns Ctr EH37 .197 F7
Violet Bank **4** EH48...141 B6
Violet Terr EH11.....120 E5
Vivian Terr EH4.....92 C4
Vogrie Cres S EH23...195 D8
Vogrie Ctry Pk* EH23 .175 D3
Vogrie PI EH23.....195 D8
Vogrie Rd EH23.....195 D7
Voil Rd FK9.....2 A3
Vorlich's Gn KY1....17 C3
Vorlich Cres EH54....192 A7
Vorlich Dr FK1.....81 E7
Vorlich PI FK1.....2 A3
Vorlich Way
  Dunfermline KY11.....30 B1
  Inverkeithing/Dunfermline KY11.....30 B1
Vrackie PI KY11.....30 B1

W
Waddell St FK2.....39 C2
WADINGBURN.....151 F1
Wadingburn La EH18...151 F1
Wadingburn Rd EH18 .172 E8
Waggon Rd Bo'ness EH51 .63 F8
  Crossford KY11.....45 C7
  Falkirk FK2.....60 B7
  Grangemouth FK2.....82 B8
  Inverkeithing KY11.....47 C2
Wakefield Ave EH7.....94 F2
Walden Dr EH41.....220 F7
Walden PI EH41.....220 F6
Walden Terr EH41.....220 F6
Waldie Ave EH49.....85 A5
Walker Cres EH22.....152 D1
Walker Dr Bonnybridge FK4 .57 D5
  South Queensferry EH30 .68 A1
Walker PI
  Bonnyrigg and Lasswade EH18.....172 E6
  Dunfermline KY11.....29 E1
Walker Rd EH47.....181 D5
Walkers Ct EH14.....119 E1
Walkers Rigg EH14...119 E1
Walker St
  Alloa/Clackmannan FK10 .23 F2
  Cowdenbeath KY4.....13 B3
  Edinburgh EH3.....228 A3
  Kincardine FK10.....23 E3
  Kirkcaldy KY7.....17 B6
  Lochgelly KY5.....14 A6
Walkers Wynd EH14 .119 E1
Walker Terr
  East Linton EH40.....103 D7
  Edinburgh EH11.....228 A2
Walk The KY1.....18 B7
Wallace Ave EH21.....125 A4
Wallace Bldgs FK2.....60 B6
Wallace Brae Ave FK2..82 C8
Wallace Brae Bank FK2 .82 C8
Wallace Brae Dr **1** FK2 .82 C8
Wallace Brae Dr FK2...82 C8
Wallace Brae Gdns **4** FK2.....82 C8
Wallace Brae PI **3** FK2 .82 C8
Wallace Brae Rise FK2 .82 C8
Wallace Cres Denny FK6 .36 C2
  Grangemouth FK2.....82 D8
  Musselburgh EH21.....124 A6
  Plean FK7.....20 D3
  Roslin EH25.....172 A3
Wallace Ct
  Grangemouth FK3.....61 D8

Wallace Ct continued
  Stirling FK8.....2 B1
Wallace Gate FK8.....7 B8
Wallace Gdns FK9.....2 D3
Wallace High Sch FK9...2 C4
Wallacelea FK2.....82 E7
Wallace Mill Gdns EH53 .144 C6
Wallace Monument* FK9. 2 E4
Wallace PI
  Cambusbarron FK7.....6 D5
  Falkirk FK2.....60 C6
  Falkirk FK2.....8 C4
  Kingseat KY12.....12 A1
  Tranent EH33.....126 C7
Wallace Rd EH48.....141 C6
Wallacerig Gdns FK2...82 E8
Wallace St Alloa FK10...10 C7
  Bannockburn FK7.....7 E1
  Cowdenbeath KY4.....13 C3
  Falkirk FK1.....60 C6
  Falkirk FK2.....60 C6
  Grangemouth FK3.....61 D8
  Stirling FK8.....2 B1
WALLACESTONE.....82 B7
Wallacestone Brae FK2 .82 B7
Wallacestone Prim Sch FK2.....82 D7
Wallace View
  Bo'ness EH51.....63 D5
  Shieldhill FK1.....81 D7
  Tullibody FK10.....4 D3
Wall Gdns FK1.....59 C5
Wallsend Ct KY12.....28 D5
Walls PI KY11.....29 E1
Wall St FK1.....59 C5
Walstale Rd FK7.....7 A3
WALLYFORD.....125 C5
Wallyford Ind Est EH21...125 B4
Wallyford Prim Sch EH21.....125 B5
Wallyford Sta EH21...125 B5
Wallyford Toll FK11...125 C6
Walmer Ct KY12.....29 A3
Walnut Gr KY11.....46 D8
Walter Hay Ct KY11.....46 F3
Walter Scott Ave EH16 .122 B1
Wanless Ct EH21.....124 D6
Ward Ave FK2.....61 C2
Warden's CI EH1.....229 A2
WARDIE.....93 A6
Wardie Ave EH5.....93 A5
Wardieburn Dr EH5.....92 F6
Wardieburn Place E EH5 .92 F6
Wardieburn Place N EH5..92 F6
Wardieburn Place S EH5..92 F6
Wardieburn Place W EH5 .92 E6
Wardieburn Rd EH5.....92 E6
Wardieburn Street E EH5 .92 F6
Wardieburn Street W EH5 .92 E6
Wardieburn Terr EH5...92 F6
Wardie Cres EH5.....93 A6
Wardie Dell EH5.....93 A6
Wardiefield EH5.....93 A6
Wardie Gr EH5.....92 F6
Wardie House La EH5...93 A6
Wardie Pk EH5.....93 A5
Wardie Prim Sch EH5...93 A6
Wardie Rd EH5.....93 A5
Wardie Sq EH5.....93 A6
Wardie Steps EH5.....93 A6
Wardlaw Cres KY12.....26 F7
Wardlaw PI
  Edinburgh EH11.....120 E5
  Falkirk FK2.....39 C2
Wardlaw St
  Cowdenbeath KY4.....13 C3
  Edinburgh EH11.....120 E5
Wardlaw Terr EH11....120 E5
Wardlaw Way KY12.....26 F7
Ward PI EH54.....143 C5
Wardrop Cres EH48...139 E5
Ward St FK10.....10 A5
Ware Rd Dirleton EH39...53 C6
  North Berwick EH39....54 A6
Warrender Cres EH42...78 E1
Warrender Ct EH39.....54 A6
Warrender Park Cres EH9.....121 C5
Warrender Park Rd EH9..121 C5
Warrender Park Terr EH9.....121 C5
Warrender Swim Ctr EH9.....121 C4
Warren Hill EH31.....51 F2
WARRISTON.....93 C4
Warriston Ave EH3.....93 C3
Warriston Cres EH3....93 C3
Warriston Dr EH3.....93 C4
Warriston Farm Rd EH14 .147 C6
Warriston Gdns EH3...93 C4
Warriston Gr EH3.....93 C4
Warriston PI EH3.....93 C4
Warriston Rd EH7.....93 C4
Warriston Terr EH3.....93 B4
Washington La **3** EH11 .120 F6
Waterfall Wlk EH42...153 B2
Waterfront Ave EH5...92 D7
Waterfront Broadway EH5.....92 D6
Waterfront Gait EH5...92 B6
Waterfront Pk EH5.....92 B6
Waterfront Way FK9.....2 A3
Waterfurs Dr FK2.....60 A8
Waterlands Gdns ML8..215 A3
Waterloo Bank EH26 .191 F4
Waterloo PI
  Edinburgh EH1.....229 A4

Waterloo Pl continued
Elphinstone EH33 ....126 B2
Waterloo Rd RH33 ....126 D4
Water of Leith Visitor Ctr*
EH14...................120 C2
Water of Leith Walkway*
EH14...................147 D2
Waters' Cl EH6 ....94 A5
Waters End FK2 ....39 B2
Waterside
🖣 Haddington EH41.....130 B8
Linlithgow EH49 ....84 C7
Water St EH6 ....94 A5
Watertoun Rd EH9 ....121 E3
Water Yett EH49..........84 F7
Watling Ave FK1..........59 C5
Watling Cres FK1..........59 D5
Watling Dr FK1...........59 D5
Watling Gdns FK1.........59 D6
Watling St FK1............59 C5
Watson Cres EH11........120 F5
Watson Ct KY4...........12 E8
Watson Gn EH54.........143 C8
Watson Pl Armadale EH48.140 A6
Dunfermline KY12.........29 B6
Longcroft FK4 ....57 C4
Watson St
Cowdenbeath KY4 ....13 D3
Falkirk FK2 ....60 B5
Penicuik EH26 ....191 F5
Watt Ave EH48...........140 A5
Watters Cres KY5.........14 B6
Watt Gdns FK1 ....59 E6
Watt Gr EH22 ....174 E5
Watt Pl EH22.............174 B4
Watt Rd KY11.............59 D5
Watt's Cl EH21............124 B6
Watt St KY11 ....18 A7
Wauchope Ave EH16....122 E4
Wauchope Cres EH16...122 E4
Wauchope Pk EH16......122 F3
Wauchope Pl EH16 ......122 E4
Wauchope Sq EH16......122 E4
Wauchope Terr EH16....122 E4
Waugh Path EH19.......173 D8
Waughton Cotts EH40...74 F5
Waughton Steading EH40.74 E5
Waulker Ave FK8 ....1 F2
Waulkmill Dr EH26......192 A5
Waulkmill Loan EH14 ...147 E3
Waulkmill Rd EH26 .....192 A5
Waulkmill View EH26...191 F5
Wavell St FK3 ....61 C5
Waverley Bridge EH1....229 A3
Waverley Cres
Bonnyrigg FK4............58 B3
Bonnyrigg and Lasswade
EH19...................173 C7
Grangemouth FK3........61 D5
Livingston EH54...........52 A8
Stirling FK8 ....2 C1
Waverley Ct EH19........173 C7
Waverley Dr EH19 ....173 C7
Waverley House N EH31..52 A2
Waverley House S EH31..52 A2
Waverley Park Terr EH8..94 A1
Waverley Pk
Bonnyrigg and Lasswade
EH19...................173 C7
Edinburgh EH8............94 A1
Mayfield EH22...........174 D6
Redding FK2..............61 B1
Waverley Pl EH7..........94 A2
Waverley Rd
Bonnyrigg and Lasswade
EH19...................173 C7
Dalkeith EH22...........152 F2
Stenhousemuir FK5.......38 C2
Waverley Sh Ctr EH1....229 A3
Waverley St
Bathgate EH48...........141 A7
Falkirk FK2 ....60 B8
Mayfield EH22...........174 D6
Waverley Steps EH2 .....2 A4
Waverley Street Ind Units 🖪
EH48...................141 A7
Waverley Terr
Bonnyrigg and Lasswade
EH19...................173 C7
Mayfield EH22...........174 D6
Stenhousemuir FK5.......38 C2
Wayfarers Dr KY11.......47 F3
Wayfarers Pl KY11........47 F3
Wayfarers Way KY11.....47 F3
Weaver Pl EH48 ....141 B7
Weaver Row FK7 ....7 A4
Weavers Cres KY2 ....17 B6
Weaver's Knowe Cres
EH14...................147 F5
Weavers Terr KY12.......27 D1
Weavers Wlk KY12 ....29 A2
Webster Ave FK2 ....39 B3
Webster Ct EH52........115 E5
Webster Pl KY11..........46 C5
Webster's Land EH1 ....228 C2
Wedderburn St KY11 ....29 E1
Wedderburn Ct EH21...124 D3
Wedderburn Ho EH21...124 D3
Wedderburn Pl KY11.....29 D2
Wedderburn Rd KY2.....16 C7
Wedderburn St KY11.....29 D2
Wedderburn Terr EH21..124 D4
Wee Brae EH18..........152 A1
Wee Cswy KY12..........42 D8
Wee Row FK2 ....60 B6
Weir Ave KY4.............13 B2
Weir Cres EH22..........152 E2
Weir Ct EH22.............152 E2
Weir Dr FK7................8 D4

Weir St Falkirk FK1.......60 C5
Stirling FK8 ....1 F2
Wellbank FK2 ....61 B2
Well Ct EH3 ....228 A3
Wellflats Rd EH29........89 B1
Wellgate Dr FK9..........2 C7
Wellgreen La 🖫 FK8.....7 B7
Wellgreen Pl FK8 ....7 B6
Wellgreen Rd FK8 ....7 B7
Wellhead Cl EH30........89 D8
Wellheads The KY11.....45 D3
Wellington Pl EH6 ....94 A5
Wellington Sch EH26 ...208 F6
Wellington St EH7 ....93 F2
Wellmyre FK10 ....11 A3
Wellpark EH52...........114 F8
Wellpark Cres FK7........6 F4
Welpark Terr FK1.........58 A5
Well Rd Bridge of Allan FK9..2 A8
Falkirk FK1 ....59 F3
Lochgelly KY5.............14 B7
Wellside EH41...........129 F8
Wellside Ct FK1..........60 A5
Wellside Pl FK1...........60 A5
Wellview La EH54........164 F5
WELLWOOD.............13 C4
Wellwood Prim Sch KY12..29 A7
Well Wynd EH33 ....119 A6
Welsh Ct FK6.............36 E1
Welsh Gdns FK9 ....2 A8
Welsh Rd EH47..........160 F6
Wemyss Ave KY12 ....26 A8
Wemyss Ct KY11.........46 E5
Wemyssfield KY1.........17 B3
Wemyss Gdns EH21.....125 C5
Wemyss Pl
Cockenzie & Port Seton
EH32...................97 C4
Edinburgh EH3...........228 B4
Haddington EH41........130 A8
Longniddry EH32 ....98 E6
Wemyss Place Mews
EH3...................228 B4
Wemyss Rd EH32 ....98 E6
Wemyss St
Cowdenbeath KY4 ....13 D3
Rosyth KY11..............46 F5
Wemyss Terr EH32.......98 F5
Werberside Mews EH4...92 E4
Wesley Cres EH19 ....173 D7
Wesley Pl FK2.............82 B8
West Adam St EH8......229 B2
West Adniston Cotts
EH33...................127 C6
West Albert Rd KY1......17 B4
West Annandale St EH7..93 D3
West Approach Rd
Edinburgh, Dalry EH11..120 E6
Edinburgh, Fountainbridge EH3,
EH11...................228 A2
West Baldridge Rd KY12..28 E5
Westbank Ct EH33 ......127 D5
Westbank Gdns EH33...127 D5
West Bankhead Loan EH15..95 A1
Westbank Pl EH15........95 A1
Westbank Rd EH33......127 C5
Westbank St EH15........95 A1
Westbank Terr EH33 ....127 C5
West Bankton Pl EH54..164 F7
WEST BARNS............77 E1
West Barns Prim Sch
EH42...................77 F1
West Bay Ct EH39........54 B7
West Bay Rd EH39 ....54 B7
WEST BENHAR..........159 B4
West Benhar Rd ML7....159 B3
West Boreland Rd FK6...36 D2
West Bow FK1............229 A2
West Bowling Green St
EH6...................93 D5
West Bridge St FK1......60 A5
West Brighton Cres
EH15...................123 A8
West Broomhill Rd KY3..50 E8
West Bryson Rd EH11...120 F5
Westburn Ave
Cowdenbeath KY4 ....13 B2
Edinburgh EH14.........148 C8
Falkirk FK1 ....59 F4
Westburn Gr EH14......148 C8
Westburn Middlefield
EH14...................148 C8
Westburn Pk EH14......148 D8
West Burnside FK12.....115 E5
West Cairn Cres EH26..191 E6
West Caiystane Rd EH10..150 A3
WEST CALDER...........163 D2
West Calder High Sch
EH55...................164 B5
West Calder Sta EH55..163 D3
West Calder Workspace
EH55...................163 C3
West Camus Rd EH10...150 A6
West Carmuirs Loan FK5..58 F6
West Carnethy Ave EH13..149 A5
West Castle Rd EH10....121 A5
West Catherine Pl EH12..120 C7
West Cherrybank EH6...93 C6
West Church Dr FK3.....40 B1
Westcliffe Ct FK3........61 F6
West Clifton Farm Cotts
EH53...................145 D8
West Coates EH12.......120 E7
West Colinton Ho EH13..149 A6
West College St EH1....229 A2
WEST CRAIGS...........118 F7
West Craigs Ave EH12..118 F6
West Craigs Pl EH12....119 A6

West Craigs Ind Est
EH12...................118 F7
Westcraigs Pk EH48 ...138 C3
Westcraigs Rd
Blackridge EH48 ....138 D2
Harthill ML7.............159 F6
West Cres EH34..........157 E4
West Croft EH28.........117 E2
West Cromwell St EH6...93 F6
West Crosscauseway
EH8...................229 B1
West Ct
Edinburgh, Niddrie Mains
EH16...................122 E3
Edinburgh, Ravelston EH4..92 C1
West Dr Dunfermline KY12..29 B3
Stenhousemuir FK5.......38 C1
WEST END...............228 B2
West End
Cockburnspath TD13....218 F4
West Calder EH55.......163 C2
West End Gdns FK10.....10 A6
Westend Pl EH3 ....54 B7
West End Pl EH11.......120 F6
WESTER ABERDOUR....49 B6
Wester Bankton EH54..165 A7
Wester Bogie Rd KY2 ...16 B7
Wester Broom Ave EH12..92 B3
Wester Broom Dr EH12..119 C5
Wester Broom Gdns
EH12...................119 C5
Wester Broom Gr EH12..119 C5
Wester Broom Pl EH12..119 C6
Wester Broom Terr
EH12...................119 C5
Wester Cl EH6 ....93 C7
Wester Coates Ave EH12..120 E7
Wester Coates Gdns
EH12...................120 E7
Wester Coates Pl EH12..120 E7
Wester Coates Rd EH12..120 E7
Wester Coates Terr
EH12...................120 E7
Wester Cowden Cotts
EH22...................153 E3
Wester Dalmeny Steading
EH30...................89 E8
Wester Drylaw Ave EH4..92 B3
Wester Drylaw Dr EH4...92 B3
Wester Drylaw Pl EH4...92 C3
Wester Drylaw Row EH4..92 C2
Westerdunes Ct EH39...53 E7
Westerdunes Pk EH39...53 D7
Westerfield Dr KY12 ....29 F6
Westerglen Rd FK1......60 A2
Wester Hailes Ed Ctr
EH11...................119 C1
Wester Hailes Pk EH14..148 D8
Wester Hailes Rd EH14..148 D7
Wester Hailes Sta EH14..148 D8
Wester Hill EH10.........149 E8
Wester Inch Bsns Pk
EH48...................142 D8
Wester Inch Rdbt EH48..141 D4
Westerlands Dr EH48 ....7 B5
Westerlea Ct FK9 ....2 A5
Westerlea Dr FK9 ....2 A5
Westermains EH48.......139 E5
WESTER MILLERHILL...152 E7
Western Ave
Crossford KY12...........28 B1
Falkirk FK2 ....60 B6
Western Cnr EH12......120 B7
Western Gdns EH12.....120 C7
Western General Hospl
EH4...................107 C4
Western Harbour Breakwater
EH6...................93 D8
West Harbour Dr EH6...93 D8
Western Harbour Midway
EH6...................93 D8
Western Harbour Pl EH6..93 D8
Western Harbour Terr
EH6...................93 D8
Western Harbour View
EH6...................93 D8
Western Harbour Way
EH6...................93 D8
Western Pl EH12.........120 C7
Western Terr EH12......120 C7
WESTER PENCAITLAND..156 D6
Wester Row EH14.......118 E1
Wester Steil EH11.......120 E1
Westerton FK7 ....20 D8
Westerton Dr FK9........2 A7
Westerton Rd
Broxburn EH52 ....116 B5
Grangemouth FK3.......61 F7
Westerton Terr FK2......39 C3
West Fairbrae Cres EH11..119 E3
West Fairbrae Dr EH11..119 E3
West Fenton Cotts EH39..72 E8
West Fenton Gait EH31..52 C2
West Fergus Pl KY1......17 B3
West Ferryfield EH5 .....92 F5
WESTFIELD.............110 F5
Westfield EH10...........24 B3
Westfield Ave EH11.....120 C5
Westfield Bank 🖪 EH52..152 E1
Westfield Cotts EH41...129 D3
Westfield Ct EH11.......120 C5
Westfield Dr 🖬 EH22..152 E1

Westfield Gr
Crossgates KY4...........30 E6
Dalkeith EH22...........152 E1
Westfield Pk EH22......152 E1
Westfield Pl FK6.........36 E1
Westfield Prim Sch EH48.110 F4
Westfield Rd EH11......120 D5
Westfield Rdbt FK2......60 F6
Westfield St
Edinburgh EH11.........120 D5
Falkirk FK2 ....60 E5
Westfield Trad Est 🖪 FK6..36 E1
West Fountain Pl EH11..120 F6
West Garleton Holdings
EH41...................100 E4
Westgarth Ave EH13 ...149 B6
Westgate Dunbar EH42...78 D3
Mid Calder EH53........144 B3
North Berwick EH39.....54 B7
Westgate Ct 🖪 EH39...54 B7
West Gate Rd FK2........62 A8
West Glen Ave EH54 ...142 E6
West Gorgie Pk EH14...120 C4
West Gorgie Pl EH14...120 C3
West Grange Gdns EH9..121 D3
West Granton Access EH5..92 D5
West Granton Rd EH5...92 D6
Westhall Cres KY12......27 D1
Westhall Gdns
Edinburgh EH10.........121 B5
Uphall EH52..............115 A4
West Hall Rd EH52......115 E4
West Harbour Rd
Charlestown KY11........45 A4
Cockenzie & Port Seton
EH32...................97 B4
Edinburgh EH5...........92 E7
West Harwood Crofts
EH55...................184 C6
Westhaugh Rd FK9 ....1 F4
West Holmes Gdns EH21..124 B6
West Holmes Pl EH21...115 B4
West Holmes Rd EH21...115 B4
Westhouses Ave EH22...174 E5
Westhouses Dr EH22...174 E5
Westhouses Rd EH22...174 E5
Westhouses St EH22....174 E5
West James St FK12......5 A6
West Johnstone St FK12..5 A6
West La KY4...............13 B2
Westland Cotts EH17...151 E5
West Leven St KY3.......50 E8
West Link Rd FK9.........2 D5
West Links Rd EH31......51 F2
West Loan EH32 ....96 F1
West Lodge Gdns FK10...9 F8
West Lorimer Pl EH32...97 B3
West Lothian Coll EH54..143 D1
West Lothian Coll FK1...121 F2
Westmains Cotts EH41..132 A5
West Mains Cotts EH55..183 F8
West Mains Ind Est
Falkirk FK3 ....60 F7
Grangemouth FK3.......61 A7
West Mains Rd
Falkirk FK1 ....60 F7
Edinburgh EH9 ....121 F2
West Main St
Aberlady EH32...........71 C4
Armadale EH48.........139 E5
Blackburn EH47.........161 C5
Broxburn EH52 ....115 D5
Harthill ML7.............114 F4
Uphall EH52..............114 F4
Whitburn EH47 ....147 F4
West Maitland St EH12..228 A2
West March St KY1......17 D7
West Mayfield EH9.......121 E4
West Meikle Pinkerton Cotts
EH42...................107 C4
West Mill Bank EH13...149 A6
Westmill Ct EH18.......173 A8
West Mill La EH4........228 A3
Westmill Rd EH18.......173 A8
West Mill Rd EH13......148 F6
Westmill Wynd EH18...173 A8
Westminster Pl FK3......38 E4
West Montgomery Pl 🖪
EH7...................93 F2
Westmost Cl EH6 ....93 C7
Westmuir Rd EH55.......163 D2
West Murrayfield FK7...7 D1
West Netherton St KY12..29 A2
West Newington Pl 🖬
EH9...................121 E5
West Nicolson St EH8...229 B2
West Norton Pl EH7.....229 C4
WESTPANS..............125 B7
Westpark Cres FK7......59 F8
Westpark Ct FK2.........59 F8
West Park Gr EH52......115 B5
West Park Pl EH11......120 F6
WEST PILTON...........92 C5
West Pilton Ave EH4...92 C5
West Pilton Bank EH4...92 C5
West Pilton Brae EH4...92 C5
West Pilton Cres EH4...92 C6
West Pilton Crossway
EH4...................92 C5
West Pilton Dr EH4......92 D5
West Pilton Gdns EH4...92 C5
West Pilton Gn EH4.....92 C5
West Pilton Lea EH4....92 C5
West Pilton Loan EH4...92 C5
West Pilton March EH4..92 D5
West Pilton Pk EH4......92 C5

West Pilton Rd EH4......92 D5
West Pilton Rise EH4 ...92 C5
West Pilton St EH4......92 C5
West Pilton Terr EH4....92 C5
West Pilton View EH4...92 C4
West Pk Carnock KY12 ..27 C6
Lochgelly KY5 ....14 A7
Westpoint Dunbar EH42...78 C2
Garvald EH41............132 D2
West Port Dunbar EH42..78 D2
Dysart KY1...............18 A7
Edinburgh EH1...........228 C2
Linlithgow EH49 ....84 F7
West Powburn EH9......121 E3
West Preston St EH8....121 E5
West Quality St KY1.....18 A7
WESTQUARTER..........61 B2
Westquarter Ave FK2....61 B2
Westquarter Dovecot*
FK2...................61 A2
Westquarter Prim Sch
FK2...................61 A2
Westray Terr FK1.........60 C2
West Register St EH2...229 A4
West Register Street La
EH2...................229 A4
West Relugas Rd EH9...121 D3
Westreron Ho
Bridge of Allan FK9 .....2 A8
Stirling FK9 ....2 A1
West Richmond St EH8..229 B2
WESTRIGG.............138 F3
WEST SALTOUN.........157 C3
West Saltoun EH34.....157 C3
West Sands KY11.........68 C6
West Savile Gdns EH9...121 E3
West Savile Rd EH16....121 F3
West Savile Terr EH9...121 E3
West Scotland Street La 🖬
EH3...................93 C2
West Seaside EH32 .....96 F1
West Shore Bsns Ctr EH5..92 C7
West Shore Rd EH5......92 C7
West Shore Road Trad Est
EH5...................92 C7
Westside Plaza Sh Ctr
EH14...................148 D8
West Silvermills La EH3..93 B2
West St EH26............191 E4
West Stanhope Pl 🖬
EH12...................120 E7
West Telferton EH7 .....94 F1
West Terr Blackness EH49..65 D5
South Queensferry EH30..68 B1
West Tollcross EH3 .....228 B1
West Torbain KY2........16 D8
West Vennel 🖪 FK10...10 B6
Westview EH4............84 C7
Westview Cres FK10 .....4 C2
West Vows Wlk KY1.....35 B6
Westwater St KY5 ....14 B8
West Way KY11...........48 B5
West Werberside EH4...92 E4
WEST WINDYGOUL.....126 C5
West Windygoul EH33..126 C5
West Windygoul Gdns
EH33...................126 C4
West Winnelstrae EH5...92 F4
Westwood Ave KY1 ......17 E8
Westwood Cres FK2 .....2 B3
Westwood Pk EH54.....142 F7
Westwood Pl KY11.......29 E4
West Woods EH4 ....92 E3
Westwood View EH55...163 D3
West Wynd KY12 ....17 D6
Wetherby Bsns Coll EH1.229 B3
Wale Brae EH6...........93 D6
Wharry Rd FK12...........4 E7
Whauphill ML11.........217 F8
Whauphill Cres ML11...217 F8
Wheatear Ct 🖪 KY11...29 F3
Wheatfield Gr EH20.....172 A8
Wheatfield Loan EH20..151 B1
Wheatfield Pl EH11.....120 D5
Wheatfield Rd
Bo'ness EH51 ....64 C6
Edinburgh EH11.........120 D5
Wheatfield St EH11.....120 D5
Wheatfield Wlk EH20...172 B8
Wheatlands Ave EH54..58 A6
Wheatsheaf La EH22...153 A3
Whimbrel Pl KY11.......30 C4
Whinbank EH54..........143 E6
Whinhill KY11............29 C3
Whinneyknowe KY11...68 C6
Whinniehill Terr KY12...27 C6
Whinnyburn Pl KY11....46 D5
Whinny Hill Cres KY11..47 A1
Whinny Hill Rd ML7......71 C4
Whin Park Ind Est EH51..64 C6
Whin Pk EH32.............97 B3
Whinrig EH52.............115 C6
WHINS OF MILTON.......7 B2
Whins Pl EH15............95 A1
Whins Rd Alloa FK10....10 C7
Stirling FK7 ....7 B2
Winnwell Rd FK8 ....2 A1
Whirlbut Cres KY11......29 B2
Whirlbut St KY11.........29 B2

Whitburgh Mains Cotts
EH37 . . . . **176** D4
WHITBURN **161** D5
Whitburn Acad EH47. . . . **161** C7
Whitburn Rd
Bathgate EH48 . . . . **140** E3
Livingston EH54. . . . . **143** C3
Whitdale Prim Sch EH47 **161** C6
White Castle Hillfort★
EH14. . . . . **222** B7
WHITECRAIG **124** E1
Whitecraig Ave EH21. . . **124** E1
Whitecraig Cres EH21. . . **124** E1
Whitecraig Gardens E
EH21 . . . . **124** E1
Whitecraig Prim Sch
EH21. . . . . **124** E1
Whitecraig Rd EH21. . . . **124** E1
Whitecraig Terr EH21. . . **124** E1
WHITECROSS **83** F6
Whitecross Ind Pk EH49 . **83** E7
Whitecross Prim Sch
EH49. . . . . **83** F6
Whitedalehead Rd EH47 . **161** C6
Whitedales EH10 . . . . **150** C5
Whitefield Neuk KY12. . . . **29** F6
Whitefield Rd KY12. . . . . . **29** E6
Whitegates PI FK1. . . . . . . **59** C4
Whitehall Ct EH14 . . . . **92** B2
White Hart St 12 EH22. . **53** A3
Whitehead Gr EH30 . . . . . . **89** D8
Whitehill EH22. . . . . **153** F2
Whitehill Ave EH21 . . . . . **124** A4
Whitehill Dr
Blackburn EH47 . . . . **162** C8
Dalkeith EH22 . . . . **153** D2
Whitehill Farm Rd EH21. **124** A4
Whitehill Gdns EH21 . . . **124** A4
Whitehill Gr EH22. . . . . . **153** D2
Whitehill Ind Est
Blackburn EH48. . . . . **141** C2
Dalkeith EH22 . . . . **153** E2
Whitehill PI
Rosewell EH24 . . . . **172** D2
Stirling FK8 . . . . **7** A5
Whitehill Rd
Blackburn EH47 . . . . **141** C1
Edinburgh EH15. . . . . **123** D3
Rosewell EH24 . . . . **172** E1
Whitehill St EH21. . . . . . . **123** E4
Whitehill View EH47. . . . **162** C8
White Horse CI EH8. . . . . **229** C3
Whitehouse Loan EH9 . . **121** C5
Whitehouse Rd
Edinburgh EH4. . . . . **91** A4
Stirling FK7 . . . . **7** D7
Whitehouse Terr EH9 . . . **121** C5
WHITEKIRK **75** F8
Whitelaw Cres KY11 . . . . . **29** D2
Whitelaw Dr EH48 . . . . . . **141** E6
Whitelaw PI KY11 . . . . **29** D2
Whitelaw Rd KY11 . . . . **29** D2
Whitelea Cres EH48. . . . **138** D1
Whitelea Cres La EH14. . **168** C8
Whitelea Rd EH14. . . . . . **168** C8
Whiteloch Ct EH33. . . . . . **127** C5
Whiteloch Rd EH33. . . . . **127** C5
Whitemoss La EH27 . . . . **145** E2
Whitemoss Rd EH27 . . . . **145** E2
Whitemyre Ct KY12 . . . . . . **28** D5
White Pk EH11. . . . . **120** E5
Whitequarries Ind Est
EH52. . . . . **87** C7
Whitesands Geology Trail★
EH42. . . . . **107** F7
White's CI 5 EH42. . . . . **153** A3
Whiteside EH48. . . . . **140** F4
Whiteside Cotts EH48 . . **140** F4
Whiteside Ct EH48 . . . . . **140** F4
Whiteside Farm La EH48 **140** D4
Whiteside Ind Est EH48 **140** F4
Whitesideloan FK2. . . . . . **82** E8
Whites Quay KY11 . . . . . . **47** F2
White St EH47. . . . . **161** A6
Whitestone PI EH48. . . . **141** C1
Whiteyetts Cres FK10 . . . . **5** D2
Whiteyetts Dr FK10 . . . . . . **5** D2
Whiteyetts PI FK10. . . . . . . **5** D2
Whitingford EH6. . . . . **93** D5
Whitson Cres EH11. . . . . **120** B5
Whitson Gr EH11 . . . . **120** B5
Whitson Place E EH11. . . **120** B5
Whitson Place W EH11. . . **120** B5
Whitson Rd EH11 . . . . **120** B5
Whitson Terr EH11. . . . . . **120** B5
Whitson Way EH11. . . . . . **120** B5
Whitson Wlk EH11. . . . . . **120** A5
Whitten La EH49. . . . . **84** F7
Whittingehame Dr EH41 **130** C8
Whittingehame Mews
EH41. . . . . **130** C8
Whittret Knowe ML1. . . . **217** F7
Wholeflats Rd FK2, FK3. . . **62** A4
Wholeflats Rdbt FK3. . . . . **61** E5
Wholequarter La FK2. . . . . **61** B2
Whytbank Gdns KY1 . . . . . **17** B3
Whytehouse Ave KY1 . . . . **17** B3
Whyteman's Brae KY1 . . . **17** B3
Whytemans Brae Hospl
KY1. . . . . **17** B7
Whyte Melville Rd KY2. . . **17** A4
Whyte 7 FK7. . . . . **7** A1
Whyte PI EH7 . . . . **94** A1
Whytescauseway KY1 . . . **17** B3
Whyte St Harthill ML7 . . . **159** F6

Whyte St continued
Lochgelly KY5 . . . . **14** B8
Whyte Wlk KY1 . . . . **29** F4
Widows Row EH42. . . . . . . **76** B3
Wilderness Rdbt EH54 . . **164** C6
Wilderness The FK2 . . . . . **22** D4
Wilfrid Terr 6 EH8. . . . . . **94** C1
Wilkie PI FK5. . . . . **38** B2
WILKIESTON **146** A6
Wilkieston Rd EH28. . . . . **117** C2
William Black PI EH30 . . . **89** C8
William Booth PI FK7 . . . . . **7** A3
Williamfield Ave FK7. . . . . . **7** A4
Williamfield Sq 2 EH15. **123** A8
William Jameson PI EH15 . **95** A1
William Sharp PI KY4 . . . **13** D4
Williamson Ave FK2. . . . . . **39** A1
Williamson's PI FK2. . . . . . **60** C7
Williamson's Quay KY1. . . **17** C4
Williamson St FK1. . . . . . . **60** B4
William St
Dunfermline KY12 . . . . **28** E4
Edinburgh EH3. . . . . **228** A3
Kirkcaldy KY1 . . . . **17** B2
Williamstone Ct EH14 . . . **54** A6
Williamston Intc EH54 . . **144** A1
Williamston Prim Sch
EH54. . . . . **164** F8
William Street NE La
EH3 . . . . **228** A3
William Street NW La
EH3 . . . . **228** A3
William Street SE La
EH3 . . . . **228** A3
William Street SW La
EH3 . . . . **228** A2
Willow Ave
Bonnyrigg and Lasswade
EH19. . . . . **173** B6
Fauldhouse EH47 . . . . **181** F5
Willowbank EH47 . . . . **143** E6
Willowbank Row EH6 . . . . **93** D6
WILLOWBRAE. **122** D7
Willowbrae FK2. . . . . **82** D8
Willow Brae
Fauldhouse EH47 . . . . **181** F5
Plean FK7 . . . . **20** C3
Willowbrae Ave EH8. . . . **122** C8
Willowbrae Gdns EH8. . . **122** D8
Willowbrae Rd EH8 . . . . . **122** D8
Willowdean EH49 . . . . **86** C4
Willow Dell EH51. . . . . **63** D5
Willow Dr KY1. . . . . **17** B8
Willow Gr
Dunfermline KY11 . . . . **46** E8
Fauldhouse EH47 . . . . **181** F5
Livingston EH54. . . . . **144** B5
Menstrie FK11. . . . . **3** E6
Willow Grange FK2 . . . . . . **61** C1
Willowgrove House Sch
EH54. . . . . **144** B5
Willow Pk EH47. . . . . **181** F5
Willow Rd EH22. . . . . **174** E6
Willows The
Cairneyhill KY12 . . . . **27** D1
Tullibody FK10. . . . . **4** B1
Willow Tree PI EH14 . . . . **147** D3
Willow View EH47 . . . . . . **181** F5
Wilson Ave Dalkeith EH22 **153** C3
Denny FK6. . . . . **36** D2
Falkirk FK1. . . . . **59** C5
Kirkcaldy KY2 . . . . **17** B6
Polmont FK2 . . . . **61** F2
Prestonpans EH32. . . . . . . **96** F7
Wilson Bruce Ct KY5 . . . . **14** C8
Wilson Dr Bannockburn FK7. . **7** C2
Falkirk FK2. . . . . **61** A4
Wilson Gdns FK1. . . . . **59** C6
Wilson PI Bonnybridge FK4. . **58** C4
Dunbar EH42 . . . . **106** E8
Wilson Rd Allanton ML7. . **198** A8
Dunbar EH42. . . . . **106** D8
Falkirk FK1. . . . . **59** C6
Gorebridge EH23. . . . . . . **174** D1
Livingston EH54. . . . . **142** E3
Wilson's CI
1 Dunfermline KY12 . . . . . **29** A3
16 Dunfermline KY12 . . . . **60** B4
Wilson's Ct EH1 . . . . **229** B3
Wilson's Pk EH15. . . . . **95** B1
Wilson St Bairhall ML12. . **26** A8
Cowdenbeath KY4. . . . . . . **13** C4
Grangemouth FK3. . . . . . . **61** E6
Penicuik EH26 . . . . **191** E5
Townhill KY12 . . . . **29** D8
Wilson Terr
Broxburn EH52 . . . . **115** B5
Stoneyburn EH47. . . . . . . **162** A2
WILSONTOWN. **201** C2
Wilsontown Rd ML11. . . . **201** C2
Wilson Way KY11 . . . . **46** D2
Wilson Wlk 5 EH35. . . . . **126** C5
Wilton Rd Carluke ML8 . . **215** B1
Edinburgh EH16. . . . . **121** F3
WINCHBURGH **87** E2
Winchburgh Cotts EH52. . **87** F2
Winchburgh Prim Sch
EH52. . . . . **87** E2
Winchester Ave FK6. . . . . . **36** F3
Winchester Avenue Ind Est
FK6. . . . . **36** F3
Winchester Ct FK6. . . . . . . **36** F3
Winchester Dr FK6. . . . . . . **36** F2
Windlebrook KY11. . . . . . . **47** A8
Windmill Ct EH8 . . . . **229** B1
Windmill Grn KY1 . . . . **17** F8
Windmill Knowe KY4 . . . . **30** E6

Windmill La EH8 . . . . **229** B1
Windmill PI
Edinburgh EH8. . . . . **229** B1
Kirkcaldy KY1 . . . . **18** A8
Windmill Rd KY1. . . . . **17** F8
Windmill St EH8 . . . . **229** A1
Windrush Dr EH6 . . . . **93** D7
Windrush View FK10 . . . . . **5** D2
Windsor Ave FK1. . . . . **59** E4
Windsor Cres Falkirk FK1 . . **59** E4
Maddiston FK2. . . . . **83** A6
Windsor Dr Denny FK6. . . . **36** D3
Falkirk FK1 . . . . **59** F4
Penicuik EH26 . . . . **192** A6
Windsor Gdns Alloa FK10 . . **5** A8
5 Falkirk FK1. . . . . **59** F4
Musselburgh EH21. . . . . . **124** E6
Windsor Park Dr EH21. . . **124** F6
Windsor Park PI EH21. . . **124** F6
Windsor Park Sch FK1. . . . **59** E4
Windsor Park Terr EH21 . **124** F6
Windsor Pk EH21. . . . . . . **124** F6
Windsor PI
Edinburgh EH15. . . . . **123** B8
Shotts ML7 . . . . **179** E5
Stirling FK8 . . . . **7** A7
Windsor Rd Falkirk FK1. . . **59** E4
Penicuik EH26 . . . . **192** A6
Windsor Sq EH26 . . . . . . **192** A6
Windsor St Edinburgh EH7 . **93** E2
Menstrie FK11. . . . . **3** F6
Shotts ML7 . . . . **179** E5
Windsor Street La EH7 . . . **93** E2
Windsor Terr EH26. . . . . . **192** A6
Windygate KY2 . . . . **16** F1
Windygates Rd EH19. . . . . **54** B6
Windygoul Cres EH33 . . . **126** E5
Windygoul Prim Sch
EH33. . . . . **126** D4
Windyhill Ave FK10 . . . . . . **23** D6
WINDYKNOWE **140** F5
Windyknowe Cres EH48 . **140** F4
Windyknowe Pk EH48. . . **140** F5
Windyknowe Prim Sch
EH48. . . . . **140** D6
Windy Mains Farm Cotts
EH36 . . . . **177** D5
Wingate Cres EH42 . . . . . . **78** C2
Winifred Cres KY2 . . . . **17** A6
Winifred St KY2 . . . . **17** A6
Winterfield Mains EH42. . **78** A2
Winterfield PI EH42. . . . . . **78** A2
Winterthur La KY12 . . . . . **29** A4
Winton CI EH33 . . . . **126** E4
Winton Ct
Cockenzie & Port Seton
EH32. . . . . **97** C4
New Winton EH33 . . . . . . **127** B3
Tranent EH33. . . . . **126** E4
Winton Dr EH10 . . . . **150** C4
Winton Gdns EH10 . . . . . **150** C4
Winton Gr Edinburgh EH10 **150** B5
Tranent EH33. . . . . **126** E4
Wintonhill Cotts EH34. . . **127** D2
Winton Gr Holm FK-34 . . . **156** D7
Winton Loan
Edinburgh EH10. . . . . **150** C4
Tranent EH33. . . . . **127** A6
Winton Pk
Cockenzie & Port Seton
EH32. . . . . **97** C3
Edinburgh EH10. . . . . **150** B4
New Winton EH33 . . . . . . **127** B3
Winton Terr
Edinburgh EH10. . . . . **150** B5
New Winton EH33 . . . . . . **127** B3
Winton Way EH33 . . . . . . **126** D4
Wishart Ave
Bonnyrigg and Lasswade
EH19. . . . . **173** D8
North Berwick EH39 . . . . . . **54** C6
Wishart Dr FK7 . . . . **7** C4
Wishart PI Dalkeith EH22 . **152** E2
Kirkcaldy KY1 . . . . **17** F6
Tranent EH35. . . . . **155** D6
Wishaw Terr EH7 . . . . **94** B1
Wisp Gn EH15 . . . . **123** B4
Wisp The Dalkeith EH22 . **123** B1
Edinburgh EH15, EH16 . . . **123** B3
Witchbrae KY1 . . . . **29** E3
Witholm EH22 . . . . **153** E2
Wolfe Rd FK1 . . . . **60** D4
Wolfstar Farm Cotts
EH35. . . . . **155** F6
Wolrige Rd EH16. . . . . **151** A8
Wolseley Cres EH8. . . . . . . **94** C1
Wolseley PI EH8 . . . . **94** C1
Wolseley Terr 8 EH8. . . . . **94** C1
Wolsey Ave EH19 . . . . **173** C6
Wood Avens FK10. . . . . **4** B1
Woodbank KY4 . . . . **13** B2
Woodbank Crofts EH48 . **110** F2
Woodbank Gr KY12 . . . . . . **26** D7
Woodbine Terr EH6. . . . . . . **94** A3
WOODBURN **153** C3
Woodburn Ave
Dalkeith EH22 . . . . **153** C2
Redding FK2 . . . . **61** B2
Woodburn Bank EH22 . . . **153** C3
Woodburn Cres
Bonnyrigg FK4. . . . . **57** F3
Oakley KY12 . . . . **26** F7
Redding FK2 . . . . **61** B2
Woodburn Dr Alloa FK10. . . **4** F1
Dalkeith EH22 . . . . **153** B3
Woodburn Gdns
Dalkeith EH22 . . . . **153** C3

Woodburn Gdns continued
Falkirk FK2 . . . . **60** E5
Woodburn Gr EH22 . . . . . **153** C2
Woodburn Loan EH22. . . **153** C3
Woodburn Medway
EH22. . . . . **153** C3
Woodburn Pk EH22 . . . . . **153** C3
Woodburn PI EH22. . . . . . **153** C3
Woodburn Prim Sch
EH22. . . . . **153** C3
Woodburn Rd
Dalkeith EH22 . . . . **153** C3
Falkirk FK2 . . . . **60** D5
Woodburn St
Dalkeith EH22 . . . . **153** C3
Falkirk FK2 . . . . **60** E5
Woodburn Terr
Dalkeith EH22 . . . . **153** D3
Edinburgh EH10. . . . . **121** B3
Woodburn View EH22. . . **153** D3
Woodburn Way FK12. . . . . . **5** A6
Woodbush EH42 . . . . **78** E2
Woodbush Brae EH42 . . . . **78** E2
Woodbush PI EH42 . . . . . . **78** E2
Woodbush Rd EH42 . . . . . **78** E2
Wood Dr EH47. . . . . **160** F6
WOODEND **87** F7
Woodend Bsns Ctr KY4. . . **13** B1
Woodend Gdns KY11. . . . . **47** F5
Woodend Ind Est KY4 . . . . **13** B1
Woodend Pk EH33 . . . . . . **171** F3
Woodend PI KY4. . . . . **13** B2
Woodend Rd ML8. . . . . . . **215** A2
Woodend Wlk EH48. . . . . **139** E6
Woodfield Ave EH13 . . . . **148** F6
Woodfield Pk
Bilston EH25 . . . . **171** D6
Edinburgh EH13. . . . . **148** F6
Woodhall Ave EH14 . . . . . **148** D6
Woodhall Bank EH13. . . . **148** F5
Woodhall Cres EH13 . . . . **148** F5
Woodhall Ct EH14 . . . . . . **148** D6
Woodhall Dr EH14 . . . . . . **148** F5
Woodhall Millbrae EH14 **148** E6
Woodhall PI EH34. . . . . . . **156** D6
Woodhall Rd
Edinburgh EH13. . . . . **148** F5
Pencaitland EH34 . . . . . . **156** D6
Woodhall Terr EH14 . . . . **148** D6
Woodhall Farm Rd KY12 . **25** F2
Woodhead Gr EH48 . . . . . **139** D5
Woodhead PI EH48 . . . . . **140** E6
Woodhill Ct FK3. . . . . **61** D6
Woodhill Gr KY12. . . . . **28** B2
Woodhill Rd EH48 . . . . . . **138** B3
WOODLANDS **60** B4
Woodlands FK10. . . . . **5** E1
Woodlands Bank KY11. . . . **48** A3
Woodlands Cres EH48. . . **140** B5
Woodlands Cres FK1. . . . . **60** A4
Woodlands Dr
Bo'ness EH51. . . . . **63** D5
Crossford KY12. . . . . **28** A2
Grangemouth FK2. . . . . . . **82** E8
Woodlands Gr
Armadale EH48 . . . . **140** B5
Edinburgh EH15. . . . . **122** E6
Townhill KY12 . . . . **29** D7
Woodlands Pk EH54 . . . . **142** F8
Woodlands Rd KY2 . . . . . . **16** D6
Woodlands Sch EH14 . . . **147** F4
Woodlands Terr KY12 . . . . **26** B8
Woodlands The KY11 . . . . . **46** F5
Woodland View EH22 . . . **153** D4
Woodland Way FK6 . . . . . . **57** D7
Wood Lea KY10. . . . . **23** E5
Woodlea Cotts EH49 . . . . . **65** A3
Woodlea Gdns Alloa FK10. . **5** A1
Woodlea Pk Alloa FK10 . . . **10** B8
Sauchie FK10. . . . . **5** A1
Woodmill Cres KY11 . . . . . **29** D3
Woodmill High Sch KY11. . **29** E3
Woodmill PI KY11. . . . . **29** E3
Woodmill Rd KY11. . . . . . . **29** E3
Woodmill St KY11. . . . . . . **29** B3
Woodmill Terr KY11 . . . . . **29** B3
Woodmuir Cres EH55. . . . **182** E6
Woodmuir Prim Sch
EH55. . . . . **182** E6
Woodmuir Rd
Breich EH55. . . . . **182** E6
Whitburn EH47 . . . . **161** C6
Wood PI Livingston EH54. . **143** C4
Rosyth KY11. . . . . **46** E5
Wood Rd KY11 . . . . **46** C2
Woodrow EH23. . . . . **174** C1
Woodruff Gait KY12. . . . . . **28** F5
Woodrush Glade EH54 . . **164** C8
Wood's Ct EH19 . . . . **173** B7
Woodside KY4. . . . . **13** C3
Woodside KY11. . . . . **46** F5
Woodside Ct
Cambusbarron FK7 . . . . **6** D5
Falkirk FK1. . . . . **60** B3
Woodside Dr EH26 . . . . . . **191** F5
Woodside Gdns
Grangemouth FK2 . . . . **82** E8
Musselburgh EH21. . . . . . **124** E6
Woodside Gr FK5. . . . . **59** D8
Woodside PI
Bridgend EH49 . . . . **86** C4
Falkirk FK7. . . . . **8** C4
Woodside Rd Alloa FK10 . . . **4** F1
Forrestfield ML6 . . . . **137** A3
Stirling FK8 . . . . **2** A3
Tullibody FK10. . . . . **4** A1

Woodside St KY11 . . . . **46** F5
Woodside Terr
Bridgend EH49 . . . . **86** C4
Clackmannan FK10 . . . . . . **10** F4
Edinburgh EH15. . . . . **123** D7
Falkirk FK1. . . . . **60** B3
Tarbrax EH55. . . . . **203** F3
Wood St FK3. . . . . **61** C7
Woodstock PI EH16. . . . . **122** B1
Wood Terr EH48. . . . . **140** A6
Woodville Ct EH52 . . . . . **115** D4
Woodville Terr EH6. . . . . . **94** A3
Wooer St 4 FK1. . . . . **60** B4
Woolcarders Ct FK7 . . . . . . **6** D6
Woolfords Cotts EH55. . . **203** A7
Woolmet Cres EH22 . . . . . **152** B8
Woolmet PI EH14. . . . . . . **122** F3
Wordie Rd FK7. . . . . **6** F1
World's End CI EH1 . . . . . **229** B3
Wotherspoon Cres EH48 **139** F5
Wotherspoon Dr FK51 . . . . **63** D6
W Parliament Sq EH1 . . . **229** A3
Wright Ave EH48. . . . . **141** A3
Wright PI Kirkcaldy KY1 . . . **17** D7
Lochgelly KY5 . . . . **14** A8
Wright St FK2 . . . . **60** B6
Writers CI EH42 . . . . **78** D3
Writers' Mus★ EH1. . . . . . **229** A3
Wyckliffe KY12 . . . . **28** C6
Wymet Ct KY12 . . . . **29** A3
Wymet Ho KY12 . . . . **29** A3
Wyndford Ave EH52. . . . . **115** A5
Wyndford Brae EH49 . . . . . **86** E7
Wyndford PI EH52 . . . . . . **115** A5
Wynd The Alva FK12. . . . . . . **5** A7
Dalgety Bay KY11 . . . . **48** C3
Gifford EH41. . . . . **220** F6
Ormiston EH35 . . . . **155** E7
Wyre Hayes Cotts KY4 . . . . **30** F8
Wyvern Pk EH9 . . . . **121** D4
Wyvis Pk EH26 . . . . **192** A7
Wyvis PI ML7 . . . . **180** B3

X

Xcite Bathgate Sports Ctr
EH48. . . . . **141** B1

Y

Yardheads EH6 . . . . **93** F5
Yardley PI FK2. . . . . **39** A1
Yarrow Ct EH26. . . . . **192** A7
Yarrow PI FK3. . . . . **61** F6
Yeaman La EH11. . . . . **120** F6
Yeaman PI EH11. . . . . **120** F6
Yellowcraig Trail★ EH39 . **53** B8
Yester Mains Cotts EH41 **220** F5
Yester PI EH41, EH32 . . . **100** F1
Yester Prim Sch EH41. . . **220** F6
Yetholm Pk KY12 . . . . **28** F2
Yetholm Way KY2. . . . . **17** C6
Yetts The FK7 . . . . **6** C5
Yew Gr EH54 . . . . **144** B5
Yewlands Cres EH16 . . . . **151** B7
Yewlands Gdns EH16. . . . **151** B7
Yew Terr FK2. . . . . **61** A2
YIELDSHIELDS. **215** E2
Yieldshields Rd ML8 . . . . **216** D3
York Arc 4 FK3. . . . . **40** D1
York Dr KY12 . . . . **60** D6
York La 8 Edinburgh EH1. . **229** A4
2 Grangemouth FK3 . . . . . **40** D1
York PI Dunfermline KY12 . . **29** C6
Edinburgh EH1 . . . . **229** A4
Kirkcaldy KY1 . . . . **17** F8
York Rd Edinburgh EH5 . . . **93** C6
North Berwick EH39 . . . . . . **54** A7
York Sq 3 FK3. . . . . **40** D1
York St FK2 . . . . **60** D6
Young Ave EH33 . . . . **126** D5
Young Cres EH48. . . . . **140** F5
Young Ct KY4. . . . . **13** C3
Young Sq EH54 . . . . **164** B6
Youngs Rd EH52. . . . . **116** A6
Young St Edinburgh EH2. . **228** B3
West Calder EH55 . . . . . . **163** C2
Young's Terr 6 KY1. . . . . . **17** C5
Young Street North La
EH2 . . . . **228** B3
Young Street South La
EH2 . . . . **228** B3
Young Terr KY4. . . . . **13** B3
Yule PI EH47 . . . . **141** C1
Yule Terr FK7 . . . . **162** C8

Z

Zealandia Rd KY11. . . . . . . **46** B1
Zetland Dr
Grangemouth FK3. . . . . . . **61** A8
Laurieston FK2 . . . . **61** A4
Zetland PI Edinburgh EH5. . **93** B6
Lochgelly KY5 . . . . **14** A7
Skinflats FK2 . . . . **39** F3
Zetland St FK10. . . . . **11** B4
Zetland Terr FK2 . . . . **61** F2